DOCUMENTS
ON
AMERICAN FOREIGN RELATIONS
1942 — 1943

WORLD PEACE FOUNDATION

40 Mt. Vernon Street, Boston, Massachusetts

Founded in 1910

THE World Peace Foundation is a non-profit organization which was founded in 1910 by Edwin Ginn, the educational publisher, for the purpose of promoting peace, justice and good-will among nations. For many years the Foundation has sought to increase public understanding of international problems by an objective presentation of the facts of international relations. This purpose is accomplished principally through its publications and by the maintenance of a Reference Service which furnishes on request information on current international problems. Recently increased attention has been focused on American foreign relations by study groups organized for the consideration of actual problems of policy.

DOCUMENTS
ON
AMERICAN FOREIGN RELATIONS

VOL. V
JULY 1942—JUNE 1943

EDITED BY

LELAND M. GOODRICH
Director, World Peace Foundation

AND

MARIE J. CARROLL
Chief, Reference Service

32305

WORLD PEACE FOUNDATION

BOSTON

1944

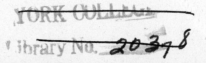

Copyright, 1944, by
World Peace Foundation

PRINTED IN THE UNITED STATES OF AMERICA

INTRODUCTION

During the year July 1, 1942 to June 30, 1943, the period covered by this volume, the foreign relations of the United States were naturally conducted with one dominant purpose in mind — the winning of the war in which this country had become totally involved as the result of the attack at Pearl Harbor. From this fact, certain consequences have followed which have affected the character and contents of this volume. In the first place, American foreign relations have been predominantly concerned with the winning of the war, and only exceptionally with those matters which figure so prominently in the peace-time relations of states. In the second place, because of the need of preserving the confidential and secret character of many documents in time of war, there are more serious gaps than would usually be the case. Nevertheless, it is hoped that by the use of rather full headnotes and by the inclusion in one or two instances of exhibits that are not strictly official in character, but nevertheless reliable, a fairly complete story has been told of the important developments.

There were two significant developments in American foreign relations which are reflected in the documents contained in this volume. On the military front, the United Nations passed from the defensive to the offensive and this change in military fortunes found expression in acts and policies in both the foreign and domestic fields. While El Alamein marked the turn of the tide in North Africa, the landing of British and American troops in French North Africa in November 1942 meant that the Anglo-American allies had definitely taken the initiative, and the Russian victory at Stalingrad a few weeks later was the turning point on the Eastern front as well. These developments, combined with a parallel show of growing power by the United States and her allies in the Pacific area, meant that the United Nations at last had the military initiative in their hands. The most effective use of this advantage required a closer coordination of national efforts and the evolution of methods of consultation and organized cooperation to that end.

But the year under review saw not alone the search for more effective means of cooperation between the United Nations in the effective prosecution of the war. There was also growing recognition of the need of increased cooperation in dealing with problems of the peace. Under-Secretary of State Welles, in his Toronto Address of February 26, 1943 (see this volume, p. 45), had suggested the technique to be followed, and in summoning the United Nations Food and Agriculture Conference, which met at Hot Springs, Virginia, May 18–June 3, 1943, the first important step was taken in the development of suitable machinery of international organization for implementing the peace-time purposes of the United Nations. The development of a comparable organization for the administration of relief and rehabilitation was in its initial stages during this period; but since the actual signing of the agreement and the setting up of UNRRA as a going concern came after June 30, 1943, it has been thought advisable to postpone the publication of the documents pertaining to this important advance in international organization to the succeeding volume of this series.

Few important changes in the organization of materials have been made in this volume. The title of Chapter II of Volume IV — *From Neutrality to Belligerency* — has been changed to *The Axis Powers*, and the chapter has been placed after *Defense and the War Effort*, which has seemed a more logical arrangement now that the transition has been accomplished. A number of subtopics relating to economic warfare which have hitherto been included in the chapter on *Trade and Finance* have been moved up to the chapter on *Defense and the War Effort* in view of the fact that they are more closely related to the prosecution of the war than to normal trade and financial policy. In general, changes in the organization of material have been kept to a minimum on the assumption that persons who customarily make use of the volumes in the series will find continuity in the general pattern of arrangement distinctly helpful.

It is our hope that this compilation of the materials bearing upon the conduct of American foreign relations during the critical period July 1, 1942 to June 30, 1943, will contribute not only to a better understanding of the contribution of the United States to the war effort but also to a greater recognition of the fact that the United States is inescapably a part of the world and must assume its full share of the responsibility in building a better world order.

Finally, we wish to express our deep appreciation of the invaluable assistance rendered by members of the staff of the World Peace Foundation, in particular to Miss Annette Chapman and to Mr. Robert J. Vernon, Jr. We are especially indebted to Mrs. Ralph de Miranda for her work in the preparation of the Index.

LELAND M. GOODRICH
MARIE J. CARROLL

February 23, 1944

CONTENTS

CHAPTER I

PRINCIPLES AND POLICY:
GENERAL STATEMENTS

(1) *The War and Human Freedom.* *Radio Address by the Secretary of State (Hull), July 23, 1942* [1]

The conflict now raging throughout the earth is not a war of nation against nation. It is not a local or regional war or even a series of such wars. On the side of our enemies, led and driven by the most ambitious, depraved, and cruel leaders in history, it is an attempt to conquer and enslave this country and every country. On our side, the side of the United Nations, it is, for each of us, a life-and-death struggle for the preservation of our freedom, our homes, our very existence. We are united in our determination to destroy the world-wide forces of ruthless conquest and brutal enslavement. Their defeat will restore freedom or the opportunity for freedom alike to all countries and all peoples.

I

From Berlin and Tokyo the assault on human freedom has spread in ever-widening circles. In some cases the victim nations were lulled into inaction by promises or by protestations of peaceful intention. In other cases they were so intimidated that no preparation for resistance was made. In all cases the invaders, before armed attack, set into motion every conceivable device of deceit, subversion, treachery, and corruption within the borders of the intended victim.

As country after country, in Europe and in Asia, was attacked in this way, it became clear that no nation anywhere was immune, that for none was safety to be found in mere desire for peace, in avoidance of provocation, in neutrality, or in distance from the centers of assault, Nation after nation learned — too late — that safety against such an attack lay only in more effective force; in superior will; in concerted action of all free nations directed toward resisting and defeating the common enemies; in applying the law of self-defense and self-preservation rather than in relying upon professions of neutrality, which, in the

---

[1] Broadcast over all national radio networks, Department of State, *Bulletin*, VII, p. 639.

face of a world-wide movement to subjugate all nations and all peoples, are as absurd and as suicidal as are such professions on the part of a citizen of a peaceful community attacked by a band of confessed outlaws.

Today twenty-eight United Nations are fighting against the would-be conquerors and enslavers of the human race. We know what is at stake. By the barbarian invaders of today nothing is spared — neither life, nor morals, nor honor, nor virtue, nor pledges, nor the customs, the national institutions, even the religion of any people. Their aim is to sweep away every vestige of individual and national rights; to substitute, the world over, their unspeakable tyranny for the ways of life developed each for itself by the various nations; to make all mankind subservient to their will; to convert the two billions of the earth's inhabitants into abject victims and tools of their insatiable lust for power and dominion.

We have seen their work in the countries they have invaded — murder of defenseless men, women, and children; rape, torture, and pillage; mass terrorization; the black system of hostages; starvation and deprivations that beggar description; the most thorough-going bondage the world has ever seen.

This is the so-called "New Order" of Hitler and the Japanese war lords — an order as old as slavery — new only in the calculated thoroughness of its cruelty; in the depth of the degradation to which it subjects its victims; in the degree to which it has revived the worst practices of the darkest ages in history.

From time immemorial attempts at conquest and enslavement have checked and harried the great onward march of men and women toward greater freedom and higher levels of civilized existence. The methods employed have been the same as those which we witness today. Ruthless, ambitious men would succeed in corrupting, coercing, or deceiving into blind obedience enough servile followers to attack or terrify peaceful and law-abiding peoples, too often unprepared to resist. In a few instances whole civilizations collapsed under the impact, and darkness descended on large portions of the world. More often, the attacks were — at great cost — defeated, and mankind resumed its onward march. Yet throughout the ages two lessons have remained unlearned.

The first is that man's innate striving for freedom cannot be extinguished. Since the world began too many men have fought, suffered, and died for freedom — and not in vain — for doubt to remain on that score. And yet, over and over again would-be conquerors and enslavers of mankind have sought to translate their mad dreams of barbarous domination into reality.

The second lesson is that liberty is truly won only when it is guarded by the same watchfulness, the same courage, the same willingness to fight for it which first secured it. Repeatedly throughout history, free men — having won the fight, having acquired precious rights and privileges which freedom brings — have dropped their guard, relaxed their vigilance, taken their freedom for granted. They have busied themselves with many things and have not noticed the beginnings of new tyrannies, the rise of new threats to liberty. They have become so abhorrent of force and cruelty that they have believed the bully and the gangster could be reformed by reason and justice or be defeated by passive resistance. And so they have been surprised and unprepared when the attacks have come again.

It is perhaps too much to expect that tyrants will ever learn that man's longing for liberty cannot be destroyed. Dreams of conquest have their roots in diseased mentality. And that malady may well be ineradicable.

But it is not too much to expect that free men may learn — and never forget — that lack of vigilance is the greatest danger to liberty; that enjoyment of liberty is the fruit of willingness to fight, suffer, and die for it; that the right to freedom cannot be divorced from the duty of defending it.

This latest assault on human freedom is, in a profound sense, a searching test for nations and for individuals. There is no surer way for men and for nations to show themselves unworthy of liberty than, by supine submission and refusal to fight, to render more difficult the task of those who are fighting for the preservation of human freedom — unless it be to align themselves, freely and voluntarily, with the destroyers of liberty. There is no surer way for men and for nations to show themselves worthy of liberty than to fight for its preservation, in any way that is open to them, against those who would destroy it for all.

In the plans of the new tyrants of the East and of the West, there is no freedom or hope for anyone. If there be some people who believe that they can expect from Hitler or the Japanese war lords greater measure of freedom or of opportunity for freedom than they now possess, they need only look at the firing squads in Poland, Czechoslovakia, Norway, France, Yugoslavia, at the concentration camps in Germany and Austria. They need only see the degradation of the forced laborers torn from every occupied country. They can learn the fraudulent quality of that brand of "freedom" from the Chinese in Nanking, from the Filipinos in Manila, from the inhabitants of the East Indies.

There is no chance for liberty for any people anywhere save through the victory of the free peoples. Never did a plainer duty to fight against its foes devolve upon all peoples who prize liberty and all who aspire to it. Never was there such an opportunity for every people, as have the people of the Philippines, to demonstrate its fitness both for the rights and the responsibilities of freedom — and, through proof given of its fitness, to create an overwhelming sentiment in every country of the world in support of its striving for liberty.

II

We, Americans, are fighting today because we have been attacked. We are fighting, as I have said, to preserve our very existence. We and the other free peoples are forced into a desperate fight because we did not learn the lessons of which I have spoken. We are forced to fight because we ignored the simple but fundamental fact that the price of peace and of the preservation of right and freedom among nations is the acceptance of international responsibilities.

After the last war too many nations, including our own, tolerated, or participated in, attempts to advance their own interests at the expense of any system of collective security and of opportunity for all. Too many of us were blind to the evils which, thus loosed, created growing cancers within and among nations — political suspicions and hatreds; the race of armaments, first stealthy and then the subject of flagrant boasts; economic nationalism and its train of economic depression and misery; and finally the emergence from their dark places of the looters and thugs who found their opportunity in disorder and disaster. The shadow of a new war fell across the world. War began in 1931 when Japan invaded China.

From the time when the first signs of menace to the peace of the world appeared on the horizon, the Government of the United States strove increasingly to promote peace on the solid foundation of law, justice, non-intervention, non-aggression, and international collaboration. With growing insistence we advocated the principles of a broad and constructive world order in political, economic, social, moral, and intellectual relations among nations — principles which must constitute the foundation of any satisfactory future world order. We practiced these principles in our good-neighbor policy, which was applicable to every part of the earth and which we sought to apply not alone in the Western Hemisphere, but in the Pacific area, in Europe, and everywhere else as well.

When hostilities broke out and wars were declared, our Government made every honorable and feasible effort to prevent spread of the conflicts and to safeguard this country against being drawn into war. But danger increased all around us. Peaceful, unoffending countries, one after another, were brought under the heel of the invader, both in Europe and in Asia. Hitler and the Japanese war lords, by their acts and their official declarations, have made it plain that the purpose of the Japanese is to conquer and dominate virtually one-half of the world with one-half of its population, while Hitler's purpose is, first to conquer continental Europe, and then to seize the British Isles, and through control of the British fleet to dominate the seven seas.

Events have demonstrated beyond question that each of the Axis powers was bent on unlimited conquest. As time went on it became manifest that the United States and the whole Western Hemisphere were ultimate targets. Conclusive proof was given by the international desperadoes themselves through the publication on September 27, 1940 of the Tripartite Pact. By that treaty of alliance Germany, Japan, and Italy in effect agreed that, if any country not then at war with one of them placed obstacles in the way of the program of conquest of any of them, the three would unite in political, military, and economic action against that country. This provision was aimed directly at the United States. One of the highest official spokesmen of the Axis powers openly proclaimed that the objective of the three partners was a new world order to be achieved by force.

Finally a realization that these plans and purposes created a state of imminent and acute danger to all remaining peaceful countries, especially to those of the Western Hemisphere, forced us to face the all-important question as to when and where the peaceful nations, including ours, should begin to resist the movements of military aggression in order to make such resistance most effective.

It was in these circumstances that our Government felt the compelling importance of adopting the policy of aid to Great Britain and to other nations which resisted aggression, as set forth in the Lease-Lend Act, submitted to Congress in January 1941. It is scarcely necessary to say that all subsequent utterances and acts of the leaders of Germany, Japan, and Italy have fully confirmed the wisdom and timeliness of the policy of this Government in thus proceeding to defend the country before it should be too late.

In December 1941, acting in concert, moving in harmony with their world-wide objective, all three launched their assault against us, the spearhead of which was at Pearl Harbor, reasoning that to achieve victory they must conquer us, and to conquer us they must strike before we were prepared to resist successfully.

When they made this concerted attack against us, the war lords of Japan and Germany must have believed that at the root of our sincere and strong desire for peace lay a lack of will and of capacity to rise in unity of purpose and to pour all our strength and energy into the battle. They have since begun to learn better at Wake and at Midway; at Bataan and at Corregidor; in the Straits of Macassar and in the Coral Sea; from the sky over Tokyo itself; again at Midway; on and over every ocean of the world traversed by our air fleets and our naval and merchant vessels; on every battlefield of the world increasingly supplied with our war materials. They will have final and conclusive answer from our expanding armies, navies, and air forces, operating side by side with our valiant allies and backed by our nation-wide industrial power and the courage, the determination, and the ingenuity of our people.

That answer is being forged in the fighting spirit which now pervades the people of this country, in the will to victory of all the United Nations.

In this vast struggle, we, Americans, stand united with those who, like ourselves, are fighting for the preservation of their freedom; with those who are fighting to regain the freedom of which they have been brutally deprived; with those who are fighting for the opportunity to achieve freedom.

We have always believed — and we believe today — that all peoples, without distinction of race, color, or religion, who are prepared and willing to accept the responsibilities of liberty, are entitled to its enjoyment. We have always sought — and we seek today — to encourage and aid all who aspire to freedom to establish their right to it by preparing themselves to assume its obligations. We have striven to meet squarely our own responsibility in this respect — in Cuba, in the Philippines, and wherever else it has devolved upon us. It has been our purpose in the past — and will remain our purpose in the future — to use the full measure of our influence to support attainment of freedom by all peoples who, by their acts, show themselves worthy of it and ready for it.

We, who have received from the preceding generations the priceless fruits of the centuries-old struggle for liberty, freely accept today the sacrifices which may be needed to pass on to our children an even greater heritage.

Our enemies confront us with armed might in every part of the globe. We cannot win this war by standing at our borders and limiting ourselves to beating off attacks. Air, submarine, and other forms of assault can be effectively defeated only if those attacked seek out and destroy the sources of attack. We shall send all the aid that we can to our gallant allies. And we shall seek out our enemies and attack them at any and every point of the globe at which the destruction of the Axis forces can be accomplished most effectively, most speedily, and most certainly.

We know the magnitude of the task before us. We know that its accomplishment will exact unlimited effort and unfaltering courage. However long the road we shall press on to the final victory.

Temporary reverses must not and will not be the occasion for weakness and discouragement. On the contrary they are the signal for all true soldiers and patriots to strike back all the harder, with that superb resolution which never yields to force or threat of force.

Fighting as we are in self-defense, in self-preservation, we must make certain the defeat and destruction of the world-invading forces of Hitler and the Japanese war lords. To do this our people and the peoples of every one of the twenty-eight United Nations must make up their minds to sacrifice time and substance and life itself to an extent unprecedented in past history.

International desperadoes like individual bandits will not abandon outlawry voluntarily. They will only be stopped by force.

III

With victory achieved our first concern must be for those whose sufferings have been almost beyond human endurance. When the armies of our enemies are beaten, the people of many countries will be starving and without means of procuring food; homeless and without means of building shelter; their fields scorched; their cattle slaughtered; their tools gone; their factories and mines destroyed; their roads and transport wrecked. Unknown millions will be far from their homes — prisoners of war, inmates of concentration camps, forced laborers in alien lands, refugees from battle, from cruelty, from starvation. Disease and danger of disease will lurk everywhere. In some countries confusion and chaos will follow the cessation of hostilities. Victory must be followed by swift and effective action to meet these pressing human needs.

At the same time all countries — those which will need relief and those more fortunate — will be faced with the immediate problems of transition from war to peace. War production must be transformed into production for the peacetime needs of mankind. In some countries the physical ravages of war must be repaired. In others, agriculture must be re-established. In all countries returning soldiers must find places in the work of peace. There will be enormous deficiencies of many kinds of goods. All countries, including ours, will need an immense volume of production. There will, therefore, exist vast opportunities for useful employment. The termination of the war effort will release, for use in peaceful pursuits, stirring enthusiasms, the aspirations and energies of youth, technical experience, and — in many industries — ample plants and abundance of tools. The compelling demands of war are revealing how great a supply of goods can be produced for national defense. The needs of peace should be no less compelling, though some of the means of meeting them must be different. Toward meeting these needs each and every nation should intensively direct its efforts to the creation of an abundance for peacetime life. This can only be achieved by a combination of the efforts of individuals, the efforts of groups, and the efforts of nations. Governments can and must help to focus the energies by encouraging, coordinating, and aiding the efforts of individuals and groups.

During this period of transition the United Nations must continue to act in the spirit of cooperation which now underlies their war effort — to supplement and make more effective the action of countries individually in re-establishing public order, in providing swift relief, in meeting the manifold problems of readjustment.

Beyond these there will lie before all countries the great constructive task of building human freedom and Christian morality on firmer and broader foundations than ever before. This task, too, will of necessity call for both national and international action.

Within each nation liberty under law is an essential requirement of progress. The spirit of liberty, when deeply imbedded in the minds and hearts of the people, is the most powerful remedy for racial animosities, religious intolerance, ignorance, and all the other evils which prevent men from uniting in a brotherhood of truly civilized existence. It inspires men to acquisition of knowledge and understanding. It is the only real foundation of political and social stability.

Liberty is more than a matter of political rights, indispensable as those rights are. In our own country we have learned from bitter experience that to be truly free, men must have, as well, economic freedom and economic security — the assurance for all alike of an opportunity to work as free men in the company of free men; to obtain through work the material and spiritual means of life; to advance through the exercise of ability, initiative, and enterprise; to make provision against the hazards of human existence. We know that this is true of mankind everywhere. We know that in all countries there has been — and there will be increasingly in the future — demand for a forward movement of social justice. Each of us must be resolved that, once the war is won, this demand shall be met as speedily and as fully as possible.

All these advances — in political freedom, in economic betterment, in social justice, in spiritual values — can be achieved by each nation primarily through its own work and effort, mainly through its own wise policies and actions. They can be made only where there is acceptance and cultivation of the concepts and the spirit of human rights and human freedom. It is impossible for any nation or group of nations to prescribe the methods or provide the means by which any other nation can accomplish or maintain its own political and economic independence, be strong, prosper, and attain high spiritual goals. It is possible, however, for all nations to give and to receive help.

That which nations can and must do toward helping one another is to take, by cooperative action, steps for the elimination of impediments and obstructions which prevent the full use by each — for the welfare of its people — of the energy and resources which are at its command. And the nations can and must, again by cooperative action under common agreement, create such facilities as will enable each to increase the effectiveness of its own national efforts.

Such cooperative action is already under way. Twenty-eight United Nations have proclaimed their adherence to a program of principles and purposes by which mankind may advance toward higher standards of national and international conduct. That program is embodied in the

Declaration made on August 14, 1941, by President Roosevelt and Prime Minister Churchill, now known as the Atlantic Charter.[1]

The pledge of the Atlantic Charter is of a system which will give every nation, large or small, a greater assurance of stable peace, greater opportunity for the realization of its aspirations to freedom, and greater facilities for material advancement. But that pledge implies an obligation for each nation to demonstrate its capacity for stable and progressive government, to fulfill scrupulously its established duties to other nations, to settle its international differences and disputes by none but peaceful methods, and to make its full contribution to the maintenance of enduring peace.

IV

For decades all nations have lived in the shadow of threatened coercion or war. This has imposed heavy burdens of armament, which in the cases of many nations has absorbed so large a part of their production effort as to leave the remainder of their resources inadequate for maintaining, let alone improving, the economic, social, and cultural standards of their people. Closely related to this has been a burden less obvious but of immense weight — the inevitable limitation that fear of war imposes on productive activity. Many men, groups of men, and even nations have dared not plan, create, or increase the means of production, fearing lest war come and their efforts thus be rendered vain.

No nation can make satisfactory progress while its citizens are in the grip of constant fear of external attack or interference. It is plain that some international agency must be created which can — by force, if necessary — keep the peace among nations in the future. There must be international cooperative action to set up the mechanisms which can thus insure peace. This must include eventual adjustment of national armaments in such a manner that the rule of law cannot be successfully challenged and that the burden of armaments may be reduced to a minimum.

In the creation of such mechanisms there would be a practical and purposeful application of sovereign powers through measures of international cooperation for purposes of safeguarding the peace. Participation by all nations in such measures would be for each its contribution toward its own future security and safety from outside attack.

Settlement of disputes by peaceful means, and indeed all processes of international cooperation, presuppose respect for law and obligations. It is plain that one of the institutions which must be established and be

[1] *Documents on American Foreign Relations, IV, 1941–42*, p. 591 (hereinafter series cited as *Documents*, etc.).

given vitality is an international court of justice. It is equally clear that, in the process of re-establishing international order, the United Nations must exercise surveillance over aggressor nations until such time as the latter demonstrate their willingness and ability to live at peace with other nations. How long such surveillance will need to continue must depend upon the rapidity with which the peoples of Germany, Japan, Italy, and their satellites give convincing proof that they have repudiated and abandoned the monstrous philosophy of superior race and conquest by force and have embraced loyally the basic principles of peaceful processes. During the formative period of the world organization, interruption by these aggressors must be rendered impossible.

One of the greatest of all obstacles which in the past have impeded human progress and afforded breeding grounds for dictators has been extreme nationalism. All will agree that nationalism and its spirit are essential to the healthy and normal political and economic life of a people, but when policies of nationalism — political, economic, social, and moral — are carried to such extremes as to exclude and prevent necessary policies of international cooperation, they become dangerous and deadly. Nationalism, run riot between the last war and this war, defeated all attempts to carry out indispensable measures of international economic and political action, encouraged and facilitated the rise of dictators, and drove the world straight toward the present war.

During this period narrow and short-sighted nationalism found its most virulent expression in the economic field. It prevented goods and services from flowing in volume at all adequate from nation to nation and thus severely hampered the work of production, distribution, and consumption and greatly retarded efforts for social betterment.

No nation can make satisfactory progress when it is deprived, by its own action or by the action of others, of the immeasurable benefits of international exchange of goods and services. The Atlantic Charter declares the right of all nations to "access, on equal terms, to the trade and to the raw materials of the world which are needed for their economic prosperity." This is essential if the legitimate and growing demand for the greatest practicable measure of stable employment is to be met, accompanied by rising standards of living. If the actual and potential losses resulting from limitations on economic activity are to be eliminated, a system must be provided by which this can be assured.

In order to accomplish this, and to establish among the nations a circle of mutual benefit, excessive trade barriers of the many different kinds must be reduced, and practices which impose injuries on others and divert trade from its natural economic course must be avoided. Equally plain is the need for making national currencies once more freely exchangeable for each other at stable rates of exchange; for a system of financial relations so devised that materials can be produced and ways may be found of moving them where there are markets created by human need; for machinery through which capital may — for the development of the world's resources and for the stabilization of economic activity — move on equitable terms from financially stronger to financially weaker countries. There may be need for some special trade arrangement and for international agreements to handle difficult surplus problems and to meet situations in special areas.

These are only some of the things that nations can attempt to do as continuous discussion and experience instruct the judgment. There are bound to be many others. But the new policies should always be guided by cautious and sound judgment lest we make new mistakes in place of old ones and create new conflicts.

Building for the future in the economic sphere thus means that each nation must give substance and reality to programs of social and economic progress by augmenting production and using the greater output for the increase of general welfare; but not permitting it to be diverted or checked by special interests, private or public. It also means that each nation must play its full part in a system of world relations designed to facilitate the production and movement of goods in response to human needs.

With peace among nations reasonably assured, with political stability established, with economic shackles removed, a vast fund of resources will be released in each nation to meet the needs of progress, to make possible for all of its citizens an advancement toward higher living standards, to invigorate the constructive forces of initiative and enterprise. The nations of the world will then be able to go forward in the manner of their own choosing in all avenues of human betterment more completely than they ever have been able to do in the past. They will do so through their own efforts and with complete self-respect. Continuous self-development of nations and individuals in a framework of effective cooperation with others is the sound and logical road to the higher standards of life which we all crave and seek.

No nation will find this easy. Neither victory nor any form of postwar settlement will of itself create a millennium. Rather we shall be offered an opportunity to eliminate vast obstacles and wastes, to make available additional means of advancing national and international standards, to create new facilities whereby the natural resources of the earth and the products of human hands and brains can be more effectively utilized for the promotion of human welfare.

To make full use of this opportunity, we must be resolved not alone to proclaim the blessings and benefits which we all alike desire for humanity but to find the mechanisms by which they may be most fully and most speedily attained and be most effectively safeguarded.

The manifold tasks that lie ahead will not be accomplished overnight. There will be need for plans, developed with careful consideration and carried forward boldly and vigorously. The vision, the resolution, and the skill with which the conditions of peace will be established and developed after the war will be as much a measure of man's capacity for freedom and progress as the fervor and determination which men show in winning the victory.

Without impediment to the fullest prosecution of the war — indeed for its most effective prosecution — the United Nations should from time to time, as they did in adopting the Atlantic Charter, formulate and proclaim their common views regarding fundamental policies which will chart for mankind a wise course based on enduring spiritual values. In support of such policies an informed public opinion must be developed. This is a task of intensive study, hard thinking, broad vision, and leadership — not for governments alone, but for parents, and teachers, and clergymen, and all those, within each nation, who provide spiritual, moral, and intellectual guidance. Never did so great and so compelling a duty in this respect devolve upon those who are in positions of responsibility, public and private.

V

For the immediate present the all-important issue is that of winning the war — winning it as soon as possible and winning it decisively. Into that we must put our utmost effort — now and every day until victory is won.

A bitter armed attack on human freedom has aroused mankind to new heights of courage, determination, and moral strength. It has evoked a spirit of work, sacrifice, and cooperative effort. With that strength and with that spirit we shall win.

(2) Radio Address by the President (Roosevelt) to the International Student Assembly, September 3, 1942 [1]

[Excerpt]

．　．　．　．　．　．

We exult in the thought that it is the young, free men and women of the United Nations and not the wound-up robots of the slave states who will mold the shape of the new world.

The delegates to this International Student Assembly represent the 29 United Nations. They also represent, in spirit at least, the younger

---

[1] Session held at Washington, D.C., September 2–5, 1942. Department of State, *Bulletin*, VII, p. 729.

generation of many other nations who, though they are not now actively at war on our side, are with us heart and soul in aspiration for a secure and peaceful world.

Before the first World War very few people in any country believed that youth had the right to speak for itself as a group or to participate in councils of state.

We have learned much since then. We know that wisdom does not come necessarily with years, that old men may be foolish and young men may be wise. But in every war it is the younger generation which bears the burden of combat and inherits all the ills that war leaves in its wake.

In the economic crises that followed the false prosperity after the first World War, many young men and women suffered even more than did their elders. For they were denied the primary opportunities for education, for training, for work, or even for food enough to build up healthy bodies. As a result, they were tempted to seek some simple remedy not only for their own individual problems but for all the problems that beset the world. Some listened to alien, siren voices which offered glib answers to all the questions. "Democracy is dead," said these voices. "Follow us, and we will teach you efficiency. We will lead you to world conquest. We will give you power over inferior races. And all that we ask you to give in return is your freedom."

Other young people in the democracies listened to gospels of despair. They took refuge in cynicism and bitterness.

However, the day finally came when all theory had to give way to fact — the terrible, tangible fact of dive bombers, panzer divisions, the actual threat to the security of every home and every family in every free country in the world. And when that fact became clear to our youth they answered the call to arms — many millions of them; and today they are determined to fight until the forces of aggression have been utterly destroyed.

What I am saying here in Washington is being heard by several million American soldiers, sailors, and marines, not only within the continental limits of the United States but in far-distant points: in Central and South America, in the islands of the Atlantic, in Britain and Ireland, on the coasts of Africa, in Egypt, in Iraq and Iran, in Russia, in India, in China, in Australia, in New Zealand, in many islands of the Pacific, and on all the seas of the world. There — in all those places — are our fighting men.

And to them I should like to deliver a special message, from their Commander-in-Chief and from the very hearts of their countrymen:

You young Americans today are conducting yourselves in a manner that is worthy of the highest, proudest traditions of our Nation.

No pilgrims who landed on the uncharted New England coast, no pioneers who forced their way through the trackless wilderness, showed greater fortitude, greater determination than you are showing now.

Neither your own fathers, in 1918, nor your fathers' fathers, in 1863 or 1776, fought with greater gallantry or more selfless devotion to duty and country than you are now displaying on battlefields far from home.

And what is more, you know why you are fighting. You know that the road which has led you to the Solomon Islands or to the Red Sea or to the coast of France is in fact an extension of Main Street, and that when you fight, anywhere along that road, you are fighting in the defense of your own homes, your own free schools, your own churches, your own ideals.

We here at home are supremely conscious of our obligations to you, now and in the future. We will not let you down.

We know that in the minds of many of you are thoughts of interrupted education, interrupted careers, delayed opportunities for getting a job. The solution of such problems cannot be left, as it was last time, to mere chance. This Government has accepted the responsibility for seeing to it that, wherever possible, work has been provided for those who were willing and able but who could not find work. That responsibility will continue after the war. And when you come home we do not propose to involve you, as last time, in a domestic economic mess of our own making.

You are doing first things first — fighting to win this war. For you know that should this war be lost all our plans for the peace to follow would be meaningless.

Victory is essential; but victory is not enough for you — or for us. We must be sure that when you have won victory you will not have to tell your children that you fought in vain — that you were betrayed. We must be sure that in your homes there will not be want, that in your schools only the living truth will be taught, that in your churches there may be preached without fear a faith in which men may deeply believe.

The better world for which you fight — and for which some of you give your lives — will not come merely because we shall have won the war. It will not come merely because we wish very hard that it would come. It will be made possible only by bold vision, intelligent planning, and hard work. It cannot be brought about overnight but only by years of effort and perseverance and unfaltering faith.

You young soldiers and sailors, farmers and factory workers, artists and scholars, who are fighting our way to victory now, all of you will have to take your part in shaping that world. You will earn it by what you do now; but you will not attain it if you leave the job for others to do alone. When you lay aside your gun at the end of the war, you cannot at the same time lay aside your duty to the future.

What I have said to our American soldiers and sailors applies to all the young men and women of the United Nations who are facing our common enemies. There is a complete unanimity of spirit among all the youth of all kinds and kindreds who fight to preserve or to regain their freedom.

In Norway and Holland, Belgium and France, Czechoslovakia and Poland, Serbia and Greece there is a fighting spirit that defies the harsh oppression, the barbarous cruelty and terrorism of the Nazis. Although disarmed, the unconquerable people still strike at their oppressors. Although forbidden to know the truth, they listen at the risk of their lives to radio broadcasts from afar; and, by word of mouth and by secret newspaper passed from one patriot to another, they still spread the truth. When the time comes for these peoples to rise, Hitler's "new order" will be destroyed by the hands of its own victims.

Today the embattled youth of Russia and China are realizing a new individual dignity, casting off the last links of the ancient chains of imperial despotism which had bound them so long.

This is a development of historic importance. It means that the old term "Western Civilization" no longer applies. World events and the common needs of all humanity are joining the culture of Asia with the culture of Europe and of the Americas to form for the first time a real world civilization.

In the concept of the Four Freedoms, in the basic principles of the Atlantic Charter, we have set for ourselves high goals, unlimited objectives.

These concepts and these principles are designed to form a world in which men, women, and children can live in freedom and in equity and, above all, without fear of the horrors of war. For no soldiers or sailors in any of our forces today would so willingly endure the rigors of battle if they thought that in another 20 years their own sons would be fighting still another war on distant deserts or seas or in faraway jungles or skies.

We have profited by our past mistakes. This time we shall know how to make full use of victory. This time the achievements of our fighting forces will not be thrown away by political cynicism and timidity and incompetence.

There is still a handful of men and women in the United States and elsewhere who mock and sneer at the Four Freedoms and the Atlantic Charter. They are few in number, but some of them have the financial power to give our enemies the false impression that they have a large following among our citizenry. They play petty politics in a world crisis. They fiddle with many sour notes while civilization burns. These puny prophets decry our determination to implement our high concepts and sound principles. And the words of these little men of little faith are quoted with gleeful approval by the press and radio of our enemies.

We are deeply aware that we cannot achieve our goals easily. We cannot attain the fullness of all our ideals overnight. We know that this is to be a long and hard and bitter fight — and that there will still be an enormous job for us to do long after the last German, Japanese, and Italian bombing planes have been shot to earth.

But we do believe that with divine guidance we can make — in this dark world of today and in the new post-war world — a steady progress toward the highest goals that men have ever imagined.

We of the United Nations have the technical means, the physical resources, and, most of all, the adventurous courage and the vision and the will that are needed to build and sustain the kind of world order which alone can justify the tremendous sacrifices now being made by our youth.

But we must keep at it; we must never relax, never falter, never fear; and we must keep at it together.

We must maintain the offensive against evil in all its forms. We must work and we must fight to insure that our children shall have and shall enjoy in peace their inalienable rights to freedom of speech, freedom of religion, freedom from want, freedom from fear.

Only on those bold terms can this total war result in total victory.

(3) *Address by the Acting Secretary of State (Welles) at the World Trade Dinner of the Twenty-ninth National Foreign Trade Convention, Boston, Massachusetts, October 8, 1942* [1]

[Excerpt]

Just a year has passed since I last had the privilege of addressing the National Foreign Trade Convention.

During the short space of these 12 months the people of the United States have passed through some of the most portentous events they have known in their entire history. They have experienced the most far-reaching changes in their national life which they have yet undergone. They are confronting the gravest dangers they have ever yet had to face. They are now engaged in the greatest war that mankind has suffered.

And yet as we look back over the record of these past 12 months, I think we may well feel proud that we are American citizens.

. . . .

Democracies may take long to prepare for war or to engage in war, but, when the free men and women of a democracy such as ours are at war to preserve their liberty and their faith, they will never fail to excel

[1] Broadcast over the Blue Network; *ibid.*, p. 808.

the regimented slaves of the dictators. We are fighting for our own independence and for the right to live in a decent and a peaceful world. The hosts of Hitler, of the Japanese war lords, and of the Italian Fascist racketeers are being slaughtered because of the insane delusion of their masters that they could make the resources of the world their own individual loot.

Of the outcome of this gigantic contest I have not the shadow of a doubt.

For I am not one of those few who believe that "we are losing this war." I not only believe that we are going to win this war, but I know that however long the struggle may be, however mountainous the obstacles that must yet be overcome, the American people will never lay down their arms until the final and complete victory is won by the United Nations.

In the grim struggle which lies before us we are fighting side by side with the other partners of the United Nations.

Never in the long centuries of modern history have men and women fought more gloriously than have the armies of the Soviet Union. Their epic and successful resistance to the onslaughts of Hitler's forces a year ago not only gave the lie to Hitler's boasts that he could crush the Russian Army but constituted in itself the major triumph of the United Nations in the war until that time. And once more through the long summer of 1942 the Soviet heroes have held firm.

We don't hear Hitler tell the German people this year that the Soviet Union will quickly crumble before his offensive. He doesn't dare. For he knows that the German people have learned to their bitter cost that Hitler's promises in this case, as they will soon learn they are in every case, are but the empty lies of a rapidly deflating demagogue.

The United States and its associates among the United Nations mus render the utmost measure of assistance to the Soviet Union. Whether that assistance be through the furnishing of arms, equipment, or supplies, or whether that assistance be by means of the diversion of German armies forced upon Hitler through the creation of a new theater of operations, the fullest measure of every means of help will be given. The surest way to insure the defeat of Hitler is to give this help and to give it unstintingly at the earliest possible moment.

The amazing efforts of the British air force in its all-out attacks upon Germany have long since shown the German people how much value they can attach to the assurances given them by the Nazi leaders that Germany would never be bombed. The havoc and devastation created by these British flyers, now joined by our own air forces, are crippling war plants, munitions factories, shipyards, and railways and gravely impairing the German effort to maintain the earlier levels of war production.

Nor can we here in the United States ever fail to remember with profound gratitude and renewed encouragement that 11 of the other republics of the Americas are joined with us, side by side, in the war and that 7 other republics have severed all relations with the Axis and are rendering their neighbors who are at war every form of cooperation and assistance. It is true that the remaining 2 [1] republics of the 21 have still refrained from carrying out the unanimous recommendations of the Inter-American Conference of Rio de Janeiro, in which they themselves joined, that all of the Americas sever all relations with the Axis, and are still permitting their territory to be utilized by the officials and the subversive agents of the Axis as a base for hostile activities against their neighbors. As a result of the reports on Allied ship movements sent by these agents, Brazilian, Cuban, Mexican, Colombian, Dominican, Uruguayan, Argentine, Chilean, Panamanian, and United States ships have been sunk without warning while plying between the American Republics, and as a result many nationals of these countries have lost their lives within the waters of the Western Hemisphere. But I cannot believe that these 2 republics will continue long to permit their brothers and neighbors of the Americas, engaged as they are in a life-and-death struggle to preserve the liberties and the integrity of the New World, to be stabbed in the back by Axis emissaries operating in the territory and under the free institutions of these 2 republics of the Western Hemisphere.[2]

Not until freedom was in mortal danger throughout the earth did liberty-loving nations fully learn the lesson of collaboration. Had that lesson been learned earlier, had the United Nations found their unity in anticipation of attack rather than under the urgent pressure of attack, the maximum effectiveness of our war effort would have been reached far more speedily. It is now evident that in the cooperation and unity of the United Nations lies our ultimate victory. I believe that it is equally true that in the continuance and timeliness of that cooperation also lies our hope for an honest, a workable, and a lasting peace.

The unity which the free peoples have achieved to win their war must continue on to win their peace. For since this is in truth a people's war it must be followed by a people's peace. The translation into terms of reality of the promise of the great freedoms for all people everywhere is the final objective. We must be beforehand in charting the course toward that objective. The clearer we can make the outlines of the peace, the firmer will be our determination to attain it, the stronger our will to win the war.

One hears it said that no thought should be given to the problems of

---

[1] Argentina and Chile. Chile later severed diplomatic relations with the principal Axis powers on January 20, 1943 (Department of State, *Bulletin*, VIII, p. 83).

[2] See p. 422 for political repercussions from this statement.

the peace, nor to the problems of the transitional period between war and established peace, until after the war has been won.

The shallowness of such thinking, whether sincere or sinister, is apparent.

In many cases it is due, I think, to what Plato terms "double ignorance": when a man is ignorant that he is ignorant.

It does not detract from our war effort, nor from the single-minded drive of the Nation towards the ultimate victory, that our people should be thinking of, and planning for, the kind of world of the future in which peace can be maintained and in which men and women can live out their lives in security and free from fear.

Such efforts, in my judgment, contribute directly to the drive towards victory.

The setting up now of efficient machinery to deal with such problems as relief and rehabilitation, for example, which will accompany victory, cannot fail to strengthen the resolve of all liberty-loving peoples, including those in areas now occupied by the enemy, to bring the conflict to the speediest possible conclusion; it cannot fail to make them realize that the sort of world for which we are striving is worth the sacrifices of war, is worth the cost of victory.

It is clear to all of us, I think, that the United Nations must maintain their unity beyond the immediate task of prosecuting the people's war in order to prepare for and insure to the people their peace.

Point four of the Atlantic Charter promises "to further the enjoyment by all States, great or small, victor or vanquished, of access, on equal terms, to the trade and to the raw materials of the world which are needed for their economic prosperity."

This promise, and the balance of the Charter, the United Nations adopted as their own by their common declaration of last January 1.[1]

How do they propose to make it real?

Some things at least are clear.

Access to raw materials does not mean and cannot mean that every nation, or any nation, can have the source of all of them within its borders. That is not the way the world was put together. Coal and iron in combination are found in few locations. Much of the nickel of the world is in one great Canadian deposit. Neither coffee nor cork will grow in the United States. No nation can be self-sufficient by changes in its boundaries, and those who try by force to do so, as the Axis leaders have tried, bring on themselves inevitably only their own destruction. The path to plentiful supplies does not lie through physical control of the sources of supply.

The problem of raw materials is not exclusively, or even primarily, a problem of colonial or undeveloped areas. The great mineral deposits

[1] For text see *Documents, IV, 1941–42,* p. 203.

exist chiefly in countries that are already self-governing, such as the United States, the Soviet Union, Canada, Germany, Sweden, South Africa, Mexico, Brazil. Access to raw materials does not mean possession of a colony. It means effective power to buy in the world's markets.

The legal right to export raw materials has seldom been restricted by producing countries. True, the United States and other countries sometimes have been guilty of forbidding the export of certain things needed for production elsewhere, for fear that others might obtain the means to trespass on their markets. But those cases were rare. Countries producing raw materials desired normally to sell their surplus, and the problem usually was to find a profitable market. The right to buy was real and satisfied peace-loving peoples. Belgium, Denmark, Sweden, Switzerland, Czechoslovakia, Norway, not to speak of the United States and England, bought in the years between the wars great quantities of foreign raw materials, and none of them claimed that they needed greater resources to live. The countries that complained and shrieked that they must have colonies or die have shown now by their conduct that what they wanted was not prosperity and peace but the materials for making war.

For war, indeed, one cannot count on overseas supplies, and an aggressor must first corner all he can of coal and iron and oil and copper, in the ground or out of it.

But the Atlantic Charter does not propose to aid aggression. It proposes, on the contrary, to make sure that aggression does not happen, and to that end the United Nations will create the necessary instruments — and this time they will be effective instruments and must be firmly used — to make it certain that any power that again threatens to enslave its neighbors is denied the means to do so. The materials of war must be denied to any future Hitler.

The access to raw materials of which the Charter speaks is access for the purposes of peace. For that purpose it matters little in whose territory particular resources are found. Access means the right to buy in peaceful trade, and it exists whenever that right is effective and secure.

What forces then have interfered with that right in the past or may interfere with it in the future?

Most raw materials are not subject to monopolistic practices because producers are too numerous; but there have been charges in the past, and there are charges now, that in certain cases the producers of some commodities, with the support of the governments to which they owed allegiance, have managed, by what our Sherman Law calls combinations in restraint of trade, to reduce supplies and enhance prices beyond reasonable levels or to discriminate among their customers. A world devoted to increased production and fair and fruitful exchange of all kinds of useful goods cannot tolerate such practices.

But monopoly in the field of raw materials is not the major problem. Most materials are plentiful in peace, and their producers want to sell them to any customer who has the means to buy. The real problem of consumers has always been the means of payment. In the world that emerges from the war that problem will be very serious indeed.

When this war ends much of the world will be impoverished beyond anything known in modern times.

Relief cannot go on forever, and the day must come as soon as possible when the devastated areas again are self-supporting. That will require enormous shipments from abroad, both of capital goods and of the raw materials of industry. For these early reconstruction shipments no immediate means of payment will be visible. That means large financing, much of it long-term. The United Nations must arrange that too. But finally comes payment, both of whatever interest burden the loans carry and for the current purchases of raw materials and other imports. I need not tell this audience that international payments, on that scale, can be made only in goods and services. There is no other way. Access to raw materials comes in the end to access to the great buying markets of the world. Those who expect to export must take the world's goods and services in payment.. I hope that the United States is ready, now, to act upon that lesson.

The United Nations have agreed to act upon it, and in mutual-aid agreements with a growing number of them we and they have promised to direct our common efforts to increased production, employment, and the exchange and consumption of all kinds of useful goods. We and they have promised further to attack the problem by removing discriminations in the treatment of international trade and by reducing unwarranted and artificial tariff barriers. The future prosperity and peace of the world, and of the United States, depend vitally on the good faith and the thoroughness with which we and they together carry out those promises.

During the war as fully as we can, and more fully after we have destroyed the madmen who seek to rule the world by force and terror, we of the United Nations will go forward in a loyal partnership to carry out the pledges we have made to each other and the world.

There is no limit, then, to the material prosperity which is within the reach of the United States, and of mankind. The great thing that has happened in our time is that mankind at long last has taught itself enough of the means and techniques of production, of transport, and of scientific agriculture so that it is technically possible to produce and to distribute on this planet the basic physical necessities of health and decent living for all of the world's people. What remains — and it is a great and formidable task — is so to remake our relations with each other, in loyal and cooperative effort, that the great productive forces which are within our sight may function freely for the benefit of all. It is within our power to make a mighty start upon that road; we have laid down the principles of action; it is for the people of the United States to determine whether their Government is to be authorized to carry on.

For 12 tragic years after the close of the last World War the United States withdrew from almost every form of constructive cooperation with the other nations of the earth.

We are reaping the bitter cost of that isolation.

For I am persuaded that, after the victory is won, so long as the power and influence of the United States are felt in the councils of the world, so long as our corporation is effectively offered, so long can one hope that peace can and will be maintained.

The blessings we have inherited from our forefathers do not constitute an inheritance that we may only passively enjoy. They can only be preserved by sacrifice, by courage, by resolution, and by vision.

If the American people prove themselves worthy of their ancestors, if they still possess their forefathers' dauntless courage and their ability to meet new conditions with wisdom and determination, the future of this Nation will rest secure and our children and our children's children will be able to live out their lives in safety and in peace.

(4) *Radio Address by the President (Roosevelt), October 12, 1942* [1]

[Excerpt]

.   .   .   .   .   .

We celebrate today the exploit of a bold and adventurous Italian — Christopher Columbus — who with the aid of Spain opened up a new world where freedom and tolerance and respect for human rights and dignity provided an asylum for the oppressed of the old world.

Today, the sons of the new world are fighting in lands far distant from their own America. They are fighting to save for all mankind, including ourselves, the principles which have flourished in this new world of freedom.

We are mindful of the countless millions of people whose future liberty and whose very lives depend upon permanent victory for the United Nations.

There are a few people in this country who, when the collapse of the Axis begins, will tell our people that we are safe once more; that we can tell the rest of the world to "stew in its own juice"; that never again will we help to pull "the other fellow's chestnuts from the fire"; that the

---

[1] From the Office of the Secretary to the President. The address was delivered following a trip of inspection of camps, training stations and war factories. It primarily dealt with matters related to the conduct of the war.

future of civilization can jolly well take care of itself insofar as we are concerned.

But it is useless to win battles if the cause for which we fought these battles is lost. It is useless to win a war unless it stays won.

We, therefore, fight for the restoration and perpetuation of faith and hope throughout the world.

The objective of today is clear and realistic. It is to destroy completely the military power of Germany, Italy and Japan to such good purpose that their threat against us and all the other United Nations cannot be revived a generation hence.

We are united in seeking the kind of victory that will guarantee that our grandchildren can grow and, under God, may live their lives, free from the constant threat of invasion, destruction, slavery and violent death.

(5) *The Realist Base of American Foreign Policy. Address by Assistant Secretary of State Berle at the Fifth Annual Meeting of the Alabama State Chamber of Commerce, Birmingham, October 15, 1942* [1]

In war, as in peace, sound foreign policy must be based on the solidest political and economic facts. Unless this is true, it is difficult to be victorious in war and impossible to organize peace after victory. The salient points are well known; but they bear repeating.

The United States is productive, strong, and independent and proposes to stay so. She has found that the best means of remaining productive, strong, and independent is to maintain disinterested friendship with all other nations; and that this policy works best when all other nations are themselves productive, independent, and as strong as their circumstances permit. We have no wish to acquire the territory or dominate the affairs of other nations, and no peace-loving nation need fear us. Equally, we propose to handle our affairs so that we need fear nobody.

Every once in so often certain other nations become possessed of a wild desire to conquer as much of the globe as they can. The present war comes directly out of such a plan. The Nazi-Japanese combination intended to do just that. The United States and our neighbor nations of the New World were a direct target in this wild scheme. We have had to join with other law-abiding nations to defend ourselves. We propose to finish the job. The present policy of this Government is to make war — war to the victorious end. New methods are needed, and new factors must be considered.

As the world has grown smaller — and you can go around the world today without great difficulty in 10 days — schemes of conquest are no

[1] Department of State, *Bulletin*, VII, p. 831.

longer certain to be checked by the Atlantic and the Pacific Oceans. These oceans, now, can be crossed quite easily. Today, an occasional air raid probably would not seriously threaten our existence. But tomorrow — that is another story. No student of aviation fails to point out that we are only beginning to learn what air power can do. On the drafting boards of the aviation designers there are already plans which make present air warfare and air transport look as obsolete as a sailing ship looks alongside an ocean liner.

Both in this war and after it our foreign policy must take account of that fact. It changes our whole point of view. In the last war, and in the present war, the German explosion of conquest was met by barriers: the British and French land armies and the sea, held by the British and American Navies. These barriers borrowed time for us: time to produce munitions, to organize armies and air force, and to meet our better-prepared enemies on even terms. But the future does not offer to lend us time. It puts us in a permanent front line. If you imagine two or three hundred Pearl Harbors occurring all over the United States, you will have a rough picture of what the next war might look like — if we let a "next war" start. This is a new factor, and we have to take account of it also, and so use victory that a new war cannot start.

In our great international crises, certain nations habitually wind up on the same side as the United States.

First in our thinking are the unity and coherence of the American family of nations. This hemisphere, following a great ideal, has steadily drawn together in friendship at a time when other continents were breaking apart into groups of enemies. How strong and deep this habitual friendship can be is notably illustrated by the great part which Brazil is playing in the present conflict.

And, during a century and a quarter, though Britain has been a great maritime power, a great competitor, and our nearest overseas neighbor among the great powers, we have lived at peace with Britain and have twice been her ally. No dispute has arisen which could not be solved by reason and common sense. I think our relationship with Britain rests on something more solid than cousinly sentiment. Great Britain, in the last analysis, has found that a strong United States is a great buttress of a world in which Britain can live. We, on our side, have found that a strong and serene British Commonwealth of Nations is a great guaranty of the kind of world in which we want to live. Year after year we have come to work together in all essential matters. Neither of us fears the other; neither of us has sacrificed independence. We do not even forego our right to puff, grunt, complain about, and argue with each other. In all crises we necessarily and instinctively hang together, and both of us have been safer and better off on that account.

Another great power which has habitually joined with us is Russia, though few Americans have realized that fact until lately. When the country was young, the mere existence of Russia prevented Napoleon from becoming a world conqueror; and this fact made us safe. Later, and in the difficult days of our Civil War, Russia stood by the United States as a great counterweight against interference in this hemisphere by any European power. In the first World War, at the sacrifice of her own armies, Russia twice carried out a general military push which enabled the Western nations to draw breath and equip themselves for final triumph. Today, a defense of unparalleled bravery, symbolized by the deathless name of Stalingrad, has probably proved the turning-point in the Nazi drive for world power.

Since the appearance of the Far East in Western affairs, we have had an historic friendship for China and she for us. The cornerstone of any American policy in the Far East must be close working-relations with the Chinese nation — a very great nation, devoted to a world at peace. The struggle carried on by Generalissimo Chiang Kai-shek and the Chinese people has made it possible for this country to meet a Japanese attack, timed to coincide with the Nazi attack; and China saved us in the East as Russia and Britain have saved us in the West.

You may say that these countries have only acted in their own interest and are defending themselves. That is true. We have done the same. The point is that their own interests and their own self-defense have regularly proved of vital importance to us in maintaining our national interest and our self-defense — not once but over and over again in our history.

Out of these relationships has now been forged the greatest union history has ever seen: the United Nations.

The greatest tribute to the strength of the United Nations recently has been the violent attempt of the Axis to break it up. You have heard Axis propaganda attempt to make Russia believe that Britain and the United States would let her down. At the same time German lies were spread that Russia would betray her allies. Meanwhile the poison squad was busily endeavoring to sow dissension between Britain and the United States. Most of this propaganda has missed its mark; its real importance is to show the Nazi fear of these great, friendly nations when they unite.

They have united, in their common interest, to an amazing degree. I want to trace some of the outlines of their united effort.

Modern war is a continuous process. It involves organizing and maintaining a continuous belt line from the farms and the munitions factories to the fighting fronts. All of this huge belt line has to work all the time and work in gear. If any part of it breaks down, all the fighting fronts are endangered.

For that reason the United Nations have already forged a huge international economic system. That system exists now and is working. This war runs through all the continents and includes fronts in the Arctic Aleutians and the African tropics. It ranges from the Solomon Islands to the Russian steppes and is fought in the Egyptian desert and in the Channel ports. When supply has to flow to all these fronts you can see that the economics of war are international by their very nature.

It has been necessary to organize production on an international basis so that supplies, civilian and military, may be planned ahead, may be created for tomorrow, and may be gathered for today. No one country could possibly achieve this. There are, accordingly, combined boards which plan the utilization of the raw-materials resources of the United Nations. Such a board is working in Washington now, and a counterpart exists in London.

Raw materials are useful only as they produce supplies and munitions. Last June there was created a Combined Production and Resources Board, which shall "take account of the need for maximum utilization of the productive resources available to the United States, the British Commonwealth of Nations, and the United Nations."

There is a Combined Food Board to work in collaboration toward the best utilization of food resources and to formulate plans for the development, expansion, and purchase of necessary food.

Since supplies must reach the place where they are needed, there is a Combined Shipping Board, which, in essence, pools the shipping of the allied maritime powers.

When it comes to arms, the language of the agreement is worth repeating: "The entire munitions resources of Great Britain and the United States will be deemed to be in a common pool." Out of this pool all the United Nations must draw their war supplies, save Russia, who has supplies of her own but needs all re-enforcement from the pool that ships can carry and ports receive. The Munitions Assignment Board has the huge task of allocating the weapons of war to the fighting fronts.

Were it not for this vast machinery, the war would probably have been over long ago. Were it not that this machinery is truly international, the free fighting nations would have been weakened one by one to the point of defeat and hammered into submission for lack of munitions or starved into impotence for lack of supply.

This is the "commerce" of wartime: a commerce such as the world has never seen. This commerce matches armor against danger; maintains distribution and supply behind the lines. This commerce says, in a word, that the combined resources of all the free nations shall be devoted to the common defense and shall be laid on the line when and where they are needed.

During the period of war this is the machinery that must support the economic life of all the United Nations, including ourselves. Sometimes we have been criticized because the huge machine did not get into action more rapidly. Much of this criticism is sound and useful. But it must be remembered that all this huge design of wartime life has been built within a period of nine months. It will increase in effectiveness until the war is over.

When victory comes — as come it will — this vast machinery will be the way by which the civilian population of most of the world gets its supplies. The organization will be there and standing; it will have under its direct charge the resources of most of the world.

I ask you to remember this, because we shall have the problem, when peace is won, of keeping and holding that peace through an extremely difficult period. You cannot expect order in a hungry world — and the world will be very hungry indeed. The machinery which has been built up to supply us during wartime will have to be used, in large measure, to keep us supplied until the commerce of peace can be re-established. There will be no other way. Until new arrangements can be made to reopen the flow of trade and commerce, to start production out, to repair the wrecked plants, and replace the broken machines, we shall have to rely for a time on the war supplies while we are working to re-establish the business of peace.

The technique of that period of transition must be planned and thought out soon, for this time we cannot risk the breaking of all ranks which took place in 1918 when Germany collapsed. Then the Allied machinery stopped at once; Europe and, to some extent, America were shaken in the convulsion of a great economic crisis. In the ensuing confusion the victory of World War I was literally frittered away.

In that transition period it will be necessary by a combined effort to make arrangements — and make them quickly — so that nations generally can use their resources and their manpower to satisfy their peoples' needs.

Since no country wants to be on either the giving or receiving end of an international breadline, this means economic arrangements which permit nations to get into production as rapidly as possible and put their resources to work. They literally must increase their resources by trade and commerce, for no other peaceful way has yet been devised.

For that reason the trade routes and markets of the world have to be reopened. The endless barriers, restrictions, and hurdles by which trade has been slowly strangled in the last 20 years will have to be removed. This rule goes for everyone, including America. No country can expect to cut itself off from general commerce without harming its neighbors a great deal and itself most of all.

To do this, however, we must squarely face one fact and arrange to meet it. Open trade and life-giving commerce cannot exist unless you have a financial system so arranged that the goods can move — and do — and so handled that business can be done — and is.

For the transition period at least, financial arrangements must therefore be worked out so that our neighbors in this world community can set up in business again. It will be essential for them; it will be sound commerce for us.

Perhaps an illustration close to home may be useful. At the close of our Civil War the South was exhausted and her economic life was broken. The capital and credit of the country were concentrated in the North. Endeavors were made at that time by some enlightened citizens to try to put some of this northern capital and credit to work in the Southern States. But most of the northern bankers at that time did not have the vision or the courage to do the job, and there was no central banking system able to move in. Instead, the money and credit which could and should have rebuilt the ruined areas went into the fantastic speculations of the Goulds, the Jim Fiskes, and the Daniel Drews and caused the wild scandals of the New York Stock Exchange.

Re-establishment of the South was unnecessarily delayed for an entire generation. Nor did the rest of the country escape; it had to suffer the hardships of the long panic which began in 1873. It took the country 30 years to recover from that mistake.

I do not see that the task is impossible. We have the resources. If it is desired to use gold as a financial base, as many people do, we have at our command by far the greatest share of the world's gold. What is more important, we have the production and the goods available to back up our finance. We shall be in a position to make and deliver almost anything which is required to give to our neighbor countries a new start in international economic life. At the very time this is most needed we shall want to keep our plants busy, our people employed, and to provide jobs for the returning soldiers. With ordinary intelligence we should be able to assist the general situation, to everyone's advantage.

A good many years ago we discovered that the trade and commerce of this country could be paralyzed by a system of banking and finance which was not sufficiently elastic. It took three panics to teach us that lesson: the panic of 1893, the panic of 1903, and the panic of 1907. In all those panics we saw trade within this country drop to nothing, though the goods were there; we saw men out of work, though the work was there to be done; we saw banks fail, though the assets were there; we saw hardship in the midst of obvious plenty. Then we finally learned our lesson and passed the Federal Reserve Act of 1914.

The existence of that act and the creation of the parallel agency of the Reconstruction Finance Corporation made it possible to end the depression of 1929 just as soon as a government was chosen which had the will and the determination to do it.

Somewhat the same problem exists in the international field. Perhaps it is not amiss to suggest that business and financial men begin to do some thinking as to how the methods which have proved successful within the United States may be applied so that the trade and commerce which are necessary for the health and for the peace of the world may be re-established and kept going.

Because of this a good many observers, both practical bankers and students, have been advancing the idea that we could profitably extend some of the principles of reserve banking to the international field. Certainly, experience suggests that this is a logical line of development. After World War I the various financial systems of the victorious powers endeavored to go it alone, fighting each other at times, cooperating at times, in much the same way that governments made shifting alliances and had shifting antagonisms. The United States particularly endeavored to do this, and the fiasco of American foreign finance is an unpleasant memory, unhappily kept alive by reams of defaulted bonds and unsuccessful international schemes. Had that same capital and energy been used with intelligence and care and in sound cooperation with other countries, there is great reason to believe that the results would have been better for us; and that the economics of the world would have been more productive; and, most important of all, that there would have been more employment, better wages, and a higher standard of living for workers and producers.

This time we shall have to do it better. For purposes of common defense we have erected an economic machine for war supply capable of developing the entire world. In the light of this experience it should not be too difficult to create institutions capable of handling the finance of transition and turning the processes of reconstruction into permanent processes of international trade.

I have stressed the possibility of creating a system of international finance because that is likely to be the first problem which arises. It is not the only problem and not at all the most dramatic and most appealing. It is one step which we can consider seriously because we already know the technique. If we solve that question we shall have a tool in our hands with which we may be able to attack other and still greater problems.

At the beginning of this essay we noted that the foreign policy of the United States was based on the strength and independence of this country — but also on the disinterested and cooperative friendship with other nations. We found that certain groups of countries in all major crises have tended to draw together, linked by common interest. We have found that this was true in political crises, as it is today in the great and bitter experience of war.

Let it never be said that cooperation is the child only of war. The first World War taught us that military victory depended on united action. The last two decades have shown us that united action is no less essential if victory is to mean peace. The second World War has given us a vision of limitless economic power achieved by cooperation. We must not again lightly throw away that power in the moment of triumph, when arms are grounded and we embark on the task of healing the world.

(6) Address by the Under Secretary of State (Welles) before the New York Herald-Tribune Forum, New York City, November 17, 1942 [1]

Tonight we of the United Nations have the right to look ahead, not only with hope and with passionate conviction but with the assurance which high military achievement affords to the ultimate victory which will presage a free world.

None of us are so optimistic as to delude ourselves into the belief that the end is in sight; or that we have not still before us grave obstacles, dark days, reverses, and great sacrifices yet to be undergone. But the tremendous initial effort, in the case of our own country, of transforming the inertia of a democracy of 130 millions of people at peace into the driving, irresistible energy of 130 millions of American citizens aroused and united in war, has been successfully made.

The first months of confusion and of crosscurrents are past. The men and women of the United States are now enabled to see for themselves the development of the strategic moves in which their Commander-in-Chief and their military and naval leaders are engaged. They are able to appreciate the amazing nature of the feat realized in the occupation of North Africa and to recognize the time and the extent of the preparation required for this gigantic task.

They now realize that the prodding of our self-appointed pundits who were constantly demanding the creation of a second front was not required and that the carefully thought-out plans for the second front now in being had long since been conceived and were already in process of realization while the clamor of these critics went on.

They can now fully evaluate the lack of vision and of knowledge of those who demanded the abandonment of our whole policy toward the French people, at the very moment that that policy was afforded the striking opportunity of proving its full worth — its full worth to the cause for which we fight and its full worth in preserving the soul of France during the darkest days she has ever known: France, the birthplace of so many of those principles of human liberty for which we and the people of France once more battle today.

They realize that we have in North Africa but one objective — the defeat of the Axis forces — which will bring with it the liberation of the people of France. During these first days all arrangements which we

[1] Ibid., p. 939.

may make with Frenchmen in North Africa are solely military in character and are undertaken — properly — by the American and British military commanders. It is the hope of all of us that all Frenchmen who represent or who are part of the forces of resistance to Hitler will unite as one in the support of our military endeavor.

And so the clouds are lifting — the clouds of doubt and of disparagement and of lack of self-confidence. We can all see more clearly how inevitable has now become the final conquest of the armies of that criminal paranoiac whom the German people were so benighted as to acclaim as their leader; how crushing will at long last be the defeat which the Japanese hordes and their military leaders will suffer in just retribution for the treacherous barbarity which they have been inflicting upon the world during the past 11 years.

How can we achieve that free world, the attainment of which alone can compensate mankind for the stupendous sacrifices which human beings everywhere are now being called upon to suffer?

Our military victory will only be won, in Churchill's immortal words, by blood and tears, and toil and sweat.

It is just as clear that the free world which we must achieve can only be attained, not through the expenditure of toil and sweat alone but also through the exercise of all the wisdom which men of today have gained from the experience of the past, and by the utilization not only of idealism but also of the practical knowledge of the working of human nature and of the laws of economics and of finance.

What the United Nations' blueprint imperatively requires is to be drafted in the light of experience and of common sense, and in a spirit of justice, of democracy, and of tolerance, by men who have their eyes on the stars but their feet on the ground.

In the fundamentals of international relationships there is nothing more fatally dangerous than the common American fallacy that the formulation of an aspiration is equivalent to the hard-won realization of an objective. Of this basic truth we have no more tragic proof than the Kellogg-Briand pact.

It seems to me that the first essential is the continuous and rapid perfecting of a relationship between the United Nations so that this military relationship may be further strengthened by the removal of all semblance of disunity or of suspicious rivalry, and by the clarification of the free-world goals for which we are fighting, and so that the form of international organization determined to be best suited to achieve international security will have developed to such an extent that it can fully operate as soon as the present military partnership has achieved its purpose of complete victory.

Another essential is the reaching of agreements between the United Nations before the armistice is signed upon those international adjustments, based upon the universal principles of the Atlantic Charter and pursuant to the pledges contained in our mutual-aid agreements with many of our allies, which we believe to be desirable and necessary for the maintenance of a peaceful and prosperous world of the future.

We all envisage the tragic chaos and anarchy which will have engulfed Europe and a great part of the rest of the world by the time Hitler's brief day is done and when he and his accomplices confront their judges. The United Nations' machinery for relief and rehabilitation must be prepared to operate without a moment's delay to alleviate the suffering and misery of millions of homeless and starving human beings if civilization is to be saved from years of social and moral collapse.

"No one will go hungry or without the other means of livelihood in any territory occupied by the United Nations, if it is humanly within our powers to make the necessary supplies available to them. Weapons will also be supplied to the peoples of these territories to hasten the defeat of the Axis." This is the direction of the President to the Lend-Lease Administrator, to General Eisenhower, and to the Department of State, and it is being carried out by them to the full extent of their power and resources. The other United Nations, each to the full extent of its ability, will, I am sure, cooperate whole-heartedly in this great task.

Through prearrangement certain measures such as the disarmament of aggressor nations laid down in the Atlantic Charter must likewise be undertaken rapidly and with the utmost precision.

Surely we should not again resort to the procedures adopted in 1919 for the settlement of the future of the world. We cannot afford to permit the basic issues by which the destiny of humanity will be determined, to be resolved without prior agreement, in hurried confusion, by a group of harassed statesmen, working against time, pressed from one side by the popular demand for immediate demobilization and crowded on the other by the exigencies of domestic politics.

If we are to attain our free world — the world of the four freedoms — to the extent practicable, the essential principles of international political and economic relations in that new world must be agreed upon in advance and with the full support of each one of the United Nations, so that agreements to be reached will implement those principles.

If the people of the United States now believe as a result of the experience of the past 25 years that the security of our Republic is vitally affected by the fate of the other peoples of the earth, they will recognize that the nature of the international political and economic relations which will obtain in the world, after victory has been achieved, is to us a matter of profound self-interest.

As the months pass, two extreme schools of thought will become more and more vocal: the first, stemming from the leaders of the group which preached extreme isolation, will once more proclaim that war in the rest of the world every 20 years or so is inevitable, that we can stay out if we so desire, and that any assumption by this country of any form of responsibility for what goes on in the world means our unnecessary involvement in war; the other, of which very often men of the highest idealism and sincerity are the spokesmen, will maintain that the United States must assume the burdens of the entire globe, must see to it that the standards in which we ourselves believe must immediately be adopted by all the peoples of the earth and must undertake to inculcate in all parts of the world our own policies of social and political reform whether the other peoples involved so desire or not. While under a different guise, this school of thought is in no way dissimilar in theory from the strange doctrine of incipient "bear the white man's burden" imperialism which flared in this country in the first years of this century.

The people of the United States today realize that the adoption of either one of these two philosophies would prove equally dangerous to the future well-being of our Nation.

Our free world must be founded on the four freedoms: freedom *of* speech and *of* religion — and freedom *from* want and *from* fear.

I do not believe that the two first freedoms — of speech and of religion — can ever be assured to mankind, so long as want and war are permitted to ravage the earth. Freedom of speech and of religion need only protection; they require only relief from obstruction.

Freedom from fear — the assurance of peace — and freedom from want — the assurance of individual personal security — require all the implementation which the genius of man can devise through effective forms of international cooperation.

Peace — freedom from fear — cannot be assured until the nations of the world, particularly the great powers, and that includes the United States, recognize that the threat of war anywhere throughout the globe threatens their own security — and until they are jointly willing to exercise the police powers necessary to prevent such threats from materializing into armed hostilities.

And since policemen might be tyrants if they had no political superiors, freedom from fear also demands some form of organized international political cooperation, to make the rules of international living and to change them as the years go by, and some sort of international court to adjudicate disputes. With effective institutions of that character to insure equity and justice, and the continued will to make them work, the peoples of the world should at length be able to live out their lives in peace.

Freedom from want requires these things:

People who want to work must be able to find useful jobs, not sometimes, not in good years only, but continuously.

These jobs must be at things which they do well and which can be done well in the places where they work.

They must be able to exchange the things which they produce, on fair terms, for other things which other people, often in other places, can make better than they.

Efficient and continuous production and fair exchange are both necessary to the abundance which we seek, and they depend upon each other. In the past we have succeeded better with production than exchange. Production is called into existence by the prospects for exchange, prospects which have constantly been thwarted by all kinds of inequalities, imperfections, and restrictions. The problem of removing obstacles to fair exchange — the problem of distribution of goods and purchasing power — is far more difficult than the problem of production.

It will take much wisdom, much cooperative effort, and much surrender of private, shortsighted, and sectional self-interest to make these things all come true. But the goal is freedom from want — individual security and national prosperity — and is everlastingly worth striving for.

As mankind progresses on the path toward the goal of freedom from want and from fear, freedom of religion and of speech will more and more become a living reality.

Never before have peace and individual security been classed as freedom. Never before have they been placed alongside of religious liberty and free speech as human freedoms which should be inalienable.

Upon these four freedoms must rest the structure of the future free world.

This time there must be no compromise between justice and injustice; no yielding to expediency; no swerving from the great human rights and liberties established by the Atlantic Charter itself.

In the words of our President: "We shall win this war, and in Victory, we shall seek not vengeance, but the establishment of an international order in which the spirit of Christ shall rule the hearts of men and of nations."

We won't get a free world any other way.

(7) *Address by the Under Secretary of State (Welles) at the Dedication of the Sara Delano Roosevelt Memorial, December 6, 1942* [1]

[Excerpt]

. . . .

We are gathered together in these dedication ceremonies on the eve of the first anniversary of that treacherous attack upon the United

---

[1] Delivered at St. Paul's Church, Eastchester, Mount Vernon, N.Y., and broadcast over the facilities of the National Broadcasting Company; *ibid.*, p. 991.

States which involved our people in this great World War which has engulfed all the continents of the earth.

It is a solemn moment as we think back over the crowded history of these past 12 months, during which our united people and their Government have made the supreme effort to preserve the freedom with which this land of ours has been blessed and to turn the tides of battle toward the ultimate victory of the great cause which we uphold: the cause of human liberty.

We think back to those first difficult months when we had to achieve the readjustment of our national life in all its phases so as to insure an all-out war effort, and of the months thereafter when the long and difficult task of translating military and naval plans into accomplishment had to be realized. Now at the end of this 12-month period the strategy which our Government has been devising has become clear. The successes of our military and naval forces and of those of the peoples who are fighting at our side have instilled in us new hope and renewed conviction. It may well be, however, that a dark and anxious time may yet have to be traversed before the ultimate victory, which we know we will attain, is won. Until that time, the efforts, the devotion, and the sacrifices of every one of us must be consecrated to the supreme task of winning the war.

But there are many of us today who are thinking back further than the anniversary of Pearl Harbor. They are thinking back over the past quarter of a century and are asking themselves whether this shattering world upheaval in which all mankind is engaged was in fact inevitable.

They are asking themselves: If, at the conclusion of the last World War, the Government of the United States, in association with the other governments of free peoples, had sought the ideal which Woodrow Wilson once held up before the eyes of the people of this country — "a universal dominion of right by such a concert of free peoples as shall bring peace and safety to all nations and make the world itself at last free" — would this tragedy have come to pass?

The foreign policy of any nation must inevitably be a policy of self-interest. The foreign policy of the United States should ever be a policy based upon that course and upon those principles which, in the judgment of the American people themselves, will most clearly further the individual interest of their country and the general welfare of the people of the United States.

And I think a question that we can well afford to ask ourselves on the eve of the anniversary of our entrance into the present war is whether the policy pursued by the people of the United States during the years subsequent to the end of the last World War has proved in any sense to be to the interest or to the individual advantage of the American people. During that period we refused to assume the slightest measure of responsibility for the maintenance of world order. During the greater portion of that period we divorced ourselves from almost every form of cooperation with other powers, and as a people and as a government we stood aside while the forces which resulted in Hitlerism and all that which Hitlerism implies were shaping themselves. We stood aside, pretending to ourselves that the United States could keep itself secure and free from danger even if all the rest of the world went up in flames.

From the standpoint of narrow and selfish self-interest alone, there are two straight questions which we might well ask ourselves.

The cost of our participation in the war and of our military and naval production will burden the United States with a staggering national debt which must be paid by the taxpayers of this country. To win this struggle we are necessarily diverting the greater portion of our tremendous productive capacity into channels of destruction, not those of construction, and the debt burden which will have been created will inevitably affect the manner of life of every one of us and will inevitably diminish the opportunity for the progressive advancement of the generation to come.

Would we not as a people have been better advised if we had been willing 20 years ago to join with the other free peoples of the earth in promoting an international order which would have maintained the peace of the world and which could have prevented the rise of those conditions which have resulted in the total war of today? Is it conceivable that the material sacrifices which we might have been called upon to undertake to maintain world order in those earlier years could have involved a thousandth part of the material sacrifices which we are called upon today to undertake?

And the second question we may well ask ourselves is a question which hits straight at every family in the United States which has a father, or a son, or a brother serving this country today in the armed forces of the United States. Had the American people been willing a generation ago to bear their fair share of responsibility for the maintenance of world order, would our men today be forced to offer up their lives in order that they may insure the preservation of the independence and the security of their fellow citizens?

Already we hear again the voices of those who decry all forms of practical international cooperation. Already we can see the efforts of those who would make this fundamental issue, the issue of our national future, a question of party politics. Already we can once more follow the machinations of those special-privilege interests which would again turn the policy of the United States into one of narrow isolation because of their belief that they themselves would profit through such a course.

Surely this is a question which transcends the bounds of any aspect of party and any claim of material advantage by a special few.

Today we are fighting this war in the closest collaboration with the governments joined with us. Our military operations, so successfully carried out recently on different fronts, have required effective cooperation and understanding with our allies. The very conduct of the war makes it indispensable that this form of agreement as to the strategy of our military and naval undertakings be continued by all the governments of the United Nations. Our own security depends upon it.

We realize now that in this war this form of association of free peoples, struggling to preserve their liberty, is vitally necessary for the safety of our nation.

Do we realize that an association of the free peoples of the United Nations when the war is won is just as essential to the future security of this country?

Surely we must assure ourselves when we achieve the victory for which we are fighting that this free people of ours, joined with the other free peoples who are fighting at our side, will see to it that the necessary measures of international cooperation are undertaken so that this catastrophe will not occur again.

In this shrine dedicated to the freedoms which we, the American people, by an inalienable right enjoy, we may well dedicate ourselves to the supreme task of the creation in the future of a world in which all peoples may in truth be free — free from the fear of war and assured of the right to live out their lives in safety and in peace.

(8) *Statement of the Secretary of State (Hull) on Issue of Publication Entitled "Peace and War," January 2, 1943* [1]

We are issuing today a publication entitled "Peace and War," prepared in the Department of State.[2] It is an introduction to a collection of documents concerning the foreign relations of the United States during the fateful decade 1931–1941. This book and the collection of documents which is in the process of publication present a record of policies and acts by which the United States sought to promote conditions of peace and world order and to meet the world-wide dangers resulting from Japanese, German, and Italian aggression as those dangers arose.

That record shows, I think, that throughout this period our Government consistently advocated, practiced, and urged upon other countries principles of international conduct on the basis of which the nations of the world could attain security, confidence, and progress. Much was accomplished in the face of immense difficulties. It is for the establishment of those principles that we and our associates are fighting today.

[1] *Ibid.*, VIII, p. 4.
[2] *Peace and War: United States Foreign Policy, 1931–1941.* Washington, United States Government Printing Office, 1942, Department of State Publication 1853, 144 p.

I am convinced that, had those principles been adopted and applied by the nations of the world, all legitimate grievances and controversies between nations could have been satisfactorily adjusted by peaceful processes and without resort to force. We and all mankind would have been spared the horrors of this world-enveloping war thrust upon us by the criminal ambitions of the leaders of Japan, Germany, and Italy, who — intent upon conquest — rejected all principles of law, justice, fair-dealing, and peaceful negotiation and resorted to the sword.

In making this information more fully available to the people of the United States, we earnestly hope that a study of it will help our citizens to a clearer understanding of the problems and tasks which have confronted us, of those which confront us now, and of those which will confront us in the crucial days ahead.

There will be confident hope for the future provided our people and other peoples hold fast to the eternal principles of law, justice, fair-dealing, and morality which we have constantly proclaimed and sought to apply, and which must underlie any practicable program of peaceful international collaboration for the good of all.

Our people and the peoples of the United Nations will need to have in the future, as they have today, a unity of purpose and a willingness to make appropriate and indispensable contributions toward the achievement of military victory and toward the establishment and maintenance of a peace that will endure. With unity of purpose and common effort, there can be achieved a peace that will open to all mankind greater opportunity than has ever before existed for welfare and progress in every avenue of human endeavor.

(9) *Message of the President (Roosevelt) to the Congress on the State of the Nation, January 7, 1943* [1]

[Excerpt]

MR. VICE PRESIDENT, MR. SPEAKER, MEMBERS OF THE SENATE AND OF THE HOUSE OF REPRESENTATIVES:

The Seventy-eighth Congress assembles in one of the great moments in the history of this nation. The past year was perhaps the most crucial for modern civilization; the coming year will be filled with violent conflict — yet with high promise of better things.

. . . . . .

[Here follows an appraisal of the events of 1942.]

We should never forget the things we are fighting for. But, at this critical period of the war, we should confine ourselves to the larger

[1] Department of State, *Bulletin*, VIII, p. 15; *Congressional Record*, vol. 89, pt. 1, p. 45.

objectives and not get bogged down in argument over methods and details.

We, and all the United Nations, want a decent peace and a durable peace. In the years between the end of the first World War and the beginning of the second World War, we were not living under a decent or a durable peace.

I have reason to know that our boys at the front are concerned with two broad aims beyond the winning of the war; and their thinking and their opinion coincide with what most Americans here back home are mulling over. They know, and we know, that it would be inconceivable — it would, indeed, be sacrilegious — if this nation and the world did not attain some real, lasting good out of all these efforts and sufferings and bloodshed and death.

The men in our armed forces want a lasting peace, and, equally, they want permanent employment for themselves, their families, and their neighbors when they are mustered out at the end of the war.

Two years ago I spoke in my Annual Message of four freedoms.[1] The blessings of two of them — freedom of speech and freedom of religion — are an essential part of the very life of this nation; and we hope that these blessings will be granted to all men everywhere.

The people at home and the people at the front — men and women — are wondering about the third freedom, freedom from want. To them it means that when they are mustered out, when war production is converted to the economy of peace, they will have the right to expect full employment — for themselves and for all able-bodied men and women in America who want to work.

They expect the opportunity to work, to run their farms, their stores, to earn decent wages. They are eager to face the risks inherent in our system of free enterprise.

They do not want a post-war America which suffers from under-nourishment or slums — or the dole. They want no get-rich-quick era of bogus "prosperity" which will end for them in selling apples on a street corner, as happened after the bursting of the boom in 1929.

When you talk with our young men and women, you will find they want to work for themselves and their families; they consider they have the right to work; and they know that after the last war their fathers did not gain that right.

When you talk with our young men and women, you will find that with the opportunity for employment they want assurance against the evils of all major economic hazards — assurance that will extend from the cradle to the grave. This great Government can and must provide this assurance.

[1] *Documents, III, 1940–41*, p. 26.

I have been told that this is no time to speak of a better America after the war. I am told it is a grave error on my part.

I dissent.

If the security of the individual citizen or the family should become a subject of national debate, the country knows where I stand.

I say this now to this Seventy-eighth Congress, because it is wholly possible that freedom from want — the right of employment and the right of assurance against life's hazards — will loom very large as a task of America during the coming two years.

I trust it will not be regarded as an issue, but rather as a task for all of us to study sympathetically, to work out with a constant regard for the attainment of the objective, with fairness to all and with injustice to none.

In this war of survival we must keep before our minds not only the evil things we fight against but the good things we are fighting for. We fight to retain a great past, and we fight to gain a greater future.

Let us remember that economic safety for the America of the future is threatened unless a greater economic stability comes to the rest of the world. We cannot make America an island in either a military or an economic sense. Hitlerism, like any other form of crime or disease, can grow from the evil seeds of economic as well as military feudalism.

Victory in this war is the first and greatest goal before us. Victory in the peace is the next. That means striving toward the enlargement of the security of man here and throughout the world and, finally, striving for the fourth freedom, freedom from fear.

It is of little account for any of us to talk of essential human needs, of attaining security, if we run the risk of another World War in 10 or 20 or 50 years. That is just plain common sense. Wars grow in size, in death and destruction, and in the inevitability of engulfing all nations, in inverse ratio to the shrinking size of the world as a result of the conquest of the air. I shudder to think of what will happen to humanity, including ourselves, if this war ends in an inconclusive peace and another war breaks out when the babies of today have grown to fighting age.

Every normal American prays that neither he nor his sons nor his grandsons will be compelled to go through this horror again.

Undoubtedly a few Americans, even now, think that this nation can end this war comfortably and then climb back into an American hole and pull the hole in after them.

But we have learned that we can never dig a hole so deep that it would be safe against predatory animals. We have also learned that if we do not pull the fangs of the predatory animals of this world, they will multiply and grow in strength and they will be at our throats once more in a short generation.

Most Americans realize more clearly than ever before that modern war equipment in the hands of aggressor nations can bring danger over-night to our own national existence or to that of any other nation, or island, or continent.

It is clear to us that if Germany and Italy and Japan — or any one of them — remain armed at the end of this war or are permitted to rearm, they will again, and inevitably, embark upon an ambitious career of world conquest. They must be disarmed and kept disarmed, and they must abandon the philosophy and the teaching of that philosophy which has brought so much suffering to the world.

After the first World War we tried to achieve a formula for permanent peace, based on a magnificent idealism. We failed. But by our failure we have learned that we cannot maintain peace at this stage of human development by good intentions alone.

Today the United Nations are the mightiest military coalition in history. They represent an overwhelming majority of the population of the world. Bound together in solemn agreement that they themselves will not commit acts of aggression or conquest against any of their neighbors, the United Nations can and must remain united for the maintenance of peace by preventing any attempt to rearm in Germany, in Japan, in Italy, or in any other nation which seeks to violate the Tenth Commandment, "Thou shalt not covet."

There are cynics and skeptics who say it cannot be done. The Ameri-can people and all the freedom-loving peoples of this earth are now demanding that it must be done. And the will of these people shall prevail.

The philosophy of the Axis powers is based on profound contempt for the human race. If, in the formation of our future policy, we were guided by the same cynical contempt, then we should be surrendering to the philosophy of our enemies and our victory would turn to defeat.

The issue of this war is the basic issue between those who believe in mankind and those who do not — the ancient issue between those who put their faith in the people and those who put their faith in dictators and tyrants. There have always been those who did not believe in the people, who attempted to block their forward movement across history, to force them back to servility and suffering and silence.

The people have now gathered their strength. They are moving forward in their might and power, and no force, no combination of forces, no trickery, deceit, or violence can stop them now. They see before them the hope of the world: a decent, secure, peaceful life for all men everywhere.

I do not prophesy when this war will end.

But I do believe that this year of 1943 will give to the United Nations a very substantial advance along the roads that lead to Berlin and Rome and Tokyo.

I tell you it is within the realm of possibility that this Seventy-eighth Congress may have the historic privilege of helping greatly to save the world from future fear.

Therefore, let us — all of us — have confidence; let us redouble our efforts.

A tremendous, costly, long-enduring task in peace as well as in war is still ahead of us.

But as we face that continuing task we may know that the state of this nation is good, the heart of this nation is sound, the spirit of this nation is strong, the faith of this nation is eternal.

(10) *Address by the President (Roosevelt) before the White House Correspondents' Association, Washington, D. C., February 12, 1943* [1]

[Excerpts]

.   .   .   .

In every battalion and in every ship's crew you will find every kind of American citizen representing every occupation, every section, every origin, every religion, every political viewpoint.

Ask them what they are fighting for, and every one of them will say: "I am fighting for my country." Ask them what they really mean by that and you will get what, on the surface, may seem to be a wide variety of answers.

One will say he is fighting for the right to say what he pleases and to read and listen to what he likes.

Another will say he is fighting because he never wants to see the Nazi swastika flying over the First Baptist Church on Elm Street.

Another soldier will say he is fighting for the right to work and earn three square meals a day for himself and his folks.

A fourth soldier will say he is fighting in this World War so that his children and grandchildren will not have to go back to Europe, or Africa or Asia to do this ugly job all over again.

But all these answers really add up to the same thing: every American fights for freedom. And today the personal freedom of every American and his family depends, and in the future will increasingly depend, upon the freedom of his neighbors in other lands.

For today the whole world is one neighborhood. That is why this war, which had its beginnings in seemingly remote areas, has spread to every continent and most of the islands of the sea, involving the lives and the liberties of the entire human race. And unless the peace that

[1] From office of the Secretary to the President; Department of State, *Bulletin*, VIII, p. 145. This address was given following the President's return from the Casablanca Conference and a visit to the North African front. It was broadcast over a nation-wide hook-up.

follows recognizes that the whole world is one neighborhood and does justice to the whole human race, the germs of another World War will remain as a constant threat to mankind.

.   .   .   .

It was made clear to us at Casablanca that all Frenchmen outside of France are uniting in one great paramount objective — the complete liberation of France and of all the French people who now suffer the torture of the Nazi yoke. As each day passes a spirit of unselfishness is more greatly uniting all Frenchmen who have the opportunity to strike a blow for liberation.

In the years of the American and French revolutions the fundamental principle guiding our democracies was established. The cornerstone of our whole democratic edifice was the principle that from the people and the people alone flows the authority of government.

It is one of our war aims, as expressed in the Atlantic Charter, that the conquered populations of today be again the masters of their destiny. There must be no doubt anywhere that it is the unalterable purpose of the United Nations to restore to conquered peoples their sacred rights.

French sovereignty rests with the people of France. Its expression has been temporarily suspended by German occupation. Once the triumphant armies of the United Nations have expelled the common foe, Frenchmen will be represented by a government of their own popular choice.

It will be a free choice in every sense. No nation in all the world that is free to make a choice is going to set itself up under the Fascist form of government, or the Nazi form of government or the Japanese warlord form of government. Such forms are the offspring of seizure of power followed by the abridgement of freedom. Therefore, the United Nations can properly say of these forms of government two simple words: "Never again."

The right of self-determination included in the Atlantic Charter does not carry with it the right of any government to commit wholesale murder or the right to make slaves of its own people or of any other peoples in the world.

And the world can rest assured that this total war — this sacrifice of lives all over the globe — is not being carried on for the purpose or even with the remotest idea of keeping the Quislings or Lavals in power anywhere on this earth.

.   .   .   .

In an attempt to ward off the inevitable disaster, the Axis propagandists are trying all of their old tricks in order to divide the United Nations. They seek to create the idea that if we win this war, Russia,

England, China and the United States are going to get into a cat-and-dog fight.

This is their final effort to turn one nation against another, in the vain hope that they may settle with one or two at a time — that any of us may be so gullible and so forgetful as to be duped into making "deals" at the expense of our Allies.

To these panicky attempts to escape the consequences of their crimes we say — all the United Nations say — that the only terms on which we shall deal with any Axis government or any Axis factions are the terms proclaimed at Casablanca: "Unconditional Surrender." In our uncompromising policy we mean no harm to the common people of the Axis nations. But we do mean to impose punishment and retribution in full upon their guilty, barbaric leaders.

The Nazis must be frantic indeed if they believe that they can devise any propaganda which would turn the British and American and Chinese governments and peoples against Russia — or Russia against the rest of us.

The overwhelming courage and endurance of the Russian people in withstanding and hurling back the invaders — and the genius with which their great armies have been directed and led by Mr. Stalin and their military commanders — all speak for themselves.

The tragedy of the war has sharpened the vision of the leadership and peoples of all the United Nations and I can say to you from my own full knowledge that they see the utter necessity of our standing together after the war to secure a peace based on principles of permanence.

You can be quite sure that if Japan should be the first of the Axis partners to fall, the total efforts and resources of all the United Nations would be concentrated on the job of crushing Germany.

And, on the other hand, lest there be any question in Nazi or Japanese minds that we are wholly one in the prosecution of the war to a complete victory all over the world, the Prime Minister wished to make a formal agreement that if Germany should be conquered before Japan, all British Empire resources and manpower would, of course, join with China and us in an out-and-out final attack on Japan. I told him that no formal statement or agreement along these lines was in the least bit necessary — that the American people accept the word of a great English gentleman — and that it was obvious and clear that all of us are completely in accord in our determination to destroy the forces of barbarism in Asia and in Europe and in Africa. In other words — our policy toward our Japanese enemies is precisely the same as our policy toward our Nazi enemies: it is a policy of fighting hard on all fronts and ending the war as quickly as we can on the uncompromising terms of unconditional surrender.

Today is the anniversary of the birth of a great, plain American.

The living memory of Abraham Lincoln is now honored and cherished by all of our people, wherever they may be, and by men and women and children throughout the British Commonwealth, and the Soviet Union, and the Republic of China, and in every land on earth where people love freedom and will give their lives for freedom.

President Lincoln said in 1862, "Fellow Citizens, we cannot escape history. We of this Congress and this administration will be remembered in spite of ourselves. No personal significance or insignificance can spare one or another of us. The fiery trial through which we pass will light us . . . in honor or dishonor, to the latest generation."

Today, eighty years after Lincoln delivered that message, the fires of war are blazing across the whole horizon of mankind — from Kharkov to Kunming — from the Mediterranean to the Coral Sea — from Berlin to Tokyo.

Again — we cannot escape history. We have supreme confidence that with the help of God honor will prevail. We have faith that future generations will know that here, in the middle of the twentieth century, there came the time when men of good will found a way to unite and produce and fight to destroy the forces of ignorance, intolerance, slavery and war.

(11) *Address by the Under Secretary of State (Welles) at the University of Toronto, Canada, February 26, 1943* [1]

[Excerpt]

.   .   .   .

When the war ends similar problems will face us both. We shall both confront the task of demobilization, and we shall both endeavor to make sure that the young men — and the young women — who are discharged from military service have a real chance to find useful and productive employment. Both of us prefer a system of free enterprise, and we shall both desire to lighten government controls as rapidly as the phenomenon of scarcity vanishes and conditions permit free enterprise to play its proper role. Both of us will find our industries still working largely on war orders, and the problems of conversion will be urgent. Both of us will want to make our contribution to the relief and reconstruction of the devastated countries, and we shall want to make that contribution in the way which will help the peoples of those regions get back to health and strength and to self-reliance as rapidly as possible. We shall both be interested in possible international arrangements about gold, and currencies, and international investment. And we shall both desire to increase the economic interchange between us and with others on the most fruitful basis possible.

[1] Department of State, *Bulletin*, VIII, p. 179.

On all these questions we can talk usefully together as we have agreed to do. Our discussions will become even more useful as we undertake to conduct them in an even larger framework, the framework of the whole United Nations. There is no disagreement anywhere as to what the United Nations want. They want full employment for their people at good wages and under good working conditions and the other physical and institutional arrangements that add up to freedom from want. But differences of opinion doubtless exist within and between the several countries as to the means to be adopted — divergencies may arise as to the desirability or efficacy of particular policies or measures.

An examination of the causes of any disagreement will usually reveal that it exists mainly because people are considering the question from different viewpoints, that the parties are basing their judgments on different or incomplete facts and different considerations. If both parties had the same facts and considerations in mind, and if each knew fully the reasons behind the position taken by the other, there would much more quickly be a meeting of minds.

This is true not only of individuals but also of nations, and it suggests the need for joint as well as separate study of the facts and considerations relating to proposals aimed at attaining the desired ends. I believe that if the United Nations were to set up machinery for the purpose of assembling and studying all international aspects of problems under the general heading of freedom from want, and for assembling all the pertinent facts and considerations relating thereto, and for jointly analyzing all facts and considerations relating to measures or policies proposed for furthering the end in view, the controversies and conflicts of policy which have so long embittered relations in the international economic field, and therefore generally, might largely disappear. If the analysis were thorough enough and the problems of each country were fully understood by the others, solutions could be found that would serve the interests of all concerned. Nothing is more clear to my mind than this: if all aspects of an economic problem were explored, it would become apparent that the basic interests of all countries are largely common interests, that each country's economic problems are related to and inseparable from those of the others.

A United Nations' study such as I have in mind would explore in a careful, thorough, and systematic way world problems in the economic field, toward the solution of which much progress must be made if we are to have anything approaching the goal of freedom from want in our own countries or elsewhere. People and governments here and everywhere are studying these problems, are searching for solutions. The plans of one government or group of governments may seem sound enough in the light of their own interests but may contain flaws which are visible only from the viewpoint of other governments or countries.

If the study to which I have referred did no more than detect and focus attention on such flaws, if it did no more than prevent the crystallization in one country or group of countries of ideas which are objectionable from the viewpoint of others, it would serve a highly useful purpose. It is, however, my hope and belief that a United Nations' undertaking such as I have suggested would be able to formulate plans and recommendations of a constructive sort — to find, so to speak, common denominators which, in the net, would be advantageous to all. Failing to begin such organized study and discussion now, there is danger that divergent views and policies may become crystallized, to the detriment of the common war effort, and to the detriment of efforts to bring about a peace that will be more than a brief and uneasy interlude before another even more horrible and more destructive war devastates and depopulates the world.

My Government believes that the initiation of such studies is already overdue. If we do not make a start now, there is danger that we shall be brought together to make the peace with as many plans as there are governments. The day of complete victory cannot come too soon; we all give thanks to God for every advance we make toward that goal, at every sign of weakness in our enemies. Between now and that day we must endeavor to prepare ourselves to meet the responsibilities and to make the most of the opportunities that peace will bring.

I am glad to say that my Government intends at once to undertake discussions with other members of the United Nations as to the most practical and effective methods through which these vitally necessary conferences and consultations between us all can be held. It is my conviction that from these meetings a large measure of agreement will already be found to exist, that solutions will be available for such divergencies as may be apparent, and that in the last analysis it will be found that what may even appear to be fundamental obstacles can be resolved in the interest of the welfare of us all.

What the people of the United States are striving for, I am persuaded, is exactly what the people of Canada are striving for. They seek the attainment of the noble objectives set forth in the Atlantic Charter. They seek to achieve these ends, not because of any altruistic motives, not through the dictates of any theoretical idealism, but rather because they believe that the attainment of these objectives will be in their own self-interest — and I believe that in my own country we have learned through the bitter experience of the past quarter of a century that the most practical form of self-interest is enlightened self-interest.

We have seen beyond the shadow of any doubt that a policy of international cooperation which far too many told us 24 years ago was a policy of suicidal sentimentality, was in fact a policy of advantageous hard-headed realism.

Most of us have learned a great truth that is beginning to dawn upon the consciousness of many peoples in all parts of the globe, and that is that the real self-interest of one nation coincides with the permanent, with the ultimate, self-interests of other nations.

For there is no people which will not benefit more by peace than by war. The preservation of peace and the practice of human tolerance must come to be recognized by every nation and by every government as the indispensable requisites of all peoples. Never again can humanity permit dictator demagogues once more to proclaim the alleged virile glories of war or the cruel falsehood that there exists a master race.

No rational man or woman today can question the fact that had the nations of the world been able to create some effective form of international organization in the years that followed the close of the last great World War, and had been able to bulwark that organization with judicial and police powers, the devastating tragedy which humanity today is undergoing would have been avoided. From the standpoint of material self-interest alone, leaving aside every moral consideration, the lot of every one of our fellow citizens would have been far better. No one can appraise the cost of the present war in terms of life and human suffering. But we can appraise its cost in material terms, and we know that as a result of this material cost the standard of living of every individual in every region of the world will be impaired.

If at the conclusion of this war the Governments of the United Nations are not afforded by their peoples the opportunity of collaborating together in effective policies of recovery, or of assuming a joint responsibility for making completely sure that the peace of the world is not again violated, there can be no result other than utter disaster. The structure of our civilization is not so tough as to make it conceivable that it would resist a repetition of the present holocaust.

We have evolved here in the New World a system of international relationships which constitutes perhaps the highest achievement in the sphere of practical international living which civilized man has so far created. From the historical standpoint it is very recent indeed, but it has grown, gradually perhaps but nevertheless steadily, throughout the period of the individual life of the democracies of the Americas. It is a system in which the smallest state is just as free to determine its own destiny as the largest state. It is a system where the smallest state feels just as secure as the largest state because of its knowledge that its independence and integrity are a matter of vital concern to its more powerful neighbors and because of its assurance that should its liberties be jeopardized by aggression coming from without the Western Hemisphere, its more powerful neighbors will take the action necessary to repel that danger.

Every region of the world possesses its own peculiar problems, its own special advantages, and its own inherent difficulties. We hear much of the age-old rivalries which have persisted in Europe and in other quarters of the globe. But I think that we of the Americas can say that if 22 independent democracies such as those which occupy North, Central, and South America — of different races, of different languages, and of different origins — can achieve the measure of progress which we now have achieved toward a peaceful and humane relationship and toward profitable economic cooperation, that same form of relationship can be achieved in all regions of the world.

The creation of that same kind of decent international relationship by all peoples is the objective today of the United Nations. I am confident that after the unconditional surrender of our common enemies that objective will be attained.

Through our continued cooperation the peace of the world can be maintained, for with the defeat and total disarmament of the Axis powers there can be no further conflict — if the United Nations stand together.

We cannot permit this time that the supreme sacrifice which our sons and our brothers are making in the defense of our liberties shall be made in vain. Only through our combined efforts can we make certain that the victory which we will win in battle can become in fact the victory of peace.

(12) *The Tools of Future Peace. Address by Assistant Secretary of State Berle before the Rotary Club of Reading, Pennsylvania, April 4, 1943* [1]

All of us in the State Department welcome any opportunity to meet representative groups of Americans and to take counsel with them. The State Department is the country's first line of defense. It meets foreign problems long before they become acute. It endeavors so to handle affairs that world peace shall be promoted, American interests protected, and the future made as secure as the situation permits. The State Department must make arrangements so that the work of our fighting forces is as easy as possible. When peace approaches, it must bring into existence those agreements which are most likely to make for an enduring peace.

The American State Department has no secret agents. Its work is done in the open. The proposals it makes are submitted to the public opinion of the country, usually through direct submission to the Congress of the United States. We never have gone in for the practice of foreign affairs as described by popular fiction writers. The State Department is the smallest and least expensive department in Washington.

---

[1] Broadcast through facilities of the National Broadcasting Company; *ibid.*, p. 289.

Anyone has a right to ask us what we are doing, and everyone gets a prompt and clear answer.

I am proud to have been a member of the Department during the past few years. I think the record would show that, as the World War approached, the country was as well prepared diplomatically as American processes permitted.

II

Let me give a single illustration.

When the Nazi and Japanese war lords in all seriousness concocted their mad scheme to conquer the entire world, we had reason to believe that the United States of necessity would be part of their plans of conquest.

On the Atlantic side, with which I have had most to do, you would find there are two great avenues of attack on the United States. One of them is called, in our trade, the "Northern Bridge." This is the passage from the continent of Europe to England, from England to Iceland, from Iceland to Greenland, and so to the North American Continent.

The other great avenue of approach is sometimes called the "Atlantic Narrows." This is the narrowest part of the Atlantic Ocean and lies between the shoulder of Africa, with Dakar at its point, and the shoulder of South America, where lies the Brazilian city of Natal.

These are two arms, encircling a huge Atlantic lake. Under the old rules of land and naval warfare neither of these passages was dangerous. But some of us who have studied aviation, and particularly the rise of the German *Luftwaffe*, felt that both of these passages could be used by a determined enemy for surprise thrusts at the United States. If we had time to make arrangements and prepare, of course thrusts could be blocked. But if we were not ready, we should find the enemy on our flanks — and the whole Nazi plan of campaign was to thrust before the enemy was ready and, if possible, to prevent him from being ready by fifth-column activities, propaganda, dirty politics, and every other method known to these evil men. We know now that the Nazis planned attack by both routes.

We tackled both problems. If you followed the news as events took place you will recall that from 1936, at the Buenos Aires Conference, to the present, President Roosevelt, Secretary Hull and Under Secretary Welles, and the State Department worked steadily at bringing the other American Republics into a unified plan of defense of the hemisphere. We offered our aid and full cooperation. By 1939, before the war broke out, we had every reason to believe that any Nazi thrust across the Atlantic Narrows from Africa toward South America would be met with stiff resistance; and we firmly expected to be there, helping.

On the northern side we endeavored to strengthen the hands of the British. We had an added reason for doing this. Alone among the great powers, Great Britain had not waited for an attack by the Nazi and Fascist powers. She guaranteed the existence of Poland and served notice on Hitler that if he continued his career of world-conquest he would have to fight not only weak antagonists but England as well. When war did come, in September 1939, we gave to Britain such assistance as we could and shortly thereafter began an all-out rearmament program of our own. When in April of 1940, almost exactly three years ago, Denmark was invaded, with the assistance of the Danish Minister in Washington we began discussions designed to give us the right to protect Greenland. We set up a joint staff group to work out a common defense of Canada. We undertook the defense of Greenland and shortly after, first with the British and later alone, we took over the defense of Iceland. This made safe the Northern Bridge.

The fall of France in 1940 had left Britain alone — the only country to oppose the Nazi forces then raging unchecked on the continent of Europe. Britain for a century has been traditionally our friend; and she also is the great island fortress lying athwart the Northern Bridge. During the summer of 1940 we rushed supplies for the defense of Britain by every means in our power. Both in honor and in self-interest we could have done no less.

At that same time we took note of the fact that though France had been conquered the great French Empire in North Africa had retained a certain amount of freedom of action. We went to work to make sure that North Africa did not enter into the German orbit. The French Government at Vichy of course was virtually imprisoned by the Germans and was being led by cajolery and threat toward the Axis camp. Until an allied army landed in Europe not very much could be done except to hinder and delay the Germans, and this we did at Vichy. But in North Africa we could make connections in the hope that that great territory would one day rejoin the liberty-loving countries of the world. In terms of defense this meant added protection against a German thrust in the direction of South America. In terms of ultimate victory it meant the possibility of entry into the Mediterranean for allied armies and planes.

Thanks in part to these operations, and in greater part to the bravery of the British people, both the Northern Bridge and the Southern Narrows are now secure. With the landing of our troops in North Africa last November that operation was complete; and with it the character of the war changed. The Nazi attackers were now forced to the defense. Instead of being able to strike at will, they can be struck at will — which is not nearly as much fun.

III

This brief bit of history may serve to give you some idea of the kind of thinking and work the State Department has to do. You will recall that it has not always been easy. There were those who attacked us for being unduly friendly to Britain — and I think those critics know now that they were wrong. There were those — there still are — who attacked us for fighting a rear-guard action at Vichy instead of abandoning old Marshal Pétain outright to the Axis.[1] There were others who criticized our maintaining our staffs in North Africa instead of leaving the field clear for the Germans. Most of those people realize now, I think, that the policy followed was wise.

Certainly the hundreds of thousands of American boys who landed in North Africa know that it was sound policy to work things out so that resistance there was slight and so that they could get at the business of fighting the Axis, who is our enemy, instead of fighting Frenchmen, who are not. This kind of work has to continue until the war is ended.

But besides this the State Department has the primary responsibility for working toward the agreements on which an ultimate peace must be made. In speaking of this I do not wish to give the impression that the war is nearly over. I am clear that Germany has wholly lost the war. But to say that Germany has lost the war does not mean that we have yet won it. The toughest part still lies ahead: a road of blood and sorrow which we must travel relentlessly to the victorious end. In justice to our children we can do no less. We cannot condemn another generation to do this all over again a few years later.

IV

The accords of peace must be submitted to the processes of American public opinion. Their bases are simple, and they are well understood.

There are four great freedom-loving powers in the world. They are the United States, Great Britain, Russia, and China. On these four the great structure of a reorganized and peaceful world must inevitably rest.

With Britain we have the ties of a friendship which has been uninterrupted for nearly a century and a half. This is partly due to the friendly understanding which exists between peoples which speak the same language and which have, beyond all others, the great tradition of democracy. But this friendship has likewise been founded on the fact that, in final analysis, British interests and ours have run together: the thing that was best for the United States was likewise best for Britain. We have been stiff competitors in trade — and both of us have prospered on competition. We have toughly argued questions of commercial

---

[1] For documents relating to our policy, see this volume, p. 535.

policy, and probably will do so again. But whenever a crisis approaches, our two great countries draw together automatically.

A strong and victorious Russia is also necessary to the United States. Let me give a bit of history here which ought to be better known in America. If you follow it you will see that in the last century and a half the existence of a strong Russia has proved a major guaranty of American safety.

In the days when Napoleon attempted to conquer the earth his plans included a large slice of the Western Hemisphere. He was never able to realize those plans, principally because a strong Russia which was not partial to his schemes made it impossible for him to divert sufficient force to make good his conquests; and the defeat of Napoleon began with his retreat from Moscow, just as the defeat of Hitler began with his retreat from Stalingrad.

Again, during our Civil War, certain European countries showed a dangerous desire to take advantage of our misfortune and to seize territory in the Americas. One of them actually set up a Hapsburg emperor on the throne in Mexico. At that time the Russian fleet stood by, thanks to the wise diplomacy of Mr. Seward, then Secretary of State, acting under the guidance of Abraham Lincoln. This discouraged other European nations from taking advantage of our own tragic struggle and safeguarded the American Continent.

Again, in the War of 1914, the Russian pressure on the East Front undoubtedly prevented Germany from crushing France as she did crush France in 1940. The time which Russia then bought for the Allies at the expense of her own men and blood made it possible for Britain, France, and the United States to meet the Germans in the north of France and roll the German armies backward to defeat.

Finally, the Russian resistance during the past 20 months has without doubt proved the turning point in the present World War. Both Britain and we would have been hard put had Russia abandoned her resistance in 1941 and 1942.

I think it is thus clear that Russia is an essential part of the chain of American history. This does not mean that we have always felt that we should care to adopt the Russian form of government. We were not interested in the Czarist government at the time of the Napoleonic Wars or at the time of the Civil War. We were glad when the Russians liberated themselves from the rule of the Czars. Americans are not communist, nor ever likely to be. But we recognize that Russia's form of government is a matter for Russia to choose; and none but the ignorant fail to recognize the many advances made for the Russian people by the communist government.

The fourth great cornerstone is, of course, China. She is the oldest and proudest representative of the Asiatic peoples, with a majestic history. She has also been a power for peace and a steady friend of freedom-loving forces in the western world. She has met the rise of Japanese militarism with a steadfast resistance like that of Washington at Valley Forge. Under impossible circumstances she has stood off one of the strongest of modern military powers.

Friendship between China and the United States is and must be the sheet anchor of our policy in the Pacific Ocean. Wisdom, justice, and mere common sense require that China shall be the great Eastern power in the framework of peace.

With these four are the gallant company of the other 27 United Nations — and of certain of these a special word must be said. When a great country resists another great country it hopes and intends to be victorious. But when a small nation fights against overwhelming power for its liberty the immediate result is terrible catastrophe. It must expect to be overwhelmed by impossible odds. It must rely on the tenacity of its people, continuing to resist even after its enemy has conquered its armies. It must place its faith in the victory of freedom-loving peoples and in the justice of the world. Many of the United Nations are small countries, weak by military standard, but everlastingly strong in patriotism and in spirit. In combination, their resistance, heroic beyond measure, has made possible the victory we hope to attain.

V

In union, the United Nations, grouped around the United States, Britain, Russia, and China, will be invincible in war. It is my conviction that the same union, carried forward into peace, will make possible the reorganization of a peaceful world.

No one nation can maintain peace by itself, just as no one nation can make itself safe by its own efforts. The attempt to do so would exhaust even the strongest country in a short space of years. It follows that we must work out ways of staying together; and our success in doing it will be the greatest guaranty we can give our children that they in their mature years will not go through the travail of another war.

For that very reason our enemies have used every trick of propaganda to endeavor to create division among the United Nations. From reports reaching us we know indeed that the Nazis and the Japanese war lords have already lost faith in their ability to win a military victory. But they hope to escape the stern justice which awaits them by dividing the freedom-loving countries and so achieving a compromise peace. They will fail, of course; but we know the methods they expect to use.

One such method is the attempt to create in Britain and in the United States fear of Soviet Russia. This is based on the fact that both Britain and the United States are not communist and that their civilizations are firmly built on individualist lines instead of on the collective model. Vague rumors, accordingly, are spread of huge imperial plans supposed to be harbored by Soviet Russia, in the hope that fools will thereby slacken aid to the Russian arms. These efforts of Nazi propaganda are often helped by trouble-makers; for both in Britain and in the United States there are meddlers or loose thinkers or plain liars who like to circulate wild stories, always without evidence, that public officials are not sufficiently friendly to Russia — or else, that they are too friendly to Russia. In Washington we know both kinds of rumors very well. I make two piles on my desk every morning. One of them is for the type of letter that says, "Beware of Russia" — coming usually from some misguided person who has heard some propaganda scare story. The other pile is for the type of letter or report which says that there is a plot or conspiracy among public officials to hamstring Russia — again, usually from well-meaning but misguided people who have swallowed propaganda from people who, for reasons of their own, want to create trouble between the Russians and ourselves. The latter type, recently, has frequently been built around tales that Britain or the United States or various officials in one or the other were engaged in constructing buffer states against Russia or in building belts of states designed to be hostile to Russia, known by the French name of *cordon sanitaire*.

Of course, the briefest look at the facts swamps both kinds of propaganda. Soviet Russia, when she is victorious, as she will be, and when she has cleared her lands of Nazi troops, as she will, faces a titanic job in rebuilding her own country. She will not, in our judgment, become the victim of any urge to seize great additions to her already huge empire. What she will want — and ought to want — is safety and security for her own country, which has been invaded by barbarians, with the bloodiest results, twice in 25 years. In her reconstruction she will be entitled to all the cooperation we can give; and while she is fighting, the limit of our help is the limit of our capacity. The military operations which have taken place have been of material assistance; and I am convinced that they will be increasingly useful.

The other story which relates to buffer states is built out of plain ignorance. Buffer states used to be dear to the secret diplomacy of a century ago; they were countries set up to keep apart great powers which could not get along together. Today the idea of a buffer state is as dead as a dodo. You cannot have buffer states in air warfare. Any buffer state, or any belt of buffer states, which could be built around Russia could be flown over by a modern air force in a few minutes and probably demolished in a few hours.

The other typical propaganda line is the story that Britain is scheming and plotting to seize the trade of the world and that America must beware. It is true that Britain is a trading nation. She will need all the trade she can get to repair the damage done her by German bombs. American businessmen themselves, for that matter, hope to have expanded trade when the war is over. But neither Britain nor the United States is able to exclude the other from the world markets; and neither country would if she could. The record shows that when British trade expands ours expands likewise, and that when the prosperity of either country fades away both countries suffer. Britain is one of our best markets, just as the United States is one of the best British markets. We are far more likely to collaborate than we are to exclude.

VI

We can dismiss, I think, the lies circulated by propagandists and trouble-makers. We must, indeed; for we have a great deal of very serious and difficult work to do. The job of building, patiently, quietly, and technically, a world peace is beginning now and will probably last a long time. The guiding principles are very simple:

> World peace must be insured;
> World commerce must be kept moving;
> World opportunity must be kept open.

While the principles are simple enough, the actual task brings in a huge range of questions. They will emerge in general discussion from time to time. Some of them you already know: we are at work on the simplest steps of economic cooperation.

The United Nations, in this case at the initiative of the United States and Great Britain, have begun to exchange ideas on the subject of stabilized currency.[1] If commerce is to revive, there has to be some kind of stable money to make commerce possible.

Discussions are about to begin on the problem of food [2] — a problem which interests every one of us and will do so even more as war takes its toll.

Preliminary studies are being made looking toward a solution of the vast, new problem opened up by civil aviation.

These three discussions are merely the forerunners of a great number of questions which will have to be discussed by experts who can state problems and suggest solutions, and placed before public opinion so that a true meeting of minds may be had. The nature of all the various problems may change and shift as the war goes on; but we are making sure that the hour of victory will not find us unprepared.

I am sure that in spite of the vastness of the task we shall achieve a great measure of success. The American continents have written a happy page in international history through experience in cooperative

---

[1] See this volume, p. 650.   [2] *Ibid.*, p. 297.

action between the 21 republics and between the United States and Canada. The development of the great inter-American experiment through the years reached the point where we had achieved peace without empire and where the smallest nation on this hemisphere could cooperate with the largest without fear.

An equally happy page has been written in the development of the British family of nations, the commonwealth which includes Britain, Canada, Australia, New Zealand, and the Union of South Africa. Here are nations independent yet bound together by common ideals, common interests, and common desires.

The pressures of war have brought these great groups of nations together and have brought them into ever closer relations with the peoples of Europe and of Asia. In our own lifetime we have seen the problems of organization and peace solved between these huge groups. We have reason to hope that they can be solved with other nations and groups of nations as well.

VII

Below these huge problems are always people: your family and mine; our various friends; boys and girls getting through school, getting married, getting jobs, raising families; mature men and women, bearing their part; older men and women, nearing the sunset of life. No one can look soundly and sensibly at foreign affairs unless he looks straight through the screen of governments and diplomats and treaties and pacts, and sees clearly the millions of people, known and unknown, who are striving to live, to work, to serve their country and their kind, to be themselves.

The object of all this huge struggle must be greater security and greater opportunity for all these people, even to the least. When we realize this, it is plain that the selfish interest, the narrow nationalist, the trickster who wants a cheap advantage, the imperialist who wishes to seize the countries of others have no permanent place in modern history.

(13) *Letter from the President (Roosevelt) to the President of the American Society of International Law, Read at the Annual Meeting of the Society, April 30, 1943* [1]

[Excerpt]

. . . .

With war raging on all seas and in far-flung lands, we are face to face with the proposition that the alternative to such shocking destruction

---

[1] A copy of the letter was furnished by Honorable Frederic R. Coudert, to whom it was addressed.

as exists today is a definite body of law accepted and followed by nations in their relations with each other. It is not sufficient to hope that international problems will automatically adjust themselves. We know too well that progress is achieved the hard way. Men on the battlefields are dying that civilization may be saved and that law by which we have learned to govern our conduct toward our neighbor, and not force, shall prevail. The body of law under which our civilization must advance must be a steadily growing one, tempered by past experience but capable of fulfilling the needs of a rapidly changing world. The world must have such law for its dependence. It cannot permit a recurrence of the present reign of lawlessness.

. . . .

(14) *Address by Francis B. Sayre, Special Assistant to the Secretary of State, before the American Society of International Law, Washington, D. C., April 30, 1943* [1]

[Excerpt]

. . . .

You have just heard the words of a great President.[2] I should like to add to these the words of another war President. May I recall to you the words of Woodrow Wilson, spoken at the end of the first World War on May 9, 1919 in the course of his address before the International Law Society at Paris.

"I thought it a privilege to come here tonight," he said, "because your studies were devoted to one of the things which will be of most consequence to men in the future, the intelligent development of international law. In one sense, this great, unprecedented war was fought to give validity to international law, to prove that it has a reality which no nation could afford to disregard; that, while it did not have the ordinary sanctions, while there was no international authority as yet to enforce it, it nevertheless had something behind it which was greater than that, the moral rectitude of mankind. . . .

"In a sense the old enterprise of national law is played out," he went on to say. "I mean that the future of mankind depends more upon the relations of nations to one another, more upon the realization of the common brotherhood of mankind, than upon the separate and selfish development of national systems of law; so that the men who can, if I may express it so, think without language, think the common thoughts of humanity, are the men who will be most serviceable in the immediate future."

I think all of us listening to these words tonight feel the lift of Woodrow Wilson's lofty spirit. All of us alike realize, as the world is coming to realize through fire and suffering, that we cannot hope for enduring peace, we cannot hope for human progress except as we build our law and our institutions upon the conscience of mankind, upon the underlying eternal principle of right as distinct from wrong, upon justice and

[1] Department of State, *Bulletin*, VIII, p. 370.   [2] See this volume, p. 57.

morality and the eternal verities of life. For the world in which we live is a moral world; and sooner or later nations and civilizations built upon unrestrained force and stark materialism and selfish unconcern for humanity are bound as inevitably as the rising of the sun to crash in disaster.

If civilization is to go forward the pathway is clear: First, the inarticulate conscience of mankind, humanity's understanding of right and morality as distinguished from evil, must be formulated and enshrined in written or unwritten objective standards and principles and rules for the guidance of human conduct. Without common standards and formulations of accepted fundamentals of ethics and morals, groups of men can never successfully work together or attain peace. Second, there must be a common determination to defend this body of accepted principles against violation and attack, even, when necessary, at the point of the sword and to the death.

In the latter task we are now engaged. The winning of the present war in spite of its staggering and terrifying cost in human life and material resources is an absolute necessity if civilization is to go forward. For if those who seek to build upon justice and morality and concern for the welfare of others prove unable to develop sufficient strength and power to overcome the opposing forces of inhumanity, of brutishness, of primitive savagery, our civilization has no justification for survival. In that event the Nazis would be right. Their thesis that the Christian ethic weakens and softens and is therefore impractical and injurious to the race would be proven correct. It would be better for mankind to begin anew.

We of the United Nations believe exactly the reverse. We know that the protection of individual liberties which the Axis powers scorn makes for matchless strength in nations and in empires. If we look back through the pages of history we find that power and mastery have come to those nations and those peoples which have developed an understanding and a tolerance for other peoples, which have organized protective care for the weak as against the strong, which have sought to safeguard and strengthen the rights of the individual irrespective of his race or color or physical strength or weakness. It is this concept of individual liberties which justifies the right of our civilization to survive, and it is from this ideal that the United Nations are drawing and will continue to draw the strength and unflagging devotion by which the Axis will be crushed into final defeat.

The practical way, if not the only way, to guard individual liberties is through the development of a body of law based upon even-handed justice.

The great ideal of justice to all alike before the law upon which much of England's greatness has been built and which constituted our own

American birthright existed long before Magna Charta. It existed long before Justinian. But it is highly significant that the two greatest bodies of law which the world has ever known — the Roman law and the English common law, enshrining this great principle — constituted the foundations upon which were built two of the greatest empires which the world has known. And it is equally significant that the strength of these empires has rested primarily not upon the mere physical strength of their armies and their soldiers but upon their legal systems, upon their understanding and regard for the rights of other peoples, and upon their progress in learning the great art of governing subject races.

No nation can possibly hold alien peoples in permanent subjection by mere brute force. All history proves the contrary to be true. The strength of the British Commonwealth today lies largely in the self-governing Dominions, bound to it no longer by force but by ties of understanding and common faith in spiritual ideals. World power rests upon understanding and tolerance, and it can be built only upon respect for the rights of the individual human personality.

What Rome and England achieved for their own empires through the building up of their great systems of law for the protection of the weak against the strong and the guaranty of impartial justice to all alike, must in a sense be undertaken now for humanity. The whole world must build up a body of practice and of law giving expression to the conscience of mankind so far as it relates to the rights of nations and of peoples. Such rights must be based henceforth upon universal justice rather than upon sheer physical force.

Obviously such a task can be achieved by no people single-handed. It can be achieved only by the joint and cooperative effort of all nations and peoples who believe in human brotherhood. And in such a movement it is natural that all the world should turn in hope to America, born of the struggle to make men free. The building of the peace will be a task to try men's souls; and unless we clearly realize the supreme struggle which lies ahead and consecrate ourselves to the coming task with the same devotion now displayed on the battlefront, we cannot hope to win the objectives for which we are fighting.

· · · · · · · ·

(15) *Address by the Under Secretary of State (Welles) at the Commencement Exercises of the North Carolina College for Negroes, Durham, North Carolina, May 31, 1943* [1]

[Excerpt]

· · · · · · ·

The people of the United States realized today, I am convinced, that what we have utterly failed to do in the past was, in the truest and most

---

[1] Department of State, *Bulletin*, VIII, p. 479.

practical sense, "to mind our own business." They cannot fail to see also that had we been willing to play our part in keeping the peace of the world since the last World War the cost to us in life and treasure would have been but an infinitesimal part of the cost required of us today so that we can achieve that victory which we must gain if the United States is to survive as a free nation.

This long-range problem of post-war policy is fundamentally a question of our own self-interest.

I know that men and women are thinking this problem through in every section of this country. The more opportunity which is given for public discussion of these vital issues, the more light which is thrown upon the specific aspects of the complexities which are involved, the more assurance will there be that the answer to be given by our democracy will be a wise one. It has always seemed to me that if the American people had had more time for study and discussion of the basic policy at stake in 1919, and if the issue itself had not become enmeshed in the web of bitter partisan politics, a more realistic and a more enlightened course would have been followed by this country during the past generation.

It is my individual view that it would be premature at this stage for this Government to attempt to define with precision and in detail any exact plan of international cooperation upon which the American people would be expected to pass.

We all of us must agree that certain conditions are going inevitably to obtain at the conclusion of the war.

For a number of years, particularly in Europe, social and economic conditions will be in a state of flux. In some of the presently Axis-occupied countries there will be political instability. Both in these countries as well as in the Axis countries millions will be starving and other millions must be repatriated to the homes from which they have been driven. Throughout the world there will be a chaotic, and in some areas an anarchic, state of affairs.

During this period — and no one can today estimate how long it may be — order will have to be maintained by those of the United Nations which will have to assume these necessary functions.

It is during that transition period, as well as during the remaining period of the war, that the opportunity may presumably be afforded to the United Nations to undertake the more specific elaboration of the form of international organization upon which they may jointly determine.

We all of us remember that the agreements which in their entirety comprise the inter-American understanding upon which Pan Americanism rests, and through which the regional solidarity of the American Republics has had its being, were not brought into existence in a day.

They were not achieved by means of an initial blueprint. On the contrary, the objectives sought were only achieved over a period of many years, and it required an actual act of aggression against one of the American Republics, the United States, to bring about the final consummation of the regional understanding of the Western Hemisphere.

It may well be that the surest course for the United Nations to pursue would be the construction of an international organization by the same method of gradual evolution. By permitting sufficient elasticity of operation at the outset of the transition period, the practical experience undergone by the United Nations during the war as well as after the victory is won will presumably demonstrate clearly the type of organization which will most efficiently guarantee the securing of the basic objectives which they seek.

It seems clear though, as a result of the tragic lesson which humanity has learned from the events of the past 25 years, that any form of international organization, in order to function successfully, must be premised upon the recognition of a few cardinal principles:

There must be, through international agreement, a combination of armed forces made available by the powers which are prepared to do so, which may be used regionally or on a broader scale, and which can and will prevent aggression, render international conflict impossible, and, in general, see to it that the peace of the world is maintained inviolate;

An international tribunal to which international controversies can be referred and in which international confidence can be safely placed;

An efficient international method for the outlawing of certain kinds of armaments and for the inspection of all national armaments;

The creation of appropriate and practical technical organizations to deal with economic and financial matters and to advise the members of the United Nations thereon, so that autarchic commercial and financial policies will not be pursued by individual powers and so that the post-war period may be an epoch of economic cooperation and of rising living standards, rather than a time of cut-throat competition and of falling living standards for us all;

The recognition — not merely in words, but in practice, as in the Western Hemisphere — of the principle of the equal sovereignty of all states, whether great or small. And, together with this, the establishment of the principle that the path must be prepared for the freedom and self-government of all peoples who desire their liberty, as soon as they are able to assume that right;

Finally, in the kind of world for which we fight, there must cease to exist any need for the use of that accursed term "racial or religious minority." If the peoples of the earth are fighting and dying to preserve and to secure the liberty of the individual under law, is it conceivable that the peoples of the United Nations can consent to the re-establishment of any system where human beings will still be regarded as belonging to such "minorities"? The equality of individuals, like the equality of peoples, cannot in fact be granted by fiat. Equality depends on their own achievements and upon their own intrinsic worth. But to equality of human rights and to equality of opportunity every human being is by Divine right entitled. That is the essence of our democratic faith. If that cornerstone is laid in the foundation of the new world of the United Nations, the blot of the concept of minorities upon the fabric of our civilization will be erased.

.   .   .   .

(16) *Address by the President (Roosevelt) to the Delegates to the United Nations Conference on Food and Agriculture, The White House, June 7, 1943* [1]

It gives me great pleasure to welcome to the White House you who have served so splendidly at the epoch-making United Nations Conference on Food and Agriculture.

I use that word *epoch-making* advisedly. The Conference could not have failed to be significant because it was the first United Nations conference. But it has succeeded even beyond our hopes; it is truly epoch-making because, in reaching unanimity upon complex and difficult problems, you have demonstrated beyond question that the United Nations really are united, not only for the prosecution of the war but for the solution of the many and difficult problems of peace. This Conference has been a living demonstration of the methods by which the conversations of nations of like mind contemplated by Article VII of the mutual-aid agreement [2] can and will give practical application to the principles of the Atlantic Charter.

You have been dealing with agriculture, the most basic of all human activities, and with food, the most basic of all human needs. Twice as many people are employed in work on food and agriculture as in work in all other fields combined. And all people have, in the literal sense of the word, a vital interest in food.

That a child or adult should get the nourishment necessary for full health is too important a thing to be left to mere chance.

You have recognized that society must accept this responsibility. As you stated in your declaration: "The primary responsibility lies with each nation for seeing that its own people have the food needed for health and life; steps to this end are for national determination. But

[1] *Ibid.*, p. 518. The Conference was held at Hot Springs, Virginia, May 18–June 3. For documents pertaining to the work of the Conference, see this volume, p. 297.

[2] See *Documents, IV, 1941–42*, p. 237.

each nation can fully achieve its goal only if all work together." On behalf of the United States I accept this declaration.

You have gone beyond the general recognition of principles to deal in specific terms with specific tasks and projects.

You have examined the needs of all countries for food and other agricultural products, both as they will exist in the short-run period of recovery from the devastation of war and as they will exist over the longer run, when our efforts can be fully devoted to expanding the production of food so that it will be adequate for health the world over.

You have surveyed with courage and with realism the magnitude of these problems and have reached unanimous agreement that they can and must and will be solved.

It is true that no nation has ever had enough food to feed all its people as we now know human beings should be fed. But neither have nations representing over 80 per cent of the world's two billion inhabitants ever before been joined together to achieve such an aim. Never before have they set out to bend their united efforts to the development of the world's resources so that all men might seek to attain food they need.

For the short run you have pointed out steps which have to be taken both in increasing supplies and in maintaining economy of use and coordination of distribution.

In considering our long-range problems you have surveyed our knowledge of the inadequacy in the quantity and quality of the diet of peoples in all lands. You have pooled our knowledge of the means of expanding our output, of increasing our agricultural efficiency, and of adjusting agricultural production to consumption needs. In the fields of both production and consumption you have recognized the need for the better utilization of the knowledge we now have and for extending still further the boundaries of our knowledge through education and research.

You have called upon your governments individually and collectively to enlarge and improve their activities in these fields.

For the perfection and rapid execution of these plans, you have recommended the creation of a permanent United Nations organization. To facilitate and hasten the creation of that organization, and to carry on the work you have begun until its creation, you have established an Interim Commission. The Government of the United States is honored that you have asked that the Interim Commission have its seat in Washington, and will be glad to take the preliminary action for the establishment of that Commission which you have entrusted to it.

Finally, you have expressed your deep conviction that our goal in this field cannot be attained without forward action in other fields as well. Increased food-production must be accompanied by increased industrial-production and by increased purchasing power. There must be measures for dealing with trade barriers, international exchange stability, and international investment. The better use of natural and human resources must be assured to improve the living standard and, may I add, the better use of these resources without exploitation on the part of any nation. Many of these questions lie outside the scope of the work you have undertaken, but their solution is nonetheless essential to its success. They require, and shall receive, our united attention.

In the political field these relationships are equally important. And they work both ways. A sound world agricultural program will depend upon world political security, while that security will in turn be greatly strengthened if each country can be assured of the food it needs. Freedom from want and freedom from fear go hand in hand.

Our ultimate objective can be simply stated: It is to build for ourselves, for all men, a world in which each individual human being shall have the opportunity to live out his life in peace; to work productively, earning at least enough for his actual needs and those of his family; to associate with the friends of his choice; to think and worship freely; and to die secure in the knowledge that his children and their children shall have the same opportunities.

That objective, as men know from long and bitter experience, will not be easy to achieve. But you and I know also that throughout history there has been no more worthwhile, no more inspiring, challenge.

That challenge will be met.

You have demonstrated beyond question that free peoples all over the world can agree upon a common course of action and upon common machinery for action. You have brought new hope to the world that through the establishment of orderly international procedures for the solution of international problems there will be attained freedom from want and freedom from fear. The United Nations are united in the war against fear and want as solidly and effectively as they are united on the battlefront in this world-wide war against aggression.

And we are winning by action and unity.

CHAPTER II

DEFENSE AND THE WAR EFFORT

[See *Documents, IV, 1941–42*, p. 125.]

From the outbreak of war in Europe down to December 7, 1941, the United States was not a belligerent. We were nevertheless increasingly conscious of the perils of our position and during this period were committed to a policy of "total defense." [1] Since December 8, our policy has been to wage "total war." [2] That means that we are committed to subordinating every aspect of our national action to winning the war, recognizing nevertheless that as has been often pointed out, war is not an end in itself but rather a means to an end, and that the operations incident to the winning of the war must be subordinated, in so far as the attainment of the more immediate objective is not jeopardized, to the larger purposes for which we must continue to strive after the war is won.

Since the activities of the Government have been of necessity so completely subordinated in the period under review to the purpose of winning the war, the title of this chapter might with some propriety be applied to the whole book. Certainly, the greater part of the documents included in this volume could, without too much violence to the demands of logic, be brought under this head. Our relations with foreign countries, and our policies and actions in dealing with questions of international trade and finance, are for the most part immediately concerned with winning the war.

The actual coverage of this chapter is more modest than its title might justify. The selection of exhibits has been guided by the following considerations of purpose: (1) to convey an idea of the character and scope of modern war; (2) to show the essential unity of our war effort; (3) to acquaint the reader with some of the things which are being done as part of the purely national war effort which will have a bearing on post-war international problems and particularly on the way in which we meet them. While some documents to which reference is made are not included as exhibits because of their predominantly domestic character, citations to official sources are given to aid the reader in making use of them.

1. REQUIREMENTS AND COSTS OF TOTAL WAR

(1) *The First Year on the Home Front. Report from the Office of War Information, December 5, 1942* [3]

The first year of war was the year of the production race — the race to catch up with the advantage which long preparation had given to our enemies, and to surpass that advantage. We have caught up, and we are beginning to pass our adversaries. But the race is still a long way from the finish line, and many hurdles remain to be cleared.

[1] *Message of the President to the Congress, July 10, 1940.* Senate Doc. No. 188, 77th Cong., 2d sess., p. 68.

[2] See this volume, p. 70.

[3] From the Office of War Information; *New York Times*, December 6, 1942.

In that year, these things had to be done: raising, equipping, training and transporting an army; producing a huge volume of weapons, materials and food for our own fighting forces and those of our Allies; and refashioning our civilian economy to permit it to function with maximum efficiency.

It would have been difficult enough to do these jobs if there had been time to work out the basic plans and the details of organization and function. But there was no time. The enemy, knowing that this year was to be crucial, was pressing on every front. Our tasks had to be carried forward in a hurry. It was necessary to meet the requirements of the next day and yet provide the basic plant and organization for the still greater requirements of the next year.

Viewed in this light, the over-all accomplishments of the past year have been considerable, despite mistakes and shortcomings in details.

Measured against the yardstick of the President's production goals of last January, we produced a great deal, but not enough in every category.

In the year 1942 we shall have produced approximately:

> 49,000 planes
> 32,000 tanks and self-propelled artillery
> 17,000 anti-aircraft guns larger than 20 mm.
> 8,200,000 tons of merchant shipping

While we have reached the goal in merchant shipping, we have fallen behind in other categories. Yet there are compensating factors. An increasing proportion of our planes are heavy bombers. In addition to the tanks and self-propelled artillery, many thousands of scout cars and half- and full-track carriers have been produced which are an essential to a well-rounded mechanized force as are tanks themselves. Many, many thousands of anti-aircraft machine guns have been turned out.

Moreover, the total volume of production for war has reached tremendous heights. In 1942 we shall have expended some 47 billions for munitions and war construction, which is substantially above the most optimistic estimate of our production possibilities a year ago.

The record is impressive, but there is no cause for contentment, either in the total figures or in the fact that we are now outproducing the Axis in armaments. The difficulties which lie ahead are as many or more than those which have been surmounted.

A year ago the overriding problem was that of conversion of peacetime industry. By and large that is no longer a problem. Some months ago the proper flow of raw materials was the great problem. That is still with us, but steps have been taken which should go far towards giving us a workable solution. The foremost task now is to bring into balance the myriad components of the program through proper scheduling and production controls.

The production tasks of 1942 seem easy compared to those which lie ahead. In 1942 we were still living off our peacetime fat. We are now close to the bare muscle and we can only proceed by toughening and increasing that muscle. In the next year our program calls for so great an increase in munitions production that we shall have to produce two-thirds again as much as we did in 1942. We are pressing closer to the limits of our resources in materials, transportation and power. And in the next year we shall have to press close to the limit of our ultimate resource — manpower.

A year ago 7,000,000 persons were employed in war work. Now the total has risen to 17,500,000. In 1943 we will need to add at least 5,000,000 to our working and fighting forces. And by the end of that year nearly all of our working population will be engaged in war work or in civilian work geared to the war.

In the year past our manpower problem was not one of national shortage, but of local shortages and bottlenecks in critical areas, aggravated by labor pirating and hoarding and discriminatory practices in the hiring of Negroes, workers from minority groups and women. In the next year local shortages will merge into a national shortage which will require not only additions to the labor supply from women and older and younger people, but extensive transfers from non-war industry and the most efficient utilization of our present labor force.

Our transportation facilities carried the greatest volume of traffic in history and both our railroads and trucking systems set fine records. The next year will see even greater burdens cast on them, with little, if any, additional equipment available. Rubber-borne transportation, truck, bus and private automobiles, presents one of our gravest problems, and stringent tire conservation measures have been undertaken to assure against a breakdown which might vitally impair our productive effort.

Food and fiber production reached a record high in 1942. Food production was 12 per cent above 1941 and 40 per cent above the war year of 1918. A large proportion of this production was in proteins and fats, necessities in time of war — meat, milk, eggs, soybeans.

Increase or even maintenance of this high level will not be an easy matter. Shortages of labor and farm machinery are inevitable, although deferment of essential farm workers and operators from military call will ease the former. In the meantime, the food needs of our armed forces are mounting to such an extent that military and lend-lease buying will take 25 per cent of our farm output. Shortages have developed in some products and will develop in others. Yet an adequate over-all diet can be assured.

The part played by management, labor and the farmers in our production achievements cannot be overestimated. The doubts and hesitancies which impeded conversion of industry went overboard soon after the beginning of the year and conversion was accomplished in much less time than many had feared. Labor voluntarily surrendered the right to strike, and its leaders have loyally kept their agreement. Labor-management committees in some 1800 plants have given us the basis for effective cooperation and for participation by labor in the productive process. Still, some unauthorized strikes remain, as do the lingering traces of business-as-usual in various corners of the production effort.

The refashioning of our civilian economy has taken much effort. Effective stabilization of the civilian economy was delayed for many months over disagreement as to means and methods. By March 15, 1942 the cost of living had risen some 15 per cent over the end of 1939. But price regulation instituted in April held down the increases in prices subject to control to $\frac{6}{10}$ of one per cent as of October 15. Wage stabilization, one of the great issues of the year, has reached the stage of solution. Growing shortages of rubber, meat, sugar, coffee, and gasoline and fuel oil in the East brought the necessity of rationing these and some other commodities to insure an orderly and fair distribution of our supplies. The total volume of goods available to civilian consumers has steadily grown smaller. In the plenty of peacetime we can permit anyone to buy as much as he wants because some will always remain for those who come last. In the scarcity of war, those who cannot stock up must be able to secure their share along with their richer neighbors. For the coming year efforts will be directed towards guaranteeing the essentials of civilian living to prevent such faltering of the civilian economy as will impair the war effort.

The campaign of the home front has had to be carried on in many other sectors. Unprecedented sums of money have been raised through taxes and public financing. In the first ten months of 1942, over 13 billion dollars was collected in taxes, and over 33 billion dollars was raised through the sale of bonds and other government obligations. Provision has had to be made for expanding health, sanitary and welfare services; more housing has been and still is needed for war workers; a civilian defense organization of 10,000,000 volunteers has been built; the safeguarding of our shores and establishments from spies and saboteurs has required constant vigilance.

Not the least of our hosts of problems have been those of governmental organization. New organizations have been created for production, manpower, economic stabilization, the handling of labor disputes and wages, price control, economic warfare, war information, and other matters. A network of combined boards has worked to fuse effectively our resources with those of the other United Nations. Controversy still revolves over organizational problems, and some of them will continue to be with us in the coming year. It took generations to build our structure of peacetime government. Now we are trying, as we must, to build a wartime government in a year or two.

Our country has done a great deal in this one year. Under any ordinary standards we would be entitled to indulge in some degree of satisfaction. The standards of war, and in particular of this war, are much too exacting for any feeling of satisfaction. Next year calls for greater tasks and presents us with equal, if not greater, obstacles. The record of the past may give us this much assurance — that we have no cause for feeling that the job ahead cannot or will not be done.

(2) *Budget Message of the President (Roosevelt) Submitted to the Congress, January 11, 1943* [1]

[Excerpt]

To THE CONGRESS OF THE UNITED STATES:

I am transmitting herewith a war Budget exceeding 100 billion dollars for the fiscal year beginning July 1, 1943. Last year I called the Budget an instrument for transforming a peace economy into a war economy. This Budget presents the maximum program for waging war.

We wage total war because our very existence is threatened. Without that supreme effort we cannot hope to retain the freedom and self-respect which give life its value.

Total war is grim reality. It means the dedication of our lives and resources to a single objective: Victory.

Total war in a democracy is a violent conflict in which everyone must anticipate that both lives and possessions will be assigned to their most effective use in the common effort — the effort for community survival — Nation survival.

In total war we are all soldiers, whether in uniform, overalls, or shirt sleeves.

BUDGETING FOR TOTAL WAR

WAR EXPENDITURES

The huge and expanding rate of war expenditures shows our determination to equip our fighting forces and those of our Allies with the instruments of war needed for victory. Monthly expenditures for war purposes amounted to 2 billion dollars just after Pearl Harbor; they now exceed 6 billion dollars and they will average more than 8 billion dollars a month during the fiscal year 1944. For the whole of the current fiscal year total war expenditures are now estimated at 77 billion dollars; for the next fiscal year, at 100 billion dollars. These estimates include the net outlays

[1] From the Office of the Secretary to the President; *Congressional Record*, vol. 89, pt. 1, p. 98–102.

of Government corporations for war purposes and assume only a small rise in prices.

Victory cannot be bought with any amount of money, however large; victory is achieved by the blood of soldiers, the sweat of working men and women, and the sacrifice of all people. But a 100-billion-dollar expenditure program does reflect a national effort of gigantic magnitude. It calls for vision on the part of those in charge of war production, ingenuity of management, and the skill, devotion, and tenacity of the men on the farms and in the factories. It makes possible the expansion of our armed forces necessary to offensive operations, the production of planes and munitions to provide unquestioned superiority, and the construction of ships which will make it possible for us to strike at the enemy wherever he may be. It reflects the determination of the civilians to "pass the ammunition." Moreover, consumers' goods and services will have to be produced in an amount adequate to maintain the health and productivity of the civilian population. And all of this will have to be done while we are withdrawing millions of men from production for service in the armed forces.

Some persons may believe that such a program is fantastic. My reply is that this program is feasible. If the Nation's manpower and resources are fully harnessed, I am confident that the objective of this program can be reached, but it requires a complete recognition of the necessities of total war by all — management, labor, farmers, consumers, and public servants — regardless of party. Production short of these military requirements would be a betrayal of our fighting men.

This Budget does not include the detailed estimates of war expenditures which would reveal information to our enemies. An additional reason for such action at this time is that rapid developments on far-flung battle fronts make it impossible to submit a detailed war Budget for a year ending 18 months hence. I shall continue, however, to report on the broad categories of war expenditures. The following table summarizes our present estimates of war expenditures from general and special accounts and by Government corporations.

Estimates of total expenditures for war, fiscal years 1943 and 1944

[Billions]

Object of Expenditure	Fiscal 1943	Fiscal 1944
Munitions	$43	$66
Military and civilian pay, subsistence, and travel	15	21
Industrial construction	6	2
Other construction	8	5
Other, including agricultural lend-lease	5	6
Total	$77	$100

This spring I shall submit the necessary information upon which the Congress can base war appropriations for the fiscal year 1944.[1] In the meantime there are available about 170 billion dollars of unspent war appropriations and authorizations; about two-thirds of this amount is already obligated or committed. Further appropriations will soon be needed to permit letting of contracts with industry for the next year.

THE PROCUREMENT OF MUNITIONS

Total mobilization of all our men and women, all our equipment, and all our materials in a balanced production program will enable us to accomplish the production goals underlying this war Budget.

Manpower. — Marked progress has been made in mobilizing manpower. In spite of the increase in the armed services, industrial production rose by 46 per cent, and agricultural production by 15 per cent between calendar years 1940 and 1942. Industrial production has not been delayed and crops have not been lost because of lack of manpower except in a few isolated cases. More than 10 million people have been added to the employed or the armed forces since the summer of 1940, 7 million of whom were unemployed and more than 3 million of whom are additions to the Nation's labor and armed forces.

Manpower mobilization is now entering a much more difficult phase. During the calendar year 1943 approximately 6 million people will be needed above present requirements for the armed services and war production. This number can be obtained by transferring from less essential work, and by drawing into the working force people who have not recently sought employment. Vigorous action is required to mobilize and train our reserve of women and young people, to accelerate the transfer of workers to essential industries, and to reduce harmful turnover and migration of workers in essential industries. It also requires prevention of labor hoarding and elimination of hiring restrictions based on sex, creed, or race. I reiterate my previous recommendation for a unified and adequate rehabilitation service to make available a million persons for war industry and to restore to civil employment persons who are being disabled in the armed forces.

Manpower needs of the armed forces and of war production during the calendar year 1943 can be met without impairment of essential civilian requirements. I stress the important distinction between "essential requirements" and the thousand and one things that are nonessentials or luxuries. The production of these nonessentials wastes manpower at a time when careful economy and greater efficiency in the use of our manpower resources is imperative. Private thought and public discussion of this subject are very necessary.

[1] See this volume, p. 80, 89.

Equipment. — Were it not for an unprecedented program of conversion and the building up of a new war industry during the past two and one-half years, we could not expect to fulfill the war-production program outlined in this Message.

Some progress, but not enough, has been made in spreading war contracts more widely among medium-sized and smaller plants. Further efforts are necessary. In certain cases, of course, saving of manpower and materials requires concentration in those plants best equipped to produce a given commodity.

Materials. — Furthermore, war production is limited by our supply of raw materials. The available materials must be transformed into the maximum of striking power. The production of less urgent or the wrong quantity of items, or poor scheduling of production in any single plant or in the munitions program as a whole, results in waste of precious materials. The Nation's war production must be so scheduled that the right items are produced in the right amounts at the right time.

War contracts. — The procurement program must achieve maximum production with minimum waste and with the speed essential in time of war. This is the controlling objective not only for the original negotiation of contracts but also for the renegotiation required by law. The law provides for the prevention or recapture of excessive profits, thus supplementing and reinforcing the objectives of the excess-profits tax. I believe that control of the costs of production is of equal importance.

The proper negotiation and renegotiation of contracts must strive to reconcile the avoidance of excessive profits with the maintenance of incentives to economical management.

FARM AND FOOD PROGRAM

Food is a primary weapon of war. An adequate food supply is, therefore, a basic aspect of a total war program. I have placed in the hands of the Secretary of Agriculture full responsibility for determining and fulfilling the food requirements in this war. Our agricultural production is larger than ever in our history but the needs of our armed services and our Allies are so great that a shortage of certain foods is inevitable. The production of the less-needed commodities must be reduced, while the production of commodities for war and essential civilian use must be increased. It is imperative also that this increased demand for food be adjusted to available supplies. There will be sufficient volume in our bill of fare but less variety. That may hurt our taste but not our health.

To facilitate this program, I am recommending appropriations for Aids to Agriculture totaling 837 million dollars for the fiscal year 1944. Among the major items included in the 837-million-dollar total are 400 million for Conservation and Use of Agricultural Land Resources;

194 million for Parity Payments on the 1942 crops; and 96 million for Exportation and Domestic Consumption of Surplus Commodities. Other large items included are 64 million dollars for payments under the Sugar Act; 38 million for the Farm Security Administration; and 31 million for reductions in interest rates on farm mortgages.

Prior to the 1943 appropriation acts, annual appropriations for parity payments were made a year in advance of actual need, and acreage allotments for the year ahead were used as a factor in determining payments on the crops of the current year. In the 1943 Budget and appropriation acts, provisions were made to insure that all factors used in determining the amount of parity payments on the crops of a given year would pertain to the program of that year. Also, to bring this item into conformity with our general budgetary practice, the annual cash appropriation for parity payments was omitted, but the Secretary was authorized to incur contractual obligations assuring the cooperating producers of cotton, corn, wheat, rice, and tobacco that such payments would be made, if and as necessary, on their 1942 crops.

The appropriation now requested, therefore, is simply the amount estimated to be necessary to compensate the producers of corn, wheat, and certain minor types of tobacco for the disparity between the market returns from the normal yield of their 1942 allotted acreage and the parity price return from that production. It is expected that no parity payments will be necessary on the 1942 crops of cotton, rice, and most types of tobacco.

Since the established national policy is to assure the cooperating producers of these basic crops parity prices on the normal yields of their allotted acreages, I am again recommending that the authority to incur contractual obligations for such payments on future crops be renewed.

On the other hand, I am recommending a reduction of 50 million dollars in the appropriation for Conservation and Use of Agricultural Land Resources. I am also directing the Secretary of Agriculture to utilize the 400 million dollars still provided under this heading as fully and effectively as the basic law will permit to encourage greater production of the crops essential to the war effort. This fund will not be used for restriction of production except of less-needed crops. Payments will be made only to those producers who comply fully in their plantings with the stated war-production goals.

For Exportation and Domestic Consumption of Agricultural Commodities the Budget includes only the permanent annual appropriation of 30 per cent of customs revenues provided by law, plus reappropriation of unobligated balances. The food-stamp plan, which is a major item of the current program, will be discontinued shortly. Although other items such as school lunch and school milk projects and the direct distribution of surplus commodities are somewhat expanded, there will be an over-all reduction of about 30 million dollars.

Provision for operations under the Farm Tenant Act and for Loans, Grants, and Rural Rehabilitation are continued on about the same level as for the current year. Small farms, like other small war plants, must be encouraged to make a maximum contribution to the war. I hope the Congress will give as much sympathetic consideration to these smaller and poorer farmers as it has given to the smaller and poorer industrial concerns.

Because no one can immediately foresee all the needs we may encounter in fulfilling our essential war requirements for agriculture, various loan and purchase operations, involving contingent liabilities which cannot be exactly predetermined, may be necessary.

CIVILIAN CONSUMPTION

In spite of a 100-billion-dollar war program, civilians can be supplied with an average of about $500 worth of goods and services during the next year. This implies an average reduction of almost 25 per cent in civilian consumption below the record level of the calendar year 1941. Even then most of us will be better fed, better clothed, and better housed than other peoples in the world. Do not let us assume from that statement, however, that there is no need for great improvement in the living conditions of a large segment of our population.

It is the responsibility of the Government to plan for more production of essential civilian goods and less of nonessential goods. Production and distribution of goods should be simplified and standardized; unnecessary costs and frills should be eliminated. Total war demands simplification of American life. By giving up what we do not need, all of us will be better able to get what we do need.

In order to distribute the scarce necessities of life equitably we are rationing some commodities. By rationing we restrict consumption, but only to assure to each civilian his share of basic commodities.

The essentials for civilian life also include a good standard of health and medical service, education, and care for children in wartime as well as in peace.

THE STABILIZATION PROGRAM

We must assure each citizen the necessities of life at prices which he can pay. Otherwise, rising prices will lift many goods beyond his reach just as surely as if those goods did not exist. By a concerted effort to stabilize prices, rents, and wages we have succeeded in keeping the rise in the cost of living within narrow bounds. We shall continue those efforts, and we shall succeed. By making effective use of all measures of control, we shall be able to stabilize prices with only a limited use of subsidies to stimulate needed production.

Some would like to see the controls relaxed for this or that special group. They forget that to relax controls for one group is an argument to relax for other groups, thereby starting the cost-of-living spiral which would undermine the war effort and cause grave post-war difficulties. Economic stabilization for all groups — not for just the other fellow — is the only policy consistent with the requirements of total war. I have read of this bloc, and that bloc, and the other bloc, which existed in past Congresses. May this new Congress confine itself to one bloc — a national bloc.

Stabilization goes beyond effective price control. Under war conditions a rise in profits, wages, and farm incomes unfortunately does not increase the supply of goods for civilians; it merely invites the bidding up of prices of scarce commodities. The stabilization of incomes and the absorption of excess purchasing power by fiscal measures are essential for the success of the stabilization program. I am confident that the Congress will implement that program by adequate legislation increasing taxation, savings, or both. Thus, we will help to "pay as we go" and make the coming peace easier for ourselves and our children.

CIVILIAN CONTROLS IN TOTAL WAR

Total war requires nothing less than organizing all the human and material resources of the Nation. To accomplish this all-out mobilization speedily, effectively, and fairly we have had to adopt extensive controls over civilian life. We use the Selective Service System to man the armed forces. We are systematizing the movement of labor to assure needed manpower to war industries and agriculture. We regulate prices, wages, salaries, and rents; we limit consumer credit; we allocate scarce raw materials; and we ration scarce consumer goods — all to the end of providing the materials of war and distributing the sacrifices equitably.

Such regulations and restrictions have complicated our daily lives. We save rubber, metal, fats — everything. We fill out forms, carry coupons, answer questionnaires. This is all new. We have overdone it in many cases. By trial and error we are learning simpler and better methods. But remember always that reaching the objective is what counts most. There is no easy, pleasant way to restrict the living habits — the eating, clothing, heating, travel, and working habits — of 130 million people. There is no easy, pleasant way to wage total war.

About 400,000 civilian employees of the Federal Government are engaged in the task of civilian administration for total war. They direct and schedule war production; handle the procurement of food, munitions, and equipment for our armed forces and our Allies; supervise wartime transportation; administer price, wage, rent, labor, and material controls and commodity rationing; conduct economic and propaganda offensives against our enemies; and do necessary paper work for the armed forces.

Besides these Government employees, millions of men and women volunteers — who draw no pay — are carrying out tasks of war administration, many of them after long hours at their regular occupation. These patriotic citizens are serving on draft boards, on war price and ration boards, in the civilian defense organization, the war bond campaign, and many other activities. They deserve the gratitude of their countrymen.

More than 1,600,000 — or approximately three-fifths — of all Federal civilian employees are engaged directly in war production. They build and load ships, make guns and shells, repair machines and equipment, build arsenals and camps, sew uniforms, operate airports and signal systems. These are the workers in navy yards, arsenals, storage depots, military airfields, and other operating centers. It is scarcely ethical to try to make people believe that these workers are holding down armchair or unnecessary Government jobs.

This huge organization, created overnight to meet our war needs, could not be expected to function smoothly from the very start. Congressional committees and many individuals have made helpful suggestions. Criticism is welcome if it is based on truth. We will continue our efforts to make the organization more fully effective.

.   .   .   .

Financing Total War

THE NEED FOR ADDITIONAL FUNDS

Financing expenditures which will exceed 100 billion dollars is a task of tremendous magnitude. By meeting this task squarely we will contribute substantially to the war effort and clear the ground for successful reconstruction after the war. An adequate financial program is essential both for winning the war and for winning the peace.

Financing total war involves two main fiscal problems. One problem is to supply the funds currently required to pay for the war and to keep the increase in Federal debt within bounds. The second problem is caused by the disbursement of 100 billion dollars a year to contractors, war workers, farmers, soldiers, and their families, thus adding many billions to the people's buying power, at a time when the amount of goods to be bought is declining steadily. A large portion of this excess buying power must be recovered into the Treasury to prevent the excess from being used to bid up the price of scarce goods and thus undermine the stabilization program by breaking price ceilings, creating black markets, and increasing the cost of living.

We cannot hope to increase tax collections as fast as we step up war expenditures or to absorb by fiscal measures alone all excess purchasing power created by these expenditures. We must, therefore, provide a substantial portion of the needed funds by additional borrowing, and we must also use direct controls, such as price ceilings and rationing, for the protection of the consumer. Nevertheless, the more nearly increases in tax receipts follow increases in expenditures, the better we safeguard our financial integrity and the easier the administration of price control and rationing. All of these measures are interrelated. Each increase in taxes and each increase in savings will lessen the upward pressure on prices and reduce the amount of rationing and other direct controls we shall need.

The revenue acts of the past three years, particularly the Revenue Act of 1942, have contributed greatly toward meeting our fiscal needs. In the fiscal year 1944, total general and special receipts under present law are estimated at 35 billion dollars, or almost six times those of the fiscal year 1940. But the increase in expenditures has been even more rapid.

I believe that we should strive to collect not less than 16 billion dollars of additional funds by taxation, savings, or both, during the fiscal year 1944.

On the basis of present legislation, we expect to meet 34 per cent of total estimated Federal expenditures by current receipts during the fiscal year 1944. If the objective proposed in this Message is adopted, we shall meet approximately 50 per cent of expenditures during the fiscal year 1944.

THE NEED FOR A BALANCED AND FLEXIBLE REVENUE SYSTEM

I hope that the Congress in working out the revenue program will consider that the fiscal measures must be designed not only to provide revenue, but also to support the stabilization program as well by deterring luxury or nonessential spending. The cost of the war should be distributed in an equitable and fair manner. Furthermore, care should be taken that the fiscal measures do not impair but actually promote maximum war production. Finally, it is more important than ever before to simplify taxation both for taxpayers and for those collecting the tax, and to put our taxes as far as feasible on a pay-as-you-go basis.

I cannot ask the Congress to impose the necessarily heavy financial burdens on the lower and middle incomes unless the taxes on higher and very large incomes are made fully effective. At a time when wages and salaries are stabilized, the receipt of very large net incomes from any source constitutes a gross inequity undermining national unity.

Fairness requires the closing of loopholes and the removal of inequities which still exist in our tax laws. I have spoken on these subjects on several previous occasions.

The Congress can do much to solve our problem of war finance and to support the stabilization program. In the past, wars have usually been paid for mainly by means of inflation, thereby shifting the greatest burden to the weakest shoulders and inviting post-war collapse. We seek to avoid both. Of necessity, the program must be harsh. We should remember, however, that it is a war for existence, and not taxation, which compels us to devote more than one-half of all our resources to war use. An effective program of war finance does not add to the total sacrifices necessitated by war, but it does assure that those sacrifices are distributed equitably and with a minimum of friction.

We should remember, furthermore, that helping to finance the war is the privilege mainly of those who still enjoy the receipt of incomes as civilians during the war. It is a modest contribution toward victory when we compare it with the contribution of those in the fighting forces.

By the end of the current fiscal year, the public debt will total 135 billion dollars. By June 30, 1944, it will be about 210 billion dollars under existing revenue legislation. Before the present debt limit of 125 billion dollars is reached, the Congress will be requested to extend that limit. To do this is sound, for such a debt can and will be repaid. The Nation is soundly solvent.

Preparing for Total Victory

Preparing for total victory includes preparing the base on which a happier world can be built. The tremendous productive capacity of our country, of all countries, has been demonstrated. Freedom from want for everybody, everywhere, is no longer a Utopian dream. It can be translated into action when the fear of aggression has been removed by victory. The soldiers of the fighting forces and the workmen engaged in military production want to be assured that they will return to a life of opportunity and security in a society of free men.

The economic stabilization program, although born of war necessity, will greatly facilitate post-war reconstruction. A determined policy of war taxation and savings will aid in making post-war problems manageable by reducing the volume of additional borrowing and supporting the stabilization program. Because of the unavoidable magnitude of interest-bearing debt, taxes probably will never revert to their pre-war level. But substantial reduction from the war level will, nevertheless, be possible and will go hand in hand with a greater human security if the underlying fiscal structure is kept sound.

I shall be happy to meet with the appropriate committees of the Congress at any and all times in regard to the methods by which they propose to attain the objectives outlined in this Message. We are at one in our desire quickly to win this war and to avoid passing on to future generations more than their just share of its sacrifices and burdens.

JANUARY 6, 1943. FRANKLIN D. ROOSEVELT.

(3) Comparative Statement of Receipts and Expenditures for the Fiscal Years 1944, 1943 and 1942 [1]

This table gives expenditures and receipts for the fiscal years 1942 and 1943 (actual), and 1944 (as estimated in January 1943, and as revised in July 1943). It also shows the effect of these financial operations on the Federal debt. It is to be noted that while appropriations are the legal basis for incurring obligations and for the subsequent expenditure of cash, the figures for actual cash payments do not correspond with the appropriation figures. Thus while appropriations for war activities for the years 1942, 1943 and 1944 were roughly 111, 75 and 98 billion dollars respectively, actual expenditures for the years 1942 and 1943 were roughly 28 and 75 billion dollars, and for 1944 were estimated in July 1943 to be roughly 100 billion dollars. This is due to the fact that money appropriated is not necessarily spent in the year for which it is appropriated or in which obligations are incurred.

These statistics on the relative outlays for war and other activities and on the great increase in the public debt afford striking evidence of the financial effect of total war on the national economy and suggest some of the problems which the country will have to face in the post-war period. They are the monetary expression of the war effort.

CLASSIFICATION	1944		1943 ACTUAL	1942 ACTUAL
	REVISED ESTIMATES JULY 1943	BUDGET ESTIMATES JANUARY 1943		
GENERAL AND SPECIAL ACCOUNTS				
RECEIPTS:				
Direct taxes on individuals	$18,795,000,000	$13,750,600,000	$7,077,427,667	$3,695,340,678
Direct taxes on corporations	14,080,400,000	14,915,000,000	9,995,930,353	5,021,578,716
Excise taxes	4,021,380,000	3,915,380,000	3,796,648,587	3,127,631,235
Employment taxes . . .	2,105,000,000	1,982,000,000	1,507,919,214	1,194,046,889
Customs	333,700,000	204,300,000	324,290,778	388,948,427
Miscellaneous receipts .	1,014,215,000	639,215,000	906,117,131	277,376,297
Adjustment to daily Treasury statement basis .	—	—	− 223,688,228	− 37,007,418
Total receipts . .	40,349,695,000	35,406,695,000	23,384,645,502	13,667,914,824
Deduct:				
Net appropriation for Federal old-age and survivors insurance trust fund	1,631,750,000	1,525,450,000	1,103,002,793	868,853,203
Post-war credits for excess-profits tax and Victory tax	570,000,000	800,000,000	210,000,000	—
Net receipts . . .	38,147,945,000	33,081,245,000	22,071,642,709	12,799,061,621

[1] Based on Table 2 appended to the *Statement by the President on the Summation of the 1944 Budget*, issued by the Office of the Secretary to the President for publication August 1, 1943.

| CLASSIFICATION | 1944 | | 1943 ACTUAL | 1942 ACTUAL |
	REVISED ESTIMATES JULY 1943	BUDGET ESTIMATES JANUARY 1943		
GENERAL AND SPECIAL ACCOUNTS				
EXPENDITURES:				
War activities: [1]				
War Department . .	56,000,000,000	62,000,000,000	42,265,037,019	14,097,466,382
Navy Department . .	28,000,000,000	24,000,000,000	20,888,349,025	8,579,588,976
U.S. Maritime Commission	4,200,000,000	4,300,000,000	2,775,752,114	929,451,092
War Shipping Administration	2,500,000,000	1,900,000,000	1,104,980,535	132,171,176
Other	6,300,000,000	4,800,000,000	5,074,743,511	2,272,387,464
Total war activities	97,000,000,000	97,000,000,000	72,108,862,204	26,011,065,090
Interest on the public debt .	2,700,000,000	3,000,000,000	1,808,160,396	1,260,085,336
Other activities	4,340,820,000	4,128,924,923	4,265,326,041	5,220,156,972
Total expenditures	104,040,820,000	104,128,924,923	78,182,348,641	32,491,307,398
Excess of expenditures, general and special accounts	65,892,875,000	71,047,679,923	56,110,705,932	19,692,245,777
GOVERNMENT CORPORATIONS AND CREDIT AGENCIES				
NET EXPENDITURES (from checking accounts):				
War activities	3,000,000,000	2,693,000,000	2,975,711,476	2,254,949,959
Redemption of obligations in the market	2,894,588,000	1,772,123,000	688,141,664	1,809,413,050
Other activities	[a] 1,166,588,000	309,000,000	[a] 1,470,167,674	[a] 439,638,755
Net expenditures .	4,728,000,000	4,774,123,000	2,193,685,466	3,624,724,254
TRUST ACCOUNTS				
RECEIPTS	4,845,331,400	4,666,197,150	3,939,498,582	3,190,884,100
EXPENDITURES . . .	4,811,700,000	4,631,402,115	3,606,797,088	3,071,664,796
Excess of receipts over expenditures	33,631,400	34,795,035	332,701,494	119,219,304
THE PUBLIC DEBT				
Public debt at beginning of year	136,696,090,330	134,830,142,661	72,422,445,116	48,961,443,535
Net increase in public debt during year	69,303,909,670	74,919,007,888	64,273,645,214	23,461,001,581
Public debt at end of year .	206,000,000,000	209,749,150,549	136,696,090,330	72,422,445,116

[1] Expenditures from Lend-Lease (Defense Aid) appropriations are included under the various agencies.
[a] Excess of receipts over expenditures.

2. ADMINISTRATIVE POWERS AND ORGANIZATION

[See *Documents, IV, 1941-42*, p. 126.]

Generally speaking, the administrative problems which became critical during this period were problems arising from the necessity of integrating the total activities of the people of the country into one unified effort. In order to meet this need for the more effective use of available resources for war purposes while keeping to a minimum those dislocations and abnormalities likely to have bad effects in the post-war period, it became necessary to revise, in some respects radically, the existing administrative set-up.

The War Production Board, as originally established by Executive Order of the President on January 16, 1942,[1] continued during the period under consideration as the agency responsible for the general direction of the war procurement and production program. To strengthen the Board in dealing with the threatened rubber shortage, and on the basis of recommendations made by the Rubber Survey Committee,[2] the President, by Executive Order No. 9246, September 17, 1942,[3] gave to the Chairman of the Board "full responsibility for and control over the Nation's rubber program in all of its phases" and created within the War Production Board, a Rubber Director, appointed by and responsible to the Chairman. The organization and distribution of functions within the War Production Board were established by General Administrative Order No. 2–85, March 19, 1943.[4]

Problems of production and distribution became critical in respect to products other than rubber as the result of special demands and difficulties of production and procurement incident to the war. To deal with the problem of petroleum products, the President established by Executive Order No. 9276, December 2, 1942,[5] the Petroleum Administration for War, which was vested with authority to "establish basic policies and formulate plans and programs to assure for the prosecution of the war the conservation and most effective development of petroleum in the United States and its territories and possessions." When, as the result of cessations of work in the coal-mining industry, a shortage of coal threatened the country, the President, by Executive Order No. 9332, April 19, 1943,[6] established within the Department of the Interior, the Solid Fuels Administration for War, headed by an Administrator vested with authority of like nature and extent over solid fuels.

War demands for food and the need of preparing in advance to meet relief requirements, combined with manpower shortages and certain maladjustments incidental to priorities and price control, threatened an actual shortage of important foods both during the war and in the post-war period. To meet this situation, the President, by Executive Order No. 9280, December 5, 1942,[7] vested in the Secretary of Agriculture certain powers in connection with the determination of food requirements and the production and distribution of food. By Executive Order No. 9322, March 26, 1943,[8] the Food Production Administration (except the Farm Credit Administration), the Food Distribution Administration, the Farm Credit Corporation and the Extension Service were consolidated within the Department of Agriculture into an Administration of Food Production and Distribution, under the direction and supervision of an Administrator appointed by and responsible to the President, and vested with the powers given the Secretary of Agriculture under the Executive Order of December 5, 1942. By Executive Order No. 9334, April 19, 1943,[9] the name of the agency was changed to War Food Administration.

As the result of increased demands for manpower in connection with all aspects of the war effort, the situation became increasingly critical during the period under review. By Executive Order No. 9139, April 18, 1942,[10] the President had established a Manpower Commission to serve as a coordinating agency. By

---

[1] For text of order, and other information bearing on organization and functions of the Board, see *Documents, IV, 1941–42*, p. 161.

[2] House Doc. No. 836, 77th Cong., 2d sess.   [3] 7 *Fed. Reg.*, p. 7379.

[4] War Production Board, *Manual of Policy and Procedures; United States Government Manual* (Summer, 1943), p. 119.   [5] 7 *Fed. Reg.*, p. 10091.

[6] 8 *ibid.*, p. 5355.   [7] 7 *ibid.*, p. 10179.   [8] 8 *ibid.*, p. 3807.

[9] *Ibid.*, p. 5423.   [10] *Documents, IV, 1941–42*, p. 142.

Executive Order No. 9247, September 17, 1942,[1] certain additional functions in connection with employment service and training were transferred to the Commission. By Executive Order No. 9279, December 5, 1942 [2] the Selective Service System was transferred to the War Manpower Commission and its administration was made subject to the supervision and direction of the Chairman.

Perhaps the most critical problem that the Administration had to face during the year under review so far as the "home front" was concerned was that presented by the increasing pressure of purchasing power, unabsorbed into the war effort, on the available supply of goods. The threat of inflation was recognized as serious both from the point of view of the war effort and from the point of view of post-war adjustment. A separate agency to deal with problems of inflation and civilian supply was first created on April 11, 1941, when the President by Executive Order No. 8734 [3] created the Office of Price Administration and Civilian Supply. By Executive Order No. 8875, August 28, 1941,[4] the name of the agency was changed to Office of Price Administration, and the functions of allocating civilian supply were transferred to the Office of Production Management. The Emergency Price Control Act of 1942, approved by the President, January 30, 1942,[5] created the Office of Price Administration as an independent agency. The purposes of the Office were declared to be, among others, to stabilize prices and to prevent speculative, unwarranted and abnormal increases in prices and rents and to eliminate and prevent profiteering, hoarding, speculation and other disruptive practices resulting from abnormal market conditions or scarcities caused by or contributing to the national emergency. Following rising pressure from certain interested groups for increased prices and wages, President Roosevelt, in a message to Congress on September 7, 1942,[6] pointed out the seriousness of the inflation threat which faced the country and asked that the Congress pass legislation under which the President would be specifically authorized to stabilize the cost of living, including the price of all farm commodities. The President stated that in case the Congress failed to act by October 1, he would accept the responsibility, asserting that he had "the powers, under the Constitution and under Congressional acts, to take measures necessary to avert a disaster which would interfere with the winning of the war." [7]

By Act of October 2, 1942,[8] the Emergency Price Control Act of 1942 was extended to June 30, 1944, and the President was authorized to stabilize prices, wages and salaries affecting the cost of living. By Executive Order No. 9250, October 3, 1942,[9] the President established the Office of Economic Stabilization, under an Economic Stabilization Director, in the Office for Emergency Management, and also set up within the Office of Economic Stabilization an Economic Stabilization Board with which the Director was to advise and consult. The Director was given the authority, with the approval of the President, to "formulate and develop a comprehensive national economic policy relating to the control of civilian purchasing power, prices, rents, wages, salaries, profits, rationing, subsidies, and all related matters — all for the purpose of preventing avoidable increases in the cost of living, cooperating in minimizing the unnecessary migration of labor from one business, industry, or region to another, and facilitating the prosecution of the war," and "to issue directives on policy to the Federal departments and agencies concerned." The guiding policy of the Director was declared to be "to stabilize the cost of living in accordance with the Act of October 2, 1942." General directives for the stabilization of wages, prices and salaries were set forth in Executive Order No. 9328, April 8, 1943,[10] and the Economic Stabilization Director was authorized to exercise "all powers and duties conferred upon the President" by the Act of October 2, 1942.

[1] 7 *Fed. Reg.*, p. 7379.   [2] *Ibid.*, p. 10177; see this volume, p. 92.
[3] 6 *Fed. Reg.*, p. 1917.   [4] *Ibid.*, p. 4483.   [5] 56 Stat. 29.
[6] *Congressional Record*, vol. 88, pt. 5, p. 7042.   [7] *Ibid.*, p. 7285.
[8] 56 Stat. 765.   [9] 7 *Fed. Reg.*, p. 7871.   [10] 8 *ibid.*, p. 4681.

Broad powers to ration commodities among consumers were delegated to the Office of Price Administration by the Chairman of the War Production Board, under the terms of Directive 1, issued January 24, 1942.[1] By Executive Order No. 9125, April 7, 1942,[2] the President delegated to the Price Administrator certain enforcement authority with respect to rationing, acting under Title III of the Second War Powers Act, approved March 27, 1942.[3]

The administrative organization as it had thus far developed was criticized rather generally on the ground that the responsibility rested upon the President, already overtaxed by other demands upon his time and energy, to coordinate the different aspects of the war effort on the home front. The Office of War Mobilization was established with a view to relieving the President personally of a major part of this responsibility.

For further information on the evolution and details of administrative powers and organization for meeting the emergency requirements of the war effort, consult *United States Government Manual*, issued by the Division of Public Inquiries, Office of War Information.

(1) *Executive Order No. 9347 Establishing the Office of War Mobilization, May 27, 1943* [4]

By virtue of the authority vested in me by the Constitution and the statutes of the United States, particularly by the First War Powers Act, 1941,[5] as President of the United States and as Commander-in-Chief of the Army and Navy, and in order to provide for the more effective coordination of the mobilization of the nation for war, it is hereby ordered as follows:

I

There is established in the Office for Emergency Management of the Executive Office of the President an Office of War Mobilization which shall be under the direction of a Director of War Mobilization (hereinafter referred to as Director), to be appointed by the President.

II

There is established in the Office of War Mobilization the War Mobilization Committee (hereinafter referred to as the Committee), of which the Director shall be the Chairman and with which he shall advise and consult. The Committee shall consist, in addition to the Director, of the Secretary of War, the Secretary of the Navy, the Chairman of the Munitions Assignments Board, the Chairman of the War Production Board, and the Director of Economic Stabilization. The Chairman shall request the heads of other agencies or departments to participate in the deliberations of the Committee whenever matters specially affecting such agencies or departments are under consideration. It shall be

---

[1] Executive Order No. 9040, 7 *Fed. Reg.*, p. 527.
[2] 7 *Fed. Reg.*, p. 2719.
[3] 56 Stat. 177. See *Documents, IV, 1941–42*, p. 128.
[4] From the Office of the Secretary to the President; 8 *Fed. Reg.*, p. 7207.
[5] See *Documents, IV, 1941–42*, p. 126.

the duty of the heads of the agencies and departments to supply necessary data to the Director and the Committee.

III

It shall be the function of the Office of War Mobilization, acting in consultation with the Committee and subject to the direction and control of the President,

(a) To develop unified programs and to establish policies for the maximum use of the nation's natural and industrial resources for military and civilian needs, for the effective use of the national manpower not in the armed forces, for the maintenance and stabilization of the civilian economy, and for the adjustment of such economy to war needs and conditions;

(b) To unify the activities of Federal agencies and departments engaged in or concerned with production, procurement, distribution or transportation of military or civilian supplies, materials, and products and to resolve and determine controversies between such agencies or departments, except those to be resolved by the Director of Economic Stabilization under Section 3, Title IV of Executive Order 9230; and

(c) To issue such directives on policy or operations to the Federal agencies and departments as may be necessary to carry out the programs developed, the policies established, and the decisions made under this Order. It shall be the duty of all such agencies and departments to execute these directives, and to make to the Office of War Mobilization such progress reports as may be required.

IV

The Office of War Mobilization may perform the functions, exercise the powers, authority and discretion conferred on it by this Order through such officials and such agencies and in such manner, as the Director, subject to the provisions of this Order, may determine. The Director shall receive such compensation as the President shall provide, and within the limits of funds which may be made available, may employ necessary personnel and make provision for supplies, facilities and services necessary to discharge his responsibilities.

All prior executive orders insofar as they are in conflict herewith are amended accordingly.

(a) Statement by the President (Roosevelt) Accompanying Executive Order No. 9347, May 27, 1943 [1]

To unify more closely the work of the war agencies concerned with the production, procurement, transportation and distribution of military and civilian supplies, materials and products, I am creating the Office of War Mobilization which will be under the direction of Justice James F. Byrnes.

[1] From the Office of the Secretary to the President; *New York Times*, May 29, 1943.

Justice Byrnes will be assisted by a War Mobilization Committee composed of the Secretary of War, the Secretary of the Navy, the Chairman of the Munitions Assignment Board, the Chairman of the War Production Board and the Economic Stabilization Director. The Committee has been purposely kept small so that it can function most effectively. But the heads of the various departments and agencies will be asked to sit with the Committee whenever matters of special concern to their departments or agencies are under consideration.

The Committee will lay down unified policies and develop integrated programs and will see that the policies established and programs developed are expedited. In addition to its regular meetings, the Committee will meet from time to time with me in the Cabinet room.

We are entering a phase of the war effort when we must streamline our activities, avoid duplication and overlapping, eliminate interdepartmental friction, make decisions with dispatch, and keep both our military machine and our essential civilian economy running in team and at high speed.

Justice Byrnes is resigning as Economic Stabilization Director to become Director of the Office of War Mobilization. Judge Fred M. Vinson, of Kentucky, now a member of the U. S. Circuit Court of Appeals, will succeed Justice Byrnes as Economic Stabilization Director. Judge Vinson was a member of Congress for fourteen years and for eight years of that period a member of the House Ways and Means Committee.

3. MILITARY AND NAVAL POLICIES AND ESTABLISHMENTS

A. Financial Statistics

(1) *Appropriations and Contract Authorizations, by Appropriation Acts, for the Navy Department and War Department, Military Activities, for the Fiscal Years 1942, 1943 and 1944, as of July 12, 1943* [1]

NAVY DEPARTMENT

APPROPRIATING ACTS AND DATE APPROVED	BUREAU OF AERONAUTICS	OTHER	TOTAL
Fiscal Year 1942			
Pub. No. 48, May 6, 1941:			
Appropriations	$ 434,980,400	$ 2,980,541,350	$ 3,415,521,750
Contract authorizations . . .	——	31,448,894	31,448,894
Pub. No. 150, Jul. 3, 1941:			
Appropriations	482,046,600	201,340,000	683,386,600
Coast Guard appropriations transferred from Treasury Dept. pursuant to E. O. 8929, Nov. 1, 1941 . .	——	50,721,320	50,721,320
Contract authorizations . . .	10,000,000	——	10,000,000
Pub. No. 247, Aug. 25, 1941:			
Appropriations	90,000,000	1,494,795,785	1,584,795,785
Pub. No. 282, Oct. 28, 1941:			
Appropriations	——	120,996,000	120,996,000
Coast Guard transferred from Treasury Dept. pursuant to E. O. 8929, Nov. 1, 1941	——	27,544,585	27,544,585

[1] From the Executive Office of the President, Bureau of the Budget.

NAVY DEPARTMENT — *Continued*

APPROPRIATING ACTS AND DATE APPROVED	BUREAU OF AERONAUTICS	OTHER	TOTAL
Fiscal Year 1942 — Cont'd			
Pub. No. 253, Dec. 17, 1941:			
Appropriations	$309,720,000	$774,230,727	$1,083,950,727
Contract authorizations . . .	640,000,000	——	640,000,000
Pub. No. 463, Feb. 21, 1942:			
Appropriations	——	1,426,140	1,426,140
Pub. No. 528, Apr. 28, 1942:			
Appropriations	464,827,500	1,044,924,000	1,509,751,500
Contract authorizations . . .	——	25,000,000	25,000,000
Pub. No. 626, Jun. 23, 1942:			
Appropriations	——	444,984,740	444,984,740
Contract authorizations . . .	150,000,000	——	150,000,000
Pub. No. 441, Feb. 7, 1942:			
Appropriations	4,408,300,000	5,285,225,500	9,693,525,500
Pub. No. 648, Jul. 2, 1942:			
Appropriations	——	672,622	672,622
Permanent Appropriations . .	——	1,630,179	1,630,179
Coast Guard:			
Transferred from Treasury Dept. pursuant to E. O. 8929, Nov. 1, 1941:			
Appropriations	——	62,193,150	62,193,150
Contract authorizations . . .	——	6,370,000	6,370,000
Other appropriations transferred from Treasury Dept. pursuant to E.O. 8929, Nov. 1, 1941	——	83,080	83,080
Transferred to Coast Guard pursuant to E.O. 9083, Feb. 28, 1942, from:			
U. S. Maritime Commission:			
Construction Fund	——	28,000,000	28,000,000
State Marine Schools . . .	——	190,000	190,000
Department of Commerce:			
Bureau of Marine Inspection and Navigation	——	2,898,995	2,898,995
Transferred from Coast Guard pursuant to E. O. 9198, Jul. 11, 1942, to:			
Executive Office, War Shipping Administration	——	— 33,190,000	— 33,190,000
Pub. No. 763, Oct. 26, 1942:			
Appropriations	——	7,520,456	7,520,456
Pub. No. 92, Jun. 26, 1943:			
Appropriations	——	30,000,000	30,000,000
Total fiscal year 1942:			
Appropriations	$6,189,874,500	$12,526,728,629	$18,716,603,129
Contract authorizations . . .	$800,000,000	$ 62,818,894	$ 862,818,894

NAVY DEPARTMENT — *Continued*

APPROPRIATING ACTS AND DATE APPROVED	BUREAU OF AERONAUTICS	OTHER	TOTAL
Fiscal Year 1943			
Pub. No. 441, Feb. 7, 1942:			
Appropriations:			
Annual	$1,436,418,585	$12,608,921,389	$14,045,339,974
Permanent — (revised) . .	——	2,360,900	2,360,900
Contract authorizations . . .	——	500,000,000	500,000,000
Transferred to Coast Guard, pursuant to E.O. 9083, Feb. 28, 1942, from:			
U. S. Maritime Commission:			
State Marine Schools . . .	——	360,417	360,417
Department of Commerce:			
Bureau of Marine Inspection and Navigation	——	3,030,980	3,030,980
Treasury Department:			
Bureau of Customs . . .	——	52,400	52,400
Transferred from Coast Guard, pursuant to E. O. 9198, Jul. 11, 1942, to:			
Executive Office of the President:			
War Shipping Administration	——	48,360,417	48,360,417
Pub. No. 626, Jun. 23, 1942:			
Appropriations	——	209,440,000	209,440,000
Pub. No. 763, Oct. 26, 1942:			
Appropriations	3,822,000,000	1,766,568,308	5,588,568,308
Pub. No. 11, Mar. 18, 1943:			
Appropriations	——	793,668	793,668
Pub. No. 20, Mar. 31, 1943:			
Appropriations	——	3,836,176,119	3,836,176,119
Contract authorizations . . .	——	449,740,400	449,740,400
Pub. No. 92, Jun. 26, 1943:			
Appropriations	——	172,439,000	172,439,000
Pub. No. 140, Jul. 12, 1943:			
Appropriations	——	751,140	751,140
Total Fiscal Year 1943:			
Appropriations	$5,258,418,585	$18,552,533,904	$23,810,952,489
Contract authorizations . . .	——	$ 949,740,400	$ 949,740,400
Fiscal Year 1944 [1]			
Pub. No. 92, Jun. 26, 1943:			
Appropriations:			
Annual	$4,583,725,000	$22,851,062,198	$27,434,787,198
Permanent	——	2,568,000	2,568,000
Contract authorizations . . .	2,000,000,000	——	2,000,000,000

[1] Indefinite contract authorizations for construction of the expanded navy, according to estimates of the Navy Department, will call for appropriations after the fiscal year 1944 amounting to more than $14,000,000,000.

WAR DEPARTMENT, MILITARY ACTIVITIES

APPROPRIATING ACTS AND DATE APPROVED	AIR CORPS	OTHER	TOTAL
Fiscal Year 1942			
Pub. No. 139, Jun. 30, 1941:			
Appropriations	$ 4,342,253,322	$ 6,042,568,302	$10,384,821,624
Contract authorizations . . .	104,258,995	78,886,700	183,145,695
Pub. No. 150, Jul. 3, 1941:			
Appropriations	—	6,500,000	6,500,000
Pub. No. 247, Aug. 25, 1941:			
Appropriations	204,007,800	4,084,949,863	4,288,957,663
Pub. No. 353, Dec. 17, 1941:			
Appropriations	779,000,000	6,597,026,583	7,376,026,583
Pub. No. 422, Jan. 30, 1942:			
Appropriations	9,041,373,090	3,484,499,384	12,525,872,474
Pub. No. 463, Feb. 21, 1942:			
Appropriations	—	793,284	793,284
Pub. No. 474, Mar. 5, 1942:			
Appropriations	167,440,000	23,318,297,900	23,485,737,900
Pub. No. 528, Mar. 28, 1942:			
Appropriations	8,515,861,251	8,878,816,092	17,394,677,343
Pub. No. 648, Jul. 2, 1942:			
Appropriations	—	481,377	481,377
Pub. No. 763, Oct. 26, 1942:			
Appropriations	—	330,670	330,670
Total, fiscal year 1942:			
Appropriations	$23,049,935,463	$52,414,263,455	$75,464,198,918
Contract authorizations . . .	$ 104,258,995	$ 78,886,700	$ 183,145,695
Fiscal Year 1943			
Pub. No. 649, Jul. 2, 1942:			
Appropriations	$11,317,416,790	$31,502,586,277	$42,820,003,067
Pub. No. 678, Jul. 25, 1942:			
Appropriations	—	3,298	3,298
Pub. No. 11, Mar. 18, 1943:			
Appropriations	—	688,711	688,711
Pub. No. 140, Jul. 12, 1943:			
Appropriations	—	272,715	272,715
Total Fiscal Year 1943:			
Appropriations	$11,317,416,790	$31,503,551,001	$42,820,967,791
Fiscal Year 1944			
Pub. No. 108, Jul. 1, 1943:			
Appropriations	$23,655,481,000	$35,379,358,673	$59,034,839,673

B. Mobilization of Manpower

(1) " Selective Training and Service Act of 1940." Amendments Adopted November 13, 1942 [1]

Only those amendments of special significance are given. For other amendments, see text of the *Selective Training and Service Act of 1940*, as amended,

[1] *The Selective Training and Service Act of 1940*, as Amended. Second Printing of Second Edition, January 15, 1943.

given in convenient form in the *Selective Service Manual*, prepared and distributed by the Director of Selective Service, under the jurisdiction of the War Manpower Commission. The more important sections of the Act, as then in effect, were carried in *Documents, III, 1940–41*, p. 672 and *IV, 1941–42*, p. 135.

The most significant change made in the Act during the period under review was the lowering of the draft age from 20 to 18 by the Act of November 13, 1942. In his radio address of October 12, 1942 President Roosevelt said:

"All of our combat units that go overseas must consist of young, strong men who have had thorough training. A division that has an average age of twenty-three or twenty-four is a better fighting unit than one that has an average age of thirty-three or thirty-four. The more of such troops we have in the field, the sooner the war will be won, and the smaller will be the cost in casualties.

"Therefore, I believe that it will be necessary to lower the present minimum age limit for Selective Service from twenty years down to eighteen. We have learned how inevitable that is — and how important to the speeding up of victory."

Action by Congress followed promptly. Bills introduced by Senator Chan Gurney (South Dakota) in the Senate (S. 2748) [1] and Representative James W. Wadsworth (New York) in the House (H. R. 7528) contained provisions for the amendment of the Act to this effect. Secretary of War Stimson supported the enactment of H. R. 7528 in a letter dated October 13, 1942, addressed to Representative May (Kentucky), Chairman of the House Committee on Military Affairs.[2] Secretary Stimson, General Marshall, and General Hershey testified before the Committee in support of the bill. Secretary Stimson, in a prepared statement before the House Committee on Military Affairs, reaffirmed his support of the bill, while giving to the Committee estimates that had been reached by the General Staff regarding the size of the army for 1943.[3] After considering the bill in Executive session, the House Committee reported unanimously an amended bill which came before the House after the Committee on Rules had adopted a rule limiting debate and permitting a vote on the age limit, the principal provision of the bill. Opposition to the bill focused on a proposal requiring that each inductee under the age of twenty years be given twelve months military training before being ordered to combat. This proposal was opposed by General Marshall in a letter to Representative Wadsworth read on the floor of the House, October 17, 1942 [4] on the ground that it would be completely disruptive of the army's training program. The bill, with amendments agreed to in the Committee of the Whole, was passed by the House on October 17, 1942 — yeas 345, nays 16, not voting 66.[5]

The Senate passed H. R. 7528, after amending it, on October 24, 1942 by a vote of 58 yeas and 5 nays [6] and requested a conference with the House to consider the amendments. The conference report (House Report No. 2624) was agreed to by the House on November 10, 1942 [7] and by the Senate on November 12,[8] and signed by the President (as Public Law 772) and approved November 13.

President Roosevelt, by Proclamation No. 2572 [9] set the dates for registration of male citizens and every other male person residing in the United States under the provisions of the Selective Service and Training Act, as amended.

---

[1] *Congressional Record*, vol. 88, pt. 7, p. 8563; S. 2748 was reported with amendment (Senate Report No. 1644) on October 19, 1942 (legislative day, October 15) and debated. It was indefinitely postponed and H. R. 7528 was passed in lieu (*ibid.*, pt. 6, p. 8315; pt. 7, p. 8654).

[2] *Hearings before the Committee on Military Affairs*, House of Representatives, on H. R. 7528, 77th Cong., 2d sess., p. 26.

[3] *Ibid.*, p. 2.

[4] *Congressional Record*, vol. 88, pt. 6, p. 8270.

[5] *Ibid.*, p. 8308.

[6] *Ibid.*, pt. 7, p. 8654.

[7] *Ibid.*, p. 8747.

[8] *Ibid.*, p. 8774.

[9] 7 *Fed. Reg.*, p. 9474.

SEC. 3.[1] (a) Except as otherwise provided in this Act, every male citizen of the United States, and every other male person residing in the United States, who is between the ages of eighteen and forty-five at the time fixed for his registration, shall be liable for training and service in the land or naval forces of the United States: . . . *Provided further,*[2] That no man, without his consent, shall be inducted for training and service under this Act after he has attained the forty-fifth anniversary of the day of his birth.

. . . .

SEC. 5.[3] (f) Any person eighteen or nineteen years of age who, while pursuing a course of instruction at a high school or similar institution of learning, is ordered to report for induction under this Act during the last half of the academic year at such school or institution, shall, upon his request, have his induction under this Act postponed until the end of such academic year.

. . . .

(k) [4] Every registrant found by a selective service local board, subject to appeal in accordance with section 10 (a) (2), to be necessary to and regularly engaged in an agricultural occupation or endeavor essential to the war effort, shall be deferred from training and service in the land and naval forces so long as he remains so engaged and until such time as a satisfactory replacement can be obtained: *Provided,* That should any such person leave such occupation or endeavor, except for induction into the land or naval forces under this Act, his selective service local board, subject to appeal in accordance with section 10 (a) (2), shall reclassify such registrant in a class immediately available for military service, unless prior to leaving such occupation or endeavor he requests such local board to determine, and such local board, subject to appeal in accordance with section 10 (a) (2), determines, that it is in the best interest of the war effort for him to leave such occupation or endeavor for other work.

. . . .

SEC. 15. (a) [5] When used in this Act —
(a) The term "between the ages of eighteen and forty-five" shall refer to men who have attained the eighteenth anniversary of the day of their birth and who have not attained the forty-fifth anniversary of the day of their birth; and other terms designating different age groups shall be construed in a similar manner.

---

[1] It was amended to read in its present form by Public Law 772, 77th Cong., approved November 13, 1942.
[2] Added by section 5 of Public Law 772.
[3] Amended by section 2 of Public Law 772.
[4] Added by section 4 of Public Law 772.
[5] Amended by section 3 of Public Law 772.

(a) Agreements Regarding the Service of Nationals of One Country in the Armed Forces of Another Country, as of June 30, 1943 [1]

The Selective Training and Service Act of 1940, as amended, provides that with certain exceptions every male citizen of the United States and every other male person residing in the United States between the ages of eighteen and sixty-five shall register. The Act further provides that, with certain exceptions, registrants within specified age limits are liable for active military service in the United States armed forces. During World War I the United States Government entered into conventions with certain associated powers permitting nationals of co-belligerent countries to enlist in the armed forces of their own country. In a series of executive agreements with co-belligerent countries the United States Government has agreed to such an arrangement in this war. Under the terms of these agreements, aliens, who are nationals of co-belligerent countries and who have not declared their intention to become citizens, may elect to serve in the forces of their respective countries, and in case they are already serving in the armed forces of the United States, may elect to transfer to the armed forces of their own countries. The details are to be worked out directly between the War Department and the Selective Service System on the part of the United States Government and the appropriate authorities of the foreign governments. Reciprocal treatment is provided for.

The first of these agreements was entered into with the Canadian Government and became effective April 6, 1942 (see *Documents, IV, 1941–42*, p. 448). Subsequent agreements with other countries have been identical in content, except for the agreement with Mexico (see this volume, p. 437).

A list of agreements in effect with co-belligerent countries, with the effective date of each, regarding the services of nationals of one country in the armed forces of the other country follows:

AUSTRALIA, July 18, 1942	(E.A.S. 303)
BELGIUM, August 4, 1942	(E.A.S. 304)
BRAZIL, April 30, 1943	(E.A.S. 327)
CANADA, April 6, 1942	(E.A.S. 249)
CUBA, January 11, 1943	(E.A.S. 321)
EL SALVADOR, May 15, 1943	(E.A.S. 325)
GREECE, March 2, 1943	(E.A.S. 322)
INDIA, May 27, 1942	(E.A.S. 308)
MEXICO, January 22, 1943	(E.A.S. 323)
NEW ZEALAND, July 2, 1942	(E.A.S. 305)
NETHERLANDS, July 8, 1942	(E.A.S. 306)
NORWAY, December 24, 1942	(E.A.S. 319)
POLAND, January 27, 1943	(E.A.S. 320)
UNION OF SOUTH AFRICA, June 11, 1942	(E.A.S. 310)
UNITED KINGDOM, April 30, 1942	(E.A.S. 307)
YUGOSLAVIA, May 18, 1942	(E.A.S. 309)

(2) Executive Order No. 9279 Providing for the Most Effective Mobilization and Utilization of the National Manpower and Transferring the Selective Service System to the War Manpower Commission, December 5, 1942 [2]

The requirements of total war have placed an increasing strain on the manpower resources of the United States. The principle of compulsory military

[1] Based on list appearing in Department of State, *Bulletin*, VIII, p. 175, and data obtained from the *Bulletin* and the *Executive Agreement Series*.
[2] 7 *Fed. Reg.*, p. 10177.

service was adopted even before the United States became a belligerent. Other countries at war have found it necessary to apply the principle of selective compulsory service to the meeting of other war manpower needs. In the United States such extreme measures were, in the period under review, effectively resisted, though a bill was introduced in Congress by Senator Austin (S. 666) [1] and by Representative Wadsworth (H. R. 1742)[2] to provide for compulsory general service on a selective basis and Secretary Stimson in his radio address of March 9, 1943 gave his support to such a measure.

The first attempt through administrative action to coordinate measures taken, in meeting manpower requirements with a view to the more effective utilization of available manpower resources was the establishment of the War Manpower Commission on April 18, 1942.[3] In his radio address of October 12, 1942,[4] President Roosevelt recognized the need of rationing manpower, though the measures he recommended fell short of governmental compulsion. The Manpower Subcommittee of the Senate Special Committee to Investigate the National Defense Program, in a report filed with the Senate on November 12, 1942,[5] analyzed the problem, and made certain specific recommendations. It advised against the use of coercion. To meet the increasing need for coordinated action, the President by Executive Order No. 9279, December 5, 1942, transferred to the War Manpower Commission functions hitherto performed by other agencies, including the administration of the Selective Service System.

In order to promote the most effective mobilization and utilization of the national manpower and to eliminate so far as possible waste of manpower due to disruptive recruitment and undue migration of workers, and by virtue of the authority vested in me by the Constitution and Statutes, including the First War Powers Act, 1941, and the Selective Training and Service Act of 1940, as amended, as President of the United States, and as Commander-in-Chief of the Army and the Navy, it is hereby ordered as follows:

1. The War Manpower Commission (established by Section 1 of Executive Order No. 9139, dated April 18, 1942 [6]) shall consist of a Chairman appointed by the President and one representative, designated subject to the approval of the Chairman, of each of the following departments and agencies: The Department of War, the Department of the Navy, the Department of Agriculture, the Department of Labor, the Federal Security Agency, the War Production Board, the United States Civil Service Commission, the National Housing Agency, and such other executive departments and agencies as the President shall determine; and a joint representative of the War Shipping Administration and the Office of Defense Transportation, designated by the Chairman of the War Manpower Commission (hereinafter referred to as the Chairman).

2. (a) The Selective Service System created and established for the purpose of carrying out the provisions of the Selective Training and

---

[1] *Congressional Record*, vol. 89, pt. 1, p. 666.

[2] *Ibid.*, p. A730.

[3] Executive Order No. 9139, 7 *Fed. Reg.*, p. 2919; *Documents, IV, 1941–42*, p. 142.

[4] *New York Times*, October 13, 1942.

[5] Senate Report No. 480, Part 11, 77th Cong., 2d sess.

[6] 7 *Fed. Reg.*, p. 2919.

Service Act of 1940, as amended, and all of its functions, powers, duties, personnel (including the Director of Selective Service), records, property, and funds (including all unexpended balances of appropriations, allocations, or other funds available for the administration of said Act, as amended) are transferred to the War Manpower Commission in the Office for Emergency Management of the Executive Office of the President, and shall be administered under the supervision and direction of the Chairman. The local boards and appeal boards of the Selective Service System shall, subject to the supervision and direction of the Chairman, continue to exercise the functions, powers, and duties vested in them by the Selective Training and Service Act of 1940, as amended.

(b) The functions, powers, and duties of the Director of Selective Service, including authority delegated to him by the President under the provisions of the Selective Training and Service Act of 1940, as amended, are transferred to the Chairman and may be exercised through the Director of Selective Service and such other officers, agents, and persons and in such manner as the Chairman may determine.

(c) The Chief of Finance, United States Army, shall act as the fiscal, disbursing, and accounting agent of the Chairman in carrying out the provisions of the Selective Training and Service Act of 1940, as amended.

3. The Secretary of War and the Secretary of the Navy shall, after consultation with the Chairman, determine the number of men required to be selected each month in order to fulfill the total respective requirements of the Army and Navy as approved by the President. The Chairman shall furnish the required number of men through the Selective Service System.

4. After the effective date of this Order no male person who has attained the eighteenth anniversary and has not attained the thirty-eighth anniversary of the day of his birth shall be inducted into the enlisted personnel of the armed forces (including reserve components), except, under provisions of the Selective Training and Service Act of 1940, as amended; but any such person who has, on or before the effective date of this Order, submitted a bona fide application for voluntary enlistment may be enlisted within ten days after said date.

5. Insofar as the effective prosecution of the war requires it, the Chairman shall take all lawful and appropriate steps to assure that (a) all hiring, rehiring, solicitation, and recruitment of workers in or for work in any establishment, plant, facility, occupation, or area designated by the Chairman as subject to the provisions of this section shall be conducted solely through the United States Employment Service or in accordance with such arrangements as the Chairman may approve; and (b) no employer shall retain in his employ any worker whose services are more urgently needed in any establishment, plant, facility, occupation, or area designated as more essential by the Chairman pursuant to this section.

6. The Secretary of War and the Secretary of the Navy shall take such steps as may be necessary to assure that all training programs for the armed forces (including their reserve components) and the Women's Army Auxiliary Corps, which are carried on in non-Federal educational institutions, conform with such policies or regulations as the Chairman, after consultation with the Secretary of War and the Secretary of the Navy, prescribes as necessary to insure the efficient utilization of the Nation's educational facilities and personnel for the effective prosecution of the war.

7. The Chairman shall (a) issue such policies, rules, regulations, and general or special orders as he deems necessary to carry out the provisions of this Order, (b) take steps to prevent and relieve gross inequities or undue hardships arising from the exercise of the provisions of Section 5 of this Order insofar as he finds so doing will not interfere with the effective prosecution of the war, and (c) establish such procedures (including appeals) as are necessary to assure a hearing to any person claiming that any action, taken by any local or regional agent or agency of the War Manpower Commission pursuant to Section 5 of this Order and said Executive Order No. 9139, is unfair or unreasonable as applied to him.

8. (a) The Chairman may perform the functions and duties and exercise the powers, authority, and discretion conferred upon him by this Order or any other Order of the President through such officers, agents, and persons and in such manner as he shall determine.

(b) The Chairman may avail himself of the services and facilities of such Executive departments and agencies as he determines may be of assistance in carrying out the provisions of this Order. He may accept the services and facilities of State and local agencies.

9. Subject to appeal to the President or to such agent or agency as the President may designate, each Executive department and agency shall so utilize its facilities, services, and personnel and take such action, under authority vested in it by law, as the Chairman, after consultation with such department or agency, determines necessary to promote compliance with the provisions of this Order or of policies, directives, or regulations prescribed under said Executive Order No. 9139.

10. The Chairman shall appoint a Management-Labor Policy Committee to be selected from the fields of labor, agriculture, and industrial management, and shall consult with the members thereof in carrying out his responsibilities. The Chairman may appoint such other advisory committees composed of representatives of governmental or private groups or both as he deems appropriate.

11. The Chairman shall be ex officio an additional member of the Economic Stabilization Board established by Executive Order No. 9250, dated October 3, 1942.[1]

[1] 7 Fed. Reg., p. 7871.

12. All prior Executive Orders, insofar as they are in conflict herewith, are amended accordingly. All prior regulations, rulings, and other directives relating to the Selective Service System shall remain in effect, except insofar as they are in conflict with this Order or are hereafter amended by regulations, rulings, or other directives issued by or under the direction of the Chairman.

13. This Order shall take effect immediately and shall continue in force and effect until the termination of Title I of the First War Powers Act, 1941.

(3) *The Size of the Army. Radio Address by the Secretary of War (Stimson), March 9, 1943* [1]

Tonight I wish to speak to you about the subtle danger which, unless guarded against, may destroy our present bright hopes for a decisive victory. It arises out of a mental attitude which is quite prevalent among our people, including many of the best of them, and has danger of which most of them are quite unconscious.

We are raising and training a magnificent army. We are constructing and manning a superb navy. The fine young men of both these forces are now just beginning to meet the enemy and have already shown their mettle. They are equal to their tasks. Man for man they have proved themselves superior in skill, initiative and resourcefulness to the men of the Axis nations which we are fighting. There is no trouble with that section of the American people who are in uniform either on the land, on the sea or in the air.

Nor does the trouble exist among millions of patriotic citizens at home, who have given up their dearest to the dangers of this war and who are cheerfully devoting themselves to patriotic tasks and sacrifices here and are thus trying in every way to hasten and push forward the war effort.

It is hard to analyze the attitude to which I refer. It doubtless arises from various causes and it manifests itself in many ways. Some call it the spirit of "business as usual" but that definition is not broad enough. Very often it appears in patriotic people who do not realize what we are up against and who honestly do not understand the purpose and necessity of some of the war measures which their Government is taking. But the attitude is just as dangerous even when it is innocent. I think it can accurately be called the attitude of trying to win the war — the most fierce and dangerous war which has ever confronted the United States — in some easy manner and without too much trouble and sacrifice.

Abraham Lincoln met it in the Civil War even after that war had been going on for over a year and many bloody battles had been fought. He said to a caller at the White House in September, 1862, "The fact is the

[1] Bureau of Public Relations, War Department.

people have not made up their minds that we are at war with the South. They have not buckled down to the determination to fight this war through; or they have got the idea into their heads that we are going to get out of this fix somehow by strategy. . . . They have no idea that this war is to be carried on and put through by hard, tough fighting; that it will hurt somebody; and no headway is going to be made while this delusion lasts."

Today this attitude which Lincoln described manifests itself when we say:

The Russians have destroyed so many Germans that Germany will not be able to carry on any more offensives;

Or when we say: ·

The German people are cracking;

Or when we say:

The best way to win the war is to give our Allies plenty of weapons to fight for us;

Or when we say:

If we make too big a military effort we shall so dislocate our economy that we shall never recover; we shall create a permanent dictatorship and lose our historic freedom;

Or when we say other things which at bottom represent merely wishful thinking or the dread of personal sacrifices and the desire to find a better way out.

I believe that this attitude towards hard fighting on our part really underlies much of the criticism which is being directed today against the proposed size of our Army. On the other hand, I also realize that the Army plans involve many factors of great complexity and that the doubt in many minds is perfectly honest and patriotic. Such minds are entitled to all the light which we can give them. It is my purpose tonight to try to explain to you how the size of the army was fixed; the kind of army we are training and the purposes for which it is designed; and why it is impossible to reduce its size or interrupt its training without the gravest danger to our ultimate victory.

I

The Numerical Size of the Army

We are planning to have raised by the end of this year 1943 an army of 8,200,000 men composed of 7,500,000 enlisted men and 700,000 officers. This number will include an air force of about two and a half million. It also will include the Women's Army Auxiliary Corps of upwards of 150,000.

These figures were not arrived at by guess work; they were the product of months of study by the General Staff and the War College. They were also the product of joint planning with the Navy over the future work of both these services. The proposed size of the Army, the Navy, the Coast Guard and the Marine Corps were all determined at the same time, and all of these forces were balanced within themselves and against each other, and also in connection with the available manpower, the estimated capacity of production of equipment, and the estimated availability of shipping for their transport. These figures have received the approval of the joint chiefs of staff of the Army and the Navy and finally of the President. They have thus had the benefit of all the brains, accumulated research, and judgment which our governmental machinery provides for that purpose. They have not been worked out in disregard of but in full reference to our program of shipbuilding and production of equipment.

When we look at the estimated size of the forces of our enemies which are in the field against us, our numbers certainly do not look relatively too large. I realize that the figures of the hostile forces are estimates only but they are based upon the best information available to those whose business it is to make such estimates. In Europe the estimated forces of the Germans and their allies show about 14,000,000 men under arms. Russia and Britain together have a much smaller number. In Asia the Japanese have more than 3,000,000 men. These figures represent the aggregate of individuals in the various forces.

When we compare the *combat* units of the various forces the disparity between us is even greater. Our plans are to produce about one hundred American divisions of ground forces, together with their auxiliary troops. Germany is estimated to have approximately three hundred divisions, Italy 80 divisions, Germany's European satellites another 80 divisions, and Japan about 86 more. This makes an aggregate of about 546. Making all allowances for error these figures certainly make our ground forces seem of very modest size in comparison.

II

The Character and Objective of the Army

It is not the purpose of our military leaders to create a huge defensive army, awaiting in the United States such unknown and uncertain opportunities for its use as may hereafter occur. Their plans are much more wise than that. The Army is being raised on the fundamental and correct theory that we shall at once take the offensive and seize a number of priceless opportunities which are already opening up for us to end the war as quickly as possible.

III

The Nature of the Training Necessary to Meet These Objectives of the Army

To successfully meet these priceless opportunities we have put into effect the most carefully planned and coordinated program of military training which has ever existed in the United States.

The training contemplated by this program for the individuals is a process covering a long time. The Germans think two years necessary for such training of their men. We believe that our men can do it in one year but that is a minimum. Furthermore, the recruits are not all taken into the Army at the same time and all graduated at the same time. Such a method would be impossible for any country, even one as rich and powerful as the United States. And furthermore it would not meet the changing requirements of war. It would be too rigid and inflexible. Each of the reception centers and training schools takes in a succession of new classes and these groups are passed along the steps of the course until the final product in the shape of army divisions is produced at the end. During each group's training the men are first instructed in the schooling of the individual soldier, are then crystallized into small and later large units for training in cooperative team action in modern warfare, and finally large divisional combat forces emerge from the other end of the system, each highly trained for its specific task. Every month the requisite number of men to form a certain number of divisions is taken into the reception centers at the entrance to the machine and every month at the other end that number of divisions is emerging highly trained for the various objectives to which they are to be assigned.

Anyone who studies this system as it is now running will be astounded at the careful planning which has been required as well as at the smooth continuity of the process of training which it has produced. It is now proceeding under the highest pressure of perfected action. Nothing like it has ever existed in this country before. It represents a great stream of training towards a carefully thought out goal. It has taken over two years to develop and construct this system; to train the instructors of its schools and to develop the immense overhead necessary for its smooth operation; and to construct the cantonments and other buildings for its use. Almost every unit in it has been devised and fitted into its place in accordance with the program of the size of the army to be completed by December 1943, which I described a few minutes ago.

The first point to be borne in mind about this system of training is that the whole structure is complex and interrelated. Men are taught in a large number of different kinds of schools for different purposes of warfare. For example, in the ground forces there are special schools for infantry, artillery, tank warfare, anti-aircraft gunnery, anti-tank gunnery, Signal Corps work with all its ramifications of scientific specialties, mechanics' schools, Quartermasters' schools and many more. In the Air Corps exists a similar large group of different schools for different purposes and specialties. The number of the graduates of these several schools must conform to the number required in the final produce of combat forces and all must be taught to work with each other in carrying out the war task of the final division or combat force to which each belongs.

The second point to be remembered is that the whole process takes at least a year. If you interrupt the steady flow of entrants to the schools in March 1943, the effect of this break will be produced a year later and then, if it proves a mistake, cannot be corrected for at least another year.

IV

THE DISASTROUS RESULTS OF INTERRUPTING THIS PROCESS

In the light of the foregoing description of the purpose and process of our Army's training, I think one can see more easily the danger of meddling with that process. Plan and process are tied together. The plan contemplates a succession of carefully directed blows at our enemies. The size and character of these blows and the aggregate forces which are necessary have been carefully thought out. Just as our present offensives are being carried out by men who have been through a year's training, the men now being brought into the Army are to be trained for campaigns a year ahead. Our main object is to continuously build up a force which will strike without interruption and with cumulative effect. That purpose can be thwarted by a mistake made now.

The various critics who today are asking that we should slow up or interrupt our work fail to realize the far-reaching effect of interruption. Furthermore they do not understand the psychology of combat. They do not realize that battles are won by continuous rapid blows upon an enemy and that when an enemy begins to show signs of demoralization these blows must be continued and, if possible, redoubled in order that he may not have time to reform his forces. Once the enemy is checked or shaken on the field of battle, he must be constantly pursued and hammered until he is completely beaten or surrenders. The very fact that it is known that we have trained forces ready to do this tends towards his demoralization.

On the other hand, the commander who after an initial success stops and gives his broken opponent time to reform and reorganize only finds that he must fight his battle over again. If after the battle of Gettysburg, the Federal commander had been able to pursue and destroy his defeated enemy, the length of the Civil War might have been shortened by more than a year. On the other hand, the fact that in 1918 Foch was ready to remorselessly follow up and shatter the German enemy who had been shaken at Soissons on July 18th and again at St. Quentin on August 8th, permitted the last great war to be finished in November 1918 instead of lasting over into 1919 as had been expected.

I speak with careful consideration when I say that if we should halt this great training establishment which we have now built and timed according to the present timetable of the war, we should deal a heavier blow to our hopes of a complete final victory than by any loss which we are likely to sustain on the field of battle.

V

Another argument of our critics is that by constructing too large an Army we are making undue inroads into our limited manpower; that we are taking necessary workers from the factories which are providing Army equipment and machines; and that we are similarly slowing down the construction of merchant shipping which is necessary to carry the Army and its supplies across the ocean. As I have already said, this argument ignores the careful study which has been given to this subject by our President and his military advisers. As between them and their critics I think it is the safer bet to trust the former. But there is this further answer to this argument which I think is conclusive. The argument depends upon the assumption that there is no elasticity in the efficiency of the civilian industries which are producing weapons and ships; that every man-hour taken away from industry and put into the Army must result in exactly the same ultimate loss in rapidity of production.

Every thoughtful citizen who will give any real consideration to the problem will know that such an assumption is not true. Only those who believe that our industry and our farming and our general civilian activity are really keyed to an all-out war are entitled to make this argument. It is the duty of every citizen to examine into his own life and his own community and see whether production in industry and on the farm cannot be increased enormously in efficiency; whether absenteeism, threatened strikes, general complacency, insistence of "business as usual," or even insistence on hoped-for standards of living, are not going a long way to prevent what could be accomplished by an all-out war effort. If you are content with the present situation and with the present results in industry, in agriculture, and in our civilian life, then I suggest that you go to one of our great camps and see our boys in uniform working. I suggest that you read the detailed dispatches from

Tunisia and the Southwest Pacific about the fighting efforts of our soldiers. I suggest that you compare your comforts of life with theirs, and then ask yourself again — are you content? I hope and pray that it will not require tragic disaster to bring our people to a realization of the facts. The great wave of patriotic ardor which was shown so dramatically in the weeks after Pearl Harbor must not fall away into arguments of rights, wages, profits, and relative advantage of one man over another.

The Armed Forces, the men who are going into actual combat, have placed their house in order. Their spirit and their program are all that patriotism and careful planning can effect. I now ask whether industry and agriculture should not likewise be put on a more efficient wartime basis. When you are driving a team of horses and one of them goes lame, you do not lame the other horse to equalize the team. You try to get two sound horses.

I fully understand that we must have essential food and necessary goods for civilian consumption. I am well aware of the difficulties in getting machinery and employees which our farmers and manufacturers are now experiencing, but I am convinced that with the initiative, resourcefulness and willingness to sacrifice of the American people, these problems can be solved without crippling their Armed Forces.

For myself I have reached the conclusion that one of the reasons why industry and agriculture and the whole civilian population have not moved more rapidly towards an all-out effort is that we have relied almost entirely on voluntary cooperation. This voluntary cooperation would work with a large part of our population as soon as they clearly understood the need for it. But the effect of the recalcitrant or thoughtless few is so great upon the minds and efforts of others that I am convinced that the only way to accomplish the result which we must all reach, is through a General Service Act. This has proved true in England and I believe it is now true here.

The issue between the proponents of the Army program and its critics in my opinion largely narrows down to this difference: the leaders of the Army are trying, by shortening the war, to save the lives of thousands of young Americans — lives vital to the future of this country. The opponents of the Army program are trying to avoid present trouble — the inconveniences and relatively minor sacrifices which would be involved in a more thorough and drastic reorganization of our industrial and civilian life for the remaining period of this war. I firmly believe that when the true situation is understood by the American people, there will be no doubt as to their decision. Even if, as Lincoln said in 1862, they have not yet truly realized what it means to be at war, they will soon do so. And when they have done so, they will be ready to make any sacrifice for victory.

C. Size of the Navy

(1) *Annual Report of the Secretary of the Navy (Knox), June 30, 1942* [1]

[Excerpts]

The fiscal year which ended on June 30, 1942 was, for the United States Navy, one of gigantic demands whose ultimate fulfillment can be accomplished only through the most gigantic measures. It is the intent of this report to convey to the President and the Nation that the Navy views its task with the fullest realism and will continue to relax no effort until every enemy has been driven from every ocean and sea.

Under the impact of unprecedented war, fiscal 1942 dissipated all previously conceived beliefs that a two-ocean Navy would be enough. Now it is realized that no Navy will be sufficient which permits less than the most ships and planes, equipped with the hardest hitting weapons, and manned by the best trained officers and men, in any area throughout the world where enemy forces may be met.

All the Navy's efforts, all its planning, and all its huge expansion in a year of multi-billion expending have been concentrated on that eventual goal, and by the close of the fiscal year long strides had been made in the direction of total adequacy to fight — and win — the four-dimensional war of our enemies' choosing, viz.: land, sea, air, and the blending of all of them into the amphibious.

. . . .

Meanwhile, the shipbuilding program was revised in consequence of far-reaching legislation enacted subsequent to the outbreak of hostilities. The Naval Expansion Act of July 19, 1940, had provided for a total increase of 1,425,000 combatant and auxiliary tons, but with the impact of European and Asiatic war, this total was supplemented by the acts of December 17, 1941, December 23, 1941, and May 13, 1942, to provide for an additional 350,000 tons of combat ships and 800,000 tons of auxiliary vessels. Moreover, there was pending before Congress at the close of the fiscal year further legislation (culminating in the act of July 9, 1942), sanctioning the construction of 3,100,000 tons of combat and auxiliary units over and above the grand total previously authorized. Thus, under stress of global requirements, the original plan for the construction of a two-ocean Navy has been amplified to provide for the creation of a giant armada capable of seeking out and driving the enemy from all the world's ocean ways.

The over-all ship production program was scheduled for completion in 1947, but speeded-up construction has broken all previous records

[1] *Annual Report of the Secretary of the Navy for the Fiscal Year 1942.* Washington, U. S. Government Printing Office, 1942. 56 p.

and it is now expected that, except for some large units upon which work has been suspended due to material shortages and the length of time required to build, the entire authorized tonnage will have been commissioned and put into active service before the close of 1945.

.   .   .   .

As regards the 18,082 civilians employed in the Navy Department and Marine Corps Headquarters, it should be remarked that when the present naval expansion program is concluded and when the lend-lease and defense-aid requirements of our Allies have been fulfilled, this number will be reduced to a level compatible with the needs of the Department in the exercise of its normal functions. The same holds true of the present civilian field force. This is not to infer, however, that we shall be able to return to the old low levels of 1938. The Department must be guided in its plans for post-war retrenchment by the requirements of a permanently enlarged fleet.

D. Detailing Military Personnel to Service with Foreign Governments

(1) *An Act to Authorize the President to Detail Officers and Enlisted Men of the United States Army, Navy and Marine Corps to Assist the Governments of the Latin American Republics in Military and Naval Matters, as Amended October 1, 1942* [1]

Article I, section 9, clause 8, of the Constitution prohibits any person holding any office of trust or profit under the United States from accepting any present, emolument, office, or title from any king, prince, or foreign state without the consent of Congress. On April 19, 1910, the Congress gave its consent to the detail of army officers to Cuba and Panama to assist those countries in their military problems (36 Stat. 624). Again, by the Act of May 19, 1926 (44 Stat. 565), as amended by the Act of May 14, 1935 (45 Stat. 218), the Congress authorized the President to detail officers and enlisted men of the United States Army, Navy, and Marine Corps to assist the Governments of North America, Central America, South America, and certain other friendly nations.

The exigencies of the present war compelled an extension of our interests in the military efforts of foreign countries beyond the boundaries of the Western Hemisphere. The amendment of the 1926 act to permit the detailing of military personnel beyond the limits of the Western Hemisphere was requested by the War Department. In a letter to the Speaker of the House of Representatives dated July 29, 1942, Secretary of War Stimson stated that a request had been received from one foreign government and that it was felt to be of the utmost importance that the President should be in the position of being able to meet this and other similar requests.

That the President of the United States be, and hereby is, authorized, upon application from the foreign governments concerned, and whenever in his discretion the public interests render such a course advisable, to

[1] Act of May 19, 1926 (44 Stat. 565), as amended by Act of May 14, 1935 (45 Stat. 218), as amended by Act of October 1, 1942 (Public Law 722, 77th Cong.).

detail officers and enlisted men of the United States Army, Navy, and Marine Corps to assist the governments of the republics of North America, Central America, and South America and of the republics of Cuba, Haiti, Santo Domingo, and the Commonwealth of the Philippine Islands, *and, during war or a declared national emergency, the governments of such other countries as the President deems it in the interest of national defense to assist,*[1] in military and naval matters: *Provided,* That the officers and enlisted men so detailed be, and they are hereby, authorized to accept from the government to which detailed offices and such compensation and emoluments thereunto appertaining as may be first approved by the Secretary of War or by the Secretary of the Navy, as the case may be: *Provided, further,* That while so detailed such officers and enlisted men shall receive, in addition to the compensation and emoluments allowed them by such governments, the pay and allowances whereto entitled in the United States Army, Navy, and Marine Corps and shall be allowed the same credit for longevity, retirement, and for all other purposes that they would receive if they were serving with the forces of the United States. (Act of May 19, 1926 (44 Stat. 565), as amended by the Act of May 14, 1935 (49 Stat. 218).

4. LEND–LEASE

[See *Documents, III, 1940–41,* p. 711; *IV, 1941–42,* p. 169.]

A. Extension of Lend-Lease Act

The Lend-Lease Act, officially designated An Act to Promote the Defense of the United States, was enacted by the Congress as a measure of national defense on March 11, 1941,[2] a little less than nine months before the attack at Pearl Harbor. The action constituted an implementation of the resolve of our Government that the United States should become an "arsenal of democracy" in the fight against Axis aggression. It gave assurance that the flow of supplies would not be interrupted by a lack of dollar exchange.

Under the Act, the President is authorized "in the interest of national defense" to procure and provide "defense articles" and "defense information" for the government of any country whose defense he deems "vital to the defense of the United States." Defense articles and defense information are defined to include all types of goods and services necessary to the waging of total war. The Act provides that "the terms and conditions under which any such foreign government receives any aid . . . shall be those which the President deems satisfactory, and the benefit to the United States may be payment or repayment in kind or property, or any other direct or indirect benefit which the President deems satisfactory." By the terms of Sec. 3, par. (c) of the Act, the powers conferred were to terminate on June 30, 1943, or after the passage of a concurrent resolution by the two Houses of Congress before that date declaring that the powers conferred were no longer necessary to the national defense.

With the national emergency continuing, with Lend-Lease generally recognized as an important instrument for the prosecution of the war and with the

[1] The words in italics are the words inserted by the Act of October 1, 1942.
[2] Public Law 11, 77th Cong.; *Documents, III, 1940–41,* p. 712.

administration of Lend-Lease receiving general approval, the possibility of terminating the Act by concurrent resolution or allowing the authority to lapse by Congressional inaction was not seriously considered.

H. R. 1501 (A bill to extend for one year the provisions of An Act to Promote the Defense of the United States, approved March 11, 1941) was introduced by Mr. Bloom, Chairman of the House Committee on Foreign Affairs, on January 26, 1943. The bill was referred to the Committee on Foreign Affairs and hearings were held over a period of about four weeks.[1] Among those appearing before the Committee were Secretary of War Stimson, Secretary of the Navy Knox, Secretary of Agriculture Wickard, Assistant Secretaries of State Acheson and Berle, and Lend-Lease Administrator Stettinius. The Committee also had before it a report submitted to Congress by the Lend-Lease Administrator on January 25, 1943 on operations under the Lend-Lease Act, from the passage of the Act, March 11, 1941, to December 31, 1942.[2] The Committee unanimously reported the bill favorably without amendment on February 26, 1943.[3]

An identical bill (S. 813) was introduced by Mr. Connally in the Senate on March 2 (legislative day, March 1), and referred to the Senate Committee on Foreign Relations. No substantial controversy developed with respect to the bill. The Committee heard only the Administrator of the Office of Lend-Lease Administration and the Secretary of the Navy.[4] It had before it the hearings before the House Committee on Foreign Affairs. The bill was unanimously reported favorably and without amendment on March 10 (legislative day, March 9), 1943.[5]

On March 10, 1943, the House passed the bill (H. R. 1501) by a vote of 407 to 6,[6] and on March 11, 1943, the Senate concurred by a vote of 82 to 0.[7] It was signed by the President on March 11, 1943. The act as adopted provided for a one-year extension of the authority originally conferred to June 30, 1944.[8]

Subsection (c) of Section 3 was amended by the insertion of "June 30, 1944" for "June 30, 1943" and of "July 1, 1947" for "July 1, 1946" and subsection (b) of Section 6 by insertion of "June 30, 1947" for "June 30, 1946."

(1) Statement by the Lend-Lease Administrator (Stettinius) before the House Committee on Foreign Affairs, January 29, 1943 [9]

[Excerpt]

The Committee also had before it a report to the Congress prepared by the Lend-Lease Administrator on operations under the Lend-Lease Act from the passage of the Act, March 11, 1941 to December 31, 1942.[10] The Administrator was one of the two persons to submit a statement to and testify before the Senate Committee on Foreign Relations.

. . . .

[1] *Hearings before the Committee on Foreign Affairs, House of Representatives, on H. R. 1501 [Extension of Lend-Lease Act]*, January 29, February 2, 3, 4, 8, 9, 10, 15, 16, 17, 23, 1943, 78th Cong., 1st sess.

[2] House Doc. No. 57, 78th Cong., 1st sess.

[3] House Report No. 188, 78th Cong., 1st sess.

[4] *Hearings before the Committee on Foreign Relations, U. S. Senate, on S. 813 [Extension of Lend-Lease Act]*, March 1 and 2, 1943, 78th Cong., 1st sess.

[5] Senate Report No. 99, 78th Cong., 1st sess.

[6] *Congressional Record*, vol. 89, pt. 2, p. 1815.

[7] *Ibid.*, p. 1853.

[8] Public Law 9, 78th Cong.

[9] *Hearings before the Committee on Foreign Affairs, House of Representatives, on H. R. 1501 [Extension of Lend-Lease Act]*, 78th Cong., 1st sess., p. 2.

[10] House Doc. No. 57, 78th Cong., 1st sess.

The American people and the Congress considered the Lend-Lease Act vital to our security in the spring of 1941 when we were not at war. I think there can be few who would contend that lend-lease is not an essential military instrument today.

That act, passed by the Congress in a time of peril, was an expression by the American people of their will to oppose the Axis in its attempt to dominate the free peoples of the world. The years preceding the debate on the Lend-Lease Act had been years of retreat and defeat. Japan had overrun Manchuria; Germany had seized Austria and Czechoslovakia. Poland had fallen, and the Axis armies had blitzed their way through Norway, Belgium, and the Netherlands. France had fallen. The *Luftwaffe* was over Britain.

There was no assurance in the sombre beginning of 1941 that Britain could hold out alone. With Dunkerque Britain had lost the major part of her equipment. We know now how pitifully small was her stock of weapons and supplies — so small in fact that 1,000,000 old World War Lee-Enfield rifles, 190,000,000 rounds of ammunition, 895 pieces of artillery and 60,000 machine guns sent by our Government out of its World War stocks were a major contribution to the equipment of her army, and to the sustenance of her spirit in those dark days. Airplanes, tanks, and other munitions ordered by Britain in 1939 and 1940 had hardly begun to arrive.

But British, French, Dutch, and Chinese cash purchase orders for plant expansion and for munitions, placed in the United States in 1939 and 1940, had stimulated our industries to take the first steps toward conversion to war. Bombers, tanks, and ships cannot be bought off the shelf. We had begun the long, hard work of building and equipping plants, of designing, retooling, and testing. To turn industry from peace to war takes time. That time was necessary — necessary to the defense of the United States today. To a large extent we and our allies are fighting today with the machines, the planes, and weapons ordered in 1940 and 1941.

Fortunately, the American people and the Congress had determined to help. What would have happened had we not done so? Can anyone seriously believe that there could have been a Libyan or a North African offensive in 1942 if Britain had been bombed into submission? Or would we now be fighting Hitler on the shores of South America or possibly Maine and Florida?

The American people and the Congress determined in 1941 that the support of Britain, in what Prime Minister Churchill called her finest hour, was necessary to the defense of this country. Britain desperately needed planes and tanks and guns, and she could not pay for them. Her dollar exchange had run low, and she could no longer place orders in this country, which was then her only source of additional war *matériel*.

The issue before the Congress in March 1941 was this: Should the American people stand by and say, no munitions unless the cash — the nonexistent cash — were put on the barrel head?

That issue was met in the most practical kind of way. We would supply the tools of war and discuss the terms of settlement later. The American people and the Congress of a democratic country understood our danger and met the Nazi challenge. The democracies had had enough of too little and too late. Today we can be thankful for that vision and that foresight.

The Axis had counted on our not helping our friends when their tills ran empty. They had propagandized against us so much as the country of the money bags that they came to believe that legend themselves.

The Lend-Lease Act was the answer of the American people and the Congress to both our friends and our enemies. It meant that supplies would go where they were needed, with reference only to need, and not to dollars. It meant that we could really begin to arm, and to organize our economy and our people against Axis aggression.

Within 16 days after the passage of the Lend-Lease Act, the Congress appropriated $7,000,000,000 to carry out its provisions.

Soon after this appropriation was passed in the spring of 1941, about $2,000,000,000 was allocated for the production of aircraft, over half a billion dollars for new shipways and new ship construction, and more than $1,700,000,000 was allocated for the construction or expansion of munitions plants and the purchase of other munitions. What was produced under these early orders fought many months later in the great battles of 1942, Leningrad, Stalingrad, and Tunisia.

LEND-LEASE AND THE POOLING OF RESOURCES

In the period of almost 2 years since the passage of the Lend-Lease Act the world scene has changed enormously. In June 1941, Hitler's armies struck east against the Soviet Union. In December, Pearl Harbor was attacked by the Japanese, and Hitler and Mussolini declared war against us. The conflict had spread to the corners of the earth. With the entry of the United States into war, and with Britain, Russia, China, and the United States fiercely fighting a defensive and delaying action against Axis aggression, it became imperative for the United Nations to combine their resources and manpower as rapidly and as efficiently as possible.

Lend-lease has become an essential part of the coordinated process of supplying our armed forces and those of our allies. The system for allocating United Nations supplies to the different theaters of war according to military need rests in large measure on lend-lease and lend-lease in reverse. The flow of war supplies from the factories to the fighting fronts proceeds without being impeded by considerations of finance. Lend-lease, in fact, fulfilled the President's original pledge to remove the dollar sign from war supply. Lend-lease in reverse has removed the symbol of the pound sterling, the franc, and the Chinese dollar. To paraphrase the President, money cannot take the place of munitions at the fighting fronts.

There is only one war. What we send to fight in Russia or the Middle East, the bombers based in Britain or Australia or India, the tanks which have just fought across 1,300 miles of desert in 90 days, these are part of our war effort. The guns, the food, and the camps we receive all over the world as lend-lease in reverse are a vital factor in the supply of our troops. Mutual aid among the Allies, on the supply side as on the battlefields, is an essential part of our organization for waging war — an organization of nations united in their determination to force an unconditional surrender of the Axis powers.

In the last war there was no real pooling of the resources of the United States and its allies. The United States paid in dollars all the necessary expenses for its Army in France and England. In the year and one-half that the United States Army was in the war total expenditures of the United States in France exceeded two and a quarter billion dollars.

The situation in the present war is wholly different. Weapons, food, industrial equipment for Russia, China, the United Kingdom, and the other allied countries are provided by the United States principally under lend-lease. To the extent of the resources at their command, these countries in turn provide the armed forces of the United States with equipment, food, shelter, and all necessary services as lend-lease in reverse.

When I speak of the pooling of the resources of the United Nations and when I refer to the battle of the world between the United Nations and the Axis powers, I wish to emphasize the magnitude of our supply problem.

·   ·   ·   ·   ·   ·   ·

(2) *Statement by Assistant Secretary of State Acheson before the House Committee on Foreign Affairs, February 3, 1943* [1]

[Excerpt]

·   ·   ·   ·   ·   ·   ·

Our foreign policy has two basic objectives: To help in winning the war and to prepare for an enduring peace. The powers created in the Lend-Lease Act and the programs of action which have been developed

[1] Department of State, *Bulletin*, VIII, p. 187 (see corrigendum, *ibid.*, p. 209); *Hearings before, the Committee on Foreign Affairs, House of Representatives, on H. R. 1501 [Extension of the Lend-Lease Act]*, 78th Cong., 1st sess., p. 81.

under it are of crucial importance in our work to fulfil both these purposes. Lend-lease has become the cornerstone of our wartime relations with friendly powers. The lend-lease agreements under which the lend-lease programs are conducted in war also lay foundations upon which peace can be built. Lend-lease is an indispensable instrument of our foreign policy today.

This is a war of alliance, and it can be won only if all the resources of all the allies are pooled in ways which permit the fighting forces of the United Nations to hit the enemy hardest where it hurts him most. We must fight over supply lines which reach to and from every remote corner of the earth. Shipping is one of our most serious shortages, but it is not the only one. To overcome supply difficulties more complex than any ever faced before, the United Nations must combine more completely and more effectively than allies have ever yet done.

In this task lend-lease is essential, for lend-lease is the most expeditious way in which we can join America's technological genius and industrial might with the fighting men of our allies already in the field against the enemy. Reciprocal lend-lease is the most expeditious way in which our allies can, in turn, provide, on the spot, weapons and food and other necessities for our own fighting men overseas.

At home and abroad, lend-lease provides the mechanism whereby the total needs of all United Nations forces can be considered together and procured together, without financial complications and with maximum efficiency.

The organization of our wartime economic controls and our lend-lease machinery allocate supplies on the basis of military need, not financial ability. Lend-lease has facilitated the organization of our domestic economy for war and has helped to establish our supply relations with friendly governments on a sound, simple basis. It has required the concentration of procurement for foreign governments in the hands of our own Government departments; it has provided workable channels through which the requests of foreign governments can be considered and decided.

[Here follows an extended discussion of the agreements that had been negotiated.]

The act provides that the benefit to the United States from the lend-lease program "may be payment or repayment in kind or property, or any other direct or indirect benefit which the President deems satisfactory." The President's Fourth Report to the Congress on Lend-Lease operations, dated March 11, 1942,[1] puts the matter simply.

---

[1] House Doc. No. 661, 77th Cong., 2d sess.

The first benefit we receive, he said, is one that needs no explanation — it is the direct military assistance to American security which results from the fight our allies are waging against the common enemy. To aid them in that fight has always been the basic purpose of the Lend-Lease Act; whatever other significance it may have, lend-lease was designed as a military weapon, and it has proved a most successful one. The lend-lease materials we send abroad are part of our own effort in the ruthless war which the Axis is waging against us. "The major benefit we will receive for our lend-lease aid," the President has said, "will be the defeat of the Axis."

The second benefit to the United States, the President has pointed out, is the reciprocal aid we receive from our allies. It is now a major factor in the supply of our forces abroad, in the maintenance abroad of our merchant marine, and in the flow of vital industrial and military information on which our war production and our war tactics largely depend. The equipment and maintenance of our forces abroad from the production of Britain, Australia, New Zealand, the French, Belgian, and Dutch colonies, and of China, has become an immense and steadily growing element in our war effort. The information we have been given about the radio detection of approaching planes, to mention one among many items, is of value beyond measure not only to our soldiers and sailors but to all of us.

In this connection, specific reciprocal-aid agreements have been made which apply the principle of Article II of the master agreements to the particular problem of supplying our armed forces in the field. Reciprocal-aid agreements were formally executed with the United Kingdom, Australia, New Zealand, and Fighting France, on September 3, 1942, and with Belgium on January 30, 1943. In addition, negotiations are now under way looking to the execution of similar agreements with others of the United Nations. The texts of the reciprocal-aid agreements thus far negotiated are to be found in appendix XI of Mr. Stettinius' current report to Congress.[1]

"These agreements," the President said in his Sixth Report to Congress,[2] "rest on the simple principle that each participant provide the other with such articles, services, facilities, or information as each may be in a position to supply for the joint prosecution of the war. The rule to be followed in providing mutual aid is that the war production and war resources of each nation should be used by all United Nations forces in ways which most effectively utilize the available materials, manpower, production facilities, and shipping space. Reciprocal aid represents the most economical use of the war resources of the United Nations. It means that we are husbanding time and transport to use resources

[1] *Ibid.*, No. 57, 78th Cong., 1st sess.   [2] *Ibid.*, No. 839, 77th Cong., 2d sess.

where they are. It means also, of course, that the peoples of Britain, Australia, and New Zealand, already on short rations, are freely sharing what they have with our troops."

In the nature of things, the bulk of the reciprocal aid we receive is in the form of supplies and services for American troops overseas. This aid of course has increased. Until very recently few of us had any idea of the really huge volume of assistance being rendered under these agreements. Major Spiegelberg has given you from first-hand experience an account of this development.[1]

A third direct benefit to the United States from the lend-lease program stipulated for by our master agreements is the pledge made by our allies that they will work with us, and, in the words of Article VII, with all other countries of like mind, for the economic objectives set out in that article. Article VII, which is repeated in substance in all our lend-lease agreements, reads as follows in the agreement with Great Britain:

In the final determination of the benefits to be provided to the United States of America by the Government of the United Kingdom in return for aid furnished under the act of Congress of March 11, 1941, the terms and conditions thereof shall be such as not to burden commerce between the two countries, but to promote mutually advantageous economic relations between them and the betterment of world-wide economic relations. To that end, they shall include provision for agreed action by the United States of America and the United Kingdom, open to participation by all other countries of like mind, directed to the expansion, by appropriate international and domestic measures, of production, employment, and the exchange and consumption of goods, which are the material foundations of the liberty and welfare of all peoples; to the elimination of all forms of discriminatory treatment in international commerce, and to the reduction of tariffs and other trade barriers; and, in general, to the attainment of all the economic objectives set forth in the joint declaration made on August 14, 1941, by the President of the United States of America and the Prime Minister of the United Kingdom.

At an early convenient date, conversations shall be begun between the two Governments with a view to determining, in the light of governing economic conditions, the best means of attaining the above-stated objectives by their own agreed action and of seeking the agreed action of other like-minded Governments.

It is to this article that the Under Secretary of State referred when he spoke of the first master agreement as the most important milestone on the road to the objectives set forth in the Atlantic Charter. The greatest economic benefit we can seek in the post-war world is the benefit which we receive as one of the great commercial nations from a high level of employment everywhere and a high volume of useful international trade.

The program envisaged by Article VII has two aspects. On the one hand it contains the pledge that the terms and conditions of the final

---

[1] See *Hearings before the Committee on Foreign Affairs, House of Representatives, on H. R. 1501 [Extension of Lend-Lease Act]*, 78th Cong., 1st sess., p. 49–80.

lend-lease settlement shall be such as not to burden commerce between the signatories but to promote mutually advantageous economic relations between them and the betterment of world-wide economic relations. In the light of our long and bitter experience with the international transfer problems of the 1920's, the President here declares one aspect of the relationship to which lend-lease transactions give rise. It is not a relationship which requires or permits of a settlement which will burden the commerce between the parties or between either of them and other nations. It does require settlement by action which will expand production and employment and the exchange and consumption of goods.

By this provision, the President has said, we have affirmatively declared our intention to avoid a repetition of our international debt experience during the 'twenties. We shall not seek the method of settlement by payment in gold or goods which in the past has proved an insurmountable burden to the trade of the world. On such terms we would have no hopes for the revival of trade on which all our post-war plans must rest and little hope for the survival after the war of the United Nations.

There is another ground, the President has said, for this provision of the master agreements. I quote here from the President's fifth lend-lease message to Congress: [1]

A lend-lease settlement which fulfils this principle will be sound from the economic point of view. But it will have a greater merit. It will represent the only fair way to distribute the financial costs of war among the United Nations.

The real costs of the war cannot be measured, nor compared, nor paid for in money. They must and are being met in blood and toil. But the financial costs of the war can and should be met in a way which will serve the needs of lasting peace and mutual economic well-being.

All the United Nations are seeking maximum conversion to war production, in the light of their special resources. If each country devotes roughly the same fraction of its national production to the war, then the financial burden of war is distributed equally among the United Nations in accordance with their ability to pay. And although the nations richest in resources are able to make larger contributions, the claim of war against each is relatively the same. Such a distribution of the financial costs of war means that no nation will grow rich from the war effort of its allies. The money costs of the war will fall according to the rule of equality in sacrifice, as in effort.

Closely linked with the provisions of Article VII, that the settlement should not burden commerce, are its affirmative provisions for agreement on "appropriate international and domestic measures" to assure the expansion of production and employment. The President has said in this connection: [1]

... If the promise of the peace is to be fulfilled, a large volume of production and trade among nations must be restored and sustained. This trade must be

[1] House Doc. No. 799, 77th Cong., 2d sess., p. 22.

solidly founded on stable exchange relationships and liberal principles of commerce. The lend-lease settlements will rest on a specific and detailed program for achieving these ends, which are, as Article VII of the agreements with Great Britain, China, and Russia point out, "the material foundations of the liberty and welfare of all peoples."

Cooperative action among the United Nations is contemplated to fulfil this program for economic progress, in the many spheres where action is needed. It is hoped that plans will soon develop for a series of agreements and recommendations for legislation, in the fields of commercial policy, of money and finance, international investment, and reconstruction.

We must seek the reduction of trade barriers and of other obstacles to trade, both on our side and on the side of other nations. Reducing trade barriers is an indispensably necessary first step toward our goal of full employment. With hampering limitations on trade reduced, we can look forward to success in the use of positive means of enlarging investment, employment, and production.

These are not the only benefits, large as they are, to be expected from the program of lend-lease assistance. That program may well involve arrangements for benefits to the United States of other than an economic character. As the war develops, it may be expected that arrangements of this nature will become pertinent and will be made.

The test of foreign policy in time of war is the effectiveness with which it contributes to the winning of the war and the extent to which it prepares the way for a decent and lasting peace. The lend-lease program is today a vital part of the foreign policy of the United States. It has been proved an effective means of supplying the fighting fronts of the United Nations. It is an integral part of our organization for waging war. Lend-lease agreements have been entered into from time to time to meet the changing needs of our system of war supply, and additional agreements will be made in the future to deal with the problems of the war as they emerge. The powers conferred on the President in the Lend-Lease Act are and must be sufficiently broad to give the flexibility we need in adapting our lend-lease program to the demands of war.

(3) Statements and Testimony before the House Committee on Foreign Affairs in the Course of Hearings Held January 29 through February 23, 1943 [1]

Selected statements and testimony on certain issues raised in the course of the hearings are here given because of the light they throw not only on administration policy but also upon possible lines of attack on the Lend-Lease program. The record of the hearings before the House Committee was available to the members of the Senate Committee on Foreign Relations at the time brief hearings were held by that Committee on the bill.

[1] Hearings before the Committee on Foreign Affairs, House of Representatives, on H. R. 1501 [Extension of Lend-Lease Act], 78th Cong., 1st sess.

(a) Nature of Lend-Lease Assistance. Testimony of Assistant Secretary of State Acheson, February 3, 1943 [1]

[Excerpts]

. . . .

ASSISTANT SECRETARY ACHESON. That was exactly it, and not only this article, but all of the articles were to make clear the nature of the relationship into which we and the other signing party were entering. We were not entering into a commercial transaction. It was not a transaction in which we sold something and for which they promised to pay a price. We entered into a relationship through which the resources of this country and the other countries could be made available to the fighting forces for the purpose of carrying on a war, those to be transferred as effectively and quickly as they possibly could to the fighting forces and the supporting industrial forces behind the fighting forces.

In discussing these matters and negotiating these matters with our allies, the question was, of course, What is this relationship; is it a relationship of debtor and creditor? These agreements undertake to make clear what it is. It is a relationship of mutual aid to the full extent and capacity of each country to render aid for the purpose of winning the war, and is bound up with the ultimate benefits which we hope to receive under the agreements, as well as with the immediate benefits we are receiving, such, for example, as the reciprocal lend-lease, of which you heard yesterday.

The ultimate benefits will be in the larger field covered by the economic article, Article VII, and also by all other arrangements which may be entered into in the security and in the political field.

. . . .

MR. VORYS. . . .

What do we accomplish in lease-lend by leaving the dollar sign off of the transactions? Now, I realize that we made a lot of mistakes after the last war and then proceeded to attempt to rectify those by making adjustments. But what is baffling to me is to think of an economy in our country that is still based on a dollar sign and to contemplate an international relationship where we cannot even see where we are at in the terms of our own thinking. Why can we not, or why could we not have done all this by means of loans and credits with an understanding that the dollar balance did not express the whole story? What objection is there to doing it that way?

MR. ACHESON. You mean what is the objection to going forward with loans or credits instead of with lend-lease?

MR. VORYS. Yes, loans and credits, with the understanding, certainly necessary in wartime, that the balance be struck or the arrangement to be made will be taken up later. What is the objection to proceeding along in that way?

MR. ACHESON. I should think there would be two that would occur to me right away. One is that you have not accomplished anything if you proceed on something which looks as though it were a loan or a credit but is not a loan or a credit. You have merely created a very confusing situation.

The second thing is in the mechanism of doing that you simply provide, "We are now extending a certain buying power to the other signatory power" and you immediately take out of the control of our Government what it now has, which is the direction of all purchases for war purposes in the United States. That is one of the more important things about lend-lease, that through this

[1] *Ibid.*, p. 93, 102–3.

arrangement our procurement divisions procure for everybody. Instead of having 6 or 7 or 20 purchasing missions in this country all of them dealing with these vital materials and creating competition and expense and confusion we have a channel through the appropriate procurement division of the Government acts itself. That is a most important thing. So far as changing from the lend-lease concept to your idea of a credit, which would not really be a credit, because although a loan in form it would be understood that repayment would not really be expected, as for that, I should think it would simply create confusion.

(b) Equality of Sacrifice. Testimony of Assistant Secretary of State Acheson, February 4, 1943 [1]

[Excerpt]

In his prepared statement Assistant Secretary of State Acheson had quoted President Roosevelt as follows:[2]

"All the United Nations are seeking maximum conversion to war production, in the light of their special resources. If each country devotes roughly the same fraction of its national production to the war, then the financial burden of war is distributed equally among the United Nations in accordance with their ability to pay. And although the nations richest in resources are able to make larger contributions, the claim of war against each is relatively the same. Such a distribution of the financial costs of war means that no nation will grow rich from the war effort of its allies. The money costs of the war will fall according to the rule of equality in sacrifice, as in effort."

In the course of Mr. Acheson's testimony, Mr. Mundt had asked if a statement contained in an article appearing in *Newsweek* to the effect that the per capita cost of the war in Great Britain was $440.00 as compared with $840.00 in the United States was erroneous.

MR. ACHESON. Well, Mr. Mundt, you know I am not an economist nor a statistician but I listened to your question the other day and it seemed to me there were some observations which even a layman might make on the figures which you discussed.

MR. MUNDT. I would be pleased to have them because I have some correspondence and phone calls with reference to this matter. I do not uphold Professor Robey's contention nor do I deny it but I think it should be corrected, do you not, if the impression gets out to the country that we are contributing twice as much per capita, it is not going to be desirable. .

MR. ACHESON. Well, I think if you want to really go into this matter of conversion of various economies to war purposes you would do well to get peopel trained in that work to testify, either from the Bureau of the Budget or the Economic Advisor of the Department of State. But I should like to make some observations.

MR. MUNDT. I would be happy to have you do so.

MR. ACHESON. You quoted from the article the other day as I recall it, the per capita expenditures in the United States was $840.

MR. MUNDT. $840 and $440.

MR. ACHESON. Yes; in Great Britain, $440. Then, as I recall it, that figure for British per capita expenditures was compared with the amount of appropriation for which the President has asked for the coming fiscal year, that is, for 1944.

MR. MUNDT. That is, for the $109,000,000,000 budget.

[1] *Ibid.*, p. 121–3.
[2] From the President's fifth lend-lease message to Congress, *ibid.*, p. 88.

MR. ACHESON. I should think a layman would want to point out at the threshold that you are comparing different things and different years. First we should have that clearly in mind. He is comparing a past year of actual expenditure in Great Britain with a future year's estimated appropriation in the United States. Those things are different.

Now in the second place comparing actual pound expenses per capita in the United Kingdom with actual dollar expenditures per capita in the United States for the same year is misleading unless you also bring into the comparison the actual per capita income in Great Britain during the same year and the actual per capita income in the United States for the same year. If you do that you will then see that any differences of the price level will be washed out and you will get the proportion of the national income in each country which is going for governmental expenses.

Now a hasty examination of the figures in that respect shows that the total central government expenses in the United States were $274 per capita in the fiscal year 1942. They are estimated to be $649 for the fiscal year 1943 and $827 for the fiscal year 1944.

The total central government expenses in Great Britain were $400 per capita in the fiscal year 1942 and are estimated to be $424 for the fiscal year 1943, taking $4 as the nominal conversion rate of the pound. No estimate is available for 1944.

When you compare this with the income for the two countries for the same period you find the total Federal expenses in the United States were 34 percent of national income for the fiscal year 1942. Our estimated expenses will probably be 66 percent for the fiscal year 1943 and about 76 percent for the fiscal year 1944.

The total central government expenses in the United Kingdom were 73 percent of the British national income for the fiscal year 1942; they will probably remain the same in the fiscal year 1943, and will rise slowly to about 75 percent or thereabouts in the fiscal year 1944. So that the comparison to make as to Government spending is between 73 percent for the British and 34 percent for us in the fiscal year 1942, and between 73 percent for the British and 66 percent for us in the fiscal year 1943. As for the fiscal year 1944, the fraction in each country will probably be about the same.

There are other comparisons which are also interesting. What I have just given is the comparison of the total Government expenditures to total income. But total government expenditures in dollars as compared with total income in dollars is not the most accurate way of comparing the financial burden of the war effort in the two countries, since expenditure figures contain many items, like debt service and so on, which do not represent goods and services for the war effort. The most significant ratio in this connection is the ratio of goods and services used in the war compared to the total of available goods and services. Using this ratio, we get the same general results, but on a more meaningful level. The British have been ahead of us, we are catching up, and we will both soon be close to the same absolute maximum in our conversion to war. For the calendar year 1942, our first full year in the war, we devoted about 33 percent of the total of available goods and services to the war, the British some 46 percent. During this year we shall both approach 50 percent, and thereafter remain together at or near that figure, which is probably close to a maximum, in view of the physical limitations on that process of conversion.

(c) Powers of the President to Achieve the Broad Economic Purposes Set Forth in Article VII of the Master Lend-Lease Agreements. Testimony of Assistant Secretary of State Acheson, February 3, 1943 [1]

[Excerpts]

MR. CHIPERFIELD. Mr. Acheson, I hope Dr. Eaton's dream comes true, but knowing him as I do I know he is also interested as I am in a practical and workable peace that will have the full confidence and approval of the American people. I want to ask you one or two questions with reference to Article VII and I am confining myself to that article.

In executing the terms of Article VII did you rely on any statutory authority for entering into that part of the master agreements?

MR. ACHESON. That is section 3 (*b*) of the Lend-Lease Act.

MR. CHIPERFIELD. Three (*d*)?

MR. ACHESON. Three (*b*).

MR. CHIPERFIELD. Of the Lend-Lease Act?

MR. ACHESON. Yes.

MR. CHIPERFIELD. Now, did you rely on the so-called Reciprocal Trade Act?

MR. ACHESON. No.

MR. CHIPERFIELD. I do not have that act before me, I am sorry.

MR. ACHESON. I have that right here. Section 3 (*b*) of the Lend-Lease Act provides:

The terms and conditions upon which any such foreign government receives any aid authorized under subsection (*a*) shall be those which the President deems satisfactory, and the benefit to the United States may be payment or repayment in kind or property, or any other direct or indirect benefit which the President deems satisfactory.

Now, repayment in kind or property, as I said in the statement, is covered by Article II. Article II provides that the other signatory Government will furnish us with whatever it is able to furnish us and under that article we are getting repayment in kind or property.

MR. CHIPERFIELD. Then you are not relying on any broad authority of the President as Commander-in-Chief?

MR. ACHESON. We are relying on section 3 (*b*) of the act.

MR. CHIPERFIELD. Frankly what has been bothering me is whether or not we perhaps have not provided by this Lend-Lease Act for authority to the President, so far at least as the economic part of a world war settlement is concerned, to enter into peace terms without the approval of either the Senate or any approval of the Congress. What comment do you have as to that?

MR. ACHESON. I should say that you have not done that and that you need not have any worry about it.

MR. CHIPERFIELD. That was in the back of my mind where Article VII here says —

to reduce tariffs and accomplish all the economic objectives of the Atlantic Charter, and so on.

[1] *Ibid.*, p. 100–1, 109–10.

And I was wondering if that gave the President authority to make Executive agreements to obtain those objectives and that we would not have anything as a Congress to say about it.

Mr. Acheson. I should think certainly not. I do not understand that section 3 (b) in any way changes the constitutional powers of Congress or of the executive branch, or alters established constitutional procedures. Action by this Government to reduce tariffs, for example, will be accomplished, as it must be accomplished under the Constitution, by an act of Congress approved by the President.

. . . .

Mr. Acheson. Yes, Mr. Eberharter, I think the constitutional situation is very clear. The President has control over our relations with foreign nations. He has the sole power of negotiation. No one can tell him what to do or how to do it. He does the negotiating. Now, in this agreement what he has tried to do broadly is to stop a tendency which might very easily develop of having a series of closed economies, closed against us and against one another, and to say to the other countries, "You must agree to sit down with us and work out an arrangement which will have the effect of increasing the whole volume of production in the world, of consumption and employment and reducing the barriers of trade and doing away with the discrimination." And they agree that they will do that. They are not holding out any of their special arrangements as being sacred or being protected from these negotiations. They agree to go into it and work this thing out. It is the President's constitutional function to carry out that negotiation. Now, whatever may be agreed upon may be carried out only as the article itself says, by appropriate national and international measures. Those must be taken according to the constitutional form of each of the countries. In this country some of these actions may take the form of a treaty. We know our constitutional procedure for that. Some of them could take the form of legislation, and we know what our constitutional procedure is for that. But there is nothing in section 3 (*b*) or in this agreement which in any way tends to curtail the power of the Congress or of the President or of the Senate as the treaty-ratifying body.

Mr. Eberharter. Then it is more or less in the nature of a statement of broad principles, or, you might say of broad objectives, which this country is committing itself to when the time comes to make the peace perhaps with reference only to one phase, and that is the phase of the cooperation among the United Nations?

Mr. Acheson. Yes; it is a commitment not in the legal but in the political field. It is a commitment that our Chief Executive will sit down with the chief executives of other countries and negotiate arrangements which are not going to be bilateral closed arrangements but will be open to everybody and have for their purpose the enlargement of consumption and production, and trade, and the reduction of impediments to those developments in trade. After that is done each one of these countries will have to submit the program to be carried out according to its own constitutional procedures, and they may carry it out or they may not but it is beyond the power of any man, certainly as the Government of the United States is organized, to do more than that, and it is entirely within the province of the President under the Constitution to agree to that form of procedure.

(d) Congressional Approval of Agreements Determining Benefits to Be Received by the United States. Testimony of Assistant Secretary of State Acheson, February 3, 1943 [1]

[Excerpt]

MR. VORYS. What objection would there be to a provision in the extension of lease-lend that the agreements determining the final benefit should be subject to approval by the Congress or by a concurrent resolution, let us say, just as lease-lend was enacted?

MR. ACHESON. I think in answer to that question you ought to consider what the agreements are; what is necessary in the course of the war and the effect of that sort of proposal which you would make. You are thinking presumably about the master agreements. We have a great many other agreements, too, those with the South American countries about which I have spoken. Those are agreements in which there is a final determination. There you are dealing with specific amounts and with specific items. In these agreements the issues are easily imaginable and a definite conclusion is altogether possible. But it has to be done quickly. It would be most undesirable to have a discussion of that kind in the Congress, or an approval. It is a matter which must be negotiated by the Executive in any event. It is primarily connected with the prosecution of the war and clearly any matters of that sort ought to be left as they are. When you get to the final agreements —

MR. VORYS. The master agreements is what I had in mind.

MR. ACHESON. The master agreements. There they may be quite different from what you are imagining. You tend to think of a final agreement as a document complete in itself. That is not likely to be the case. In the first place, we have in one sense a final agreement, which is that all the reciprocal aid which we receive is taken into consideration in whatever is done at the end of the whole matter to clear up the account. There ought not to be any question about the fact that is true. That should be final and absolute.

MR. VORYS. Pardon me. Will you excuse me? There ought not to be any question about what?

MR. ACHESON. About the fact that whatever is turned over to us under reciprocal aid is taken into consideration in the final settlement and that should not be subject to the approval of anybody. It is so inherently right that no doubt ought to be thrown in the minds of other countries that what they are doing for us is similar in nature to what we are doing for them. So that that is in one sense a final determination right there. Similarly in Article IV or V there is a question of return. Now, there again is something in the nature of a final determination already: that whatever the President wants returned and thinks useful for the United States shall be returned, and that is the end of that transaction.

We should not get into the perfectly hopeless situation of attempting to value a gun when it was given to the Russians and then saying "it is subject to depreciation and wear and tear and one of the wheels was hit by a shell and therefore it is worth half as much as when it was turned over to you." That is not the purpose of lend-lease. So what is done in that respect should not be required to be subject to the approval of Congress.

Then when you come to more intangible — well, first of all, let us come to very tangible things. You can imagine it may be necessary in the course of the

[1] *Ibid.*, p. 105–7.

conduct of military operations to decide that certain materials turned over for a specific purpose and used or lost in the fulfillment of that purpose are to be regarded as written off. Suppose, for instance, the combined chiefs of staff were discussing an expedition somewhere. Should this expedition be by American troops or by British troops? That ought to be determined solely on the military circumstances. There ought not to be any other consideration entering into it. We should not be in a position of saying, "We will let you have American troop ships to carry your troops, but if any of them are lost in the course of this operation you will have to pay us for them." That ought to be out.

Similarly, equipment or whatever equipment is most available ought to be used. And if the operation was sizable it might be desirable, I do not say it is, but I am saying the kind of thing that might be a final determination, that everything that is used in this operation shall be regarded as paid for by the fact that it is used. That is one type of thing might happen.

Then you come to the considerations that we are talking about in Article VII. It says:

> To that end they shall include provision for agreed action by the United States of America and the United Kingdom open to participation by all other countries of like mind, directed to the expansion, by appropriate international and domestic measures, of production, employment, and the exchange and consumption of goods, which are the material foundations of the liberty and welfare of all peoples; to the elimination of all forms of discriminatory treatment in international commerce, and to the reduction of tariff and other trade barriers; and, in general, to the attainment of all the economic objectives set forth in the Joint Declaration made on August 12, 1941, by the President of the United States of America and the Prime Minister of the United Kingdom.

These problems involve matters which have to be negotiated between the Executives of the two nations and carried out by the appropriate constitutional procedures in each case. So far as concerns forward action by this Government in the broad field of economic policy, as I said a few moments ago, the Lend-Lease Act does not in my opinion give the President any powers which he does not have independently of the act, nor does it take away from the Congress any of its authority over economic policy, either domestic or international. Some of the issues likely to arise during the implementation of Article VII are issues which under constitutional procedure should be settled by treaty. Some are issues which should be settled by Executive agreement, and others are of course problems which can be dealt with only by legislation. You may be assured that those issues will be presented and decided in each case according to our normal constitutional procedures.

MR. CHIPERFIELD. Will the gentleman yield?

MR. VORYS. Yes.

MR. CHIPERFIELD. In other words, you are not going to make an agreement that will reduce tariffs, say, on wheat, without having some legislation — that is, the approval of Congress — on that particular item?

MR. ACHESON. That is right, Mr. Chiperfield. So that in the final settlement, so far as they call for such action in the future, we will be subject to congressional action. Only the Congress can do or take that action. Nobody else can. So when you say final settlement must be subject to the approval of Congress, it may mean a whole lot of things some of which may be covered by matters entirely within the executive power of the President with which you ought not to interfere, as, for instance, the acquisition of bases somewhere which for military reasons are necessary for the security of the United States. That ought to be an action taken by or within the executive power of the President as Commander-in-Chief. So that by putting in this phrase which looks as though on the surface it was reasonable and the right thing to do, you may be accomplishing purposes quite contrary to your intention. And you will not be increasing the control of Congress over those matters which the Constitution has put within its power.

(e) Right to Commercial Air Bases as Benefit to Be Received. Statement of Assistant Secretary of State Berle, February 15, 1943 [1]

[Excerpt]

. . . .

The Department of State, the War Department, the Navy Department, the Civil Aeronautics Board, and the Department of Commerce have been giving consideration over many months to the problem of protecting American rights in the post-war aviation. By direction of the Secretary of State a committee was constituted consisting of Hon. Robert Lovett, Assistant Secretary of War; Hon. Artemus Gates, Assistant Secretary of the Navy; Hon. Wayne Taylor, Under Secretary of Commerce; Hon. Welch Pogue, Chairman of the Civil Aeronautics Board; and myself to coordinate this work. Prior to coming here this morning I consulted the committee, and this statement is made not only on behalf of the State Department but also on behalf of the committee.

Fields constructed in foreign countries with lend-lease funds constitute a very small proportion of a much larger number of fields, which have been constructed by other agencies. Without exception these fields have been developed under military necessity, in locations determined by our own military authorities, and primarily for our own operations.

It has not been considered feasible or desirable to make our active conduct of the war in this regard conditional upon the grant to us of permanent rights in these fields. It was not considered feasible or desirable to take the view that we would not take necessary steps for our own active prosecution of the war against a dangerous enemy, unless we could obtain permanent advantages at the expense of the countries which permitted the entry of our men and planes.

Wars cannot be won in this way.

Nevertheless, the Governments principally concerned have recognized that civil aviation will be an extremely important factor in post-war life. By reason of that fact these Governments, and particularly the Government of Great Britain, expect that agreements will be reached in due course on a fair and equitable basis, adequately recognizing the interests of their respective countries in post-war civil aviation.

With specific reference to landing rights in air fields built with lend-lease funds for the use of our military forces, one point must be made clear. Access to these fields, through the air over countries of our allies, necessarily involves discussion of the larger question of the extent to which we are prepared to afford access to landing fields in our own country. Plainly, it cannot be expected that our planes shall be accorded rights of landing, service, and commercial access in foreign countries if we adopt the policy of denying access to the planes of those countries reaching our shores. With this in mind there has been a general understanding that agreements on an equitable basis would be reached in due time.

[1] *Ibid.*, p. 209–10.

The committee will realize that the location of these fields has been determined by considerations of military necessity, rather than commercial desirability. It may be expected that some of these fields will have commercial usefulness after the war; many will cease to be important or interesting when the
particular campaign in which they are useful has been concluded. The fields
cannot be dealt with on an over-all or inclusive basis, but have to be considered
in each case in the light of probable traffic.

The subject of reverse lend-lease was extensively explored in the Hearings
before the House Committee on Foreign Affairs. Mr. Stettinius explained the
situation at some length in his prepared statement to the Committee (See
above, p. 106.) In his report to Congress, covering the period March 11, 1941
to December 31, 1942,[1] he further developed the extent of "lend-lease in reverse."
Major George A. Spiegelberg, Recorder, General Purchasing Board in the Office
of the General Purchasing Agent, European Theatre of Operations, submitted a
prepared statement on the amount and character of reverse lend-lease to the
Committee and gave further information in answer to questions.[2]

At a later date a statement was prepared by the Administrator and was submitted to the Subcommittee of the House Committee on Appropriations, when
that committee was considering the Defense Aid (Lend-Lease) Supplemental
Appropriation Bill, May 4, 1943 (see this volume, p. 241). Reference to it is
included here because of its full and comprehensive character even though it
was not before the House Committee on Foreign Affairs at the time that the
extension of the Lend-Lease Act was under consideration.

(4) *Report from the House Committee on Foreign Affairs on Bill to Extend for One Year the Provisions of the Lend-Lease Act, February 26, 1943* [3]

[Excerpts]

BENEFITS TO BE CONSIDERED IN FINAL SETTLEMENTS UNDER THE LEND-LEASE ACT

The Master Agreements provide the framework and the underlying
principles upon which the United States should be ready to enter upon
negotiations for a final settlement under the Lend-Lease Act. Section 3 (*b*) of the act provides that the terms and conditions upon which
any foreign government received lend-lease aid —

shall be those which the President deems satisfactory, and the benefit to the
United States may be payment or repayment in kind or property, or any other
direct or indirect benefit which the President deems satisfactory.

[1] House Doc. No. 57, 78th Cong., 1st sess.
[2] *Hearings before the Committee on Foreign Affairs, House of Representatives, on
H. R. 1501 [Extension of Lend-Lease Act]*, 78th Cong., 1st sess., p. 49.
[3] House Report No. 188, 78th Cong., 1st sess.

The first and principal direct benefit which has accrued from this act has been the facilitating of unselfish and efficient joint action in the war and making possible joint efforts in securing a just and lasting peace.

The second of the direct benefits we receive under the lend-lease program is the great volume of aid through lend-lease in reverse with which our forces abroad are equipped and supplied, and our war effort at home materially assisted. Reverse lend-lease aid has facilitated the most economic use of available shipping and other resources, and has saved very large sums of money which would otherwise have had to be appropriated.

A third direct benefit to be received under the act is the return under the provisions of Article V of the Agreements, of such defense articles as the President may deem of use to the United States.

A fourth direct benefit is the program of economic action to which Article VII of the Agreements looks forward. In purely economic terms the greatest benefit the United States can seek in the post-war world is what we can receive, as one of the great commercial nations, from a high level of employment everywhere, and a large volume of useful international trade. Favorable economic policies adopted by other nations after negotiations under Article VII are benefits which should be considered by the President under section 3 (b).

Article VII does not in any way alter the constitutional relationship of Congress and the President in the field of economic policy. It does not reduce tariff barriers, nor remove discriminations, nor set up machinery to secure an expansion of employment, production, and consumption. It does, however, bind the signatories to confer together, with all other countries of like mind, to determine the best means of attaining the economic objectives which it sets forth. Those conversations will concern all the subjects dealt with in Article VII, without limitation or exception. The results of negotiations undertaken in accordance with this provision are then to be referred for action to the proper constitutional authority in each of the countries concerned.

With reference to the United States, it is to be expected that the conversations under Article VII will give rise to a series of proposals for forward action in the field of economic policy, some in the form of treaties, some of executive agreements, and some of suggestions for legislation. The form chosen for any particular proposal in this field will follow normal constitutional practice, and is not affected by the terms of the Lend-Lease Act. This the President has indicated in his Fifth Report to the Congress on Lend-Lease Operations, dated June 11, 1942, where he said, with reference to the purposes of Article VII:

It is hoped that plans will soon develop for a series of agreements and recommendations for legislation, in the fields of commercial policy, of money and finance, international investment and reconstruction.

Article VII thus sets the stage for the economic negotiations on which many of our hopes for post-war prosperity depend. The achievement of that prosperity will not be possible unless the signatories to the Master Agreements agree upon a settlement which, in the language of Article VII, will be of such a nature "as not to burden commerce."

The committee is of the opinion that a lend-lease settlement which will not burden commerce cannot be based solely upon payment in gold or in goods as a benefit. This conclusion seems apparent in the light of the history of the war-debts problem during the 'twenties, and of the purpose of Congress in passing the Lend-Lease Act in its present form, rather than providing for a loan or series of loans. As Secretary Stimson pointed out in his testimony, the World War of 1914–18 was the only important instance in modern history when assistance to allies was granted in the form of loans. The results of that experiment are known to all. The method of settlement by payment in gold or in goods has in the past proved self-defeating and destructive, and would after this war seriously interfere with the achievement of the conditions of world economic order on which the prosperity of this country largely depends.

This policy for the settlement has another justification, as the President has said:

A lend-lease settlement which fulfills this principle will be sound from the economic point of view. But it will have a greater merit. It will represent the only fair way to distribute the financial costs of war among the United Nations.

The real costs of the war cannot be measured, nor compared, nor paid for in money. They must and are being met in blood and toil. But the financial costs of the war can and should be met in a way which will serve the needs of lasting peace and mutual economic well-being.

All the United Nations are seeking maximum conversion to war production, in the light of their special resources. If each country devotes roughly the same fraction of its national production to the war, then the financial burden of war is distributed equally among the United Nations in accordance with their ability to pay. And although the nations richest in resources are able to make larger contributions, the claim of war against each is relatively the same. Such a distribution of the financial costs of war means that no nation will grow rich from the war effort of its allies. The money costs of the war will fall according to the rule of equality in sacrifice, as in effort.[1]

The committee is of the opinion that the question of political benefits under the Lend-Lease Act, which the existing Master Agreements do not touch, is of great importance. In the field of security and political relationships there is a vast and complicated area which involves considerations going far beyond the Lend-Lease Act alone. The problem of air and naval bases as they bear on the security of the United States,

---

[1] *Fifth Report to the Congress on Lend-Lease Operations, June 11, 1942*, House Doc. No. 799, 77th Cong., 2d sess., p. 22.

to take one example, or of air rights generally, are problems which in their ramifications can be taken up only as the general development of our foreign policy permits.

PROCEDURE FOR DETERMINATION OF BENEFITS

In our opinion the original intention of Congress contemplated both the broad and inclusive meaning which this committee attaches to the phrase "direct and indirect benefit" in section 3 (*b*) of the Act and the procedure which is being followed for determining what these benefits should be. The powers conferred on the President by section 3 (*b*) are executive and administrative powers, closely linked to his duties as the Commander-in-Chief and the representative of the Nation in the field of international affairs.

Your committee desires to state at this point that an important portion of the time spent in the hearings upon this bill, in both open and executive session, has been devoted to a thorough discussion of the functions to be performed by the Congress in connection with the final agreements to be entered into by the United States and other nations, flowing from the operations of this act or further developments arising from this war. In those discussions your committee has been assured by responsible representatives of the State Department and others holding positions of authority in the executive branch of the Government that, in their judgment, all agreements of a permanent nature with other nations flowing from this act and post-war developments, must of necessity be handled in accordance with the normal course of our constitutional procedure. Confident that it is the intent of the Congress as well as the administration that the constitutional procedure pursued since the beginning of our Government shall continue to prevail, your committee stands ready to cooperate in any and every effort to achieve a peace which shall bless us and our descendants. The proposals for forward action in the economic field contemplated by Article VII must be handled in accordance with the normal course of our constitutional procedure, by statutes, treaties, or executive agreements, as may prove proper. The powers of the Senate in the field of treaties are unimpaired, as are those of the Congress in the field of legislation. Section 3 (*b*) of the Act clarifies the President's essential Executive powers in the administration of the lend-lease program.

. . . .

CONCLUSION

The Committee is convinced that the Lend-Lease Act should be extended. Lend-lease aided in sustaining and strengthening the United Nations in days of defeat and retreat. Lend-lease has helped and will continue to help in equipping and supplying the armed forces of the United Nations now beginning a relentless offensive. Lend-lease has made it possible for the resources of the United Nations to be pooled and made available at the points where they can do most harm to the enemy.

As an essential part of our mechanism for waging war, the Lend-Lease Act has operated with brilliant effectiveness. As an experiment in cooperative effort by the partners in a war of alliance, the Lend-Lease Act has been one of the most inspiring achievements of the war. For any group of nations to fight an enemy which is both disciplined and ruthless requires mutual trust and close cooperation. Lend-lease has been a powerful agency in developing that relationship.

The cooperative efforts of free people have achieved through lend-lease and reverse lend-lease an instrument which is more effective than the Axis method of conscripting the supplies and resources of vassal states. There is no substitute for belief in the cause of freedom and the determination of free people to retain that freedom. Lend-lease is not only in the democratic tradition, it will prove a vital factor in the inevitable victory of the United States and the United Nations.

(5) *Report from the Senate Committee on Foreign Relations, on Bill to Extend for One Year the Provisions of the Lend-Lease Act, March 10, 1943* [1]

[Excerpt]

BENEFITS OF THE LEND-LEASE PROGRAM

Lend-lease is considered as a weapon of war. In 1941, we chose the lend-lease device as the means of providing military assistance to friendly nations, because we wished to promote resistance to the Axis powers. Instead of granting loans or credits the Congress voted the President power to transfer defense articles, services, or information as the war situation required, on the terms and conditions specified in section 3 (*b*) of the act, which provides that the benefits shall be —

those which the President deems satisfactory, and the benefit to the United States may be payment or repayment in kind or property, or any other direct or indirect benefit which the President deems satisfactory.

After almost 2 years' experience with active lend-lease operations, the chief benefits which the United States is receiving, and will in the future receive under the act, now seem manifest. While a final settlement of the lend-lease records is deferred, under the lend-lease agreements, until the progress of events makes the problem clearer, certain elements of that settlement can safely be set forth at this time.

[1] Senate Report No. 99, 78th Cong., 1st sess.

The security of the United States is benefited under our lend-lease program first and principally by the use of lend-lease supplies in the war which the Axis has undertaken to wage against us. What we send to our allies for their use in war is part of our own war effort.

The purpose of weapons, and the materials from which they are made, is to inflict harm upon the enemy. When we send these materials to our allies, as when we send them to our own troops and factories, the benefit we seek and receive is their use against the enemy. This is not a commercial transaction. It is a military move.

There is no adequate way to value such military moves in dollars, pounds, or rubles. There is no way to compare the price of an American tank with the life of its Russian, British, or Australian crew. Our supplies which go to the war are paid for on the battlefield in the damage they do our enemies.

A second benefit accruing to the United States under the lend-lease program is the assistance rendered to our forces abroad by our allies as lend-lease in reverse.[1] Our allies have helped in important ways to supply the needs of our armed forces and our merchant marine from their own stores and production. In Britain and the Middle East, Australia, New Zealand, India, and China, and in the areas controlled by the French National Committee, and by the Governments of Belgium and the Netherlands, our forces are sustained on reverse lend-lease to the limit of their resources. It is a striking tribute to the efficacy of this program that our Army in the United Kingdom is now spending in the neighborhood of only $25,000 a month for its incidental supplies not covered by lend-lease in reverse, and that our forces in the south and southwest Pacific among other things are supplied with almost their entire food requirements and provisioning of ships. A detailed description of the type of aid received by our forces abroad as lend-lease in reverse was reported to the committee, and to the Foreign Affairs Committee of the House, and is discussed elsewhere in this report.

Lend-lease in reverse has proved to be more than a financial benefit to our military and maritime appropriations. It is a visible symbol of the way in which the materials of the United Nations, like their men, are pooled in a single gigantic effort against the Axis. That sharing of resources is an element of solidarity in the grand alliance of the United Nations, and a hopeful portent for our future.

In the third place, the United States will be benefited under the act by the return of such articles not consumed or destroyed in the course

---

[1] As a practical matter, it has proved impossible to give dollar values for the bulk of the supplies and services thus rendered us. The staffs in the field are instructed simply to transmit descriptions in physical terms, on the basis of which adequate records can be maintained in Washington. In the nature of the lend-lease relationship, it is difficult to keep records in any other form.

of the war, as the President may deem to be of use to the United States. While the volume and condition of lend-lease supplies at the end of the war is utterly unpredictable, it is fair to assume that such supplies as remain may be of real value, either in keeping the peace, aiding relief work abroad, or in supplementing our stocks at home.

During the hearings before congressional committees, it was indicated that potential benefits under the lend-lease program might result from Article VII of the master lend-lease agreements with Great Britain, the Soviet Union, China, and seven other of our chief allies. It is stated in the British agreement, for example, that the terms and conditions of that settlement under section 3 (b) of the act shall be such:

as not to burden commerce between the two countries, but to promote mutually advantageous economic relations between them and the betterment of world-wide economic relations. To that end, they shall include provision for agreed action by the United States of America and the United Kingdom, open to participation by all other countries of like mind, directed to the expansion, by appropriate international and domestic measures, of production, employment, and the exchange and consumption of goods, which are the material foundations of the liberty and welfare of all peoples; to the elimination of all forms of discriminatory treatment in international commerce, and to the reduction of tariffs and other trade barriers; and in general, to the attainment of all the economic objectives set forth in the joint declaration made on August 12, 1941, by the President of the United States of America and the Prime Minister of the United Kingdom.

At an early convenient date, conversations shall be begun between the two Governments with a view to determining, in the light of governing economic conditions, the best means of attaining the above-stated objectives by their own agreed action and of seeking the agreed action of other like-minded governments.[1]

Article VII indicates the type of economic action which may be contemplated. It is not a commitment which binds either of the legislative bodies of this Government. For example, Article VII does not authorize the reduction of tariffs or commit the United States to other measures which under the Constitution must be adopted by the Congress or by either branch thereof.

So far as action by the United States is concerned, it is to be expected that conversations under Article VII will result in proposals of policy which will be dealt with in each case according to the normal course of our constitutional procedure. Nothing in section 3 (b) of the Lend-Lease Act, or Article VII of the lend-lease agreements, affects the way in which this Government will decide the kinds of economic action it will take. The committee believes that there is no authority in the Lend-Lease Act to warrant any general post-war commitments or post-war policies in agreements made under the terms of the Lend-Lease Act.

One final class of benefits to be considered in relation to section 3 (b)

[1] See discussion in *Hearings before the Committee on Foreign Affairs, House of Representatives, on H. R. 1501*, 78th Cong., 1st sess., p. 87–8, 98–101, 105–11, 117–23.

may be mentioned. The problem of air and naval bases as they affect the security of the United States, to take one example, goes far beyond the field of lend-lease alone, yet its solution may give rise to some lend-lease benefits under section 3 (*b*). This problem is believed to be an integral part of the United Nations' general problem of winning the war.

CONCLUSION

There is no substantial controversy now over the renewal of the Lend-Lease Act. It has permitted the establishment of a method of procurement which is today an integral part of our wartime machinery of supply. Its utility to the United Nations has been reflected in every theater of the war. Under the act, aid is provided to the nations opposing the Axis in a manner which will make the most effective use of our resources. The renewal of the Lend-Lease Act is clearly necessary for the immediate prosecution of our war of alliance.

The Lend-Lease Act is more than a convenient way to facilitate the flow of supply to its fronts where they will prove most effective. It is a positive instrument establishing the wartime relations of allies on the sound foundation of cooperative effort in a common cause.

B. Amount, Form and Allocation of Lend-Lease Aid

In the period July 1, 1942 to June 30, 1943 the President, under the terms of the Lend-Lease Act of March 11, 1941, sec. 5 subsection b (Public Law 11, 77th Cong.) has transmitted the following reports to Congress: sixth report, September 11, 1942 (House Doc. No. 839, 77th Cong., 2d sess.); seventh report, December 11, 1942 (House Doc. No. 904, 77th Cong., 2d sess.); eighth quarterly, March 11, 1943 (House Doc. No. 129, 78th Cong., 1st sess.); and report for period ended April 30, 1943, May 25, 1943 (House Doc. No. 209, 78th Cong., 1st sess.). The Lend-Lease Administrator, Edward R. Stettinius, Jr., under the authority vested in him by Executive Order No. 8926, October 28, 1941, and pursuant to the direction of the President, submitted a *Report to the 78th Congress on Lend-Lease Operations from the Passage of the Act, March 11, 1941 to December 31, 1942*, dated January 25, 1943 (House Doc. No. 57, 78th Cong., 1st sess.).

(1) *Total Lend-Lease Appropriations and Transfer Authorizations, as of July 31, 1943* [1]

Lend-Lease Appropriations to the President

First Lend-Lease Appropriation	$ 7,000,000,000
Second Lend-Lease Appropriation	5,985,000,000
Third Lend-Lease Appropriation (Fifth Supp. 1942) . . .	5,425,000,000
Fourth Lend-Lease Appropriation	6,273,629,000
TOTAL	$24,683,629,000

[1] *Eleventh Report to Congress on Lend-Lease Operations, July 31, 1943.* Washington, Office of Lend-Lease Administration, p. 40.

Transfers Authorized from Other Appropriations

War Department — Third Supplemental, 1942	$ 2,000,000,000
War Department — Fourth Supplemental, 1942	4,000,000,000
War Department — Fifth Supplemental, 1942	11,250,000,000
War Department — Sixth Supplemental, 1942	2,220,000,000
War Department — Military Appropriation Act, 1943 . . .	12,700,000,000
Navy Department — Second Supplemental, 1943	3,000,000,000
Departments Other Than War — Third Supplemental, 1942 .	800,000,000
TOTAL	$35,970,000,000

NOTE. — In addition to the foregoing, Congress has with certain limitations authorized the leasing of ships of the Navy and merchant ships constructed with funds appropriated to the Maritime Commission without any numerical limitation as to the dollar value or the number of such ships which may be so leased. (See for example, Public Law 1, 78th Congress, approved February 19, 1943, and Public Law 11, 78th Congress, approved March 18, 1943.)

(2) *Lend-Lease Exports, March 1941 through June 30, 1943*

The total of Lend-Lease Aid through June 1943 was $12,922,932,000, which figure consisted of $10,883,946,000 of goods transferred and $2,038,986,000 for services rendered.[1] These figures do not include the value of goods consigned to United States commanding generals for subsequent transfer in the field to lend-lease countries.

The figures in the table below do not include (1) articles transferred to foreign countries but used in the United States, such as trainer planes for the instruction of United Nations' pilots; (2) some ships which leave the United States under their own power; (3) some goods consigned to United States commanding generals for subsequent transfer to lend-lease countries; (4) materials which have been transferred but not yet exported; (5) goods purchased outside the United States and sent directly to lend-lease countries; and (6) some other items of relatively small amount.

The figures include the value of planes flight-delivered which were not included in data presented in previous Reports to Congress.

(Millions of Dollars)

	UNITED KINGDOM	U.S.S.R.	AFRICA, MIDDLE EAST AND MEDITER-RANEAN AREA	CHINA, INDIA, AUSTRALIA, AND NEW ZEALAND	OTHER	TOTAL
MUNITIONS						
Ordnance	192	70	133	103	52	550
Ammunition	374	246	218	163	53	1,054
Aircraft and Parts . .	507	522	249	196	188	1,662
Tanks and Parts . .	369	183	204	127	43	926
Motor Vehicles and Parts	143	316	183	147	35	824
Watercraft	125	56	17	12	17	227
Total	1,710	1,393	1,004	748	388	5,243

[1] *Ibid.*, p. 9.

	UNITED KINGDOM	U.S.S.R.	AFRICA, MIDDLE EAST AND MEDITER-RANEAN AREA	CHINA, INDIA, AUSTRALIA, AND NEW ZEALAND	OTHER	TOTAL
INDUSTRIAL ITEMS						
Machinery	260	188	73	78	10	609
Metals	425	302	110	131	16	984
Petroleum Products .	310	15	43	62	5	435
Other	223	130	72	65	36	526
Total	1,218	635	298	336	67	2,554
AGRICULTURAL PRODUCTS						
Foods	1,213	373	57	30	27	1,700
Other Agricultural Products	317	43	4	19	2	385
Total	1,530	416	61	49	29	2,085
TOTAL EXPORTS	4,458	2,444	1,363	1,133	484	9,882

5. ECONOMIC WARFARE

A. Trading with the Enemy

[See *Documents, IV, 1941–42*, p. 760.]

(1) *Transactions Involving Trade or Communication with Enemy Nationals. General Ruling No. 11, March 18, 1942, as Amended September 22, 1942 and November 8, 1942* [1]

For text of original General Ruling No. 11, see *Documents, IV, 1941–42*, p. 769. The principal change involved the extension of the provisions of the Trading with the Enemy Act to that portion of continental France unoccupied by the Germans before November 11, 1942.

(1) No license or other authorization now outstanding or hereafter issued, unless expressly referring to this general ruling, shall be deemed to authorize any transaction which, directly or indirectly, involves any trade or communication with an enemy national.

(2) As used in this general ruling and in any other rulings, licenses, instructions, etc.:

(*a*) The term "enemy national" shall mean the following:

(*i*) The Government of any country against which the United States has declared war (Germany, Italy, Japan, Bulgaria, Hungary, and Rumania) and any agent, instrumentality or representative of the foregoing Governments, or other person acting therefor, wherever situated (including the accredited representatives of other Govern-

[1] Treasury Department, *Documents Pertaining to Foreign Funds Control*, p. 23; 7 *Fed. Reg.*, p. 7518, 9119.

ments to the extent, and only to the extent, that they are actually representing the interests of the Governments of Germany, Italy and Japan and Bulgaria, Hungary and Rumania); and

(*ii*) The government of any other blocked country having its seat within enemy territory, and any agent, instrumentality, or representative thereof, or other person acting therefor, actually situated within enemy territory; and

(*iii*) Any individual within enemy territory and any partnership, association, corporation or other organization to the extent that it is actually situated within enemy territory; and

(*iv*) Any person whose name appears on The Proclaimed List of Certain Blocked Nationals and any other person acting therefor.

(*b*) The term "enemy territory" shall mean the following:

(*i*) The territory of Germany, Italy, Japan, Bulgaria, Hungary, and Rumania; and

(*ii*) The territory controlled or occupied by the military, naval or police forces or other authority of Germany, Italy or Japan.

(*iii*) The territory so controlled or occupied shall be deemed to be the territory of Albania; Austria; that portion of Belgium within continental Europe; Bulgaria; that portion of Burma occupied by Japan; that portion of China occupied by Japan; Czechoslovakia; Danzig; that portion of Denmark within continental Europe; Estonia; that portion of France within continental France; French Indo-China; Greece; Hong Kong; Hungary; Latvia; Lithuania; Luxemburg; British Malaya; that portion of the Netherlands within continental Europe; that portion of the Netherlands East Indies occupied by Japan; Norway; that portion of the Philippine Islands occupied by Japan; Poland; Rumania; San Marino; Thailand; that portion of the Union of Soviet Socialist Republics occupied by Germany; Yugoslavia; and any other territory controlled or occupied by Germany, Italy or Japan.

(*c*) The term "The Proclaimed List of Certain Blocked Nationals" shall mean "The Proclaimed List of Certain Blocked Nationals" as amended and supplemented, promulgated pursuant to the President's Proclamation of July 17, 1941.

(*d*) The term "trade or communication with an enemy national" shall mean the sending, taking, bringing, transportation, importation, exportation, or transmission of, or the attempt to send, take, bring, transport, import, export or transmit

(*i*) any letter, writing, paper, telegram, cablegram, wireless message, telephone message or other communication of any nature whatsoever, or (*ii*) any property of any nature whatsoever, including any goods, wares, merchandise, securities, currency, stamps, coin, bullion, money, checks, drafts, proxies, powers of attorney, evidences of ownership, evidences of indebtedness, evidences of property, or contracts

directly or indirectly to or from an enemy national after March 18, 1942; *provided, however,* that the date November 8, 1942 shall be substituted for the date of March 18, 1942 with respect to trade and communication with those enemy nationals who became enemy nationals only by reason of the amendment of this general ruling on November 8, 1942.

(3) This general ruling shall not be deemed to affect any outstanding specific license insofar as such license expressly authorizes any transaction which involves trade or communication with any person whose name appears on The Proclaimed List of Certain Blocked Nationals.

(4) Any transaction prohibited by section 3 (*a*) of the Trading with the Enemy Act, as amended, is licensed thereunder unless such transaction is prohibited pursuant to section 5 (*b*) of that Act and not licensed by the Secretary of the Treasury. In this connection, attention is directed to the General License under section 3 (*a*) of the Trading with the Enemy Act, issued by the President on December 13, 1941.

(a) Standards of Conduct for United States Concerns Doing Business in Latin America. Public Circular No. 18A of the Treasury Department, April 13, 1943 [1]

(1) *Subject and Scope.* Public Circular No. 18 [2] prescribes the standard of conduct to be observed with respect to transactions involving enemy nationals. This public circular supplements Public Circular No. 18 and prescribes the standard of conduct to be observed by United States concerns located within Latin America with respect to transactions involving other nationals of blocked countries. It does not purport to prescribe standards for concerns *not located within* Latin America.

(2) *Authorized Transactions by United States Concerns Located Within Latin America.* Subject to the exceptions noted in paragraph (3), United States concerns located within Latin America are authorized to engage in transactions involving blocked nationals located within the generally licensed trade area, or within Spain, Portugal, Switzerland or Sweden, without further license. Such United States concerns will, of course, be expected to comply with all local controls in engaging in such transactions.

(3) *Transactions by United States Concerns Located within Latin America Which Are Not Authorized.* The following transactions shall not be engaged in

[1] From the Office of the Secretary of the Treasury; 8 *Fed. Reg.*, p. 4877.

[2] *Documents, IV, 1941–42*, p. 769; 7 *Fed. Reg.*, p. 2503. Par. 2 of Public Circular No. 18, dated March 30, 1942, reads as follows:

"(2) Any person within the Western Hemisphere who is subject to the jurisdiction of the United States shall not engage in any financial, business, trade or other commercial transaction which is directly or indirectly with, by, on behalf of, or for the benefit of an enemy national, except as specifically authorized by the Secretary of the Treasury, by means of regulations, rulings, instructions, licenses or otherwise."

by any United States concern located within Latin America except pursuant to general or specific licenses issued by the Treasury Department:

(a) Any transaction involving a dollar account of a blocked national located outside the generally licensed trade area, if such account is held on the books of a United States concern located within Latin America which is a bank or other financial institution;

(b) Any transaction involving an enemy national (see Public Circular No. 18).

In addition to the foregoing, the Treasury Department or any United States Mission in the other American Republics at any time may stipulate that any particular transaction or class of transactions requires a specific license. Any such stipulation shall be binding upon all persons having notice thereof.

(4) *Filing of Applications.* Applications for specific licenses to engage in any transaction may be filed with any United States diplomatic and consular officer in the other American Republics or with a Federal Reserve Bank in the United States.

(5) *Definitions.*

(a) The term "transaction involving a blocked national" shall include any transaction with, by, on behalf of, or at the direction of a blocked country or national thereof, or which involves property in which such national or country has an interest.

(b) The term "United States concern located within Latin America" shall mean any person subject to the jurisdiction of the United States located within Latin America, and the term "person subject to the jurisdiction of the United States" shall have the meaning prescribed in Public Circular No. 18.

(c) The term "generally licensed trade area" shall have the meaning prescribed in General License No. 53.

RANDOLPH PAUL,
Acting Secretary of the Treasury.

(2) *Transmission of Messages to or from Enemy Territory. Statement of the Department of State, March 1, 1943* [1]

The transmission to or from enemy territory of private messages or of documents intended for private use is subject to the restrictions hereinafter indicated, which have been prescribed in consultation with the Secretary of the Treasury, the Director of Censorship, and the Alien Property Custodian, to whom the President has delegated certain of his powers and authority under the Trading with the Enemy Act to license acts, transactions, and communications prohibited by sections 3 (a) and 3 (c) of the act.

1. *Documents.* The United States Government does not permit, by open mail, diplomatic channels, or otherwise, directly or indirectly, the transmission from the United States to enemy territory or from enemy territory to the United States of documents intended for private use, such as birth, marriage, or death certificates; divorce decrees; legal

[1] Department of State, *Bulletin*, VIII, p. 296.

notices concerning estates, lawsuits, etc.; powers of attorney; affidavits-deeds to real property; miscellaneous legal documents concerning prop; erty or litigation; commissions to take testimony or other documents pertaining to depositions; subpoenas, citations, complaints, or other forms of legal process; or forms submitted in connection with claims for pensions, disability allowances, insurance benefits, etc.

2. *Messages.* With the exceptions stated in paragraphs 3 and 4 below, the United States Government does not permit, by open mail, telephone, telegraph, diplomatic channels, or otherwise, directly or indirectly, the transmission from the United States to enemy territory or from enemy territory to the United States of private messages such as those pertaining to private property, business, estates, or the discharge of financial obligations. (The direct or indirect transfer of funds to enemy territory for the payment of charges arising in connection with private American property, real or personal, in enemy territory, such as taxes, rent, salaries of custodians, insurance premiums, repairs, and cost of packing or storage is likewise prohibited.)

3. *Communication through Red Cross facilities.* Brief paraphrased messages of a personal nature, including welfare and whereabouts inquiries, may be transmitted by telegraph or, where possible, by mail to or from enemy territory through the facilities of the International Red Cross, the American Red Cross, and other national Red Cross societies or those of other organizations or societies licensed by the Director of Censorship. All such messages are subjected to censorship before being forwarded. They are restricted to subjects of a personal nature, such as the welfare and whereabouts of friends or relatives, and will not be transmitted if they contain references to business or financial matters. The facilities of the International Red Cross and other Red Cross societies are available to all persons regardless of nationality. For further information concerning the transmission of messages through Red Cross facilities, application may be made to the nearest chapter of the American Red Cross.

4. *Communication through official channels.* Only in exceptional circumstances will the Department of State undertake the transmission to enemy territory by official telegrams of messages of a personal nature. If satisfied that efforts have been made to communicate through Red Cross facilities and that such efforts have proved unsuccessful, the Department will accept for transmission to enemy territory by telegraph in behalf of nationals of the United States and at their expense brief messages restricted, like those transmitted through Red Cross facilities, to subjects of a personal nature. Before being forwarded, such messages will be paraphrased by the Department of State and subjected to censorship. Only in similar exceptional circumstances will the diplomatic and consular representatives of the Swiss Government protecting American

interests in enemy territory transmit by official telegrams messages of a personal nature from enemy territory to the United States.

5. *Communication with prisoners of war and internees.* The foregoing restrictions upon the transmission to or from enemy territory of private messages and documents intended for private use are not construed as modifying or limiting the provisions of title III, section IV, of the convention relating to the treatment of prisoners of war, signed at Geneva on July 27, 1929. Information concerning the procedure to be followed in communicating with prisoners of war or with civilian internees in enemy territory may be obtained by addressing the Office of the Provost Marshal General, War Department, Washington, D. C.

6. *Enemy territory.* The term *enemy territory* as used herein shall be understood to mean enemy territory as defined in General Ruling 11, issued on March 18, 1942 by the Treasury Department pursuant to Executive Order 8389, as amended. It includes Germany; Italy; Japan; Albania; Austria; that portion of Belgium within continental Europe; Bulgaria; that portion of Burma occupied by Japan; that portion of China occupied by Japan; Czechoslovakia; Danzig; that portion of Denmark within continental Europe; Estonia; that portion of France within continental Europe occupied by Germany or Italy; French Indo-China; Greece; Hong Kong; Hungary; Latvia; Lithuania; Luxemburg; British Malaya; Monaco; that portion of the Netherlands within continental Europe; that portion of the Netherlands East Indies occupied by Japan; Norway; that portion of the Philippine Islands occupied by Japan; Poland; Rumania; San Marino; Thailand; that portion of the Union of Soviet Socialist Republics occupied by Germany; Yugoslavia; and any other territory controlled or occupied by Germany, Italy, or Japan.

B. Export Control

[See *Documents, II, 1939–40,* p. 786–801; *III, 1940–41,* p. 473–98; and *IV, 1941–42,* p. 718–40.]

The system of export control now in operation as a part of the total war effort was developed under the authority of sec. 6 of the Act of July 2, 1940 [1] which authorized the President, whenever he "determines that it is necessary in the interest of national defense to prohibit or curtail the exportation of any military equipment or munitions, or component parts thereof, or machinery, tools, or material or supplies necessary for the manufacture, servicing or operation thereof," to "prohibit or curtail such exportation, except under such rules and regulations as he may prescribe." This act was passed at a time when the United States was a non-belligerent, and was therefore conceived at the time as a measure to provide for national defense by measures short of war. During the period before Pearl Harbor, the system of export control based on this act was elaborated in great detail with the result that upon the outbreak of war there was available a largely perfected instrument for carrying on an important phase of economic warfare. Exhibits in Volumes II, III and IV of this series have

[1] Public Law 703, 76th Cong., 54 Stat. 712.

shown the evolution of this system. The exhibits in Volume IV, 1941–42, p. 718–40, give a fairly detailed picture of the organization of export control and the way in which it operated after a period of actual war experience.

The over-all responsibility for the administration of export control remained during this period with the Board of Economic Warfare, as provided by Executive Order No. 8900 and Administrative Order No. 1, September 15, 1941,[1] acting in cooperation with the Department of State.

The rules and regulations in force as of June 30, 1942, determining articles and materials subject to export control, and prescribing the conditions under which export licenses, including intransit licenses, are to be issued, are listed in the *Federal Register* of July 2, 1942.[2] A general Revision of Export Regulations, dated January 27, 1943, appeared in the *Federal Register* of February 4, 1943.[3] Subsequent amendments may be found by consulting the Index of the *Federal Register* (Monthly, Quarterly and Annual) under *Economic Warfare, Board of.*

The two significant changes introduced during the period under review were (1) the adoption of a revised plan of export control incorporating principles of decentralization and cooperation applicable to trade with Latin American countries and (2) the adoption of purchasing-mission programs in our relations with certain other countries, including most British Empire areas.

(1) *Decentralization Plan of Export Procedure. Announcement of the Board of Economic Warfare, March 3, 1943* [4]

Decentralization Plan A of Export Control was adopted in order to give the other American Republics an opportunity to cooperate in the selection of commercial goods to be exported from the United States and in order to bring about closer correlation of available cargo space and essential supplies. It was based on agreements entered into with the Governments of the American Republics. The cancellation of general licenses provided for in the earlier system of export control became effective two months after the effective date of Decentralization Plan A for each country.

A. *The Plan will operate as follows:*

1. The Government of each country will designate one of its agencies (hereinafter referred to as "country agency") with which all parties desiring to import articles and materials from or by way of the United States will file applications for Import Recommendations. These Import Recommendations and the procedure outlined hereafter are to replace the present certificates of necessity procedure or similar devices now in use.

2. The Embassy or Legation of the United States and the Country Agency will collaborate in this program.

3. The Board of Economic Warfare will inform the Country Agency of the quantities of material in short supply which it is estimated can be supplied to that country for a stated period.

[1] 6 *Fed. Reg.*, p. 4795, 4818. The Economic Defense Board, to which this authority was delegated under these orders was renamed the Board of Economic Warfare by Executive Order No. 8982, December 17, 1941 (6 *Fed. Reg.*, p. 6530).

[2] 7 *ibid.*, p. 4952–5019.

[3] 8 *ibid.*, p. 1494–1577. Corrections of this General Revision appeared at p.1879, 2773.

[4] *Current Export Bulletin* No. 79.

4. The Country Agency will, as soon as practicable, establish a list of *all* articles and materials which are importable, and for which the Country Agency will issue Import Recommendations. This list will include allocated as well as non-allocated materials according to the needs of the country and the availability of shipping space.

In lieu of the foregoing, the Country Agency may establish a list of articles the importation of which will not be approved and for which Import Recommendations will not be issued. Import Recommendations will be issued for all articles not on such a list.

5. Importers will apply to the Country Agency for Import Recommendations covering the materials which they wish to import and will supply the Country Agency with such information as is required.

6. The Country Agency will examine, select and issue Import Recommendations for those materials which it deems most essential for the war effort and the economy of the country. The total quantity of Import Recommendations issued will be limited by the estimates of available supply and shipping tonnage.

7. The Country Agency will issue information describing in detail the method of applying for Import Recommendations, the places at which applications may be filed and other pertinent regulations.

8. If the Country Agency issues an Import Recommendation a copy, marked No. 4, will be sent to the applicant-importer with instructions to forward that copy to the exporter.

9. The exporter will file a license application with the Board of Economic Warfare in the usual manner attaching to it the Import Recommendation Form copy No. 4 which he received from the importer.

10. Under this program the Country Agency will issue Import Recommendations for all shipments to its respective country, and unless an export license application is accompanied by the corresponding Import Recommendation it will not be acted upon.

11. All general licenses for shipment to countries included in this plan will be cancelled, including GIT and the special general license provisions for medicinals, with the exception of General License GUS, Shipments Valued at $25 or Less, Personal Baggage, General License for Ship's Stores, return of empty containers, photographic films, plates and paper, technical data, newspapers and publications, as set forth in Comprehensive Export Schedule No. 11.

12. The Board of Economic Warfare will endeavor to issue export licenses for which the Country Agency has issued Import Recommendations. The Board of Economic Warfare reserves the right to reject an application for an export license even though accom-

panied by an Import Recommendation and to grant an export license without an Import Recommendation when it deems such action necessary to the best interests of the war effort.

B. *The Importer in the Country of Destination will be responsible for the following:*

1. The importer will keep himself informed of the regulations of the Country Agency.
2. The importer will place orders as usual with his respective exporters.
3. Upon the announcement by the Country Agency that it will consider applications for Import Recommendations the importer will file Import Recommendation applications with the Country Agency and will supply such additional information to the Country Agency as may be requested.
4. Upon filing an application for an Import Recommendation, the importer will submit satisfactory evidence to the Country Agency that he has placed an order for the material with the exporter named thereon.
5. The Country Agency will either reject or issue Import Recommendations. Rejected applications will be returned to the importer and will require no further action on his part. When Import Recommendations are issued the importer is required to proceed in accordance with his undertaking as set forth on the Import Recommendations and to follow instructions issued by the Country Agency.
6. The Country Agency's issuance of an Import Recommendation will not constitute a guarantee that an export license will be granted. Circumstances may prevent the issuance of an export license.
7. The importer having received copy No. 4 of the Import Recommendation will mail it to the exporter with the confirmation copy of his order.

C. *The Exporter will act in the following manner:*

1. The exporter will receive the order and copy No. 4 of the Import Recommendation from the importer.
2. The exporter will apply to the Board of Economic Warfare for an export license for the materials covered by the Import Recommendation issued to the importer and the exporter will attach to the license application the Import Recommendation which he received from the importer, inserting the number of the Import Recommendation in the upper part of the space provided for the description of the material.

3. Import Recommendations, accompanied by corresponding license applications, must be filed with the Board of Economic Warfare, Washington, D. C. within sixty days from the date they were issued by the Country Agency. If the exporter finds it impossible to file an export license application with the Import Recommendation within sixty days of its issuance a letter should be addressed to the Board of Economic Warfare explaining the circumstances. In order to permit the material being secured in time, particularly on CMP materials, it is asked that these special requests be reduced to a minimum.

4. Upon receipt of a license the exporter will proceed with his commercial and financial arrangements in the customary manner. The Board of Economic Warfare will have no participation in these arrangements.

5. Rejected license applications may be appealed in accordance with existing procedures as set forth in Comprehensive Export Schedule No. 11 and subsequent Current Export Bulletins.

D. *Multiple Commodity Licenses — Related Commodities under One License*

Importers applying for Import Recommendations may include in one application related commodities destined to one consignee as described in Comprehensive Export Schedule No. 11, pages 92 to 93. Categories 92, 93, 94 and 95 have been deleted from this list.

E. *Effective Date of Plan*

In subsequent bulletins the Office of Exports will announce the countries for which the foregoing procedure will be followed, and the respective dates on which the procedure will become operative. Until such announcement is made, exporters in the United States and importers abroad should continue to follow existing procedures.

(SIGNED) A. N. ZIEGLER, J.A.G.D.
Acting Chief of Office
Office of Exports

(a) *Effective Dates of Decentralization Plan A. Announcement of Board of Economic Warfare, March 5, 1943* [1]

Decentralization Plan A, announced in Current Export Bulletin No. 79, will become operative in the following countries in accordance with the details set forth below. The second column indicates the Country Agency designated by each country. The fourth column designates the date until which licenses may be issued without Import Recommendations. On and after that date all Certificates of Necessity will be considered as cancelled, and Import Recommendations must accompany all export license applications.

[1] *Current Export Bulletin* No. 80.

Country	Country Agency	Effective Date of Decentralization Plan A	Licenses May Be Issued Without Import Recommendations Until:
Bolivia	Ministry of National Economy, La Paz	April 1, 1943	June 1, 1943
Colombia	Superintendencia Nacional de Importaciones, Bogotá	May 1, 1943	July 1, 1943
Costa Rica	Oficina de Defensa Economica, San José	April 1, 1943	June 1, 1943
Ecuador	Oficina de Prioridades y Distribución de Importaciones, Quito	April 1, 1943	June 1, 1943
El Salvador	Comite de Coordinación Economica, San Salvador	April 1, 1943	June 1, 1943
Guatemala	Sección de Coordinación Economica Financiera de Guatemala, Guatemala	April 1, 1943	June 1, 1943
Honduras	Oficina de Control de Materiales Estrategicos, Tegucigalpa	April 1, 1943	June 1, 1943
Mexico	Comito Coordinador de las Importaciones, Mexico	To be announced	To be announced
Nicaragua	Junta de Control de Precios y Comercio, Managua	April 1, 1943	June 1, 1943
Panama	Comisión de Control de Importacion, Ministerio de Agricultura y Comercio, Panama	April 1, 1943	June 1, 1943
Paraguay	Department of Industry and Commerce, Ministry of Agriculture, Asunción	April 1, 1943	June 1, 1943
Peru	Repartición Comercial, Ministerio de Hacienda y Comercio, Lima	April 1, 1943	June 1, 1943
Uruguay	Controlador de Exportaciones e Importaciones, Montevideo	May 1, 1943	July 1, 1943
Venezuela	Comisión de Control de Importaciones, Caracas	April 1, 1943	June 1, 1943

The cancellation of general licenses as announced in *Current Export Bulletin* No. 79, Paragraph 11, will become effective for each country two months after the effective date of Decentralization Plan A for each country. Shipments which are on dock, on lighter, laden aboard the exporting carrier or in transit to ports of exit prior to the effective date of cancellation of general licenses may be exported under the previous general license provisions.

Exporters are urged to submit the Import Recommendations with their applications at the earliest possible time.

Notwithstanding the fact that general licenses will remain in effect for a two months' period after the effective date of Plan A in each country, exporters intending to ship such commodities are strongly urged to apply to the Office of Exports for export licenses for these commodities in order that they may have valid licenses under which their cargo can move if it does not clear port by the expiration date of the General Licenses.

. . . .

(Signed) A. N. Ziegler, J.A.G.D.
Acting Chief of Office
Office of Exports

(b) *Procedure for Exports to Argentina. Announcement of the Board of Economic Warfare, February 27, 1943* [1]

I. A procedure has been designed to determine the essential needs of Argentina for all materials to be imported from or by way of the United States.

Effective April 1, 1943, exportations to Argentina may no longer be made under general license, with certain exceptions, and this procedure will apply to allocated as well as non-allocated materials.

After April 1, 1943, applications for individual licenses will not be considered for shipments to Argentina except under the procedure herein outlined.

Intransit shipments to Argentina through the United States will also be governed by this procedure.

II. This plan of procedure will be carried out in the following manner:

A. Procedure to be followed in Argentina:

1. Importers wishing to import any commodity from or by way of the United States into Argentina will first apply to the Central Bank of Argentina for a Certificate of Necessity, and will submit such information as may be required by the Central Bank of Argentina.
2. The Central Bank of Argentina will issue information describing in detail the method of applying for Certificates of Necessity and other pertinent information.
3. The Central Bank of Argentina will issue Certificates of Necessity for those commodities deemed essential to the national economy of Argentina. The issuance of these Certificates of Necessity will be limited by estimates of available supply and transportation facilities.
4. The Embassy of the United States and the Central Bank of Argentina will collaborate in this procedure.
5. Certificate of Necessity, if issued, will be delivered to the importer by the Central Bank of Argentina.
6. All articles and materials for the maintenance and repair and for the operation of the meat-packing plants (*frigeríficos*) and of the mines producing tungsten and beryllium for the fulfillment of bulk contracts for the war effort will not require Certificates of Necessity. Operations materials for the meat-packing plant to be used in filling other than bulk contracts for the war effort, however, will require Certificates of Necessity.

B. Procedure to be followed by the *importer* in Argentina:

1. The importer will keep himself informed of the regulations issued by the Central Bank of Argentina.
2. The importer will place his orders as usual with his exporters.
3. The Central Bank of Argentina will either refuse or issue Certificates of Necessity. Rejected applications will be returned to the importer and will require no further action on his part.
4. If the Central Bank of Argentina issues a Certificate of Necessity it will be delivered to the importer, who will then forward it to his exporter.
5. Upon receipt of notification from the exporter that he has been granted an export license the importer will complete any portion of the transaction still pending.

[1] *Current Export Bulletin* No. 77.

C. Procedure to be followed by the *exporter:*

1. The exporter will receive the original copy of the Certificate of Necessity from the importer.
2. The exporter will apply to the Office of Exports, Board of Economic Warfare, Washington, D. C. for an export license for the materials covered by the Certificate of Necessity issued to the importer, and the exporter will attach to the license application the original Certificate of Necessity.
3. Upon receipt of an export license the exporter will proceed with his commercial and financial arrangements in the customary manner. The Board of Economic Warfare will have no participation in these arrangements.
4. Rejected license applications may be appealed in accordance with the procedure set forth in Comprehensive Export Schedule No. 11 and subsequent Current Export Bulletins.
5. Beginning April 1, 1943, each application for an export license to Argentina must be accompanied by a Certificate of Necessity when presented to the Board of Economic Warfare. Effective March 31, 1943, all outstanding Certificates of Necessity, issued in 1942, for which licenses have not been granted, will expire.

III. All general licenses for shipment to Argentina, as of April 1, 1943, are hereby cancelled, including GIT and the special general license provisions for medicinals, with the exception of General License GUS, Shipments Valued at $25 or Less, Personal Baggage, General License for Ship's Stores, return of empty containers, photographic films, plates and paper, technical data, newspapers and publications, as set forth in Comprehensive Export Schedule No. 11.

Shipments which are on dock, on lighter, or laden aboard the exporting carrier prior to April 1, 1943, may be exported under the previous general license provisions.

IV. The Board of Economic Warfare will endeavor to issue export licenses and shipping space permits pursuant to applications accompanied by Certificates of Necessity, but may deny such applications when it deems such action necessary in the interest of the prosecution of the war.

The Board of Economic Warfare likewise may grant export licenses without receiving Certificates of Necessity in order to meet emergency needs relating to exports essential to the production and transportation of war materials.

(SIGNED) A. N. ZIEGLER, J.A.G.D.
Acting Chief of Office
Office of Exports

(c) *Agreement with Canada on the Programing of Exports to the Other American Republics. Announcement of the Department of State, May 22, 1943* [1]

An agreement has been reached with the Government of Canada whereby exports from the United States and Canada to the other American Republics will be jointly programed.

[1] Department of State, *Bulletin*, VIII, p. 454.

Effective June 1, 1943, Canada will participate in the decentralized export-control plan, the purpose of which is to assure that goods exported to the other American Republics will be utilized to the best interest of the war effort and to maintain the essential economy of those countries. The procedure provides for the joint programing of exports within the available supply of scarce materials and within the available shipping space.

The joint programing of exports will follow as far as possible the specific requests or recommendations of the importing countries. Agencies have already been created in the other American Republics which certify within the available supply and shipping tonnage orders for goods to be exported from the United States. This procedure is now to be extended to exports from Canada to those countries. The American diplomatic missions and the Canadian representatives in the other American Republics will cooperate closely in this action.

The operational details of integrating this export program are being worked out by the Department of State, the Board of Economic Warfare, and Canadian officials.

It is the underlying policy of both Governments that in the operation of the decentralization plan no advantage should be taken by nationals of either country at the expense of the other.

(2) *Purchasing Mission Program Licenses. Announcement of the Board of Economic Warfare, March 10, 1943* [1]

The system of purchasing-mission-program licensing, superseding the system of general licenses hitherto in force,[2] was worked out jointly by the Department of State, the Office of Lend-Lease Administration and the Board of Economic Warfare, in agreement with the purchasing missions of the foreign governments concerned, to make possible closer coordination in procurement and shipping. Under the plan United States exporters are provided with advance information with which to schedule available business in accordance with known essential requirements.

The program-licensing procedure was adopted to make the most essential use of scarce materials and shipping space and to coincide with the provisions of the Controlled Materials Plan and with allocations by the War Production Board.

The Board of Economic Warfare in collaboration with the Office of Lend-Lease Administration will shortly announce Program Licenses for foreign government purchasing agencies. The Program Licenses will replace the present Unlimited Licenses, described on pages 83 through 86 of Comprehensive Export Schedule No. 11, and also replace certain General Licenses and individual license procedure for countries in the C group.

The present holders of Unlimited Licenses are the Amtorg Trading Corporation, the Belgian Congo Purchasing Commission, the British Ministry of Supply Mission, the Netherlands Purchasing Commission and the Universal Trading Corporation.

All commodities now subject to War Production Board control will be covered by the Program License corresponding to WPB programs. Other commodities will be covered by dollar and tonnage limitations so that non-essential cargo will not crowd out essential cargo.

[1] *Current Export Bulletin* No. 81.   [2] *Documents, IV, 1941–42*, p. 730.

The following are the essential features of the proposed program-licensing procedure:

1. Before a Program License which is issued to a foreign government purchasing mission or agency will become effective, a program proposal of exports essential to the particular destination must be submitted by the mission or agency to the appropriate United States Government agency. The submission of separate program proposals for each destination will be required if any Program License is to cover more than one destination.

2. Quarterly requirements will be determined after consideration of the program proposals by the appropriate United States agencies. The Office of Lend-Lease Administration or the Board of Economic Warfare, depending upon the destination involved, will present the requirements to the War Production Board or other agencies controlling the allocation of supplies and shipping and quarterly programs for the foreign government agencies will be determined.

3. A ceiling stated in the program license for any commodity will determine the maximum exports of that commodity under the license. The Office of Lend-Lease Administration, acting under its statutory authority, may approve requisitions for any part of the total amount specified in the program. The amounts which are supplied by Lend-Lease will be deducted in order to show the licensable remainder. The Program and Program License may be amended by the appropriate United States agencies.

4. A certifying agency will be designated in each Program License to authorize exports under the Program License. The form of the release certificates and applications therefor will be determined by the Board of Economic Warfare.

5. Exporters may appeal to the Board of Economic Warfare in cases of rejected export proposals.

6. The foreign government purchasing agency will maintain such accounts and submit such reports as may be required by the Office of Lend-Lease Administration and the Board of Economic Warfare.

7. Export release certificates may be issued only when the "end-use" of the commodity to be exported is in accordance with the "end-use" listed on the original program. If the ultimate "end-use" is changed, a request for an amendment of the program must be filed by the agency with the Office of Lend-Lease Administration or with the Board of Economic Warfare.

The Board of Economic Warfare will consider each program license separately and on its merits, and include such detailed arrangements in each case as appear necessary. The program licensing procedure is being adopted to make the most essential use of scarce materials and shipping space, and to coincide with the provisions of the Controlled Materials

Plan and allocations by the War Production Board. The Program License will be amended as changing conditions necessitate.

(a) Program License for Certain British Empire Destinations. Announcement of the Board of Economic Warfare, April 12, 1943 [1]

The procedure outlined below applies, for certain British Empire destinations, the principles of program licensing as announced in *Current Export Bulletin* No. 81. Until other program licenses for other destinations are announced, current procedures may be followed for those other destinations.

Under the program license procedure, the Board of Economic Warfare has issued a license to The British Supply Council in North America authorizing the exportation to British Empire destinations (except Canada, Newfoundland, Labrador and the Middle East) of specified kinds and quantities of commodities for specified end-uses. The British Supply Council, in accordance with the wishes of the missions for the various parts of the Empire, will act as certifying agency with respect to all British Empire destinations which are under the Program License.

The program-licensing procedure is being adopted to make the most essential use of scarce materials and shipping space, and to conform with the provisions of the Controlled Materials Plan and allocations by the War Production Board. The issuance of Release Certificates to exporters will not only give final clearance for shipments to be made from the United States, but will also indicate that an import license has been issued by the country of destination. One of the reasons for adopting this procedure is to expedite shipments to these destinations. Another is to achieve unified programs for the export of commercial and Lend-Lease shipments.

REVOCATION OF CERTAIN GENERAL AND UNLIMITED LICENSES

1. The Unlimited License heretofore in effect for the British Ministry of Supply Mission was revoked as of April 6, 1943, with the provision that exportations may be made under this Unlimited License until July 1, 1943, pursuant to release certificates valid on April 6, 1943. Release certificates issued under this Unlimited License which were valid on March 31, 1943, will remain valid until July 1, 1943, regardless of their expiration date.

None of the above provisions applies to the Unlimited License which continues in effect for the following Middle East destinations: Anglo-Egyptian Sudan, Cyprus, British Somaliland, Palestine and Trans-jordan, Aden (including Perim and Sokotra Islands) and Egypt.

2. All general licenses for exports to those destinations in the British Empire on "List A" attached will be cancelled as of April 30, 1943, including the special general license provisions for medicinals, but with the exception of the General Intransit License, General License GUS, and the general licenses for shipments valued at $25 or less, personal baggage, ship stores, plane stores, fuel and supplies, return of empty containers, technical data, newspapers and publications, metal drums and containers, as set forth in Comprehensive Export Schedule No. 11, and photographic films, plates and paper, as set forth on page 97 thereof. The cancellation of these general licenses shall not become effective for the commodities on "List B" attached until June 30, 1943. Shipments of commodities to the destinations on "List A" attached that are now entitled to the provisions

[1] *Current Export Bulletin* No. 89.

of General Licenses, which are on dock, on lighter, laden aboard the exporting carrier or in transit to a port of exit pursuant to an actual order for export prior to the effective dates of these changes may be exported under the previous general license provisions. Shipments moving to a vessel subsequent to the effective dates of change pursuant to ODT permits issued prior to such dates may also be exported under the previous General License provisions.

3. *Individual licenses.* No further applications should be filed for individual licenses to export commodities to the British Empire (excluding Newfoundland, Labrador, and the Middle East). Those licenses valid on March 31, 1943, will remain valid until July 1, 1943, regardless of their expiration date. All outstanding individual licenses to export to the above destinations will become invalid on July 1, 1943, if issued prior to April 1, 1943.

.   .   .   .

(b) Countries or Regions Covered by Program Licenses, as of July 1, 1943

License No.	Country or Region	Agency	Date of Announcement
1	British Empire (exclusive of Canada, Newfoundland, Labrador, Middle East [1]	British Supply Council in North America	Apr. 12, 1943
2	Belgian Congo [2]	Belgian Congo Purchasing Commission	Apr. 14, 1943
3	Newfoundland [3]	Newfoundland Supply Liaison	Apr. 19, 1943 [4]
4	Netherlands West Indies [5]		May 25, 1943
5	Madagascar [6]		May 25, 1943
6	U.S.S.R. [7]	Government Purchasing Commission of the Soviet Union	Jul. 1, 1943

(3) Regulation Issued by the Secretary of State (Hull) Governing the Export of Arms, Ammunition, and Implements of War, December 10, 1942 [8]

Pursuant to the authority vested in the Secretary of State by section 12 of the joint resolution approved November 4, 1939, as amended (54 Stat. 10; 56 Stat. 19; 22 U.S.C. 452), and to the proclamation issued pursuant thereto,[9] the regulations governing the international traffic in arms,

[1] *Current Export Bulletin* No. 89.
[2] *Ibid.*, No. 90.
[3] *Ibid.*, No. 92.
[4] Announced that program license would be issued on or about May 20, 1943.
[5] *Current Export Bulletin* No. 97.
[6] *Ibid.*
[7] *Ibid.*, No. 103.
[8] 7 *Fed. Reg.*, p. 10424.
[9] Proclamation 2549 of April 9, 1942 (7 *Fed. Reg.*, p. 2769; *Documents, IV, 1941–42,* p. 737).

ammunition, and implements of war promulgated by him on June 2, 1942 (7 *Fed. Reg.*, p. 4216) are hereby augmented by the following § 201.41:

§ 201.41 *Unlimited export and import licenses.* When the Secretary of State has determined that the issuance of unlimited export and import licenses will materially aid the war effort, he will issue such licenses to appropriately registered persons authorizing the exportation or importation, or both, by such persons of arms, ammunition, and implements of war, subject to specific terms imposed by him. No exportation or importation of arms, ammunition, or implements of war, shall be made, or attempted to be made, under the authority of such an unlimited license without compliance with the specific terms thereof and the special provisions and instructions pertaining thereto and with the regulations of this part.

C. Foreign Funds Control

[See *Documents, III, 1940–41*, p. 533–43; *IV, 1941–42*, p. 740–52.]

The system of foreign funds control as a measure of economic pressure and subsequently of economic warfare was developed during the period preceding our actual participation in the war as a belligerent. After the declarations of war against the Axis powers by Congress, the system was refined and perfected but remained substantially as before. The pertinent documents down to March 30, 1943, have been brought together and made available to the public by the United States Treasury Department in a publication entitled *Documents Pertaining to Foreign Funds Control.* The documents included in this section are those that are most significant in the light that they throw on developments and problems faced during the period under review.

(1) *German Attempts to Extort Ransom Payments for Persons in Occupied Countries. Department of State Release, November 24, 1942* [1]

Information in the possession of the Government of the United States indicates that the German authorities are developing an organized business of selling exit permits from occupied countries. In practice, the Germans are attempting to obtain from relatives and friends of persons in these countries the payment of ransom, payment being made in neutral currency useful to the German war effort. Similar information has been received by the British and Netherlands Governments.

The manner in which this system of extortion is carried on is described in a report to the Department by one of our missions abroad in the following terms:

The ransom system as practiced at present seems to be an extension of the practice instituted by the Nazi Government whereunder emigrants were permitted to leave Germany if the state were compensated on their departure by all of their visible wealth, with the exception of a small percentage, usually

[1] Department of State, *Bulletin*, VII, p. 962.

reduced in effect to about ten or twelve and one-half percent, which the emigrant was permitted to retain and to export abroad. It is very apparently designed to provide foreign exchange for the furtherance of the German war effort (though there may be reason for suspicion that individual members of the Nazi Party may personally profit by it). The United States is looked upon as the most fruitful source of the expected funds; and banking agents, or other intermediaries, have been canvassing means for circumventing American laws and the Treasury Regulations governing money exports, in an effort to provide the ransom sums demanded.

In the hostage and ransom system the victims are subjected to terrorization whereby their desire to find refuge in one of the United Nations or a neutral country is immeasurably increased. First, they are made the victims of unbearable restrictions designed to make life not worth living, usually under confinement in vile concentration camps; and, second, they are faced with the threat of deportation to domains in Eastern Europe, with the prospect of an unknown and possibly horrible fate awaiting them there.

The system seems to have been applied particularly to persons in the Netherlands and has developed to the scale of a regular traffic. The sums demanded vary according to the financial resources of the victims. Amounts as high as $75,000 for a single person have been quoted. These sums are required to be paid into an account in the name of some intermediary in a bank in a neutral country, from which the money is eventually transferred to the credit of the German Reichsbank.

Methods of combating this barbaric and inhuman practice have been the subject of discussion between the United States Government, the British Government, and the Government of the Netherlands. All three Governments are agreed as to the need for energetic measures to repress this traffic. The most effective means of dealing with extortion is to prevent the extortioner from benefiting from his viciousness. If the Germans can be prevented from obtaining the sums they are demanding for the release of hostages, their incentive to find new victims will be removed. Yielding to these attempts at extortion merely encourages the Nazis to employ them against other helpless victims.

The three Governments have also had in mind the substantial benefit which would accrue to the German war effort if this traffic were permitted to develop. The degraded methods which the Germans are using are a measure of their desperation for foreign exchange and serve to indicate both the difficulty which the enemy is having in producing goods for exportation to the neutral countries and the effectiveness of the United Nations' financial blockade.

Warning is hereby given that any person in a country to which the Proclaimed List of Certain Blocked Nationals [1] applies who acts as a broker or agent in this traffic will immediately be included in that list and thereby be publicly designated as an enemy. Furthermore, persons

---

[1] See this volume, p. 132.

in such countries who pay ransom are warned that they are assisting the enemy in his war effort and are rendering themselves liable to treatment as enemies.

One of the purposes of the freezing-control regulations administered by the Treasury Department is to prevent practices of this sort. The Department understands that no licenses under the freezing regulations have been granted to persons in the United States to make such payments and that the Treasury Department has investigated a number of cases of attempts to extort ransom payments from persons in this country. It would be a violation of the freezing regulations and of the Trading with the Enemy Act to make such a payment without a license, and the Department is informed by the Treasury Department that in case of such a violation all appropriate sanctions would be invoked against the persons participating.

(2) *Transmitting of United States Currency to Mexico Prohibited. General Ruling No. 14 of the Treasury Department, August 14, 1942* [1]

The sending, mailing, exporting, or otherwise transmitting of any United States currency out of the United States directly or indirectly to Mexico on and after August 14, 1942 is hereby prohibited, except as specifically licensed or otherwise authorized by the Secretary of the Treasury.

(a) *Press Release No. 37 of the Treasury Department, August 14, 1942* [2]

The Secretary of the Treasury today announced that the Government of Mexico and the Government of the United States have, in cooperation, taken steps to further supplement the measures aimed at preventing the disposition within the Western Hemisphere of currency looted by the Axis.

The Government of Mexico has prohibited the importation into that country of all United States currency other than bills of two-dollar denomination and United States coins. At the same time all United States currency presently within Mexico has been ordered into the Bank of Mexico and associated banks. Such currency will not be released by the Mexican Government but in those cases in which persons who have turned over such currency can prove that the currency was legitimately acquired and free from Axis taint, the peso equivalent will be turned over to the person surrendering the United States currency. It was announced that persons failing to turn in United States currency in their possession would be treated as enemies of Mexico within the meaning of the Mexican laws dealing with trading with the enemy and enemy property.

In order to supplement the Mexican decree the Treasury announced that on and after August 14, 1942, it would be illegal to export to Mexico any United

---

[1] Treasury Department, *Documents Pertaining to Foreign Funds Control*, p. 28; 7 *Fed. Reg.*, p. 6417.

[2] Treasury Department, *Documents Pertaining to Foreign Funds Control*, p. 100.

States currency other than coins and bills of two-dollar denomination. Furthermore, all United States currency brought into this country from Mexico on and after August 14, 1942 (except coins and bills of two-dollar denomination), will be required to be surrendered to the United States customs authorities at the border. Such currency will be turned over to the Federal Reserve Banks in accordance with the procedure established under General Ruling No. 5, as amended.

The effect of this joint measure of the United States and Mexican Governments is to prevent use being made of Mexico as a place in which Axis agents may dispose of dollar currency looted abroad.

Treasury spokesmen stated that the new regulations would in no way interfere with the legitimate activities of residents on either side of the United States-Mexico border who have long been accustomed to using pesos and dollar currency without distinction on both sides of the international line. The exemptions provided in both the Mexican and United States rulings will allow pesos to enter and leave the United States and American two-dollar bills and coins to enter and leave Mexico freely.

It was further said that the new regulations would not affect the free passage across the border of checks, drafts, traveler's checks and other credit instruments in the same manner as has been true up to the present time. Likewise nothing contained in the present regulations will prevent Americans from maintaining bank accounts in Mexican banks or Mexicans from maintaining accounts in banks within the United States. Such accounts, many of which now exist, will remain entirely unaffected.

This action supersedes the previous Treasury Department ruling which had allowed any person arriving in the United States from Mexico to bring with him up to $250 in United States currency regardless of the denomination of the bills imported.

It was pointed out that tourists going from the United States to Mexico would be subject to no inconvenience whatsoever in connection with the new rulings, provided that before departing for Mexico they converted such funds as they intended taking with them into traveler's checks, bank drafts, or other credit instruments or into two-dollar bills or coins.

Treasury spokesmen stated that the two-dollar bill had been eliminated from the restrictions imposed on the importation and exportation of other United States currency to and from Mexico by reason of the fact that very few such bills have fallen into Axis hands whereas it is known that large amounts of United States currency of other denominations have come under the control of the aggressors.

The Treasury also announced that any person leaving the United States going through Mexico en route to any other country would be allowed to carry United States currency in any denomination having an aggregate value of $250, plus $250 for each accompanying dependent.

D. Proclaimed List of Certain Blocked Nationals

[See *Documents, IV, 1941–42*, p. 752.]

(1) *Revisions of the Proclaimed List of Certain Blocked Nationals, as of June 30, 1943*

The Proclaimed List of Certain Blocked Nationals was originally issued together with subsequent revisions and supplements, under the authority of the President's Proclamation No. 2497, dated July 17, 1941.[1] The original list was issued on the same day and contained the names of more than 1800 persons and business institutions in the other American Republics.[2] Prior to Revision I, seven supplements were issued.[3]

REVISION	SUPPLEMENT	DATE	FEDERAL REGISTER	
		1942	vol.	page
I		Feb. 7	7	855
I	1	" 28	"	1618
I	2	Mar. 27	"	2439
I	3	Apr. 11	"	2777
I	4	May 1	"	3293
II		" 12	"	3587
II	1	" 22	"	3867
II	2	Jun. 2	"	4222
II	3	" 19	"	4639
II	4	Jul. 17	"	5545
II	5	" 31	"	5970
III		Aug. 10	"	6282
III	1	" 28	"	6847
III	2	Sept. 18	"	7422
III	3	Oct. 10	"	8165
III	4	" 30	"	8845
IV	CUMULATIVE	Nov. 12	"	9510
IV	1	" 20	"	9671
IV	2	Dec. 18	"	10761
		1943		
IV	3	Jan. 16	8	832
IV	4	Feb. 12	"	2006
IV	5	Mar. 13	"	3137
IV	6	Apr. 9	"	4753
V		" 23	"	5435
V	1	May 7	"	6017
V	2	Jun. 4	"	7533

(2) *"The Generally Licensed Trade Area" and Transactions Therein. General License No. 53, as Amended, May 18, 1943* [4]

For text of General License No. 53 as it read before amendment, see *Documents, IV, 1941-42*, p. 756. The new material introduced by the amendment of May 18, 1943 consists of section (3) and the exception clause contained in par. (c) of section (4) [formerly numbered (3)].

(1) A general license is hereby granted licensing all transactions ordinarily incident to the importing and exporting of goods, wares and merchandise between the United States and any of the members of the

[1] *Documents, IV, 1941-42*, p. 753; 6 *Fed. Reg.*, p. 3555; Department of State, *Bulletin*, V, p. 42.
[2] 6 *Fed. Reg.*, p. 3557.
[3] *Ibid.*, p. 3773, 4915, 5722, 6204, 6351, 6732; 7 *ibid.*, p. 334.
[4] From the Office of the Secretary of the Treasury; 8 *Fed. Reg.*, p. 6595.

generally licensed trade area or between the members of the generally licensed trade area if (*i*) such transaction is by, or on behalf of, or pursuant to the direction of any national of a blocked country within the generally licensed trade area, or (*ii*) such transaction involves property in which any such national has at any time on or since the effective date of the Order had any interest, provided the following terms and conditions are complied with:

(*a*) Such transaction is not by, or on behalf of, or pursuant to the direction of (*i*) any person whose name appears on "The Proclaimed List of Certain Blocked Nationals," or (*ii*) any blocked country or national thereof not within the generally licensed trade area;

(*b*) Such transaction does not involve property in which (*i*) any person whose name appears on "The Proclaimed List of Certain Blocked Nationals," or (*ii*) any blocked country or national thereof not within the generally licensed trade area, has at any time on or since the effective date of the Order had any interest; and

(*c*) Any banking institution within the United States, prior to issuing, confirming or advising letters of credit, or accepting or paying drafts drawn, or reimbursing themselves for payments made, under letters of credit, or making any other payment or transfer of credit, in connection with any importation or exportation pursuant to this general license, or engaging in any other transaction herein authorized, shall satisfy itself (from the shipping documents or otherwise) that: (*i*) any such transaction is incident to a bona fide importation or exportation and is customary in the normal course of business, and that the value of such importation or exportation reasonably corresponds with the sums of money involved in financing such transaction; and (*ii*) such importation or exportation is or will be made pursuant to all the terms and conditions of this license.

(2) Subject to all other terms and conditions of this general license any national of a blocked country doing business within the United States pursuant to a license is also hereby authorized, while so licensed, to engage in any transaction referred to in paragraph (1) to the same extent that such national is licensed to engage in such transaction involving persons within the generally licensed trade area who are not nationals of a blocked country.

(3) This General License shall also authorize any transaction engaged in by a bank within the generally licensed trade area pursuant to the order of or for the account of any national of a blocked country within the generally licensed trade area to the same extent, and under the same circumstances, as though such transaction were solely for the account of such bank; provided, however, that this paragraph shall not

be deemed to permit any payment, transfer or withdrawal from any blocked account; and provided further that the following terms and conditions are complied with:

(a) Such transaction is not by, or on behalf of, or pursuant to the direction of (i) any person whose name appears on "The Proclaimed List of Certain Blocked Nationals," or (ii) any blocked country or national thereof not within the generally licensed trade area;

(b) Such transaction does not involve property in which (i) any person whose name appears on "The Proclaimed List of Certain Blocked Nationals," or (ii) any blocked country or national thereof not within the generally licensed trade area, has at any time on or since the effective date of the Order had any interest.

(4) As used in this general license:

(a) The term "generally licensed trade area" shall mean the following:

   (i) the American Republics, i.e., (1) Argentina, (2) Bolivia, (3) Brazil, (4) Chile, (5) Colombia, (6) Costa Rica, (7) Cuba, (8) The Dominican Republic, (9) Ecuador, (10) El Salvador, (11) Guatemala, (12) Haiti, (13) Honduras, (14) Mexico, (15) Nicaragua, (16) Panama, (17) Paraguay, (18) Peru, (19) Uruguay, and (20) Venezuela;

   (ii) the British Commonwealth of Nations, i.e., (1) the United Kingdom (England, Wales, Scotland and Northern Ireland), (2) the British Dominions (Canada, Australia, New Zealand, the Union of South Africa and Newfoundland), (3) Eire, (4) the Isle of Man, (5) India, (6) Egypt, (7) Anglo-Egyptian Soudan, (8) Iraq, (9) all colonies and protectorates under the British Crown, and (10) all mandated territories administered by the United Kingdom or by any British Dominion;

   (iii) the Union of Soviet Socialist Republics;

   (iv) the Faroe Islands;

   (v) the Netherlands West Indies;

   (vi) the Belgian Congo and Ruanda-Urundi;

   (vii) Greenland;

   (viii) Iceland;

   (ix) (1) Syria and Lebanon; and (2) the New Hebrides Islands; and

   (x) (1) French Equatorial Africa, including the Cameroons; (2) New Caledonia; (3) Tahiti; (4) the French Establishments in India;

   Provided, however, that the term "generally licensed trade area" shall not include any territory which is controlled or occupied by the military, naval, or police forces or other authority of Japan, Germany, or Italy, or allies thereof.

(b) The term "member" of the generally licensed trade area shall mean any of the foreign countries or political subdivisions comprising the generally licensed trade area.

(c) The term "any national of a blocked country within the generally licensed trade area" shall mean any national of a blocked country who was situated within and doing business within such area on and since June 14, 1941 except that with respect to transactions authorized by paragraph (3) hereof, such terms shall mean any national of a blocked country who is situated within such area.

(d) The term "The Proclaimed List of Certain Blocked Nationals" shall mean "The Proclaimed List of Certain Blocked Nationals" as amended and supplemented promulgated pursuant to the proclamation of July 17, 1941.

RANDOLPH PAUL
Acting Secretary of the Treasury

E. Treatment of Enemy Property

[See *Documents, IV, 1941–42*, p. 830.]

(1) *Executive Order No. 9193 Amending Executive Order No. 9095* [1] *Establishing the Office of Alien Property Custodian and Defining Its Functions and Duties and Related Matter, July 6, 1942* [2]

By virtue of the authority vested in me by the Constitution, by the First War Powers Act, 1941, by the Trading with the Enemy Act of October 6, 1917, as amended, and as President of the United States, it is hereby ordered as follows:

Executive Order No. 9095 of March 11, 1942, is amended to read as follows:

1. There is hereby established in the Office for Emergency Management of the Executive Office of the President the Office of Alien Property Custodian, at the head of which shall be an Alien Property Custodian appointed by the President. The Alien Property Custodian shall receive compensation at such rate as the President shall approve and in addition shall be entitled to actual and necessary transportation, subsistence, and other expenses incidental to the performance of his duties. Within the limitation of such funds as may be made available for that purpose, the Alien Property Custodian may appoint assistants and other personnel and delegate to them such functions as he may deem necessary to carry out the provisions of this Executive Order.

2. The Alien Property Custodian is authorized and empowered to take such action as he deems necessary in the national interest, including, but not limited to, the power to direct, manage, supervise, control or vest, with respect to:

[1] *Documents, IV, 1941–42*, p. 830; 7 *Fed. Reg.*, p. 1971.
[2] From the Office of the Secretary to the President; 7 *Fed. Reg.*, p. 5205.

(a) any business enterprise within the United States which is a national of a designated enemy country and any property of any nature whatsoever owned or controlled by, payable or deliverable to, held on behalf of or on account of or owing to or which is evidence of ownership or control of any such business enterprise, and any interest of any nature whatsoever in such business enterprise held by an enemy country or national thereof;

(b) any other business enterprise within the United States which is a national of a foreign country and any property of any nature whatsoever owned or controlled by, payable or deliverable to, held on behalf of or on account of or owing to or which is evidence of ownership or control of any such business enterprise, and any interest of any nature whatsoever in such business enterprise held by a foreign country or national thereof, when it is determined by the Custodian and he has certified to the Secretary of the Treasury that it is necessary in the national interest, with respect to such business enterprise, either (i) to provide for the protection of the property, (ii) to change personnel or supervise the employment policies, (iii) to liquidate, reorganize, or sell, (iv) to direct the management in respect to operations, or (v) to vest;

(c) any other property within the United States owned or controlled by a designated enemy country or national thereof, not including in such other property, however, cash, bullion, moneys, currencies, deposits, credits, credit instruments, foreign exchange and securities except to the extent that the Alien Property Custodian determines that such cash, bullion, moneys, currencies, deposits, credits, credit instruments, foreign exchange and securities are necessary for the maintenance or safeguarding of other property belonging to the same designated enemy country or the same national thereof and subject to vesting pursuant to section 2 hereof;

(d) any patent, patent application, design patent, design patent application, copyright, copyright application, trademark or trademark application or right related thereto in which any foreign country or national thereof has any interest and any property of any nature whatsoever (including, without limitation, royalties and license fees) payable or held with respect thereto, and any interest of any nature whatsoever held therein by any foreign country or national thereof;

(e) any ship or vessel or interest therein, in which any foreign country or national thereof has an interest; and

(f) any property of any nature whatsoever which is in the process of administration by any person acting under judicial supervision or which is in partition, libel, condemnation or other similar proceedings and which is payable or deliverable to, or claimed by, a designated enemy country or national thereof.

When the Alien Property Custodian determines to exercise any power and authority conferred upon him by this section with respect to any of the foregoing property over which the Secretary of the Treasury is exercising any control and so notifies the Secretary of the Treasury in writing, the Secretary of the Treasury shall release all control of such property, except as authorized or directed by the Alien Property Custodian.

3. Subject to the provisions of this Executive Order, all powers and authority conferred upon me by sections 3(a) and 5(b) of the Trading with the Enemy Act, as amended, are hereby delegated to the Secretary of the Treasury or any person, agency, or instrumentality designated by him; *provided, however*, that when any property or interest, not belonging to a foreign government or central bank, shall be vested by the Secretary of the Treasury, such property or interest shall be vested in, and dealt with by, the Alien Property Custodian upon the terms directed by the Secretary of the Treasury. Except as otherwise provided herein, this Executive Order shall not be deemed to modify or amend Executive Order No. 8389, as amended,[1] or the President's Proclamation of July 17, 1941,[2] or Executive Order No. 8839, as amended,[3] or the regulations, rulings, licenses and other action taken thereunder, or in connection therewith.

4. Without limitation as to any other powers or authority of the Secretary of the Treasury or the Alien Property Custodian under any other provision of this Executive Order, the Secretary of the Treasury and the Alien Property Custodian are authorized and empowered, either jointly or severally, to prescribe from time to time, regulations, rulings and instructions to carry out the purposes of this Executive Order. The Secretary of the Treasury and the Alien Property Custodian each shall make available to the other all information in his files to enable the other to discharge his functions, and shall keep each other currently informed as to investigations being conducted with respect to enemy ownership or control of business enterprises within the United States.

5. The Alien Property Custodian is authorized to issue appropriate regulations governing the service of process or notice upon any person within any designated enemy country or any enemy-occupied territory in connection with any court or administrative action or proceeding within the United States. The Alien Property Custodian also is authorized to take such other and further measures in connection with representing any such person in any such action or proceeding as in his judgment and discretion is or may be in the interest of the United States. If, as a result of any such action or proceeding, any such person obtains,

---

[1] 6 *Fed. Reg.*, p. 2897, 3715, 6348, 6785.
[2] *Ibid.*, p. 3555.
[3] *Ibid.*, p. 3823, 4795.

or is determined to have, an interest in any property (including money judgments), such property, less an amount equal to the costs and expenses incurred by the Alien Property Custodian in such action or proceeding, shall be subject to the provisions of Executive Order No. 8389, as amended, *provided, however,* that this shall not be deemed to limit the powers of the Alien Property Custodian under section 2 of this Order; and *provided further,* that the Alien Property Custodian may vest an amount of such property equal to the costs and expenses incurred by the Alien Property Custodian in such action or proceeding.

6. To enable the Alien Property Custodian to carry out his functions under this Executive Order, there are hereby delegated to the Alien Property Custodian or any person, agency, or instrumentality designated by him all powers and authority conferred upon me by section 5(b) of the Trading with the Enemy Act, as amended, including, but not limited to, the power to make such investigations and require such reports as he deems necessary or appropriate to determine whether any enterprise or property should be subject to his jurisdiction and control under this Executive Order. The powers and authority conferred upon the Alien Property Custodian by Executive Order No. 9142 [1] shall be administered by him in conformity with the provisions of this Executive Order.

7. In the exercise of the authority herein delegated, the Alien Property Custodian shall be subject to the provisions of Executive Order No. 8839 of July 30, 1941, and shall designate a representative to the Board of Economic Warfare in accordance with section 6 thereof.

8. All records and other property (including office equipment) of the Treasury Department which are used primarily in the administration of powers and duties to be exercised by the Alien Property Custodian, and such personnel as is used primarily in the administration of such powers and duties and which was hired by the Treasury Department after September 1, 1941 (including officers whose chief duties relate to the administration of such powers and duties), as the Secretary of the Treasury and the Alien Property Custodian shall jointly certify for transfer, shall be transferred to the Office of the Alien Property Custodian. In the event of disagreement concerning the transfer of any personnel, records, or property, the determination shall be made by the Director of the Bureau of the Budget, pursuant to the formula here prescribed. Any personnel transferred pursuant to this Executive Order shall be transferred without loss of such Civil Service status or eligibility therefore as they may have.

9. This Executive Order shall not be deemed to modify or amend Executive Order No. 8843 of August 9, 1941,[2] and the regulations, rulings, licenses and other action taken thereunder. Any and all action hereto-

---

[1] 7 *ibid.,* p. 2985.   [2] 6 *ibid.,* p. 4035.

fore taken by the Secretary of the Treasury or the Alien Property Custodian, or by any person, agency, or instrumentality designated by either of them, pursuant to sections 3(a) and 5(b) of the Trading with the Enemy Act, as amended, or pursuant to prior Executive Orders, and any and all action heretofore taken by the Board of Governors of the Federal Reserve System pursuant to Executive Order No. 8843 of August 9, 1941, are hereby confirmed and ratified.

10. For the purpose of this Executive Order:

(a) The term "designated enemy country" shall mean any foreign country against which the United States has declared the existence of a state of war (Germany, Italy, Japan, Bulgaria, Hungary and Rumania) and any other country with which the United States is at war in the future. The term "national" shall have the meaning prescribed in section 5 of Executive Order No. 8389, as amended, *provided, however,* that persons not within designated enemy countries (even though they may be within enemy-occupied countries or areas) shall not be deemed to be nationals of a designated enemy country unless the Alien Property Custodian determines: (i) that such person is controlled by or acting for or on behalf of (including cloaks for) a designated enemy country or a person within such country; or (ii) that such person is a citizen or subject of a designated enemy country and within an enemy-occupied country or area; or (iii) that the national interest of the United States requires that such person be treated as a national of a designated enemy country. For the purpose of this Executive Order any determination by the Alien Property Custodian that any property or interest of any foreign country or national thereof is the property or interest of a designated enemy country or national thereof shall be final and conclusive as to the power of the Alien Property Custodian to exercise any of the power or authority conferred upon me by section 5(b) of the Trading with the Enemy Act, as amended.

(b) The term "business enterprise within the United States" shall mean any individual proprietorship, partnership, corporation or other organization primarily engaged in the conduct of a business within the United States, and any other individual proprietorship, partnership, corporation or other organization to the extent that it has an established office within the United States engaged in the conduct of business within the United States.

11. The Secretary of the Treasury or the Alien Property Custodian, as the case may be, shall, except as otherwise agreed to by the Secretary of State, consult with the Secretary of State before vesting any property or interest pursuant to this Executive Order, and the Secretary of the Treasury shall consult with the Secretary of State before issuing any Order adding any additional foreign countries to section 3 of Executive Order No. 8389, as amended.

12. Any orders, regulations, rulings, instructions, licenses or other actions issued or taken by any person, agency or instrumentality referred to in this Executive Order, shall be final and conclusive as to the power of such person, agency, or instrumentality to exercise any of the power or authority conferred upon me by sections 3(a) and 5(b) of the Trading with the Enemy Act, as amended; and to the extent necessary and appropriate to enable them to perform their duties and functions hereunder, the Secretary of the Treasury and the Alien Property Custodian shall be deemed to be authorized to exercise severally any and all authority, rights, privileges and powers conferred on the President by sections 3(a) and 5(b) of the Trading with the Enemy Act of October 6, 1917, as amended, and by sections 301 and 302 of Title III of the First War Powers Act, 1941, approved December 18, 1941. No person affected by any order, regulation, ruling, instruction, license or other action issued or taken by either the Secretary of the Treasury or the Alien Property Custodian shall be entitled to challenge the validity thereof or otherwise excuse his actions, or failure to act, on the ground that pursuant to the provisions of this Executive Order, such order, regulation, ruling, instruction, license or other action was within the jurisdiction of the Alien Property Custodian rather than the Secretary of the Treasury or vice versa.

13. Any regulations, rulings, instructions, licenses, determinations, or other actions issued, made or taken by any agency or person referred to in this Executive Order, purporting to be under the provisions of this Executive Order or any other proclamation, order or regulation, issued under sections 3(a) or 5(b) of the Trading with the Enemy Act, as amended, shall be conclusively presumed to have been issued, made or taken after appropriate consultation as herein required and after appropriate certification in any case in which a certification is required pursuant to the provisions of this Executive Order.

(a) Statement Issued by the Office of the Secretary to the President with Reference to Executive Order No. 9193, July 6, 1943 [1]

The President has signed an executive order allocating powers and functions between the Alien Property Custodian and the Secretary of the Treasury with respect to property of enemy, neutral, and occupied countries and their nationals. The Executive Order provides for the following division:
1. The Alien Property Custodian will handle:
   (a) Enemy-owned or controlled businesses (including dummies) operating in the United States and the dollar balances and other assets of such businesses.

[1] From the Office of the Secretary to the President.

(b) Businesses owned or controlled by nationals of neutral or occupied countries and which are now under Treasury regulation where the Alien Property Custodian certifies that it is necessary in the national interest for him to assume control in order (*i*) to protect the property; (*ii*) to remove personnel or supervise employment policies; (*iii*) to liquidate, reorganize or sell the business; (*iv*) to manage the business; or (*v*) to vest the business.

(c) All other enemy property except dollar balances, bullion and securities unless the dollars, bullion or securities of an enemy are needed by the Alien Property Custodian in the management of other property taken from the same enemy.

(d) All *foreign*-owned patents, copyrights, and trademarks.

(e) Foreign ships (particularly that group of enemy-owned ships which the United States has libeled and are now involved in judicial forfeiture proceedings).

(f) All forms of property and claims of enemy nationals involved in estates, trusts, receivership proceedings, etc. The Alien Property Custodian would also handle the representation of the interest of enemy nationals and persons in occupied countries in judicial and administrative proceedings in the United States and the Alien Property Custodian will issue regulations governing the service of process on such persons.

2. The Treasury will continue to handle:
(a) The dollar balances, bullion and securities of governments or nationals except those which belong to an enemy business.

(b) All property of the occupied and neutral countries and their nationals except those particular business enterprises where the Alien Property Custodian determines that it is necessary in the national interest for him to assume control.

(c) All transactions or business dealings with countries frozen under the freezing orders including the control of all trade and commercial communications with the enemy and enemy-controlled countries.

(d) All other phases of freezing control which it has handled in the past or which may hereafter arise.

3. Both the Alien Property Custodian and the Treasury will be given full powers under section 5(b) of the Trading with the Enemy Act, as amended by the First War Powers Act, to enable them to discharge their respective functions with the further stipulation that should the Secretary of the Treasury have occasion to vest any property (other than the assets of foreign governments and central banks), such property will be vested in and dealt with by the Alien Property Custodian upon the terms directed by the Secretary of the Treasury. Appropriate provision is made for consultation with the State Department before either the Treasury or the Alien Property Custodian does any vesting.

4. The Secretary of the Treasury also retains the powers under section 3(a) of the Trading with the Enemy Act, as amended, in order to enable the Treasury to continue its present control over transactions involving trade and communication with the enemy.

(2) Prohibition of Certain Transactions Respecting Patents and Trademarks. General Order No. 11, Issued by the Alien Property Custodian (Crowley), November 17, 1942 [1]

Under the authority of the Trading with the Enemy Act, as amended, and Executive Order No. 9095, as amended,[2] and pursuant to law, the undersigned hereby issues the following regulation:

§ 503.11 *General Order No. 11.* (a) The following transactions are hereby prohibited, except as authorized by the Alien Property Custodian by means of regulations, rulings, instructions, orders, licenses, or otherwise, if such transactions are by, or on behalf of, or pursuant to the direction of any foreign country designated in section 3 of Executive Order No. 8389, as amended, or any national thereof, or such transactions involve property in which any foreign country designated in section 3 of Executive Order No. 8389, as amended, or any national thereof, has at any time on or since the effective date of Executive Order No. 8389, as amended, had any interest of any nature whatsoever, direct or indirect:

(1) The filing and prosecution in the United States Patent Office of applications for Letters Patent or for the registration of Trademarks;

(2) The receipt of Letters Patent or Trademark Registrations issued by the United States Patent Office;

(3) The execution of, or the recording of, any assignment, grant, encumbrance, license, or other agreement of, under, or with respect to any invention, or any patent, trademark, or application therefor, issued by, or filed in or intended for filing in, the United States Patent Office.

(b) The terms "foreign country" and "national" shall have the meanings defined in sections 5D and 5E, respectively, of Executive Order No. 8389, as amended.

Regulation No. 1,[3] published November 19, 1942, exempted certain persons from the prohibitions of General Order No. 11 and Regulation No. 2[4] of the same date provided for the issuance of general licenses and prescribed the conditions under which these might be obtained. This regulation was published in amended form on June 6, 1943.[5]

(3) Prohibition of Certain Transactions Respecting Interests in Works Subject to Copyright. General Order No. 13, Issued by the Alien Property Custodian (Crowley), November 17, 1942 [6]

Under the authority of the Trading with the Enemy Act, as amended, and Executive Order No. 9095, as amended, and pursuant to law, the undersigned hereby issues the following regulation:

---

[1] 7 *Fed. Reg.*, p. 9475.   [2] See this volume, p. 156.
[3] 7 *Fed. Reg.*, p. 9477.   [4] *Ibid.*   [5] 8 *ibid.*, p. 291.   [6] 7 *ibid.*, p. 9476.

§ 503.13 *General Order No. 13.* (*a*) The following transactions are hereby prohibited, except as authorized by the Alien Property Custodian by means of regulations, rulings, instructions, orders, licenses, or otherwise, if such transactions are by, or on behalf of, or pursuant to the direction of, or are entered into with any foreign country designated in section 3 of Executive Order No. 8389, as amended, or any national thereof:

(1) The execution of, or the recording of, any application for copyright or renewal thereof under the copyright laws of the United States;

(2) The execution of, or the recording of, any assignment, grant, encumbrance, license or other agreement with respect to any interest in any work subject to copyright in the United States.

(*b*) For the purposes of this order:

(1) The term "foreign country" shall have the meaning defined in section 5D of Executive Order No. 8389, as amended;

(2) The term "national" shall have the meaning defined in section 5E of Executive Order No. 8389, as amended;

(3) "Interest" in a work subject to copyright shall mean ownership, part ownership, or claim of ownership, in whole or in part, of any subsisting copyright or claim of copyright, and any right, license, privilege or property in or to or with respect to such work; and any right, title or interest in, to or under any contract or other instrument, and any royalty, share of profits, license fees, or other emolument or compensation reserved with respect thereto. Such interest shall also include but not by way of limitation, any interest as hereinbefore described which is held or claimed as trustee, agent, representative or nominal proprietor.

Regulation No. 1,[1] published November 19, 1942, exempted certain persons from the prohibitions of General Order No. 13, and Regulation No. 2,[2] of the same date, provided for general licenses. Regulation No. 3[3] published established conditions under which these might be obtained.

(4) *General Orders Issued by Alien Property Custodian, as of June 30, 1943*[4]

General orders and regulations are published in the *Federal Register.* Besides tne general orders (listed below) and regulations, the Alien Property Custodian had issued (as of June 30, 1943) nearly 2000 vesting orders by which the Alien

---

[1] *Ibid.*, p. 9477.
[2] *Ibid.*
[3] 8 *ibid.*, p. 1.
[4] From the Office of the Alien Property Custodian.

Property Custodian has taken title to property. These are also published in the *Federal Register.*

| G.O. Number | Date Published in Federal Register | | | Volume | Number | Page |
	Month	Day	Year			
2	Jun.	23	1942	7	122	4634
3	"	"	"	"	122	4635
4	Jul.	21	"	"	142	5539
5	Aug.	11	"	"	157	6199
6	"	"	"	"	157	6199
7	Oct.	17	"	"	205	8376
8	"	"	"	"	205	8377
11 *	Nov.	19	"	"	227	9476
12	"	"	"	"	227	9476
13	"	"	"	"	227	9476
14	Dec.	17	"	"	246	10546
15	Jan.	6	1943	8	3	223
17	Dec.	29	1942	7	253	10906
18	Feb.	9	1943	8	27	1707
20	Feb.	10	"	"	29	1780
21	Mar.	17	"	"	53	3245
22	May	28	"	"	105	7095
26	Jun.	9	"	"	113	7628

* Regulation No. 1 under General Order No. 11, published November 19, 1942; No. 2 as amended, under General Order No. 11, published January 8, 1943.

F. Capture and Disposition of Prizes

(1) *An Act to Facilitate the Disposition of Prizes Captured by the United States during the Present War, and for Other Purposes, Approved August 18, 1942* [1]

Be it enacted by the Senate and House of Representatives of the United States of America in Congress assembled, That the district courts shall have original jurisdiction of all prizes captured during the present war on the high seas if said capture was made by authority of the United States or was adopted and ratified by the President of the United States and the prize was brought into the territorial waters of a cobelligerent or was taken or appropriated for the use of the United States on the high seas or in such territorial waters, including jurisdiction of all proceedings for the condemnation of such property taken as prize.

SEC. 2. The venue of any proceeding brought under the jurisdiction conferred by this Act shall be in the judicial district selected by the Attorney General, or his designee, for the convenience of the United States.

SEC. 3. The jurisdiction of prizes brought into the territorial waters of a cobelligerent shall not be exercised under authority of this Act, nor

[1] Public Law 704, 77th Cong., originating as H. R. 7211.

shall prizes be taken or appropriated within such territorial waters for the use of the United States, unless the government having jurisdiction over such territorial waters consents to the exercise of such jurisdiction or to such taking or appropriation.

SEC. 4. In any case, whether or not brought under the jurisdiction conferred by this Act, the power to take or appropriate property for the use of the United States as provided by sections 4624 and 4625 of the Revised Statutes (title 34, U. S. C., secs. 1140, 1141) may be exercised by the War Shipping Administration with the approval of the Secretary of the Navy or his designee, or by such other officers or agencies as the President may designate.

SEC. 5. The district courts are authorized to appoint special prize commissioners to exercise abroad in cases arising under this Act the duties prescribed for such commissioners. Said courts may appoint such number of such special commissioners, and having such qualifications, as said courts may deem proper, without regard for the requirements of section 4621 of the Revised Statutes, as amended (U. S. C., title 34, sec. 1137), except that for each case arising under the jurisdiction conferred by this Act there shall be at least one special commissioner who shall be a naval officer, active or retired, approved by the Secretary of the Navy, who shall receive no other compensation than his pay in the Navy, and who shall protect the interests of the Department of the Navy in the prize property. Said courts may confer on such special commissioners such additional powers and duties, to be performed abroad or in the United States, as they may deem necessary or proper for carrying out the purposes of this Act.

SEC. 6. The district courts may adopt such rules to govern the exercise of the jurisdiction conferred by this Act as they may deem necessary or proper for carrying out the purposes thereof. All provisions of law relating to capture as prize or to the taking or appropriation of captures for the use of the United States, to the extent that such provisions are consistent with the provisions of this Act, shall be applicable in the exercise of the jurisdiction herein conferred.

SEC. 7. A cobelligerent of the United States which consents to the exercise of the jurisdiction herein conferred with respect to prizes of the United States brought into its territorial waters and to the taking or appropriation of such prizes within its territorial waters for the use of the United States shall be accorded, upon proclamation by the President of the United States, like privileges with respect to prizes captured under authority of such cobelligerent and brought into the territorial waters of the United States or taken or appropriated in the territorial waters of the United States for the use of such cobelligerent. Reciprocal recognition and full faith and credit shall be given to the jurisdiction acquired by courts of a cobelligerent hereunder and to all proceedings had or judgments rendered in exercise of such jurisdiction.

SEC. 8. Nothing in this Act shall be construed to impair or diminish the jurisdiction of any court of the United States under any other provisions of law, but the provisions of this Act shall be in addition thereto.

Acting under the authority conferred by section 2 of the Act, the Attorney General has selected the following judicial districts wherein proceedings under the jurisdiction conferred by the Act may be brought:

"(a) As to prizes captured on the Atlantic or Arctic Oceans or the connecting waters of either, the Southern District of New York

"(b) As to prizes captured on the Pacific or Indian Oceans or the connecting waters of either, the Northern District of California." [1]

Acting under the provisions of sections 3 and 7 of the above act, the President proclaimed that the Governments of the United Kingdom [2] and New Zealand [3] shall be accorded like privileges with respect to prizes captured under the authority of the said Governments and brought into the territorial waters of the United States or taken or appropriated in the territorial waters of the United States for the use of the said Governments.

6. PUBLIC INFORMATION AND PROPAGANDA

[See *Documents, IV, 1941–42*, p. 185.]

The order defining the foreign information activities of the Office of War Information became necessary because of uncertainty as to where the line was to be drawn in this field between the activities of the Office of War Information, as established by Executive Order No. 9182, June 13, 1942 [4] and the Office of Strategic Services, established by Military Order of the President, June 13, 1942. [5] The problem presented is one special aspect of the larger problem of delimiting the respective functions of military and civilian authorities in time of war.

(1) *Executive Order No. 9312 Defining the Foreign Information Activities of the Office of War Information, March 9, 1943* [6]

Under and by virtue of the authority vested in me by Title I of the First War Powers Act, 1941, approved December 18, 1941 (Public Law 354 — 77th Congress), and as Commander-in-Chief of the Army and Navy and as President of the United States, it is hereby ordered as follows:

1. The Office of War Information will plan, develop, and execute all phases of the federal program of radio, press, publication, and related

---

[1] Order No. 3725, Office of the Attorney General, August 26, 1942 (7 *Fed. Reg.*, p. 7103).

[2] Proclamation 2575, dated January 30, 1943 (8 *Fed. Reg.*, p. 1429).

[3] Proclamation 2582, dated April 1, 1943 (8 *Fed. Reg.*, p. 4275).

[4] *Documents, IV, 1941–42*, p. 189.

[5] *Ibid.*, p. 160.

[6] 8 *Fed. Reg.*, p. 3021.

foreign propaganda activities involving the dissemination of information. The program for foreign propaganda in areas of actual or projected military operations will be coordinated with military plans through the planning agencies of the War and Navy Departments, and shall be subject to the approval of the Joint Chiefs of Staff. Parts of the foreign propaganda program which are to be executed in a theater of military operations will be subject to the control of the theater commander. The authority, functions and duties of the Office of War Information shall not extend to the Western Hemisphere, exclusive of the United States and Canada.

2. The military order of June 13, 1942, establishing the Office of Strategic Services, is hereby modified to the extent necessary to make this order effective.

CHAPTER III

THE AXIS POWERS

1. AMERICAN POLICY TOWARD ENEMY STATES AFTER THE WAR

Apart from the statements of the broad principles of our post-war policy which have been made from time to time,[1] with an occasional specific mention of their applicability to the defeated nations, there had been up to the end of the period under review few indications by responsible persons of the specific line of policy which the United States intends to pursue toward the defeated Axis powers.

It has been made clear by the President, the Secretary of State and other responsible officials that our immediate military purpose is complete victory, involving the destruction of the political systems which we regard as responsible for the wars of military aggression which have engulfed us. One of the clearest statements of this purpose is to be found in the address of Under Secretary of State Welles, on Memorial Day, 1942, when he said:

"We must utterly and finally crush the evil men and the iniquitous systems which they have devised that are today menacing our existence and that of free men and women throughout the world." [2]

In his radio address of October 12, 1942, the President said:

"The objective of today is clear and realistic. It is to destroy completely the military power of Germany, Italy and Japan to such good purpose that their threat against us and all the other United Nations cannot be revived a generation hence." [3]

In his message to Congress, January 7, 1943, the President went somewhat further in indicating his view regarding our policy toward the defeated Axis powers. He said:

"It is clear to us that if Germany or Italy or Japan — or any one of them — remain armed at the end of this war or are permitted to rearm, they will again, and inevitably, embark upon an ambitious career of world conquest. They must be disarmed and kept disarmed, and they must abandon the philosophy and the teaching of that philosophy which has brought so much suffering to the world." [4]

At the conclusion of the Casablanca Conference, speaking informally to the Press, President Roosevelt stated that he and Prime Minister Churchill were agreed that the only terms on which they would deal with "any Axis Government or any Axis factions" were "Unconditional Surrender." [5]

One point on which there has been considerable speculation has been whether under Point 3 of the Atlantic Charter ("they respect the right of all peoples to choose the form of Government under which they will live,") the peoples of the Axis countries are to be allowed to choose whatever form of government they will. In his address before the White House Correspondents' Association, February 12, 1943, following his return from the Casablanca Conference, President Roosevelt dealt with this point by asserting: [6]

"No nation in all the world that is free to make a choice is going to set itself up under the Fascist form of government, or the Nazi form of government or the

---

[1] See Chap. I, this volume. [2] *Documents, IV, 1941–42*, p. 74.
[3] See this volume, p. 22. [4] *Ibid.*, p. 38. [5] *Ibid.*, p. 254. [6] *Ibid.*, p. 42.

Japanese war-lord form of government. Such forms are the offspring of seizure of power followed by the abridgement of freedom. Therefore, the United Nations can properly say of these forms of government two simple words: 'Never again.'

"The right of self-determination included in the Atlantic Charter does not carry with it the right of any government to commit wholesale murder or the right to make slaves of its own people or of any other peoples in the world."

Furthermore, the President emphasized in this address, in repeating the terms of "unconditional surrender," that "in our uncompromising policy we mean no harm to the common people of the Axis nations. But we do mean to impose punishment and retribution in full upon their guilty, barbaric leaders." Specific statements on this latter point were made on August 21[1] and October 7, 1942.[2]

A. Italy

(1) Address by Assistant Secretary of State Berle at the Joint Meeting of the Mazzini Society and the Italian-American Labor Council, New York City, November 14, 1942 [3]

MY FRIENDS:

It is altogether fitting that you, Americans of Italian ancestry, have gathered here tonight to take counsel concerning Italy. You have sprung from the loins of that country, you honor her language, and seek now to preserve Italian nationhood and the Italian soul.

You have asked what Americans of Italian ancestry, speaking with the voice of America, can say to the plain people of Italy.

We are divided today from the masses of Italy by a battle line. But if for a moment we could cross that battle line, and could speak to them face to face, we should say this:

You are Italians, enslaved today by Fascist masters who secured and held power by the methods and with the ethics of gangsters.

These Fascist masters, in their turn, have betrayed the country to Nazi tyrants beyond the Alps, and have sold you as mercenary soldiers to fight the battles for Hitler.

You seek to be free, and you ask how freedom can be secured.

Freedom is not a gift: it is an achievement. You must attain it yourselves. But, when that freedom is won, certain pledges have been made to you and to the world.

The first right which grows from the achievement of freedom is the right to maintain and preserve it, in friendly and law-abiding relations with the other nations of the world.

We know, and you know, that you have much to undo, in the hard but splendid road toward liberty. No nation can lose its freedom for 20 years without suffering the consequence of that loss. Italy has been led into grievous and terrible ways. Fascist dictatorship appeared first

---

[1] *Ibid.*, p. 176.   [2] *Ibid.*, p. 177.
[3] Department of State, *Bulletin*, VII, p. 925.

in Italy. It subjugated Italians by terrorism, torture, imprisonment, the lies of a controlled press, by murder. This Fascist leadership led an Italian army to conquer Abyssinia; stabbed a defeated France in the back; seized the quiet country of Albania; invaded Greece, a friendly neighbor; and maintains uneasy armies in Yugoslavia.

Like all evil conceptions, the Fascist domination of Italy at length is destroying itself. They were forced to call to their help the Nazi tyrants from beyond the Alps. For this help they paid a price: the liberty of Italy. Their Nazi ally now treats them as a conquered country of serfs. Its secret police is in every village, and Nazi officers sit in every Fascist Ministry of State. Cynically, Hitler used Italian youth as his mercenary soldiers in Russia and in Egypt. When his commanders were defeated in Egypt two weeks ago, they took all available supplies and, deserting, left Italian soldiers to perish miserably in the Egyptian deserts while the German contingents saved themselves.

Today Italy is short of food and Italian children want milk. Yet her food is taken against her will for Germans, who already have more than she. Marshal Goering cynically stated that all Europe, which includes Italy, would starve to death before Germans went hungry. It will be remembered that in the last World War Americans fed Italy, and the young men in your armies, as children, drank American milk.

As the march of dictatorship in Europe began in the Mediterranean, so the march of freedom has at length also begun in the Mediterranean.

In 10 days of unparalleled drama, British forces, supported by Americans, overthrew Marshal Rommel in Egypt, cut his army to pieces, and are now driving the shattered fragments across the Libyan waste. Hard upon this victory came an American expedition which in 4 short days accomplished the liberation of all North Africa, from the Atlantic shoulder of Morocco to the coasts of Tunis. The armies of the United Nations stand within gunshot of the Italian shore.

In the truest sense, the armies under the United Nations flags are armies for the liberation of Italy; they are the allies and friends of the mute, plain people from the Alps to Sicily, just as they are the allies and friends of the plain people of France and of your neighbors, the Yugoslavs and the Greeks.

In this new military situation Italy once more enters the valley of decision. She must decide whether she will exhaust her remaining men, and let her nationhood ebb out as servant of a decaying Nazi state; or whether she will cleanse herself from the evil into which her Fascists have led her, rescue herself from that slavery into which she has been delivered by the bullies and cowards who have dominated her for two decades.

Plainly, there can be no compromise with the cult of Fascist slavery, nor with any of the men who have carried it on. A treaty with Fascists could be nothing more than a trap for fools. There can be no peace with those who deny the right of peace. There can be no faith in those who insist that good faith must go out of the world. There can be no compromise between free men and slave-masters. Until the Fascist domination of Italy is ended, and while Italians, however blindly, follow Fascist leadership, there can be no valid dealing save by force alone.

Nevertheless, we in America insist on hoping that the day will come when we can once more welcome into the brotherhood of civilization a free and friendly Italian nation, giving again to the world the fruit of her shining culture and her spendid traditions.

The Italy of history, of the arts, of science, of unparalleled music and poetry, the Italy which peacefully conquered in the glorious competition of thought and ideas — that Italy must be saved, for who can imagine a world without her?

The United Nations have made a pledge to Italy, as to the entire world. It was drawn on a warship in the Atlantic by President Roosevelt in consultation with Prime Minister Churchill, and proclaimed on August 14, 1941. On New Year's Day of this year, all the United Nations accepted this pledge as their basis of hope for a better future of the world:

[Here follows the text of the Atlantic Charter.]

Pledge was thus given not only to the victors but also to the vanquished.

No American seeks to destroy or impair the nationhood of Italy. When Italy, freed from her Fascist gangsters, is able once more to speak to the world, and as the armies of the United Nations achieve that victory which cannot fail, the pledge of the United Nations will be redeemed. This pledge does not contemplate a punitive peace: the aim is justice, not revenge.

A just peace must mean an end of danger from aggression. Secretary Hull, speaking for the Government of the United States, has insisted on surveillance of aggressor nations until there is convincing proof that their peoples "have repudiated and abandoned the monstrous philosophy of superior race and conquest by force and have embraced loyally the basic principles of peaceful processes." In the United States, Americans of all origins live in peace and friendship with many millions of Italian ancestry. We know that under right leadership this people can give that convincing proof. The Italian people now, while the struggle is still in progress, can give unquestioned evidence that the philosophy of conquest and force has been conclusively put aside, by joining the struggle against Nazi and Fascist tyranny.

This is little to ask. It asks of the people of Italy that they shall not condemn themselves and their children to further slaughter; that they shall accept the peaceful arrangements of peaceful peoples; that they shall submit only to those restraints which must bind on free peoples if freedom is to remain in the world. In the truest sense, the Italian nation is offered a freedom beyond the wildest Fascist dreams: freedom of religion, freedom of thought, freedom from want, and freedom from fear; the freedom of farm and vineyard; peace in the olive groves; quiet workmanship in factory and shop; freedom again to work, to hope, and to live. She is asked to accept those obligations which make these freedoms equally possible for her neighbors.

For Italy, the meaning of victory by the United Nations is this:

Final destruction of the Fascist and Nazi tyranny which has oppressed her;

Opportunity to her people to give convincing proof that she has abandoned the philosophy of superior race and of conquest by force and has loyally embraced the basic principles of peaceful processes;

Enjoyment, with all other states, of access on equal terms to the trade and raw materials of the world which are needed for economic prosperity;

Opportunity to collaborate in securing for all improved labor standards, economic advancement, and social security;

Opportunity to work for the objectives to which the free nations of the world are pledged.

The destiny of the Italian people rests in their own hands.

In this hour of decision, who is the true Italian patriot? Not he who clings desperately and afraid to the chains of the Nazis, who have already declared him to be an inferior breed. Not he who in silence forgets the traditions of his heroes, and allows himself to be driven like a sheep to the slaughter to serve the warlords of Berlin. The Italian patriots of today will be those who now repeat achievements of their great forerunners, who drive out tyranny, who reestablish firm and loyal government, who make their people free, who lead Italy once more into the family of civilized nations.

To those true patriots who undertake the liberation of Italy, we say, You do not act alone. The armies of America and of the United Nations are close at hand, and behind them the full strength of the most powerful nations in the world.

The voice of free Italy has been stilled for two decades. Convincing proof that Italy has repudiated the monstrous philosophies which have spread death and terror and pestilence throughout the world must be given by Italians who drive out the traitors and foreigners who have led her to the rim of destruction.

When the voice of the true Italy is heard again, we shall hear Garibaldi, Cavour, Mazzini, Matteotti, De Bosis, and Rosselli speak from beyond the grave, saying: "Here again is our nation; these are our people."

B. Japan

(1) *Address by the Former American Ambassador to Japan (Grew), Syracuse, New York, September 18, 1942* [1]

[Excerpt]

MR. MAYOR, LADIES AND GENTLEMEN:

In November 1939, at a time when the Japanese Army was floundering unsuccessfully in China, I wrote in my diary:

To await the hoped-for discrediting in Japan of the Japanese Army and the Japanese military system is to await the millennium. The Japanese Army is no protuberance like the tail of a dog, which might be cut off to prevent the tail from wagging the dog. It is inextricably bound up with the fabric of the entire nation. Certainly there are plenty of Japanese who dislike the Army's methods; there is plenty of restiveness at the wholesale impressment of young men to fight in China, at the death and crippling of many, and at the restrictions and handicaps in everyday life entailed by the expenses of the China campaign. But that the Army can be discredited in the eyes of the people to a degree where its power and prestige will become so effectively undermined as to deprive it of control, or at least of its preponderant influence in shaping national policy, is an hypothesis which I believe no one conversant with Japan and the Japanese would for a moment entertain. Should a *coup d'état* occur in Japan through social upheaval, there is little doubt that it would lead immediately to a ruthless military dictatorship.

That entry in my diary was almost three years ago. A good deal of water has run under the mill since then, but those comments are just as true today as they were then — except in one fundamental respect. I then wrote that the Japanese Army was inextricably bound up with the life of the people, and when I wrote of the Army I alluded to the whole great military machine which includes the Navy too. So it is today. From every village and farm and factory and home, sons and brothers and fellow workers have been taken for military or naval service throughout the nation. That whole machine is closely integrated with every phase of the national life. But I also wrote at that time that that military machine could not be discredited in the eyes of the people. Today I amend that statement. The Japanese military machine can and will be discredited in the eyes of the Japanese people, and we, the United States of America, will bring that about.

Two questions. First, why? Answer: because until it is so discredited, permanent peace never can and never will be restored in the Pacific area. Second, how? Answer: by utter and complete defeat by the armed forces of the United States of America and of the other United Nations. Only when that Japanese military machine is rendered physically impotent, physically incapable of carrying on its far-flung campaign of crushing

[1] *Ibid.*, p. 763.

and conquering and enslaving — yes, literally enslaving — those who
fall beneath the wheels of its ruthless and utterly pitiless car of juggernaut, only then will the Japanese people as a whole come to the realization that crime does not pay, that they have been forced to follow false
gods, and that the ways of peace are in all respects preferable to the ways
of war. And when that time comes — as it assuredly will come in due
course — many a Japanese, many a patriotic and loyal Japanese, loyal
to his Emperor, loyal to the spirits of his ancestors, and loyal to his
nation, yet who did not want this war, who had nothing whatever to do
with the bringing on of this war, will sigh with profoundest relief. And
this I say with 10 long years of intimate knowledge and experience of
Japan and all her works.

.   .   .   .

2. ACQUISITIONS OF TERRITORY BY THE AXIS POWERS

(1) *Status of Austria. Statement of the Secretary of State (Hull), July
27, 1942* [1]

At the Secretary's press conference on July 27 a correspondent stated that
there appeared to be some confusion with respect to the view of this country as
to the present status of Austria and asked for clarification on this point.

It is probable that such confusion, if it exists, has arisen from administrative steps which may have been taken by this Government in pursuance of its own laws designed to afford adequate protection to this
country's interests in dealing with the situation presented by the imposition of military control over Austria and residents of Austria by Germany. This Government very clearly made known its opinions as to
the manner in which the seizure of Austria took place and the relation
of that seizure to this Government's well-known policy toward the
taking of territory by force. This Government has never taken the position that Austria was legally absorbed into the German Reich.

(2) *Continued Resistance of Albania to Italian Occupation. Statement
of the Secretary of State (Hull), December 10, 1942* [1]

The Government of the United States is not unmindful of the continued resistance of the Albanian people to the Italian forces of occupation. The effort of the various guerilla bands operating against the
common enemy in Albania is admired and appreciated. The Government
and people of the United States look forward to the day when effective
military assistance can be given these brave men to drive the invader
from their homes.

[1] *Ibid.*, p. 660.   [1] *Ibid.*, p. 998.

Consistent with its well-established policy not to recognize territorial conquest by force, the Government of the United States has never recognized the annexation of Albania by the Italian crown. The joint declaration of the President and the British Prime Minister, made on August 14, 1941, known as the "Atlantic Charter," provides as follows:

> Third, they respect the right to all peoples to choose the form of government under which they will live; and they wish to see sovereign rights and self-government restored to those who have been forcibly deprived of them.

The restoration of a free Albania is inherent in that statement of principle.

3. PUNISHMENT OF WAR CRIMINALS

On October 25, 1941, the President made a public statement condemning the execution of hostages by the Nazis.[1] In a statement of the same date Prime Minister Churchill associated himself with the President's statement.[2] Representatives of nine occupied countries meeting at London adopted on January 13, 1942, a declaration calling for the punishment of war criminals.[3]

(1) *Crimes against Civilian Populations in Occupied Countries. Statement of the President (Roosevelt), August 21, 1942* [4]

The Secretary of State recently forwarded to me a communication signed by the Ambassador of the Netherlands and the Ministers of Yugoslavia and Luxemburg on behalf of the Governments of Belgium, Greece, Luxemburg, Norway, Netherlands, Poland, Czechoslovakia, Yugoslavia, and the French National Committee in London, calling attention to the barbaric crimes against civilian populations which are being committed in occupied countries, particularly on the continent of Europe.

In this communication, attention was invited to the declaration signed in London on January 13, 1942 by the representatives of nine governments whose countries are under German occupation. This declaration affirmed that acts of violence thus perpetrated against the civilian populations are at variance with accepted ideas concerning acts of war and political offenses as these are understood by civilized nations; stated that the punishment, through the channel of organized justice of those guilty and responsible for these crimes, is one of the principal war aims of the contracting governments; and recorded the determination of the contracting governments in a spirit of international solidarity to see to it that those guilty and responsible, whatever their nationality, are handed over to justice and tried and that the sentences pronounced are carried out.

---

[1] *Documents, IV, 1941–42*, p. 662.   [2] *Ibid.*   [3] *Ibid.*, p. 663.
[4] Department of State, *Bulletin*, VII, p. 709.

The communication which I have just received from the chiefs of mission of the Netherlands, Yugoslavia, and Luxemburg states that these acts of oppression and terror have taken proportions and forms giving rise to the fear that as the defeat of the enemy countries approaches, the barbaric and unrelenting character of the occupational regime will become more marked and may even lead to the extermination of certain populations.

As I stated on October 25, 1941:

The practice of executing scores of innocent hostages in reprisal for isolated attacks on Germans in countries temporarily under the Nazi heel revolts a world already inured to suffering and brutality. Civilized peoples long ago adopted the basic principle that no man should be punished for the deed of another. Unable to apprehend the persons involved in these attacks the Nazis characteristically slaughter fifty or a hundred innocent persons. Those who would "collaborate" with Hitler or try to appease him cannot ignore this ghastly warning.

The Nazis might have learned from the last war the impossibility of breaking men's spirit by terrorism. Instead they develop their *lebensraum* and "new order" by depths of frightfulness which even they have never approached before. These are the acts of desperate men who know in their hearts that they cannot win. Frightfulness can never bring peace to Europe. It only sows the seeds of hatred which will one day bring fearful retribution.

The Government of the United States has been aware for some time of these crimes. Our Government is constantly receiving additional information from dependable sources, and it welcomes reports from any trustworthy source which would assist in keeping our growing fund of information and evidence up to date and reliable.

The United Nations are going to win this war. When victory has been achieved, it is the purpose of the Government of the United States, as I know it is the purpose of each of the United Nations, to make appropriate use of the information and evidence in respect to these barbaric crimes of the invaders, in Europe and in Asia. It seems only fair that they should have this warning that the time will come when they shall have to stand in courts of law in the very countries which they are now oppressing and answer for their acts.

(2) Cooperation with United Nations Commission to Investigate War Crimes. Statement of the President (Roosevelt), October 7, 1942 [1]

On August 21 I said that this Government was constantly receiving information concerning the barbaric crimes being committed by the enemy against civilian populations in occupied countries, particularly on the continent of Europe.[2] I said it was the purpose of this Government, as I knew it to be the purpose of the other United Nations, to

[1] *Ibid.*, p. 797.   [2] See this volume, p. 176.

see that when victory is won the perpetrators of these crimes shall answer for them before courts of law.

The commission of these crimes continues.

I now declare it to be the intention of this Government that the successful close of the war shall include provision for the surrender to the United Nations of war criminals.

With a view to establishing responsibility of the guilty individuals through the collection and assessment of all available evidence, this Government is prepared to cooperate with the British and other Governments in establishing a United Nations Commission for the Investigation of War Crimes.

The number of persons eventually found guilty will undoubtedly be extremely small compared to the total enemy populations. It is not the intention of this Government or of the Governments associated with us to resort to mass reprisals. It is our intention that just and sure punishment shall be meted out to the ringleaders responsible for the organized murder of thousands of innocent persons and the commission of atrocities which have violated every tenet of the Christian faith.

The President designated the Honorable Herbert Claiborne Pell, former American Minister to Portugal and Hungary, as the representative of the United States on the United Nations Commission for the Investigation of War Crimes. Announcing this appointment on June 29, 1943, the White House said: "It is hoped that the Commission, which will have its headquarters at London, will be able to take concrete steps looking to the punishment of agents of the Axis powers who have perpetrated atrocious crimes against their innocent victims." [1]

4. RESPONSIBILITY FOR THE TREATMENT OF JEWS AND OTHER SUBJECT PEOPLES

(1) *Message of the President (Roosevelt) to the President of the American Jewish Congress, Dr. Stephen A. Wise, Read at Madison Square Garden, New York City, July 21, 1942* [2]

July 17, 1942.

Dear Dr. Wise:

Americans who love justice and hate oppression will hail the solemn commemoration in Madison Square Garden as an expression of the determination of the Jewish people to make every sacrifice for victory over the Axis powers. Citizens, regardless of religious allegiance, will share in the sorrow of our Jewish fellow citizens over the savagery of the Nazis against their helpless victims. The Nazis will not succeed in exterminating their victims any more than they will succeed in enslaving mankind. The American people not only sympathize with all victims

[1] Department of State, *Bulletin*, IX, p. 3.
[2] *Congress Weekly*, vol. 9, August 14, 1942, p. 1; *New York Times*, July 22, 1942.

of Nazi crimes but will hold the perpetrators of these crimes to strict accountability in a day of reckoning which will surely come.

I express the confident hope that the Atlantic Charter and the just world order to be made possible by the triumph of the United Nations will bring the Jews and oppressed people in all lands the four freedoms which Christian and Jewish teachings have largely inspired.

(2) German Policy of Extermination of the Jewish Race. Department of State Release on Statement of Allied Governments, December 17, 1942 [1]

The attention of the Belgian, Czechoslovak, Greek, Luxemburg, Netherlands, Norwegian, Polish, Soviet, United Kingdom, United States, and Yugoslav Governments and also of the French National Committee has been drawn to numerous reports from Europe that the German authorities, not content with denying to persons of Jewish race in all the territories over which their barbarous rule has been extended the most elementary human rights, are now carrying into effect Hitler's oft-repeated intention to exterminate the Jewish people in Europe. From all the occupied countries Jews are being transported in conditions of appalling horror and brutality to eastern Europe. In Poland, which has been made the principal Nazi slaughterhouse, the ghettos established by the German invader are being systematically emptied of all Jews except a few highly skilled workers required for war industries. None of those taken away are ever heard of again. The able-bodied are slowly worked to death in labor camps. The infirm are left to die of exposure and starvation or are deliberately massacred in mass executions. The number of victims of these bloody cruelties is reckoned in many hundreds of thousands of entirely innocent men, women, and children.

The above-mentioned Governments and the French National Committee condemn in the strongest possible terms this bestial policy of cold-blooded extermination. They declare that such events can only strengthen the resolve of all freedom-loving peoples to overthrow the barbarous Hitlerite tyranny. They reaffirm their solemn resolution to insure that those responsible for these crimes shall not escape retribution and to press on with the necessary practical measures to this end.

(3) Concurrent Resolution Condemning Outrages Inflicted upon Civilians in the Nazi-Occupied Countries, Agreed to by the House of Representatives, March 18, 1943 [2]

WHEREAS the American people view with indignation the atrocities inflicted upon the civilian population in the Nazi-occupied countries,

---

[1] Department of State, *Bulletin*, VII, p. 1009.

[2] *Congressional Record*, vol. 89, pt. 2, p. 1723; originated as S. Con. Res. 9, Senate Report No. 252, passed the Senate, March 9, 1943, 78th Cong., 1st sess. (*ibid.*, p. 1723).

and especially the mass murder of Jewish men, women, and children; and

WHEREAS this policy of the Nazis has created a reign of terror, brutality, and extermination in Poland and other countries in Eastern and Central Europe: Now, therefore, be it

Resolved by the Senate (the House of Representatives concurring), That these brutal and indefensible outrages against millions of helpless men, women, and children should be, and they are hereby, condemned as unworthy of any nation or any regime which pretends to be civilized:

Resolved further, That the dictates of humanity and honorable conduct in war demand that this inexcusable slaughter and mistreatment shall cease and that it is the sense of this Congress that those guilty, directly or indirectly, of these criminal acts shall be held accountable and punished in a manner commensurate with the offenses for which they are responsible.

(4) *The Jewish Massacres and German Responsibility. Address by Assistant Secretary of State Berle, Boston, Massachusetts, May 2, 1943* [1]

[Excerpt]

We are assembled, as Americans, to consider the greatest tragedy in modern history.

There is now no question that the German Reich, by deliberate policy and by detailed organization, has undertaken to exterminate the Jewish religion and the Jewish people on the continent of Europe. She has carried out these measures within the borders of Germany proper. She has exerted pressure on the satellite states to compel them to take like measures. She has set aside certain localities in Europe as human abattoirs. She has detailed specific groups of men as slaughterers.

The statement that this is done by the German Reich is made advisedly. Undeniably, the extermination of the Jews was and is an idea dear to Hitler and to the little group of degenerates who have been his intimates and counselors. Unquestionably this policy is identified with the so-called "Nazi Party." But the time has passed when we can pretend that this series of horrors constitutes the sole guilt of any small group of German rulers, or of any single German party. No group of rulers, no party, could have conceived, organized, and carried out a program of general civilian slaughter without at least the tacit acquiescence of a large part of the German people. Had there been any general disapproval, any

---

[1] Delivered at a mass meeting to protest against the inhuman treatment of civilians by the Germans in German-occupied Europe, particularly of the Jews. The address was delivered on behalf of Mr. Berle, whose illness prevented him from attending, by Robert G. Hooker, Jr., Executive Assistant to Mr. Berle. (Department of State, *Bulletin,* VIII, p. 395.)

spontaneous revulsion of horror, any general practice of pity or kindliness, such a program could not continue.

It is no doubt true that there are Germans, and many of them, who do not approve; but they have preferred the easier course of silence. It seems to be the fact that there have been cases of Germans in high station and low who have done their feeble best to mitigate some part of this devil's work of cruelty.

We have accounts of revolt by contingents of German soldiers against orders to act as human slaughterers. We have heard stories of German officers who turned from this filthy work in disgust. We know of cases of civilians who have risked a good deal to befriend a few hunted wretches.

These, we must assume, have been the nonrepresentative Germans, since their feelings and their voices found little effective echo among their countrymen. We may as well face the fact that for the first time in modern history a supposedly civilized nation has formulated, planned, and is systematically carrying out a program of national murder.

We cannot but realize that this fact and this guilt, now generalized throughout the German people, must constitute one of the basic considerations in dealing with the German people in the hour of their final and conclusive defeat, and of the complete and unconditional surrender which can be their only refuge from the implacable warfare of the armies of the United Nations.

The so-called "satellite states" must share their responsibility too. It is no secret that personalities and groups in certain of these states have been anxiously seeking to establish contact with various of the United Nations, in the hope of obtaining easier terms of peace when the Nazi machine finally goes to pieces. They foresee, now, a time in the not distant future when their countries will be judged for the part they have played in this bitter drama. Can it be doubted that their right to survive as nations must turn, in part at least, on the degree of guilt which they have been willing to assume in this criminal business?

I believe we are forced to this conclusion by the undisputed facts of the case. These continuing massacres in Germany, in Rumania, in Hungary, and more recently in Bulgaria were not the hidden acts of small groups. The orders were not given and carried out in secret. The killing was not done by stealth. The knowledge of the plans was general; their execution was done in the light of day. A civilian populace looked on, accepted the situation, continued to support the government which had created it, continued to accept instructions from the officials who carried it out, continued to regard, with apparent unconcern, the degradation of their civilization and their culture. There is no record that an underground was anywhere formed to make headway against the Nazi rulers. There is nothing to suggest that groups of valiant men met here and there to raise their voices in protest.

There were and are groups in the German Reich today quite capable of putting a stop to this criminal degeneracy. The German Army claims to have one of the oldest and proudest military traditions in Europe; and their officers like to consider themselves as gentlemen, somewhat removed and apart from the Nazi canaille. Yet, so far as we know, parts of the German Army actively executed these massacres; the remainder stood idly by without lifting a finger.

Is it conceivable that, had there been any national will or national conscience which condemned this awful and evil thing — is it conceivable that a group of men of power and influence would not have met and said, "Let there be an end of this *Schweinerei*"?

You know how these things work. If the national policy is really at variance with the national will, the senior who receives the order protests against its issue; his immediate subordinates make it plain that they do not wish to execute the commands; the juniors make it plain to their commanding officers that execution of such an order will not be carried out. In a swift crystallization of will, the group suddenly forms; the word goes out; and the most ruthless and despotic dictator hesitates and at length recalls orders which are likely to recoil on his own head.

We have waited in vain for such a protest. We know that in older days there was a Germany which would not have tolerated this sort of thing. We know that a nation which could build an underground opposition capable of checking Napoleon, which could make headway against the corrupt absolutism of the Holy Alliance, which could lead in developing the trade-union movement in Europe — we know that such a nation once had within it the innate capability of refusing to permit any small group of leaders to impose upon it the sickening bloodguilt of the massacres of the past few months.

Inevitably, in God's good time, the fate of the German people and of the people of the satellite states will rest in the hands of the United Nations. These will have to determine whether the German people are capable of acting as a civilized nation. I am very clear that one piece of evidence which must enter into the final judgment will be whether the German people have been able and willing to stop this wickedness, or whether they can only take refuge in whining excuses of fear. I believe in the day of surrender we shall have the right to ask, "What did you do to prevent the guilt of the Nazi criminals from becoming the guilt of the German people?"; and by their fruits shall they be judged.

As this sickening spectacle has progressed, many have come to the governments of the United Nations asking whether something cannot be done. I should be less than frank if I did not give you the blunt and cruel conclusion which is the only honest answer. Nothing can be done to save these helpless unfortunates, except through the invasion of

Europe, the defeat of the German arms, and the breaking, once and for all, of the German power. There is no other way.

．　．　．　．　．　．　．

For by every means in our power we must swiftly put ourselves in a position where we can give life, as the only answer to those who have chosen to give death. We must in strength be willing and able to render justice where justice has been denied. We must be able not merely to fix responsibility but to make sure that the responsibility when fixed is carried out.

We must make it plain to the world that no nation which attempts the murder of a people can have or hold any position in the work of the world until that crime is purged, until such reparation as can be made is done, and until the genius of law and the spirit of humanity are restored as the ruling concepts in the life of the nations.

5. TREATMENT OF PRISONERS OF WAR AND INTERNED CIVILIANS

A. Exchange of Nationals

(1) *German Violation of Exchange Agreement. Department of State Release, July 1, 1942* [1]

The German Government has withdrawn the previously agreed safe conducts for future voyages of the S.S. *Drottningholm* between New York and Lisbon and has thereby violated the exchange agreement. This Government informed the German Government through the Swiss Government by note "that the German Government, by unilateral action, has violated the agreement entered into between this Government and the German Government for the exchange of their nationals in that it has withdrawn the safe conduct previously given for the several round-trip voyages of the *Drottningholm* between New York and Lisbon. As the assurance of this safe conduct was an essential part of the Exchange Agreement between the two Governments, this Government must consider the agreement as terminated by the act of the German Government."

(2) *German Action with Respect to Americans Formerly Stationed in France. Department of State Release on the Press Conference of the Under Secretary of State (Welles), February 11, 1943* [2]

Following the military occupation of Unoccupied France on November 11, 1942, American diplomatic and consular officers, press correspondents, Red Cross representatives, and relief workers who were located in France found themselves

---

[1] *Ibid.*, VII, p. 579.   [2] *Ibid.*, VIII, p. 149.

in an anomalous situation. While we had severed diplomatic relations with the Vichy Government, there was no state of war. On the other hand, we were at war with Germany, and the German Government, on the ground that the terms of the armistice agreement with France of June 22, 1940 [1] had been violated, ordered the military occupation of Unoccupied France.

The American group had been assembled at Lourdes, France, pending negotiations with the Vichy Government, carried on through the Swiss Government, for the exchange of nationals. On January 11, the State Department announced that it had been advised by the Legation at Bern that the German Government had thrown a detachment of S.S. troops around the American group, and that it apparently intended to transfer them to Germany, and to take upon itself negotiations then in progress. This action was protested by the Department of State on January 11.[2] The position of the German Government apparently was that the American group should not be allowed to depart until the whereabouts of the German Armistice Commission in Africa and the German Consul in Algiers was made known, and arrangements were made for the return of these persons. The American Government took the position that the members of the German Armistice Commission should be treated as prisoners of war.

At his press conference on February 11, 1943 the Under Secretary of State, Mr. Sumner Welles, said there were one or two facts that he would like to ask the members of the press conference to think about since they were of particular importance and he wondered if the people of this country realized the full significance of what he had in mind. Mr. Welles said that he was talking about the action of the German Government in not only refusing to permit the diplomatic personnel of the United States who had been stationed at Vichy to leave France but also the action of the Hitler government in taking that considerable number of American diplomatic officers and putting them in concentration in Germany. As the press would probably remember, Mr. Welles continued, the reason for the action taken was that the German Government insisted that as part of the exchange involved, not only should the United States Government permit the members of the French Embassy staff here to return but also that we should permit the German members of the German Armistice Commission in North Africa, who had been taken at the time of the American occupation in North Africa, to be returned to Germany as a part of the exchange. Frankly, said Mr. Welles, that was one of the cheapest efforts of international blackmail that he had yet known. After pointing out that the German Armistice Commission was composed of military and civilian members, Mr. Welles said that this Government agreed to permit the civilian members of the German Armistice Commission to be returned as a part of the exchange thereto properly in accordance with every principle of international conduct and law. The military members, Mr. Welles said, were regarded in a different category and not susceptible to that part of the exchange transaction. In conclusion, Mr. Welles said that that is the reason why our American diplomatic officials are now in concentration in Germany,

[1] *Documents, II, 1939-40*, p. 427.   [2] Department of State, *Bulletin*, VIII, p. 42.

and he thought it was important that that fact be known and thoroughly known.

When asked if we had made any protest to the Germans through the Swiss, Mr.Welles said that we had made numerous protests on the subject. In reply to a question as to whether there was any further action that the Government could take, Mr. Welles said not for the moment and added that he would put it that way.

Replying to a correspondent who asked if the military members were considered prisoners of war, Mr. Welles said that military members were considered by the War Department as prisoners of war.

A correspondent asked if the Under Secretary could elaborate to any extent on the treatment being accorded the American diplomats in Germany and began to point out that Mr. Welles spoke of a concentration camp. Mr. Welles interrupted to say that he did not say "concentration camp" but had said "in concentration." Mr. Welles said that he understood that the American diplomats were lodged in a hotel in western Germany and the reports so far would seem to indicate that they were obtaining good treatment. When asked if there was no prospect of their coming home, Mr. Welles said not for the time being for the reasons stated.

A correspondent asked if that meant that our friends in Hershey, Pa., would have to stay there a while longer. Mr. Welles said that it seemed that way.

When asked how many were involved, Mr. Welles said that the correspondents would be given the appropriate figure. (The total number of the American group in Germany is 139, of which 95 are personnel of the State, War, and Navy Departments and the remainder, journalists and Red Cross and other relief workers. The Germans involved in the prospective exchange total 71, of which 47 are military personnel and 24 civilians.)

(3) *Exchange of American and Japanese Nationals. Department of State Release on the Status of Negotiations, May 22, 1943* [1]

For the information of the relatives and friends of American civilians held in the Far East by the Japanese authorities, the Department of State announces that it has received a communication from the Japanese Government giving reason to hope that a second exchange of approximately 1,500 American civilians for an equal number of Japanese civilians held in the United States may be arranged. The first exchange,[2] involving the same number of civilians, took place last summer, the chartered Swedish motor vessel *Gripsholm* being used to transport the

---

[1] *Ibid.*, p. 442.   [2] See note, *Documents, IV, 1941–42*, p. 815.

Japanese from the United States to Lourenço Marques in Portuguese East Africa, where the exchange took place, and the liberated Americans, who were received there from Japanese vessels, being brought home on the *Gripsholm*. While arrangements were being made for that exchange the Department entered into negotiations with the Japanese Government for a second and further exchanges. It has continuously pursued those negotiations in the hope that an agreement could be reached mutually acceptable to both Governments. In its latest proposal the Department suggested that a minimum of three more exchanges be agreed on, which would involve the repatriation of 1,500 on each exchange. The reply of the Japanese Government indicates that that Government prefers for the time being to limit consideration to one exchange, involving the repatriation of 1,500 persons on each side, and that subsequent exchanges be left for future consideration.

The Japanese Government has expressed its desires with respect to the composition of the Japanese passenger list for the second exchange. The Department is now engaged, with the assistance of the other Government agencies concerned, in identifying and locating Japanese for inclusion in the passenger list. The work entails in many cases search throughout the United States for Japanese who have been named by the Japanese Government for inclusion in the exchange. Some may already have departed from the United States. Others cannot be identified until the English spellings of their Japanese names, by which they are known here, are ascertained. However, progress is rapidly being made in composing the passenger list. Until that task is completed and final and definite arrangements for the exchange have been made with the Japanese Government, the Department cannot indicate the date when the exchange may be accomplished.

As in the first exchange, there will be included a number of citizens of the other American Republics and of Canada on a proportionate basis with citizens of the United States. Similarly, a number of Japanese from the other American Republics and from Canada will be included with Japanese from the United States.

(4) *Repatriation of American Prisoners of War Held in Japanese Custody. Department of State Release, May 25, 1943* [1]

Relatives and friends of Americans held as prisoners of war by the Japanese military authorities have inquired of various agencies of the Government concerning the prospects for their early repatriation, suggesting in most cases that Japanese prisoners of war be offered in exchange for the Americans.

---

[1] Department of State, *Bulletin*, VIII, p. 472.

There are three distinct categories of American nationals in Japanese custody, namely:

(1) Prisoners of war, that is, members of the American armed forces who have been captured by the Japanese armed forces,

(2) Sanitary and religious personnel captured while serving with the armed forces, and

(3) Civilians in Japan or Japanese-occupied or controlled territory, the majority of whom have been interned.[1]

. . . .

There is no customarily accepted practice among nations nor provision of international law or conventions for the return or exchange during war of able-bodied members of the armed forces of one belligerent captured by the forces of the opposing belligerents. It is a major objective of warfare to deplete as rapidly as possible the forces of the enemy, and it has so far been deemed inexpedient for military reasons to propose the release and return of able-bodied prisoners of war. In the circumstances, there is no immediate prospect of obtaining the release and return to the United States of able-bodied members of the American armed forces taken prisoners of war by the Japanese.

The only prisoners of war whose release and return to their own country is provided for and sanctioned by international agreement and practice are the seriously sick and seriously wounded who are no longer capable of contributing to the enemy war effort. The release and return of such prisoners is provided for in the Geneva Prisoners of War Convention of 1929,[2] which both Japan and the United States are applying in this war. Steps are already under way for implementing the relevant provisions of that convention. Military operations and the difficulties of transportation through military zones are the principal obstacles at present in the way of such a movement.

Negotiations are also under way for the release and return of such captured sanitary and religious personnel as may not be needed to care for their compatriots who are prisoners of war.

Every endeavor is being made to obtain the release as quickly as possible of those eligible therefor, and all feasible steps are being taken to provide for the well-being of all our nationals of whatever category in enemy hands until such time as they can be offered an opportunity to return to their homes in the United States.

---

[1] The status of negotiations for an exchange of civilian nationals between the United States and Japan was discussed in a press release of May 22, 1943; see this volume, p. 185.

[2] *Treaties, Conventions* etc., 1923–1937, IV, p. 5224. See also *Documents, IV, 1941–42*, p. 813.

B. Relief of Civilian Internees and Prisoners of War in Japan

Immediately following the Japanese occupation of the Philippine Islands, efforts were made by the American Red Cross to locate a neutral ship of sufficient cargo capacity and cruising radius for the carriage of prisoner-of-war supplies to the Far East, including the Philippine Islands. These were to be in addition to various relief supplies carried on the first voyage from the United States of the motorship *Gripsholm*, under the terms of the American-Japanese exchange agreement.

In the spring of 1942 a suitable vessel was located, the Swedish ship *Vasaland*, then at Gothenburg. Efforts made by the American Red Cross through the International Red Cross to secure the assent of the German authorities to the departure of this ship from the Baltic proved fruitless, following which the *Kanangoora*, a Swedish vessel now on the Pacific coast, was chartered with the expectation that it could be used for this purpose.

Supplementing the repeated efforts of the American Red Cross, made through the intermediary of the International Red Cross, to obtain from the Japanese Government a guaranty of safe conduct for this ship to carry relief supplies for American prisoners of war and civilian internees in Japanese custody, messages dated July 30, August 29, and September 18, 1942, respectively, were sent by the Secretary of State to the Japanese Government through the Swiss Government representing American interests in Japan.

(1) *Instruction from the Department of State to the American Minister in Bern, Switzerland (Harrison), July 30, 1942* [1]

Please request that Swiss Minister Tokyo be instructed to press for consent of Japanese Government to voyage from San Francisco to Manila via Kobe, Shanghai and Hong Kong of Swedish motorship *Kanangoora* which is being chartered by American Red Cross and operated by the International Red Cross to carry supplies for prisoners of war and civilian internees in the Far East. Please expedite report.

(2) *The Acting Secretary of State (Welles) to the Japanese Government, August 29, 1942* [2]

1. The Japanese Government has agreed to apply the provisions of the Geneva Prisoners of War Convention of 1929 to American prisoners of war and civilian internees. Article 37 of that Convention provides for the receipt by prisoners of supplies of food and clothing supplemental to those which it is the duty of the detaining power to furnish, in as much as it states that prisoners shall be allowed to receive parcels intended to supply them with food or clothing. It further states that such parcels shall be delivered to the prisoners.

2. The American Red Cross assumed that the Japanese Government would grant safe conduct for a Red Cross ship to transport supplemental supplies of food and clothing destined to American and other prisoners

---

[1] Department of State, *Bulletin*, VII, p. 768.   [2] *Ibid.*, p. 741.

of war and civilian internees in Japanese custody as German and Italian Governments have done and are continuing to do for supplies being sent for prisoners and internees in their custody. Accordingly, the American Red Cross chartered the neutral Swedish motorship *Kanangoora* to carry such supplies and the ship is now ready to sail from San Francisco with the supplies. It is to be operated by the International Red Cross Committee, a representative of which, who will be a citizen of a neutral country, will be the only person on board besides the Swedish citizens composing the crew.

3. The American Red Cross has requested, through the channels of the International Red Cross Committee, the consent of the Japanese Government for the voyage of the ship to Manila via Kobe, Shanghai and Hong Kong, with the supplies. The United States Government also has officially asked for that consent through the channels of the Swiss Government representing the interests of the United States in Japan. Through both channels the Japanese Government has now replied refusing such consent. It states that it does not object, however, to such shipments on vessels exchanging Japanese and United States nationals at Lourenço Marques.

4. The motorship *Gripsholm* used by the United States Government in the exchange of Japanese and Americans at Lourenço Marques does not have sufficient cargo-carrying capacity to transport the amount of supplies which it is desired to send to prisoners and internees in the Far East. Moreover, the exchange ship does not provide a means of continued transportation of such supplies. Additional shipping must therefore be employed if the prisoners and internees are to receive supplementary supplies as provided for by the Convention.

5. If the Japanese Government will not permit the *Kanangoora* to proceed on its proposed voyage to the Far East with the supplies in question, then the United States Government proposes that the Japanese Government agree that the *Kanangoora* or other Red Cross ship shall proceed fron the United States with the supplies to Macao or to Lourenço Marques, to which port the Japanese Government will similarly send a Red Cross ship to receive the supplies and transport them for delivery to the prisoners and internees. The United States Government desires to point out in this connection that it is incumbent upon the Japanese Government to facilitate by whatever means may be available, the delivery of parcels intended for prisoners in fulfillment of the obligation of the detaining power to allow prisoners to receive parcels and to deliver the parcels to them as provided by Article 37 of the Geneva Prisoners of War Convention.[1] The United States Government, while looking to the Japanese Government to fulfill its obligations under the Convention in this matter, is fully conscious of its own obligations thereunder.

[1] *Treaties, Conventions*, etc., 1923–1937, IV, p. 5224.

(3) *The Secretary of State (Hull) to the Japanese Government,
September 18, 1942* [1]

The Government of the United States has noted the Japanese Government's statement that it has never refused and will not refuse in the future to accept and to deliver parcels containing foodstuffs and clothing as provided for under Article 37 of the Geneva Prisoners of War Convention and is gratified to have official confirmation that supplies sent by the American Red Cross on the exchange ships will be distributed to American prisoners of war and civilian internees in Japan, in the Philippines, and in other areas under Japanese occupation.

The Government of the United States also has noted the statement of the Japanese Government that it must maintain for the moment its refusal to allow, for strategic reasons, any vessel to cross the western Pacific and that the Japanese Government has no intention of sending to Lourenço Marques Japanese ships other than the exchange vessels.

The Government of the United States desires, however, to point out that the supplies already sent to the Philippine Islands are insufficient in quantity adequately to satisfy the continuing needs of American prisoners of war and civilian internees detained by the Japanese authorities there. Furthermore, sufficient cargo space is not available on the exchange vessels to permit the shipment of sufficient supplementary supplies to serve the continuing needs of American nationals detained by the Japanese authorities in the Philippine Islands and in other areas under Japanese occupation.

The Government of the United States, therefore, proposes again that the Japanese Government consent to the appointment of a neutral International Red Cross Committee delegate in the Philippine Islands to whom funds might be sent from the United States to be used in the purchase of local produce for distribution among American nationals in Japanese custody there. This Government confidently expects that as soon as the strategic reasons which the Japanese Government states are at present influencing it in refusing to permit neutral vessels to cross the western Pacific are no longer controlling, the Japanese Government will give safe conduct for the shipment of supplementary supplies from this country. Until that time, however, it is only by opening a means whereby funds may be provided to and used by a neutral Red Cross representative in the Philippine Islands that American nationals in Japanese custody in the Philippines may be furnished on a continuing basis the supplementary supplies which prisoners of war are entitled to receive under the Convention, which both Governments have agreed reciprocally to apply and to extend to civilian internees. In this connection, this Government desires to point out that the dietary habits of

[1] Department of State, *Bulletin*, VII, p. 768.

Americans are different from those of the Japanese people and that this Government is accordingly anxious to supplement the basic Japanese rations by supplies of a type more characteristic of the usual American diet.

The attention of the Japanese Government is drawn to the fact that International Red Cross Committee delegates are permitted to function freely in the continental United States and the Territory of Hawaii in the distribution of relief among persons of Japanese nationality detained in the United States and Hawaii.

The Government of the United States desires to know urgently whether or not the Japanese Government will henceforth grant full reciprocity in these respects.

6. ALLEGED VIOLATIONS OF THE LAWS OF WAR

(1) *Opinion of the Supreme Court of the United States in the Case of* Ex parte *Quirin et al. (Saboteur Cases), October 29, 1942* [1]

[Excerpt]

The seven petitioners, born in Germany, and with the exception of Haupt, admittedly citizens of Germany, together with Dasch, were trained in sabotage methods in Germany. Four of them, acting under instructions from the German High Command, were landed from a submarine on Long Island, during the hours of darkness, on or about June 13, 1942, carrying with them a supply of explosives, fuses, and incendiary and timing devices. While landing they wore German Marine Infantry uniforms or parts of uniforms. Immediately after landing they buried their uniforms and other articles mentioned and proceeded in civilian dress to New York City. The other four landed in like manner on Ponte Vedra Beach, Florida, and proceeded in like manner to Jacksonville. They were subsequently taken into custody by agents of the Federal Bureau of Investigation in New York or Chicago and brought to trial before a Military Commission set up by the President by Order of July 2, 1942 [2] to try petitioners for offenses against the law of war and the Articles of War. The case came before the Supreme Court on a petition for a writ of habeas corpus based on the contention that the President was without power to order the petitioners to be tried by a military tribunal for the offense with which they were charged. The Court filed a *per curiam* opinion on July 31, 1942, denying the petition,[3] and filed a full opinion October 29, 1942. In the excerpt below, the Court considers the charge of unlawful belligerency, and concludes that the specifications are sufficient to charge the petitioners with this offense, trial of which is within the jurisdiction of the Commission. Footnotes are omitted.

From the very beginning of its history this Court has recognized and applied the law of war as including that part of the law of nations which prescribes, for the conduct of war, the status, rights and duties of enemy nations as well as of enemy individuals. By the Articles of War, and especially Article 15, Congress has explicitly provided, so far as it may constitutionally do so, that military tribunals shall have jurisdiction to try offenders or offenses against the law of war in appropriate cases.

[1] 317 U. S. (1942), 1.   [2] 7 *Fed. Reg.*, p. 5103.   [3] 317 U. S. (1942), 18, footnote.

Congress, in addition to making rules for the government of our Armed Forces, has thus exercised its authority to define and punish offenses against the law of nations by sanctioning, within constitutional limitations, the jurisdiction of military commissions to try persons for offenses which, according to the rules and precepts of the law of nations, and more particularly the law of war, are cognizable by such tribunals. And the President, as Commander-in-Chief, by his Proclamation in time of war has invoked that law. By his Order creating the present Commission he has undertaken to exercise the authority conferred upon him by Congress, and also such authority as the Constitution itself gives the Commander-in-Chief, to direct the performance of those functions which may constitutionally be performed by the military arm of the nation in time of war.

An important incident to the conduct of war is the adoption of measures by the military command not only to repel and defeat the enemy, but to seize and subject to disciplinary measures those enemies who in their attempt to thwart or impede our military effort have violated the law of war. It is unnecessary for present purposes to determine to what extent the President as Commander-in-Chief has constitutional power to create military commissions without the support of Congressional legislation. For here Congress has authorized trial of offenses against the law of war before such commissions. We are concerned only with the question whether it is within the constitutional power of the National Government to place petitioners upon trial before a military commission for the offenses with which they are charged. We must therefore first inquire whether any of the acts charged is an offense against the law of war cognizable before a military tribunal, and if so whether the Constitution prohibits the trial. We may assume that there are acts regarded in other countries, or by some writers on international law, as offenses against the law of war which would not be triable by military tribunal here, either because they are not recognized by our courts as violations of the law of war or because they are of that class of offenses constitutionally triable only by a jury. It was upon such grounds that the Court denied the right to proceed by military tribunal in *Ex parte Milligan*,[1] *supra*. But as we shall show, these petitioners were charged with an offense against the law of war which the Constitution does not require to be tried by jury.

It is no objection that Congress in providing for the trial of such offenses has not itself undertaken to codify that branch of international law or to mark its precise boundaries, or to enumerate or define by statute all the acts which that law condemns. An Act of Congress punishing "the crime of piracy, as defined by the law of nations" is an appropriate exercise of its constitutional authority, Art. I, § 8, cl. 10, "to

[1] 4 Wall 2, 110–13, 119, 132.

define and punish" the offense, since it has adopted by reference the sufficiently precise definition of international law. *United States* v. *Smith*, 5 Wheat. 153; see *The Marianna Flora*, 11 Wheat. 1, 40–41; *United States* v. *Brig Malek Adhel*, 2 How. 210, 232; *The Ambrose Light*, 25 F. 408, 423–28; 18 U.S.C. § 481. Similarly, by the reference in the 15th Article of War to "offenders or offenses that . . . by the law of war may be triable by such military commissions," Congress has incorporated by reference, as within the jurisdiction of military commissions, all offenses which are defined as such by the law of war (compare *Dynes* v. *Hoover*, 20 How. 65, 82), and which may constitutionally be included within that jurisdiction. Congress had the choice of crystallizing in permanent form and in minute detail every offense against the law of war, or of adopting the system of common law applied by military tribunals so far as it should be recognized and deemed applicable by the courts. It chose the latter course.

By universal agreement and practice, the law of war draws a distinction between the armed forces and the peaceful populations of belligerent nations and also between those who are lawful and unlawful combatants. Lawful combatants are subject to capture and detention as prisoners of war by opposing military forces. Unlawful combatants are likewise subject to capture and detention, but in addition they are subject to trial and punishment by military tribunals for acts which render their belligerency unlawful. The spy who secretly and without uniform passes the military lines of a belligerent in time of war, seeking to gather military information and communicate it to the enemy, or an enemy combatant who without uniform comes secretly through the lines for the purpose of waging war by destruction of life or property, are familiar examples of belligerents who are generally deemed not to be entitled to the status of prisoners of war, but to be offenders against the law of war subject to trial and punishment by military tribunals. See Winthrop, Military law, 2d ed., pp. 1196–97, 1219–21; Instructions for the Government of Armies of the United States in the Field, approved by the President, General Order No. 100, April 24, 1863, §§ IV and V.

Such was the practice of our own military authorities before the adoption of the Constitution, and during the Mexican and Civil Wars.

Paragraph 83 of General Order No. 100 of April 24, 1863, directed that: "Scouts or single soldiers, if disguised in the dress of the country, or in the uniform of the army hostile to their own, employed in obtaining information, if found within or lurking about the lines of the captor, are treated as spies, and suffer death." And Paragraph 84, that "Armed prowlers, by whatever names they may be called, or persons of the enemy's territory, who steal within the lines of the hostile army, for the purpose of robbing, killing, or of destroying bridges, roads, or canals, or of robbing or destroying the mail, or of cutting the telegraph wires, are not entitled to the privileges of the prisoner of war." These and related provisions have been continued in substance by the Rules of Land Warfare promulgated by the War Department for the guidance of the Army. Rules of 1914, Par. 369–77; Rules of 1940, Par. 345–57. Paragraph 357 of the 1940 Rules provides that "All war crimes are subject to the death penalty, although a lesser penalty may be imposed." Paragraph 8 (1940) divides the enemy population into "armed forces" and "peaceful population," and Paragraph 9 names as distinguishing characteristics of lawful belligerents that they "carry arms openly" and "have a fixed distinctive emblem." Paragraph 348 declares that "persons who take up arms and commit hostilities" without having the means of identification prescribed for belligerents are punishable as "war criminals." Paragraph 351 provides that "men and bodies of men, who, without being lawful belligerents" "nevertheless commit hostile acts of any kind" are not entitled to the privileges of prisoners of war if captured and may be tried by military commission and punished by death or lesser punishment. And paragraph 352 provides that "armed prowlers . . . or persons of the enemy territory who steal within the lines of the hostile army for the purpose of robbing, killing, or of destroying bridges, roads, or canals, of robbing or destroying the mail, or of cutting the telegraph wires, are not entitled to be treated as prisoners of war." As is evident from reading these and related Paragraphs 345–347, the specified violations are intended to be only illustrative of the applicable principles of the common law of war, and not an exclusive enumeration of the punishable acts recognized as such by that law. The definition of lawful belligerents by Paragraph 9 is that adopted by Article 1, Annex to Hague Convention No. IV of October 18, 1907, to which the United States was a signatory and which was ratified by the Senate in 1909. 36 Stat. 2295. The preamble to the Convention declares:

"Until a more complete code of the laws of war has been issued, the High Contracting Parties deem it expedient to declare that, in cases not included in the Regulations adopted by them, the inhabitants and the belligerents remain under the protection and the rule of the principles of the law of nations, as they result from the usages established among civilized peoples, from the laws of humanity, and the dictates of the public conscience."

Our Government, by thus defining lawful belligerents entitled to be treated as prisoners of war, has recognized that there is a class of unlawful belligerents not entitled to that privilege, including those who, though combatants, do not wear "fixed and distinctive emblems." And by Article 15 of the Articles of War Congress has made provision for their trial and punishment by military commission, according to "the law of war."

By a long course of practical administrative construction by its military authorities, our Government has likewise recognized that those who during time of war pass surreptitiously from enemy territory into our own, discarding their uniforms upon entry, for the commission of hostile acts involving destruction of life or property, have the status of unlawful combatants punishable as such by military commission. This precept of the law of war has been so recognized in practice both here and abroad, and has so generally been accepted as valid by authorities on international law that we think it must be regarded as a rule or principle of the law of war recognized by this Government by its enactment of the Fifteenth Article of War.

(2) Japanese Trial and Execution of American Aviators. Statement of the President (Roosevelt), April 21, 1943 [1]

On April 18, 1942, American bombers carried out an attack on strategic objectives in Japan, in the course of which crews of two of the American bombers were captured by the Japanese. The captured members of the crews were not accorded treatment as prescribed by the Prisoners of War Convention, signed at Geneva, July 27, 1929,[2] which the Japanese Government had stated its intention to respect during the present hostilities, but rather were tried and punished, in some cases by the death penalty, presumably for having violated the laws of war by engaging in the bombing of undefended cities, prohibited by Article XXV of the Annex to the Convention Respecting the Laws and Customs of War on Land, signed at The Hague, October 18, 1907.[3]

It is with a feeling of deepest horror, which I know will be shared by all civilized peoples, that I have to announce the barbarous execution by the Japanese Government of some of the members of this country's armed forces who fell into Japanese hands as an incident of warfare.

The press has just carried the details of the American bombing of Japan a year ago. The crews of two of the American bombers were captured by the Japanese. On October 19, 1942 this Government learned from Japanese radio broadcasts of the capture, trial, and severe punishment of those Americans. Continued endeavor was made to obtain confirmation of those reports from Tokyo. It was not until March 12, 1943 that the American Government received the communication given by the Japanese Government stating that these Americans had in fact been tried and that the death penalty had been pronounced against them. It was further stated that the death penalty was commuted for some but that the sentence of death had been applied to others.

This Government has vigorously condemned this act of barbarity in a formal communication sent to the Japanese Government. In that communication this Government has informed the Japanese Government

---

[1] Department of State, *Bulletin*, VIII, p. 337.

[2] Senate Doc. No. 134, 75th Cong., 3d sess.; *Treaties, Conventions*, etc., 1923–1937, IV, p. 5224.

[3] *Treaties, Conventions*, etc., 1776–1909, II, p. 2269. This convention was not ratified by Japan and therefore is not binding on the United States and Japan except insofar as it states rules of customary international law.

that the American Government will hold personally and officially responsible for these diabolical crimes all of those officers of the Japanese Government who have participated therein and will in due course bring those officers to justice.

This recourse by our enemies to frightfulness is barbarous. The effort of the Japanese warlords thus to intimidate us will utterly fail. It will make the American people more determined than ever to blot out the shameless militarism of Japan.

I have instructed the Department of State to make public the text of our communication to the Japanese Government.

(a) Communication of the United States Government to the Japanese Government, April 12, 1943 [1]

The Government of the United States has received the reply of the Japanese Government conveyed under date of February 17, 1943, to the Swiss Minister at Tokyo to the inquiry made by the Minister on behalf of the Government of the United States concerning the correctness of reports broadcast by Japanese radio stations that the Japanese authorities intended to try before military tribunals American prisoners of war, for military operations, and to impose upon them severe penalties including even the death penalty.

The Japanese Government states that it has tried the members of the crews of American planes who fell into Japanese hands after the raid on Japan on April 18 last, that they were sentenced to death and that, following commutation of the sentence for the larger number of them, the sentence of death was applied to certain of the accused.

The Government of the United States has subsequently been informed of the refusal of the Japanese Government to treat the remaining American aviators as prisoners of war, to divulge their names, to state the sentences imposed upon them or to permit visits to them by the Swiss Minister as representative of the protecting Power for American interests.

The Japanese Government alleges that it has subjected the American aviators to this treatment because they intentionally bombed non-military installations and deliberately fired on civilians, and that the aviators admitted these acts.

The Government of the United States informs the Japanese Government that instructions to American armed forces have always ordered those forces to direct their attacks upon military objectives. The American forces participating in the attack on Japan had such instructions and it is known that they did not deviate therefrom. The Government of the United States brands as false the charge that American aviators intentionally have attacked non-combatants anywhere.

With regard to the allegation of the Japanese Government that the

---

[1] Department of State, *Bulletin*, VIII, p. 337.

American aviators admitted the acts of which the Japanese Government accuses them, there are numerous known instances in which Japanese official agencies have employed brutal and bestial methods in extorting alleged confessions from persons in their power. It is customary for those agencies to use statements obtained under torture, or alleged statements, in proceedings against the victims.

If the admissions alleged by the Japanese Government to have been made by the American aviators were in fact made, they could only have been extorted fabrications.

Moreover, the Japanese Government entered into a solemn obligation by agreement with the Government of the United States to observe the terms of the Geneva Prisoners of War Convention. Article 1 of that Convention provides for treatment as prisoners of war of members of armies and of persons captured in the course of military operations at sea or in the air. Article 60 provides that upon the opening of a judicial proceeding directed against a prisoner of war, the representative of the protecting Power shall be given notice thereof at least three weeks prior to the trial and of the names and charges against the prisoners who are to be tried. Article 61 provides that no prisoner may be obliged to admit himself guilty of the act of which he is accused. Article 62 provides that the accused shall have the assistance of qualified counsel of his choice and that a representative of the protecting Power shall be permitted to attend the trial. Article 65 provides that sentence pronounced against the prisoners shall be communicated to the protecting Power immediately. Article 66 provides, in the event that the death penalty is pronounced, that the details as to the nature and circumstances of the offense shall be communicated to the protecting Power, for transmission to the Power in whose forces the prisoner served, and that the sentence shall not be executed before the expiration of a period of at least three months after such communication. The Japanese Government has not complied with any of these provisions of the Convention in its treatment of the captured American aviators.

The Government of the United States calls again upon the Japanese Government to carry out its agreement to observe the provisions of the Convention by communicating to the Swiss Minister at Tokyo the charges and sentences imposed upon the American aviators, by permitting the Swiss representatives to visit those now held in prison, by restoring to those aviators the full rights to which they are entitled under the Prisoners of War Convention, and by informing the Minister of the names and disposition or place of burial of the bodies of any of the aviators against whom sentence of death has been carried out.

If, as would appear from its communication under reference, the Japanese Government has descended to such acts of barbarity and manifestations of depravity as to murder in cold blood uniformed members of the American armed forces made prisoners as an incident of warfare, the American Government will hold personally and officially responsible for those deliberate crimes all of those officers of the Japanese Government who have participated in their commitment and will in due course bring those officers to justice.

The American Government also solemnly warns the Japanese Government that for any other violations of its undertakings as regards American prisoners of war or for any other acts of criminal barbarity inflicted upon American prisoners in violation of the rules of warfare accepted and practiced by civilized nations as military operations now in progress draw to their inexorable and inevitable conclusion, the American Government will visit upon the officers of the Japanese Government responsible for such uncivilized and inhumane acts the punishment they deserve.

(3) *Use of Poison Gas. Statement of the President (Roosevelt), June 8, 1943* [1]

From time to time since the present war began there have been reports that one or more of the Axis powers were seriously contemplating use of poisonous or noxious gases or other inhumane devices of warfare.

I have been loath to believe that any nation, even our present enemies, could or would be willing to loose upon mankind such terrible and inhumane weapons. However, evidence that the Axis powers are making significant preparations indicative of such an intention is being reported with increasing frequency from a variety of sources.

Use of such weapons has been outlawed by the general opinion of civilized mankind. This country has not used them, and I hope that we never will be compelled to use them. I state categorically that we shall under no circumstances resort to the use of such weapons unless they are first used by our enemies.

As President of the United States and as Commander-in-Chief of the American armed forces, I want to make clear beyond all doubt to any of our enemies contemplating a resort to such desperate and barbarous methods that acts of this nature committed against any one of the United Nations will be regarded as having been committed against the United States itself and will be treated accordingly. We promise to any perpetrators of such crimes full and swift retaliation in kind, and I feel obliged now to warn the Axis armies and the Axis peoples, in Europe and in Asia, that the terrible consequences of any use of these inhumane methods on their part will be brought down swiftly and surely upon their own heads. Any use of gas by any Axis power, therefore, will immediately be followed by the fullest possible retaliation upon munition centers, seaports, and other military objectives throughout the whole extent of the territory of such Axis country.

[1] *Ibid.*, p. 507.

CHAPTER IV

THE UNITED NATIONS

[See *Documents, IV, 1941–42*, p. 198.]

1. MEMBERSHIP AND BASIC PRINCIPLES OF COLLABORATION

A. Unilateral Reaffirmation and Interpretation

The basic principles of the United Nations were set forth in the Declaration by United Nations, January 1, 1942.[1] This Declaration, besides committing the signatories to the employment of "its full resources, military or economic, against those members of the Tripartite Pact and its adherents with which such government is at war," and "to cooperate with the Governments signatory hereto and not to make a separate armistice or peace with the enemies," carried acceptance in its preamble of the "program of purposes and principles embodied in . . . the Atlantic Charter." [2]

Serious doubts have been expressed from time to time as to the interpretation to be placed on these general statements of purposes and principles, and in particular, as to the world-wide application of the Charter. Prime Minister Churchill, in his statement in the House of Commons, September 8, 1941,[3] used words tending to support a more limited application. Mr. Wendell Willkie in statements made during and following his round-the-world trip criticized the failure to make clear that the principles of the Charter applied to the peoples of Asia. There have been demands for a "Pacific Charter" and for a "World Charter."

Commenting on the Charter on August 14, 1941,[4] Secretary of State Hull said: "It is a statement of basic principles and fundamental ideas and policies that are universal in their practical application." In his radio address of July 23, 1942,[5] the Secretary used these words: "The pledge of the Atlantic Charter is of a system which will give every nation, large or small, a greater assurance of stable peace, greater opportunity for the realization of its aspirations to freedom, and greater facilities for material advancement. But that pledge implies an obligation for each nation to demonstrate its capacity for stable and progressive government, to fulfill scrupulously its established duties to other nations, to settle its international differences and disputes by none but peaceful methods, and to make its full contribution to the maintenance of enduring peace."

Asked for comment at his press conference on Mr. Wendell L. Willkie's radio address of October 26 in which he suggested the need of a "Pacific Charter" or a "World Charter," President Roosevelt replied that both he and Secretary Hull had made it clear that "the Atlantic Charter applies to all humanity." He added that the agreement had been called the Atlantic Charter because of the place at which it was signed.[6]

[1] *Documents, IV, 1941–42*, p. 203.
[2] For text, see *ibid.*, p. 10.
[3] *Ibid.*, p. 213.
[4] *Ibid.*, p. 12.
[5] See this volume, p. 1.
[6] *New York Times*, October 28, 1942.

(1) *First Anniversary of the Signing of the Atlantic Charter. Message of the President (Roosevelt) to the Prime Minister of the United Kingdom (Churchill), August 14, 1942* [1]

A year ago today you and I, as representatives of two free nations, set down and subscribed to a declaration of principles common to our peoples. We based, and continue to base, our hopes for a better future for the world on the realization of these principles. This declaration is known as the Atlantic Charter.

A year ago today the nations resisting a common, barbaric foe were units or small groups, fighting for their existence.

Now, these nations and groups of nations in all the continents of the earth have united. They have formed a great union of humanity, dedicated to the realization of that common program of purposes and principles set forth in the Atlantic Charter, through world-wide victory over their common enemies. Their faith in life, liberty, independence and religious freedom, and in the preservation of human rights and justice in their own lands as well as in other lands, has been given form and substance and power through a great gathering of peoples now known as the United Nations.

Freedom and independence are today in jeopardy — the world over. If the forces of conquest are not successfully resisted and defeated there will be no freedom and no independence and no opportunity for freedom for any nation.

It is, therefore, to the single and supreme objective of defeating the Axis forces of aggression that the United Nations have pledged all their resources and efforts.

When victory comes, we shall stand shoulder to shoulder in seeking to nourish the great ideals for which we fight. It is a worthwhile battle. It will be so recognized through all the ages, even amid the unfortunate peoples who follow false gods today.

We reaffirm our principles. They will bring us to a happier world.

(2) *Anniversary of the Signing of the Declaration by United Nations. Statement of the President (Roosevelt), January 1, 1943* [2]

One year ago 26 nations signed at Washington the Declaration by United Nations.[3]

The world situation at that moment was grim indeed. Yet on that last New Year's Day, these nations, bound together by the universal

---

[1] Department of State, *Bulletin,* VII, p. 697.
[2] *Ibid.,* VIII, p. 3.   [3] *See Documents, IV, 1941-42, p. 203.*

ideals of the Atlantic Charter, signed an act of faith that military aggression, treaty violation, and calculated savagery should be remorselessly overwhelmed by their combined might and the sacred principles of life, liberty, and the pursuit of happiness be restored as cherished ideals of mankind. They thus created the mightiest coalition in history, mighty not only for its overwhelming material force but still more for its eternal spiritual values. Three other nations have since joined that coalition.

The unity thus achieved amidst dire danger has borne rich fruit. The United Nations are passing from the defensive to the offensive.

The unity achieved on the battleline is being earnestly sought in the not less complex problems on a different front. In this as in no previous war men are conscious of the supreme necessity of planning what is to come after — and of carrying forward into peace the common effort which will have brought them victory in the war. They have come to see that the maintenance and safeguarding of peace is the most vital single necessity in the lives of each and all of us.

Our task on this New Year's Day is threefold: first, to press on with the massed forces of free humanity till the present bandit assault upon civilization is completely crushed; second, so to organize relations among nations that forces of barbarism can never again break loose; third, to cooperate to the end that mankind may enjoy in peace and in freedom the unprecedented blessings which Divine Providence through the progress of civilization has put within our reach.

(a) Informal Remarks of the President (Roosevelt) Regarding Peace Objectives, January 1, 1943 [1]

Of course, as I think has been intimated before, there are a great many objectives when peace comes, so that we won't go back to the old menace of the pre-war period — a great many things the United Nations ought to and I think will remain united for.

However, there is one thing which at the present time stands out as the most important war objective, and that is to maintain peace, so that all of us, in going through this war, including the men on the fighting fronts and on the seas, will not have to go through a world cataclysm again — that they will have some reasonable assurance that their children won't have to go through it again. Almost all the other things we hope to get out of the war are more or less dependent on the maintenance of peace — all kinds of planning for the future, economic and social, and so forth and so on. It isn't much use if there is going to be another

---

[1] These remarks were made at the President's press conference, following the release to the press of the formal statement above; Department of State, *Bulletin*, VIII. p. 3.

world war in 10 years, or 15 years, or 20 years. All the planning for the future is dependent, obviously, on peace.

In an address before the White House Correspondents' Association on February 12, 1943, the President elaborated on the interpretation to be given to Point 3 of the Atlantic Charter with special reference to the situation in French North Africa.[1]

(3) *Address of the President of the Soviet of the People's Commissars of the Soviet Union (Stalin) to the Moscow Soviet, November 6, 1942* [2]

[Excerpt]

. . . .

(4) *The fighting alliance of the U.S.S.R, Great Britain and the United States of America against Hitlerite Germany and her allies in Europe.* It may now be considered indisputable that in the course of the war imposed upon nations by Hitlerite Germany, a radical demarcation of forces and formation of two opposite camps has taken place — the camp of the Italo-German coalition and the camp of the Anglo-Soviet-American coalition. It is equally indisputable that these two opposite coalitions are guided by two different and opposite programs of action. The program of action of the Italo-German coalition may be described by the following points:

Racial hatred; domination of "chosen" nations; subjugation of other nations and seizure of their territories; economic enslavement of subjugated nations and spoliation of their national wealth; destruction of democratic liberties; institution of the Hitlerite regime everywhere.

The program of action of the Anglo-Soviet-American coalition is:

Abolition of racial exclusiveness; equality of nations and integrity of their territories; liberation of enslaved nations and the restoration of their sovereign rights; the right of every nation to arrange its affairs as it wishes; economic aid to nations that have suffered and assistance to them in attaining their material welfare; restoration of democratic liberties; destruction of the Hitlerite regime.

The effect of the program of action of the Italo-German coalition has been that all occupied countries of Europe — Norway, Denmark, Belgium, Holland, France, Poland, Czechoslovakia, Yugoslavia, Greece and occupied regions of the U.S.S.R. — are burning with hatred of the Italo-German tyrants, are causing all the damage they can to the Germans and their allies and are waiting for a favorable opportunity to take revenge on their conquerors for the humiliations and violence they are suffering.

In this connection, one of the characteristic features of the present

----

[1] See this volume, p. 42.

[2] Embassy of the Union of Soviet Socialist Republics, *Information Bulletin*, No. 135, November 12, 1942, p. 4; *New York Times*, November 7, 1942.

moment is the progressively growing isolation of the Italo-German coalition and the depletion of its moral and political reserves in Europe, its growing weakness and disintegration. The effect of the program of action of the Anglo-Soviet-American coalition has been that all occupied countries in Europe are full of sympathy for the members of this coalition and are prepared to render them all the help of which they are capable.

In this connection, another characteristic feature of the present moment is that the moral and political reserves of this coalition are growing from day to day in Europe — and not only in Europe — and that that coalition is progressively winning millions of sympathizers, ready to join it in fighting against Hitler's tyranny. If the relative strength of these two coalitions is examined from the standpoint of human and material resources, one cannot help reaching the conclusion that the Anglo-Soviet-American coalition has an indisputable advantage.

[Here follows a review of the measures taken by the coalition to win the war.]

There can be no doubt that all these facts point to progressive rapprochement between the U.S.S.R., Great Britain and the United States of America and their uniting in a fighting alliance against the Italo-German coalition.

It follows that the logic of things is stronger than any other logic. There can be only one conclusion, namely, that the Anglo-Soviet-American coalition has every chance of vanquishing the Italo-German coalition and certainly will vanquish it.

(5) *Our tasks.* The war has torn off all veils and laid bare all relationships. The situation has become so clear that nothing is easier than to define our tasks in this war. In an interview with the Turkish General Erkilet, published in the Turkish newspaper *Cumhuriet*, that cannibal Hitler said: "We shall destroy Russia so that she will never be able to rise again." That would appear clear although rather silly. It is not our aim to destroy Germany, for it is impossible to destroy Germany, just as it is impossible to destroy Russia. But the Hitlerite state can and should be destroyed. And our first task in fact is to destroy the Hitlerite state and its inspirers.

In the same interview with the same general, that cannibal Hitler went on to say: "We shall continue the war until Russia ceases to have an organized military force." That would appear clear although illiterate. It is not our aim to destroy all organized military force in Germany, for every literate person will understand that that is not only impossible in regard to Germany, as it is in regard to Russia, but also inadvisable from the point of view of the victor. But Hitler's army can and should be destroyed.

Our second task, in fact, is to destroy Hitler's army and its leaders. The Hitlerite scoundrels have made it a rule to torture Soviet war prisoners, to slay them by the hundreds and to condemn thousands of them to death by starvation. They outrage and slaughter the civilian population of occupied territories of our country, men and women, children and old folk, our brothers and sisters. They have made it their aim to enslave or exterminate the population of the Ukraine, Byelorussia, the Baltic Republics, Moldavia, the Crimea and the Caucasus. Only villains and scoundrels bereft of all honor and fallen to the state of beasts can permit themselves such outrages toward innocent, unarmed people.

But that is not all. They have covered Europe with gallows and concentration camps, have introduced a vile "system of hostages." They shoot and hang absolutely innocent citizens taken as "hostages," because some German beast was prevented from violating women or robbing citizens. They have converted Europe into a prison of nations. And this they call "the new order in Europe."

We know who are the men guilty of these outrages, the builders of "the new order in Europe," all those newly-baked governor generals or just ordinary governors, commandants and subcommandants. Their names are known to tens of thousands of tormented people. Let these butchers know that they will not escape the responsibility for their crimes or elude the avenging hand of the tormented nations.

Our third task is to destroy the hated "new order in Europe," and to punish its builders.

Such are our tasks.

Comrades, we are waging a great war of liberation. We are not waging it alone, but in conjunction with our Allies. It will end in our victory over the vile foes of mankind, over the German-fascist imperialists. On its standard is inscribed: "Hail the victory of the Anglo-Soviet-American fighting alliance! Hail the liberation of the nations of Europe from Hitler's tyranny! Hail the liberty and independence of our glorious Soviet motherland! Execration and death to the German-fascist invaders, to their state, their army, their 'new order in Europe'!"

Glory to our Red Army!

Glory to our Navy!

Glory to our men and women guerrillas!

(4) Address of the Prime Minister of the United Kingdom (Churchill) at the Lord Mayor's Dinner, London, November 10, 1942 [1]

[Excerpt]

In this address, delivered shortly after the beginning of the joint Anglo-American invasion of French North Africa on November 8, Mr. Churchill interpreted that event in words that have now become classic:

"Now, this is not the end. It is not even the beginning to the end. But it is, perhaps, the end of the beginning."

[1] New York Times, November 11, 1942.

A brief survey of the military and political situation in French North Africa was followed by a statement of British policy toward France leading into a statement of Great Britain's broader intentions.

.   .   .   .

For ourselves we have no wish but to see France free and strong, with her empire gathered round her and with Alsace-Lorraine restored. We covet no French possession. We have no acquisitive designs or ambitions in North Africa or any other part of the world. We have not entered this war for profit or expansion but only for honor and to do our duty in defending the right.

Let me, however, make this clear, in case there should be any mistake about it in any quarter: we mean to hold our own. I have not become the King's First Minister in order to preside over the liquidation of the British Empire. For that task, if ever it were prescribed, someone else would have to be found, and under a democracy I suppose the nation would have to be consulted.

I am proud to be a member of that vast commonwealth and society of nations and communities gathered in and around the ancient British monarchy, without which the good cause might well have perished from the face of the earth.

Here we are and here we stand, a veritable rock of salvation in this drifting world. There was a time not long ago when for a whole year we stood all alone. Those days, thank God, have gone.

We now move forward in a great and gallant company. For our record we have nothing to fear. We have no need to make excuses or apologies. Our record pleads for us and we shall get gratitude in the breasts of every man and woman in every part of the world.

As I have said, in this war we have no territorial aims. We desire no commercial favors, we wish to alter no sovereignty or frontier for our own benefit.

We have come into North Africa shoulder to shoulder with our American friends and allies for one purpose and one purpose only. Namely, to gain a vantage ground from which to open a new front against Hitler and Hitlerism, to cleanse the shores of Africa from the stain of Nazi and Fascist tyranny, to open the Mediterranean to Allied sea power and air power, and thus effect the liberation of the peoples of Europe from the pit of misery into which they have been passed by their own improvidence and by the brutal violence of the enemy.

These two African undertakings, in the East and in the West, were part of a single strategic and political conception which we had labored long to bring to fruition and about which we are now justified in entertaining good and reasonable confidence. Taken together they were a grand design, vast in its scope, honorable in its motive and noble in its aim.

British and American forces continue to prosper in the Mediterranean. The whole event will be a new bond between the English-speaking people and a new hope for the whole world.

.   .   .   .

(5) Radio Address of the Prime Minister of the United Kingdom (Churchill), London, March 21, 1943 [1]

[Excerpt]

.   .   .   .

There will certainly be large numbers of men not only abroad but at home who will have to be brought back to their families and to their jobs or to other equally good jobs. For all these, after full provision has been made for the garrisoning of guilty countries, return to something like home and freedom will be their hearts' desire. However vigorously the war against Japan is prosecuted, there will certainly be a partial demobilization following on the defeat of Hitler and this will raise the most difficult and intricate problems, and we are taking care in our arrangements to avoid the mistakes which were so freely committed last time.

Of course, these ideas may be completely falsified by events. It may be that Japan will collapse before Hitler, in which case quite another layout will be necessary. As, however, many people wish ardently to discuss the future, I adopt for this purpose tonight what seems to me the most likely situation.

On this assumption, it would be our hope that the United Nations, headed by three great victorious powers, the British Commonwealth of Nations, the United States and Soviet Russia, should immediately begin to confer upon the future world organization, which is to be our safeguard against further wars, by effectually disarming and keeping disarmed the guilty states, by bringing to justice the grand criminals and their accomplices, and by securing the return to devastated and subjugated countries of mechanical resources and artistic treasures of which they have been pillaged.

We shall also have a heavy task in trying to avert widespread famine in some, at least, of the ruined regions. We must hope and pray that unity of the three leading victorious powers will be worthy of their supreme responsibility and that they will think not only of their own welfare but of the welfare and future of all. One can imagine that under a world institution embodying or representing the United Nations, and some day all the nations, there should come into being a Council of Europe and a Council of Asia.

[1] *Christian Science Monitor*, March 22, 1943.

As according to the forecast I am outlining, the war against Japan will still be raging, it is upon the creation of the Council of Europe and the settlement of Europe that the first practical task will be centered. Now this is stupendous business. In Europe lie most of the causes which have led to these two world wars. In Europe dwell historic parent races from whom our western civilization has been so largely derived. I believe myself to be what is called a good European and I should deem it a noble task to take part in reviving and restoring the fertile genius and true greatness of Europe.

I hope we shall not lightly cast aside all the immense work which was accomplished by the creation of the League of Nations. Certainly we must take as our foundation of the lofty conception of freedom the law and morality which was the spirit of the League. We must try — I am speaking of course only for ourselves — to make the Council of Europe, or whatever it may be called, into a really effective league with all strongest forces concerned woven into its texture, with a high court to adjust disputes and with forces, armed forces, national or international or both, held ready to enforce these decisions and prevent renewed aggression and preparation of future wars.

Anyone can see that this council, when created, must eventually embrace the whole of Europe and that all the main branches of the European family must some day be partners in it. What is to happen to the large number of small nations whose rights and interests must be safeguarded? Here let me ask what would be thought of an army that consisted only of battalions and brigades and which never formed any of the larger and higher organizations like army corps? It would soon get mopped up.

It would, therefore, seem to me at any rate worthy of patient study that side by side with the great powers there should be a number of groupings of states or confederations which would express themselves through their own chosen representatives, the whole making a council of great states and groups of states.

It is my earnest hope, though I can hardly expect to see it fulfilled in my lifetime, that we shall achieve the largest common measure of the integrated life of Europe that is possible without destroying the individual characteristics and traditions of its many ancient and historic races. All this will, I believe, be found to harmonize with the high permanent interests of Britain, the United States and Russia. It certainly cannot be accomplished without their cordial and concerted agreement and direct participation. Thus and thus only will the glory of Europe rise again.

This does not mean that many tentative discussions are not taking place between the great nations concerned or that the whole vast problem of European destiny — for that is what I am speaking of now — is not a subject of ceaseless heart-searchings.

We must remember, however, that we in Britain and the British Commonwealth of Nations, although almost a world in ourselves, will have to reach agreements with great and friendly equals and also to respect and have care for the rights of weaker and smaller states, and that it will not be given to any one nation to achieve full satisfaction of its individual wishes.

.   .   .   .

The emphasis placed by Mr. Churchill in this address on the primary responsibility resting on the United Kingdom, Soviet Russia and the United States to guide the post-war world drew a protest from Dr. E. N. Van Kleffens, the Foreign Minister of the Netherlands, one of the small powers most ready to challenge an assumption of special prerogatives by the so-called great powers. When questioned on the issue at his press conference of March 25, Secretary of State Hull refused to commit himself. He said the Atlantic Charter spoke clearly on the issue raised.[1]

B. Supplementary Agreements between All or Certain of the United Nations

[For agreements in connection with Lend-Lease operations, see *Documents, IV, 1941-42*, p. 235; this volume, p. 217.]

(1) *Declaration of Certain of the United Nations Regarding Forced Transfers of Property in Enemy-Controlled Territory, January 5, 1943* [2]

The Union of South Africa, the United States of America, Australia, Belgium, Canada, China, the Czechoslovak Republic, the United Kingdom of Great Britain and Northern Ireland, the Union of Soviet Socialist Republics, Greece, India, Luxemburg, the Netherlands, New Zealand, Norway, Poland, Yugoslavia and the French National Committee:

Hereby issue a formal warning to all concerned, and in particular to persons in neutral countries, that they intend to do their utmost to defeat the methods of dispossession practiced by the governments with which they are at war against the countries and peoples who have been so wantonly assaulted and despoiled.

Accordingly the governments making this declaration and the French National Committee reserve all their rights to declare invalid any transfers of, or dealings with, property, rights and interests of any description whatsoever which are, or have been, situated in the territories which have come under the occupation or control, direct or indirect, of the governments with which they are at war or which belong or have belonged, to persons, including juridical persons, resident in such territories. This warning applies whether such transfers or dealings have taken the form

[1] *New York Times*, March 26, 1943.
[2] Department of State, *Bulletin*, VIII, p. 21.

of open looting or plunder, or of transactions apparently legal in form, even when they purport to be voluntarily effected.

The governments making this declaration and the French National Committee solemnly record their solidarity in this matter.

(2) *Casablanca Agreement on "Unconditional Surrender" Terms. Address of the President (Roosevelt) before The White House Correspondents' Association, Washington, D. C., February 12, 1943* [1]

[Excerpt]

In a press conference, at the close of the Casablanca Conference (see p. 254), the President, borrowing a phrase from a letter of General Grant to the Confederate commander of Forts Henry and Donelson during the American Civil War, called the meeting the "Unconditional Surrender" conference, and declared that with this end in view, plans were laid for the complete military defeat of the Axis powers. It was stated in the official communiqué that Premier Stalin had been fully informed of the military proposals.[2]

· · · · · · ·

In an attempt to ward off the inevitable disaster, the Axis propagandists are trying all of their old tricks in order to divide the United Nations. They seek to create the idea that if we win this war, Russia, England, China and the United States are going to get into a cat-and-dog fight.

This is their final effort to turn one nation against another, in the vain hope that they may settle with one or two at a time — that any of us may be so gullible and so forgetful as to be duped into making "deals" at the expense of our Allies.

To these panicky attempts to escape the consequences of their crimes we say — all the United Nations say — that the only terms on which we shall deal with any Axis government or any Axis factions are the terms proclaimed at Casablanca: "Unconditional Surrender." In our uncompromising policy we mean no harm to the common people of the Axis nations. But we do mean to impose punishment and retribution in full upon their guilty, barbaric leaders.

· · · · · ·

(a) *Order of the Day of the Supreme Commander-in-Chief, Marshal of the Soviet Union (Stalin), May 1, 1943* [3]

[Excerpt]

This statement is given here because of the light it throws on Stalin's attitude toward the Casablanca formula.

· · · · · ·

[1] *Ibid.*, p. 145.   [2] See this volume, p. 251.
[3] Embassy of the Union of Soviet Socialist Republics, *Information Bulletin*, No. 47, May 4, 1943, p. 1.

Secondly, the crisis in the Fascist camp finds expression in that the Fascists begin to speak more frequently about peace. To judge by the reports of the foreign press, one can arrive at the conclusion that the Germans would wish to obtain peace with Britain and the U.S.A. on the condition that the latter two draw away from the Soviet Union, or on the contrary, they would wish to obtain peace with the Soviet Union under the condition that it draw away from Britain and the U.S.A. Themselves treacherous to the marrow, the German imperialists have the nerve to apply their own yardstick to the Allies, expecting some one of the Allies to swallow the bait.

Obviously it is not from fine living that the Germans babble about peace. The babble about peace in the Fascist camp only indicates that they are going through a grave crisis.

But of what kind of peace can one talk with the imperialist bandits from the German-Fascist camp who have flooded Europe with blood and studded it with gallows? Is it not clear that only the utter routing of the Hitlerite armies and the unconditional surrender of Hitlerite Germany can bring peace to Europe? Is it not because the German Fascists sense the coming catastrophe that they babble about peace? The German-Italian Fascist camp is experiencing a grave crisis and faces catastrophe.

* * * * * * * *

C. Adherences to the Declaration by United Nations

(1) *Adherence of Ethiopia. White House Press Release, October 9, 1942* [1]

The adherence of Ethiopia to the Declaration by United Nations preceded by nearly two months the actual declaration of war by Ethiopia against the principal of the Axis powers. On December 1, the Emperor proclaimed that a state of war existed between the Government of Ethiopia and the Governments of Italy, Germany, and Japan.[2]

The President has received the following cablegram from Haile Selassie, Emperor of Ethiopia:

"My Government and people are anxious to assume the obligations of the United Nations pact. We, the first nation to regain its freedom and independence, wish to place the military and economic resources of our country at the disposal of those nations who gladly sacrifice all for liberty and justice."

The President replied as follows:

"I have received Your Majesty's telegram stating that your Government and people are anxious to assume the obligations of the Declaration by United Nations and that Ethiopia desires to place its military and economic resources at the disposal of the nations which gladly sacrifice all for liberty and justice.

"It is gratifying to accept the adherence of Ethiopia to the Declaration by United Nations; to welcome as one of the United Nations the first state to regain its territory after temporary occupation by an Axis

[1] Department of State, *Bulletin*, VII, p. 805.   [2] *Ibid.*, p. 1009.

aggressor. You may be sure that there is deep appreciation for your offer to place at the disposal of the United Nations the military and economic resources of Ethiopia for use in the struggle against the common enemy."

(2) Adherence of Iraq. Exchange of Communications between the Minister of Iraq (Jawdat) and the Secretary of State (Hull) [1]

The Government of Iraq declared war against Germany, Italy and Japan to take effect as from midnight on January 16–17, 1943.[2]

(a) The Minister of Iraq (Jawdat) to the Secretary of State (Hull), January 16, 1943

SIR:

Now that my Government has been compelled, in defense of the national integrity of Iraq, to declare that there exists a state of war between Iraq on the one hand and Germany, Italy and Japan on the other, it considers that the time has come to subscribe more concretely to the common program of purposes and principles embodied in the Atlantic Charter. Those purposes and principles coincide with the aspirations of the people of Iraq. At this time when the greater part of the civilized world is striving for liberty and independence, Iraq desires to make its contribution in the struggle against the common enemy. My country thus takes pride in associating itself with the United Nations which are battling for liberty and the preservation of civilization.

I have the honor to inform you that in accordance with instructions received from my Government, Iraq formally adheres, by means of this communication, to the Declaration by United Nations, dated January 1, 1942.

I take [etc.]

(b) The Secretary of State (Hull) to the Minister of Iraq (Jawdat), January 22, 1943

SIR:

I have the honor to acknowledge the receipt of your note of January 16, 1943, stating that as your Government has been compelled, in defense of the national integrity of Iraq, to declare the existence of a state of war with Germany, Italy, and Japan, it desires to subscribe more concretely to the purposes and principles embodied in the Atlantic Charter; that those purposes and principles coincide with the aspirations of the people of Iraq; that Iraq desires to make its contribution in the struggle against the common enemy; and that accordingly Iraq formally adheres to the Declaration by United Nations.

[1] *Ibid.*, VIII, p. 83.   [2] *Ibid.*, p. 42.

It is very gratifying that Iraq is taking a position at the side of the freedom-loving nations which have pledged themselves to employ their full resources in the struggle against the powers seeking to dominate the world. On behalf of the Government of the United States, as depository for the Declaration, I take great pleasure in welcoming Iraq into the ranks of the United Nations.

Accept [etc.]

(3) Adherence of Brazil. Exchange of Communications between the Brazilian Ambassador (Souza) and the Acting Secretary of State (Welles) [1]

Following the sinking of five Brazilian vessels by presumably Axis submarines, the Government of Brazil declared war against Germany, Italy and Japan on August 22, 1942.[2]

(a) The Brazilian Ambassador (Souza) to the Acting Secretary of State (Welles), February 8, 1943

MR. SECRETARY:

I have the honor to communicate to Your Excellency in compliance with instructions received from my Government that by act of the 6th of this month Brazil declares its formal adherence to the Declaration of the United Nations and to the Atlantic Charter, to which the said Declaration refers.

In conveying the advice to Your Excellency of this decision of the Brazilian Government, and also in accordance with the above instructions, I should very much appreciate the favor of your good offices to the end that the same be transmitted to the other signatory nations of the foregoing Declaration.

I take [etc.]

(b) The Acting Secretary of State (Welles) to the Brazilian Ambassador (Souza), February 20, 1943

EXCELLENCY:

I have the honor to acknowledge the receipt of your note of February 8, 1943 stating that on February 6 Brazil declared its formal adherence to the Declaration by United Nations, and to the Atlantic Charter to which the Declaration refers.

There is genuine satisfaction that Brazil has formally associated itself with the other United Nations which have subscribed to the principles of the Atlantic Charter and have pledged themselves to employ their full resources in the common struggle against the brutal forces seeking to

[1] *Ibid.*, p. 208. [2] *Ibid.*, p. 710.

subjugate the world. The Government of the United States, as depository for the Declaration, is indeed gratified to welcome Brazil into the ranks of the United Nations.

In accordance with your request, this Government will transmit to the other United Nations the notice of Brazil's adherence to the Declaration. Accept [etc.]

(4) *Adherence of Bolivia. Exchange of Telegrams between the Minister of Foreign Affairs of Bolivia (Elio) and the Secretary of State (Hull)* [1]

(a) *The Minister of Foreign Affairs of Bolivia (Elio) to the Secretary of State (Hull), April 27, 1943*

In harmony with the decree issued by my Government on the 7th day of the current month and year declaring a state of war between Bolivia and the nations of the Axis, a decision adopted to safeguard the national sovereignty and integrity my Government considers that the time has come to contribute in a more complete manner to the program of purposes and principles of the Atlantic Charter, purposes and principles which coincide with the aspirations and sentiments of the Bolivian people. In this hour when the greater part of the civilized world is fighting for its liberty and its independence Bolivia desires to increase its efforts in the struggle against those who do not recognize right and aim at rule by force and violence. My country feels proud thus to associate itself with the United Nations in their sacrifices for liberty and for the preservation of civilization from the dangers which threaten it because of the action of the anti-democratic systems. I therefore have the honor to inform Your Excellency that in accordance with instructions received from my Government Bolivia formally adheres by means of this communication to the declaration of the United Nations bearing date of January 1, 1942.

I repeat [etc.]

(b) *The Secretary of State (Hull) to the Minister of Foreign Affairs of Bolivia (Elio), April 30, 1943*

I have received your telegram of April 27, 1943, stating that in harmony with the Bolivian Government's decree of April 7 declaring a state of war between Bolivia and the Axis nations, the Bolivian Government considers that the time has come to contribute more completely to the program of purposes and principles of the Atlantic Charter; that now when the greater part of the civilized world is fighting for liberty and independence, Bolivia desires to increase its efforts in the struggle; and

[1] *Ibid.*, p. 374.

that accordingly Bolivia formally adheres to the Declaration by United Nations of January 1, 1942.

It is a source of genuine satisfaction for the Government of the United States, as depository for the Declaration, to welcome Bolivia as one of the United Nations; to see Bolivia thus associated with thirty-one other freedom-loving nations which have pledged themselves to employ their full resources in the struggle against the common enemies.

Please accept [etc.]

D. United Nations and Associated Nations

(1) *List of United Nations and Associated Nations, as of June 30, 1943*

The distinction between United Nations and Associated Nations was made by the Department of State in announcing the list of nations that had received invitations to attend the United Nations Conference on Food and Agriculture [1] and in announcing the submission to certain foreign governments of a draft agreement for a United Nations Relief and Rehabilitation Administration.[2]

Included in the category of United Nations are those nations which have declared war on one or more of the Axis powers and have also formally adhered to the Declaration by United Nations. Apparently included in the category of Associated Nations, are those nations, principally certain of the Latin American Republics, which have at least severed relations with one or more of the Axis powers, which have accepted, explicitly or implicitly, the basic principles for which the United Nations are fighting, and which have been accepted as associates by the principal United Nations.

It would appear that inclusion in the United Nations dates from the time of formal adherence to the Declaration by United Nations and not from the date of declaration of war.[3]

UNITED NATIONS

Original Signatories of Declaration by United Nations, January 1, 1942:

Australia	India
Belgium	Luxemburg
Canada	Netherlands
China	New Zealand
Costa Rica	Nicaragua
Cuba	Norway
Czechoslovakia	Panama
Dominican Republic	Poland
El Salvador	Union of South Africa
Greece	Union of Soviet Socialist Republics
Guatemala	United Kingdom
Haiti	United States
Honduras	Yugoslavia

[1] *Ibid.*, p. 298. [2] *Ibid.*, p. 523.
[3] *Ibid.*, p. 298. Bolivia had, at the time the invitation to attend the United Nations Conference on Food and Agriculture was extended, declared war but not formally adhered to the Declaration.

Nations That Subsequently Adhered to Declaration by United Nations:

Bolivia	April 27, 1943
Brazil	February 6, 1943
Ethiopia	October 9, 1942
Iraq	January 16, 1943
Mexico	June 5, 1942
Philippine Commonwealth	June 10, 1942

ASSOCIATED NATIONS

Chile	Liberia
Colombia	Paraguay
Ecuador	Peru [1]
Egypt	Uruguay
Iceland	Venezuela
Iran	

2. PROSECUTION OF THE WAR

A. Lend-Lease

[See *Documents, III, 1940–41*, p. 711; *IV, 1941–42*, p. 169, 225.]

Documents and exhibits bearing on the more definitely national aspects of Lend-Lease, including the extension of the Lend-Lease Act for a one-year period, are given in Chapter II, p. 105. The documents and exhibits presented below relate more exclusively to the relations of the United States with foreign nations. While Lend-Lease is to be regarded as an instrument for the prosecution of the war, it has been made abundantly clear that it is also regarded as an instrument for creating a better world. The Lend-Lease agreements entered into with foreign countries contain provisions bearing definitely on problems of the post-war period.

1. SITUATION AS REGARDS COUNTRIES ELIGIBLE FOR LEND–LEASE ASSISTANCE AND AGREEMENTS REACHED

[1] By telegram of February 8, 1943 to Secretary of State Hull the Government of Peru "affirmed its adherence to the principles of the Atlantic Charter." (*Ibid.*, p. 154.)

(1) *Status of Nations — Lend-Lease Countries and United Nations, as of June 30, 1943* [1]

Country	Declared Eligible for Lend-Lease Aid	Lend-Lease Agreement Signed	Reciprocal Lend-Lease Agreement Signed	United Nations Declaration Signed
Argentina	May 6, 1941	—	—	
Australia	Nov. 11, 1941	Feb. 23, 1942	Sept. 3, 1942	Jan. 1, 1942
Belgium	Jun. 13, 1941	Jun. 16, 1942	Jan. 30, 1943	"
Bolivia	May 6, 1941	Dec. 6, 1941	—	Apr. 27, 1943
Brazil	"	Mar. 3, 1942	—	Feb. 6, 1943
Canada	Nov. 11, 1941		—	Jan. 1, 1942
Chile	May 6, 1941	Mar. 2, 1943	—	
China	"	Jun. 2, 1942	—	Jan. 1, 1942
Colombia	"	Mar. 17, 1942		
Costa Rica	"	Jan. 16, 1942	—	Jan. 1, 1942
Cuba	"	Nov. 7, 1941	—	"
Czechoslovakia	Jan. 5, 1942	Jul. 11, 1942	—	"
Dominican Rep.	May 6, 1941	Aug. 2, 1941	—	"
Ecuador	"	Apr. 6, 1942	—	—
Egypt	Nov. 11, 1941	—	—	—
El Salvador	May 6, 1941	Feb. 2, 1942	—	Jan. 1, 1942
Ethiopia	Dec. 7, 1942	—	—	Oct. 9, 1942
Fighting France	Nov. 11, 1941	—	Sept. 3, 1942	—
French North and West Africa	Nov. 13, 1942	—	—	—
Greece	Mar. 11, 1941	Jul. 10, 1942	—	Jan. 1, 1942
Guatemala	May 6, 1941	Nov. 16, 1942	—	"
Haiti	"	Sept. 16, 1941	—	"
Honduras	"	Feb. 28, 1942	—	"
Iceland	Jul. 1, 1941	Nov. 21, 1941		
India	Nov. 11, 1941	—	—	Jan. 1, 1942
Iran	Mar. 10, 1942	—	—	
Iraq	May 1, 1942	—	—	Jan. 16, 1943
Liberia	Mar. 10, 1942	Jun. 8, 1943	—	
Luxemburg	—	—	—	Jan. 1, 1942
Mexico	May 6, 1941	Mar. 18, 1943	—	Jun. 5, 1942
Netherlands	Aug. 21, 1941	Jul. 8, 1942	Jun. 14, 1943	Jan. 1, 1942
New Zealand	Nov. 11, 1941	Feb. 23, 1941	Sept. 3, 1942	"
Nicaragua	May 6, 1941	Oct. 16, 1941	—	"
Norway	Jun. 4, 1941	Jul. 11, 1942	—	"
Panama	May 6, 1941		—	"
Paraguay	"	Sept. 20, 1941	—	—
Peru	"	Mar. 11, 1942	—	
Philippines	—	—	—	Jun. 10, 1942
Poland	Aug. 28, 1941	Jul. 1, 1942	—	Jan. 1, 1942
Saudi Arabia	Feb. 18, 1943	—	—	
South Africa	Nov. 11, 1941	—	—	Jan. 1, 1942
Turkey	Nov. 7, 1941	—	—	
United Kingdom	Mar. 11, 1941	Feb. 23, 1942	Sept. 3, 1942	Jan. 1, 1942
United States	—			"
U.S.S.R.	Nov. 7, 1941	Jun. 11, 1942	—	"
Uruguay	May 6, 1941	Jan. 13, 1942	—	—
Venezuela	"	Mar. 18, 1942	—	
Yugoslavia	Nov. 11, 1941	Jul. 24, 1942	—	Jan. 1, 1942

[1] *Eleventh Report to Congress on Lend-Lease Operations for the Period Ended July 31, 1943*, p. 41.

2. AGREEMENTS FOR MUTUAL AID PURSUANT TO THE LEND-LEASE ACT OF MARCH 11, 1941

(1) *Agreement between the Governments of the United States and Poland, Signed July 1, 1942* [1]

The text of the agreement followed in all substantial respects the text of the agreement signed with the Government of the United Kingdom, signed February 23, 1942,[2] with an additional paragraph inserted in the preamble registering acceptance of the purposes and principles of the Atlantic Charter. For the convenience of the users of this volume, the full text is given below.

Whereas the Governments of the United States of America and Poland declare that they are engaged in a cooperative undertaking, together with every other nation or people of like mind, to the end of laying the bases of a just and enduring world peace securing order under law to themselves and all nations;

And whereas the Governments of the United States of America and Poland, as signatories of the Declaration by United Nations of January 1, 1942, have subscribed to a common program of purposes and principles embodied in the Joint Declaration made on August 14, 1941 by the President of the United States of America and the Prime Minister of the United Kingdom of Great Britain and Northern Ireland, known as the Atlantic Charter;

And whereas the President of the United States of America has determined, pursuant to the Act of Congress of March 11, 1941, that the defense of Poland against aggression is vital to the defense of the United States of America;

And whereas the United States of America has extended and is continuing to extend to Poland aid in resisting aggression;

And whereas it is expedient that the final determination of the terms and conditions upon which the Government of Poland receives such aid and of the benefits to be received by the United States of America in return therefor should be deferred until the extent of the defense aid is known and until the progress of events makes clearer the final terms and conditions and benefits which will be in the mutual interests of the United States of America and Poland and will promote the establishment and maintenance of world peace;

And whereas the Governments of the United States of America and Poland are mutually desirous of concluding now a preliminary agreement in regard to the provision of defense aid and in regard to certain considerations which shall be taken into account in determining such terms and conditions and the making of such an agreement has been in all respects duly authorized, and all acts, conditions and formalities which it may have been necessary to perform, fulfill or execute prior to the mak-

[1] Department of State, *Bulletin*, VII, p. 577; *Executive Agreement Series* 257.
[2] *Documents, IV, 1941–42*, p. 235.

ing of such an agreement in conformity with the laws either of the United States of America or of Poland have been performed, fulfilled or executed as required;

The undersigned, being duly authorized by their respective Governments for that purpose, have agreed as follows:

ARTICLE I. The Government of the United States of America will continue to supply the Government of Poland with such defense articles, defense services, and defense information as the President of the United States of America shall authorize to be transferred or provided.

ARTICLE II. The Government of Poland will continue to contribute to the defense of the United States of America and the strengthening thereof and will provide such articles, services, facilities or information as it may be in a position to supply.

ARTICLE III. The Government of Poland will not without the consent of the President of the United States of America transfer title to, or possession of, any defense article or defense information transferred to it under the Act of March 11, 1941 of the Congress of the United States of America or permit the use thereof by anyone not an officer, employee, or agent of the Government of Poland.

ARTICLE IV. If, as a result of the transfer to the Government of Poland of any defense article or defense information, it becomes necessary for that Government to take any action or make any payment in order fully to protect any of the rights of a citizen of the United States of America who has patent rights in and to any such defense article or information, the Government of Poland will take such action or make such payment when requested to do so by the President of the United States of America.

ARTICLE V. The Government of Poland will return to the United States of America at the end of the present emergency, as determined by the President of the United States of America, such defense articles transferred under this Agreement as shall not have been destroyed, lost or consumed and as shall be determined by the President to be useful in the defense of the United States of America or of the Western Hemisphere or to be otherwise of use to the United States of America.

ARTICLE VI. In the final determination of the benefits to be provided to the United States of America by the Government of Poland full cognizance shall be taken of all property, services, information, facilities, or other benefits or considerations provided by the Government of Poland subsequent to March 11, 1941, and accepted or acknowledged by the President on behalf of the United States of America.

ARTICLE VII. In the final determination of the benefits to be provided to the United States of America by the Government of Poland in return for aid furnished under the Act of Congress of March 11, 1941, the terms and conditions thereof shall be such as not to burden commerce between the two countries, but to promote mutually advantageous economic relations between them and the betterment of world-wide economic relations. To that end, they shall include provision for agreed action by the United States of America and Poland, open to participation by all other countries of like mind, directed to the expansion, by appropriate international and domestic measures, of production, employment, and the exchange and consumption of goods, which are the material foundations of the liberty and welfare of all peoples; to the elimination of all forms of discriminatory treatment in international commerce, and to the reduction of tariffs and other trade barriers; and, in general, to the attainment of all the economic objectives set forth in the Joint Declaration made on August 14, 1941, by the President of the United States of America and the Prime Minister of the United Kingdom.

At an early convenient date, conversations shall be begun between the two Governments with a view to determining, in the light of governing economic conditions, the best means of attaining the above-stated objectives by their own agreed action and of seeking the agreed action of other like-minded Governments.

ARTICLE VIII. This Agreement shall take effect as from this day's date. It shall continue in force until a date to be agreed upon by the two Governments.

Signed and sealed at Washington in duplicate this first day of July, 1942.

FOR THE GOVERNMENT OF THE UNITED STATES OF AMERICA:

CORDELL HULL
Secretary of State of the
United States of America

FOR THE GOVERNMENT OF POLAND:

JAN CIECHANOWSKI
Ambassador of Poland
at Washington

———

During the period under review, agreements containing substantially the same provisions have been signed with the following governments: The Netherlands, July 8, 1942;[1] Greece, July 10, 1942;[2] Czechoslovakia, July 11, 1942;[3] Norway, July 11, 1942;[4] Yugoslavia, July 24, 1942;[5] Liberia, June 8, 1943.[6] The agreements with the Governments of Norway and Liberia were subject to certain supplementary understandings which are recorded below.

In addition, two supplementary agreements were entered into with the Government of the United Kingdom relating to specific technical problems which arose in connection with the carrying out of the agreement of February 23, 1942.[7]

[1] Department of State, *Bulletin*, VII, p. 604; *Executive Agreement Series* 259.
[2] *Ibid.*, p. 602; *E.A.S.* 260.   [3] *Ibid.*, p. 607; *E.A.S.* 261.
[4] *Ibid.*, p. 609; *E.A.S.* 262.   [5] *Ibid.*, p. 647; *E.A.S.* 263.
[6] *Ibid.*, VIII, p. 515; *E.A.S.* 324.
[7] For text of this agreement, see *Documents, IV, 1941-42*, p. 235.

3. AGREEMENTS SUPPLEMENTARY TO MASTER AGREEMENTS

(1) *Interchange of Patent Rights, Information, Inventions, Designs, or Processes. Agreement between the Governments of the United States of America and the United Kingdom, Signed at Washington, August 24, 1942* [1]

The Government of the United States of America and the Government of the United Kingdom of Great Britain and Northern Ireland, in further fulfillment of the policy set forth in their agreement of February 23, 1942 on the principles applying to mutual aid in the prosecution of the war against aggression,[2] have considered the interchange of patent rights, information, and similar matters, and have authorized their representatives to agree as follows:

ARTICLE I. Each Government, in so far as it may lawfully do so, will procure and make available to the other Government for use in war production patent rights, information, inventions, designs, or processes requested by the other Government. In the case of the United States of America, the law authorizing such procurement and transfer is now the Act of the Congress of the United States approved March 11, 1941 (Public 11, 77th Congress).[3] Each Government will bear the cost of the procurement of such patent rights, information, inventions, designs, or processes from its own nationals. In this Agreement the term "nationals" shall include all corporations and natural persons domiciled, resident, or otherwise within the jurisdiction of the Government concerned (as well as the Government itself and all of its agencies), except natural persons who are exclusively citizens or subjects of the country of the other Government. The basic principle as to which Government shall undertake and bear the cost of procurement in doubtful cases shall be decided in accordance with whether dollar or sterling costs are necessarily involved. In the former case the Government of the United States of America will effect acquisition and in the latter case the Government of the United Kingdom will effect acquisition, but each Government will pay the remuneration and other expenses of its own representatives incurred in connection with communicating any research or manufacturing information to the other Government.

ARTICLE II. All patent rights so acquired shall be acquired and used for the purposes of, and until the termination of, the war only, unless otherwise expressly provided, except that contracts entered into (for the production, use or disposition of articles) which cannot be terminated without penalty, may be completed, and all articles on hand at the termination of the war, or completed as permitted herein, may be used

---

[1] *Executive Agreement Series* 268.
[2] *Ibid.*, 241; *Documents, IV, 1941–42*, p. 235.
[3] 55 Stat. 31 (Lend Lease Act); see *Documents, III, 1940–41*, p. 712.

and disposed of. Information, inventions, designs, or processes so acquired and not covered by patents or patent applications shall be acquired upon such terms as may most expeditiously make such information, inventions, designs, or processes available for the purposes of the war, with provision, to the extent practicable, for the limitation of the use thereof for the purposes of and until the termination of the war. When the information, invention, design, or process is of a category for which the other Government requests secrecy upon security grounds, each Government will take such steps as it deems practicable to ensure the appropriate degree of secrecy in manufacture and use. The term "termination of the war," for the purposes of this Agreement, shall mean the date when the Government of the United States of America and the Government of the United Kingdom have ceased to be jointly engaged in actual hostilities against a common enemy, or such other date as may be mutually agreed upon, and shall not be dependent on the date of the signing of a peace treaty.

ARTICLE III. Such acquisition by the Government of the United States of America will be effected in accordance with regular Lend-Lease procedure (or its then current equivalent) and will be financed under such program, except that other procedure may be used in those instances where no expenditure of funds is necessary.

ARTICLE IV. Such acquisition by the Government of the United Kingdom will be effected on the basis of written requests submitted by any authorized department or agency of the Government of the United States of America to the British Supply Council (or to such other agency of the Government of the United Kingdom as may be designated from time to time). Copies of all such requests will be furnished to the Office of Lend-Lease Administration. The British Supply Council will furnish to that Office reports as to all patent rights, information, inventions, designs, or processes obtained and transferred to the agency requesting the same and the acquisition cost thereof, if any.

ARTICLE V. In so far as is found practicable in the circumstances of each case, adequate licenses or assignments and contract rights shall be acquired by each Government, in accordance with the requests of the other Government, and transferred to the other Government. Where desirable each Government will sponsor necessary relationships and permit dealings between the original grantor and the ultimate user. It is contemplated that normally the rights obtained should, subject to the limitations contained in Article II of this Agreement, among other things, include:

(a) The right to make, to have made, to use, and to dispose of, articles embodying the subject-matter of the patent rights, information, inventions, designs, or processes, so acquired, including the right to use and practice any of the aforesaid.

(b) Provision for securing to the recipient Government or its designees all necessary personal expert services and supplementary information.

(c) Permission to transfer, assign, license, or otherwise dispose of, any or all of the rights and privileges acquired, to the other Government, with further permission to the latter to transfer, assign, license, or otherwise dispose of any or all of the same to contractors, sub-contractors, or other appropriate designees of the recipient Government, for war production purposes only.

(d) The reservation on the part of the acquiring Government that it, and parties in interest holding under it, shall have the right at any time to contest the validity of any patent rights acquired.

(e) Whenever practicable, a guarantee by the licensor or patentee as to the validity of his patent, in respect of which the license is granted, with an indemnity against any infringement claims.

(f) Provision for the exchange of information, between the licensor or patentee and ultimate licensee, as to improvements or the results of research on the subject-matter of the license, together with the use of any patents which may be obtained in respect of such improvements, with a further provision that the like information and right to use additional patents shall simultaneously be furnished to both Governments.

ARTICLE VI. Subject to the provisos set out in Article VII hereunder, the Government of the United Kingdom agrees and undertakes to indemnify and save harmless the Government of the United States of America against all claims asserted by corporations or subjects of the United Kingdom arising as a result of the use and practice of any patent rights, inventions, information, designs, or processes furnished by the Government of the United Kingdom to the Government of the United States of America and used by the latter Government pursuant to the provisions of Article II of this Agreement, or arising as a result of production, use, or disposition, by or on behalf of the Government of the United States of America, of articles:

(a) Supplied to the Government of the United Kingdom under Lend-Lease or equivalent procedure; or

(b) Embodying the subject-matter of patent rights, information, inventions, designs, or processes furnished (or which purport to have been furnished) by the Government of the United Kingdom to the Government of the United States of America and used by the Government of the United States of America pursuant to the provisions of Article II of this Agreement; or

(c) So produced, used, or disposed of, pursuant to a request made or authority given by the Government of the United Kingdom to the Government of the United States of America;

provided always that the Government of the United States of America will, whenever in its judgment practicable, avail itself of any indemnity from a third party of which it shall have the benefit, in lieu of the indemnity from the Government of the United Kingdom contained in this Agreement. The Government of the United Kingdom will not look to the Government of the United States of America for any corresponding indemnity against claims asserted by nationals of the United States in the United Kingdom.

ARTICLE VII. The indemnity by the Government of the United Kingdom to the Government of the United States of America shall be subject to the following conditions, namely:

(a) That the Government of the United States of America, as soon as practicable after receiving notice of any claim by which a liability might fall upon the Government of the United Kingdom under the indemnity, will notify the Government of the United Kingdom of such claim having been made.

(b) That the Government of the United States of America will not make any compromise or settlement out of court with any such claimant, without the prior knowledge and concurrence of the Government of the United Kingdom.

(c) That, in all cases in which no prior compromise or settlement of a claim shall have been made, as in paragraph (b) of this Article, and the claim becomes the subject of legal proceedings in the United States Court of Claims, or other appropriate United States Court, the Government of the United Kingdom will (if it shall so request) be permitted to assist the Government of the United States of America in defending any such proceedings.

ARTICLE VIII. The Government of the United Kingdom shall not be liable in respect of claims asserted by nationals of the United States of America in the United States as a result of the use and practice of any patent rights, information, inventions, designs, or processes, or as a result of production, use, or disposition of articles embodying the subject-matter of any of the aforesaid.

ARTICLE IX. In order to avoid conflict with the understanding contained in this Agreement, departments or agencies of the Government of the United States of America which negotiate contracts for production in the United States pursuant to specifications furnished by or on behalf of the Government of the United Kingdom, will not require contractors in the United States to give indemnities to the Government of the United States of America which would be likely to result in efforts by the contractors to obtain an offsetting indemnity from the Government of the United Kingdom; the Government of the United Kingdom assumes a reciprocal obligation toward the Government of the United States of America.

ARTICLE X. Anything contained in this Agreement to the contrary notwithstanding, any obligations heretofore or hereafter undertaken by the Government of the United Kingdom pursuant to the provisions of Section 7 of the Act of the Congress of the United States approved March 11, 1941 (Public 11, 77th Congress), as such obligations may be interpreted by the President of the United States of America or by a United States court of competent jurisdiction, shall be performed by the Government of the United Kingdom.

ARTICLE XI. All payments made by the Government of the United States of America and the Government of the United Kingdom, respectively, in carrying out the terms of this Agreement shall be accounted for by the appropriate agencies of the two Governments as aid extended and benefits received by the Government of the United States of America in accordance with the Act of the Congress of the United States approved March 11, 1941 (Public 11, 77th Congress) and the agreement between the two Governments entered into at Washington on February 23, 1942.

ARTICLE XII. Each Government will give to the other Government all possible information and other assistance required in connection with computing any payments to be made to nationals of the other Government with respect to the use of their patent rights, information, inventions, designs or processes.

ARTICLE XIII. A joint committee of representatives of the Government of the United States of America and of the Government of the United Kingdom shall be established for the purpose of dealing with problems arising in connection with operations under this Agreement and of making appropriate recommendations to proper authorities with respect thereto.

ARTICLE XIV. License agreements, or other contractual obligations between nationals of the United States of America on the one hand and nationals of the United Kingdom on the other hand, existing on January 1, 1942, and continuing in effect, or any claim for royalty arising thereunder, shall not be deemed to be within the scope of this Agreement.

ARTICLE XV. This agreement shall be deemed to have been in effect and operation as from January 1, 1942. Each Government shall have the option to terminate this Agreement as from any date specified in a notice given by the Government exercising such option to the other Government, which date shall be not less than six months from the giving of such notice, and the provisions of this Agreement shall cease to be effective from the date so specified, but without prejudice to any liability which may then already have been incurred, or which may thereafter arise, pursuant to any obligations undertaken by either Government by virtue of this Agreement.

Signed and sealed in duplicate at Washington this twenty-fourth day of August, 1942.

FOR THE GOVERNMENT OF THE UNITED STATES OF AMERICA:

CORDELL HULL   [SEAL]
Secretary of State of the
United States of America

FOR THE GOVERNMENT OF THE UNITED KINGDOM OF GREAT BRITAIN AND NORTHERN IRELAND:

HALIFAX   [SEAL]
His Majesty's Ambassador Ex-
traordinary and Plenipoten-
tiary at Washington

(2) *Certain Problems of Marine Transportation and Litigation. Agreement between the United States of America and the United Kingdom, Signed at London, December 4, 1942, and Exchange of Notes of Same Date* [1]

The Government of the United States of America and the Government of the United Kingdom of Great Britain and Northern Ireland being desirous of defining, in so far as certain problems of marine transportation and litigation are concerned, the manner in which shall be provided mutual aid in the conduct of the war including the aid contemplated by the Agreements concluded between them at Washington on the 23rd February, 1942,[2] and the 3rd September, 1942,[3] have agreed as follows: —

ARTICLE 1. (1) Each contracting Government agrees to waive all claims arising out of or in connection with negligent navigation or general average in respect of any cargo or freight owned by such Government and in respect of any vessel (including naval vessel) owned by such Government against the other contracting Government or any cargo, freight or vessel (including naval vessel) owned by such other Government or against any servant or agent of such other Government or in any case where such other Government represents that such claim if made would ultimately be borne by such other Government.

(2) Each contracting Government agrees on behalf of itself and of any organization which is owned or controlled by it and operating for its account or on its behalf to waive all claims for salvage services against the other contracting Government or against any cargo, freight or vessel

[1] *Executive Agreement Series* 282.
[2] *Ibid.*, 241; *Documents, IV, 1941–42*, p. 235.
[3] *Executive Agreement Series* 270; this volume, p. 234.

(including naval vessel) owned by such other Government or in any case where such other Government represents that such salvage claim if made would ultimately be borne by such other Government.

(3) Each contracting Government agrees to waive all claims for loss of or damage to cargo owned by such Government and arising out of the carriage thereof or for loss of or damage to any cargo or vessel owned by one contracting Government and caused by the shipment or carriage of cargo owned by the other contracting Government against such other Government or against any servant or agent of such other Government or against any vessel (including naval vessel) owned by such other Government or in any case where such other Government represents that the claim if made would ultimately be borne by such other Government.

(4) Each contracting Government undertakes not to make any claim in respect of any vessel or cargo insured by it to which it may be entitled by virtue of any right of subrogation either —

(a) directly against the other contracting Government; or

(b) in any case where such other Government represents that such claim if made would ultimately be borne by such other Government.

(5) Each contracting Government agrees to extend the principles of this Agreement to such other maritime claims as may from time to time be agreed between them.

ARTICLE 2. Where in any case claims arise which are not required to be waived by this Agreement in addition to or in conjunction with claims which are so required to be waived and it is necessary in any proceedings including proceedings for the limitation of liability that claims be marshalled or for the proper assessment of any salvage or general average that values should be estimated, the provisions of this Agreement shall not apply but claims which would otherwise be required to be waived under this Agreement shall be asserted. Any recoveries, however, shall be waived by the Government entitled to such recoveries or at the option of such Government shall be dealt with in such other way as will give effect to the purposes of this Agreement.

ARTICLE 3. (1) For the purpose of this Agreement the expression "vessel owned by a contracting Government" includes a vessel on bare boat charter to a contracting Government or requisitioned by a contracting Government on bare boat terms or otherwise in the possession of a contracting Government (except to the extent that the risk of loss or liability is borne by some person other than either contracting Government).

(2) In order to carry out the full intention of the provisions of Article 1 of this Agreement each contracting Government will so arrange in connection with bare boat charters to it that the owners or persons interested

through such owners shall not have or assert any claims of the character specified in Article 1.

ARTICLE 4. Each contracting Government upon the request of the other will provide undertakings for the release of vessels or cargo owned by the other contracting Government from judicial proceedings in Courts in the United States of America or in the United Kingdom as the case may be where such release will promote the war effort and the requesting Government so represents, upon compliance with the following conditions: —

(a) upon the tender of such request due authority will be conferred by the Government interested in such vessel or cargo upon the law officers of the Government furnishing the undertaking to appear on their behalf and to conduct the defence of such proceedings in so far as such vessel or cargo is concerned, to settle or compromise any such suit, to assert or settle and compromise any claim to which the requesting Government may be entitled in respect of the subject-matter of the suit and to make and receive payments in respect thereof; and

(b) the requesting Government upon tendering such a request will assure the other Government of its full cooperation in making defense to such suit and asserting such claims including the making available of witnesses and evidence and including preparation for trial.

Unless otherwise agreed, each contracting Government will reimburse or account to the other for any payment made or received by the one Government on behalf of the other.

ARTICLE 5. Nothing in this Agreement shall be construed as a waiver of the right of either contracting Government in appropriate cases to assert sovereign immunity.

ARTICLE 6. (1) This Agreement, which shall come into force on the date of signature, shall apply in respect of all claims arising before the date of this Agreement but remaining unsettled at such date or which may arise during the currency of this Agreement.

(2) This Agreement shall remain in force until the expiration of six months from the date upon which either of the contracting Governments shall have given notice in writing of their intention to terminate it.

IN WITNESS whereof the undersigned, duly authorized to that effect by their respective Governments, have signed the present Agreement and have affixed thereto their seals.

DONE in London in duplicate, this fourth day of December, 1942.

[SEAL]   JOHN G. WINANT.

[SEAL]   ANTHONY EDEN.

(a) *The American Ambassador (Winant) to the British Secretary of State for Foreign Affairs (Eden)*

SIR:

With reference to Article IV of the agreement signed today between the Government of the United Kingdom of Great Britain and Northern Ireland and the Government of the United States of America relating to certain problems of maritime transportation and litigation, I have the honor to state that for the present and until further notice it is the intention of my Government that the accounting contemplated by that Article will be accomplished under the Act of Congress of March 11, 1941[1] to the extent authorized under that Act.

Accordingly, the Government of the United States will in appropriate cases make such payments as are necessary in the course of operations under the agreement according to its procedure in the administration of that Act and will receive any moneys which may accrue in the course of such operations as a benefit under that Act and Article VI of the agreement between our two Governments dated February 23, 1942.

Accept, Sir, [etc.]

(b) *The British Secretary of State for Foreign Affairs (Eden) to the American Ambassador (Winant)*

YOUR EXCELLENCY,

I have the honor to acknowledge receipt of your note of today's date referring to Article IV of the agreement signed today between our two Governments relating to certain problems of marine transportation and litigation. In reply I wish to state that for the present and until further notice my Government intends that the accounting required by Article IV shall be on the same basis as the payments contemplated in Your Excellency's note and that the Government of the United Kingdom will make any payments required by the agreement and receive any moneys accruing under it as reciprocal aid according to the terms of the agreement between our two Governments dated the 23rd February, 1942.

I have the honor [etc.]

(3) *Exchange of Notes between the Governments of the United States and Norway, Supplementing the Agreement of July 11, 1942, Effected July 11, 1942*[2]

This exchange of notes concerns the application of certain provisions of the Agreement in relation to the operation of the Norwegian merchant fleet for the benefit of the United Nations in the common war effort and consultations at the end of the present emergency.

[1] 55 Stat. 31.   [2] Department of State, *Bulletin*, VII, p. 612.

(a) The Ambassador of Norway (Morgenstierne) to the Secretary of State (Hull)

EXCELLENCY:

I have the honor to refer to the conversations between representatives of the Royal Norwegian Government and the Government of the United States of America in connection with the negotiation of the Agreement on the Principles Applying to Mutual Aid in the Prosecution of the War Against Aggression signed this day.

During the course of these conversations the Norwegian representatives have referred to the fact that the Royal Norwegian Government has been driven from its country by Hitler, whose forces are in occupation of the country and are despoiling its resources; they have pointed out that the principal national asset remaining at the disposal of their Government is the Norwegian Merchant Fleet, which that Government is operating for the benefit of the United Nations in the common war effort; that for the protection and maintenance of that Fleet, it is necessary to install armaments and other protective devices and equipment upon its vessels, and to repair damage and replace losses thereto occasioned by acts of war and operation under war conditions; that it will also be necessary for the Royal Norwegian Government, when the invader has been driven from its territory, to ensure the maintenance of reestablished peaceful conditions, and that, for this reason, the need of the Royal Norwegian Government for arms and equipment will not necessarily cease with the general cessation of hostilities.

The conversations referred to have disclosed a mutual understanding on the part of the Royal Norwegian Government and the Government of the United States of America with respect to the application of certain provisions of the Agreement signed this day, as follows:

1. Armaments and other protective devices and equipment installed upon Norwegian ships subsequent to December 7, 1941 shall, under the provisions of the Agreement signed this day, remain the property of the Government of the United States of America. The installation of such armaments, protective devices, and other equipment shall be at the expense and for the account of the Government of the United States of America, which shall bear any risk of loss, or damage, and shall not be regarded as giving rise to any financial obligation on the part of the Royal Norwegian Government. Such armaments may if found mutually desirable be manned by American gun crews.

2. The repair under the Lend-Lease Act, subsequent to December 7, 1941, of damage to Norwegian ships which is caused by acts of war or by operation under war conditions, as well as repair and replacement necessitated by operation under war conditions shall be made at the expense and for the account of the Government of the United States of

America, and shall not be regarded as giving rise to any financial obligation on the part of the Royal Norwegian Government. The repair of damage not caused by acts of war or not necessitated by operation under war conditions shall be made at the expense and for the account of the Royal Norwegian Government or the appropriate agency designated by it.

3. The Government of the United States of America recognizes that the Norwegian Merchant Fleet not only constitutes an important contribution to the war effort of the United Nations but is likewise one of the principal national assets of the Royal Norwegian Government and, accordingly, that the latter Government which is operating its Fleet for the benefit of the United Nations in the common war effort, should be assisted in replacing ships lost in the service of the United Nations. Accordingly, the Government of the United States of America will continue to review the situation with the Royal Norwegian Government with a view to assisting that Government in a program of replacement as soon as conditions permit. The two Governments agree that negotiations to this end should be commenced without delay and should be pressed to a conclusion as promptly as possible.

4. In the application of Article V of the Agreement relating to the return at the end of the present emergency of articles transferred under the Agreement, the Government of the United States of America will take into account the circumstance that when the invader has been driven from Norway it will be necessary for the Royal Norwegian Government to ensure the maintenance of reestablished peaceful conditions. Accordingly, the Government of the United States of America and the Royal Norwegian Government will consider, and will consult with each other with respect to the possible retention by the latter of such military equipment as may be considered necessary for those purposes.

Accept [etc.]

(b) The Secretary of State (Hull) to the Ambassador of Norway (Morgenstierne)

Excellency:

I have the honor to acknowledge the receipt of your note of today's date concerning the conversations between representatives of the Government of the United States of America and the Royal Norwegian Government in connection with the negotiation of the Agreement on the Principles Applying to Mutual Aid in the Prosecution of the War Against Aggression signed this day, and to confirm the statement contained therein of the understanding of the two Governments with respect to the application of certain provisions of the Agreement.

Accept [etc.]

(4) Exchange of Notes between the Governments of the United States and Liberia, Supplementing the Agreement of June 8, 1943, Effected June 8, 1943 [1]

The exchange of notes confirms the understanding of the two Governments of the relation between the Mutual Aid Agreement of June 8, 1943 [2] and the agreement regarding defense areas in Liberia, concluded at Monrovia on March 31, 1942.[3]

(a) The Consul General of Liberia (Walker) to the Special Representative of the United States (Villard)

SIR:

I have the honor to refer to the Agreement [3] signed in the city of New York on this day, between the Government of the United States of America and the Government of the Republic of Liberia on the principles applying to mutual aid under the Lend-Lease Act of the United States of America of March 11, 1941, and to set forth the understanding of the Government of the Republic of Liberia of the relationship between this Agreement and the Agreement concluded between our Governments on March 31, 1942, as follows:

The Agreement signed this day states in terms of general principles the basis on which aid under the Act of March 11, 1941 is to be furnished to the Republic of Liberia.

The provisions of Article V of the Agreement of March 31, 1942, and the accompanying letter of the same date addressed by the Special Representative of the President of the United States of America to the President of Liberia, are interpreted as setting forth specific applications of the general principles contained in the Agreement signed this day, and especially of Article I, and as enumerating the defense aids which the Government of the United States of America has undertaken, for the time being, to supply the Government of the Republic of Liberia, under the Lend-Lease Act and otherwise.

If the Government of the United States of America concurs in the foregoing, I would suggest that the present note and your reply to that effect be regarded as placing on record the understanding of our two Governments in this matter.

Accept [etc.]

(b) The Special Representative of the United States (Villard) to the Consul General of Liberia (Walker)

SIR:

I have the honor to acknowledge the receipt of your note of today's date concerning the relationship between the Agreement signed in the

---

[1] *Ibid.*, VIII, p. 517.   [2] *Ibid.*, p. 515; *Executive Agreement Series* 324.
[3] *Executive Agreement Series* 275; this volume, p. 601.

city of New York on this day between the Government of the Republic of Liberia and the Government of the United States of America and the Agreement concluded between our Governments on March 31, 1942.

In reply I am glad to inform you that the Government of the United States of America agrees with the understanding of the Government of the Republic of Liberia as expressed in that note. In accordance with the suggestion contained therein, your note and this reply will be regarded as placing on record the understanding between our two Governments in this matter.

Accept [etc.]

4. AGREEMENTS FOR AND EXTENT OF RECIPROCAL LEND-LEASE AID

(1) Sixth Report of the President (Roosevelt) to Congress on Lend-Lease Operations, September 11, 1942 [1]

[Excerpt]

. . . .

Ever since we began giving aid to our allies, our allies have been giving aid to us. On September 3, 1942, this informal pooling of resources was made formal in signed agreements with United Kingdom, Australia, New Zealand, and Fighting France.

With these agreements, the program of reciprocal aid to our forces enters upon a new phase.

The agreements rest on the simple principle that each participant provide the other with such articles, services, facilities, or information as each may be in a position to supply for the joint prosecution of the war. The rule to be followed in providing mutual aid is that the war production and war resources of each nation should be used by all United Nations' forces in ways which most effectively utilize the available materials, manpower, production facilities, and shipping space.

The agreements signed on September 3 carry forward the application of these principles in certain important ways. They specify, in the first instance, that while each participant retains the right of final decision with reference to its own war production and war resources, decisions as to the most effective use of resources shall, so far as possible, be made in common, pursuant to common plans for winning the war. In the second place, they provide, as to financing the provision of such aid, that the general rule to be applied is that as large a portion as possible of the articles and services which each participant may authorize to be

[1] House Doc. No. 839, 77th Cong., 2d sess., p. 14.

provided to the other shall be in the form of reciprocal aid, so that the need of each for the currency of the other may be reduced to a minimum.

The agreements then go on to specify certain specific types of assistance which are being provided and will increasingly be provided for our armed forces abroad: Military equipment, munitions, and military and naval stores; supplies, materials, facilities, and services for the forces, except for the pay and allowance of such forces, administrative expenses, and such local purchases as may be made outside the usual channels. The construction of military projects, tasks, and other capital works will be facilitated under this program of reciprocal aid, both in the territories of the participants in the agreement, and wherever those territories are a more practicable source of supply than the United States or another of the United Nations.

The program of reciprocal lend-lease has become a very material and important aspect of our supply problem. It puts the idea of pooling all our resources for war in its most dynamic form. It is more than a gracious and much appreciated gesture of good will. Reciprocal aid represents the most economical use of the war resources of the United Nations. It means that we are husbanding time and transport to use resources where they are. It means, also, of course, that the peoples of Britain, Australia, and New Zealand, already on short rations, are freely sharing what they have with our troops.

Under reciprocal lend-lease General MacArthur's men are receiving munitions, uniforms, food, and shelter from the Australians. Similarly, United States forces are receiving aid from New Zealand. The Fighting French in Equatorial Africa and New Caledonia are furnishing us with materials, facilities, and services. In Great Britain we are receiving a formidable amount of munitions and supplies. Guns and camps, aircraft and military stores have been turned over to our troops. In July alone, a quarter of a million British workmen were engaged on construction for the American Army.

.   .   .   .

The last Lend-Lease Report to Congress [1] set forth a principle for distributing the financial burden of the war among the United Nations in accordance with their ability to contribute to the common pool. The passage of the Lend-Lease Act meant that the dollar sign would not stand in the way of our aid to the other United Nations. The reciprocal aid agreements and the arrangements between the United Kingdom and the Soviet Union demonstrate that the lend-lease policy is becoming a model for assistance furnished by our allies.

[1] Fifth Report, House Report No. 799, 77th Cong., 2d sess.

(2) *Agreement for Reciprocal Lend-Lease Aid to the United States and Its Armed Forces, Concluded between the Governments of the United Kingdom and the United States, by Exchange of Notes, Dated September 3, 1942* [1]

An agreement specifying the principles and procedures applicable to the provision of aid to the United States and its armed forces by the Government of the United Kingdom was concluded on September 3 by an exchange of notes between the Secretary of State and the British Ambassador, Lord Halifax.

This agreement formalized the principles and procedures applicable to the provision of aid to the armed forces of the United States by the other parties on the same terms as those under which the United States supplies aid to them in accordance with the provisions of the Lend-Lease Act. In advance of a formal agreement, such aid was provided on these terms as occasion required from the time of the passage of the Lend-Lease Act. This aid rapidly increased in importance as the intensity of the American war effort increased in the various theaters of operations concerned.

The agreement specified that the general principle governing the provision of mutual aid was that the war production and war resources of each contracting party should be used in ways which most effectively utilized the available materials, manpower, production facilities, and shipping space. The agreement further specified that a maximum of the articles and services provided by each party to the other should be in the form of reciprocal aid so that the need of each for the currency of the other might be reduced to a minimum. The United Kingdom agreed to provide the armed forces of the United States with military equipment, munitions, military and naval stores, other supplies, materials, facilities, and services when they can most effectively be procured in that country.

(a) *Note from the British Ambassador (Halifax) to the Secretary of State (Hull)*

SIR:

In the United Nations declaration of January 1, 1942, the contracting governments pledged themselves to employ their full resources, military or economic, against those nations with which they are at war and in the Agreement of February 23, 1942, each contracting government undertook to provide the other with such articles, services, facilities or information useful in the prosecution of their common war undertaking as each may be in a position to supply. It is further the understanding of the Government of the United Kingdom of Great Britain and Northern Ireland that the general principle to be followed in providing mutual aid as set forth in the said Agreement of February 23, 1942, is that the war production and the war resources of both Nations should be used by the armed forces of each and of the other United Nations in ways which most effectively utilize the available materials, manpower, production facilities and shipping space.

With a view, therefore, to supplementing Article 2 and Article 6 of the Agreement of February 23, 1942, between our two Governments for

[1] Department of State, *Bulletin*, VII, p. 734; *Executive Agreement Series* 270.

the provision of reciprocal aid, I have the honor to set forth below the understanding of the Government of the United Kingdom of Great Britain and Northern Ireland of the principles and procedures applicable to the provision of aid by the Government of the United Kingdom of Great Britain and Northern Ireland to the armed forces of the United States and the manner in which such aid will be correlated with the maintenance of those forces by the United States Government.

1. While each Government retains the right of final decision, in the light of its own potentialities and responsibilities, decisions as to the most effective use of resources shall, so far as possible, be made in common, pursuant to common plans for winning the war.

2. As to financing the provision of such aid, within the fields mentioned below, it is the understanding of the Government of the United Kingdom of Great Britain and Northern Ireland that the general principle to be applied, to the point at which the common war effort is most effective, is that as large a portion as possible of the articles and services which each Government may authorize to be provided to the other shall be in the form of reciprocal aid so that the need of each Government for the currency of the other may be reduced to a minimum.

It is accordingly the understanding of the Government of the United Kingdom of Great Britain and Northern Ireland that the United States Government will provide, in accordance with the provisions of, and to the extent authorized under, the Act of March 11, 1941, the share of its war production made available to the United Kingdom. The Government of the United Kingdom will provide on the same terms and as reciprocal aid so much of its war production made available to the United States as it authorizes in accordance with the Agreement of February 23, 1942.

3. The Government of the United Kingdom will provide the United States or its armed forces with the following types of assistance as such reciprocal aid, when it is found that they can most effectively be procured in the United Kingdom or in the British Colonial Empire:

(a) Military equipment, munitions and military and naval stores.

(b) Other supplies, materials, facilities and services for the United States forces, except for the pay and allowances of such forces, administrative expenses, and such local purchases as its official establishments may make other than through the official establishments of the Government of the United Kingdom as specified in paragraph 4.

(c) Supplies, materials and services needed in the construction of military projects, tasks and similar capital works required for the common war effort in the United Kingdom or in the British Colonial Empire, except for the wages and salaries of United States citizens.

(d) Supplies, materials and services needed in the construction of such military projects, tasks and capital works in territory other than the

United Kingdom or the British Colonial Empire or territory of the United States to the extent that the United Kingdom or the British Colonial Empire is a more practicable source of supply than the United States or another of the United Nations.

4. The practical application of the principles formulated in this note, including the procedure by which requests for aid by either Government are made and acted upon, shall be worked out as occasion may require by agreement between the two Governments, acting when possible through their appropriate military or civilian administrative authorities. Requests by the United States Government for such aid will be presented by duly authorized authorities of the United States to official agencies of the United Kingdom which will be designated or established in London and in the areas where United States forces are located for the purpose of facilitating the provision of reciprocal aid.

5. It is the understanding of the Government of the United Kingdom of Great Britain and Northern Ireland that all such aid, as well as other aid, including information, received under Article 6 of the Agreement of February 23, 1942, accepted by the President of the United States or his authorized representatives from the Government of the United Kingdom will be received as a benefit to the United States under the Act of March 11, 1941. In so far as circumstances will permit, appropriate record of aid received under this arrangement, except for miscellaneous facilities and services, will be kept by each Government.

If the Government of the United States concurs in the foregoing, I would suggest that the present note and your reply to that effect be regarded as placing on record the understanding of our two Governments in this matter.

I have [etc.]

(b) *Note from the Secretary of State (Hull) to the British Ambassador (Halifax)*

EXCELLENCY:

I have the honor to acknowledge the receipt of your note of today's date concerning the principles and procedures applicable to the provision of aid by the Government of the United Kingdom of Great Britain and Northern Ireland to the armed forces of the United States of America.

In reply I wish to inform you that the Government of the United States agrees with the understanding of the Government of the United Kingdom of Great Britain and Northern Ireland as expressed in that note. In accordance with the suggestion contained therein, your note and this reply will be regarded as placing on record the understanding between our two Governments in this matter.

This further integration and strengthening of our common war effort gives me great satisfaction.

Accept [etc.]   ———

On the same date, September 3, 1942, agreements specifying the principles and procedures applicable to the provision of aid to the United States and its armed forces by the Governments of Australia and New Zealand were concluded by exchange of notes between the Secretary of State and the Australian and New Zealand Ministers.[1] These agreements contained substantially the same provisions as the agreement with the Government of the United Kingdom. In addition they made applicable to the relations between the Government of the United States, on the one hand, and the Governments of Australia and New Zealand, on the other, the principles of the agreement between the Government of the United States and the United Kingdom, signed February 23, 1942.[2]

A similar agreement concerning the provision of aid by Fighting France was concluded in London on September 3 by an exchange of notes between Brigadier General John E. Dahlquist, Acting Military Representative of the United States of America, and M. Maurice de Jean, representing the French National Committee. Because of its special features, the text of this is given below.

Agreements similar to those concluded with the Governments of the United Kingdom, Australia and New Zealand were reached by exchange of notes between the Government of the United States and the Governments of Belgium [3] and the Netherlands under dates of January 30 and June 14, 1943, respectively. The Netherlands agreement is reproduced below.

(3) *Agreement for Reciprocal Lend-Lease Aid to the United States and Its Armed Forces, Concluded between the Acting Military Representative of the United States (Dahlquist) and M. Maurice de Jean, Representing the French National Committee, London, September 3, 1942* [4]

(a) *Note from the French National Committee to the Acting Military Representative of the United States (Dahlquist)*

The French National Committee sets forth below its understanding of the principles governing the provision of reciprocal aid by the United States of America to Fighting France and by Fighting France to the United States:

1. The United States of America will continue to supply Fighting France with such defense articles, defense services, and defense information as the President shall authorize to be transferred or provided.

---

[1] *Ibid.*, p. 736. The texts of these agreements have been published as *Executive Agreement Series* 271 and 272 respectively.

[2] *Documents, IV, 1941–42*, p. 235.

[3] Department of State, *Bulletin*, VIII, p. 102; *Executive Agreement Series* 313.

[4] Department of State, *Bulletin*, VII, p. 739; *Executive Agreement Series* 273.

2. Fighting France will continue to contribute to the defense of the United States of America and the strengthening thereof and will provide such articles, services, facilities or information as it may be in a position to supply.

3. The fundamental principle to be followed in providing such aid is that the war production and war resources of Fighting France and of the United States of America should be used by the armed forces of each in the ways which most effectively utilize available materials, manpower, production facilities and shipping space. While each retains the right of final decision, in the light of its own potentialities and responsibilities, decisions as to the most effective use of resources shall, so far as possible, be made in common, pursuant to common plans for winning the war.

4. As to financing the provision of such aid, within the fields mentioned below, it is the Committee's understanding that the general principle to be applied, to the point at which the common war effort is most effective, is that as large a portion as possible of the articles and services to be provided by each to the other shall be in the form of reciprocal aid.

It is accordingly the Committee's understanding that the United States Government will provide, in accordance with the provisions of, and to the extent authorized under, the Act of March 11, 1941, the share of its war production made available to Fighting France. Fighting France will provide on the same terms and as reciprocal aid so much of its war production made available to the United States as it authorizes in accordance with the principles enunciated in this note.

5. Within the territories under the control of Fighting France, or within the same theater of operations, the National Committee will provide the United States or its armed forces with the following types of assistance, as such reciprocal aid, when it is found that they can most effectively be procured in territory under the control of Fighting France:

(a) Military equipment, munitions and military and naval stores;

(b) Other supplies, materials, facilities and services for the United States forces, except for the pay and allowances of such forces, administrative expenses, and such local purchases as its official establishments may make other than through the official establishments of Fighting France as specified in paragraph 6.

(c) Supplies, materials and services, except for the wages and salaries of United States citizens, needed in the construction of military projects, tasks and similar capital works required for the common war effort in territory under the control of Fighting France, or in the same theater of operations, to the extent that such territory is the most practicable source of supply.

6. The practical application of the principles formulated in this note, including the procedure by which requests for aid are made and acted upon, shall be worked out by agreement as occasion may require through

the appropriate military or civilian administrative authorities. Requests by the United States forces for such aid will be presented by their duly authorized authorities to official agencies of Fighting France which will be designated or established in the areas where United States forces are located for the purpose of facilitating the provision of reciprocal aid.

7. It is the Committee's understanding that all such aid accepted by the President of the United States or his authorized representatives from Fighting France will be received as a benefit to the United States under the Act of March 11, 1941. In so far as circumstances will permit, appropriate record of aid received under this arrangement, except for miscellaneous facilities and services, will be kept by each.

If the Government of the United States concurs in the foregoing, the present note and a reply to that effect will be regarded as placing on record the understanding in this matter.

(b) *Note from the Acting Military Representative of the United States (Dahlquist) to the French National Committee*

The Government of the United States of America agrees with the understanding of the National Committee, as expressed in the English text of the Committee's note of today's date, concerning the principles and procedures applicable to the provision of aid by Fighting France to the armed forces of the United States of America and, in accordance with the suggestion contained therein, that note and this reply will be regarded as placing on record the understanding in this matter.

(4) *Agreement for Reciprocal Lend-Lease Aid to the United States and Its Armed Forces, Concluded between the Governments of the United States and the Kingdom of the Netherlands, by Exchange of Notes, Dated June 14, 1943* [1]

(a) *The Netherlands Ambassador (Loudon) to the Secretary of State (Hull)*

SIR:

In the United Nations' declaration of January 1, 1942, the contracting governments pledged themselves to employ their full resources, military or economic, against those nations with which they are at war; and in the Agreement of July 8, 1942 between the Governments of the United States and of the Netherlands, on the Principles Applying to Mutual Aid in the Prosecution of the War against Aggression, each contracting government undertook to provide the other with such articles, services, facilities, or information useful in the prosecution of their common war effort as it might be in a position to supply. It is the understanding of the

[1] Department of State, *Bulletin*, VIII, p. 594; *Executive Agreement Series* 326.

Government of the Kingdom of the Netherlands that the general principles to be followed in providing mutual aid as set forth in the said Agreement of July 8, 1942 is that the war production and the war resources of both Nations should be used by each in ways which most effectively utilize the available materials, manpower, production facilities and shipping space.

With a view, therefore, to supplementing the Agreement of July 8, 1942, I have the honor to set forth below the understanding of the Government of the Kingdom of the Netherlands of the principles and procedures applicable to the provision of aid by the Government of the Kingdom of the Netherlands to the armed forces of the United States and the manner in which such aid will be correlated with the maintenance of those forces by the United States Government.

1. The Government of the Kingdom of the Netherlands, retaining the right of final decision, in the light of its own potentialities and responsibilities, will provide the United States or its forces with the following types of assistance as such reciprocal aid, when and to the extent that it is found that they can most effectively be procured in territory of the Kingdom of the Netherlands:

(a) Supplies, materials, facilities, information and services for the United States forces except for the pay and allowances of such forces, administrative expenses, and such local purchases as its official establishments may make other than through the official establishments of the Government of the Netherlands as specified in paragraph 2.

(b) Supplies, materials, information and services needed in the construction of military projects, tasks and similar capital works required for the common war effort in territory of the Kingdom of the Netherlands, except for the wages and salaries of United States citizens.

(c) Supplies, materials, information and services needed in the construction of such military projects, tasks and capital works in territory other than territory of the Kingdom of the Netherlands or territory of the United States, to the extent that territory of the Kingdom of the Netherlands is a more practicable source of supply than the United States, or another of the United Nations.

2. The practical application of the principles formulated in this note, including the procedure by which requests for aid by either Government are made and acted upon, shall be worked out as occasion may require by agreement between the two Governments, acting when possible through their appropriate military or civilian administrative authorities. Requests by the United States Government for such aid will be presented by duly authorized authorities of the United States to official agencies of the Netherlands which will be designated or established in Washington, or in the areas where United States forces are located, for the purpose of facilitating the provision of reciprocal aid.

3. It is the understanding of the Government of the Kingdom of the Netherlands that all such aid, as well as other aid, including information, received under Article 6 of the Agreement of July 8, 1942, accepted by the President of the United States or his authorized representatives from the Government of the Netherlands will be received as a benefit to the United States under the Act of March 11, 1941. In so far as circumstances will permit, appropriate record of aid received under this arrangement will be kept by each Government.

If the Government of the United States concurs in the foregoing, I would suggest that the present note and your reply to that effect be regarded as placing on record the understanding of our two Governments in this matter and that for clarity and convenience of administration this understanding be considered to be effective as from July 8, 1942, the date of the Agreement of the two Governments on the principles of mutual aid.

Accept [etc.]

(b) The Secretary of State (Hull) to the Netherlands Ambassador (Loudon)

EXCELLENCY:

I have the honor to acknowledge the receipt of Your Excellency's note of today's date concerning the principles and procedures applicable to the provision of aid by the Government of the Kingdom of the Netherlands to the armed forces of the United States of America.

In reply I wish to inform you that the Government of the United States agrees with the understanding of the Government of the Kingdom of the Netherlands as expressed in that note. In accordance with the suggestion contained therein, your note and this reply will be regarded as placing on record the understanding between our two Governments in this matter.

This further integration and strengthening of our common war effort gives me great satisfaction.

Accept [etc.]

(5) Reverse Lend-Lease Aid Received by American Forces in All Theaters. Statement of the Administrator of Lend-Lease (Stettinius), before the Subcommittee of the House Committee on Appropriations, May 4, 1943 [1]

The principle of mutual aid which has operated in the British Isles since the early months of 1942 has been increasingly extended to other theaters where our allies find themselves in a position to meet the

---

[1] *Hearings before the Subcommittee of the House Committee on Appropriations, on the Defense Aid (Lend-Lease) Supplemental Appropriation Bill,* 78th Cong., 1st sess., p. 30.

demands of American forces. Reciprocal aid has been supplied the United States whenever and wherever our forces needed supplies and our allies could possibly provide them. In all parts of the world — the United Kingdom, Russia, Australia, China, New Zealand, New Caledonia, Fiji, Iceland, India, the Belgian Congo, North Africa, British East and South Africa, Iran, Iraq, Syria, the Caribbean — American military and naval forces and our merchant marine have received every type of available commodity or service which could satisfy their needs. While the flow of lend-lease goods going abroad has steadily increased, reciprocal benefits from our Allies, also granted without payment, have grown steadily.

THE UNITED KINGDOM

The United Kingdom has continued to furnish United States armed forces with a great diversity of supplies and services of every kind and description. In terms of ships' tons — a ship's ton is 40 cubic feet or a dead-weight ton, whichever occupies less space — the following is the most accurate picture which can be given of the articles and equipment received from the British from June 1, 1942, to March 31, 1943:

Articles and equipment:	In Ships' Tons
Engineer Corps	249,471
Quartermaster Corps	731,301
Signal Corps	7,371
Ordnance Department	115,716
Transportation Corps	3,757
Medical Corps	85,983
Air Force	139,541
Miscellaneous supplies	29,541
Total	1,362,681

There is excluded from the above total the dead weight of materials provided by the British for construction intended exclusively for American forces. This total is 2,177,384 tons. The British have officially estimated that, when completed, this construction program alone will have entailed an expenditure of $600,000,000.

Following is a brief description of the nature of the articles and equipment afforded the various services:

[Here follows a detailed listing.]

In connection with the foregoing, it must be borne in mind that articles and equipment constitute only a portion of the reciprocal aid afforded United States forces in the European theater of operations by the British Government. In addition, to mention only some of the reciprocal aid received, the following should be referred to:

(a) Transfer of existing billets to United States troops.

(b) Transfer of existing air fields to the United States Air Force.

(c) Requisitioning of thousands of buildings for depots, headquarters, offices, and officers' quarters.

(d) British civilian labor directly employed by United States forces and paid by the British; the number varies in amount from 12,000 to 25,000 individuals so employed.

(e) British civilian labor indirectly employed for United States forces, the number of whom it is impossible to estimate with any degree of accuracy.

(f) · Sea transport of all United States Army personnel and freight.

(g) Rail and motor transport of all United States personnel and freight, including motor transport necessary within depot areas.

(h) All official mail, telephone, and telegraph communication within the United Kingdom.

(i) All damage to Government and private property as a result of training and maneuvers.

(j) All available British supplies for United States commissary stores. These supplies are resold for cash to United States troops by the United States Army and the proceeds retained.

(k) Maintenance and servicing (excluding pay of staff) of all Red Cross hostels, clubs, and operational buildings as well as supply of necessary Red Cross motorcars.

(l) All expenses incident to the publication of United States Army European theater of operations daily and weekly newspaper.

(m) All official printing except that done at United States Army printing plant.

As the need for additional articles, equipment, services, and facilities becomes apparent, arrangements are made with the British to procure the required article or service under reverse lend-lease.

Special attention should, perhaps, be focused on foodstuffs as an illustration of the readiness of the British Government to supply American forces in lines of production which are in great scarcity. The table below shows the amounts of foodstuffs procured by American forces as reciprocal aid in 1942 and the first quarter of 1943 and the planned procurement for the year 1943.

It should not be inferred that the United Kingdom has limited itself to the territory of the British Isles in providing reverse lend-lease to our armed forces. Increasingly, all over the world, in the Dominions, in the British Colonial Empire, and even in non-British countries, the United Kingdom has set up various mechanisms to assist in supplying the needs of the American Army and Navy and of American shipping, generally.

The extent to which reciprocal aid enhances the fighting effectiveness of our armed forces was well illustrated during the invasion of North Africa.

A part of our initial landing forces was equipped and supplied with articles of war turned over to them by the British. Among other things, they received more than 3,800 tons of ammunition, enough artillery for an entire division, some 80,000 tons of coal, 2,000 tons of British rations,

		1942	JANUARY – MARCH, 1943	TOTAL, 1943
"C" biscuits . . .	pounds	——	645,000	1,310,000
Hard candy. . . .	"	——	——	256,000
Cereal, assorted . .	"	——	1,234,000	8,489,000
Cinnamon	"	1,800	26,000	108,000
Cocoa.	"	——	782,000	3,865,000
Vanilla extract. . .	"	9,300	40,000	148,000
Natural wheat flour .	"	626,000	16,251,000	81,170,000
White flour	"	——	——	7,400,000
Fruit	"	336,000	360,000	2,935,000
Baking powder . .	"	23,000	95,000	639,000
Potatoes	"	1,492,000	5,435,000	57,350,000
Bread.	"	1,797,000	4,920,000	61,955,000
Salt	"	15,000	1,704,000	6,883,000
Sauce concentrate .	"	73,000	44,000	251,000
Sugar	"	896,000	7,274,000	46,463,000
Tea	"	186,000	327,000	1,107,000
Vegetables	"	3,024,000	3,500,000	51,100,000
Vinegar	"	352,000	369,000	2,171,000
Green coffee . . .	"	12,000	792,000	11,221,000
"D" rations . . .		——	226,500	3,059,000
Spaghetti	pounds	——	328,000	1,417,000
Fresh yeast	"	——	17,500	95,600
Corn on cob . . .	dozen	——	——	866,000
Soft drinks, full demand	"	——	——	4,170,000

medical maintenance units for hundreds of thousands of men, and 30,000 tons of engineering equipment. In addition, United States troops fighting with the British First Army have been supplied entirely by the United Kingdom with all items used jointly by American and British forces.

As examples, there may be cited the revolving fund which the British provide in sterling and against which all the ships operating under the War Shipping Administration are at liberty to draw for the cost of repairs, fueling, and general conditioning. Under a slightly different system, in New Zealand and Australia, repairs and fueling of War Shipping Administration vessels are made available.

Throughout the Empire the British Treasury pays all British commercial companies for oil supplied to War Shipping Administration ships. Currently, discussions are under way for the establishment of a system whereby the dollar expenditures of American vessels in small British ports will be repaid by the British upon the presentation of certified receipts.

Our Navy receives its oil free of charge from all commercial suppliers in the British Empire (with the exception of Trinidad where special arrangements prevail). In addition, American naval vessels receive a great variety of supplies, including tools, grease guns, cranes and hoists, pipe and fittings, valves, radio equipment, refrigeration materials, paints and varnishes, manila rope, steel plating, lumber, food and drink, store-keeping supplies and charts and maps.

In the Middle East, specifically in Palestine, the Persian Gulf, Egypt, Eritrea, and Syria, the British have been supplying the United States forces with local currency with which to purchase material and labor. The providing of these currencies typifies the spirit of reverse lend-lease generally, since they are not made available to us under any specific agreement but merely because it was felt, at the time our troops went into these areas, that the British were in a better position to procure these particular currencies than were the Americans. Dock installations, hospitals, cantonments, have been provided for American use by the British by this means.

More recently in Kenya, the Gold Coast and east and central Africa, the British have satisfied the needs of American forces on an *ad hoc* basis. Sudan railways are carrying supplies and equipment for American forces and the Public Works Department of the Anglo-Egyptian Sudan is providing materials and labor for necessary military installations. It is expected that the British Overseas Airways Corporation will shortly begin to transport United States personnel and freight to and from points in Africa without payment.

AUSTRALIA

Australia provides a notable example of a country drawing upon limited resources to meet the needs of United States forces. The extent of her aid is reflected in many phases of civilian life — in food shortages, despite her position as a great agricultural producer, in clothing ration-ing, in severe curtailment of travel facilities.

In 1942 Australia supplied American forces in the South and South-west Pacific with the bulk of the foodstuffs they required on a ration scale comparable to the basic allowance of the American Army. For nearly 4 months civilians went without potatoes so that this scale could be maintained. For 6 months, dried and citrus fruits, pork products, tomatoes and tomato juices, chocolate and other foodstuffs have been virtually unobtainable by civilians, although all of these foods have remained on our Army ration. For reasons of military security, it is not possible to give the exact poundage of foodstuffs to be procured as reciprocal aid in 1943, but it will be several times as great as last year. The weight of dry provisions alone will be much greater than that of all foodstuffs, dry and fresh, during the past year. Whereas United States forces absorbed only 2.3 per cent of canned meat production in 1942, they will take 35 per cent this year and will take amounts ranging up to 100 per cent of other canned-goods production.

Although clothing rationing has been introduced, the Australian Government is undertaking an extensive clothing production program for United States forces. Items to be supplied include garrison caps, blouses, shorts, gloves, battle jackets, neckties, overcoats, woolen shirts, shoes, socks, sweaters, and trousers.

The rubber tire requirements of American forces are now met from Australian production. Recreational needs of American soldiers have been met by an Australian program which calls for every type of game and accessory from boxing gloves and horseshoes to chess sets and medicine balls — in all, more than 320,000 items of such equipment. Numerous hospitals, including the newest and most modern in the country, have been given to the United States Army for its exclusive use. More than 100,000 acres of land and more than 7,000,000 square feet of floor space have been provided American forces. Air, rail, and water passenger fares and freight charges and cable and telegraphic charges are met by the Commonwealth Government — all as part of a reciprocal-aid program which consumes over 10 per cent of the Australian war budget.

NEW ZEALAND

The Government of New Zealand is likewise providing goods and services under reciprocal aid to American forces throughout the Pacific area. In a country of less than 2,000,000 people, the scope and volume of such aid is remarkable.

All kinds of foodstuffs are supplied, the bulk of them in fresh meats, butter, cheese, and vegetables, where storage facilities are available, and canned meats, dairy products, and biscuits, where preserved foods are necessary. New Zealand is increasing its productive capacity in dehydrated foods, chiefly in butter, milk, and certain vegetables, in order better to provide for the needs of the American forces. As in Australia, shortages have been occasioned by military requirements; meanwhile, the Government continues to expand its reverse lend-lease procurement above the level of foodstuffs supplied in 1942.

Quantities of clothing, including shoes, blankets, and other textiles, have been supplied. In terms of American production, the amounts involved are small, but they necessitate a rationing system so severe as to limit the supply of clothing to less than one full outfit per person per year.

New Zealand has undertaken an extensive program for the construction of hospitals, camps, warehouses, and other capital projects for the exclusive use of the American forces, or for their use in conjunction with the New Zealanders. The estimated cost of this construction as of February 28, 1943, was $22,000,000, with substantial additions planned for the fiscal year beginning last April.

The value of reciprocal aid, including construction as of February 28, 1943, was officially estimated by New Zealand officials at $31,825,000. The estimate for the fiscal year ending March 31, 1944, is $65,000,000.

RUSSIA

Our ally, Russia, needs its resources to maintain its armies on a 2,000-mile fighting front. But Russian authorities have met without payment both routine and extraordinary expenditures in North Russian ports for ships carrying lend-lease goods. Supplies and services thus provided have included fuel, food, wharfage, medical aid, laundry work, lighterage, shore transportation, repairs, tug service, and pilotage.

INDIA

The United States has not yet concluded a reciprocal-aid agreement with the Government of India. Such aid as we have received to date results from on-the-spot agreements reached by our military commanders in the area. The greater part of the aid received consists of varied types of construction projects, including a number of air fields, complete with all buildings and facilities, and numerous hospitals. Considerably over 800,000 square feet of floor space in building accommodations have been made available for such purposes as radio stations, butcher shops, warehouses, enlisted men's barracks, officers' quarters, mess halls, motor repair shops, laboratories, recreation buildings, etc. The Indian Government has even turned over one building to house a bottling plant to supply soft drinks to our forces.

In view of the critical tanker situation and the great distances involved, the transfer of fuels to American forces by the Indian Government assumes significance. We have received substantial quantities of aviation gasoline, motor gasoline, lubricating oil, and lesser amounts of other petroleum products. A part of the motor fuel has found a use in the hundreds of trucks and passenger cars given our troops without payment as reciprocal aid.

In addition, United States Army groups have been afforded postal, telegraphic, and telephone facilities, water and electric power, furnishings for buildings, and items of clothing, including mosquito and gas-proof outfits.

The network of reverse lend-lease is literally girdling the world. It is likely that in a majority of cases, the United States will grant greater aid, measured in dollar values, than she will receive. It would be most unusual to find the case otherwise — for we draw upon the richest resources and the greatest productive machine in the world. We give more because we have more to give, in accordance with the principle that each nation shall contribute to the war in accordance with its ability.

Reciprocal aid has not hitherto generally been valued because in wartime the burden of ascertaining and agreeing upon values has been too great, but we do know that our allies have made very great contributions.

B. Coordination of the War Effort

1. CONFERENCES ON POLICY AND OVER-ALL STRATEGY

During the period under review, the close cooperation between Anglo-American political and military leaders initiated during the preceding year [1] was continued and further developed. While there was apparent success in the coordination of the policies and military plans of the Governments of the United States and of the United Kingdom, both in the European and the Pacific areas, there was lacking a corresponding measure of cooperation between the Anglo-American leaders and their opposite figures in the Soviet Union. In fact, the outstanding problem of the coordination of the United Nations war effort seemed to be that of bringing the Soviet Union into the scheme of consultation and practical cooperation.

(1) *Conference of British and American Officials, London, July 1942. Announcement of the Secretary to the President, September 8, 1942* [2]

In the course of conversations between President Roosevelt and M. Molotov, People's Commissar of Foreign Affairs, in Washington in late May and early June 1942, "full understanding was reached with regard to the urgent tasks of creating a second front in Europe in 1942." [3] The demand for a second front in Europe was pressed by the Soviet leaders at this time with especial urgency in view of the impending German offensive which it was assumed would be directed toward cutting off the Soviet Union's principal source of oil and which the Soviet leaders may have entertained some doubts of being able to resist successfully.

The President and Prime Minister Churchill subsequently met in Washington, June 19–26, 1942, with their principal military advisers, to discuss the future conduct of the war. [4] It was during this conference that word came of the serious British military set-back in North Africa which momentarily threatened Alexandria and the Suez Canal. General agreement was apparently reached concerning the military plan to be pursued. The Joint Statement of the President and the Prime Minister following the Conference, together with subsequent statements by the President, the British Prime Minister and other responsible officials, gave little indication, however, that it was part of the Anglo-American plan of operations to open a second front in Europe of the kind demanded by the Soviet leaders during the summer or fall of 1942. The Soviet demand, however, became more urgent with the opening of the German offensive in early June which in the course of the summer met with a large measure of success and threatened the key city of Stalingrad, capture of which would have placed the German Army in the position to cut off Russia's principal source of oil.

In July, top-ranking American military leaders and civilian advisers to President Roosevelt went to London to confer with Prime Minister Churchill and his principal advisers and to take necessary decisions regarding future military operations, presumably within the broad program of action agreed upon by the President and Prime Minister Churchill during their June conference. Announcement of this conference was not made until September 8.

The representatives of the United States Government were Harry L. Hopkins, Personal Representative of the President; General George C.

---

[1] See *Documents, IV, 1941–42*, p. 239.
[2] Department of State, *Bulletin*, VII, p. 750; *New York Times*, September 9, 1942.
[3] *Documents, IV, 1941–42*, p. 243.   [4] *Ibid.*, p. 241.

Marshall, Chief of Staff of the Army; and Admiral Ernest J. King, Chief of Naval Operations. The American Chiefs of Staff and Mr. Hopkins held important meetings covering a period of 10 days with the British Chiefs of Staff and the British Prime Minister. At these conferences the whole conduct of the war was thoroughly canvassed and, with the approval of the President, the necessary decisions regarding military operations were made.

Stephen Early, Secretary to the President, was in London at the same time for conferences with Brendan Bracken, British Minister of Public Information.

On the return trip from London the American conferees visited Iceland and inspected the American bases there.

(a) Statement of the Prime Minister of the United Kingdom (Churchill) in the House of Commons, September 8, 1942 [1]

[Excerpt]

. . . Decisions of importance were taken affecting the whole future general conduct of our operations not only in Europe but throughout the world. These decisions were in accordance with the wishes of President Roosevelt, and they received his final approval. Thus, by the end of July complete agreement on war policy and war plans had been reached between Great Britain and the United States. This agreement covers the whole field of the war in every part of the world, and also deals with the necessary productive and administrative measures which are required to enforce the combined policy and strategy which has been agreed upon. . . .

(2) Conference of the Prime Minister of the United Kingdom (Churchill) and the Chairman of the Council of the People's Commissars of the U.S.S.R. (Stalin), August 12–15, 1942. Joint Communiqué, August 17, 1942 [2]

In addition to those whose names appear in the communiqué, the following British and American officials took part in the discussions connected with the Conference: General Sir Archibald P. Wavell, the British Commander-in-Chief in India; Major-General Russell Maxwell, United States Commander in the Middle East; Air Chief Marshal Sir Arthur William Tedder, Commander-in-Chief of the Royal Air Force in the Middle East; Brigadier General S. P. Spalding, United States officer charged with Russian Lend-Lease matters in Washington; and Loy W. Henderson, Assistant Chief of European Affairs in the United States Department of State.

Mr. Harriman, personal representative of President Roosevelt at the Conference, was reported to have said: [3]

[1] House of Commons, Parliamentary Debates, 5th series, vol. 383, col. 87; New York Times, September 9, 1942.
[2] Embassy of the Union of Soviet Socialist Republics, Information Bulletin, No. 100, August 20, 1942.
[3] New York Times, August 18, 1942.

"The President of the United States appointed me to accompany the Prime Minister of Great Britain during this most important visit to Moscow at this decisive moment. The President will be in agreement with all the decisions that have been taken here by Mr. Churchill. America will stand hand in hand at the front with Russia."

Negotiations have taken place in Moscow between the Chairman of the Council of People's Commissars of the U.S.S.R., Joseph Stalin, and the Prime Minister of Great Britain, Winston Churchill, in which Mr. Harriman, representing the President of the United States of America, participated.

There took part in the discussions: The People's Commissar of Foreign Affairs, V. M. Molotov, and Marshal K. E. Voroshilov, from the Soviet side; the British Ambassador, Sir A. Clark Kerr, the Chief of the Imperial General Staff, Sir A. Brooke, and other responsible representatives of the British armed forces and the Permanent Under-Secretary of State for Foreign Affairs, Sir Alexander Cadogan, from the British side.

A number of decisions were reached covering the field of the war against Hitlerite Germany and her associates in Europe. This just war of liberation both Governments are determined to carry on with all their power and energy until the complete destruction of Hitlerism and any similar tyranny has been achieved.

The discussions, which were carried on in an atmosphere of cordiality and complete sincerity, provide an opportunity of reaffirming the existence of close friendship and understanding between the Soviet Union, Great Britain and the United States of America in entire accordance with the Allied relationships existing between them.

(a) *Letter of the President of the People's Commissars of the U.S.S.R. (Stalin) to Mr. Henry C. Cassidy of The Associated Press, Moscow, October 4, 1942* [1]

This letter, while written at a later date and not directly related to the Moscow Conference, brings into bold relief the divergence between the Anglo-American position and the Soviet position on the questions of a second front in Europe and the adequacy of assistance given to the Soviet Union by her Anglo-American allies. This fundamental disagreement the Moscow Conference apparently did little to resolve.

DEAR MR. CASSIDY:
Owing to pressure of work and the consequent inability to grant you an interview, I shall confine myself to a brief written answer to your questions.
"1. What place does the possibility of a second front occupy in Soviet estimates of the current situation?"

[1] Embassy of the Union of Soviet Socialist Republics, *Information Bulletin*, No. 119, October 6, 1942; *New York Times*, October 5, 1942.

Answer: A very important place, one might say, a place of first-rate importance.

"2. To what extent is Allied aid to the Soviet Union proving effective and what could be done to amplify and improve this aid?"

Answer: As compared with the aid which the Soviet Union is giving to the Allies by drawing upon itself the main forces of the German Fascist armies, the aid of the Allies to the Soviet Union has so far been little effective. In order to amplify and improve this aid, only one thing is required: that the Allies fulfill their obligations fully and on time.

"3. What remains of the Soviet capacity for resistance?"

Answer: I think that the Soviet capacity of resisting the German brigands is in strength not less, if not greater, than the capacity of Fascist Germany or any other aggressive power to secure for itself world domination.

With respect,

J. Stalin.

(b) *Protocol Regarding the Delivery of Military Equipment to the Soviet Union by the United States and Great Britain, Signed October 6, 1942. Department of State Release, October 6, 1942* [1]

The agreements to which this protocol gave formal expression were understood to call for delivery to Soviet Russia by the United States of $3,000,000,000 worth of equipment and material. This total was revealed by Foreign Commissar Molotov in a speech after his return to Moscow from his visit to Washington in May 1942.[2] Both President Roosevelt and Prime Minister Churchill refused to discuss the extent of Anglo-American assistance which was planned, in spite of the widespread discussion of the second front question.

There was signed on October 6 by the Honorable Sumner Welles, the Acting Secretary of State, His Excellency Maxim Litvinoff, the Ambassador of the Soviet Union in Washington, and Sir Ronald Campbell, British Minister in Washington, a protocol regarding the delivery by the United States and Great Britain to the Soviet Union of military equipment, munitions, and raw materials.

This protocol gives formal expression to agreements, already in effect for some months, which provide for the continuance without interruption of the supply program inaugurated at the Moscow Conference a year ago.[3]

(3) *The Casablanca Conference, January 14–26, 1943. Communiqué Cabled from Casablanca, Morocco, January 26, 1943* [4]

The invasion of French North Africa by Anglo-American forces on November 7, following the successful offensive against German and Italian forces by the British 8th Army under General Sir Bernard L. Montgomery, marked the assumption of the offensive by Allied military forces, and the final fruition of plans which had been in the process of formulation and decision in June and July at the Washington and London conferences.

[1] Department of State, *Bulletin*, VII, p. 805.
[2] *New York Times*, October 7, 1942.
[3] *Documents, IV, 1941–42*, p. 253.
[4] Department of State, *Bulletin*, VIII, p. 93.

At the same time that the Anglo-American forces were taking the initiative, it became increasingly clear that the Germans would be unable to attain their military objectives on the Eastern front. In fact, by the middle of November, the Soviet counteroffensive was beginning to get under way which was eventually to wipe out all the German gains of the summer of 1942 and place Axis armies on the defensive on the Eastern European front as well.

The Casablanca Conference, therefore, was unique in the line of Anglo-American conferences in that the anti-Axis forces were visibly on the offensive in Europe. There was the promise of achievement to support the terms which President Roosevelt and Prime Minister Churchill agreed should be imposed upon the enemy: "Unconditional Surrender."

It is to be noted that the Conference was essentially an Anglo-American affair. Though Premier Stalin was invited to attend and was kept informed of proposals, and the President and the Prime Minister were in communication with Generalissimo Chiang Kai-shek, the goal of a conference of the "Big Four" was not yet reached.

The President of the United States and the Prime Minister of Great Britain have been in conference near Casablanca since January 14.

They were accompanied by the combined Chiefs of Staff of the two countries; namely —

FOR THE UNITED STATES:

Gen. George C. Marshall, Chief of Staff of the United States Army; Admiral Ernest J. King, Commander-in-Chief of the United States Navy; Lt. Gen. H. H. Arnold, commanding the United States Army Air Forces; and

FOR GREAT BRITAIN:

Admiral of the Fleet Sir Dudley Pound, First Sea Lord; Gen. Sir Alan Brooke, Chief of the Imperial General Staff; and Air Chief Marshal Sir Charles Portal, Chief of the Air Staff.

These were assisted by:

Lt. Gen. B. B. Somervell, Commanding General of the Services of Supply, United States Army; Field Marshal Sir John Dill, head of the British Joint Staff Mission in Washington; Vice Admiral Lord Louis Mountbatten, Chief of Combined Operations; Lt. Gen. Sir Hastings Ismay, Chief of Staff to the Office of the Minister of Defense, together with a number of staff officers of both countries.

They have received visits from Mr. Murphy (Robert Murphy, United States Minister to French North Africa) and Mr. MacMillan (Harold MacMillan, British Resident Minister for Allied Headquarters in North Africa); from Lt. Gen. Dwight D. Eisenhower, Commander-in-Chief of the Allied Expeditionary Force in North Africa; from Admiral of the Fleet Sir Andrew Cunningham, naval commander of the Allied Expeditionary Force in North Africa; from Maj. Gen. Carl Spaatz, air commander of the Allied Expeditionary Force in North Africa; from Lt. Gen. Mark W. Clark, United States Army (Commander of the United States Fifth Army in Tunisia), and, from Middle East Headquarters, from

Gen. Sir Harold Alexander, Air Chief Marshal Sir Arthur Tedder and Lt. Gen. F. M. Andrews, United States Army.

The President was accompanied by Harry Hopkins (Chairman of the British-American Munitions Assignments Board) and was joined by W. Averell Harriman (United States Defense Expediter in England).

With the Prime Minister was Lord Leathers, British Minister of War Transport.

For 10 days the combined staffs have been in constant session, meeting 2 or 3 times a day and recording progress at intervals to the President and the Prime Minister.

The entire field of the war was surveyed theater by theater throughout the world, and all resources were marshaled for a more intense prosecution of the war by sea, land, and air.

Nothing like this prolonged discussion between two allies has ever taken place before. Complete agreement was reached between the leaders of the two countries and their respective staffs upon war plans and enterprises to be undertaken during the campaigns of 1943 against Germany, Italy, and Japan with a view to drawing the utmost advantage from the markedly favorable turn of events at the close of 1942.

Premier Stalin was cordially invited to meet the President and the Prime Minister, in which case the meeting would have been held very much farther to the east. He was unable to leave Russia at this time on account of the great offensive which he himself, as Commander-in-Chief, is directing.

The President and the Prime Minister realized up to the full the enormous weight of the war which Russia is successfully bearing along her whole land front, and their prime object has been to draw as much weight as possible off the Russian armies by engaging the enemy as heavily as possible at the best selected points.

Premier Stalin has been fully informed of the military proposals.

The President and the Prime Minister have been in communication with Generalissimo Chiang Kai-shek. They have apprised him of the measures which they are undertaking to assist him in China's magnificent and unrelaxing struggle for the common cause.

The occasion of the meeting between the President and the Prime Minister made it opportune to invite General Giraud (General Henri Honoré Giraud, High Commissioner of French Africa) to confer with the Combined Chiefs of Staff and to arrange for a meeting between him and General de Gaulle (General Charles de Gaulle, Fighting French Commander). The two generals have been in close consultation.

The President and the Prime Minister and their combined staffs, having completed their plans for the offensive campaigns of 1943, have now separated in order to put them into active and concerted execution.

(a) *Unofficial Report of Remarks of the President (Roosevelt) and the Prime Minister of the United Kingdom (Churchill) to Press Correspondents at the Conclusion of the Conference, January 26, 1943* [1]

[Excerpt]

. . . .

The President pointed out to correspondents that the successful landings in French North Africa which had changed the whole outlook of the war since November 8 were a realization of plans he and Mr. Churchill had formulated at Washington as far back as last June.

Now the time had come for a review of events in the light of progress made in various theaters of war, and for drawing up plans in regard to steps to be taken in 1943.

Premier Stalin was cordially invited to attend these talks which if he had accepted would necessarily have been held considerably farther eastward.

But the Russian leader replied that, although he greatly desired to come, he could not leave his country owing to his duties as Commander-in-Chief of the Soviet forces engaged in transforming the grim Russian defense into sweeping advances of the winter offensive.

The Soviet Premier has been kept posted on the progress of the discussions relating to events which have already drawn off some of the enormous weight of combat Russia has been sustaining, and Generalissimo Chiang Kai-shek has been informed of the measures the United Nations propose to undertake to aid China in the struggle with Japan, now in its sixth bitter year.

The range of military studies in which Mr. Roosevelt and Mr. Churchill have been engaged with their service chiefs was described by the President as without precedent in history.

It concerns the retention of the inestimably valuable initiative obtained in North Africa and the offensive now to be pursued relentlessly in all parts of the world until the Axis powers and their satellites are conquered.

The President contrasted the possibilities for personal detailed conferences between allies widely separated geographically now and in World War I.

Here the men actually in control of operations in the different theaters of the war had been living in closest touch with each other and threshed out details in their respective tasks.

The combined staffs had proceeded on the principle of the pooling of all of the resources of the United Nations.

The main work of the committees has been to bring the war to a successful conclusion, but due regard has been paid to economic questions, particularly in North Africa where the Allies are now based and the President in some remarks he made following Mr. Churchill's talk said that the intention was to see French North Africa through its difficult period and keep it going in regard to food until the next harvest is gathered in.

Now the staff chiefs are going their various ways to put 1943 plans into what the official communiqué described as "active and concerted execution."

President Roosevelt emphasized that the future plans of the Allies are keyed onto the necessity of lending the utmost possible aid to the Russian offensive.

[1] *Christian Science Monitor*, January 27, 1943, p. 10. The account is that of Mr. R. Maillard Stead, Military Correspondent of the *Monitor*, accredited to the American Headquarters in North Africa.

This is being done by throwing a maximum strain on German manpower and going on with the process of inexorable attrition of German matériel now being carried out with notable success in Mediterranean regions.

At the same time within the scope of this policy all possible help is to be given to the Chinese.

The Axis is now finding itself with the disadvantages the democracies formerly had of having to meet heavy defensive demands on a widening perimeter, so that the Axis has the utmost difficulty to obtain adequate concentration of military power in any one sector.

Peace is to come, Mr. Roosevelt said, by total elimination of German, Italian, and Japanese war power. This doesn't mean destruction of the people in those unhappy countries, but total and merciless destruction of the machinery they have built up for imposing totalitarian doctrines on the world.

In this connection the President reminded his listeners of the famous American General, Ulysses Simpson Grant, whose initials U.S. were adapted to express his resoluteness in the nickname "Unconditional Surrender" Grant. The democracies' war plans were to compel the "unconditional surrender" of the Axis.

Mr. Churchill, who didn't refer to typewritten notes as did Mr. Roosevelt, said he was in entire agreement with everything Mr. Roosevelt had said. The Prime Minister declared that nothing could come between the two of them who were now such firm friends, and he described the conference here as the happiest in his long experience of such meetings.

· · · · · · ·

(4) Visit to Washington of the Secretary of State for Foreign Affairs of the United Kingdom (Eden), March 12–30, 1943. Unofficial Report of the Remarks of the President (Roosevelt) at Press Conference, March 30, 1943 [1]

[Excerpt]

To achieve the effective prosecution of coalition war, the maximum coordination of the military efforts of allied powers was admittedly necessary. Equally necessary was agreement between the members of the coalition on broad political purposes, as it is only within the framework of such agreement that the measure of mutual confidence and community of interests could be attained which was indispensable to the pooling and most effective use of national resources.

The apparent divergence of the viewpoint of the Anglo-American allies on the one hand and the Soviet Union on the other on the question of a second front in Western Europe, already referred to, undoubtedly reflected a more deep-seated divergence of attitudes resulting possibly from distrust, lack of understanding, the pursuit of different political objectives and conflicting national interests.

This division was high-lighted by the blunt statement of Admiral Standley, the American Ambassador to Moscow, to the British and American press representatives on March 8, in which he said that he had failed to find any reference in the Soviet press to the material help Russia was receiving from America, not only through Lend-Lease, but also through the Red Cross and American-Russian Relief. The Soviet authorities, he said, seemed "to be trying to create the impression that they are fighting the war alone." [2] Though these words brought prompt reactions from Washington and Moscow of a reassuring nature,[3] there was no question of the underlying tension which the statement reflected.

[1] *New York Times*, March 31, 1943 special dispatch by Harold Callender.
[2] *The Bulletin of International News*, March 20, 1943, p. 288; *New York Times*, March 9, 1943; this volume, p. 523.
[3] See this volume, p. 524–6.

The visit of Foreign Minister Eden was quite obviously connected with the search on the part of the Anglo-American allies for the basis of a better understanding and closer cooperation with Soviet Russia, not only in the prosecution of the war but in meeting post-war problems as well.

. . . .

Commenting upon the visit to Washington of Anthony Eden, British Foreign Secretary, who departed today for Canada, President Roosevelt at his press conference this afternoon said discussions of post-war problems would continue with Russia and other members of the United Nations, and he gave an extremely optimistic picture of the degree of accord not only between the British and American Governments but among the United Nations as a whole as it has been manifested in conferences held so far.

"If you want to be didactic and put it in terms of figures," said the President, permitting his words to be quoted directly, "I would say that so far, in all the conferences we have held with other members of the United Nations, we are about 95 per cent together. That is an amazing statement. It happens to be true."

Asked whether the statement included Russia and China, Mr. Roosevelt said it did, but he declined to make any forecast of the time and manner of the further conversations with the Russian Government which, he said, he expected to take place in the very near future.

The President emphasized that the talks were by no means confined to the United Kingdom and the United States but that the interchanges between officials of these two countries were one small part of a long series of conferences with the other United Nations. He said that intimate discussions had already taken place with China and one or two South American republics, and he recalled that Mr. Eden had been in Russia, where he saw Premier Joseph Stalin, Foreign Commissar Vyacheslav M. Molotov and other members of the Soviet Government. Mr. Roosevelt permitted the inference that he still hoped for an opportunity to meet Mr. Stalin.

The President indicated that the discussions with the British Foreign Secretary had included all parts of the world, not only, or mainly, Europe. But he agreed that if one enemy blew up, it would be necessary to concentrate first upon the tasks presented by that situation.

Mr. Roosevelt began by saying that it had been decided not to issue a formal statement about Mr. Eden's sixteen-day visit to this country, and that Mr. Eden had asked him to speak informally to the press instead.

The President said they were in entire agreement after they had discussed everything in the nature of current military and political affairs and other questions arising out of the war and relating to the present and future. He said he could speak for both himself and Mr. Eden in saying that the talks disclosed a very close similarity of outlook on the part of the two governments, a fruitful meeting of minds on all matters discussed.

He said they considered particularly the practical problems that would arise for all the United Nations upon the surrender of the enemy, primarily the safeguarding of the world against future aggressions. He said the conversations with Mr. Eden had been exploratory and that their purpose was not to take final decisions, which were impossible at this stage, but to reach a large measure of general agreement on objectives and thus to take time by the forelock. He thought this was a great aid toward the future conferences of the United Nations.

The President characterized the recent talks as one method of working toward the unity of the United Nations, which, he said, was going along extremely well, and he thought there were some who ought to take note of this. The other method, he said, was that of more formal gatherings, such as the forthcoming food conference, a later meeting on relief, another to explore financial tasks and possibly another on minerals and oil.

Mr. Roosevelt recalled that in 1918 the war ended suddenly when little preparatory work had been done, and he said that at Paris in 1919 people who thought they were experts were rushing around digging things out much like a lady who was told at noon that she would leave at three o'clock on a month's trip. This was why he thought the method now being followed was valuable in an exploratory way and as a method of getting to know each other.

The President deprecated talk of treaties or pacts in connection with the recent conversations, contending that much could be done through gentlemen's agreements. He added that there were thirty-one gentlemen involved in the United Nations discussions.

. . . .

(5) Conference of the President (Roosevelt) and the Prime Minister of the United Kingdom (Churchill), May 11–29, 1943 [1]

This was the fifth of a series of meetings between the President and the Prime Minister for the purpose of discussing broad plans of war strategy and relevant questions of policy. The Prime Minister arrived at a time when the end of the Axis resistance in North Africa was in close sight. On May 13, the German High Command announced that "the heroic struggle has today found its honorable end."

It therefore became necessary to plan ensuing stages of the Mediterranean campaign. With North Africa in Allied hands and the Mediterranean route open to Allied shipping, though still threatened from Sicily so long as that island remained in Axis control, there were obvious possibilities both as regards the European war and as regards the war in the Pacific. The opening of a military front on the continent of Europe became an early possibility, material aid could be brought to Soviet Russia more quickly and in larger quantities, and the shortening of lines of communication opened up the possibility of more vigorous action against Japan.

There had been widespread sentiment in the United States that the war against Japan had been neglected and there was need of reassurance that Japan would not be allowed so to strengthen her position as to make her dislodgment and the cause of Free China appear hopeless.

(a) Announcement of the Secretary to the President, May 11, 1943 [2]

The White House announced on the evening of May 11, 1943 the arrival in Washington of Prime Minister Winston Churchill, of Great Britain, to meet with President Roosevelt, whose guest he will be for the duration of his visit. The Prime Minister was accompanied by British military and naval experts, including Gen. Sir Alan Brooke, Chief of the Imperial General Staff; Admiral of the Fleet Sir Dudley Pound, First Sea Lord; Air Chief Marshal Sir Charles Portal; Field

[1] Department of State, Bulletin, VIII, p. 427.
[2] Ibid., p. 427.

Marshal Sir Archibald P. Wavell, Commander-in-Chief of British Forces in India; Admiral Sir James Somerville, Commander-in-Chief of the Eastern Fleet; Air Marshal Sir Richard Pierse, commanding British air officer in India; Lord Leathers, Minister of War Transportation; Lord Cherwell, Paymaster General and Statistical Officer of the Prime Minister; Lt. Gen. Sir Hastings L. Ismay, Chief Staff Officer to the Minister of Defense; and Brig. Gen. E. I. C. Jacob, Assistant Secretary (Military) of the British War Cabinet.

(b) *Address of the Prime Minister of the United Kingdom (Churchill) before the Joint Session of Congress, May 19, 1943* [1]

[Excerpts]

. . . .

Last time I came at a moment when the United States was aflame with wrath at the treacherous attack upon Pearl Harbor by Japan and at the subsequent declarations of war upon the United States made by Germany and Italy. For my part I say quite frankly that in those days after our long, and for a whole year lonely, struggle I could not repress in my heart a sense of relief and comfort that we were all bound together by common peril, by solemn faith and high purpose to see this fearful quarrel through at all costs to the end. That was an hour of passionate emotion, an hour most memorable in human records, an hour, as I believe, full of hope and glory for the future.

The experiences of a long life and the promptings of my blood have wrought in me the conviction that there is nothing more important for the future of the world than the fraternal association of our two peoples in righteous work, both in war and in peace. So, in January 1942, I had that feeling of comfort and I therefore prepared myself in a confident and steadfast spirit to bear the terrible blows which were evidently about to fall on British interests in the Far East, which were bound to fall upon us from the military strength of Japan during a period when the American and British Fleets had lost for the time being the naval command of the Pacific and Indian Oceans. One after another in swift succession very heavy misfortunes fell upon us and upon our allies, the Dutch, in the Pacific theater. The Japanese have seized the land and islands they so greedily coveted. The Philippines are enslaved. The lustrous, luxuriant regions of the Dutch East Indies have been overrun. In the Malay Peninsula and at Singapore we ourselves suffered the greatest military disaster, or at any rate the largest military disaster, in British history.

[1] *Congressional Record*, vol. 89, pt. 4, p. 4619; *New York Times*, May 20, 1943.

Mr. President and Mr. Speaker, all this has to be retrieved and all this and much else will have to be repaid.

And here let me say this: Let no one suggest that we British have not at least as great an interest as the United States in the unflinching and relentless waging of war against Japan; and I am here to tell you that we will wage that war side by side with you in accordance with the best strategic employment of our forces while there is a breath in our bodies and while blood flows in our veins.

A notable part in the war against Japan must, of course, be played by the large armies and by the air and naval forces now marshalled by Great Britain on the eastern frontiers of India. In this quarter there lies one of the means of bringing aid to hard-pressed and long-tormented China. I regard the bringing of effective and immediate aid to China as one of the most urgent of our common tasks. It may not have escaped your attention that I brought with me to this country and to this conference Field Marshal Wavell and the other two Commanders-in-Chief from India. Now they have not traveled all this way simply to concern themselves about improving the health and happiness of the Mikado of Japan. I thought it would be good that all concerned in this theater should meet together and thresh out in friendly candor and heart to heart all the points that arise, and there are many. You may be sure that if all that was necessary was for an order to be given to the great army standing ready in India to march toward the Rising Sun and open the Burma Road that order would be given this afternoon. The matter is, however, somewhat more complicated and all movements or infiltration of troops into the mountains and jungles to the northeast of India is very strictly governed by what your American military men call the science of logistics.

But, Mr. President and Mr. Speaker, I repudiate, I am sure with your sympathy, the slightest suspicion that we should hold anything back that can be usefully employed, or that I and the Government I represent are not as resolute to employ every man, gun, and airplane that can be used in this business as we have proved ourselves ready to do in other theaters of the war.

.   .   .   .

. . . Surveying the whole aspect of the air war, we cannot doubt that it is a major factor in the process of victory. That, I think, is established as a solid fact. It is similarly all agreed between us that we should at the earliest moment bring our joint air power to bear upon the military targets in the homelands of Japan. The cold-blooded execution of United States airmen by the Japanese Government is a proof not only of their barbarism but of the dread with which they regard this possibility. It is the duty of those charged with the direction of the war to overcome at the earliest moment the military, geographical, and political difficulties and begin the process, so necessary and desirable, of laying the cities and other munition centers of Japan in ashes. For in ashes they must surely lie before peace comes back to the world.

That this objective holds a high place in the present conference is obvious to thinking men, but no public discussion would be useful upon the method or sequence of events which should be pursued in order to achieve it. Let me make it plain, however, that the British will participate in this air attack on Japan in harmonious accord with the major strategy of the war. That is our desire. And the cruelties of the Japanese enemy make our airmen all the more ready to share the perils and sufferings of their American comrades.

．　．　．　．　．　．　．

(c) *Statement of the President (Roosevelt), Released to the Press, May 27, 1943* [1]

[Excerpt]

．　．　．　．　．　．

The conference of the Combined Staffs in Washington has ended in complete agreement on future operations in all theaters of the war. . . .

2. COMBINED WAR STAFFS AND UNIFIED COMMANDS

[See *Documents, IV, 1941–42,* p. 244.]

(1) *Unity of Command. Biennial Report of the Chief of Staff of the United States Army (Marshall), July 1, 1941 to June 30, 1943 to the Secretary of War* [2]

[Excerpt]

．　．　．　．　．　．

9. *Unity of Command*

Under the direction of the President, the Joint Chiefs of Staff, composed of the Chief of Staff to the Commander-in-Chief of the United States Army and Navy, the Chief of Staff of the United States Army, the Commander-in-Chief of United States Fleet and Chief of Naval Operations, and the Commanding General, Army Air Forces, are responsible for coordination between the Army and Navy, and in operations for which the United States has sole or primary responsibility, they are charged with the strategic conduct of the war. The Combined Chiefs of Staff, composed of the above United States members and four representatives of the British Chiefs of Staff, insure complete coordination of the war effort of Great Britain and the United States. A development of the Joint Chiefs of Staff and Combined Chiefs of Staff organizations is

[1] *New York Times,* May 27, 1943.
[2] Release copy received from the War Department, *Notes,* p. 5–7.

the unity of command principle which places the responsibility and authority for a contemplated operation under one commander directly responsible to the Joint Chiefs of Staff or the Combined Chiefs of Staff. When a joint or combined force commander has been designated and the units composing his force are assigned, his command responsibilities are the same as if the forces involved were all of one service or one nation. He exercises his command through the commanders of forces which have been assigned him, and normally in operations this will consist of the assignment of their respective missions. In carrying out its mission the tactics and technique of the force concerned are the responsibility of the commander of the subordinate force.

Allied to the principles of unified command is the mechanism of operational planning on a joint and combined level. The command function of the President as Commander-in-Chief of the United States forces is exercised through the United States Chiefs of Staff. The British Chiefs of Staff function in a similar manner under the Prime Minister and his War Cabinet. The United States Chiefs of Staff have organized planning and supporting agencies consisting of representatives from the Army and Navy and, where applicable, from other interested governmental agencies. These United States supporting agencies assist and advise the Joint Chiefs of Staff in matters of strategy, operational and administrative planning, psychological warfare, intelligence, transportation, the assignment of materials of war, communications, meteorology, weapons, petroleum, civil affairs and other matters. Most of the supporting agencies of the Joint Chiefs of Staff organization have a British counterpart with which they work, thus forming combined agencies to advise and assist the Combined Chiefs of Staff. An outstanding example of the success of this system is the complete harmony of action of the American and British forces in the Mediterranean area under the command of General Eisenhower.

. . . .

3. INTERNATIONAL COMMISSIONS, COMMITTEES AND BOARDS CONCERNED WITH THE PROSECUTION OF THE WAR

[See *Documents, IV, 1941–42*, p. 248, 351, 436.]

A list of the International Commissions, Committees, Boards, etc. concerned with the War on which the United States has representation was given in the Department of State *Bulletin* of January 16, 1943.[1] In this list the names of the organizations are given, the participating states, the location, basic facts regarding establishment and purpose and personnel as of the date of the preparation of the list. Organizations on which the United States was represented as of June 30, 1943 having to do with the prosecution of the war or related post-war problems are as follows:

Allied Supply Council (United States and Australia), established May 1942.

Anglo-American Caribbean Commission (United States and Great Britain), established March 9, 1942

[1] Department of State, *Bulletin*, VIII, p. 66.

The Combined Chiefs of Staff (United States and Great Britain), established February 6, 1942

Combined Food Board (United States and Great Britain), established June 9, 1942

Combined Production and Resources Board (United States, Great Britain, and Canada),[1] established June 9, 1942

Combined Raw Materials Board (United States and Great Britain), established January 26, 1942

Combined Shipping Adjustment Board (United States and Great Britain), established January 26, 1942

The Emergency Advisory Committee for Political Defense (Inter-American), established January 28, 1942

Inter-Allied Committee on Post-War Requirements (Leith-Ross Committee) (United States, Great Britain, Australia, Belgium, Canada, Czechoslovakia, Free France, Greece, Luxemburg, Netherlands, New Zealand, Norway, Poland, Union of South Africa, Union of Soviet Socialist Republics, and Yugoslavia), established September 24, 1941

Inter-American Commission for Territorial Administration (United States, Argentina, Brazil, Colombia, Costa Rica, Dominican Republic, Ecuador, El Salvador, Guatemala, Haiti, Honduras, Mexico, Nicaragua, Panama, Peru, Uruguay, Venezuela), established January 8, 1942

Inter-American Defense Board (United States, Argentina, Bolivia, Brazil, Chile, Colombia, Costa Rica, Cuba, Dominican Republic, Ecuador, El Salvador, Guatemala, Haiti, Honduras, Mexico, Nicaragua, Panama, Paraguay, Peru, Uruguay, Venezuela), established January 28, 1942

Inter-American Development Commission, established June 3, 1940

Inter-American Financial and Economic Advisory Committee (United States, Nicaragua, El Salvador, Argentina, Bolivia, Brazil, Chile, Colombia, Costa Rica, Cuba, Dominican Republic, Ecuador, Guatemala, Haiti, Honduras, Mexico, Panama, Paraguay, Peru, Uruguay, Venezuela), established October 3, 1939

Inter-American Juridical Committee, established January 28, 1942

Inter-American Maritime Technical Commission (United States, El Salvador, Argentina, Brazil, Chile, Colombia, Cuba, Ecuador, Mexico, Peru, Uruguay), established November 14, 1941

Intergovernmental Committee on Political Refugees (United States, United Kingdom, Argentina, Australia, Belgium, Bolivia, Brazil, Canada, Chile, Colombia, Costa Rica, Cuba, Denmark, Dominican Republic, Ecuador, France, Guatemala, Haiti, Honduras, Ireland, Mexico, Netherlands, New Zealand, Nicaragua, Norway, Panama, Paraguay, Peru, Sweden, Switzerland, Uruguay, and Venezuela), established July 14, 1938

Joint Brazil-United States Defense Commission, established August 1942

Joint Commission for Political Prisoners and Refugees (United States and Great Britain), established April 29, 1943

Joint Economic Committees (United States and Canada), established June 17, 1941

Joint Mexican-United States Defense Commission, established January 12, 1942

Joint Mexican-United States Commission for Economic Cooperation, established May 19, 1943

---

[1] On November 10, 1942 the Office of War Information announced that Canada had become a full member of the Board because of the "very close relations" in the production field which already existed among Canada, the United States and the United Kingdom (*ibid.*, p. 68).

Joint War Production Committee (United States and Canada), established November 5, 1941

Material Coordinating Committee (United States and Canada), established May 14, 1941

Middle East Supply Center (United States and Great Britain), established April 1941

Munitions Assignments Board (United States and Great Britain), established January 26, 1942

Pacific War Council (United States, Australia, Canada, China, Netherlands, New Zealand, Philippine Commonwealth, United Kingdom), established March 30, 1942

Permanent Joint Board on Defense (United States and Canada), established August 17, 1940

United Nations Information Board (Australia, Belgium, Canada, China, Czechoslovakia, Free Denmark, Fighting France, Great Britain, Greece, India, Luxemburg, Netherlands, New Zealand, Norway, Philippines, Poland, Union of South Africa, United States of America, Yugoslavia), established September 1940 [1]

3. RELIEF AND REHABILITATION

A. Action of United States Government

1. OFFICE OF FOREIGN RELIEF AND REHABILITATION OPERATIONS

In September 1941, the Department of State initiated formal studies on problems of relief and rehabilitation and displaced persons in the Special Research Division.

The concept and scope of the problems were first voiced publicly by Secretary Hull in a world-wide broadcast on July 23, 1942 [2] in which he said:

"With victory achieved our first concern must be for those whose sufferings have been almost beyond human endurance. When the armies of our enemies are beaten the people of many countries will be starved and without means of procuring food; homeless and without means of building shelter; their fields scorched; their cattle slaughtered; their tools gone; their factories and mines destroyed; their roads and transport wrecked. Unknown millions will be far from their homes — prisoners of war, inmates of concentration camps, forced laborers in alien lands; refugees from battle, from cruelty, from starvation. Disease and danger of disease will lurk everywhere. In some countries confusion and chaos will follow the cessation of hostilities. Victory must be followed by swift and effective action to meet these pressing human needs."

On November 21, 1942, President Roosevelt announced that the Office of Foreign Relief and Rehabilitation Operations was being established in the

[1] The United Nations Information Office, formerly known as the Inter-Allied Information Center, was first established in September 1940, as a clearing-house for the information services of the allied nations then at war with the Axis powers. In August 1942, following the entry of the United States into the war and the creation of the Office of War Information, the United States became a member of the Committee which controlled the Center, and arrangements were made for periodic meetings in Washington. Membership of the Committee gradually increased, and by December 1942, 19 governments and associated powers were participating in the work. In November 1942, the organization adopted the name of the United Nations Information Board, for the controlling committee, and the United Nations Information Office, for the executive organization. Membership on the United Nations Information Board and participation in the activities of the Office are open to all United Nations.

[2] For complete text see this volume, p. 1.

Department of State and that Herbert H. Lehman, then Governor of New York State, would be appointed director. Governor Lehman was appointed Director by the Hon. Cordell Hull, Secretary of State, on December 4, 1942. The basic principles governing the program and objectives of the new operation were stated thereafter by the President on December 11, 1942, in a letter which transmitted the seventh quarterly report on Lend-Lease operations to Congress.[1]

The staff working on relief and rehabilitation problems in the Department of State was detailed to Mr. Lehman's office when he assumed his duties, and later was absorbed by his staff.

The Office of Foreign Relief and Rehabilitation Operations also took over the direction of the work of five Inter-Departmental Committees organized by the Department of State assigned to the task of surveying relief and rehabilitation needs. They were:

1. Committee on Food Relief, H. R. Tolley, Department of Agriculture, Chairman.
2. Committee on Agricultural Rehabilitation, H. R. Tolley, Department of Agriculture, Chairman.
3. Committee on Clothing Requirements and Supplies, W. A. C. Clark, Tariff Commission, Chairman.
4. Committee on Health and Medical Requirements and Supplies, Dr. J. A. Crabtree, United States Public Health Service, Chairman.
5. Committee on Essential Services and Industries, W. B. McCoy, Department of Commerce, Chairman.

At the time the Office of Foreign Relief and Rehabilitation Operations was established, these committees had completed basic studies. The reports and recommendations of the Committees were submitted to Mr. Lehman in the latter part of December 1942, and have served as the basis of preliminary estimates of the volume and value of relief requirements for Norway, Denmark, Belgium, Luxemburg, France, Italy, Albania, Yugoslavia, Poland and Greece.

(1) *Relief in Liberated Areas. Seventh Report of the President (Roosevelt) to Congress on Lend-Lease Operations, December 11, 1942* [2]

[Excerpt]

Less than a week after our landings in North Africa, the Lend-Lease Administrator was instructed, in cooperation with General Eisenhower and the State Department, to extend aid to those areas in French Africa occupied by United Nations forces.

The policy of the United States, already announced, is to provide food, medicines, and other necessities to alleviate the hunger and suffering of the people in any territory occupied by our forces, so far as it is humanly within our power to do so. Weapons will be furnished to the armed forces of these territories to hasten the defeat of the Axis.

Methods of carrying out this policy will differ between areas, and different methods may be necessary within the same area. Where commercial channels of supply have been cut off, lend-lease can be the instru-

[1] House Doc. No. 904, 77th Cong., 2d sess., p. 5.
[2] *Ibid.*, p. 24.

ment for renewing them. Where relief distribution is necessary, lend-lease can supply the materials of relief.

Steps have already been taken with respect to North Africa in execution of this policy. About $5,000,000 worth of civilian goods have been purchased for shipment to that area. Many times that amount will be procured during the coming months, to be sent as shipping space becomes available. So long as military operations continue in this area, the amount of available shipping space cannot accurately be predicted. Cargoes necessary to maintain our armies in the field will have top priority on shipping, but civilian supply will come next on the list.

Items purchased, or to be purchased, under this program include: Medical and hospital supplies ranging from anaesthetics to operating knives, sulfa drugs and antitoxins; sugar, powdered and evaporated milk, and cheese, to meet the most urgent food needs; cotton textiles, ready-made new and used clothing, and shoes; copper sulphate to increase the production of vegetables and fruits for the consumption of our troops as well as the inhabitants; coal for transportation and kerosene for lighting. The United Kingdom will participate in this program with the United States.

The United Nations will help the victims of war in liberated territories, not only out of common humanity, but for the most urgent political and military reasons. Expansion of the agricultural production of the reoccupied regions and the improvement of their transportation facilities will be of great value to our military forces. Increased food production on the spot will enable us, after meeting the requirements of the civilian population, to supply our forces with some foodstuffs, thus saving valuable shipping space. Similarly any aid that we can furnish North Africa in maintaining and increasing its exportable production of certain strategic materials, such as phosphate rock, manganese, and high-grade iron ore will be of great value to the United Nations war effort.

The program of reoccupation will require the joint efforts of many agencies of this government, and the fullest cooperation with the other United Nations. Relief and rehabilitation of the reoccupied areas will be the common responsibility of all the United Nations, and must be a combined operation in the same sense as the military operations themselves. Success in restoring the countries we free will be a powerful factor in shortening the war, giving the liberated peoples their chance to share in the victory.

The United Nations have shown that they are capable of military teamwork of a high degree. In the field of relief and rehabilitation, they have an opportunity to develop a constructive program that will have a most direct bearing on the problems of the peace.

(2) *Scope of Work of the OFRRO. Letter from the President (Roosevelt) to the Director (Lehman), March 19, 1943* [1]

MY DEAR GOVERNOR:

Pending the working out of final plans with our allies, I should like to define the scope and duties of your work as Director of the Office of Foreign Relief and Rehabilitation.

You are authorized to plan, coordinate, and arrange for the administration of this Government's activities for the relief of victims of war in areas liberated from Axis control through the provision of food, fuel, clothing, and other basic necessities, housing facilities, medical and other essential services; and to facilitate in areas receiving relief the production and transportation of these articles and the furnishing of these services.

In planning, coordinating and arranging for the administration of the above-mentioned work, you may utilize the facilities of the various government departments, agencies and officials which are equipped to assist in this field and you may issue to them such directives as you deem necessary to achieve consistency in policy and coordination in administration. You may also utilize the facilities of such private organizations and individuals as you may find helpful in your work.

Your operations in any specific area abroad will, of course, be subject to the approval of the U. S. military commander in that area so long as military occupation continues, and in matters of general foreign policy you will be guided by the directives of the Secretary of State.

Your work in the field will likewise need to be geared to that of our allies in accordance with agreements reached with regard to the administration of such functions in each area. Should a United Nations organization be established for providing relief and rehabilitation to victims of war, the Office of Foreign Relief and Rehabilitation will need adjustment to facilitate that arrangement to the maximum extent possible.

On your organization rests a grave responsibility and challenging opportunity to facilitate the progress of the war and to relieve the deep suffering of those under Axis domination. I assure you of my full cooperation and that of Federal agencies in fields related to your own.

(3) *Objectives of the OFRRO. Statement of the Director (Lehman), April 3, 1943* [2]

In a statement which he made for a Regional Institute on Public Opinion and Post-war Planning, sponsored by the New York Public Library, Mr. Lehman stated as follows the three basic objectives of OFRRO:

To supply food and other basic necessities of life to peoples in areas liberated from Axis control who have been ravaged, despoiled and starved.

[1] Department of State, *Bulletin*, VIII, p. 256.
[2] The *Office of Foreign Relief and Rehabilitation Operations, Department of State.* Washington, Division of Public Information, OFRRO, July 15, 1943, p. 3.

To help restore those peoples as quickly as possible to a position where they no longer need relief and can make their own contribution to victory over the Axis and to the relief and rehabilitation of other peoples in other areas.

And furthermore, to do this job in a manner which will place the least possible burden on food stuffs and other materials which are or may be in short supply in the United States.

In carrying out these objectives the Office of Foreign Relief and Rehabilitation Operations expects to see to it that the United States is not made a "Santa Claus" to the rest of the world and that the resources of America are not dissipated to the detriment of its citizens. Relief is being planned so that it will not cut too heavily into our own short supplies at any one time. But within this limitation, which takes into consideration the necessities and welfare of our own people, I am convinced that our measures can do a great deal to stop starvation and death and spiritual attrition among the suffering millions of the world.

The basis of our operations will be simply this: Extension of relief on the principle of demonstrated need. We must make very certain that the necessities of life are made available to the people who need succor without discrimination as to race, or color or creed and without reference to their previous political allegiance.

(4) *Administrative Organization. Descriptive Statement Prepared by Division of Public Information, July 15, 1943* [1]

The First and Second Deputy Directors of Foreign Relief and Rehabilitation Operations assist the Director in the administration of the Office and fulfill his functions when he is absent.

The Staff Council is composed of the principal members of the staff, meeting periodically under the chairmanship of the Director or Deputy Directors. It considers and advises upon the general policies of the organization and secures coordination of the functions and plans of the various Divisions of the Office.

The Office of the Director includes, in addition to the Director, a Special Assistant and two principal staff assistants. The Special Assistant serves as a general assistant to the Director and staff assistants assist in maintaining liaison with the several Divisions of the Office and are available for special administrative assignments.

The following paragraphs outline the organization and functions of the other offices and of the various divisions at the present time:

DIVISION OF STUDIES AND PROGRESS REPORTS

The principal responsibilities of the Division of Studies and Progress Reports are the following:

To anticipate operating and policy problems that will face the Director and the several Divisions of OFRRO, and to collect and analyze, or to stimulate other agencies to collect and analyze, materials and data bearing on those problems and to prepare reports and suggest solutions.

To serve as economic and statistical consultant to the Director, to the other Divisions, and to staff members.

[1] *Ibid.*, p. 6–10.

To collect and analyze statistical data on the operations of OFRRO and to prepare comprehensive periodical reports on the development of programs, policies, operations, etc., for the confidential information of the staff members and for other purposes.

To maintain a service library for OFRRO and to serve as repository of documents, reports and other information concerning foreign relief and rehabilitation; to maintain an historical record of the OFRRO; and to prepare such digests of documents, reports, and cables as the several Divisions may find useful.

To maintain a central correspondence file for OFRRO; to serve as central mail room for the receiving and dispatching of all mail; and to operate a messenger service.

DIVISION OF PROGRAM AND REQUIREMENTS

The Division of Program and Requirements is a staff unit whose work lies between research and operations. Using factual materials accumulated and developed by the Division of Studies and Progress Reports, and ideas of the several divisions of the Department of State and various other governmental and non-governmental agencies, it is responsible for providing the Office of Foreign Relief and Rehabilitation Operations with analyses of need — in general and by specific area — and proposals for action toward meeting the need.

Chief among the materials expected from this division are the following: (1) Studies of potential recipient areas, designed to determine the dimensions and priority of needs, and to provide important background information for those who will be engaged in field operations in those areas. (2) General allocation and procurement programs for the use of the Division of Supply and Transport, framed with due attention to the supply and shipping situation, in this country and in other supply areas. (3) Particular schedules of supplies to be secured and sent abroad for the assistance of certain areas at certain times. (4) Revisions of all the above materials on the basis of reports from supply authorities and OFRRO field missions.

Organizationally, the division has four branches, dealing respectively with: (1) food and agriculture, clothing, emergency shelter, essential community services; (2) medical supplies and health services; (3) engineering, transportation, industrial and commercial rehabilitation, economic and social relations, and the problem of displaced persons; and (4) requirement analysis and statistics. These branches maintain close operating contacts with other divisions of OFRRO and the Office of the Inter-Allied Committee on Post-War Requirements in London, with other agencies of the government (through technical committees such as the one on health, and through panels of area experts), and with private organizations.

DIVISION OF SUPPLY AND TRANSPORT

The Division of Supply and Transport is charged with arranging for the procurement of the necessary food, clothing, equipment and other supplies as determined by the Program and Requirements Division, and for their transportation to the countries where they are needed. This involves necessary relationships with OLLA, Lend-Lease, BEW, the Combined Boards, WPB, Treasury, Agriculture, etc., to assure:

1. Proper consideration of foreign relief and rehabilitation needs in the allocation of supplies among various claimants.
2. Procurement and storage of supplies.
3. Transportation to designated locations.

It also involves arrangements for the immediate establishment of reserves so far as possible and for the encouragement, through appropriate agencies, of production of essential materials in countries other than the United States. The Division is organized into four branches: Food, Clothing and Textiles, Equipment and Supplies, and Transportation and Warehouse, each of which will be divided into sections.

DIVISION OF FIELD OPERATIONS

This Division is set up in the home office in Washington and has charge of the missions in countries to which relief is sent or in which rehabilitation operations are to be carried out.

The home office is to direct the operations of the OFRRO in the field in accordance with plans approved by the Director. It is the channel through which the Director translates his policies and decisions to the field. It also obtains and evaluates field data from the missions in the field for the Director, the Division of Program and Requirements, the Division of Supply and Transport, the Division of Budget and Finance, the Division of Public Information and other Divisions. It has a special section to keep in touch with the families of OFRRO personnel in field missions abroad, thus contributing to the morale of the organization.

It will handle operational relations in the field with private charities in accordance with the Director's policies. It will also maintain relationships with local governments in relief areas, negotiating relief agreements where required and obtaining local contributions of local personnel and supplies to the maximum extent possible.

The field missions will receive supplies at ports of entry designated by the Division of Supply and Transport of the home office, arrange for warehousing and inland rail or water transportation, keep prescribed accounting records, establish relief distribution points, and organize, supervise and control the distribution of all supplies on the basis of established need. Rehabilitation projects and medical relief will be undertaken by special sections of the staff or the Chief of Mission abroad, upon approval of projects by the Director.

DIVISION OF BUDGET AND FINANCE

The Division of Budget and Finance was organized to control budgeting and budget expenditures, to establish, install and maintain accounting systems and financial operative records, both domestic and foreign, and subject to the jurisdiction of those government agencies which have final determination of policies, to deal with fiscal problems as they arise in the course of operations. The Division itself will not attempt to furnish an accounting or statistical staff for local operations in the field, but will establish, install and inspect systems to be used by employees of the Division of Field Operations.

The Division also maintains a procedure section to establish routines for its own work. This section is available for the services of other divisions for this same purpose.

In the budget for the year 1943–1944, which is now under consideration, it is proposed, however, to reorganize this division so that there will be established a Budget Office and a Division of Accounting Control, both responsible to the Second Deputy Director.

The Budget Office will be charged with budget estimates and analyses and with budget control. The latter function is intended to assure the Director that expenditures and purchases will be within the limits of programs which he has approved.

The Division of Accounting Control will establish and install accounting systems for the entire organization, will maintain the basic accounts for the organization, and will audit the accounts and statistical records of the Division of Field Operations and any other divisions which maintain such records.

DIVISION OF PERSONNEL AND TRAINING

The Division formulates OFRRO personnel policies for adoption by the Director and secures conformity of all personnel actions with such policies. The Division is in charge of recruiting for OFRRO, interviewing applicants and referring competent candidates to the appropriate Divisions requiring personnel, and serves as the liaison with the Department of State's Division of Departmental Personnel and Division of Foreign Service Personnel on all personnel actions and application of personal regulations. In cooperation with the Chiefs of other Divisions of OFRRO, the Chief of Personnel and Training will develop and establish a training program for all personnel on foreign assignment.

DIVISION OF INTERNATIONAL RELATIONS

The Division of International Relations has primary responsibility for arranging, in cooperation with other offices in the Department of State, for discussions and preparations relating to international plans for relief and rehabilitation. It has special responsibility for coordinating the preparatory work of this Government for the proposed meeting of the United Nations on this subject. It assists the Director of the Office as a channel of communication and liaison with international agencies and the agencies of other governments concerned with the field of relief and rehabilitation.

DIVISION OF SPECIAL RELIEF PROBLEMS

The Division of Special Relief Problems is responsible for advising the Director on matters concerning special relief problems, more particularly problems of trans-blockade and intra-blockade relief of civilian populations in territories occupied by the enemy.

DIVISION OF PUBLIC INFORMATION

The functions of the Division of Public Information in general are:

To disclose to the public at home and abroad all news and information on activities of the Office of Foreign Relief and Rehabilitation Operations consistent with sound public policy.

To contribute by the use of news and information to the understanding of the general public as to the necessity of providing food to our Allies in war and relief and rehabilitation to liberated peoples as an essential to the establishment of a stable and enduring peace.

OFFICE OF THE GENERAL COUNSEL

The General Counsel is responsible for advising the Director, his staff members and their subordinates of their legal powers and responsibilities in all operations. The Office of the General Counsel assists in the preparation of legislative bills and data for hearings and of Executive Orders, directives and other regulations for the operation of the program of OFRRO; provides the Director and his staff with legal opinions relative to the application of statutes, Executive

Orders, and administrative regulations; and is primarily responsible for drafting, examining and construing contracts, deeds, leases and other documents relating to the activities of OFRRO. The General Counsel also serves as the Director's contact on legal matters with other federal agencies and assists in general negotiations with such agencies.

COMMITTEE ON HEALTH AND MEDICAL CARE

The Office of Foreign Relief and Rehabilitation Operations has recognized from the outset the necessity of planning and executing an extensive medical and health program in theaters of relief operations. Planning for this work has been in progress since early this year and will continue throughout the operations of the Office.

The function of collecting data on health and medical conditions in prospective theaters of relief operations has been centered in a Committee on Health and Medical Care in the OFRRO. This Committee is in the structure of the Division of Planning and Requirements in the OFRRO. At the invitation of Mr. Herbert H. Lehman, Director of Foreign Relief and Rehabilitation Operations, Surgeon General Thomas Parran of the U. S. Public Health Service is Chairman of the Advisory Committee. The Committee is constructed to cross Departmental lines to provide the broadest possible Governmental approach to the health and medical care problem. Other members, serving on the Committee at Mr. Lehman's invitation are Colonel James S. Simmons, U. S. Army; Commander T. J. Carter, U. S. Navy; Dr. Alfred Cohn, Board of Economic Warfare; Professor C.-E. A. Winslow, Yale University Medical School; Dr. Frank C. Boudreau, Milbank Memorial Fund; and Mr. Selskar M. Gunn, Rockefeller Foundation. Mr. Gunn is acting as secretary to the Committee, pending appointment of a permanent secretary.

As outlined by Mr. Lehman in his invitation to this group to participate in the work, the objectives of the Committee on Health and Medical Care are as follows:

1. "To collect and analyze available information concerning disease prevalence and important health problems in areas which may be reoccupied by our armed forces.
2. "To appraise the epidemic and other disease conditions which are likely to be an important part of relief and rehabilitation.
3. "To estimate the amount and kinds of essential health and medical supplies and equipment which must be provided.
4. "To consider — at least in general terms — the numbers, skills and potential sources of personnel needed to deal with epidemic and other health problems.
5. "To consider, in conjunction with appropriate agricultural and other sources of information, the nutritional problems ahead.
6. "To advise the Director of Foreign Relief and Rehabilitation upon request concerning other aspects of public health as the occasion requires."

(5) *Relief and Rehabilitation. Address of the Director of the OFRRO (Lehman) before the Foreign Policy Association, New York City, June 17, 1943* [1]

I am honored to appear here tonight to discuss with you some of the problems of the relief and rehabilitation of victims of war and the prin-

[1] Department of State, *Bulletin,* VIII, p. 539.

ciples which should govern their solution. I was happy to avail myself of your invitation, since I am deeply convinced that the hour has now arrived for urgent national consideration of such problems and principles. The members of your distinguished organization can do much to direct national thinking toward these massive questions.

The peace which we all seek must be rooted in the first hurried work of rehabilitation and reconstruction. The dimensions of this task can best be measured by the dimensions of the disaster which has overtaken the world. The Axis has extended its despotism over the peoples of some 35 countries and hundreds of islands, the dwelling-places of more than half a billion men, women, and children. Almost all Europe lies under the dark cloud of Nazi rule; Japan has overrun the rich islands of the western Pacific and has penetrated deep toward the heart of heroic China. In occupied Europe and in enslaved Asia the picture is universally the same — starving people, impoverished land, and nations whose whole economies have been wrecked.

Food-condition statistics in the area of Axis occupation are treacherous. But official reports from Europe and Asia leave no doubt that hunger is the general rule, that starvation is commonplace, and that the area enslaved by the Axis is a breeding-place for all the diseases of the body and of the spirit that are born of starvation, suffering, and death.

Agricultural production in Europe has dropped substantially despite the desperate efforts of Germany to make Axis-dominated Europe self-supporting. As the months roll on, the manpower shortage, the wastage and deterioration of machinery, the neglect of the soil, and the increasing disorganization of the economy will cut even deeper into total food-production.

The once matchless flocks and herds of Europe have declined to figures in some cases a third below pre-war levels. Horses are disappearing at a rate that indicates that a shortage of draft animals may be a problem even more acute than the shortage of manpower in the first harvest of peace. The occupied nations have been systematically drained of their resources, raw materials, and commercial goods to serve a vicious new order. Never before has the world witnessed so ruthless a despoliation of so many in so short a time.

A problem so vast and so world embracing, obviously, does not lend itself to piecemeal solution. The problem is to devise means to harness world production, already greatly taxed by war needs, to total world want during the coming months of tremendous human crisis. We must see to it that relief flows smoothly and swiftly into measures to remove the need of relief, and that rehabilitation measures are so devised as to enable the suffering nations to begin their own reconstruction at the earliest possible moment. Our objective is to *help people* to help *themselves* and thereby to help ourselves, by making possible a world in which the four freedoms can have a chance of realization.

We have already made important strides toward meeting these complex problems. Within the last few days the Department of State has placed before the 43 governments of all the United Nations and the other nations associated with us in this war a draft agreement for creation of a United Nations Relief and Rehabilitation Administration through which the productive resources of all the nations of goodwill may shortly be mobilized to bring succor to the victims of war.[1] The Governments of the United States, Great Britain, Russia, and China already have agreed to this plan, indicating their readiness to participate wholeheartedly in an historic effort to see to it that no one shall die for the lack of bread, protection from the elements, or the minimum assistance of modern medicine.

There is fortunately a strong disposition among the nations to recognize that this problem is without parallel in history and that its solution must lie in joint and concerted efforts by all nations. It is proposed that each nation, in making its greatest possible contribution to the task, shall within its resources make not only a financial contribution but shall contribute further in the form of supplies, shipping and other transportation, personnel and services. It is, as yet, too early to predict what total amounts or what proportion any government will be called upon to supply to the joint enterprise. There are, however, precedents for action in this direction. Under the terms of the International Wheat Agreement,[2] for example, Canada and the United Kingdom, Australia, Argentina, and the United States have undertaken to contribute large quantities of wheat for use in a major offensive against starvation. There are supplies in other areas which, when fully drawn upon, will distribute the burden of world relief over many countries. At least 50 per cent, and perhaps more, of the total cereals required for European relief can readily come from areas other than the United States, and it should be noted that cereals comprise well over half the total tonnage of any table of relief food shipments.

This proposed United Nations Relief and Rehabilitation Administration represents a practical and realistic approach to a problem of great magnitude. America cannot feed the world from its own resources alone. Neither can Britain nor Russia nor China nor any one of the other American Republics. Satisfaction of the wants of the millions of suffering men, women, and children can be accomplished only by the concerted action of all the nations whose productive resources were fortunately spared the fire and destruction of modern warfare.

The imperative demands of military necessity will not, however, wait upon international conversations or protracted conferences. It may well be that in the immediate future our fighting commanders will call upon us to move in behind a front line in Europe to provide relief to

[1] See this volume, p. 285.   [2] *Ibid.*, p. 636.

newly liberated peoples. In anticipation of such a possibility, the Office of Foreign Relief and Rehabilitation Operations is proceeding with plans as an American organization, confident that the other nations of goodwill will step forward to assist and that this practical United Nations mechanism will become a reality.

The common dislike of the concept of "relief" on the part both of nations that receive and nations that give is certain to have a deep influence on the nature of these operations. In an era when political stability is dependent upon economic stability as never before, no nation will casually become a recipient of a dole. Similarly, no nation, nor group of nations, will casually commit their resources to a tremendous relief undertaking without striving to make certain that simultaneous measures are instituted to make possible the cessation of relief expenditures at the earliest possible moment.

There should be no basic misconception of the idea of relief in the minds of Americans. Relief operations in Europe after the war of 1914–18 by no means entirely took the form of gift. Where governments had cash or assets, they were required in some cases to pay cash and in other cases to pledge assets as security for loans. In other instances, governments which had no assets which could reasonably be regarded as good security, were nevertheless provided with relief and required to pay by means of loans advanced to them under conditions where the commercial soundness of the credit was highly questionable. Most of these loans were subsequently defaulted, and our Government thus was no better off than if the loans had been outright gifts. On the other hand the country receiving relief suffered an impairment of its credit and was less able to borrow for sound projects of reconstruction so long as these loans still complicated its finances. Economic recovery was thus impaired, and one of the forces was put into motion which headed the world toward the tragic cycle which led first to a gigantic depression, then to the rise of Hitler, Mussolini, and the Japanese militarists, and finally to global conflagration.

To avoid the danger of permitting relief to cause fundamental economic derangements which might generate a third world war, a careful balance must be maintained between relief by outright gift and relief by sale or exchange. None of the liberated nations will be seeking the charity of this country. But in some instances it certainly will be the course of prudence and wisdom to advance the goods for relief and rehabilitation as outright gifts. To do otherwise under some conditions would be to impair the credit and economy of the liberated nations and thus make it difficult if not impossible for such nations to procure essential credit and exchange when the initial emergency has passed and the time arrives for sound, long-term reconstruction. In other instances, however, the liberated nations will quickly reestablish governments capable, ready, and willing to purchase the foodstuffs and goods necessary for relief and rehabilitation, and operations of the relief and rehabilitation agency can and should proceed on a commercial basis. In still other instances, the operation undoubtedly must be an admixture of both procedures. But in all situations, the technique of salvage and rehabilitation must constantly be oriented toward the objective of reconstituting the economy of the recipient nation. That is the way to put an end to relief. That is what *we* want. That is what the suffering peoples of the liberated nations will have richly earned.

For these reasons, the President, pending the creation of the United Nations Relief and Rehabilitation Administration, has assigned my office the task not alone of establishing "soup kitchens" and carrying on direct relief, but also of assisting war-stricken peoples in reviving their own production of essential goods and services as rapidly as possible. In each liberated area which the President may designate, the Office of Foreign Relief and Rehabilitation Operations is to distribute relief goods and goods to facilitate the production of basic civilian necessities, whether those goods be given away, sold, or bartered. In such way we achieve a single supply line to each liberated area and avoid inconsistency and confusion in policy and administration.

The lessons learned in the quarter century during which this war was in the making demonstrate beyond question that the United States and the United Nations have no alternative but to undertake this task. The motives that impel us to this work are readily demonstrable, even without reference to the deep moral motives which of themselves alone would be a justification for assisting those who are suffering and dying.

In the initial stages, our activities are so closely integrated with the military that relief operations actually are conducted by the army itself or under its close supervision. The work will, of course, be subject to the approval of the military commander so long as military operations require. The importance of civilian supply behind the lines was clearly demonstrated by the North African campaign where the provision of the essentials of life to civilians in the war theater was a military and political necessity, closely related to the whole campaign strategy. What was true in North Africa will be equally true, in magnified scope and under much more urgent conditions, on the continents of Europe and Asia.

It is not military necessity alone, however, that compels us to undertake relief and rehabilitation measures. Millions of people have been plundered, despoiled, and starved. Unless the United States, in concert with the other United Nations, extends a helping hand to these peoples, we can anticipate with certainty that the liberated areas for decades will suffer from disrupted economies, crushing burdens of unemployment, shattering inflations, and the internal turmoil which adds up to chaos.

If we have learned anything from the decades just behind us it is this: That we cannot, even if we would, make ourselves secure in a world in which millions of men, women, and children are dying of want or by epidemic. Let us recognize frankly that freedom from want is a basic component of any enduring peace and that if America is to have any hope of lasting peace and a stable world economy it must help see to it that the liberated peoples of the world are restored as rapidly as possible to a self-sustaining basis.

That is merely enlightened self-interest.

We cannot live with security in a world half rich, half pauperized. International trade cannot flourish or sound economic expansion take place in a world tormented by expectations of the violence that is born of suffering and misery. And the United States, in the period after this war, will need the outlets of a total world market unless our economy is to face a terrific contraction in a shattering post-war depression. We in America must not lose sight of the fact that, once this war has ended, we again will be the greatest producers in the world and will want world markets for our grain, our cotton, our tobacco, and other agricultural staples as well as our steel, our automobiles, and the thousands of products of our mills and factories.

The relief and rehabilitation of war-stricken nations is the necessary first step toward a balanced economy in which a high level of consumption will prevent the piling up of those great stocks of surplus goods which would otherwise be quickly accumulated after this war in all the primary producing countries. Relief and rehabilitation is but the opening phase of the post-war era. The long-range reconstruction which follows this phase must be conducted on the basis of world trade. By emergency relief and rehabilitation measures now we can make it possible for the liberated peoples of Europe and Asia to become in succeeding years the customers for our goods. Thus by restoring the basic economic equilibrium of these peoples we can hope to create demand which will provide jobs for the millions of fighting men who will be streaming home from our victorious armies to take jobs in an industry converting back to production for peace.

The costs of such a program will be great, even though they will be diminutive when projected against the total costs of this war or the total costs of another depression. The outlays will represent an investment for a new world in which productive facilities will have an opportunity to operate to make possible prosperous conditions at home and to diminish suffering and want abroad. This war right now is costing the American taxpayer about a billion dollars every three days. The cost in life and spiritual value is incalculable. The knowledge that America and other United Nations are prepared to extend relief and rehabilitation to the victims of war and to sustain the spirit of resistance among the down-trodden people of Europe and Asia when the hour of freedom strikes, will help to transform those people into a cohesive group, ready and willing to cooperate in the battle of liberation. Should America's readiness to bring relief to the weary peoples of Europe and Asia shorten the war by but a week or two, the United States will have saved far more on war costs than the total outlays which can be anticipated in the field of relief and rehabilitation.

The deepest aspiration of the peoples of Europe and Asia will be for an opportunity to rebuild their own lives toward a system of stability and order. Unless they are helped in the initial stages to help themselves, this opportunity for sound reconstruction may be lost. It would be folly for this country and the United Nations to pour out their total substance in a complete effort for victory and hesitate to expend the final dollars which would make possible the realization of the objectives for which they fought — the establishment of a stable world economy and of a peace that will endure.

The cry of nations and their peoples for assistance in the first hours of liberation will present democracy with a supreme test. The fate of all United Nations' attempts to insure banishment of these global wars may well be determined by the success of the first joint action in relief and rehabilitation administration. This work of binding up the wounds of those who suffer, or preventing and halting death by starvation, exposure, disease, and neglect, transcends the realm of political allegiances and can give full expression to the highest principles and instincts of all peoples. If the nations of the world should fail to work in mutual cooperation for these high principles, what hope could we hold for political cooperation to banish war? If it is true that nations learn to work together by actually working together, then the joint effort of the United Nations to help the liberated peoples of the world may well provide the experience which will make possible the more gigantic enterprises to come.

It is given to us, twice within the span of a lifetime, to attempt to devise a peace in which all men can live in freedom from fear and want. We failed last time. We dare not fail again.

(6) Continuation of Relief Work by Private Organizations. Joint Statement of the Director of the OFRRO (Lehman), the Chairman of the President's War Relief Control Board (Davies), and the Chairman of the American Red Cross (Davis), January 11, 1943 [1]

The President has declared that to the task of bringing to bear directly against the enemy the full strength of the material resources and manpower of the United Nations, there is added another task. This task,

[1] Department of State, *Bulletin*, VIII, p. 37.

continuously growing, is to supply medicines, food, clothing and other necessities of life to the peoples who have been plundered, despoiled, and starved. Every possible aid will be given, therefore, to help restore each of the liberated countries to soundness and strength so that each may make its full contribution to the United Nations' victory and to the peace which will follow.

The united resources and services of Government, supplemented by those of the American Red Cross and the International Red Cross organization, and by the voluntary efforts of all people will be required for the relief of distressed civilians in the countries associated with America in this war. While the resources and services of Government will be drawn upon to furnish the primary supplies for mass emergency relief of civilian populations, voluntary organizations rendering essential services will also need to be maintained.

Since the outbreak of war in September 1939, foreign relief has been effected materially through many voluntary relief agencies serving the people of Great Britain, France, Belgium, the Netherlands, Norway, Poland, Czechoslovakia, Yugoslavia, Greece, Russia, China and other war-torn countries.

Relief work of this character is supplemental to supplies and services already extended by the Government and which, through operations of the Office of Foreign Relief and Rehabilitation Operations, will be extended on a steadily increasing scale. It is likewise supplemental to work performed by the American Red Cross. Continuation of such voluntary relief work is essential not only as an expression of the generous sympathies of the American people but also as a distinctive service that quasi-public and voluntary agencies can render to complement public resources and services. There are many essential services which can be provided by private agencies that cannot be provided by the Government.

As in the past, private relief agencies will be licensed by and registered with the President's War Relief Control Board.

Mr. Herbert H. Lehman, Director of Foreign Relief and Rehabilitation Operations, announced on April 5, 1943 [1] that some personnel and resources of private organizations are being utilized to a limited extent in initial relief operations in North Africa.

Mr. Lehman emphasized, however, that the necessity for unified operations in the field combined with the extraordinary difficulties of transportation to relief theaters severely restrict and will continue to restrict the extent to which the Office of Foreign Relief and Rehabilitation Operations can utilize personnel and services of non-governmental relief or philanthropic groups.

"Four men in the employ of the American Friends Service Committee have been attached to the staff of Mr. Fred K. Hoehler, Director of Relief in North

[1] *Ibid.*, p. 295.

Africa for OFRRO," Mr. Lehman said. "They are Mr. Leslie O. Heath, Mr. Kendal Kimberland, Mr. Eric Johnson, and Mr. David Hartley. Under the control and supervision of Mr. Hoehler these workers of the American Friends Service Committee are providing essential relief for refugees in French North Africa.

"In connection with making available these services, the American Friends Service Committee in Philadelphia has turned over to my office 25 tons of new and used clothing and bedding for distribution among needy civilians in French North Africa. This gift was accepted by the Treasury Department for my office and will be shipped to Mr. Hoehler in North Africa."

Mr. Lehman said that Mr. James G. Vail, foreign-service secretary of the American Friends Service Committee, additionally has turned over $25,000 to the Treasury Department for use of the Office of Foreign Relief and Rehabilitation Operations in North Africa. The American Jewish Joint Distribution Committee, through its honorary chairman, Mr. Paul Baerwald, also has turned over $25,000 to the Treasury Department for use of OFRRO operations in the North African theater, he said. Under terms of acceptance of both gifts, use of the funds will be under complete control of Mr. Lehman's office and the chief of the relief mission in the field and will be used for provision of relief on the basis of need without consideration of race, nationality, or political affiliation.

He emphasized additionally that American Red Cross personnel also has provided very material assistance in the initial relief operations in North Africa. Distribution of milk to children in Algeria and French Morocco has been accomplished by American Red Cross personnel working under the direction of Mr. Hoehler, he said.

It was pointed out that use of non-governmental organizations in North Africa on a limited scale was in line with the joint statement given above.

B. Relief and Rehabilitation Operations in North Africa

The military occupation of French North Africa made it immediately necessary for the Government of the United States, acting in cooperation with the Government of the United Kingdom and French authorities in North Africa, to initiate work of relief and rehabilitation in that area. On January 29, it was announced by the Department of State that Mr. Fred K. Hoehler had arrived in Algeria to serve as Director of Relief in North Africa for the Office of Foreign Relief and Rehabilitation Operations. It was stated that Mr. Hoehler would report to and work under the general direction of Mr. Robert D. Murphy, Personal Representative of the President, in Mr. Murphy's capacity as Chief Civilian Affairs Officer on General Eisenhower's staff in North Africa.[1] Mr. Hoehler was designated as Director of Relief in North Africa after the death in an airplane crash of Mr. William Hodson while en route to Algeria.

(1) Relief Operations in Tunisia. Department of State Releases, June 1 and 26, 1943

(a) Press Release of June 1, 1943 [1]

The Office of Foreign Relief and Rehabilitation Operations announced on June 1 that its operations in Tunisia now have been centralized at field-mission headquarters in the city of Tunis.

[1] Ibid., p. 103.   [1] Ibid., p. 492.

Members of the OFRRO field mission, assisting the military detachment which has primary responsibility for relief during the initial stages of liberation, moved into major cities of Tunisia immediately after cessation of military operations. Distribution of food and clothing to civilian populations of Tunisia was begun in such centers as Sousse, Sfax, and Gabes even before the final allied victory in Tunisia.

Mr. Fred K. Hoehler, Chief of Mission for OFRRO in North Africa, appointed Mr. E. Reeseman Fryer to take charge of Tunisian operations. Mr. Fryer is assisted by a civilian staff of 10 OFRRO field workers, additional personnel assigned by the military, and national personnel assigned by the local French authorities. Mr. Paul W. Gordon, also a member of the OFRRO North African mission, is assisting Mr. Fryer, supervising activities to assist the military in southern Tunisia.

Mr. Fryer, who has been attached to the Tunisian mission since late last winter, was formerly deputy director of the War Relocation Authority and previously was regional director of that agency at San Francisco. Prior to that service he was general superintendent of the Navajo Office of Indian Affairs at Window Rock, Ariz. His home is in San Francisco.

Preliminary reports from the field indicate that plans for distribution of essential supplies to distressed civilians in Tunisia were executed close on the heels of Allied military operations in that area. While Mr. Gordon was cooperating with military authorities of the British and United States Armies in southern Tunisia and Tripolitania, Mr. Hoehler dispatched two teams of field men with truck convoys provided by the Army into areas where military action had made it essential that local supplies of food and clothing be supplemented by relief material as a matter of military and political necessity.

Initial reports to Mr. Herbert H. Lehman, Director of Foreign Relief and Rehabilitation Operations, from Mr. Hoehler show that small stockpiles of essential food and clothing assembled by OFRRO in cooperation with the military in or near Tunisia were utilized for primary civilian needs. This stockpile, which by the time of the major military offensive approximated 10 thousand tons, was comprised of cotton cloth, condensed and powdered milk, flour, sugar, and clothing.

Hoehler's reports, based on his own surveys and those of Mr. Herbert W. Parisius of Elroy, Wis., Chief Agricultural Expert on the OFRRO North African staff, indicate that prospects for supply of civilians in Tunisia are much better than had been anticipated prior to the Allied victory over the Axis forces.

Mr. Parisius, who is chairman of a committee on agricultural production and requirements of the North African Economic Board in connection with his assignment from Mr. Lehman, reported that preliminary surveys indicate that there may be 30 thousand tons of olive oil available in Tunisia, although some parts and repairs will be necessary for pressing plants which process this important vegetable oil. Mr. Parisius reported that prospects for cereal harvest in Tunisia are good.

The liberation of Tunisia had shifted emphasis of the relief program to that area from Algeria and French Morocco. The Office of Foreign Relief and Rehabilitation Operations, however, had conducted only relatively few minor operations in Algeria and French Morocco, chiefly the provision, with the cooperation of the American Red Cross, of milk rations daily to 147 thousand children between the ages of 18 months and 14 years in those two areas. With the closing of the school year, this milk program was scheduled to be virtually discontinued on May 31. Grants of milk will be continued, however, through hospitals and clinics to children in urgent need of such supplemental ration whose parents or guardians are unable to make other provisions for them. The OFRRO field mission is continuing its work in behalf of the inmates of refugee camps and is setting up camps to house sick and disabled refugees where they will have complete freedom under the care of a physician, provisions, and other assistance. The rapid release of refugees from internment camps during the last 60 days is gradually reducing the need for the OFRRO program of providing for the essential needs of able-bodied refugees. During the last 6 weeks, however, OFRRO field representatives visited camps in Algeria and French Morocco, distributing food and clothing to supplement the supply of the residents and rendering essential assistance to place refugees in jobs as they were released. The OFRRO has been assisted in its work with refugees by the American Friends Service Committee, which had representatives in the area.

(b) Press Release of June 26, 1943 [1]

The Office of Foreign Relief and Rehabilitation Operations announced June 26 that preliminary reports from its North African mission emphasize that the great bulk of its operations in Tunisia is being conducted on a commercial basis rather than on a direct contribution basis.

It was announced that Mr. Fred K. Hoehler, Chief of the OFRRO mission in North Africa, would depart soon from that area for other assignments. He will be succeeded in North Africa by Mr. E. R. Fryer, of San Francisco, formerly an official of the Office of Indian Affairs and the War Relocation Authority. Mr. Fryer has been in active charge of relief operations in Tunisia since immediately after the Allied occupation of that territory. Mr. Herbert W. Parisius, Chief Agricultural Officer on the staff of the OFRRO mission, has also left North Africa for the United States. Some 20 other members of the mission will remain in North Africa for the present to carry on the program instituted by Mr. Hoehler.

The principal relief task remaining in North Africa today is in Tunisia. In that region the OFRRO mission, working through the North African Economic Board, has brought into action several programs designed to re-establish civilian life and affairs without delay and with economy in expenditures of funds and supplies. First and most important of the measures taken is a chain of "relief stores" providing outlets for relief supplies such as dried milk, sugar, tea, coffee, and cloth or clothing in virtually all the newly liberated Tunisian cities. This system, amounting to an American merchandising system and novel in North African life, makes the Controleur Civil, or civil administrator, in each area responsible for the conduct of the stores and places the actual handling of relief goods in native hands, American personnel confining its activities to supervision.

A kind of "relief rationing" system was created to go along with the relief stores. Although in such cities as Tunis, Sfax, and Sousse, people were in need of food and clothing, in general they had enough money to care for their needs if supplies were on hand and distribution established on an equitable and non-discriminatory basis. Along with his general responsibility for the conduct of the stores, the Controleur Civil, consequently, was requested to issue tickets on a family basis authorizing purchases in the stores. Two kinds of tickets are issued, one for families of three or less and one for families of four or more people. Tunisians appear to like the plan and to appreciate that it makes greater supplies available for people in need of direct relief. Besides Tunis, relief stores are now in operation in Sfax, Sousse, Gabes, and at about a dozen smaller localities, such

[1] *Ibid.*, p. 587.

as Mateur, Medjes el Bab, Souk el Kemis, Souk el Arba, Jedeida, and Massicault.

Some direct or "gift" relief has been necessary. In Tunisia, for example, there were some 80,000 displaced persons, many of whom had taken refuge in the city of Tunis. These people came from communities all over northern Tunisia. In the city also were about 1,500 Jewish people who had taken refuge there from the Nazi military control in Bizerte. There were also a large number of European refugees of various nationalities, including Italians, who had come from many points in Tunisia. For each of these groups the OFRRO mission made appropriate arrangements through local leaders and existing social agencies to provide for urgent needs in food and clothing and for returning the people to their homes or in finding quarters for them with friends or relatives.

Not all relief for these groups is on a direct basis, but milk for the Arab children, totaling 2,000 servings a day at present and gradually increasing, is being provided. Arrangements for this service were made through the Sheik of Medina, official head of the Moslem population for the district of Tunis. All the milk is consumed at the point of distribution and is occasionally supplemented by rice or some other food which is consumed with the milk.

The needs of Jewish refugees in Tunis are served by four centers where the people receive health inspections and milk, sugar, rice, and clothing for the children and the sick. The OFRRO staff is assisting the Jewish community in evacuating these people from the centers to their own homes or in finding other places for them to live, and it is expected that within a relatively short time the need for the service will have been eliminated. The groups of Europeans are being similarly assisted through existing social agencies accustomed to caring for the needs of each national group. Wherever possible existing means and native personnel are utilized to the utmost.

Meanwhile, and in part through other divisions of the North African Economic Board, longer-range plans for assisting the French in reconstituting normal life in the region are being put into effect. Efforts are being made, for example, to restore the fishing industry of the Tunisian coast and to provide the means for re-establishing the important olive oil industry of the southern areas. As to agriculture, Mr. Parisius found the prospects for this year's grain harvest in Tunisia to be so good that the provision of food from Allied sources for an extended period is regarded now as most unlikely.

The relief situation in the remainder of North Africa is also becoming stabilized. A short time ago a regional office for the mission was established in western Algeria at Oran. A member of the staff operating from this office is assisting the Army in finding employment for former inmates of refugee camps in military labor battalions and in civilian jobs. Also operating from the Oran base is Dr. Dudley A. Reekie, an officer of the United States Public Health Service, serving with the OFRRO mission as a public health official. Upon the request of the public health office of the city of Oran and the American Consul in residence there, Dr. Reekie is aiding in the establishment of a modern health department for that city. Dr. Michael L. Furcolow, another officer of the United States Public Health Service and similarly attached to the relief mission, made a survey of health conditions in Tunis immediately following occupation by Allied military forces. Health conditions in Tunis, he reports, are not abnormal.

The OFRRO mission has concerned itself since its arrival in North Africa last January with the disposition and care of inmates of the various internment camps for political refugees in Algeria and French Morocco. All the inmates of the camps have now been liberated, and the majority have found employment in military labor activities or in civilian occupations.

A number of the refugees, however, were discovered to be sick or otherwise disabled, and for these the OFRRO mission is establishing rest camps, where proper food and medical care can be provided until strength is restored or other suitable disposition made of their cases. One of these camps is at Fouke Marine in Algeria. Accommodations for other of these unfortunate victims of the war are being found in homes in the environs of Oran, Algiers, and Casablanca.

The general program for the free distribution of milk to school children in French Morocco, Algeria, and portions of Tunisia, which has been conducted in cooperation with the American Red Cross, was discontinued by agreement with the French authorities upon the close of the school year at the end of May. In the period, beginning early in January of this year, in which the program was in effect, about 200,000 children received daily servings of dried or evaporated milk. Today, a decided improvement in growth and weight is reported for the great majority of a group of children tested by the Red Cross to show results of the program. During the summer months, a special and limited program in milk distribution will be maintained for children, nursing mothers, and others who are in special need of this type of nourishment. It is estimated that about 80,000 servings per day will be provided during the summer for such purposes in all North Africa. In addition, the refugee Arab children in Tunis will continue to receive milk until their evacuation is completed, while special arrangements have also been made with social agencies and health authorities in Algeria and Tunisia to provide milk for other groups of refugee children.

A feature of relief operations in North Africa is that the need for charitable relief has been much less than expected. Agricultural prospects are good in Tunisia and at least up to normal expectations in Algeria and French Morocco. While "black market" activities and hoarding are continuing to cause inequities in the distribution of local supplies, it is felt in general that the revival of normal trade will soon eliminate the need for relief supplies in major proportions from outside sources.

In North Africa the mission of the Office of Foreign Relief and Rehabilitation Operations has functioned as the Division of Public Welfare and Relief of the North African Economic Board. Mr. Hoehler, as chief of the OFRRO mission, has also served as chief of the Division of Public Welfare and Relief.

(2) *Liberation of Political Prisoners and Refugees in Africa. Statement of the Joint Commission for Political Prisoners and Refugees, Algiers, Department of State Release, June 24, 1943* [1]

The Joint Commission for Political Prisoners and Refugees reported today that according to its records all persons who were interned in concentration camps, incorporated into work companies or whose residence was confined to restricted areas in French North and West Africa before November 8, 1942 have now been liberated.

This Commission was set up in January, under the joint chairmanship of the United States and British Consuls General in Algiers, to assist in the release, relief and repatriation of these prisoners and refugees. The liberation has proceeded in orderly manner over the past few months, as swiftly as military security investigations and the making of

[1] *Ibid.*, p. 589.

arrangements for maintenance of internees after their release would permit. Today's report marked the climax of months of effort, involving close cooperation between British, American and French authorities, for the solution of a complex problem.

Special local assistance in the manifold details pertaining to the gradual liquidation of the internment camps was provided by a field party of the Commission, which visited the camps several times. The field party included representatives of the United States and British Consuls General, the French High Command, and the Public Welfare and Relief Division of the North African Economic Board (this division is the operating agency in North Africa of the United States Office of Foreign Relief and Rehabilitation Operations) and the International Red Cross.

The Commission also reported that all those who were released from work companies on February 12, 1943, given the status of civilian workers at current wage rates, employed by the Mediterranean Niger Railway or the coal mines of Kenadaa, and whose residence was restricted to the area in which they worked, have been given complete liberty to leave this region and accept work where they wish. With the exception of a few individuals who, of their own free will, signed contracts with one or the other of these companies and prefer to remain, all the former internees and members of work companies have left this region.

The former internees, members of work companies and persons in forced residence have all been provided with useful occupations of their own choice. A large number have signed contracts for work as civilian employees with the American armed forces. They are employed in various capacities, are paid at current wage rates for the types of work they do and are not organized in any military formations. Another large group have joined the British pioneer battalions, a noncombatant labor unit of the British Army, in which they receive the pay, rations, and quarters of British soldiers. A considerable number have been absorbed into local industry in employment of their own choice.

The situation of the Spanish Republican refugees who have signified their desire to proceed to Mexico presented a serious problem since the internment camps and work companies have been totally liquidated and definite arrangements regarding their departure for Mexico have not been completed. This problem was resolved through the excellent cooperation of the American Army which agreed to employ them under work contracts with the understanding that the contracts would terminate when arrangements were made for their transportation to Mexico.

In addition to assisting in the liberation of all persons from internment camps and work companies, the Joint Commission for Political Prisoners and Refugees obtained from the French authorities an agreement that on the presentation of a contract of employment either with the American Army or private industry, identity and ration cards would be immediately issued. This provision is especially important, since it legalizes the civil status not only of persons released from internment camps, but also of a large number of internees who at one time or another had escaped from camps and were in constant danger of being either returned to the camps or sent to prison. The identity cards are being issued with a minimum of red tape, at reduced rates, and, in the case of destitute persons gratis.

Released internees who were unable to work on account of advanced age or physical disabilities are being cared for by the public welfare and relief division of NAEB with funds contributed by private sources. Special rehabilitation camps are being developed for them. This division also has provided clothing, food and funds to relieve the immediate needs of persons released from camps who arrived at Casablanca, Oran and Algiers to begin work. Many of them were given assistance in finding living accommodations.

During the visits to internment camps the field party of the Joint Commission for Political Prisoners and Refugees also visited prisons in which political prisoners were confined. There are now in prison approximately two hundred foreign refugees who, although they have been duly sentenced by courts, should be considered as political prisoners since the offenses consist chiefly of infractions of discipline in internment camps or political demonstrations involving violence. The greater part of these prisoners are Spanish Republican refugees. The French authorities agreed to liberate from prisons all Spanish Republican refugees for the purpose of proceeding to Mexico. The Joint Commission suggested, however, that these prisoners should be liberated and allowed to make their own dispositions. Dr. Jules Abadie, former Secretary of the Interior and now Commissioner of National Education, Justice and Public Health, has given an assurance that an amnesty will be granted to these prisoners after their cases have been examined in regard to military security. The granting of these amnesties has been delayed by the temporary confusion resulting from the transition from the High Command to the French Committee of National Liberation, but is expected soon.

C. United Nations Relief and Rehabilitation Administration

On June 10, 1943 a draft agreement for a United Nations Relief and Rehabilitation Administration was placed by the Department of State before the governments of all the United Nations [1] and the other nations associated with them in

[1] The following nations, in addition to the United States, had signed the United Nations Declaration of January 1, 1942: Great Britain, the Soviet Union, China, Australia, Belgium, Bolivia, Brazil, Canada, Costa Rica, Cuba, Czechoslovakia, the Dominican Republic, El Salvador, Ethiopia, Greece, Guatemala, Haiti, Honduras, India, Iraq, Luxemburg, Mexico, the Netherlands, New Zealand, Nicaragua, Norway, Panama, the Philippines, Poland, South Africa, and Yugoslavia.

the war.[1] These nations were informed that the draft agreement had been drawn up in consultation with the British Government, the Soviet Government, and the Chinese Government, and that the draft proposal met with the approval of these four Governments. The other Governments were assured, however, that the plan was still tentative and that no action would be proposed until they all had had an opportunity for full consideration and discussion of the suggested line of approach.

The text of the draft agreement submitted provided for the immediate establishment of a central United Nations agency to assume responsibility for the relief and rehabilitation of the victims of war. It was apparently intended that preliminary discussions among all the United Nations and the nations associated with them would speedily clear the way for a meeting of all these nations at which a definite agreement would be reached providing for joint action on relief and rehabilitation. No definite arrangements, however, had been made at the time for a meeting of the United Nations and the other nations involved on the subject of this draft proposal, and no arrangements were planned until all the powers had had an opportunity to consider and discuss the draft agreement fully.

D. The Refugee Problem

On the work of the Evian Conference, July 6–14, 1938, and the organization of the Intergovernmental Committee on Political Refugees, see *Documents, I, 1938–39*, p. 437. On the subsequent history of the Committee and the development of United States policy, see *Documents, II, 1939–40*, p. 586; *III, 1940–41*, p. 587.

The present war has created an unprecedented refugee problem. It has become apparent that the problem is of such dimensions that it cannot be handled by any one government alone. The Bermuda Conference must be regarded as a first step in the evolution of a program of broad international action. It is interesting as one of the early examples of the cautious approach to international problems, first on a bilateral basis, then on a broadened multilateral basis, which appears to be the deliberate policy of the United States Government, not only in dealing with the problems of coordinated prosecution of the war but also in meeting the problems of the post-war world as well.

(1) *The Secretary of State (Hull) to the Ambassador of the United Kingdom (Halifax), February 25, 1943* [2]

The Secretary of State presents his compliments to His Excellency the British Ambassador and has the honor to refer to the British Embassy's *aide-mémoire* of January 20, 1943,[3] relating to the situation of persons fleeing from persecution for religious, racial and political reasons and to the necessity for intergovernmental relief action in their behalf.

It is evident that the problem of the refugees in question cannot be solved in a satisfactory manner by any one of the Governments of the United Nations group nor of the neutral countries. It has been, and is,

---

[1] The nations associated with the United Nations in this war were: Chile, Colombia, Ecuador, Egypt, Iceland, Iran, Liberia, Paraguay, Peru, Uruguay, and Venezuela.

It was also announced that the draft agreement was being brought to the attention of the appropriate French authorities.

[2] Department of State Release, March 3, 1943; *Bulletin*, VIII, p. 202.

[3] Not released by the Department of State.

the traditional policy of this country to seek every available means by which to extend to oppressed and persecuted peoples such assistance as may be found to be feasible and possible under the laws of the United States. In pursuance of that policy, this Government has been and is taking steps to extend assistance in a large measure to those European people who have been subjected to oppression and persecution under the Hitler regime. The measures of assistance afforded have assumed several forms, as follows:

1. Joint and several declarations of official attitude of condemnation of the policies and acts of the Axis Governments and their satellites in oppression or persecution of religious, racial and political minorities;

2. The appropriation and expenditure of large amounts of public and private funds for the relief of persons in need as a result of oppression and persecution because of their racial origin or religious or political beliefs;

3. The application of the immigration laws of the United States in the utmost liberal and humane spirit of those laws;

4. The calling by the President of the United States of the first Intergovernmental Conference at Evian-London in 1938 for the purpose of seeking a solution of refugee problems. There may be repeated here the statement made in that Conference by the Honorable Myron Taylor on behalf of this Government, as follows:

In conclusion, I need not emphasize that the discrimination and pressure against minority groups and the disregard of elementary human rights are contrary to the principles of what we have come to regard as the accepted standards of civilization. We have heard from time to time of the disruptive consequences of the dumping of merchandise upon the world's economy. How much more disturbing is the forced and chaotic dumping of unfortunate peoples in large numbers. Racial and religious problems are, in consequence, rendered more acute in all parts of the world. Economic retaliation against the countries which are responsible for this condition is encouraged. The sentiment of international mistrust and suspicion is heightened and fear, which is an important obstacle to general appeasement between nations, is accentuated.

The problem is no longer one of purely private concern. It is a problem for intergovernmental action. If the present currents of migration are permitted to continue to push anarchically upon the receiving States and if some Governments are to continue to toss large sections of their populations lightly upon a distressed and unprepared world, then there is catastrophic human suffering ahead which can only result in general unrest and in general international strain which will not be conducive to the permanent appeasement to which all peoples earnestly aspire.

At the Evian-London Conference and through the Intergovernmental Committee which grew out of that Conference, this Government exerted its most earnest efforts to persuade the various countries represented to provide asylum for as many refugees from the Axis countries as the laws of the several countries would permit. This Government has also approached other countries for the purpose of finding places of settlement for refugees with funds of the United States origin being made available.

5. As shown by the records of the Department of State, from the advent of the Hitler regime in 1933 until June 30, 1942, 547,775 visas were issued by American diplomatic and consular officers to natives of nationals of the various countries now dominated by the Axis powers, the great majority of which persons were refugees from Nazi persecution. Of this number 228,964 were issued in the war years 1939–1942. Many more than that number of visas were authorized during this latter period, the aliens in whose behalf such authorizations were given having been unable to depart from their places of foreign residence to reach the United States. Yet, of the number actually issued, practically all of the aliens who received them during the war years 1939–1942 have actually arrived in the United States and have remained here, many of them having entered in a temporary status and not yet having departed.

6. Over 5,000 visas were authorized for the admission into the United States and permanent residence here of refugee children coming from France, Spain and Portugal under arrangements with certain private persons and organizations in the United States for their care. Visas were also authorized for the parents accompanying them, in certain cases. This Government has sought the friendly assistance of the Government of Switzerland to effect the release from France of such of these children who have not been permitted to leave France, for entry into Spain where visas may be issued to them by the American consular officers.

7. Since the entry of the United States into the war, there have been no new restrictions placed by the Government of the United States upon the number of aliens of any nationality permitted to proceed to this country under existing laws, except for the more intensive examination of aliens required for security reasons.

8. Considerable sums of money have been made available by the American Red Cross and from other American sources to the American Ambassador at Madrid for the care of refugees now in Spain pending their evacuation. A number of these refugees have already been removed to North Africa. The continuation of this movement and its extent are dependent upon military considerations.

9. The American Red Cross and other American organizations have provided assistance for refugees who have been able to reach other neutral countries, such as Iran, and have undertaken extended feeding among children, including refugee children, in France.

10. In evacuating refugees to neutral areas, the full influence of the United States diplomatic and consular representatives has been from time to time invoked, not only with the oppressor nations but with any Government concerned, on behalf of the refugees.

This Government understands that, in addition to the refugee classes under immediate consideration, the British Government has certain undertakings for the care of British evacuees and of prisoners of war. Likewise, the Government of the United States has certain similar undertakings, as follows:

1. For the successful prosecution of the war and for Hemispheric safety, the Government of the United States has offered to receive dangerous Axis nationals from a number of the American Republics where facilities for the internment or close safeguarding of such Axis nationals do not exist. A considerable number of such Axis nationals have thus been brought to the United States and arrangements are being made for the receipt of more of them.

2. This Government has a number of camps in the United States and more camps are under construction or planned for the internment or detention of civilian enemy aliens. There are being maintained in these camps thousands of such aliens.

3. This Government has also established other camps for prisoners of war which are now in use and in which, by arrangement, there will also be placed large numbers of United Nations prisoners. The accommodation of these prisoners in the United States will leave available abroad considerable quantities of food, clothing, etc., for refugees there which would otherwise be used by those prisoners abroad, while on the other hand, the maintenance of the prisoners in the United States will result in a considerable reduction of supplies available here.

4. There have been set up in the United States a number of relocation centers where approximately 110,000 persons of the Japanese race are being housed and maintained at public expense after removal from vital military areas.

The Government of the United States fully shares the concern expressed by the British Government for the situation of the refugees. It feels, in view of the facts set forth above, that it has been and is making every endeavor to relieve the oppressed and persecuted peoples. In affording asylum to refugees, however, it is and must be bound by legislation enacted by Congress determining the immigration policy of the United States.

The United States is of the opinion that further efforts to solve the problem may best be undertaken through the instrumentality already existing, the Executive Committee of the Intergovernmental Committee on Refugees. To this end it may be considered advisable in order to facilitate action by the Committee that a preliminary exploration of ways and means be undertaken informally by representatives designated by the Government of the United States and the British Government. Such exploration might be undertaken along the following lines:

A. The refugee problem should not be considered as being confined to persons of any particular race or faith. Nazi measures against minorities have caused the flight of persons of various races and faiths, as well as of other persons because of their political beliefs.

B. Wheresoever practicable, intergovernmental collaboration should be sought in these times of transportation difficulty, shipping shortage, and submarine menace, to the end that arrangements may be determined for temporary asylum for refugees as near as possible to the areas in which those people find themselves at the present time and from which they may be returned to their homelands with the greatest expediency on the termination of hostilities.

C. There should accordingly be considered plans for the maintenance in neutral countries in Europe of those refugees for whose removal provision may not be made. Their maintenance in neutral countries may involve the giving of assurances for their support until they can be repatriated, which support will necessarily come from the United Nations augmented by funds from private sources. It may also involve the giving of assurances in all possible cases by their Governments-in-exile for their prompt return to their native countries upon the termination of hostilities.

D. The possibilities for the temporary asylum of the refugees, with a view to their repatriation upon the termination of hostilities, in countries other than neutral, and their dependencies, should be explored, together with the question of the availability of shipping to effect their movement from Europe.

It is suggested that the British and United States representatives might meet at Ottawa for this preliminary exploration.

(2) The Bermuda Meeting, April 19–May 19, 1943

The United States and British Governments set the date of April 19, 1943 for the opening of the meeting of representatives of the two Governments which it was decided to hold at Bermuda to consider the refugee problem.

The United States delegation consisted of —

The Honorable Harold Willis Dodds, President of Princeton University;
The Honorable Scott Lucas, President *pro tem.* of the United States Senate and United States Senator from Illinois;
The Honorable Sol Bloom of New York, Chairman of the Committee on Foreign Affairs of the House of Representatives;
Mr. R. Borden Reams, American Foreign Service officer; *secretary.*

Dr. Dodds headed the delegation, which was accompanied by a number of technical assistants.[1]

(a) Address by the Chairman of the American Delegation (Dodds), April 19, 1943 [2]

I first wish to express to the Acting Governor and to the Government and people of Bermuda the sincere appreciation of the American Government and of the American delegation to this conference for the hospitality

[1] Department of State, *Bulletin*, VIII, p. 333.　　[2] *Ibid.*, p. 351.

and courtesies shown to us. Bermuda has long been known to Americans as one of the most beautiful and legendary spots of the world — a place in which good-fellowship and friendship may be expected as a matter of course. I personally cherish many happy memories of visits to Bermuda under more peaceful and less trying conditions. It is pleasant to find that the special bonds created between the British Empire, of which Bermuda is a part, and the United States by this common struggle against the enemies of civilization have further strengthened the ties of friendship between our peoples. We all hope to return again to Bermuda when our purpose in this war has been achieved.

It is no easy task which confronts the conference. The magnitude of this problem and the difficulties attendant upon any completely satisfactory solution of it have, I believe, on the whole been underestimated. One thing is certain. We approach this problem with the conviction that every possible effort must be made to find the best possible solution which can be presented to all the United Nations for decisions. There can be no doubt of the goodwill and intention of the British and American Governments nor of the delegations representing these Governments. What can be done will be done.

History records many instances of refugee migrations caused by oppression and tyranny, but nowhere can be found a more terrible record than that of Nazi Germany. Since the present German Government came into power in 1933 its policy has been founded consistently upon the pattern of brutal subjection, persecution, pillage, and murder of small nations and religious and racial minorities. There is no need to dwell at length upon this subject. The facts are known to all the civilized peoples of this world.

From the inception of the present refugee policy the British and American Governments have, in close consultation, endeavored to alleviate in every possible and practicable manner the unhappy plight of these unfortunate peoples. These measures have not been confined to private effort. They have included the activities of the Intergovernmental Committee which was established in 1938 as a result of the Evian Conference summoned by President Roosevelt. The activities of this committee were considerable. It might well have arrived at a satisfactory solution of the problem as it then existed had not the war intervened.

The war has had a two-fold effect upon the refugee situation. It has not only deepened the miseries of the peoples under German rule and augmented the difficulties of any attempt to relieve their suffering but has also created a wider problem of other populations and individuals who as a result of Nazi barbarism are in a plight calling for all our sympathy, consideration, and concrete action where this is practicable. Germany's ambition under Nazi ideology has resulted in a calculated policy of oppression and extermination, the effects of which extend far beyond the territories actually under its ruthless heel. This created the necessity for all possible assistance to such helpless peoples, and it is under these conditions and with this purpose that this conference convenes.

The primary fact which must be borne in mind throughout these deliberations is that we are now in the middle of a bitterly contested war. We know that we will win this war, but we also know that we cannot relax for one instant our determination to concentrate our maximum effort upon its vigorous prosecution. Any other thought would not only be foolish; it would be criminal. It would constitute a betrayal, not of our countries or of the effort of the United Nations but of civilization. Complete and final victory will, of course, afford a true and final solution to the refugee problem. We fervently hope that in the better world which will arise such problems may never again return to harass civilization.

Despite these manifest limitations there is much that can and must be done, and I believe this conference will be successful in its endeavors to survey the problem as it exists today. It is naturally impossible for me at this time to forecast the probable course of our deliberations. One thing is certain, and that is that the problem is too great for solution by the two governments here represented. The cooperation of others must be solicited. Our task will be to point the way and to offer such definite proposals as may be possible under war conditions and in the light of what the war effort of the United Nations will permit.

It might be well at this point to mention some of the efforts already made on behalf of these people.

1. The participation of the United States in joint and several declarations of official condemnation of the policies and acts of the Axis governments and their satellites in oppressing and persecuting religious, racial, and political minorities.

2. The appropriation and expenditure of large amounts of public and private funds for the relief of persons suffering oppression and persecution because of their racial origin, of religious or political beliefs.

3. The application of the immigration laws of the United States in the utmost liberal and humane spirit of those laws.

4. The call by the President of the United States of the first Intergovernmental Conference at Evian-London in 1938 for the purpose of seeking a solution of refugee problems.

5. From the advent of the Hitler regime to June 30, 1942, American diplomatic and consular officers issued 547,775 visas to persons who were natives or nationals of the countries now dominated by Axis powers. A great majority of those persons were refugees from Nazi oppression and persecution. A total of 228,964 visas were issued during the war years 1939–42.

6. The United States authorized over 5,000 visas for permanent resi-

dence here to refugee children coming from France, Spain, and Portugal under arrangements by which certain private persons and organizations in the United States would be responsible for their care. Visas were also authorized for the parents accompanying them in certain cases.

7. Considerable sums of money have been made available by the American Red Cross and from other American sources to the American Ambassador at Madrid for the care of refugees now in Spain pending their evacuation.

8. The American Red Cross and other American organizations have provided assistance for refugees who have been able to reach other neutral countries.

At this time I would like to express our full recognition of the burden assumed under the most difficult circumstances by His Britannic Majesty's Government in their efforts to alleviate the lot of those who have fallen innocent victims to the cruel philosophy of Nazi Germany. We recognize with appreciation what has already been accomplished by this other great democracy and realize fully that those accomplishments were effected during a period when the British Empire was faced with the alternative of total victory or of total extinction.

We also are fully confident that the British Government, in sending to this conference a delegation of such high distinction, has demonstrated its desire and determination to play its full part in whatever further measures of relief may be found possible.

(b) Letter from the Under Secretary of State (Welles) to the President of the Congress of Industrial Organizations (Murray), April 26, 1943 [1]

The text of Mr. Murray's letter [2] to which the Under Secretary's letter was sent in reply follows:

"Dear Mr. Secretary: "April 24, 1943.

"The membership of the Congress of Industrial Organizations, in common with all the American people, is profoundly shocked at the outrageous mass murder of the Jewish people in Axis-dominated Europe.

"In response to an appeal from the Executive of the General Federation of Jewish Labor of Palestine, it was our desire and intention to send outstanding officers of the Congress of Industrial Organizations to the current conference in Bermuda to report the sentiments of our membership. To our dismay we have been informed that this conference is behind closed doors, and that we will not be permitted to appear. We appeal to you that the voice of the people's organizations of the United Nations should be heard at this conference. The closed-door policy gives us deep concern that this conference might be a mere diplomatic nicety. We would greatly regret a repetition of the futile Evian conference.

"We urgently request that you reconsider the closed-door policy and admit our representatives to be heard on this tragic and urgent matter. In view of the public importance of this matter I am taking the liberty of releasing this letter to the press next Monday afternoon.   Sincerely yours,
                                                     PHILIP MURRAY."

[1] Ibid., p. 386.   [2] Ibid., p. 387.

My Dear Mr. Murray:

I have received this morning your letter of April 24.

I know that it is unnecessary for me to state to you that this Government has from the inception of the inhuman policy of racial discrimination and mass murder practiced by the Nazi government done everything within its power to combat this policy and likewise everything within its power to relieve the sufferings of its victims.

I am for that reason surprised that you should refer to the Evian Conference as "futile." May I remind you that that conference which was called upon the initiative of President Roosevelt was the first constructive, international movement to create intergovernmental machinery which might make it possible in a practical way to give relief to those who are suffering persecution in Europe. The conditions which have resulted from the war, and in particular military conditions, have of course made it impossible to afford relief through the agencies created as a result of the Evian Conference on as large a scale as it had been hoped might be achieved.

In your letter now under acknowledgment, you say that you have been informed that the conference now in session in Bermuda is taking place behind closed doors, and you ask that representatives of the Congress of Industrial Organizations be permitted to be heard by the delegates.

In reply may I say that the Bermuda Conference is not taking place "behind closed doors," nor is there any reason why the views, recommendations, and suggestions of the Congress of Industrial Organizations or of any other organization should not be transmitted to the delegates of the United States with full assurance that such a communication will receive the fullest and most careful consideration of the delegates.

Any organization which desires to present a communication to the conference at Bermuda may transmit it to the Department of State by which it will be transmitted to the United States delegation. This has already been done in the case of every organization or person in this country desiring to present such communications for the consideration of the conference. May I suggest, therefore, that such recommendations or advice as the Congress of Industrial Organizations desires to present to the conference be transmitted immediately to this Department in order that such communication may at once be forwarded.

In conclusion may I also say that in order that the press of the United States might have full opportunity of reporting upon the conference, the Department of State arranged for representatives of four principal press organizations of this country to proceed in company of the American delegation and these press representatives are now reporting upon the proceedings of the conference. This Department has likewise made it known that it would be glad to issue passports to any other press correspondents who desire to proceed to Bermuda in order to report upon the conference.

(c) *Joint Communiqué of United States and British Delegations, April 29, 1943* [1]

The United States and United Kingdom delegates examined the refugee problem in all its aspects including the position of those potential refugees who are still in the grip of the Axis powers without any immediate prospect of escape. Nothing was excluded from their analysis and everything that held out any possibility, however remote, of a solution of the problem was carefully investigated and thoroughly discussed. From the outset it was realized that any recommendation that the delegates could make to their governments must pass two tests: Would any recommendation submitted interfere with or delay the war effort of the United Nations and was the recommendation capable of accomplishment under war conditions? The delegates at Bermuda felt bound to reject certain proposals which were not capable of meeting these tests. The delegates were able to agree on a number of concrete recommendations which they are jointly submitting to their governments and which, it is felt, will pass the tests set forth above and will lead to the relief of a substantial number of refugees of all races and nationalities. Since the recommendations necessarily concern governments other than those represented at the Bermuda conference and involve military considerations, they must remain confidential. It may be said, however, that in the course of discussion the refugee problem was broken down into its main elements. Questions of shipping, food, and supply were fully investigated. The delegates also agreed on recommendations regarding the form of intergovernmental organization which was best fitted, in their opinion, to handle the problem in the future. This organization would have to be flexible enough to permit it to consider without prejudice any new factors that might come to its attention. In each of these fields the delegates were able to submit agreed proposals for consideration of their respective governments.

(d) *Report of the Bermuda Meeting on the Refugee Problem. Department of State Release, May 19, 1943* [2]

The delegates appointed by the American and British Governments to confer at Bermuda upon the refugee problem have now terminated their discussions and have submitted a report to their respective Governments. The two Governments have received this and are at present engaged in carrying out its recommendations. Throughout the discussions at Bermuda, the United States and British delegations as well as the two Governments worked in complete harmony and in a spirit of mutual cooperation. The report was submitted as a joint report and contains no divergence of opinion.

[1] *Ibid.*, p. 388.　　　　　　　[2] *Ibid.*, p. 456.

While the details must be regarded as confidential so long as a knowledge of the recommendations contained therein would be of aid or comfort to our enemies or might adversely affect the refugees whom all are trying to aid, certain facts may now be made public.

The two delegations accomplished the useful task of dividing suggestions and proposals for the solution of the refugee problem into two categories: (1) what was possible under existing war conditions and (2) what was impossible under these same conditions.

All suggestions were measured by two strict criteria. In the first place, nothing could be recommended that would interfere with or delay the war effort of the United Nations, and, secondly, any recommendation submitted must be capable of accomplishment under war conditions.

The shipping problem was recognized to be of the utmost urgency, and it was agreed that any plan looking to the diverting of allied shipping from the war effort to remove or care for refugees would present considerations of a military character which would disclose almost insuperable difficulties. It was also agreed that no negotiations with Hitler could be undertaken since his entire record has left no doubt that he would only agree to such solutions as would be of direct aid to the Axis war aims.

The conference was, however, able to recommend measures both for removing refugees from neutral countries and, in those cases where such removal was not possible, for giving assurances of international cooperation in the future of the refugee problem so far as it affected them.

It also recommended a number of temporary refugee havens to which refugees could be transported and maintained if and when shipping should become available. At least one such movement has been effected.

Certain measures of a financial nature to cover necessary expenses and a declaration of intention to provide for repatriation upon the termination of hostilities were also recommended.

The conference also submitted a plan for an expanded and more efficient intergovernmental organization with increased authority to meet the problems created or likely to arise under war conditions.

Some of these measures are now being put into effect and others, it is hoped, will soon be possible. It is therefore believed that the practical results of the recommendations submitted by the conference will soon become apparent.

4. POST-WAR RECONSTRUCTION

The Atlantic Charter and the Declaration by United Nations state the broad principles and purposes which the United Nations and the Associated Nations have accepted for their guidance in meeting the problems of the post-war world. As Under Secretary of State Welles stated in his Toronto address on February 26, 1943, "there is no disagreement anywhere as to what the United Nations want." But differences of opinion are bound to exist with regard to the means to be adopted to attain these ends.

The theory which has underlain the approach to specific post-war problems, as evidenced by the holding of the United Nations Food and Agriculture Conference, appears to have been stated by Mr. Welles in his Toronto address:

"An examination of the causes of any disagreement will usually reveal that it exists mainly because people are considering the question from different viewpoints, that the parties are basing their judgments on different or incomplete facts and different considerations. If both parties had the same facts and considerations in mind, and if each knew fully the reasons behind the position taken by the other, there would much more quickly be a meeting of minds. . . . I believe that if the United Nations were to set up machinery for the purpose of assembling all the pertinent facts and considerations relative thereto, and for jointly analyzing all facts and considerations relating to measures or policies proposed for furthering the end in view, the controversies and conflicts of policy which have so far embittered relations in the international economic field, and therefore generally, might largely disappear." [1]

Mr. Welles went on to state that his Government intended at once to undertake discussions with the other United Nations as to the most practical and effective methods for holding such conferences.

The problem of food and agricultural production was apparently chosen as the subject of the first of these conferences because of the fact that it combined the quality of urgent importance with the relative absence of highly controversial issues.

A. United Nations Conference on Food and Agriculture, Hot Springs, Virginia, May 18–June 3, 1943

(1) *Invitation Extended by the Government of the United States to Attend the Conference. Department of State Release, March 30, 1943* [2]

Invitations to attend the Food Conference were addressed to the following nations:

United Nations: Australia; Belgium; Brazil; Canada; China; Costa Rica; Cuba; Czechoslovakia; Dominican Republic; El Salvador; Ethiopia; Greece; Guatemala; Haiti; Honduras; India; Iraq; Luxemburg; Mexico; Netherlands; New Zealand; Nicaragua; Norway; Panama; Philippine Commonwealth; Poland; Union of South Africa; Union of Soviet Socialist Republics; United Kingdom; and Yugoslavia.

Associated Nations: Bolivia; Chile; Colombia; Ecuador; Egypt; Iceland; Iran; Liberia; Paraguay; Peru; Uruguay; and Venezuela.

On April 27 it was reported that all Governments invited to attend had accepted.[3] The French National Committee accepted an invitation to be represented.

The Government of the United States of America is of the opinion that it is desirable now for the United Nations and those nations which are associated with them in this war to begin joint consideration of the basic economic problems with which they and the world will be confronted after complete military victory shall have been attained. Accord-

---

[1] See this volume, p. 45.
[2] Department of State, *Bulletin*, VIII, p. 271.
[3] *Ibid.*, p. 388, note.

ingly, and as a first step in this direction, the Govenrment of the United States proposes to convene, on April 27 at some suitable place in the United States, a conference on food and other essential agricultural products, and hereby invites the Government of ———— to send to that conference a small number of appropriate technical and expert representatives.

The purpose of the conference is to provide an opportunity for an exchange of views and information with respect to the following topics and for exploring and seeking agreement in principle as to the most desirable and practicable means and methods of dealing with the following problems:

Plans and prospects of various countries for the post-war period regarding production, import requirements or exportable surpluses of foodstuffs and other essential agricultural products, with a view to improving progressively in each country the levels of consumption within the framework of the opportunities and possibilities of an expansion of its general economic activity. Such consideration will be entirely divorced from the question of the provision of relief.

Possibilities of coordinating and stimulating by international action national policies looking to the improvement of nutrition and the enchancement of consumption in general.

Possibilities of setting up international agreements, arrangements and institutions designed to promote efficient production of foodstuffs and other essential agricultural products and to ensure for the world adequate supplies of such products with due consideration to the attainment of equitable prices from the viewpoint of both producers and consumers.

Commercial, financial and other arrangements which will be necessary in order to enable the countries of the world to obtain the foodstuffs and other essential agricultural products which they will need and to maintain adequate markets for their own surplus production.

(2) *Arrangements for Publicity. Statement by the Chairman of the United States Delegation (Jones), April 20, 1943* [1]

The statement released to the press on April 10 said that it was anticipated "that the Conference will be as informal as possible, and in view of the fact that it will be primarily a meeting of technical experts most of the discussions will take place in technical sections or committees. Plans are being made for opening and closing plenary sessions to which press and radio representatives will be accredited." [2]

The newspapermen, members of Congress and the public became quite concerned over the alleged secrecy of the Conference, and the failure to provide suitable and fair facilities for the reporting of proceedings.

[1] *Ibid.*, p. 353.
[2] *Ibid.*, p. 298.

I think that the press reports about the secrecy of the food conference, whether intentional or not, are making a mountain out of a mole hill.

I have taken the trouble to read the transcript of the President's press conference when the subject was discussed on March 19. The President was asked whether newspapermen would be permitted to cover the food conference when it occurred.

The President replied facetiously that he hoped not, and his reply was greeted with laughter.

This report indicates the humor in which the President replied to the question. In any event, the President has never expressed to me as chairman of the delegation any views as to the publicity of the conference. I expect to discuss the matter with Secretary Hull, and I have not the slightest doubt that arrangements will be made which, while not permitting representatives of the press to attend executive sessions, at the same time will give to the press all the information as to the proceedings that our newspaper representatives would believe right under the circumstances.

_____

(a) Department of State Release, May 12, 1943 [1]

[Excerpt]

The designation of Mr. Michael J. McDermott as Chief Press Relations Officer was announced on April 10, 1943. Mr. McDermott will have three assistants, who are all members of the Conference Secretariat: Mr. Harold R. Beckley, Superintendent of the Senate Press Gallery; Mr. Peter H. De Vries, Director of Economic Information, Department of Agriculture; and Mr. Wilder Foote.

Provisions have been made for working press accommodations on the hotel grounds. The Casino Building, which is a short distance from the hotel, will be given over exclusively to representatives of the press and radio. Wire-transmission facilities have been installed within the Casino. Messrs. McDermott and Beckley will maintain headquarters there, and one or the other will be in constant touch with the correspondents.

Judge Marvin Jones has personally assured the Standing Committee of Correspondents that he will cooperate with the newspapermen covering the Conference in seeing that they are given full information about the Conference in order that the public may be fully informed. Chairman Jones said he planned to meet the press daily and that no doubt the chairmen of the other delegations will want to make similar arrangements.

The first day's general session will be open to the press, after which the Conference will resolve itself into executive committees for the work of the Conference. The correspondents will attend all other open sessions as they are held from time to time. Between the public sessions, it is hoped that periodic press conferences will be held by the chairmen of the various committees and subcommittees appointed by the Conference, whereby the press may be kept currently informed of the questions being discussed by these committees and developments toward their solution. Such arrangements are being made but, of course, will have to await the decision of the Conference as a whole before being put into effect.

[1] *Ibid.*, p. 433.

(3) *Agenda for the United Nations Conference on Food and Agriculture.*
Department of State Release, April 27, 1943 [1]

After consultation, the Governments invited to the United Nations
Conference on Food and Agriculture have agreed upon the following
agenda for the Conference, .which will meet at Hot Springs, Va., on
May 18, 1943.

This agenda is organized around the following conception of the
problem with which the conference should deal:

The agenda begins with an effort to ascertain the facts as to what are
the needs of the various peoples of the world for food and other essential
agricultural products, with due regard to differing conditions and possibilities among countries. It recognizes that in the past excessive accumulations of certain agricultural products were in fact not surpluses at all
when measured by the world's minimum needs of food and clothing;
that these so-called "surpluses" were usually the result of maldistribu-
tion and underconsumption. It then seeks to ascertain the prospects
for so organizing world agricultural production as to enable the satisfaction of these needs and to explore the measures, both domestic and
international, by which production can be enhanced and better directed
in terms of consumption. Finally, it examines the measures and conditions which are necessary to assure that what can be produced moves
into consumption.

I. Consumption levels and requirements.
   A. Food.
      1. Character and extent of consumption deficiencies in each
         country.
      2. Causes and consequences of malnutrition.
      3. Measures for improving standards of consumption (educa-
         tion, etc.).
      4. Reasonable national and international goals for improved
         food consumption.
   B. Other essential agricultural products.
      1. Pre-war consumption levels in various countries as influenced
         by prosperity or depression and by buying power of the popu-
         lation.
      2. Reasonable national and international goals for improved
         consumption with sustained employment and expanded
         industrial activity.
II. Expansion of production and adaptation to consumption needs.
   A. Measures for direction of production toward commodities the
      supply of which should be increased.

[1] *Ibid.*, p. 388.

B. Measures for shifting production out of commodities in chronic surplus.

C. Measures for improving agricultural productivity and efficiency.

D. Measures for development and conservation of agricultural resources.

E. Opportunities for occupational adjustments in agricultural populations.

III. Facilitation and improvement of distribution.

A. Relation of national and international economic policies to agricultural problems, with special reference to the facilitation of the movement of agricultural products in commerce.

  1. Expansion of international trade.

  2. Broad policies for assuring increased production and consumption in general.

B. Improvement of agricultural marketing, processing, and distribution.

C. Special measures for wider food distribution.

  1. Improvement of consumption of low-income groups.

  2. International disposition of commodities in over-supply.

D. Buffer stocks and commodity arrangements to assure equitable prices and adequate supplies.

IV. Recommendations for continuing and carrying forward the work of the conference.

(4) *Letter from the President (Roosevelt) to the Opening Session,* May 18, 1943 [1]

In your capacity as chairman of the United States delegation, and as temporary chairman of the United Nations Conference on Food and Agriculture, will you convey to the delegates assembled my heartfelt regret that I cannot be present in person to welcome them upon this historic occasion. Urgent matters in the prosecution of the war make it impossible for me to attend, and until we have won the unconditional surrender of our enemies the achievement of victory must be pressed above all else. Nevertheless, I hope that later I shall be able to meet the delegates and express to them personally my profound conviction of the importance of the task on which they are about to embark.

This is the first United Nations conference. Together, we are fighting a common enemy. Together, also, we are working to build a world in which men shall be free to live out their lives in peace, prosperity and security. The broad objectives for which we work have been stated in the Atlantic Charter, the Declaration of United Nations, and at the meeting of the twenty-one American Republics at Rio de Janeiro in

[1] *Ibid.,* p. 455.

January 1942. It is the purpose of this conference to consider how best to further these policies in so far as they concern the consumption, production and distribution of food and other agricultural products in the post-war period.

We know that in the world for which we are fighting and working the four freedoms must be won for all men. We know, too, that each freedom is dependent upon the others; that freedom from fear, for example, cannot be secured without freedom from want. If we are to succeed, each nation individually, and all nations collectively, must undertake these responsibilities: They must take all necessary steps to develop world food production so that it will be adequate to meet the essential nutritional needs of the world population. And they must see to it that no hindrances, whether of international trade, of transportation or of internal distribution, be allowed to prevent any nation or group of citizens within a nation from obtaining the food necessary for health. Society must meet in full its obligation to make available to all its members at least the minimum adequate nutrition. The problems with which this conference will concern itself are the most fundamental of all human problems — for without food and clothing life itself is impossible. In this and other United Nations conferences we shall be extending our collaboration from war problems into important new fields. Only by working together can we learn to work together, and work together we must and will.

(5) *Text of the Final Act, Signed June 3, 1943* [1]

The Governments of Australia, Belgium, Bolivia, Brazil, Canada, Chile, China, Colombia, Costa Rica, Cuba, Czechoslovakia, Dominican Republic, Ecuador, Egypt, El Salvador, Ethiopia; the French Representatives; the Governments of Great Britain, Greece, Guatemala, Haiti, Honduras, Iceland, India, Iran, Iraq, Liberia, Luxemburg, Mexico, Netherlands, New Zealand, Nicaragua, Norway, Panama, Paraguay, Peru, Philippine Commonwealth, Poland, Union of South Africa, Union of Soviet Socialist Republics, United States of America, Uruguay, Venezuela, and Yugoslavia;

Having accepted the invitation extended to them by the Government of the United States of America to be represented at a United Nations Conference on Food and Agriculture;

Appointed their respective delegates, who are listed below by countries in the order of alphabetical precedence:

[Here follows list of delegates.]

[1] *Ibid.*, p. 546; all footnotes in the Final Act appear in the original.

Who met at Hot Springs, Virginia, on May 18, 1943, under the temporary Presidency of The Honorable Marvin Jones, Chairman of the Delegation of the United States of America.

The Honorable Henrik de Kauffmann, Danish Minister at Washington, attended the sessions in response to an invitation of the Government of the United States to be present in a personal capacity.

Warren Kelchner, Chief of the Division of International Conferences, Department of State of the United States, was designated, with the approval of the President of the United States, as Secretary General of the Conference, and Ralph H. Allee, Chief, Division of Latin American Agriculture, Office of Foreign Agricultural Relations, United States Department of Agriculture, as Assistant Secretary General.

The Honorable Marvin Jones, Chairman of the Delegation of the United States of America, was elected permanent President of the Conference at the Plenary Session held on May 18, 1943.

The Executive Committee of the Conference, composed of the Chairman of the Delegations, and presided over by the President of the Conference, constituted a Steering Committee of its members composed of the following:

> Marvin Jones (U.S.A.), President of the Conference, *Chairman*
> João Carlos Muniz (Brazil)
> G. S. H. Barton (Canada)
> Kuo Ping-wen (China)
> Richard Law (Great Britain)
> Sir Girja Shankar Bajpai (India)
> Ali Jawdat (Iraq)
> Manuel J. Zevada (Mexico)
> M. P. L. Steenberghe (Netherlands)
> Alexey D. Krutikov (U.S.S.R.)
> Branko Cubrilovic (Yugoslavia)

The following three members of the Executive Committee served on the Committee on Credentials of the Conference:

> J. Rafael Oreamuno (Costa Rica), *Chairman*
> Mohammed Shayesteh (Iran)
> Anders Fjelstad (Norway)

The Drafting Committee, composed of the Chairmen of the Technical Sections and three additional members appointed by the President of the Conference, was constituted as follows under the ex-officio Chairmanship of the Conference President:

> João Carlos Muniz (Brazil)
> G. S. H. Barton (Canada)
> Kuo Ping-wen (China)
> Héctor David Castro (El Salvador)
> Richard Law (Great Britain)
> Hugues Le Gallais (Luxemburg)
> Alexey D. Krutikov (U.S.S.R.)

In accordance with the regulations adopted at the opening Plenary Session, held on May 18, 1943, the Conference was divided into four Technical Sections, with Committees, as follows:

SECTION I

Consumption Levels and Requirements

Chairman: Kuo Ping-wen (China)
Vice Chairman: Manuel J. Zevada (Mexico)
Reporter: W. R. Aykroyd (India)
Secretary: Frank G. Boudreau (U.S.A.)
Assistant Secretary: E. F. Penrose (U.S.A.)

COMMITTEE 1

Chairman: Karl Evang (Norway)
Vice Chairman: Tsou Ping-wen (China)
Vice Chairman: Miguel Etchenique (Bolivia)
Secretary: Hazel K. Stiebeling (U.S.A.)
Assistant Secretary: Katherine Bain (U.S.A.)

A. Food
  1. Character and extent of consumption deficiencies in each country
  2. Causes and consequences of malnutrition
  3. Reasonable national and international goals for improved food consumption

COMMITTEE 2

Chairman: Roberto E. MacEachen (Uruguay)
Vice Chairman: Edouard J. Bigwood (Belgium)
Vice Chairman: J. Manuel Casanueva (Chile)
Secretary: Harold A. Vogel (U.S.A.)

A. Food
  4. Measures for improving standards of consumption (education, etc.)

COMMITTEE 3

Chairman: José Garibaldi Dantas (Brazil)
Vice Chairman: Cimon P. Diamantopoulos (Greece)
Vice Chairman: Gabriel L. Dennis (Liberia)
Secretary: A. W. Palmer (U.S.A.)

B. Other essential agricultural products
  1. Pre-war consumption levels in various countries as influenced by prosperity or depression and by buying power of the population
  2. Reasonable national and international goals for improved consumption with sustained employment and expanded industrial activity

SECTION II

Expansion of Production and Adaptation to Consumption Needs

Chairman: Alexey D. Krutikov (U.S.S.R.)
Vice Chairman: Sir Girja Shankar Bajpai (India)
Reporter: Murray D. Lincoln (U.S.A.)
Secretary: F. F. Elliott (U.S.A.)
Assistant Secretary: Clayton Whipple (U.S.A.)

COMMITTEE 1

Chairman: G. S. H. Barton (Canada)
Vice Chairman: J. M. Troncoso (Dominican Republic)
Vice Chairman: Yilma Deressa (Ethiopia)
Secretary: Bushrod W. Allin (U.S.A.)

A. Measures for direction of production toward commodities, the supply of which should be increased
B. Measures for shifting production out of commodities in chronic surplus

COMMITTEE 2

Chairman: Héctor David Castro (El Salvador)
Vice Chairman: Stefan Krolikowski (Poland)
Vice Chairman: César García Alvarez (Colombia)
Secretary: Philip V. Cardon (U.S.A.)

C. Measures for improving agricultural productivity and efficiency

COMMITTEE 3

Chairman: Joaquín M. Elizalde (Philippine Commonwealth)
Vice Chairman: Roberto Alamo Ibarra (Venezuela)
Vice Chairman: París E. Menéndez (Paraguay)
Secretary: Mark L. Nichols (U.S.A.)

D. Measures for development and conservation of agricultural resources

COMMITTEE 4

Chairman: E. McCarthy (Australia)
Vice Chairman: André Liautaud (Haiti)
Vice Chairman: Marcos Carías Reyes (Honduras)
Secretary: Conrad Taeuber (U.S.A.)

E. Opportunities for occupational adjustments in agricultural populations

SECTION III

Facilitation and Improvement of Distribution

Chairman: João Carlos Muniz (Brazil)
Vice Chairman: Branko Cubrilovic (Yugoslavia)
Reporter: G. H. C. Hart (Netherlands)
Secretary: Howard S. Piquet (U.S.A.)

COMMITTEE 1

Chairman: J. P. R. Maud (Great Britain)
Vice Chairman: Jan V. Hyka (Czechoslovakia)
Vice Chairman: Gerardo Klinge (Peru)
Secretary: Frank A. Waring (U.S.A.)

A. Relation of national and international economic policies to agricultural problems, with special reference to the facilitation of the movement of agricultural products in commerce
   1. Expansion of international trade
   2. Broad policies for assuring increased production and consumption in general

COMMITTEE 2

Chairman: G. A. Duncan (New Zealand)
Vice Chairman: Eduardo Morillo Safa (Mexico)
Vice Chairman: Ramón Antonio Vega (Panama)
Secretary: Frederick L. Thomsen (U.S.A.)

B. Improvement of agricultural marketing, processing, and distribution

COMMITTEE 3

Chairman: Hervé Alphand (French Delegation)
Vice Chairman: A. P. van der Post (South Africa)
Vice Chairman: Alfredo Peñaherrera Vergara (Ecuador)
Secretary: Frederick V. Waugh (U.S.A.)
Assistant Secretary: Faith M. Williams (U.S.A.)

C. Special measures for wider food distribution
   1. Improvement of consumption of low-income groups
   2. International disposition of commodities in over-supply

COMMITTEE 4

Chairman: M. P. L. Steenberghe (Netherlands)
Vice Chairman: Hussein Bey M. Enan (Egypt)
Vice Chairman: Julio Gómez Robles (Guatemala)
Secretary: Robert M. Carr (U.S.A.)

D. Buffer stocks and commodity arrangements to assure equitable prices and adequate supplies

SECTION IV

Recommendations for Continuing and Carrying Forward the Work of the Conference

Chairman: Richard Law (Great Britain)
Vice Chairman: Amadeo López Castro (Cuba)
Reporter: F. L. McDougall (Australia)
Secretary: Loyd V. Steere (U.S.A.)
Assistant Secretary: Benjamin Gerig (U.S.A.)

The final Plenary Session was held on June 3, 1943. As a result of the deliberations, as recorded in the minutes and reports of the respective Committees and Sections and of the Plenary Sessions, the United Nations Conference on Food and Agriculture approved the following declaration, resolutions, and recommendations.

I. DECLARATION

This Conference, meeting in the midst of the greatest war ever waged, and in full confidence of victory, has considered the world problems of food and agriculture and declares its belief that the goal of freedom from want of food, suitable and adequate for the health and strength of all peoples, can be achieved.

1. The first task is to complete the winning of the war and to deliver millions of people from tyranny and from hunger. During the period of critical shortage in the aftermath of war, freedom from hunger can be achieved only by urgent and concerted efforts to economize consumption, to increase supplies and distribute them to the best advantage.

2. Thereafter we must equally concert our efforts to win and maintain freedom from fear and freedom from want. The one cannot be achieved without the other.

3. There has never been enough food for the health of all people. This is justified neither by ignorance nor by the harshness of nature. Production of food must be greatly expanded; we now have knowledge of the means by which this can be done. It requires imagination and firm will on the part of each government and people to make use of that knowledge.

4. The first cause of hunger and malnutrition is poverty. It is useless to produce more food unless men and nations provide the markets to absorb it. There must be an expansion of the whole world economy to provide the purchasing power sufficient to maintain an adequate diet for all. With full employment in all countries, enlarged industrial production, the absence of exploitation, an increasing flow of trade within and between countries, an orderly management of domestic and international investment and currencies, and sustained internal and international economic equilibrium, the food which is produced can be made available to all people.

5. The primary responsibility lies with each nation for seeing that its own people have the food needed for life and health; steps to this end are for national determination. But each nation can fully achieve its goal only if all work together.

6. We commend to our respective governments and authorities the study and adoption of the findings and recommendations of this Conference and urge the early concerted discussion of the related problems falling outside the scope of this Conference.

7. The first steps toward freedom from want of food must not await the final solution of all other problems. Each advance made in one field will strengthen and quicken advance in all others. Work already begun must be continued. Once the war has been won decisive steps can be taken. We must make ready now.

II. Interim and Permanent Commissions for Carrying Out the Recommendations of the United Nations Conference on Food and Agriculture

Whereas:

1. Freedom from want is difficult to achieve without concerted action among all like-minded nations to expand and improve production, to

increase employment, to raise levels of consumption, and to establish greater freedom in international commerce;

2. The successful carrying out of the recommendations of the Conference in the field of production, distribution, and consumption of food and other agricultural products in the post-war period will be the most important prerequisite for the achievement of freedom from want, and requires the creation by the governments and authorities here represented of a permanent organization in the field of food and agriculture; therefore

The United Nations Conference on Food and Agriculture

RECOMMENDS:

1. That the governments and authorities here represented recognize and embody in a formal declaration or agreement the obligation to their respective peoples and to one another, henceforth to collaborate in raising levels of nutrition and standards of living of their peoples, and to report to one another on the progress achieved;

2. That the governments and authorities here represented establish a permanent organization in the field of food and agriculture; and

RESOLVES:

1. That in order that every practicable step may be taken to attain these and the other appropriate objectives set forth in the declaration and specific recommendations of the Conference, an Interim Commission for carrying out the recommendations of the United Nations Conference on Food and Agriculture be established.

2. That each of the governments and authorities here represented be entitled to designate a representative on the Interim Commission, and that the Interim Commission be installed in Washington not later than July 15, 1943;

3. That the Interim Commission perform its work with due regard to the exigencies of the war, through such form of organization and personnel as it may deem appropriate; and formulate regulations covering its expenditures and submit to the member governments and authorities a budget and allocation of quota contributions;

4. That the functions of the Interim Commission be to formulate and recommend for consideration by each member government or authority:

(a) A specific plan for a permanent organization in the field of food and agriculture;

(b) The formal declaration or agreement referred to in the first recommendation, in which each participant shall recognize its obligation:

(i) To raise the levels of nutrition and standards of living of its own people;

(*ii*) To improve the efficiency of agricultural production and distribution;

(*iii*) To cooperate, so far as may be possible, with other nations for the achievement of these ends;

(*iv*) To undertake to submit periodically to the other participants, through the permanent organization, reports on the action taken and the progress achieved toward these ends;

(*c*) Such proposals or reports as are necessary to give effect to the recommendations of the Conference;

5. That in the preparation of a plan for the permanent organization the Interim Commission give full consideration to the following:

(*a*) The relation of the permanent organization to, and methods of associating it with, other institutions, national as well as international, which already exist or which may hereafter be established, in the field of food and agriculture and in related scientific, economic, and other fields;

(*b*) Provision for membership in the permanent organization, in due course, of governments not represented on the Interim Commission;

6. That in considering the functions and duties to be assigned to the permanent organization the Interim Commission take into account:

(*a*) The promotion of scientific, technological, social, and economic research;

(*b*) The collection and dissemination of information and provision for the exchange of services;

(*c*) The submission to member governments and authorities of recommendations for action with regard to the following:

(*i*) Nutrition;

(*ii*) Standards of consumption of food and other agricultural products;

(*iii*) Agricultural production, distribution, and conservation;

(*iv*) Statistics and economic studies in the field of agriculture and food, including the study of the relation of agriculture to world economy;

(*v*) Education and extension work in the field of food and agriculture;

(*vi*) Agricultural credit;

(*vii*) Problems of agricultural population and farm labor;

7. That the Interim Commission further consider the desirability of assigning to the permanent organization functions in the field of:

(*a*) Development of agricultural resources and orientation of production, where necessary;

(*b*) Agricultural commodity arrangements;

(*c*) Agricultural cooperative movements;

(*d*) Land tenure;

(e) Other subjects on which recommendations have been made by the Conference;

8. That the Interim Commission also consider the initiation of preliminary statistical investigations and research into the problems with which the permanent organization will deal;

9. That the Interim Commission be deemed to have been dissolved when the permanent organization has been established;

10. That the Government of the United States of America be invited to take whatever preliminary action may be necessary for the establishment of the Interim Commission after the United Nations Conference on Food and Agriculture has completed its work.

III. Improvement of National Diets

The United Nations Conference on Food and Agriculture

Having reviewed the information submitted by the several delegations on consumption deficiencies and the relation of food to health throughout the world and being deeply impressed by the dominant role played by adequate food in the reduction of sickness and death rates and the maintenance of health,

Declares:

1. That the first essential of a decent standard of living is the provision to all men of those primary necessities which are required to promote freedom from disease, and for the attainment of good health;

2. That the most fundamental of these necessities is adequate food which should be placed within the reach of all men in all lands within the shortest possible time;

3. That ample evidence has been presented revealing the existence of malnutrition in every country, with its inevitable consequences of preventable ill health; and

Recommends:

1. That the governments and authorities here represented:

(a) Immediately undertake [1] the task of increasing the food resources and improving the diets of their people in accordance with the principles and objectives outlined in the findings of the Conference, and declare to their respective peoples and to other governments and authorities here represented their intention of so doing;

(b) Undertake periodically to report to one another through the permanent organization recommended in Resolution II on the state

[1] Obviously this is impossible for governments whose territory is entirely or partly occupied by enemy forces.

of their national nutrition and on the steps being taken for its improvement.

IV. DIETS OF VULNERABLE GROUPS

WHEREAS:

1. There are special needs of vulnerable groups, such as pregnant and nursing women, infants, pre-school and school children, adolescents, workers, and individuals receiving low incomes;

2. Families with numerous children in low-income groups are particularly vulnerable;

3. Social, economic, and health measures of various kinds are or should be provided for these groups;

4. Wide experience has shown that direct measures to supplement inadequate diets have been economical and fruitful;

The United Nations Conference on Food and Agriculture

RECOMMENDS:

That the several governments and authorities here represented undertake positive measures for the improvement of the diets of the vulnerable groups enumerated above.

V. MALNUTRITION AND DISEASE

WHEREAS:

1. Malnutrition is responsible for widespread impairment of human efficiency and for an enormous amount of ill health and disease, reduces the resistance of the body to tuberculosis, and enhances the general incidence and severity of familiar diseases;

2. Mortality rates in infants, children, and mothers are higher in ill-fed than in well-fed populations;

3. Food consumption at a level merely sufficient to prevent malnutrition is not enough to promote health and well-being;

The United Nations Conference on Food and Agriculture

RECOMMENDS:

1. That the governments and authorities here represented:

(a) Initiate or continue the study of the relationship between malnutrition and impaired bodily health and vigor; and, in particular, investigate the role of inadequate food consumption in the causation of, and mortality from, all those diseases which constitute their most serious health problems;

(*b*) Direct their attention to the study of health and well-being and of the nutritional and related factors which are necessary to secure and maintain them;

(*c*) Consider the most effective means of disseminating knowledge of correct feeding among all sections of the population.

VI. Deficiency Diseases

WHEREAS:

1. The progressive improvement of diets will result in better health and eventually in the elimination of specific deficiency diseases, and a great deal of unnecessary suffering could be avoided if an immediate and concerted attack were made upon them;

2. Progress in our knowledge of nutrition makes it possible to seek out, treat successfully, and prevent the recurrence of the common diseases resulting from specific deficiencies in the diet;

The United Nations Conference on Food and Agriculture

RECOMMENDS:

1. That the several governments and authorities here represented undertake immediately:

(*a*) To ascertain the prevalence of specific deficiency diseases among their respective peoples;

(*b*) To deal with them by suitable dietary and therapeutic measures;

(*c*) To take appropriate steps to prevent their recurrence.

VII. National Nutrition Organization

WHEREAS:

1. A sound food and nutrition policy must be adopted by each government if national diets are to be progressively improved, specific deficiency diseases eliminated, and good health achieved;

2. Such a policy requires the guidance of a central authority with special competence and responsibility to interpret the science of nutrition in the light of national conditions and to propose to the appropriate authorities practical means for extending its benefits to all sections of society;

The United Nations Conference on Food and Agriculture

RECOMMENDS:

1. That the governments and authorities here represented:

(*a*) Undertake to establish national nutrition organizations, if such do not now exist, entrusted with the responsibility of ascertaining food-consumption habits and the nutritional status of different sections of the population; such organizations to be composed of authorities in health, nutrition, economics, and agriculture, together with administrators and consumers' representatives, etc.; to be provided with adequate funds and facilities for the efficient conduct of their work; and to have the authority to bring their recommendations to the attention of the public and to those agencies of government which deal with agriculture and the framing of economic and social policy;

(b) Re-examine and, if necessary, reorganize existing agencies and review legislation concerned with health, agriculture, and nutrition to the end that food and nutrition policies may be efficiently carried out.

VIII. EXCHANGE OF INFORMATION AND EXPERIENCE

WHEREAS:

1. Experience has shown that national nutrition organizations receive considerable benefit from periodic exchanges of views and information on methods employed, obstacles encountered, and progress achieved;

2. Governments participating in a common undertaking will wish to collaborate so that levels of food consumption may become more equitable not only among the different sections of the population in a given country but among the several nations of the world as well;

The United Nations Conference on Food and Agriculture

RECOMMENDS:

1. That the several national nutrition organizations exchange information and experience and provide mutual assistance, both directly, when desirable, and through the permanent organization recommended in Resolution II, to which they should submit periodic reports on the results of their investigations into national dietary habits and nutritional status, and on the progress achieved in raising the level of food consumption throughout the population;

2. That representatives of the several national nutrition organizations meet regularly under the auspices of the permanent organization to exchange views and to make proposals for any national and international action necessary to facilitate the progress of their work.

IX. DIETARY STANDARDS

WHEREAS:

1. It is essential that there be some measure of the extent to which food supplies should be increased, and of the character and extent of the dietary improvements which need to be carried out;

2. This measure is best provided by dietary standards or allowances based upon scientific evidence;

The United Nations Conference on Food and Agriculture

RECOMMENDS:

That the governments and authorities here represented adopt as the ultimate goal of their food and nutrition policy, dietary standards or allowances based upon scientific assessment of the amount and quality of food, in terms of nutrients, which promote health, and distinguish clearly between these standards and the more immediate consumption goals which necessarily must be based upon the practical possibilities of improving the food supply of their populations.

X. COOPERATION OF EXISTING AGENCIES

WHEREAS:

1. National nutrition organizations were established in many countries before the present war and various national and international health and nutrition agencies had achieved considerable progress in the study and improvement of diets and food-consumption levels in different countries and regions;

2. If no time is to be lost in moving toward the goals set out by the Conference, it is essential to make full use of the information and experience acquired by these agencies;

The United Nations Conference on Food and Agriculture

RECOMMENDS:

That in the establishment of the permanent organization recommended in Resolution II, in any projected regional branches of that organization, and in any national nutrition organizations, due account should be taken of the work and experience of existing international regional or national agencies concerned with food, health, and nutrition; and in any such plans, the possibility of enlisting the cooperation of such agencies should be fully explored.

XI. NON-FOOD PRODUCTS

WHEREAS:

1. Many of the non-food agricultural and marine products are constituent parts of the means to human health and welfare to an extent which merits consideration for them on a plane with food;

2. It is of great importance to consuming countries that there should be a regular and adequate supply of these commodities, and to producing countries that they should be enabled to orient their agricultural enterprises to world demand;

3. The Conference has not found it possible to reach conclusions as to the effective capacity of the world to consume specific products in future years;

4. In many countries and regions which are not well adapted to the production of food, the production of other essential agricultural and marine products and their disposal on domestic and foreign markets provide a major source of income, and the income so derived determines to a large extent the abilities of these countries and regions to secure adequate quantities of the right kinds of food;

The United Nations Conference on Food and Agriculture

RECOMMENDS:

1. That the permanent organization recommended in Resolution II:

(a) Investigate the possibility of the development by the nations of the world of national standards of minimum consumption of certain non-food agricultural and marine products, taking into account the varying climatic and other relevant conditions of the different countries;

(b) Arrange at an early date for comprehensive studies of the probable future capacity of the world to consume specific agricultural and marine products in this group, taking into account in this connection the probable effect of synthetic and other substitute products;

(c) Give special study to the development of means by which regions which are not well adapted to the production of food may share in a world-wide improvement of nutrition in keeping with the purpose of the Conference.

XII. CHANGES IN PRODUCTION IN THE SHORT-TERM PERIOD

The United Nations Conference on Food and Agriculture

RECOMMENDS:

1. That, as a first step in overcoming the general shortage of food every effort should be made by countries whose agriculture can be expanded in the short-term period, so long as this is required and so far as the conditions of individual countries require or permit, to increase the acreage under crops for direct human consumption and even to hold back the rebuilding of depleted livestock herds — essential though this rebuilding will ultimately be — as well as the production of other crops which compete for acreage with essential foods;

2. That countries whose agriculture has been impaired should, in the immediate post-war period, utilize to the full their agricultural resources to bring about a rapid increase in food production, even if this involves a departure from the use of the resources which in the long run will be required, and even if it delays a return to production policies which are desirable for technical, economic, or nutritional reasons (for instance, in Europe there may need to be a concentration in the first years on

vegetables, bread grains, and other products where production can mature quickly and which yield more calories per acre than livestock);

3. That, pursuant to the above purpose, countries which have been producing more than normal output because of freedom from enemy action should:

(a) In the short run maintain such production;

(b) Whenever possible, increase production further, provided transport and the means of production, etc., are available, to assist in meeting abnormal demands.

4. That, taking into consideration that the degree of shortage of foodstuffs which will develop after the war will depend upon the course of the war and on the harvests, it will be necessary during the period from the present until the termination of the war for each of the nations which has escaped enemy invasion to continue to stress the necessity of production of those products which are required by other nations during the war, and at the same time to produce sufficient quantities of products for home consumption, subject to the requirements of the war effort;

5. That every effort should be made now and immediately after the war by countries in a position to do so, to expand the production of farm machinery and implements, fertilizers, and other materials, including improved seeds, vital to the expansion of food production, and to cooperate in making these materials available to the agricultural producing countries, so far as the exigencies of the war permit.

XIII. COORDINATION IN THE SHORT-TERM PERIOD

WHEREAS:

1. It is the consensus of the Conference that, despite all efforts to increase production, supplies of essential foodstuffs and certain other agricultural and marine products and of the necessary instruments of production, such as fertilizers and machinery, and the means of international transportation will all be inadequate to meet basic requirements in the transition period, which may extend for several years after the cessation of hostilities;

2. It is essential for the preservation of life to secure, through equitable distribution, the maximum advantage from such supplies as may be made available;

3. It is in the interest of producers and consumers alike to avoid social and economic ills due to monopolistic practices or to violent fluctuations arising from unrestrained competition for inadequate supplies, in the prices of food, the instruments of production, and other necessities, including industrial goods;

4. It is in the common interest of all that agricultural production be soundly reestablished and expanded with all possible speed in countries

now temporarily occupied by the enemy as soon as they have been liberated;

5. These objectives can be achieved only by the concerted action of governments in the stimulation of production and in the allocation of supplies;

The United Nations Conference on Food and Agriculture

RECOMMENDS:

1. That the governments and authorities here represented, for so long after the war as shortages continue, affirm the principle of mutual responsibility and coordinated action for:

(*a*) The increased production of necessary foodstuffs and other essential agricultural and marine products by all possible means, subject only to the exigencies of war, in each country where such expansion can be accomplished economically, either now or in the future;

(*b*) The transportation, distribution, and utilization of such products;

(*c*) The prevention of speculative and violent fluctuations in the prices of food, the instruments of production, and other necessities, including industrial goods, under the conditions of scarcity that appear certain to prevail after the war;

(*d*) The post-war readjustment of agriculture to achieve a progressive and balanced expansion of production and consumption throughout the world;

2. That these governments and authorities take, individually and in concert, whether by conference or otherwise, all necessary measures, both domestic and international, to secure the application of this principle and the achievement of these objectives.

XIV.   ADJUSTMENT OF PRODUCTION IN THE TRANSITION FROM THE
SHORT-TERM TO THE LONG-TERM PERIOD

The United Nations Conference on Food and Agriculture

RECOMMENDS:

1. That countries whose agriculture has been impaired should progressively modify their short-term allocation of resources to conform more closely to the long-term plan aimed at better nutrition and greater efficiency in production (for instance, in certain parts of Europe this might mean increasing the production of milk products as herds can be reestablished, accompanied by declining production of grains);

2. That countries which will have been producing during the short-term period more than normal output because of freedom from enemy action in the war or which have undertaken new lines of production, should progressively adjust the allocation of agricultural resources to

conform to a long-term coordinated production plan for the best use of these resources on a world scale, based on better diets for their own people and on the international demand for nutritionally better food.

XV. Long-Term Production Policy

Whereas:

1. It is recognized that a secure, adequate, and suitable supply of food should be a cardinal aim in every country;

2. It is recognized that this can be achieved only as part of a world-wide policy of industrial and agricultural expansion;

3. It is recognized that in order to secure this result producers should receive a fair return for their products;

4. In order to attain the highest nutritional standards, a progressive expansion and, where necessary, reorientation in agriculture will be required;

5. It is desirable to formulate a body of principles which are applicable to agricultural policy in appropriate form in all countries;

The United Nations Conference on Food and Agriculture

Recommends:

1. (*a*) That the inherent natural and economic advantages of any area should determine the farming systems adopted and the commodities produced in that area;

(*b*) That farming systems should be so designed as:

(*i*) To maintain soil fertility at levels which will sustain yields and ensure adequate return for labor;

(*ii*) To protect crops and livestock from major pests and diseases;

(*iii*) To favor steady employment throughout the year;

(These three ends, in general and save in exceptional circumstances, can best be assured by balanced mixed rotational farming and by avoidance of single-crop production, or monoculture.)

(*c*) That production of nutritionally desirable foods which can be obtained from elsewhere only with difficulty or not at all is a special obligation of the agriculture of every country;

(*d*) In every region subject to drought (occasional or in the form of sharply marked periodic dry seasons) suitable measures should be undertaken, partly by storage and partly by diversification of production and development of water resources and cultural practices;

(*e*) Land used or likely to be required for agriculture should be protected from erosion;

(*f*) The spread of existing knowledge by education and the development of new knowledge by research should be constantly promoted, and that in these matters nations can cooperate to great advantage;

2. That, subject to these principles and with the object of expanding production of the foods needed for its people, each nation should undertake to direct its policies toward:

(*a*) Increasing the efficiency of production in present producing areas through the introduction, as rapidly as conditions permit, of better farming methods, suitable modern equipment, improved varieties of crops and strains of livestock, and soil conservation practices;

(*b*) Developing any suitable undeveloped areas, where this is economically feasible, through the use of such measures as clearing the land and large-scale drainage and irrigation projects;

(*c*) Fostering desirable changes in the pattern of production, designed to give greater emphasis to foods rich in vitamins, minerals, and proteins:

(*i*) By encouraging the production, particularly in areas near consumption centers, of such products as vegetables, fruits, milk, eggs, and meat, which are relatively perishable and high in value and which are also the foods required in greatly increased quantities for better nutrition;

(*ii*) By encouraging the expansion of livestock production in areas capable of growing or economically shipping in the necessary feedstuffs;

(*iii*) By limiting the production of bulky, easily stored and transported energy foods, in areas where they cannot be produced efficiently;

(*iv*) By encouraging the production in single-crop areas of a greater diversity of foods for home use, since these areas are, in general, distant from the sources of perishable products and are particularly in need of improved diets;

(*v*) By likewise encouraging more diversified and adequate home food production in all farming areas, so that rural people may have more and better food, while eliminating the margin between producer and consumer;

3. That, to implement these aims, having regard to its individual circumstances, each country should adopt the following measures:

(*a*) The framing of policies designed to encourage production within the country of commodities that need to be produced there in greater amounts and limit production of those that should not be produced within the country or should be produced in smaller amounts;

(*b*) The supplying of low-cost credit or other aids that would help producers to acquire necessary materials, equipment, and machinery for more efficient production and better use of the land;

(*c*) The furnishing of technical assistance to producers where this is needed;

(*d*) The development of a program of education to help producers understand better farming methods and put them into practice;

(*e*) The development of a program of research designed to meet the continuing problems of agriculture within the country;

4. (*a*) That each nation consider the possibility:

    (*i*) Of drawing up periodic reports on steps taken to implement the recommendations set out above, with particular reference to production, exports, imports, and consumption of food and other agricultural and marine products. These reports should, where practicable, be on a statistical basis;

    (*ii*) Of submitting these reports to the permanent organization recommended in Resolution II;

(*b*) That, with a view to balancing production and consumption, the permanent organization consider to what extent and by what means such reports might contribute to international collaboration both on a regional and on a world basis in the field of agricultural production.

XVI. AGRICULTURAL CREDIT

WHEREAS:

1. Capital development and adequate credit facilities are necessary if agricultural production is to be restored, increased, and intensified;

2. Agricultural credit in some countries has frequently been obtainable only at rates which the farmer could not afford to pay;

3. The agricultural communities in many countries have been unable to obtain information on the organization and development of agricultural credit systems in other countries;

4. In some countries full agricultural development has been or may be obstructed by difficulties in providing adequate capital;

The United Nations Conference on Food and Agriculture

RECOMMENDS:

1. That every endeavor be made to ensure an adequate supply of credit to agriculture;

2. That to this end full use be made of all types of suitable private, cooperative, and public credit institutions;

3. That the rate of interest be as low as possible and the conditions regarding initial cost, redemption, etc., be as favorable as possible for the borrowers, particularly with a view to helping the small farmer;

4. That, in view of the importance of agricultural credit, its requirements be duly recognized by international action taken as a result of this Conference.

XVII. Cooperative Movements

Whereas:

1. The cooperative movement has been of very great importance in many countries, both to urban and rural populations, especially in agricultural districts where farming is based on small units and in urban areas of low-income families;

2. The proper functioning of cooperative societies may facilitate adjustments of agricultural production and distribution, as members have confidence in the recommendations and guidance of their own cooperative organizations, which they know operate in the interest of their members and of society in general;

3. The democratic control and educational programs, which are features of the cooperative movement, can play a vital part in the training of good democratic citizens, and assist in inducing a sound conception of economic matters;

The United Nations Conference on Food and Agriculture

Recommends:

1. That, in order to make it possible for people to help themselves in lowering costs of production and costs of distribution and marketing:

(*a*) All countries study the possibilities of the further establishment of producer and consumer cooperative societies in order to render necessary production, marketing, purchasing, finance, and other services;

(*b*) Each nation examine its laws, regulations, and institutions to determine if legal or institutional obstacles to cooperative development exist, in order to make desirable adjustments;

(*c*) Full information as to the present development of cooperatives in different countries be made available through the permanent organization recommended in Resolution II.

XVIII. Land Tenure and Farm Labor

Whereas:

Agricultural productivity and efficiency and the well-being of the tiller of the soil depend largely upon the system of land tenure and conditions of farm labor;

The United Nations Conference on Food and Agriculture

Recommends:

1. That each nation make a careful survey of existing systems of land tenure and the other conditions of agriculture within its boundaries to ascertain whether changes in these systems and conditions are necessary

or desirable to promote the productivity and efficiency of agriculture and the welfare of its workers and that special attention be given to the position of the agricultural worker as compared with that of the worker in other industries;

2. That the permanent organization recommended in Resolution II give every assistance in this study.

XIX. EDUCATION AND RESEARCH

WHEREAS:

1. Through the inadequacy of agricultural education, existing knowledge is being very imperfectly applied to agricultural production;

2. Man's increasing demands upon the soil can be met only by the increase of knowledge;

The United Nations Conference on Food and Agriculture

RECOMMENDS:

1. That each nation adopt, and carry out as rapidly as conditions may permit, a policy for:

(a) Strengthening and expanding the educational system of its rural areas;

(b) Training scientific workers and rural leaders for service in agriculture;

(c) Establishing or developing systems of rural adult education (extension systems) designed to promote technical efficiency among producers, to develop understanding of rural problems, and to enrich rural life;

2. That each nation adopt a policy of promoting research in all the branches of science, including economics, which relate to food and agriculture, and to this end cooperate actively with other nations by the exchange of knowledge, materials, and personnel; and that, in particular, each nation agree:

(a) To promote research in the natural sciences and their application to problems of food and agriculture;

(b) To develop economic and sociological investigation of rural problems;

(c) To collaborate with other nations in the collecting and assembling of factual information and statistics of food and agriculture throughout the world;

3. That, as a necessary step in securing effective action in these directions, the permanent organization recommended in Resolution II be charged with the functions:

(a) Of providing advice, and technical and other assistance, to governments desiring this in connection with the establishment or improvement of agricultural research and education;

(b) Of facilitating international help and exchange in the supply of information, services, material, and personnel;

(c) Of assisting in the planning and conduct of any research programs upon which international collaboration has been agreed or desired;

(d) Of acting as a central agency for assembling, analyzing, and disseminating factual data on world agriculture;

(e) Of assisting in a comprehensive abstracting service covering the whole range of agricultural research;

(f) Of assisting scientific societies in the arrangement of international meetings.

XX. CONSERVING LAND AND WATER RESOURCES

WHEREAS:

1. Soil erosion has in the past destroyed or severely limited the utility of vast areas of land and will in the future, unless checked, constitute the greatest physical danger to the world's food production;

2. Failure to conserve and control water supplies and to use them efficiently has, in many areas, precluded important potential increase in food production;

3. To meet the food needs of the growing world population and to ensure high nutritional standards, all land in agricultural use or suitable for being brought into agricultural use should be adequately protected from erosion and from any other serious damage by various measures, including structural work and the insurance of satisfactory agricultural systems and husbandry practices;

4. The conserving of land and water resources should be regarded as an obligation of governments as well as individuals;

The United Nations Conference on Food and Agriculture

RECOMMENDS:

1. That each nation undertake:

(a) To survey its land and water resources with the object of ascertaining:

(i) The extent and causes of soil erosion and water losses;

(ii) The soil and moisture conservation requirements of the areas covered and the types of conservation measures most needed;

(b) To develop soil and water conservation programs based on the findings of such surveys;

(c) To assist farmers in conserving and rebuilding the fertility of the soil;

2. That the necessary implementation of these policies be effected through appropriate economic and other measures such as:

(*a*) Assisting individual producers in planning and carrying out crop rotations, crop sequences, and other suitable practices;

(*b*) Protection of forest and afforestation of unprotected watersheds where necessary, including measures for the protection of food-producing wild life, to prevent flood damage and to conserve water needed for direct human consumption and for irrigation;

(*c*) Building, or assisting in building, dams, terraces, and other structures to minimize the loss of soil fertility through erosion caused by wind or water;

(*d*) Making readily available to individual producers soil amendments, particularly phosphates and lime, that will make possible expanded production of leguminous and other soil-building crops;

(*e*) Development and employment of farming systems and husbandry practices which ensure soil conservation;

(*f*) Developing a program of research designed to determine the best methods and practices for bringing about conservation of land and water resources under various conditions;

(*g*) Developing a program of education to inform the public generally of the importance and need of conservation and to help producers to understand and put into practice better farming methods;

3. That the permanent organization recommended in Resolution II provide assistance by such means as:

(*a*) Formulation of a body of principles for the conduct of soil-conservation work;

(*b*) Collection and interchange between nations of data and information on erosion, erosion-control methods, and other pertinent matters;

(*c*) Interchange between nations of personnel technically trained in the development of conservation research and in the application of its findings.

XXI. Development and Settlement of Land for Food Production
Whereas:

1. If freedom from want is to be achieved throughout the world by full development of food-producing resources, conservation of existing lands and the development of new areas must be given primary consideration;

2. There are large areas of land capable of materially adding to the world's food supply which can be opened to food production if transportation facilities were made available and insanitary conditions and other deterrents corrected;

3. There are many areas of great extent not now producing or in a low state of production because of lack of water-conserving and storing facilities for irrigation, lack of drainage, frequent flooding by rivers, wastage by erosion, deficiencies of plant food, accumulation of alkali, or improper development;

The United Nations Conference on Food and Agriculture

RECOMMENDS:

1. That each nation undertake:

(*a*) To survey its land and water resources to determine (1) in what areas, if opened to settlement, production of food could materially be increased; (2) what areas, if supplied with additional production facilities, such as water supply for irrigation, improved drainage, or by the correction of deterrents to production, could materially increase their production of food; (3) the kind, extent, and economic possibility of developments necessary for this increase in food production;

(*b*) To develop on the basis of these findings policies of settlement and development of a program applicable to the economic, social, agricultural, and geographical needs of the nation of which it is a part, considering:

   (*i*) Physical conditions including (1) soils and climate, (2) health conditions, (3) transportation, and (4) clearing, irrigation, or drainage needs;

   (*ii*) Settlement policies, including (1) the type of farming systems to be established, (2) the scale of working by plantations, small holdings, or cooperative organization of areas for production, (3) measures to prevent speculation and exploitation, and (4) financial and other assistance;

   (*iii*) Conservation measures for sustained production of the area, including (1) agronomic and management practices, (2) conservation structures and practices, (3) protection against alkali accumulations, and (4) measures of forest conservation and reforestation;

2. That the necessary implementation of these policies and programs be given through appropriate measures applicable to conditions and needs of each region or area, including:

(*a*) A comprehensive engineering service providing for developments affecting the entire area, such as transportation, improvement of sanitary conditions, water-storage reservoirs, drainage channels, and flood protection;

(*b*) Development of a program of sound land use, including conservation measures;

(*c*) Provision for technical assistance to individual producers in planning and developing the areas under their supervision;

(*d*) Provision for financial assistance to settlers for further development and operation;

(*e*) Provision for marketing produce, including necessary processing and preservation;

3. That the permanent organization recommended in Resolution II provide assistance by such means as:

(a) The interchange between nations of pertinent data and information on erosion and methods of control, land improvements, etc.;

(b) The interchange between nations of technically trained personnel to assist in the development of conservation research, etc.

XXII. Occupational Adjustments in Rural Populations

The United Nations Conference on Food and Agriculture

Recommends:

1. That, in order to effect the necessary occupational adjustments in agricultural populations:

(a) Agricultural efficiency should be improved and new lands brought under cultivation wherever possible;

(b) Areas which have a large agricultural population in relation to their agricultural resources should:

  (i) Develop industries suitable to the area, particularly for the processing and preserving of the agricultural produce of the country, and, where feasible, for the manufacture of machinery, fertilizer, and equipment needed for agriculture;

  (ii) Be encouraged, wherever it is economically sound, to export processed articles instead of the raw product, and in particular to take advantage of any reductions of trade barriers in the importing countries;

  (iii) Be assisted in securing capital for the development of industrial and transportation facilities and for the development of export outlets for processed products;

  (iv) Be assisted in securing facilities for the importation of machinery and tools where such are necessary;

  (v) Be assisted in securing and training technical personnel;

  (vi) Undertake programs of public works and, where necessary, be assisted in securing technical advice and access to capital;

  (vii) Develop sources of employment in public and private services;

(c) Where agricultural settlements are possible, appropriate steps should be taken to facilitate the movement of people from overmanned agricultural areas;

(d) In order to help in intra-national and international migration where these are feasible:

  (i) Occupational training should be provided;

  (ii) Labor bureaus should be set up where necessary;

  (iii) Transportation, communication, housing, sanitation, health, and other public facilities necessary to effective settlement should be provided by the country receiving the migrants;

(*iv*) Steps should be taken to provide for the economic security of the migrants;

(*e*) Where emigration is possible, an international organization should support arrangements to provide adequate safeguards for the settlers and for the countries concerned, and to facilitate the movement through other appropriate means.

XXIII. INTERNATIONAL SECURITY

WHEREAS:

1. Freedom from want cannot be achieved without freedom from fear;

2. Policies of aggression and the fear of aggression have induced the uneconomic employment of human and material resources, the development of uneconomic industries, the imposition of barriers to international trade, the introduction of discriminatory trade practices, and the expenditure of huge sums on armaments;

3. These obstructions to a progressively expanding economy cannot be removed without effective collaboration among nations;

The United Nations Conference on Food and Agriculture

RECOMMENDS:

1. That the governments and authorities here represented, by virtue of their determination to achieve freedom from want for all people in all lands, affirm the principle of mutual responsibility and coordinated action to establish such conditions of international security as will make possible an expanding and balanced world economy;

2. That these governments and authorities take in concert all necessary measures to secure the application of this principle and the achievement of this objective.

XXIV. ACHIEVEMENT OF AN ECONOMY OF ABUNDANCE

WHEREAS:

1. The first cause of hunger and malnutrition is poverty.

2. The promotion of the full employment of human and material resources, based on sound social and economic policies, is the first condition of a general and progressive increase in production and purchasing power;

3. The sound expansion of industry in undeveloped and other areas, with equality of access to materials and markets, serves also to expand production and purchasing power and is therefore indispensable to any comprehensive program for the advancement of agriculture;

4. Tariffs and other barriers to international trade, and abnormal fluctuations in exchange rates, restrict the production, distribution, and consumption of foodstuffs and other commodities;

5. Progress by individual nations toward a higher standard of living contributes to the solution of broader economic problems, but freedom from want cannot be achieved without effective collaboration among nations;

The United Nations Conference on Food and Agriculture

RECOMMENDS:

1. That the governments and authorities here represented, by virtue of their determination to achieve freedom from want for all people in all lands, affirm the principle of mutual responsibility and coordinated action:

(a) To promote the full and most advantageous employment of their own and all other people and a general advance in standards of living, thereby providing for an increase in both production and purchasing power;

(b) To promote the uninterrupted development and most advantageous use of agricultural and other material resources for the establishment of an equitable balance between agriculture and industry in the interest of all;

(c) To secure for agriculture the stimulus of additional purchasing power through the sound development of industry;

(d) To assist in the achievement of these ends by all appropriate means, including the supply of capital, equipment, and technical skill;

(e) To maintain an equilibrium in balances of payments, and to achieve the orderly management of currencies and exchange;

(f) To improve the methods and reduce the cost of distribution in international trade;

(g) As an integral part of this program, to reduce barriers of every kind to international trade and to eliminate all forms of discriminatory restrictions thereon, including inequitable policies in international transportation, as effectively and as rapidly as possible;

2. That these governments and authorities take, individually and in concert, whether by conference or otherwise, all necessary measures, both domestic and international, to secure the application of this principle and the achievement of these objectives.

XXV. INTERNATIONAL COMMODITY ARRANGEMENTS

WHEREAS:

1. Excessive short-term movements in the prices of food and agricultural commodities are an obstacle to the orderly conduct of their production and distribution;

2. Extreme fluctuations of the prices of food and agricultural products aggravate general deflationary and inflationary tendencies, which are injurious to producers and consumers alike;

3. The mitigation of these influences would promote the objectives of an expansionist policy;

4. Changes in the scale and character of production to meet more effectively the world's need for food and agricultural products may in certain instances require a period of transition and international co-operation to aid producers in making necessary readjustments in their productive organization;

5. International commodity arrangements may play a useful part in the advancement of these ends but further study is necessary to establish the precise forms which these arrangements should take and whether and to what extent regulation of production may be needed;

The United Nations Conference on Food and Agriculture

RECOMMENDS:

1. That international commodity arrangements should be designed so as to promote the expansion of an orderly world economy;

2. That, to this end, a body of broad principles should, through further international discussion, be agreed upon regarding the formulation, the provisions, and the administration of such international commodity arrangements as may be deemed feasible and desirable and should include assurance that:

(a) Such arrangements will include effective representation of consumers as well as producers;

(b) Increasing opportunities will be afforded for supplying consumption needs from the most efficient sources of production at prices fair to both consumers and producers and with due regard to such transitional adjustments in production as may be required to prevent serious economic and social dislocations;

(c) Adequate reserves will be maintained to meet all consumption needs;

(d) Provision will be made, when applicable, for the orderly disposal of surpluses;

3. That international organization should be created at an early date to study the feasibility and desirability of such arrangements with reference to individual commodities and, in appropriate cases, to initiate or review such arrangements to be entered into between governments, and to guide and coordinate the operations of such arrangements in accordance with agreed principles, maintaining close relations with such programs as may be undertaken in other fields of international economic

activity to the end that the objective of raising consumption levels of all peoples may be most effectively served.

XXVI. SPECIAL NATIONAL MEASURES FOR WIDER FOOD DISTRIBUTION

WHEREAS:

1. Even in the most prosperous countries there are many families which cannot afford to buy enough good food;

2. In some countries, and at some times, hunger and semistarvation have been widespread;

3. This situation has existed even when agricultural prices have been low and when large supplies of food have piled up in warehouses or rotted in the fields, and the problem will not be fully met by general economic measures to stimulate production and trade;

The United Nations Conference on Food and Agriculture

RECOMMENDS:

1. That the governments and authorities here represented accept the responsibility of making it possible, so far as it is within their power, for each person in their respective countries who is without an adequate diet, to improve his diet in the direction of obtaining the physiological requirements of health, adopting such of the following, or other, measures as are designed to fit local conditions and institutions:

(*a*) Adequate social-security measures, such as family allowances, social insurance, and minimum wages;

(*b*) Some form of direct action to make protective foods available free, or at low prices, to groups with inadequate diets;

(*c*) Special attention to assisting such groups as pregnant women, nursing mothers, infants, children, aged persons, invalids, and low-paid persons;

2. That the diets provided under these programs be based upon the best scientific information on nutritional needs;

3. That food-distribution measures be coordinated with programs to increase food production and to bring about adjustments in agriculture and fishing which will, on the one hand, encourage the production and distribution of those foods most lacking in the diets of the country, and adapted to the soils and climates; and will, on the other hand, provide an adequate level of living to persons engaged in farming and fishing;

4. That the permanent organization recommended in Resolution II assist the several governments and authorities in making surveys of nutritional needs, in helping develop new food-distribution programs, in disseminating information concerning those programs, and in aiding to coordinate efforts in this field.

XXVII. Special International Measures for Wider Food Distribution

Whereas:

1. The provision of adequate food for all the people in each nation is primarily the responsibility of the nation concerned and that this responsibility will be met primarily by national measures;

2. Nevertheless, undernutrition may continue for long periods of time in certain countries, while they are developing their agriculture and industry, and before they are able to produce internally or acquire abroad adequate amounts of food to meet the needs of their people;

3. It is generally agreed that it would be desirable if arrangements could be made whereby a part of current world food supplies could be used to supplement the national food-distribution programs of certain countries;

4. Moreover, relatively little attention has been given in the past to the possibilities of developing special measures for wider food distribution in the international field;

The United Nations Conference on Food and Agriculture

Recommends:

1. That the permanent organization recommended in Resolution II study the possibility of devising measures to meet the needs of countries with inadequate supplies, and the machinery needed for this purpose, distinguishing between methods which would be used in the case of famines following catastrophes, and in the case of countries where the available food supplies are generally inadequate;

2. That the problems of developing special international measures for wider food distribution in the latter case be studied in connection with plans in the countries concerned for the long-term development of the national resources, and for raising the technical skill and the level of living of their workers, and that the above-mentioned permanent organization collaborate with the International Labor Office on this question.

XXVIII. Government and Other National Services in Marketing

Whereas:

Improvements in the marketing of foods and other products of agricultural or marine origin are largely dependent upon certain basic government services, including the provision of quality standards, an efficient grading and inspection service, marketing research and education designed to promote improved marketing practices, and protection of the public, through the medium of pure-food laws, against impurities or adulterations and against unfair competition and undesirable trade practices;

The United Nations Conference on Food and Agriculture

RECOMMENDS:

1. That the permanent organization recommended in Resolution II:

(a) Investigate the practicability, and, if practicable, assist in the adoption of international grade standards for agricultural and marine commodities and of providing machinery for controlling the use of any such international grade standards in international trade; [1]

(b) Give assistance to governments and other national organizations looking to the establishment in each country of adequate grade standards and technical advisory and inspection services covering appropriate products, and, if requested, advise in the promotion of the educative, administrative, and legislative action necessary to achieve this objective; [2]

(c) Promote standardization of containers, both nationally and internationally, along the lines suggested in connection with grades; [3]

(d) Assist governments to extend and improve standards of nutrient content and purity of all important foods, consider also the formulation and adoption of similar international standards to facilitate and protect the interchange of such products between countries, and agree upon international methods of determination; [4]

(e) Consider the formulation and adoption of international stand-

[1] The use of any such standards should be voluntary on the part of individual countries and, if used, any one grade should apply uniformly throughout the world.

[2] The primary purpose of grade standards is to improve the quality and permit the purchase and sale of commodities by description rather than by inspection of each lot by buyers and sellers. Such standards (1) supply the basis for a common language for describing the product marketed; (2) facilitate trading by minimizing misunderstandings concerning the quality of the products; (3) reduce losses from rejections and costs of arbitration; (4) facilitate price quotations and other market information on the basis of quality; (5) reduce or eliminate the costs of resampling or inspection in various stages of marketing; (6) improve the collateral value of warehouse receipts and thus reduce financing costs; (7) help buyers to obtain the qualities of products they need; (8) permit the distribution of the various qualities on the basis of their most advantageous outlets; and (9) facilitate payments to producers on the basis of quality, which in turn would encourage adjustments in the qualities produced on the basis of consumer demand.

[3] Standardization of containers has not developed to the same extent as has standardization of grades. Lack of standardization gives rise to waste and confusion in the distribution of food.

[4] In order to protect health and improve nutrition, minimum standards for the nutrient content, and in certain cases for the methods of preparation and for the artificial enrichment of staple foods, should be prescribed by governments. These steps should be taken in addition to any measures designed to secure the absence of toxic substances and organisms from food under the usual type of pure-food laws. International standards of labeling and packaging can help, but in general the most effective action can be taken by individual countries themselves.

ards or minimum requirements for drugs, insecticides, fungicides, fertilizers, and other materials used by agricultural producers, in order to prevent misrepresentation in their preparation and sale, and to promote the purchase of products best suited to particular uses; [1]

(f) Consider whether existing international market news services adequately supply and coordinate information and statistics on prices and supply and demand; and promote any improvements considered necessary; [2]

(g) Urge upon governments the necessity, in the interests of better nutrition and better living, for further research into:

(i) Consumer needs, including palatability, packaging, food habits, shopping habits, shopping facilities, etc.;

(ii) Improved methods, with particular reference to perishable protective foods and any commodities of which buffer or other stocks may be held, of processing, preservation, storage, packaging, and transport;

(iii) Economics of marketing, including processing and retail distribution, consumer needs, and ways in which the shopkeeper, trader, and farmer can be helped to meet these needs;

(iv) The relation of food production on the farm to market demand and nutritional requirements; and

engage in the dissemination of the information so obtained, and urge on governments the need for education of the producer, the intermediary, and the consumer in the principles of good marketing, and in marketing technique, including processing and storage;

2. That the governments and authorities here represented take steps to ensure that producers and consumers are adequately protected against trade malpractices and against exploitation in the purchase and sale of food and other products of agricultural or marine origin, and commend general and specific measures to prevent confusion as to quality and country of origin; and that the permanent organization above-mentioned assist, if requested, governments and authorities to this end, and, if appropriate, formulate international codes of trade practices. [3]

XXIX. Additions to and Improvements in Marketing Facilities

Whereas:

1. Many countries are lacking in adequate facilities for the preservation of essential foods for consumption throughout the year, and for the

---

[1] In some countries little has been done to protect agriculturists from exploitation in the purchase of materials used in agricultural production.

[2] International machinery is desirable for the dissemination of such information and for the promotion of action by governments to make available comprehensive market data.

[3] There is general approval in all countries of legislative and regulatory measures designed to protect both consumers and producers from exploitation arising from unfair trade practices, but some governments have been slow to act in such cases.

production, transport, and distribution of these foods to satisfy nutritional needs;

2. The destruction and disorganization of marketing facilities resulting from the war will make this problem particularly acute in countries which are the victims of hostilities;

3. Technological developments in food preservation, processing, and transport have been accelerated by the war and give promise of contributing materially to the solution of these problems;

The United Nations Conference on Food and Agriculture

RECOMMENDS:

1. That the governments and authorities here represented take steps to secure the provision of adequate processing, transportation, and distribution facilities required for improving the nutritional levels of their populations; and that the permanent organization recommended in Resolution II study the technical, scientific, and economic factors involved, with particular reference to developments during the war, arrange for the pooling of knowledge thus acquired, and give all possible assistance to the governments and authorities in realizing these objectives; [1]

2. That steps be taken by each country to achieve full utilization of important new technological developments in food preservation, transportation, and marketing, including especially dehydration, freezing, and ocean and air transportation; [2]

3. That the permanent organization above-mentioned take steps to obtain, collate, and disseminate information regarding conditions of marketing, processing, and storage facilities in all countries, including those devastated by war, with particular reference to any increased facilities needed and to the rehabilitation of countries devastated by

[1] The methods of attaining these objectives will vary in different countries in accordance with circumstances and may include action by governments to establish in each country central organizations responsible for the work of carrying out these objectives by means of appropriate legislation designed to assist the production, processing, and distribution of the products of their economy, using the most up-to-date technological methods adapted to the conditions peculiar to each country. Among the objectives of this action are better utilization of foods not consumed in fresh form, the avoidance of loss of the nutritive value of perishable foods, the prevention of waste, and the stabilization of marketing conditions to induce so far as possible an adequate and even flow of foods to consumers. Special attention should be given to the establishment of local markets, which must be built up hand in hand with increased local production of protective foods to ensure the commercial success of both production and marketing.

[2] The war has speeded up the development of new methods of preserving perishable foods, and of facilities for ocean and air-cargo transportation, which will have very important effects upon post-war national and international trade in foodstuffs. Many countries by means of air transport will be able to draw upon much wider areas of production for their supplies of the protective foods in concentrated form, and to transport and distribute such foods to presently inaccessible areas and among sectors of the national populations now having inadequate diets.

war, in order to promote the expansion of marketing facilities in a carefully planned rather than a haphazard manner;[1]

4. That governments examine transport deficiencies, both internally and in connection with export and import trade, which may be hindering the development of adequate and efficient marketing of foodstuffs and other agricultural and marine products and take such steps as may be necessary to rectify deficiencies; and that any international body concerned with international transport assist to this end.[2]

XXX. Increasing the Efficiency and Reducing the Cost of Marketing

WHEREAS:

1. The maintenance of food consumption among the peoples of the world at levels sufficiently high to satisfy minimum health requirements calls for the provision of greater quantities of better food at reasonable prices;

2. Except in some countries where consumers largely produce their own food supplies, a substantial part of the total cost of food to the consumer consists of marketing costs (including the costs of assembly, grading, inland and sea transport, storage, wholesale and retail distribution), processing costs, and the rewards of enterprise;

3. In some countries, the provision of unessential services increases the margin between the producer and consumer;

4. Reduction in marketing costs and margins can benefit both producer and consumer alike;

The United Nations Conference on Food and Agriculture

RECOMMENDS:

1. That the governments and authorities here represented take all practicable steps to reduce marketing, processing, storage and distribution costs, and margins between producers and consumers, particularly

---

[1] Much rebuilding and readjustment of plants and personnel required for the marketing of foodstuffs will be necessary after the war. This offers an opportunity not only to meet quickly the immediate post-war needs, but also to build a marketing system adapted to modern needs, with particular reference to the attainment of increased consumption of essential foods. This will require foresight, planning, and action designed to forestall haphazard reconstruction based on temporary expediency rather than long-term efficiency and adequacy.

[2] Transportation charges frequently absorb a large or even a prohibitive part of the price of products, and ocean shipping or internal transportation charges may be so high as to prevent the interchange of products which is necessary if consumers are to be adequately supplied. The provision of transportation and storage services under present arrangements awaits the development of adequate volume of production, yet this volume cannot be built up without the transportation and other services necessary to encourage it. These difficulties cannot be solved by individual or private initiative alone; and governments should assume the responsibility by adequate action to overcome them.

by the elimination of unessential services not required by producers or by low-income consumers.[1]

2. That the permanent organization recommended in Resolution II collect and disseminate information on marketing costs and margins in different countries and in international trade, on the factors which determine or influence such costs and margins, and on the steps taken by governments, by cooperative associations, and by private enterprise to reduce them.[2]

XXXI. Fish and Marine Products

WHEREAS:

1. Fish, marine animals, and marine products are essential in high degree to the diet of the people of many countries and play an important role in the nutrition of other countries;

2. The production of fish and marine products is vital to the economy of certain countries, and the adequate livelihood of the fisherman, like that of the farmer, depends upon a balanced world economy;

3. Consideration of questions relating to fish and marine products is important in any program designed to meet immediate and long-term food and other requirements;

The United Nations Conference on Food and Agriculture

RECOMMENDS:

That the general conclusions reached by this Conference apply, wherever appropriate, to fish and marine products, and that these subjects be considered by the permanent organization recommended in Resolution II.

---

[1] Most of the links in the chain from producer to consumer are essential but there is a tendency for extravagant services to develop. There is considerable scope for reduction of marketing costs by the elimination of unessential services, including unnecessary transport. Attention should also be directed to the possibilities of reducing marketing, processing, and distribution costs by:

(a) Assisting merchants in the adoption of more efficient methods of operation;

(b) Effecting such reorganization of marketing channels as may reduce to a minimum the number of steps involved in taking the products from the farms to consumers;

(c) Regulating the charges of transportation agencies or other factors in marketing if such charges are not kept at reasonable levels by competition;

(d) Assisting in establishing or financing on a sound commercial basis of new and more efficient processing, storage, and transportation facilities.

[2] Although each country will seek to improve the efficiency of marketing in conformity with its economic and agricultural circumstances, there is a need for some international agency which can collect, analyze, and disseminate facts and experience relating to marketing costs and margins. Such data will assist not only governments but also cooperatives and private enterprises in formulating policies aimed at reducing marketing costs and hence the margin between producer and consumer.

XXXII. RESOLUTION OF APPRECIATION TO THE PRESIDENT OF THE UNITED STATES OF AMERICA

The United Nations Conference on Food and Agriculture expresses its gratitude to the President of the United States of America, Franklin Delano Roosevelt, for his initiative in convening the present Conference, for its preparation, and for his contribution to its success. This resolution is to be embodied in the Final Act of the Conference.

XXXIII. APPRECIATION TO THE OFFICIALS OF THE CONFERENCE

WHEREAS:

1. The United Nations Conference on Food and Agriculture was able to conduct its work under conditions of exceptional efficiency;

2. This efficiency and consequent good results, in no small measure resulted from the wisdom and talents of the Chairman, the Honorable Marvin Jones, whose ideals of international solidarity were a source of inspiration and stimulus to all;

3. Without the previous and exhaustive preparation of documentary materials submitted to the Conference by the Secretariat and without its painstaking work, it would not have been possible for the Conference to attain in such a short time the results achieved;

The United Nations Conference on Food and Agriculture

RESOLVES:

1. To express to its Chairman, the Honorable Marvin Jones, its deep appreciation for the admirable manner in which he has guided the Conference and to pay to him the tribute of its gratitude; and

2. To express to the Secretary General, to the Press Relations Officer, to the Assistant Secretary General, to the Secretariat, and to the clerical staff its appreciation for the efficiency and diligence shown in preparing the numerous documentary materials and in assisting the Conference in attaining its objectives.

IN WITNESS WHEREOF, the following delegates sign the present Final Act.

DONE at Hot Springs, Virginia, on the third day of June, nineteen hundred and forty-three, in the English language, the original to be deposited in the archives of the Department of State of the United States, and certified copies thereof to be furnished by the Government of the United States of America to each of the governments and authorities represented at the Conference.

[Signatures follow here.]

CHAPTER V

THE WESTERN HEMISPHERE

1. RELATIONS WITH THE AMERICAN REPUBLICS

A. Organization and Principles

1. STATEMENTS OF AMERICAN POLICY

(1) *Message of the President (Roosevelt) to the Governing Board of the Pan American Union, April 14, 1943* [1]

Today the people of the American Republics join in celebrating an occasion that is peculiarly their own. It has given me profound satisfaction to observe from year to year the increasing significance attached in all the American Republics to the observance of Pan American Day. This reflects the progress which has been made in recent years in converting the dreams and aspirations of the founders of our continental independence into effective and harmonious means for international cooperation.

At Buenos Aires in 1936 and at Lima in 1938, the American Republics foresaw the great struggle between freedom and slavery in which we are now engaged. At those historic conferences they provided for continental security through continental solidarity by devising a practical mechanism of consultation.

Employing that mechanism in the subsequent meetings of their Ministers of Foreign Affairs — at Panamá in 1939,[2] at Havana in 1940,[3] and at Rio de Janeiro in 1942 [4] — they put forward joint recommendations which established the framework within which our system, first of continental defense against aggression, and now of continental mobilization utterly to defeat the promoters of that aggression, was worked out.

Each nation carrying out those recommendations, which represent the statesmanship and foresight of the leaders of the 21 American Republics, will assure its place in the world-wide concert of free nations which will constitute the international society of the future.

The United States is proud to be working shoulder to shoulder with its sister republics for the achievement of this great objective.

[1] Department of State, *Bulletin*, VIII, p. 321.
[2] *Documents, II, 1939–40*, p. 99.
[3] *Ibid., III, 1940–41*, p. 63.
[4] *Ibid., IV, 1941–42*, p. 279.

To all of those participating in the celebration of Pan American Day in North, Central, and South America, I send warm greetings. You may all be of good cheer, for the determination of our peoples to resist aggression and overthrow the aggressors, as well as to keep our liberties secure, is firm and unbreakable. With this spirit and this resolve we may look forward with confidence to ultimate victory.

(2) *Address by the Secretary of State (Hull) before the Pan American Union, Washington, D. C., April 14, 1943* [1]

The day of the Americas is precious in the western world. In celebrating it we pay tribute to the most successful example of cooperation between sovereign nations in modern history.

Ten years ago we had set vigorously about the task of strengthening the bonds of the American family of nations. It was high time. Had we not done so, the Western Hemisphere might have been torn to pieces as have been Europe and Asia. It was necessary to renew and reinforce the foundations of the relations between nations, especially between the nations of the Americas. Thanks to this development of inter-American solidarity, the great war now raging found the Americas politically prepared.

At Montevideo in 1933 we stated the basic principles of the good-neighbor policy, including acceptance of the rule of law; renunciation of the use of force; open and expanding commerce; abandonment of intervention. At Buenos Aires in 1936 we clarified and strengthened those principles and established the practice of consultation. At Lima in 1938 we proclaimed the doctrine of the common defense of this hemisphere. At Panamá in 1939, after war had begun in Europe, we took steps to implement that doctrine.

I remember with particular gratification the Consultation of Foreign Ministers at Havana in July 1940. Those were dark days, indeed: France had fallen, Britain stood alone against the Nazi power. The tentacles of that power were reaching toward our shores. Even as we met, the agents of the Gestapo were using lies and threats and were attempting by personal pressures to influence adversely the men who had come together to concert the measures of mutual assistance for common defense. With courage and determination, the statesmen of the Western Hemisphere agreed at Havana on a far-reaching program of such measures.

After the full force of armed assault had been loosed against us, we reached agreement at the Rio Conference on policies which called for immediate and united action in defense of this hemisphere. These policies, if carried out by all of us, will insure our common defense.

[1] Department of State, *Bulletin*, VIII, p. 322.

I wish that I might on this memorable occasion call the roll of all the splendid statesmen in each of the American nations who participated in these six historic conferences and were responsible for these marvelous achievements. Their names belong in the Hall of Fame of inter-American solidarity. Many of them are here tonight. They and their associates have given the world an example of international cooperation that shines like a beacon light in humanity's present sacrificial search for decency, freedom, and security.

On this Pan American Day in 1943 I believe I can say that measures have been perfected for the attainment of victory in the vast struggle upon which we are engaged. This does not mean that the war has been won. Far from it. We have yet to travel a long, hard road with toil and pain and sorrow. But it is now clear that there can be only one end. The United Nations' forces are advancing: in Eastern Asia, where China struggles bravely; in the Pacific, where the American forces ceaselessly pound the Japanese positions; in North Africa, where British, French, and American armies are moving forward; in Russia, where the German lines are being battered; on the oceans, on the ground, and in the air. Point after point in Germany and Italy and in Japanese-occupied areas is feeling the devastating power of the United Nations' air power.

In this great drama, amid the clash of arms, in our march toward military victory, it is more important than ever for us all to keep clearly before mankind the principles to which we have dedicated ourselves. The success of the inter-American family of nations rests on observance of the principles of sovereignty, equality, law, order, justice, morality, non-intervention, friendliness, and cooperation. We emphasized these principles insistently at a time when they were being increasingly neglected and ignored and were even subjected to scoffing and derision. We applied them resolutely at a time when they were flagrantly violated by powerful countries in several parts of the world. We were determined to keep them alive. We shall never cease in our efforts to give them strength and vitality.

These principles upon which we have built our inter-American life are no exclusive property of the continents of the Americas. They are not peculiar to this hemisphere. They are universally applicable and are open to universal adoption. We have not labored to create a region apart from the rest of the world. We have fostered the idea and the practice of a community of good neighbors whose members are — in fact cannot escape being — a part of the life of the world. The international law to which we submit ourselves is not an international law of the Americas alone but is the law of civilized nations everywhere throughout the earth. The practice of equity is not a design for a hemisphere but is a rule for living in a free and peaceful world. The liberty that we jealously safeguard as the right of every American nation, great and small, is the same liberty which we believe should be established throughout the earth.

We have been able to achieve in this hemisphere a unity of nations heretofore unknown, by holding fast to the doctrine that the rights of all nations must be respected and that the problems of any nation in our group may be laid before the whole group in the certainty that there will be a friendly hearing and sympathetic help toward a constructive result with justice ever in mind; by eliminating from our relationship every vestige of imperialism; by resisting from the outset a spread to this hemisphere of such deadly poisonous political growths as Nazism and Fascism that have developed elsewhere in the world.

The solidarity developed in this system derives not from pressure by strong powers on weaker nations but from recognition and observance of rules of self-restraint even by the strongest. We have no distinction by which the strong are above the law and the weak abide by precepts enforced upon them by greater power. Rather, we seek freedom through the self-restraint and respect for the rights of all which men and nations that are free willingly accept as fundamental to freedom itself.

Only by this highway of freedom has the life of a free community been assured to the Americas. Only by cooperating in efforts along like lines can we hope effectively to contribute to the attainment of world peace and world security.

(3) *Address by the Under Secretary of State (Welles) before the Rotary Club of New York, New York City, April 15, 1943* [1]

In this commemoration of Pan American Day we are celebrating an anniversary whose significance is yearly sinking more deeply into the consciousness of the peoples of all the Americas. Today it possesses an especial importance, for we are commemorating likewise the tenth anniversary of the dedication of the United States by President Roosevelt to the policy of the good neighbor.

It is heartening for us in the Americas to turn our thoughts today to our New World.

There fortunately shines in the Western Hemisphere the continuing light of an international relationship which derives its being from the devotion of all the American peoples to the great ideals of human liberty, of tolerance, and of democracy, and from the adherence of the governments of all the Americas to the rule of peaceful justice rather than to policies of expansion and of conquest which have in our generation found their most fitting expression in a resort to the dive bomber and the tank.

During these past 10 years the world passed through the greatest economic depression which modern civilization has known, and then was

[1] *Ibid.*, VIII, p. 323.

forced into the total war which the Axis powers have inflicted upon humanity. And yet during these same years the American Republics, meeting together as sovereign equals, for the first time laid the lasting foundations of what I think I may justly call the outstanding achievement in practical international living of all history.

One of the great leaders of the United Nations has held up to us the concept of regional councils in the Europe and in the Far East of the future. We of the Americas have already created a regional understanding. While I myself believe that the future peace and security of the world can only be assured by the ultimate creation of an international organization in which every region and every peace-loving state is represented, there is already a solid cornerstone laid for a future world order in this Western Hemisphere association of 21 sovereign and independent countries.

There is nothing novel in the principles which the American Republics established as the principles which should determine their reciprocal relations. They were the same principles of international decency, of international law, of Christian civilization which had time and again been proclaimed. But what was novel was the fact that these principles were actually put into practice and that they have really determined the actions of these 21 American Republics.

In dedicating this country to the policy of the good neighbor, President Roosevelt, in his first inaugural address, consciously laid the groundwork for practical, effective inter-American cooperation in which every American state would benefit and in which no American state would lose.

At the outset it was recognized that the great obstacle to overcome in gaining the confidence and friendship of our neighbors was their belief that the United States would intervene in their affairs whenever this suited our convenience.

There was cause for this belief in 1932. Marines still stood watch on the soil of one of our neighbors. In other countries, although the marines had been withdrawn, financial advisers vested with quasi-dictatorial powers still held sway.

In another group of countries a perpetual sword of Damocles hung over the heads of their peoples in the form of the treaty right of the United States to intervene in their internal affairs to maintain order. The result was that many of the American Republics could not call their sovereignty their own because it was susceptible of infringement at the will of the United States.

The possibility of United States intervention in the domestic concerns of the other countries of this hemisphere has been removed. Today any United States administration that undertook to intervene in the internal affairs of other American countries would not only be reversing our present policy: it would be guilty of outright violation of international engagements ratified by the Senate of the United States and now part of our public law.

At two inter-American conferences — Montevideo in 1933 and Buenos Aires in 1936 — all the American Republics solemnly outlawed intervention by one country in the affairs of another.

Pursuant to the spirit of these obligations, the last vestiges of United States intervention have been liquidated:

Every marine has been withdrawn.

All fiscal supervision in other American countries has been eliminated.

Every treaty by which the United States was granted the right to intervene in other republics of this hemisphere, for whatever purpose, has been abrogated.

There was another aspect of the policy of our government which had produced results scarcely less devastating to our relations with our neighbors than those caused by intervention and interference. I refer to the successive raising of our tariff barriers.

Today it is difficult to comprehend how we expected other countries to buy goods without our taking their products in return. Yet the results of the tariffs of 1921, 1922, and 1930 were to curtail progressively the purchasing power of other countries for our goods by diminishing the opportunities for the sale of their goods in our market. It would be a distortion of the truth to say that the economic crisis which gripped the world in its vise in the early thirties was caused solely by the tariff policy of this country. It is no distortion, however, to say that the policy of tariff increases of the United States which was carried out during the decade after the first World War had an important bearing in bringing about the adoption by other countries of similar policies. This slow strangulation of international trade was one of the chief causes of the world crisis.

The other American Republics will never forget the dislocations caused the economic life of many of them by the successive tariff increases in the United States. These countries in many cases live by the export of one or two raw materials, so that their economies are peculiarly sensitive to the fluctuations of the world market. Their inability to sell to the United States and other countries had an immediate and disastrous repercussion upon their economic welfare.

It devolved upon the country of the Western Hemisphere most responsible for this short-sighted foreign-trade policy to take the initiative in reopening the channels of international trade. This was done by the United States through the Trade Agreements Act of 1934, which was extended in 1937 and again in 1940.[1]

Under this authority agreements have been signed with 15 of the 20 other American Republics.

[1] For extension in 1943, see p. 616.

Trade with the 15 American countries with which we have agreements has shown a most heartening expansion. Our exports to these countries increased from $168,000,000 to approximately $500,000,000 in a 7-year interval. Of course not all this trade expansion was the result of the liberalization of trade-restrictive measures. Part of it is attributable to the general upswing of economic activity in the United States. But it is significant that a very large proportion — approximately three fifths — of our export trade to these countries is in items covered by the trade agreements.

These two policies, non-intervention and reciprocal trade concessions, laid the groundwork for undertaking inter-American cooperative action in many broad fields.

In economic matters, and despite the return of a substantial volume of international trade, the other American Republics were intent upon diversifying their economic life in order to relieve their dependence upon one or two key export products. They drew up programs for the development of their varied resources — agricultural, mineral, and marine. Some of these programs looked forward to improving the supply of goods available for home consumption. Others were designed to open up new fields of production. Capital was lacking to these countries, however, for carrying forward these plans, as well as technical and managerial experience. As the other American republics gained confidence in the United States they approached us for the assistance they needed to carry their plans into realization.

Our government was glad to lend this assistance. In the first place, we knew that all the American Republics had resources capable of sound development. Reports made by various Government agencies as well as by private United States businessmen showed possibilities that only awaited the application of capital, technique, and management. In the second place, we knew that a rising standard of living, desirable as it was from every other point of view, would likewise inevitably create an expanding export market for our goods. The character of our export trade might change somewhat from the simpler products to those more highly processed and fabricated, but the total volume of trade would rise as new wants were created with purchasing power able to satisfy them.

At all times this assistance has been extended with the fullest respect for the sovereignty of the other American Republics and under conditions that would afford to them every opportunity to take advantage of the experience gained by this country during its period of similar economic development. In every case, these cooperative-development arrangements under way have been carried forward efficiently and successfully and have developed lasting friendships between those involved.

At the conference of Buenos Aires for the maintenance of peace, in 1936, President Roosevelt, with remarkable foresight, laid bare the growing danger to the security of the Americas which was arising from the plans for world-conquest of the Axis powers. In order to maintain inviolate the integrity and freedom of the New World he called upon the American Republics to band together in a common front.

This call met with a ready response from every country.

The solidarity of the Americas was now formally defined as their joint recognition that an act of aggression on the part of a non-American power against any American republic would be considered as an act of aggression against every independent state of the New World. In the event of such aggression the American Republics agreed to consult and to concert with one another the necessary complementary agreements so as to organize cooperation for defense.

It is unnecessary to specify in detail the stage-by-stage development of this concept until it became the working-policy guide for the countries of the Americas. It does seem useful, however, to review the practical application of this policy to the unusual and difficult problems which confronted the American republics as a result of the outbreak of war in 1939.

The first problems of magnitude confronting the American Republics were those of an economic character.

Trade with Europe was immediately disrupted. This was particularly true for the countries which normally disposed of a large amount of their coffee in the European market. The Inter-American Economic and Financial Advisory Committee, which was established by the Meeting of Foreign Ministers in Panamá, held in September 1939, after months of effort finally devised an agreement to apportion fairly the only important remaining market, namely that of the United States, among the supplying countries. The Inter-American Coffee Agreement has proved to be an unusually successful agreement for handling a difficult surplus situation. It has operated to stabilize market conditions, to provide the consumer in the United States with adequate supplies at a fair price, and to furnish security of operation to the producers among our neighbor republics.

The shortage of shipping caused by the withdrawal of a large part of the world's maritime trade for war purposes also received the attention of the Inter-American Economic and Financial Advisory Committee. To alleviate the shipping stringency in inter-American trade this committee recommended a plan for putting into service the shipping of the Axis powers that had sought refuge at the outbreak of war in the harbors of this hemisphere. Under this recommendation 82 immobilized ships have been put back into service in the interest of all the American Republics.

After the fall of France all the American Republics felt the need of strengthening their military and naval establishments. At the same time, the United States, under the Lend-Lease Act, undertook to furnish vast assistance to the countries then engaged in fighting Axis aggression. In order to advance the attainment of these objectives the American Republics agreed not to export strategic materials but to reserve them for utilization in the manufacture of supplies necessary both for themselves and for those actively engaged in war at that time. These arrangements denied to the Axis during the latter part of 1940 and all of 1941 access to strategic materials of which they were in critical need.

After the cowardly Japanese attack upon the United States at Pearl Harbor, the Meeting of Foreign Ministers at Rio de Janeiro called for the severance of all commercial and financial intercourse, direct or indirect, between the Western Hemisphere and the Axis countries. At the Inter-American Conference on Systems of Economic and Financial Control in July 1942 the precise implementation of this recommendation was agreed upon.[1] Action to make this program effective has in general been prompt and efficient. It has thwarted the plans of the Axis for interference and aggression in this hemisphere. It has helped to dry up the funds available to the Axis not only for propaganda but for every type of underground subversive activity designed to sow discord and to overthrow the governments of the sovereign American states.

In the political field the solidarity of the Americas has been a bulwark of strength.

At the Meeting of Foreign Ministers in Havana, convened within a few weeks after the fall of France, the American Republics adopted a procedure for provisional administration of any possession of a non-American country in danger of being transferred to or utilized by Axis powers. Thus the American Republics met the very delicate problem of what they would do in the event the Axis attempted to utilize the French possessions in this hemisphere as a base for inimical activities against the New World. Fortunately, the American Republics have not been obliged to take action; but should the contingency arise they have prepared a fixed and definite procedure that would not only protect their own interests but would also insure the legitimate post-war interests of the non-American territories in question.

Immediately after the attack on the United States by Japan and the declaration of war by Germany and Italy against the United States, the Foreign Ministers of the American Republics convened at Rio de Janeiro. In their first resolution the Foreign Ministers recommended unanimously that the American Republics break their diplomatic relations with Japan, Germany, and Italy. Immediately all but two of the countries which had not already taken this action did so, and since that time one of the two remaining countries has joined in similar action.[2]

[1] See *Documents, IV, 1941–42*, p. 393.
[2] For Argentina's position, see this volume, p. 414.

Today 20 sovereign American states have carried out the commitments in which 21 voluntarily joined a year ago. The breaking of diplomatic relations by these 20 countries was an action of the highest importance to the successful prosecution of the war, far transcending the mere customary severance of diplomatic ties. It had the effect of cutting the principal artery by which the Axis was pumping life blood into its dangerous activities in the Western World. Hiding behind the cloak of diplomatic immunity, the Axis nations had been utilizing the privileges accorded them under international law to carry out a hemisphere-wide program of espionage, of sabotage, and even of attempts, all fortunately thwarted, to overturn certain governments and replace them with puppets of the Quisling type.

So long as all the American Republics have not complied with the undertakings in which they joined without reservation the Axis will still, however, have a shield for the continued conduct of activities in this hemisphere perilous to the cause which is vital to the security and independence of each of them.

This, then, is a brief recital of the achievements of the last decade in inter-American relations. These achievements are very real. They have improved the economic well-being of the people of the Western Hemisphere, and they have contributed in the highest degree to guaranteeing the freedom and independence of each one of the American Republics.

I ask you to consider for a moment the dangerous position in which the New World would be today had the good-neighbor policy not been initiated, and had it not been accepted by all the American countries as a basis for cooperation between them.

In the broad sweep of history this progress in inter-American relations will be considered only a beginning. The great opportunity still lies ahead. In the future, as in the past, progress must be by patient and careful building, stage by stage. There must be imagination, even daring, in the methods employed to attain inter-American objectives, but in this, as in life generally, progress comes from the careful application of good methods, whether to matters of the first magnitude or, what is perhaps quite as necessary, to the handling of everyday routine.

The American Republics have been bountifully endowed by nature with rich natural resources. The development of these resources under the sovereign jurisdiction of the governments of these nations, and for the benefit of their peoples, can have the effect of bringing happiness into the lives of many millions who now suffer from want. Such development will require resourcefulness and long, hard work. It is going to require a wider possession and use of land, the expansion of food-production in order to feed adequately a growing population, the improvement of labor standards, the abolition of illiteracy through free public education, the extension of public-health facilities, the investment of local and foreign capital in new types of local enterprise, and a willingness to change existing habits in order to provide new ways of living that mean a better existence for all elements of the population.

It is my belief that through the extension of the same principles of international cooperation which have already given such productive results, the American Republics can make vast strides toward the attainment of the standard of living and of individual security of which their resources, material and human, are capable. This is one of the great challenges of the post-war world to inter-American relations.

I have every confidence that this challenge will be met and that the 21 republics of the Western World will become one of the first areas of the earth to advance measurably to a life of security from want and of opportunity for each individual to develop his particular talents to the benefit of society as a whole.

Today 20 American Republics and their neighbor, Canada, are joined together in the supreme objective of bringing about as rapidly as possible the unconditional surrender of the enemies of all humanity.

When the common victory is won they will likewise join in the establishment of that just and lasting peace for which we all pray.

They recognize, I believe, that the New World can never attain that measure of security and of well-being to which it aspires except in collaboration with the other states and regions of the world.

To this collaboration the American Republics have much to bring. They have the experience of their own achievement in international living. They have proven the correctness of their great ideal that cooperation among states, premised upon the recognition of the equality of the sovereign rights of all nations, great or small, and guided by the principles which they have established, can work.

It is my most cherished conviction that in the world of the future the freedom-loving democracies of the New World will in very truth guide the feet of all men into the paths of peace.

2. THE PRINCIPLE OF JURIDICAL EQUALITY

The basic principles of the Inter-American system have been evolved over a period of years and find expression in numerous Conventions, Declarations, Resolutions and other acts. Under the direction of the Executive Committee on Post-War Problems of the Governing Board of the Pan American Union a compilation of these principles has been made, and published under the title *The Basic Principles of the Inter-American System* (Pan American Union, Washington, 1943). One of the fundamental principles governing Inter-American juridical relations is stated to be "that states are juridically equal, enjoy the same rights, and have equal capacity in their exercise." (p. 3.)

(1) *Embassy Rank for Representation between the United States and Seven American Republics. Department of State Release, March 23, 1943* [1]

The Governments of Costa Rica, the Dominican Republic, El Salvador, Guatemala, Haiti, Honduras, Nicaragua, and the United States announced on March 23 that arrangements have been made whereby the Legations maintained by the above-named American Republics in the United States and the respective Legations of the United States in those countries will be elevated to the rank of Embassy.[2] The change in status will become effective with respect to each diplomatic mission upon the presentation of the letters of credence of the first Ambassador to become chief of that mission.

As a result of the exchange of Ambassadors between the United States and the 7 other American Republics named, all the diplomatic missions of the 20 other American Republics in the United States, and all United States diplomatic missions to the other American Republics, will hereafter be embassies. This, besides signifying the steady strengthening of the bonds of friendship, culture, and commerce among the American Republics concerned, gives formal recognition to the democratic principle of juridical equality that governs the mutual relations of all the American Republics.

The letters of credence of the first ambassadors under these arrangements were presented as follows: Dominican Republic, May 4;[3] El Salvador, May 4;[4] Guatemala, May 4;[5] Haiti, May 4;[6] Honduras, May 4;[7] Nicaragua, May 4;[8] and Costa Rica, May 6.[9] The newly appointed Ambassadors of Colombia [10] and Panama [11] presented their letters of credence on May 6 and 10, respectively.

3. PRINCIPLES OF POST-WAR ORGANIZATION

The Third Meeting of the Foreign Ministers of the American Republics, held at Rio de Janeiro, January 15–18, 1942, entrusted to the Inter-American Juridical Committee [12] the task of formulating specific recommendations with respect to international organization in the juridical and political fields and in the field of international security. The Preliminary Recommendation, submitted under date of September 5, 1942, was in two parts. The first part was devoted to an analysis of the factors which have contributed to the breakdown of international law and order. The second part incorporates conclusions based on the preliminary analysis. The *Introduction* and *Conclusions* are printed below.

[1] Department of State, *Bulletin*, VIII, p. 263.
[2] Salaries at the rate of $10,000 per annum were approved in the Department of State Appropriation Act, 1943, effective March 25, 1943 (Public Law 50, 78th Cong.).
[3] Department of State, *Bulletin*, VIII, p. 413.   [4] *Ibid.*, p. 414.   [5] *Ibid.*, p. 415.
[6] *Ibid.*, p. 416.   [7] *Ibid.*, p. 417.   [8] *Ibid.*, p. 419.
[9] *Ibid.*, p. 412.   [10] *Ibid.*, p. 410.   [11] *Ibid.*, p. 431.
[12] Resolution XXV, *Documents*, *IV, 1941–42*, p. 325.

The preliminary recommendations were submitted to the Executive Committee of the Governing Board of the Pan American Union on Post-War Planning. The Committee in a report to the Governing Board recommended: [1]

"1. That the preliminary recommendations on Post-war Problems formulated by the Inter-American Juridical Committee be transmitted to the Governments for consideration.

"2. That the Governments be requested to send to the Pan American Union as soon as possible such observations and comments as they may have to make thereon, for transmission to the Committee.

"3. That the Governments be requested to forward such other projects as they may wish to present on international organization in the juridical and political fields and in the field of international security, as well as in the economic field, in order that they may be transmitted respectively to the Inter-American Juridical Committee and to the Inter-American Financial and Economic Advisory Committee."

(1) *Preliminary Recommendation on Post-War Problems, Inter-American Juridical Committee, September 5, 1942* [2]

[Excerpt]

INTRODUCTION

The Third Meeting of Foreign Ministers of the American Republics, held at Rio de Janeiro in January of this year, entrusted to the Inter-American Juridical Committee, which it created, the task of formulating specific recommendations with respect to international organization in the juridical and political fields and in the field of international security.

In consequence of limitations imposed by time and circumstances, the Committee believes it wiser to defer for the moment the formulation of the specific recommendations referred to. Instead, it has chosen to begin its work with the Preliminary Recommendation here offered, which sets forth certain ideas of a fundamental character bearing upon the establishment of international peace and the maintenance of law and order.

These ideas are necessarily based upon the experience of the past. In consequence, the first part of the document, dealing with the background of the present conflict, calls attention to the gradual deterioration of international law from its earlier character of a rule of moral conduct — a deterioration observable before the First World War and later culminating in the false ideologies created by the Axis Powers with the deliberate object of satisfying their desire to expand their territories at the expense of the rights of weaker states; it then examines the political, economic and social conditions which may be considered as factors leading to the World War of 1914, that ended only in appearance in 1918; it examines further the causes of the present war, many of which are the same as those that brought on the earlier war; and it analyzes

[1] *Preliminary Recommendation on Post-War Problems.* Pan American Union, Washington, November 1942, Report of the Executive Committee, p. 2.
[2] *Ibid.*, p. 1–2, 17–22.

briefly the reasons for the failure of the League of Nations to accomplish the objectives proclaimed in the Covenant.

The second part of the Preliminary Recommendation, drafted in the form of conclusions to be drawn from the first part, sets forth the fundamental principles which, it is believed, must guide the policy of states in the restoration of law and order after the war.

In carrying out its task the Committee gave consideration to the standards of conduct laid down in the "Reaffirmation of the Fundamental Principles of International Law," which it drafted in response to Resolution XXVIII of the Third Consultative Meeting, and which was offered to the American Governments on June 2nd of this year, for signature in the Pan American Union. For the Committee believes that the fundamental principles adopted by the American Republics can be made the basis of a just and permanent peace. At the same time the Committee took into account Resolution XXXV of the Consultative Meeting, in which the Foreign Ministers took note of the contents of the Atlantic Charter and expressed to President Roosevelt their satisfaction with the inclusion in that document of principles which constitute part of the juridical heritage of America, thus indicating the general standards by which the States of the Western Hemisphere should be guided in their search for a solution of post-war problems.

The Committee did not overlook the fact that if the supreme objective of a permanent and just peace is to be attained by the cooperation of all nations it will be necessary for each one of them to accept a responsibility proportionate to its ability to contribute to that end; and that plans of a progressive character will have to be adopted, giving first consideration to emergency measures, such as the complex problems of the period of transition between the end of hostilities and a definitive treaty of peace, and leaving sufficient latitude for the later adoption, as conditions warrant, of more permanent measures, such as the determination of the machinery of government which it will be necessary for the community of nations to adopt in order to bring about a peace based upon the principle of collective security and guaranteed by pledges of cooperative defense.

It may be observed, further, that in its analysis of the causes of the war the Committee followed, for the sake of clarity, a logical classification of its material. It was aware, however, that many of the factors separately analyzed as political, economic and social, in reality worked together in bringing about the breakdown of law and order. This same interdependence of the various causes of the war, and the desire to present a sufficiently rounded report, led the Committee to undertake a general examination of the economic factors, the specific study of which falls to the Inter-American Financial and Economic Advisory Committee.

The Committee intends to study and to formulate at a later date specific recommendations representing the detailed application of the principles set forth in the second part of this Preliminary Recommendation. In doing so it will take into account the suggestions and projects which the American Governments may present to it in accordance with the terms of Resolution XXV.

In the meantime the present Recommendation is submitted to the Governments of the American Republics in the hope that it will contribute to the creation of some measure of uniformity in their points of view with relation to international organization in the post-war period. For the Committee is of the opinion that it is of the greatest importance that the American Governments should forthwith determine upon a general line of conduct, so that they may be able when the time comes to take a united stand in meeting the problems presented and in assuming the responsibilities involved in their solution.

. . . .

Conclusions

The Inter-American Juridical Committee, taking into account the facts above set forth, indicating what the Committee believes to be the main causes of the breakdown of international law and order, and believing it necessary to make its contribution to the determination of the general principles upon which law and order should be based in the future, to the end that a just and permanent peace may be established among the nations, proposes to the Governments of the American Republics the following conclusions:

I. Priority of the Moral Law and of the Fundamental Principles of International Law Derived from It

Nations must recognize in their mutual relations the priority of the moral law, which is the same for nations as for individuals; and they must make their conduct conform to the fundamental principles derived from that law.

Existing rules of positive law must not be regarded as fixing permanently the *status quo*, but rather as the necessary basis of international order and stability pending the adoption of rules more in accord with the new needs of the international community.

II. Repudiation of the Use of Force

War must be repudiated not only as an instrument of national policy, but also as a legalized procedure for the settlement of disputes.

The community of nations, acting through its organized agents, must alone have the right to use force to prevent or resist aggression and to maintain order and respect for law.

Resistance by a nation to aggression must be limited to the defense of its territory pending effective action by the community of nations.

The acts which shall be regarded as constituting aggression must be specifically defined, as well as the conditions calling into effect the right of legitimate self-defense.

III. UNQUALIFIED OBLIGATION TO SETTLE DISPUTES BY PEACEFUL METHODS

Nations must undertake an unqualified obligation to settle their disputes by peaceful methods.

The various procedures for the peaceful settlement of international disputes must be organized in such a way as to operate automatically and progressively until a final and definitive solution of the controversy has been obtained by means of one or other of the several procedures laid down, or by means of some alternative procedure which the parties in controversy may agree to adopt.

The existing procedures of conciliation and arbitration should be reorganized so as to make them more readily and more promptly accessible.

The jurisdiction of the Permanent Court of International Justice should be extended, and procedure before the Court should be coordinated with that of regional judicial tribunals, if any should be created; the jurisdiction of these regional tribunals being determined by the place and the subject matter of the controversy.

IV. SOLIDARITY IN THE PRESENCE OF AGGRESSION

Nations have a common and joint obligation to watch over the observance of the fundamental principles of international law, and they must assume a collective responsibility for the maintenance of peace and order.

An act of aggression committed against one nation must be considered as an act of aggression against all the other members of the international community.

When once the aggressor has been determined by the competent organs of the international community, nations shall have no right to remain neutral between the parties in conflict and to treat them upon equal terms.

All nations have the duty to cooperate in making effective the sanctions which the international community may adopt against an aggressor.

V. Modification of the Conception of Sovereignty

The sovereignty of the state must be understood in a manner consistent with the supreme necessity of maintaining peace, order and justice in the international community.

In the exercise of their sovereignty nations must recognize and respect the priority of the moral law and of the fundamental principles of international law derived from it.

No nation may claim as an attribute of sovereignty the right to be the judge in its own case or the right to take the law into its own hands and assert its claims by force.

The moral unity of the international community and the effective cooperation of its members call for the coordination of their sovereignty with the fact of their interdependence.

VI. Necessity of a More Effective International Organization

The maintenance of law and order and the application and development of specific rules of international conduct demand the creation of some machinery of international government which can represent the will of the entire community and its collective interests rather than the will and the interests of its individual members, and which can carry into effect its decisions.

The period of transition between the close of the war and the establishment of the future international organization must not be prolonged beyond the time that is strictly necessary, and it must be governed as far as possible by the same principles upon which the organization itself is to be based.

VII. Character of the New Association of Nations

The international community must be organized on the basis of the cooperation of all nations.

No nation is privileged to remain aloof from the organization thus established.

Whether the organization is to be based upon the League of Nations amended and strengthened, or is to be a new legal institution, it must be so constituted as to reconcile the principle of universality of membership with the existence of regional groups formed by natural bonds of solidarity and common interests.

These regional groups or associations may adopt special rules governing the relations of their members among themselves in matters in which the common interests of the whole international community are not involved.

The functions of the new international organization must be as comprehensive as the political, economic and social needs of the community require. Existing international institutions and treaty agreements must be adjusted to meet new conditions and new needs.

VIII. A More Effective System of Collective Security

The primary objective of the new international organization must be the protection of each and all of its members against acts of violence, so that every nation may rely for its security upon the collective action of the community.

Each nation must consider that it has a vital national interest of its own in the maintenance of international law and order, and that every threat or act of violence against any one member of the community constitutes a direct attack against each and all of them.

IX. Abandonment of the System of a Balance of Power. Limitation of Armaments

The establishment of an effective system of collective security must put an end to the policy that peace can be secured by a balance of power between opposing groups of states.

Nations must recognize that a just solution of the problem of armaments is an essential condition of an adequate organization of peace.

The limitation of armaments must take place progressively and side by side with the establishment and practical development of the system of collective security, up to the point which is compatible with the maintenance by each state of domestic order and with the fulfillment of its international obligations looking to the collective action of the community.

Nations must not invoke the necessity of self-defense as a ground for increasing their national armaments beyond the extent recognized as justifiable within the system of collective security.

The manufacture of munitions of war should be an exclusive function of the state, the private manufacture and private trade in arms being opposed to the general security.

During the period of transition between the end of hostilities and the definitive establishment of peace, account must be taken of the fact that the nations which have borne the burden of the war against the aggressors may have to keep their armaments in order to re-establish order in territories where there is need to do so. But this temporary right must be exercised with the objective of facilitating the creation of the system of collective security which is to follow, keeping in mind at the same time a gradual solution of the problem of the limitation of armaments.

X. Abandonment of Political Imperialism

Political imperialism, in the sense of the acquisition of control over the will of weak nations and over undeveloped countries for political as well as for military purposes, must be abandoned.

Colonies and protectorates must be administered in accordance with the principles laid down in the Covenant of the League of Nations and reaffirmed in the Havana Convention, that the well-being and development of their peoples should form a sacred trust of civilization.

XI. ELIMINATION OF POLITICAL NATIONALISM

An essential condition of the establishment of a permanent peace will be the elimination of the spirit of exaggerated nationalism which concentrates upon the interests of the particular state to the exclusion of the interests of the community at large.

Every effort must be made to get rid of false theories of nationalism which certain governments have made use of in order to create in their peoples a belief in their superiority over other peoples and consequently, as claimed, in their right to impose their culture upon them.

Doctrinal propaganda carried on in a particular state against mutual understanding between nations must be regarded as an offense against the whole community of nations and as a threat to the general peace.

The state exists for the good of its citizens, and it may not deprive them of the rights which a man possesses because of his human personality and not because the state has conferred them upon him.

Political systems which respect human liberties must be recognized as playing an important part in the cooperation of states.

In view of the fact that moral disarmament is an important factor in promoting peace, states should direct their educational institutions so as to increase mutual understanding between them and to develop within their respective territories, and by all means in their power, sentiments of international cooperation and solidarity.

XII. ELIMINATION OF ECONOMIC IMPERIALISM

The community of nations, acting through its appropriate agencies, must supervise the exploitation of undeveloped territories.

These territories must be administered in accordance with the principle of equality of treatment, so that all states may have equal access to the raw materials which they produce and may be able to sell their manufactured goods in the markets of these territories upon equal terms.

A system of free competition should be established in these territories, which will prevent particular states from having exclusive opportunities for the investment of capital and for other forms of economic enterprise, and which will promote the gradual progress of these territories and the well-being of their native populations, while at the same time protecting the interests of the international community.

XIII. ELIMINATION OF ECONOMIC NATIONALISM

Nations must recognize their economic interdependence, and that in consequence their right to regulate their own economic activities should not be without limitations.

The future international organization must give special attention to the coordination of world economy, and must endeavor to obtain concrete solutions for the problems which it presents, seeking a means of reconciling national self-determination with the predominant interest of the whole community of nations.

Nations must make every effort to lower tariff barriers and remove other restrictions upon commerce, and to increase as far as possible the free and full exchange of articles and services among the members of the international community, so as to lessen as far as possible the inequalities of natural resources and to promote the mutual well-being of their respective peoples.

In order to bring about economic disarmament the system of ruthless competition and trade rivalries must be eliminated, and in its place must be substituted measures of cooperation looking to the general welfare of the international community.

XIV. ELIMINATION OF THE SOCIAL FACTORS OF WAR

Nations must recognize that social justice and the improvement of the conditions of life for the individual citizen have a relation to the maintenance of peace and for that reason must play an essential part in any plans of international reconstruction.

Nations must endeavor to raise the standard of life of their citizens and must guarantee to each individual a degree of economic security which will permit him to live in the sufficiency and freedom from fear necessary to enable him to develop his personality and to enjoy the benefits of spiritual and material freedom to which all men have a right.

The realization of these objectives is primarily the task of each separate state; but only by parallel international action can they be adequately secured.

Nations must organize their national industry so as to meet the needs of all the people and not merely the interests of privileged groups; and while having in mind the interests of their own peoples they must also give consideration to the interests and necessities of the international community.

The social services of the new international organization must be expanded so as to include tasks which are beyond the reach of the individual state. The work of the International Labor Office must be continued to the fullest possible extent.

Rio de Janeiro
September 5, 1942

(S) AFRANIO DE MELLO FRANCO   (S) CHARLES G. FENWICK
(S) FELIX NIETO DEL RÍO   (S) CARLOS EDUARDO STOLK
(S) PABLO CAMPOS ORTÍZ

B. Political Solidarity and Defense

1. DECLARATIONS OF WAR, SEVERANCES OF DIPLOMATIC RELATIONS AND OTHER MANIFESTATIONS OF CONTINENTAL SOLIDARITY BY THE OTHER AMERICAN REPUBLICS

[See *Documents, IV, 1941–42,* p. 336.]

Under the provisions of Resolution XV of the Final Act, signed by the Foreign Ministers of the American Republics at the Havana Meeting, July 30, 1940, any attempt on the part of a non-American state "against the integrity or inviolability of the territory, the sovereignty or the political independence of an American state" was to be considered as an act of aggression against the signatory states.[1] By the terms of Resolution I of the Rio de Janeiro Meeting, January 15–28, 1942, this declaration and the "complete solidarity" of the American Republics were reaffirmed and the American Republics "in accordance with the procedures established by their own laws and in conformity with the position and circumstances obtaining in each country in the existing continental conflict," recommended the breaking of their diplomatic relations with Japan, Germany and Italy, "since the first-mentioned State attacked and the other two declared war on an American country." [2]

By June 30, 1943, all the American Republics, with the exception of Argentina, had declared war on or severed diplomatic relations with the three principal Axis powers. Following the sinking of five Brazilian vessels, presumably by Axis submarines, the Government of Brazil declared war on Germany and Italy on August 22, 1942.[3] On January 20, 1943, the Government of Chile severed diplomatic relations with these powers and Japan.[4]

Following the declaration of war by Brazil, the members of the Inter-American Defense Board, meeting in Washington, unanimously extended to Brazil "a vote of adherence and friendship on the occasion of her declaration of war against the Axis countries." [5] The military representatives of Argentina and Chile supported the resolution, even though their two governments still maintained diplomatic relations with the Axis powers.

Additional evidence of the political solidarity of the American Republics, again with the exception of Argentina, was given by the messages of congratulation sent to the President following the successful landing of American troops in North Africa.[6]

The action of the Government of Peru in adhering to the principles of the Atlantic Charter is unique in that it is the first case where an American Republic which is not at war with one of the Axis powers and therefore is not in the position where it can adhere to the Declaration by United Nations has formally accepted the principles of the Charter. By Resolution XXXV of the Meeting of Foreign Ministers at Rio de Janeiro, note was taken of the contents of the Charter and satisfaction was expressed "with the inclusion in that document of principles which constitute a part of the juridical heritage of America." [7]

[1] *Documents, III, 1940–41,* p. 76.
[2] *Ibid., IV, 1941–42,* p. 293.
[3] Department of State, *Bulletin,* VII, p. 710.
[4] *Ibid.,* VIII, p. 83.
[5] *New York Times,* August 25, 1942.
[6] Department of State, *Bulletin,* VII, p. 908, 936.
[7] *Documents, IV, 1941–42,* p. 329.

(1) *Severances of Diplomatic Relations, Declarations of War, and Adherences to the Joint Declaration by United Nations, as of June 30, 1943* [1]

	Severances of Diplomatic Relations			Declarations of War				Adherence to the Declaration by United Nations
	Germany and Italy	Japan	Bulgaria Hungary Rumania	Vichy France	Germany and Italy	Japan	Bulgaria Hungary Rumania	
Bolivia	1-28-42	1-28-42	—	—	4-7-43	4-7-43	—	4-27-43
Brazil	1-28-42	1-28-42	[2]	—	8-22-42	—	—	2-6-43
Chile	1-20-43	1-20-43	5-18-43	5-18-43	—	—	—	—
Colombia	12-19-41	12-8-41	—	11-26-42	—	—	—	1-1-42
Costa Rica	—	—	H-5-15-42 R-5-15-42	—	12-11-41	12-8-41	—	1-1-42
Cuba	—	—	—	11-9-42	12-11-41	12-9-41	—	1-1-42
Dominican Republic	—	—	—	—	12-11-41	12-8-41	—	1-1-42
Ecuador	1-29-42	1-29-42	—	11-26-42	—	—	—	1-1-42
El Salvador	—	—	—	11-13-42	12-12-41	12-8-41	—	1-1-42
Guatemala	—	—	—	11-12-42	12-11-41	12-8-41	—	1-1-42
Haiti	—	—	—	11-10-42	12-12-41	12-8-41	—	1-1-42
Honduras	—	—	—	11-13-42	12-13-41	12-8-41	12-24-41	1-1-42
Mexico	12-11-41	12-8-41	B-12-20-41 H-12-19-41 R-12-23-41 [3]	11-9-42	5-22-42	5-22-42	—	6-14-42
Nicaragua	—	—	—	11-10-42	12-11-41	12-8-41	12-19-41	1-1-42
Panama	—	—	—	11-13-42	12-12-41	12-7-41	—	1-1-42
Paraguay	1-28-42	1-28-42	—	—	—	—	—	—
Peru	1-24-42	1-24-42	—	1-26-43 [5]	—	—	—	[4]
United States	—	—	—	—	12-11-41	12-8-41	6-5-42	1-1-42
Uruguay	1-25-42	1-25-42	—	5-12-43	—	—	—	—
Venezuela	12-31-41	12-31-41	—	11-26-42	—	—	—	—

[1] Based on table in *Bulletin of the Pan American Union*, LXXVII, p. 583, and on copy from Department of State, Division of Research and Publication.

[2] Rumania severed diplomatic relations with Brazil on March 6, 1942, and Hungary did likewise on May 2, 1942.

[3] In the statement issued by the Foreign Office on this date, Mexico stated that no diplomatic relations had existed.

[4] Adhered to principles of Atlantic Charter on February 8, 1943.

[5] The Vichy Government severed diplomatic relations with the United States on November 8, 1942.

(2) Adherence by Peru to the Principles of the Atlantic Charter

(a) Text of the Telegram Sent by the Peruvian Minister of Foreign Affairs (Solf y Muro) to the Secretary of State (Hull), February 8, 1943 [1]

[Translation]

It gives me pleasure to communicate to Your Excellency that the Government of Peru, in its unflinching decision to lend all aid to the cause defended by the United States of America and the United Nations, has approved adherence to the Atlantic Charter. Let me take this opportunity to extend to Your Excellency the renewed assurances of my high consideration.

(b) The Secretary of State (Hull) to the Peruvian Minister of Foreign Affairs (Solf y Muro), February 10, 1943 [2]

I wish to thank Your Excellency for your telegram of February 8 in which you advise me that the Government of Peru, in its unflinching decision to lend all aid to the cause defended by the United Nations, has affirmed its adherence to the principles of the Atlantic Charter. At this period in the history of the struggle for justice and freedom, it is a pleasure to know that your Government makes this declaration in order once again to make known to the world the intentions of Peru and the ideals which have so long characterized the Peruvian people.

Accept [etc.]

2. MILITARY AND NAVAL COOPERATION

In accordance with the terms of Resolution XV of the Havana Conference, July 1940, on "Reciprocal Assistance and Cooperation for the Defense of the Nations of the Americas," reaffirmed by the recommendations of the Rio de Janeiro Meeting of January 1942, various commissions were created to study the problems of continental defense. The Inter-American Defense Board, composed of military and naval technicians appointed by each of the American Republics, was set up in Washington and held its first meeting March 30, 1942.[3] The establishment of a Joint Mexican-United States Defense Commission was announced on January 12, 1942 and was formally created, on the part of the United States, by Executive Order No. 9080 of February 27, 1942.[4] The Joint Brazil-United States Defense Commission for the purpose of making staff plans for the mutual defense of the Western Hemisphere was established, also, in Washington in August 1942. A supplementary military and naval agreement was signed by Cuba and the United States on September 7, 1942 which coordinates all measures for security for the duration of the war.[5]

[1] Copy in Spanish received from the Department of State.
[2] Department of State, *Bulletin*, VIII, p. 154.
[3] *Documents, IV, 1941–42*, p. 305.
[4] *Ibid.*, p. 351.
[5] See this volume, p. 363.

(1) *Bases in the Other American Republics. Department of State Release on Remarks of the Under Secretary of State (Welles) at Press Conference, March 6, 1943* [1]

Upon opening the press conference on March 6, Mr. Welles, Acting Secretary of State, said that as a result of distortion and misconception of statements which had recently been made by officials and by private persons with regard to the policy of the United States concerning some of the naval and military activities of our Government, there apparently had grown up the complete misconception that the Government of the United States was planning to undertake permanent occupation of bases in the Western Hemisphere. That misconception, of course, said Mr. Welles, should be knocked on the head immediately as has very effectively been done by the Secretary General of the Brazilian Foreign Office, among others. Unfortunately, Mr. Welles continued, he had not yet received the full text of the speech which was made a few days ago by Ambassador Leao Velloso, the Brazilian Secretary General, but he did want to take cognizance here of the very gratifying remarks which Ambassador Velloso had made with regard to American-Brazilian friendship and particularly the phrases which he used when he referred to the old, tried and true friendship of American-Brazilian solidarity. That, said Mr. Welles, he appreciated and he heartily reciprocated.

The facts in regard to this problem, as Mr. Welles said he thought the correspondents all knew, were as follows: We are making naturally certain contributions to the military defenses of the Western Hemisphere. That contribution, Mr. Welles pointed out, is based first upon arrangements which were made between our Government and the British Government for the lease of certain areas in the West Indies and elsewhere for the construction of bases; and second, upon certain cooperative agreements entered into for the duration of the present emergency with the governments of a number of other American Republics in which our armed forces have been permitted to use certain specified areas under the sovereignty of those governments for purposes in which the governments concerned and the United States have a common interest. The common interest, Mr. Welles continued, is set forth in resolution XV, adopted at the meeting of the Ministers of Foreign Affairs of the American Republics at Havana in July of 1940. The resolution is entitled "Reciprocal Assistance and Cooperation for the Defense of the Nations of the Americas." [2]

Mr. Welles said that resolution provided among other things that in the event that acts of aggression are committed against an American nation by a non-American nation "all the signatory nations, or two or

[1] Department of State, *Bulletin*, VIII, p. 215.
[2] *Documents, III, 1940–41*, p. 76.

more of them, according to circumstances, shall proceed to negotiate the necessary complementary agreements so as to organize cooperation for defense and the assistance that they shall lend each other in the event of aggressions such as those referred to in this declaration."

The crux of the problem, said Mr. Welles, is that this complementary agreement of the other American Republics covers no rights or obligations beyond the present emergency and can, of course, in no way be said to provide for the establishment of permanent military bases by this Government. A correspondent asked in connection with the idea of obtaining permanent bases if it was not our view that that would form a part of a mutual defense after the war rather than this Government's acquiring bases of its own. Mr. Welles replied that so far as the Western Hemisphere was concerned this Government had not and does not have the intention of undertaking any action for the acquisition of any permanent bases which affect the territory of any one of the American Republics.

Asked if he could say at this time what disposition was planned for the material and other equipment which had been put into certain bases down there, Mr. Welles replied that in every case that was covered by agreements entered into between the Governments and the United States. Those arrangements were incorporated in the complementary agreements to which this resolution referred. Asked if it was public information that the material will be returned or paid for in some reciprocal way, Mr. Welles said that none of the agreements had been made public. He added that none of the lend-lease agreements had been made public beyond ourselves and the other American Republics although they had been made available to the appropriate members of the Congress. When asked if all arrangements for such bases as were now occupied in the emergency had been under lend-lease agreements, Mr. Welles replied in the negative, saying that many of them had nothing whatever to do with lend-lease agreements and were in the nature of the complementary agreements to which the resolution referred.

(2) *List of Agreements Made for Detailing of Military and Naval Missions and for Other Assistance, July 1, 1942–June 30, 1943*

[For lists of agreements made during the preceding two years, see *Documents, III, 1940–41*, p. 148 and *IV, 1941–42*, p. 352.]

Agreement with Panama. Signed, July 7, 1942. Provides for the detail of an officer of the United States Army to serve as an Adviser to the Minister of Foreign Affairs of Panama in matters pertaining to the defense of Panama; also, for the detail of officers to advise the armed forces of Panama. Effective for a period of one year, but can be extended at the request of the Government of Panama. *Executive Agreement Series* 258.

Agreement with Bolivia. Signed August 11, 1942. Provides for the detail of a United States Military Mission. Effective for a period of four years. Services of Mission may be extended at request of Government of Bolivia. *Executive Agreement Series* 267.

Agreement with Colombia. Signed September 22 and November 5, 1942. Continues in effect for a period of one year, the agreement signed November 23, 1938 and amended by supplementary agreement of August 30, 1941 for a naval mission. *Executive Agreement Series* 280.

Agreement with Dominican Republic. Signed January 25, 1943. Provides for the detail of a United States Naval Mission. Effective for a period of four years, but may be extended at request of Dominican Government. *Executive Agreement Series* 312.

Agreements with El Salvador. Effected by an exchange of Notes, signed October 14 and November 24, 1942, and also on March 25, 1943. Provides for extension, until such time as it may be replaced by another agreement, of the agreement signed March 27, 1941 for detail of a military officer.[1] *Executive Agreement Series* 281 and 316.

Agreement with Chile. Effected by an exchange of notes signed November 27, 1942, December 23, 1942 and April 14, 1943. Provides for extension of military aviation agreement of April 23, 1940 for three years beginning April 23, 1943. *Executive Agreement Series* 315.

(3) *Military and Naval Cooperation with Cuba. Department of State Release, September 7, 1942* [2]

This agreement supplemented the agreement for military and naval cooperation signed at Havana on June 19, 1942.[3]

Word has been received from the Honorable Spruille Braden, American Ambassador to Cuba, of the signature on September 7 by the Minister of State of Cuba and by the Ambassador in behalf of the United States, of an agreement on military and naval cooperation between the two Governments.

This agreement, which was negotiated on the part of the United States by representatives of the Departments of State, War, and Navy and by the highest civilian and military authorities of the Cuban Government, coordinates all the special military and naval measures between Cuba and the United States which have been taken since the beginning of the war and facilitates the taking of new measures, for the duration of the war, of military and naval security by the appropriate authorities

---

[1] *Executive Agreement Series* 214; 55 Stat. 1305.
[2] Department of State, *Bulletin*, VII, p. 750.
[3] *Ibid.*, VI, p. 553.

of the respective armed forces as the necessity arises and without the need for individual negotiations in each case.

The rapidity with which United States and Cuban authorities negotiated and concluded the agreement is conclusive evidence of the unanimity of views of the two Governments.

Although details of the agreement cannot be released for reasons of military security, it may be stated that the agreement outlines the respective responsibilities of the armed forces of the two countries in the zone affected and provides for coordination of their efforts and complete cooperation on the basis of reciprocity.

A supplementary agreement for military and naval cooperation between the United States and Cuba was signed at Havana on February 1, 1943 by Spruille Braden, American Ambassador at Havana, and J. A. Martínez, Minister of State of Cuba.[1]

3. MUTUAL AID AGREEMENTS

(1) *Statement by Assistant Secretary of State Acheson before the House Committee on Foreign Affairs, February 3, 1943* [2]

[Excerpt]

. . . .

The following American Republics have signed lend-lease agreements: The Dominican Republic (August 2, 1941); Haiti (September 16, 1941); Paraguay (September 20, 1941); Brazil (October 1, 1941, replaced by a new agreement of March 3, 1942); Nicaragua (October 16, 1941); Cuba (November 7, 1941); Bolivia (December 6, 1941); Uruguay (January 13, 1942); Costa Rica (January 16, 1942); El Salvador (February 2, 1942); Honduras (February 28, 1942); Peru (March 11, 1942); Colombia (March 17, 1942); Venezuela (March 18, 1942); Mexico (March 27, 1942; this agreement is now being revised); [3] Ecuador (April 6, 1942); Guatemala (November 16, 1942). Under them we agree to provide the other American Republics with munitions of war, in certain amounts, and they, in turn, promise to furnish us with whatever defense articles, services, or information they can supply.

Our shipments of military goods under these agreements, however, may be deferred or stopped entirely whenever, in the opinion of the Commander-in-Chief, further deliveries would not be consistent with the requirements of our own defense or that of the Western Hemisphere

---

[1] *Ibid.*, VIII, p. 501; *Executive Agreement Series* 321.
[2] *Ibid.*, p. 188; *Hearings before the Committee on Foreign Affairs, House of Representatives, on H. R. 1501 (Extension of Lend-Lease Act)*, 78th Cong., 1st sess., p. 82.
[3] Signed March 18, 1943.

as a whole. These agreements contain the safeguards called for by the Lend-Lease Act: the prohibition against retransfer of defense articles without the President's approval, and the provision for protecting the patent rights of American citizens.

These agreements have not been published — nor can they be made public now for reasons of security. To do so would reveal the program of military material designed for the defense of these countries.

These agreements provide for transfer upon a cash reimbursable basis. The amounts to be reimbursed have been determined by agreement after negotiation.

I might say further in regard to these particular agreements that they differ from the master agreements, of which I shall speak at some length later on, in that they provide for the transfer of specific amounts of materials. Not only the amounts but the exact designation of the equipment requested is contained in schedules which are attached to the documents and revised from time to time in the light of changing circumstance. For this reason it is obviously undesirable at the present time to print those agreements.

The response to the war of our southern neighbors has been magnificent. Eleven have declared war, and all but one have broken diplomatic relations with the Axis. These countries have contributed greatly to the common war effort. Hundreds of ships have borne raw materials to our factories and to those of Great Britain. We have had the use of ports and airfields and transportation facilities of all kinds. Immense development projects have been undertaken cooperatively, to make rubber, lumber, and many vital minerals available for the war. They have worked with us in combating and suppressing Axis espionage and in an elaborate program for eliminating Axis influence from the economic and financial life of the American world.

Our lend-lease aid has been an element of importance in this broad and cooperative program for strengthening the common defense and the common war effort of the Americas.

In September 1941 I made the following statement to the Appropriations Committee of the House:

The role of the other American Republics in hemispheric defense cannot be measured exclusively by their obligations and their performance under lend-lease agreements. That role must be measured in the light of their many other substantial contributions of a broad and growing program of hemispheric defense. Similarly, the benefits from our hemispheric lend-lease program cannot be gauged simply in terms of commitments embodied in formal agreements. For many of these valuable defense measures adopted by the other American Republics, even though not required by a lend-lease agreement, undoubtedly flow from our lend-lease program and the hemispheric unity which it promotes.

I believe that statement is every bit as true today as it was in the fall of 1941.

. . . .

Subsequent to the statement by Mr. Acheson, a mutual aid agreement containing substantially the same provisions as the other agreements was entered into on March 2, 1943 with the Government of Chile [1] and a new agreement was entered into on March 18, 1943 with the Government of Mexico.[2]

4. DEFENSE AGAINST SUBVERSIVE ACTIVITIES

(1) *Final Act of the Inter-American Conference of Police and Judicial Authorities, Buenos Aires, Argentina, May 27–June 9, 1942* [3]

The Inter-American Conference of Police and Judicial Authorities originated in Resolution III of the Second Meeting of the Ministers of Foreign Affairs of the American Republics held at Havana in July 1940.

In that resolution the Governing Board of the Pan American Union was requested to convoke the States, members of the Union, to an international conference, "to draft the international conventions and recommendations which it deems necessary to assure through the action of the proper authorities in each State, and through the coordination of such action with that of other States in the Continent, the most complete and effective defense against acts of an unlawful character, as well as against any other unlawful activities which may affect the institutions of American States."

At the same time the Pan American Union, prior to convening the conference, was requested to undertake certain preparatory work "by means of an inquiry among the Governments of the Continent with regard to the existing legislative or administrative provisions, as well as with respect to their opinions on the various topics which it is deemed advisable to consider."

In accordance with the recommendations contained in the foregoing resolution the Pan American Union under date of August 27, 1940 transmitted to all the Governments, members of the Union, a questionnaire on topics that might be included in the program of the conference as well as on the material to be prepared in anticipation of the meeting.

The replies received to this questionnaire were submitted to a committee of the Governing Board which had been appointed to consider the most effective manner of giving effect to the foregoing resolution. This committee submitted a report to the Governing Board, which was approved on January 8, 1941, and which recommended an extension of time to enable those Governments which had not yet replied to submit their observations and proposals on the program.

The committee submitted another report to the Governing Board at the session of June 4, 1941 to which was attached a project of Program and Regulations which were forwarded to the Governments with the request that their observations thereon be submitted on or before October 15, 1941. At that same meeting the Director General of the Pan American Union was authorized to inquire of the Government of the Argentine Republic whether it would be agreeable to that Government to have the Conference meet in Buenos Aires during 1942.

On the basis of the observations received from several Governments the committee formulated a definitive project of Program and Regulations which were approved by the Governing Board at the session held on November 5, 1941.

[1] Department of State, *Bulletin*, VII, p. 208.   [2] *Ibid.*, p. 251.

[3] Pan American Union, Washington, D.C., 1943 (Congress and Conference Series No. 38). Because of its importance and because it was not available for inclusion in Vol. IV, this document is included in Vol. V even though it antedates the period covered.

At that same meeting of November 5, 1941 the Director General informed the Board of the receipt of a communication from the Government of the Argentine Republic to the effect that it would be entirely agreeable to that Government to have the Conference meet in Buenos Aires and suggesting the month of September 1942 as the most appropriate and convenient time. The Governing Board accepted with thanks the proposal of the Argentine Government and suggested that the exact date for the opening of the Conference be fixed as soon as possible. Subsequently the Third Meeting of Ministers of Foreign Affairs held at Rio de Janeiro in January 1942 adopted a resolution reading as follows:

"That the Inter-American Conference on the Coordination of Police and Judicial Measures shall convene in Buenos Aires next May, the date for the opening of the Conference to be determined by the Argentine Government and the corresponding invitations to be sent by it."

In accordance with this resolution the Argentine Government fixed May 27 as the date for the opening of the Conference and issued invitations to the countries members of the Pan American Union.

In compliance with the resolutions adopted by the Meetings of the Ministers of Foreign Affairs of the American Republics, the Argentine Government, after consultation with the Pan American Union, invited the Governments of El Salvador, United States of America, Cuba, Chile, Guatemala, Peru, Dominican Republic, Bolivia, Ecuador, Uruguay, Venezuela, Colombia, Brazil, Haiti, Honduras, Panama, Nicaragua, Mexico, Paraguay and Costa Rica, to the Inter-American Conference of Police and Judicial Authorities to meet at Buenos Aires, the capital of the Argentine Republic, on May 27, 1942.

The invitation extended by the Government of the Argentine Republic was accepted, and the American Republics indicated below appointed the representatives whose names are set forth according to order established by ballot at the Conference.

[Here follows list of representatives.]

The inaugural session of the Conference was held on May 27, 1942, at 11 A.M. In attendance were the Minister for the Interior and the Minister for Foreign Affairs and Worship of the Argentine Republic, as also the members of the diplomatic corps, officials and guests specially invited.

The Delegate for the Argentine Republic and Provisional President, Dr. Jorge H. Frías, was appointed permanent President of the Conference. Dr. Raúl C. Migone performing the duties of Secretary General.

As a result of the debates held in the preliminary session on May 28, 1942, and in the first plenary session on May 29, 1942, it was decided to appoint the Committees on Credentials and Coordination, in accordance with the Rules and Regulations, a General Committee to classify, centralize and distribute the projects submitted to the Conference, and two Subcommittees, entrusted with the study of the matters included in the first and in the second chapters, respectively, of the program of the Conference, each Subcommittee to have two rapporteurs.

These Committees and Subcommittees were formed as follows:

[Here follows list of members.]

The International Conference for the Coordination of Police and Judicial Authorities, after the deliberations in the Committees, and after hearing the reports of the respective Rapporteurs, approved the following resolutions and recommendations at the closing session held on June 9, 1942:

I. RESOLUTION RELATIVE TO DISSEMINATION OF PROPAGANDA BY MEANS OF PUBLIC DEMONSTRATIONS

WHEREAS:

1. It is of vital importance to the American Republics to prevent the diffusion of propaganda — directed, supported or instigated by foreign governments, groups or individuals — which tends to endanger their security, their institutions and the democratic ideals which inspire them;

2. Because of their deeply disturbing influence and the dangers they represent, it is imperative to include among the acts of propaganda classified as anti-American in character, all public demonstrations and exhibitions, of any nature whatsoever, which are held within the American Republics under the auspices and in the interest of non-American States which have committed acts of aggression against American Republics; these acts of aggression have brought about the participation of some of the Republics in the war, the condemnation of the aggressor nations by all the Republics, and the application, by various means, in the presence of a common danger, of the pacts of continental solidarity, and have hardened the determination of all the American nations to dedicate themselves to the task of taking all necessary measures to safeguard their security and their common heritage of liberty and democracy;

3. As a consequence, the acts of propaganda mentioned above, which are contrary to the principles, traditions and ideals which govern and strengthen the life of the American Republics, must come within the scope of the preventive and repressive action of the police and judicial authorities of the American nations;

The Inter-American Conference of Police and Judicial Authorities

RESOLVES:

First: To declare that it is of vital importance for the police and judicial authorities of America to prevent and repress, during the present war, all public demonstrations and exhibitions, whether spoken, written, broadcast, printed or in images, or by any other means, that are contrary to the spirit of the inter-American pacts of defensive solidarity, and that are favorable to the States which have committed acts of aggression against American Republics, or to the allies of the said States in the Tripartite Pact and States subservient to them.

Second: To recommend to the American Republics which have not yet done so, that they adopt measures to protect this vital interest.

II. RESOLUTION RELATIVE TO PROPAGANDA IN EDUCATIONAL INSTITUTIONS

WHEREAS:

One of the most dangerous forms of the subversive propaganda referred to in Resolution XVII of the Third Meeting of the Ministers of Foreign Affairs of the American Republics is sometimes undertaken in primary, secondary or university educational institutions and schools which are under the direction or supervision of nationals of members of the Tripartite Pact or of States subservient to them;

The Inter-American Conference of Police and Judicial Authorities

RESOLVES:

To recommend to the Governments of the American Republics that they enact legal measures, or carefully revise existing provisions on the subject, to prevent propaganda in primary, secondary or university educational establishments and schools which are directed or supervised by nationals of the members of the Tripartite Pact or States subservient to them; that they close any school in which, by means of lessons, lectures, shows, hymns, images and photographs, special symbols, or any other means of influencing opinion, an effort is made to induce the pupils, whether children or adults, to sympathize with, or take part in, activities or aggressive acts against the democratic institutions of the Continent, or against its integrity and sovereignty; and that the application of the penalty recommended hereinabove shall be without prejudice to the application of other penalties established for the same purposes by the laws of the respective countries, such as expulsion, imprisonment, or fines.

III. RECOMMENDATION RELATIVE TO ASSOCIATIONS

The Inter-American Conference of Police and Judicial Authorities

RECOMMENDS:

That the Governments of the American Republics enact laws regulating the constitution of associations controlled, directly or indirectly, by nationals of members of the Tripartite Pact or of States subservient to them, or which seek to act in any way on behalf of, or in the political interest of, any non-American State which is not engaged at war on the side of an American Republic, and for the purpose of preventing the formation and existence of entities which conspire openly or secretly against American solidarity or the security, independence or integrity of the American nations.

IV. Resolution Relative to Fishing Vessels

Whereas:

1. The unusual frequency with which marauding submarines operate near the coasts of America, logically leads to the assumption that supply bases at great distances from their natural bases, must be available to them near where they operate, which places upon the Governments of the American countries the duty to prevent elements connected with the members of the Tripartite Pact, and States subservient to them, from rendering any form of assistance in the supplying of fuel, provisions or ammunition to such submarines;

2. The privileges granted to fishing vessels to put out to sea without a strict supervision by the respective authorities affords such elements an opportunity to give the said submarines assistance of the kind mentioned;

The Inter-American Conference of Police and Judicial Authorities

Resolves:

First: To declare that supervision over the activities of fishing vessels of every kind, whether they belong to private individuals or to commercial enterprises, and the careful examination of their cargoes at the time of their departure from and upon their arrival at American shores, would contribute to the effectiveness of American police methods during the present war.

Second: To recommend to the Governments of the American Republics that they adopt measures in accordance with the objectives set forth above.

V. Recommendation on the Enforcement of Laws and Regulations Relative to Subversive Activities and on the Creation of a Special Police Unit to Deal with Such Activities

Whereas:

1. The Governments of the twenty-one American Republics recognized, at the Third Meeting of the Ministers of Foreign Affairs of the American Republics, that activities of individuals and organizations acting on behalf of and in the interest of the members of the Tripartite Pact and of the States subservient to them, constitute an immediate

and grave threat to the individual and collective security and welfare of the American family of nations;

2. The immediate and urgent need in meeting this threat is a more vigorous enforcement throughout the Hemisphere of existing basic legislation and regulations relative to the control of activities directed against the security of the State and its institutions;

3. That, in the same manner, the constant interchange of information and personal contact between the officials charged in each country with the enforcement and administration of the above-mentioned laws and regulations, specially with respect to the control and suppression of subversive activities which transcend national frontiers in their scope and effects, would be mutually beneficial and would contribute substantially to the success of the measures taken for the effective and energetic fulfillment of existing laws against such activities;

4. That the effective prevention and repression of the above-mentioned activities requires the existence of a competent national entity, which cannot be either the ordinary police or the intelligence services, where these exist, but a special police section or unit trained in the methods of sabotage, apparent accidents in important industries, espionage, and other acts which disturb the political and economic life of the country;

5. That the said unit does not represent a political police organization in the old manner, but a special service with specific functions contributing effectively to the prevention of subversive activities directed against the external or internal security of the State in the political, economic, industrial and commercial fields;

The Inter-American Conference of Police and Judicial Authorities

RESOLVES:

First: To recommend to the Governments of the American Republics that they direct their police, military and other appropriate administrative and law-enforcing officials and departments to undertake an immediate intensification of the programs directed to the elimination of subversive elements within the respective national territory which act on behalf of, or in the interest of the members of the Tripartite Pact and of the States subservient to them.

Second: To recommend to the said Governments that they require the above-mentioned officials and departments to submit periodic reports on the measures taken under existing laws and regulations, and under such special laws and regulations as hereafter may be adopted in the light of experience and changing circumstances.

Third: To recommend that the Emergency Advisory Committee for

Political Defense consider the desirability of convoking informal inter-American meetings, regional and general in character, of the officials mentioned above, in order that they may discuss problems of common interest in the defense against subversive activities of persons acting in the interest of members of the Tripartite Pact and of States subservient to them.

Fourth: To recommend, in order to insure maximum inter-American cooperation, that the American Governments take immediate measures for the creation where they do not now exist, within the police organization, of special corps, sections or units, entitled "Political-Social Police" or with an analogous title, entrusted with the special task of preventing and discovering, through the special training of their members, the crimes of espionage, sabotage, treason, and other activities directed against the external or internal security of the State in its political, economic, industrial and commercial aspects.

VI. Recommendation Relative to the Study of a Uniform Penal Law

The Inter-American Conference of Police and Judicial Authorities

Recommends:

That, in view of the requirements of the political defense of the American Continent during the existing emergency, the Emergency Advisory Committee for Political Defense formulate and submit to the Governments of the American Republics, a draft uniform penal law relative to the prevention and repression of activities against the integrity, independence, solidarity, unity and defense of the American States.

VII. Recommendation Relative to Fraudulent Citizenship

The Inter-American Conference of Police and Judicial Authorities

Recommends:

That the American Republics enact legislation providing:

That any national of the members of the Tripartite Pact or of States subservient to them who fraudulently obtains for himself or for another person, by means of a judicial or administrative procedure conducted at his request, the nationality of the respective American Republic, shall be punished with confinement or imprisonment for from two to five years.

The sentence shall deprive him of the nationality illegally obtained, and also of the public offices obtained by virtue thereof, and shall justify his expulsion from the country or, if this is not possible, the exercise of strict vigilance over his movements by the appropriate authorities.

VIII. Resolution Concerning the Granting of Citizenship

Whereas:

The existing international situation compels the American countries to adopt restrictive measures of a temporary nature relative to the granting of citizenship in the case of persons who do not have an intention to settle in the country which shelters them;

The Inter-American Conference of Police and Judicial Authorities

Resolves:

To recommend to the Governments that, within the scope of their respective laws, they restrict the granting of legal citizenship or naturalization to all aliens who do not produce satisfactory proof of, and demonstrate upon due investigation, their legal right to citizenship, without prejudice to the granting of asylum to political refugees in accordance with national uses and international conventions.

IX. Recommendation Relative to the South American Treaty on Criminal Law of 1940

The Inter-American Conference of Police and Judicial Authorities

Recommends:

First: That the Governments of the American Republics which are not signatories of the Treaty on Criminal Law signed at Montevideo on March 19, 1940,[1] study the Treaty.

Second: That the Emergency Advisory Committee for Political Defense and the Inter-American Bar Association study the above-mentioned Treaty and make known their conclusions to the Governments mentioned in the first paragraph.

X. Recommendation on Extradition

The Inter-American Conference of Police and Judicial Authorities

Recommends:

That the American Republics agree to grant extradition of nationals of members of the Tripartite Pact and of States subservient to them who are indicted or condemned for crimes against American solidarity, or the security, integrity or defense of any American Republic, in accordance with the procedures provided for in their respective laws or in the treaties and international agreements to which they are parties.

[1] *American Journal of International Law*, XXXVII (1943), *Official Docs.*, p. 122.

XI. Resolution on the Draft Convention Relative to the Expulsion of Aliens

The Inter-American Conference of Police and Judicial Authorities

RESOLVES:

To transmit the Draft Convention Relative to the Expulsion of Aliens [1] presented by the Argentine Delegation, to the Emergency Advisory Committee for Political Defense, with the recommendation that the Committee study the draft, taking into account the requirements of the present emergency and the discussions at the present Conference.

XII. Resolution on Special Travel Documents

WHEREAS:

1. As a result of the existing international situation, many foreign residents in America are without diplomatic representation or consular protection, being unable, as a result, to obtain or renew their respective passports;

2. The laws of some countries recognize the validity of special travel documents;

The Inter-American Conference of Police and Judicial Authorities

RESOLVES:

To recommend to the Governments of the American Republics that, in addition to passports and certificates of identity recognized by bilateral agreements as valid travel documents, they recognize special travel documents issued under appropriate guarantees, including a consular visa, which are for "in transit" or for a clearly determined purpose.

XIII. Resolution on the Draft Convention Relative to the Creation of an Inter-American Police Union

WHEREAS:

1. The Delegations of Argentina, Bolivia and Nicaragua, Honduras and Peru have respectively submitted the following projects: Inter-American Police Convention; Recommendation for the Adoption of an Inter-American Identification System; Resolution on the Creation of an Inter-American Register of Police and Judicial Documents; Recommendation on the Creation of a Pan American Police Union;

2. These projects express a lofty spirit of continental solidarity, and are inspired by the desire to establish cooperation among the police and

[1] Not reproduced. See Pan American Union, Congress and Conference Series, No. 38, p. 18.

judicial authorities of the American Republics on well defined and adequate bases;

3. In view of the close relationship existing among the above-mentioned projects, the Special Committee of the present Conference has combined the basic ideas and provisions of these proposals in a single instrument;[1]

4. The said instrument, as well as the original projects, are worthy of careful study by the Governments and the respective national authorities of the American Republics before a definite convention on the subject is signed;

The Inter-American Conference of Police and Judicial Authorities
RESOLVES:

First: To transmit to the Pan American Union the draft Convention relative to the creation of an Inter-American Police Union formulated by the Special Committee of the Conference, in order that the Pan American Union may communicate it to the Governments of the American Republics and to the Emergency Advisory Committee for Political Defense, with the request that they present their observations thereon.

Second: To recommend that, in the study of this draft Convention, the Governments and the Emergency Advisory Committee consider the original proposals of the Delegations of Argentina, Bolivia and Nicaragua, Honduras and Peru, as well as the discussions which took place regarding them during the present Conference, and which are recorded in its proceedings, copies of which shall be sent to the Pan American Union by the Secretary General of the Conference in order that they may be sent by the Union to the Governments and to the Committee.

Third: To urge the Pan American Union to prepare the definite project of convention, on the bases of the said draft and of the observations presented by the Governments members of the Union, and by the above-mentioned Emergency Committee.

Fourth: That the said draft Convention be considered at a special Conference, or at the next International Conference of American States, or that, after its approval, it be open for signature by the American Republics at the Pan American Union.

XIV. RECOMMENDATION ON THE CREATION OF NATIONAL INTER-DEPARTMENTAL COMMITTEES

The Inter-American Conference of Police and Judicial Authorities
RECOMMENDS:

That the American Governments consider the desirability of establishing, as soon as possible, in their respective countries, an Interdepart-

[1] Not reproduced. See Annex to Resolution XIII, *ibid.*, p. 22.

mental Coordinating Committee, or adopt an analogous procedure for facilitating the fulfillment of the recommendations of the present Conference, and for furnishing the national liaison representative with the Emergency Advisory Committee for Political Defense, all the assistance and cooperation which may be necessary to the practical and efficient performance of his duties.

In testimony whereof, the Delegates signed this present Final Act, in Spanish, English, Portuguese and French, done in Buenos Aires, the Capital city of the Argentine Republic, on the ninth of June in the year one thousand nine hundred and forty-two.

RESERVATIONS MADE BY THE ARGENTINE DELEGATION

I. Resolution relative to propaganda by means of public demonstrations:
"That the measures recommended in the first Article should be enforced in accordance with the fundamental laws of each country."

VI. Recommendation relative to the study of a uniform penal law:
"That the Emergency Advisory Committee for Political Defense may only formulate a draft convention and not a project law."

II. Resolution relative to propaganda in educational institutions.

III. Recommendation relative to associations.

V. Recommendation on the enforcement of laws and regulations relative to subversive activities and on the creation of a special police unit to deal with such activities.

VII. Recommendation relative to fraudulent citizenship:
"That the laws and measures mentioned in the preceding resolutions and recommendations should not contain limitations in respect of the different nationality of the persons to whom they shall be applicable."

RESERVATIONS MADE BY THE CHILEAN DELEGATION

"The Delegation of Chile subscribes this Final Act of the Conference, renewing the reservations and the observations submitted during the debates in the General Committee and Subcommittees, and subject to the subsequent governmental approval."

[Here follow signatures.]

(2) *Message from the President (Roosevelt) Transmitting a Report from the Secretary of State (Hull) Requesting Legislation Providing for the Participation of the United States in the Emergency Advisory Committee for Political Defense, December 3, 1942* [1]

To THE CONGRESS OF THE UNITED STATES OF AMERICA:

I commend to the favorable consideration of the Congress the enclosed report from the Secretary of State to the end that legislation may be enacted to enable the United States to continue participation in the

---

[1] House Doc. No. 893, 77th Cong., 2d sess.

Emergency Advisory Committee for Political Defense and to authorize the appropriation of such sums as may be required for such participation by the United States in this Committee for the period of the war emergency or so long as the American Republics may deem the continuation of its activities to be essential to the welfare of the Hemisphere, but not exceeding the sum of $105,560 per annum.

FRANKLIN D. ROOSEVELT.

[Enclosure]

THE PRESIDENT:

Acts of aggression of a nonmilitary character including systematic espionage, sabotage, and subversive propaganda are being attempted by the Axis nations and their satellites against both belligerent and neutral states in the Western Hemisphere. This campaign is designed to produce the eventual disintegration of the inter-American community, the erasure of its democratic ideals and procedures, and its ultimate subservience to alien philosophy and power.

Such acts assume an importance comparable with military threats and therefore must be combatted with equal skill, thoroughness, and determination.

Definite action to defeat this menace was taken at the Third Meeting of the Ministers of Foreign Affairs, held at Rio de Janeiro in January 1942, which recommended that the Pan American Union elect prior to March 1, 1942, the Emergency Advisory Committee for Political Defense to be charged with the responsibility of guiding these protective measures on a continental scale and to be composed of 7 members functioning on behalf of all of the 21 American Republics. The resolution of the Rio de Janeiro meeting furnished the general directives for the Committee's work and provided further that the Governing Board of the Pan American Union, following consultation with the governments, should determine the specific functions of the Committee, prepare the regulations to govern its activities, and fix its budget of expenses.

Pursuant to the resolution of the Rio de Janeiro meeting, the Governing Board of the Pan American Union on February 25, 1942, designated Montevideo, Uruguay, as the seat of the Committee and asked each of the following American Republics to name one representative to serve as a member: Argentina, Brazil, Chile, Mexico, Uruguay, Venezuela, and the United States of America.

Following this request of the Pan American Union, this Government designated with the approval of the President, Mr. Carl B. Spaeth, former Chief of the American Hemisphere Division, Board of Economic Warfare, as the member of the Committee from the United States.

The Committee inaugurated its work at Montevideo on April 15, 1942, and has met regularly since that time. It is giving constant and detailed attention to a wide range of pertinent studies including the control of dangerous aliens, prevention of abuse of citizenship, regulation of transit across boundaries, and prevention of political aggression. The Committee has made recommendations to the American Republics with respect to such important problems as the registration and control of the movement of enemy aliens, the prevention of sabotage with respect to hemisphere shipping, and the creation of an inter-American office for the exchange of information on individuals or organizations engaged in subversive activities.

The activities of the Committee were recognized, endorsed, and to some extent expanded, by the Inter-American Conference of Police and Judicial Authorities held at Buenos Aires from May 27 to June 9, 1942, pursuant to resolutions of the Second and Third Meetings of the Ministers of Foreign Affairs of the American Republics. Recognizing the fact that the dynamic nature of the problem of subversive activity requires continuing consideration by a central body, the Conference of Police and Judicial Authorities referred a number of special questions to the Committee for further study and for the preparation of appropriate recommendations to the 21 American Governments.

The emergency conditions attending the establishment of the Committee and the consequent urgent necessity of arranging for this Government's participation as expeditiously as possible rendered it inadvisable to request a specific appropriation at that time. Consequently, to enable the United States to participate promptly in the inauguration of the Committee's work, an allocation was made to the Department from the emergency fund for the President for the expenses of the American citizen member of the Committee and his staff, and for a contribution by this Government to the expenses of the general secretariat of the Committee. The United States member of the Committee is assisted by technical experts from this country and additional technical services are received from the secretariat of the Committee and through the close cooperation of the liaison official in each of the American Republics.

The success and effectiveness of the Committee's work will depend very largely upon the facilities and encouragement offered by the governments of the American Republics, particularly those chosen to designate nationals to serve as active members. The position of leadership which the United States holds in the military defense of the Western Hemisphere democracies is equally apparent in the companion sphere of political defense. It is imperative therefore that appropriate steps be taken to enable this Government to assume the full share of its responsibility for the effective functioning of the Committee which should become an increasingly valuable component of the inter-American defense structure.

I have the honor, therefore, to recommend that the Congress be requested to enact legislation to enable the United States to continue participation in the Emergency Advisory Committee for Political Defense and to authorize the appropriation of such sums as may be required for such participation by the United States in this Committee for the period of the war emergency or so long as the American Republics may deem the continuation of its activities to be essential to the welfare of the hemisphere, but not exceeding the sum of $105,560 per annum.

A draft of the proposed legislation is enclosed for your convenience. Respectfully submitted.

CORDELL HULL.

DEPARTMENT OF STATE, *December 1, 1942.*

As a result of the transmission of this request, H. J. Res. 16 was introduced and adopted by both Houses of Congress, and received final approval of the President, June 19, 1943.[1] Under this resolution, expenditures up to $105,560 per annum were authorized.

C. Economic and Financial Collaboration

1. INTER-AMERICAN FINANCIAL AND ECONOMIC ADVISORY COMMITTEE

(1) *Message from the President (Roosevelt) Transmitting a Report from the Secretary of State (Hull) Requesting Appropriations for the Annual Expenses of the Inter-American Financial and Economic Advisory Committee, December 3, 1942* [2]

TO THE CONGRESS OF THE UNITED STATES OF AMERICA:

I commend to the favorable consideration of the Congress the enclosed report from the Secretary of State to the end that legislation may be enacted to authorize the appropriation of such sums as may be necessary for the payment by the United States of its proportionate share in the annual expenses of the Inter-American Financial and Economic Advisory Committee.

FRANKLIN D. ROOSEVELT

[Enclosure]

THE PRESIDENT:

It has been abundantly demonstrated in the total warfare being waged throughout the world today that economic weapons are second in importance and effectiveness only to the tangible implements of war — guns, tanks, airplanes, and ships — which modern science has perfected.

[1] Public Law 80, 78th Cong.
[2] House Doc. No. 894, 77th Cong., 2d sess.; Department of State, *Bulletin*, VIII, p. 260.

The American Republics have devised a collective economic weapon in the Inter-American Financial and Economic Advisory Committee which serves as an offensive instrument for the destruction of the enemies of democracy and freedom and which is equally important in defending the hemisphere from the same type of weapon wielded by the aggressor nations.

The Inter-American Financial and Economic Advisory Committee was established by the Pan American Union in accordance with Resolution III of the First Meeting of the Ministers of Foreign Affairs of the American Republics, held at Panamá, Panama, in September and October 1939, pursuant to agreements reached at the Inter-American Conference for the Maintenance of Peace and the Eighth International Conference of American States. The full text of the resolution is enclosed for convenience of reference.[1]

The Pan American Union installed the Committee at Washington on November 15, 1939, when the Honorable Sumner Welles, the United States member, was elected the permanent Chairman. Administrative and clerical personnel, as well as office quarters and supplies, have been furnished by the Pan American Union from its regular resources derived from the annual contributions of the states members. The Committee has met at regular intervals since the date of its inauguration and has undertaken a wide range of studies resulting in the formulation of a number of constructive recommendations to the governments of the 21 American Republics.

The Second Meeting of the Ministers of Foreign Affairs of the American Republics, held at Havana, Cuba, in July 1940, endorsed the work of the Committee and enlarged its functions as indicated in the following quoted section of Resolution XXV, Economic and Financial Cooperation.[2]

Three. Specifically, to instruct the said committee that it proceed forthwith:

(a) To cooperate with each country of this continent in the study of possible measures for the increase of the domestic consumption of its own exportable surpluses of those commodities which are of primary importance to the maintenance of the economic life of such countries;

(b) To propose to the American nations immediate measures and arrangements of mutual benefit tending to increase trade among them without injury to the interests of their respective producers, for the purpose of providing increased markets for such products and of expanding their consumption;

(c) To create instruments of inter-American cooperation for the temporary storing, financing, and handling of any such commodities and for their orderly and systematic marketing, having in mind the normal conditions of production and distribution thereof;

(d) To develop commodity arrangements with a view to assuring equitable terms of trade for both producers and consumers of the commodities concerned;

---

[1] *Documents, II, 1939–40*, p. 100.
[2] *Ibid., III, 1940–41*, p. 82.

(e) To recommend methods for improving the standard of living of the peoples of the Americas, including public health and nutrition measures;

(f) To establish appropriate organizations for the distribution of a part of the surplus of any such commodity, as a humanitarian and social relief measure;

(g) To consider, while these plans and measures are being developed, the desirability of a broader system of inter-American cooperative organization in trade and industrial matters, and to propose credit measures and other measures of assistance which may be immediately necessary in the fields of economics, finance, money, and foreign exchange.

The importance of the Committee's role in meeting effectively the problems of economic dislocation resulting from world-wide hostilities was further recognized by the Third Meeting of the Ministers of Foreign Affairs of the American Republics, held at Rio de Janeiro, Brazil, in January 1942, which adopted several resolutions and recommendations assigning specific additional tasks to the Committee, including the following: [1]

(1) The formulation of a general plan for hemispheric economic mobilization and the preparation and periodic revision of a list of basic and strategic materials (resolution II, Production of Strategic Materials). [2]

This resolution also provided that in order to enable the Committee to carry out the new duties entrusted to it, its means of operation be expanded immediately and that it be empowered to request the American governments to execute inter-American economic agreements which they had previously approved.

(2) The improvement and expansion of inter-American communication facilities — air, maritime, land, inland waterway — and the full mobilization of transportation facilities (resolution IV, Mobilization of Transportation Facilities). [3]

(3) The strengthening of the Inter-American Development Commission which had been created by the Financial and Economic Advisory Committee for the purpose of mobilizing the economic forces of the American nations, and the creation of a permanent body of technical experts to study the natural resources of each country when so requested by its government (resolution VIII, Inter-American Development Commission). [4]

(4) To serve as the recipient of decisions by the American governments concerning adherence to the Convention for the Establishment of an Inter-American Bank (resolution X, Inter-American Bank). [5]

(5) The encouragement of capital investments by any of the American Republics in one of the others, requesting the various governments to adopt the measures necessary to facilitate the flow and protection of

[1] Department of State, *Bulletin*, VI, p. 117–141.
[2] *Documents, IV, 1941–42*, p. 305.
[3] *Ibid.*, p. 318.   [4] *Ibid.*, p. 314.   [5] *Ibid.*, p. 315.

such investments within the continent (resolution XI, Investment of Capital in the American Republics).[1]

(6) Cooperation within its specialized field with the Pan American Union and the Inter-American Juridical Committee in the formulation of specific recommendations for consideration at the proposed Inter-American Technical Economic Conference which is to be convoked by the Pan American Union to study current and post-war economic problems (resolution XXV, Post-war Problems).[2]

(7) The convocation of a conference of representatives of the central banks or equivalent or analogous institutions for the purpose of determining the standards of procedure for the uniform handling of bank credits, collections, contracts of lease, and consignments of merchandise involving real or juridical persons or nationals of a state which has committed an act of aggression against the American continent. This conference was held at Washington, D. C., from June 30 to July 10, 1942,[3] and resulted in important understandings concerning a pressing problem which is faced by both belligerent and nonbelligerent American states (resolution VI, Conference to Standardize Procedure in Banking Operations Relating to Nationals of Aggressor Countries).[4]

The above-mentioned Inter-American Conference on Systems of Economic and Financial Control was the second large international meeting convoked by the Financial and Economic Advisory Committee, the first having been the Inter-American Maritime Conference, which was held at Washington, D. C., in November and December 1940.[5] The latter conference gave detailed and constructive consideration to the national regulation of maritime services, the readjustment of international shipping services to meet the problem of dislocations resulting from war conditions in Europe, and expansion and improvement of inter-American shipping facilities. Both of these conferences fulfilled in their respective fields an urgent need for international consultation and action concerning serious problems arising from the emergency situation. It is generally agreed that each was successful not only in attaining its specific objectives but also in advancing inter-American cooperation and solidarity.

Additional outstanding accomplishments of the Committee include —

(1) The drafting of the convention, charter, and bylaws of the Inter-American Bank.[6] A number of the American Republics have already adhered to the convention which is still open for signature.

---

[1] *Ibid.*, p. 316.   [2] *Ibid.*, p. 325.

[3] Department of State, *Bulletin*, VI, p. 567, and VII, p. 580; *Documents, IV, 1941–42*, p. 393.

[4] *Ibid.*, p. 313.

[5] Department of State, *Bulletin*, III, p. 224, 461, 516; *Documents, III, 1940–41*, p. 114.

[6] Department of State, *Bulletin*, III, p. 305, 512; *Documents, II, 1939–40*, p. 154.

(2) Establishment of the Inter-American Development Commission.

(3) Studies resulting in the inter-American coffee agreement [1] which is designed to stabilize the coffee market in a manner equitable both to producers and to consumers.

(4) Study and action to carry out the 12 resolutions of the Inter-American Maritime Conference convoked by the Committee.

(5) The study and redrafting of a previously prepared Convention on the Simplification and Unification of Customs Procedures and Port Formalities and the formulation of recommendations to the American Republics on this general subject.

(6) The approval and submission to the American Republics of a Draft Convention on Facilities for Commercial Travelers and Commercial Samples.

(7) Special studies of topics related to cotton, cocoa, financing of the Pan American Highway, and the relief distribution of surplus commodities.

(8) A recommendation to the Governments of the American Republics, which was approved unanimously, that legislation and systems of control be adopted regulating all exports and imports in each country.[2] In this connection, the Committee has served as a clearing house for information on all matters relating to measures taken by the United States prior to December 1941 regarding export and import control, priorities and quotas, foreign trade policies, distribution of strategic products, et cetera.

(9) The study and recommendation of a plan for the effective use of more than 100 vessels, principally Italian and German, which had been immobilized in American ports [3] and which are now being operated under this formula in the service of the inter-American trade.

(10) The formulation of recommendations concerning tariffs designed to assure the sound promotion of inter-American trade.

(11) The creation as a dependency of the Committee of the Inter-American Maritime Technical Commission which meets regularly to study current shipping problems.

(12) The preparation of a recommendation to the American governments that publication of statistical data on strategic and vitally important products be discontinued except for especially authorized official purposes.

The Inter-American Financial and Economic Advisory Committee was especially established as an integral part of the inter-American organization to meet a particular situation and is assuming an increasingly important role in the concerted efforts of the American Republics

---

[1] *U. S. Treaty Series* 970 and 979; *Documents, III, 1940–41*, p. 97; *IV, 1941–42.* p. 380.

[2] *Ibid., IV, 1941–42*, p. 384, 393. [3] *Ibid.*, p. 405.

to face with the utmost determination and unity of purpose the crisis through which the hemisphere is now passing. During the 3 years of its existence, the Committee has fully demonstrated its effectiveness as a powerful instrumentality for the protection of the inter-American economic structure during this period of great danger to the ideals and way of life of the Western Hemisphere democracies. It is imperative, therefore, that the 21 American Republics continue to encourage and assist the Committee in every appropriate way in the discharge of its manifold responsibilities.

The Chairman of the Committee addressed a communication to the Secretary of State under date of August 31, 1942,[1] indicating that in order to assure adequate resources and facilities for the efficient performance of its expanding duties, the Committee has decided to establish a separate annual budget thus relieving the Pan American Union of an increasingly heavy financial burden. There is enclosed a copy of Mr. Welles' letter transmitting the text of the Committee's resolution appending tables indicating the population and annual quotas of the respective countries and the anticipated disbursements for the first fiscal year, starting on July 1, 1942. It will be observed that the budget in the sum of $42,265.85 per annum is based upon an annual contribution by each of the 21 American Republics at the rate of 15 cents United States currency per 1,000 inhabitants. Under this formula the share of the United States would be $22,810 per annum. The Department is of the opinion that the Committee has adjusted its annual budget to conform with the strictest standards of economy compatible with the efficient discharge of its duties and responsibilities.

The United States has consistently and whole-heartedly extended its cooperation and facilities in furtherance of the Committee's work which has been carried on under the leadership of a high official of this Government. The activities of the Committee constitute an indispensable supplement to the all-out war effort of the United States and should be supported with the same realistic determination that characterizes our military contribution to the world-wide struggle against totalitarianism.

I have the honor, therefore, to recommend that the Congress be requested to authorize the appropriation of such sums as may be necessary for the payment by the United States of its proportionate share in the annual expenses of the Inter-American Financial and Economic Advisory Committee.

A draft of the proposed legislation is enclosed for your convenience.[2]

Respectfully submitted.

CORDELL HULL.

DEPARTMENT OF STATE,
December 1, 1942.

---

[1] House Doc. No. 894, 77th Cong., 2d sess., p. 6.   [2] *Ibid.*, p. 10.

In response to this request, H. J. Res. 15 was introduced and passed by both houses of Congress, and received Presidential approval on June 19, 1943.[1] Under the resolution, the expenditure of up to $23,000 was authorized for the payment of the proportionate share of the United States in the annual expenses of the Inter-American Financial and Economic Advisory Committee.

2. COMPREHENSIVE ARRANGEMENTS FOR THE PROMOTION OF ECONOMIC SOLIDARITY

[For arrangements entered into before July 1, 1942, see *Documents*, *IV*, *1941–42*, p. 356.]

(1) *Arrangements with Bolivia*

Dr. Joaquin Espada, the Bolivian Minister of Finance, and Dr. Alberto Crespo, the Bolivian Minister of National Economy, accompanied by technical experts, arrived in Washington on July 5 [2] to discuss with various agencies of the United States Government the program for economic collaboration in the preparation of which the Governments of Bolivia and the United States were then engaged.[3] The visit of the President of Bolivia to the United States early in May 1943 provided the opportunity for the exchange of views between the chief executives of the two states on matters relating to the prosecution of the war and post-war adjustments.

(a) *Economic Cooperation with Bolivia. Department of State Release, July 5, 1942* [4]

[Excerpt]

A United States Economic Mission which has recently returned from Bolivia after making a five months' survey in that country has prepared a report making recommendations covering a general plan of economic development to be undertaken by the Bolivian Development Corporation, which is now being organized. This corporation will be under joint American and Bolivian management and will be financed partially by funds from the Export-Import Bank.

Problems to be considered include the construction of highways and the development of the petroleum and agricultural resources of the country as well as the stimulation of production of such strategic materials as tin, tungsten, antimony, rubber, and quinine.

(b) *Economic and Financial Cooperation with Bolivia. Department of State Release, August 14, 1942* [5]

During their visit to the United States Dr. Joaquin Espada, Minister of Finance of Bolivia, and Dr. Alberto Crespo Gutiérrez, Minister of

---

[1] Public Law 79, 78th Cong.
[2] Department of State, *Bulletin*, VII, p. 621.
[3] *Documents, IV, 1941–42*, p. 363.
[4] Department of State, *Bulletin*, VII, p. 621.
[5] *Ibid.*, p. 702.

National Economy of Bolivia, have carried on conversations with officials of the Government of the United States concerning comprehensive arrangements for economic and financial cooperation between Bolivia and the United States.

The economic and financial discussions with the Bolivian Ministers have been based in large part upon the studies made during a six-month period in Bolivia by the United States Economic Mission under the leadership of Mr. Merwin L. Bohan, a Foreign Service officer of the United States. In addition to Mr. Bohan there were seven other members of the Mission, including experts in highway construction, agriculture, and mining. This Mission conducted a survey in Bolivia with a view to recommending a program of economic development for Bolivia which would include improved communications, increased production of basic agricultural products for export, various types of development in the Bolivian mining industry, and the development of the Bolivian petroleum industry.[1]

The discussions with Dr. Espada and Dr. Crespo have resulted in the formulation of a cooperative agreement for the financing by the two Governments of the first stage of a program of economic development through a Bolivian development corporation. The plan thus developed will be submitted to the Bolivian Congress.

In accordance with the recommendations of the Economic Mission the Government of the United States has agreed to give favorable consideration at the appropriate time to the practicability, under conditions then existing, of extending, through the appropriate credit institution, credits for the financing of the second stage of the long-term program.

The recent revision of the agreement by which the Government of the United States purchases a large part of Bolivian tin-production was an integral part of the program of economic and financial cooperation between Bolivia and the United States. Moreover, during the time that the Bolivian Ministers of Finance and National Economy have been in Washington arrangements have been completed for revision of the agreement by which the Government of the United States purchases Bolivian tungsten. The Government of the United States has likewise recently entered into an agreement with the Government of Bolivia for the purchase of Bolivian production of raw rubber.

The two Bolivian Ministers have discussed with the president of the Foreign Bondholders Protective Council, Incorporated, the possible inauguration of discussions with a view to servicing the Bolivian dollar debt, and the Ministers have informed the Secretary of State that they believe it may soon be possible to find a mutually acceptable basis for subsequent formal discussions.

---

[1] *Ibid.*, V, p. 563; VI, p. 621.

(c) United States Mission of Labor Experts to Bolivia. Statement of the Bolivian Government. Department of State Release, January 29, 1943 [1]

The Government of the United States has been informed that the Bolivian Government has issued the following statement:

"At the last Cabinet meeting it was agreed that the Ministers of Labor and Social Services and of Economy and Mines would prepare a supreme decree setting up a commission of experts responsible for studying the improvements of the conditions of health, hygiene, salaries, and security of workers in general and particularly of mine workers.

"The Minister of Foreign Relations offered the information that the Government of the United States in accordance with a request made by our Government had announced through Ambassador Guachalla its desire to cooperate in this plan sending any experts that might be necessary to study together with those designated by the Bolivian Government the workers' situation with a view to improving their conditions and increasing the production of minerals taking into account the problems of transportation, wages, mine security, and other problems pertinent to the main question.

"Coordinating these ideas the country will know within the near future the result of these studies undertaken in order to establish fixed forms for the development of a policy bettering the living conditions of the working classes."

———

In accordance with the invitation extended to the United States Government to take part in the proposed study of measures beneficial to Bolivian labor, a mission of labor experts headed by the Honorable Calvert Magruder, United States Circuit Judge, Boston, departed from Miami for Bolivia on January 30, and returned March 23, 1943. Members of the mission were Mr. Robert J. Watt, International Representative of the American Federation of Labor; Mr. Charles R. Hook, Jr., Assistant to the President of the Rustless Iron and Steel Corporation of Baltimore; Mr. Alfred Giardino, Executive Secretary of the New York State Labor Board, at present preparing a study of labor conditions in South America for the United States Department of Labor; Mr. Robert E. Mathews, attorney, of the Board of Economic Warfare; and Mr. Martin J. Kyne, Vice President of United Retail, Wholesale and Department Stores of America. Mr. Edward G. Trueblood, Second Secretary of the American Embassy in Mexico, acted as secretary to the mission.

The report of the Commission was signed on March 14, 1943, it contains chapters on education, freedom of association and collective bargaining, regulation of wages and hours of work, social insurance, placement, housing, help, accident prevention and popular nutrition. By agreement with both Governments the International Labor Office has published the report. (*Labour Problems in Bolivia*, Montreal, Canada, July, 1943.)

[1] *Ibid.*, VIII, p. 107, 134.

(d) *Visit to the United States of the President of Bolivia (Peñaranda). White House Press Release, May 14, 1943* [1]

The recent visit of the President of Bolivia as a guest of the President of the United States has been the occasion for a cordial exchange of views between the two Chief Executives on a wide range of subjects of mutual interest. Bolivia, as the latest adherent to the Declaration of the United Nations, is engaged in the production of strategic materials, including especially tin, tungsten, rubber, and quinine, which are contributing increasingly to the final defeat of the Axis powers.

Matters relating to the prosecution of the war as well as problems of the post-war period have been given special consideration, particularly so far as they affect the long-term economic interests of the two countries. The President of Bolivia and the President of the United States have agreed as to the desirability of devising methods of intensifying the cooperation between their respective countries in order to make possible a continuing supply of their products and raw materials on a stable and durable basis. These matters are currently being discussed by officials of the two Governments.

Finally, the President of Bolivia and the President of the United States have reaffirmed their faith in the principles for which the United Nations are fighting and their complete certainty in the final triumph of right and justice upon which the peace and prosperity of the international community must be based.

(2) *Arrangements with Brazil*

(a) *United States Technical Mission to Brazil. White House Press Release, September 2, 1942* [1]

[For earlier history of arrangements for economic collaboration with Brazil, see *Documents, IV, 1941–42*, p. 364.]

The President announced on September 2 that a special United States technical mission of industrial engineers, headed by Morris Llewellyn Cooke, will leave soon for Brazil to cooperate with experts of that country in developing Brazilian industry and war production.

At the request of the Brazilian Government the mission has been organized by the Board of Economic Warfare, the Department of State, and the War Production Board. The general plan of the cooperative mission was agreed upon several weeks ago, and a group of Brazilian industrial experts has already been selected to work with the United States technicians. The scope and urgency of their work have been considerably increased as a result of Brazil's declaration of war against Germany and Italy.

[1] From the Office of the Secretary to the President.

The basic objectives of the mission are: (a) to increase local production of essential products, especially those which formerly were imported from the United States, in order to save shipping space; (b) to convert local industries to the use of substitute raw materials, replacing supplies ordinarily imported; (c) to maintain and improve transportation facilities; and (d) to lay the foundation for a long-range strengthening of Brazil's whole industrial economy. The program will be directed toward a further increase in Brazil's already important contribution of vital materials for her own and the United Nations' joint war effort.

Large shipments of machinery and plant equipment will not be involved in the development program. It will be based largely on practical recommendations for the application of mass-production methods and modern industrial techniques, in addition to adjustment and conversion measures.

Fuel and power are primary problems in the Brazilian industrialization program. The mission will consider measures to increase Brazil's power production or to convert its plants to alternative fuels. Expansion of existing ore-reduction plants in Brazil will be studied, with the purpose of releasing considerable equipment in the United Nations and at the same time saving thousands of tons of vital shipping space. Textile and other general manufacturing plants will be surveyed in an effort to use Brazil's surplus textile fibers and to increase production of essential consumer goods. These and many other specific problems will be considered in the general program.

Morris Llewellyn Cooke, who will direct the United States mission, is an outstanding industrial engineer with an unusually wide range of practical experience. He has served as chairman of the Mississippi Valley Commission and of the Great Plains Commission. He was Administrator of the Rural Electrification Administration from 1935 to 1937. In 1941 Mr. Cooke was named by the President as expert for the evaluation of the United States petroleum properties expropriated by Mexico.

Through the facilities of the Brazilian Inter-American Development Commission, the Office of the Coordinator of Inter-American Affairs will cooperate in the development of an enlarged force of trained workers to man Brazil's expanding war production program.

(b) *Agreement between the Governments of the United States of America and the United States of Brazil for the Development of Foodstuffs Production in Brazil, Signed at Rio de Janeiro, September 3, 1942* [1]

On the third day of September nineteen hundred and forty-two, being present in the Ministry of Foreign Affairs, in this city of Rio de Janeiro,

[1] *Executive Agreement Series* 302. A similar agreement was entered into with Venezuela, by exchange of notes, dated May 14, 1943 (*ibid.*, 333).

on the one part Ambassador Jefferson Caffery and Mr. Nelson Rockefeller, the latter Coordinator of Inter-American Affairs, as representatives of the Government of the United States of America, and on the other part, Messrs. Oswaldo Aranha and Apolonio Sales, respectively, Ministers of Foreign Affairs and of Agriculture, as representatives of the Government of the United States of Brazil, having in view the situation created by the war and the difficulties of transportation; and considering the exchange of correspondence between the Government of the United States of America and that of Brazil,[1] consisting of notes of the 3rd and the 14th of March of the current year, telegrams from the Office of the Coordinator of Inter-American Affairs, and from the Brazilian Embassy in Washington, as well as the conversations held on the 27th of August last, between the representatives of the aforesaid Office and of the American Embassy in Rio de Janeiro and the Ministry of Agriculture, resolve to sign the present Agreement for the execution of a plan for the development of foodstuffs production in Brazil, especially in the Amazon Region, North and Northeast, including the State of Baía, in accordance with the following clauses:

CLAUSE FIRST. The work to be carried out will follow a plan which shall be drawn up by the Ministry of Agriculture, with the collaboration of North-American specialists, who will be put at the disposal of the Ministry of Agriculture for this purpose.

CLAUSE SECOND. The plan referred to in the previous Clause, is designed to increase the production of foodstuffs of vegetable and animal origin, of primary necessity, covering at least the following items:

(a) technical assistance for the increase and improvement of production of foodstuffs of animal and vegetable origin;

(b) provision of means, tools, equipment, insecticides, etc., for the increased production of foodstuffs of animal and vegetable origin;

(c) amplification of the resources of the Divisions for the Development of Animal and Vegetable Production, designed to establish an efficient extension service, in accordance with the modern agricultural techniques followed in Brazil and in the United States;

(d) development of plans, technical assistance and the execution of irrigation, drainage, and soil conservation works;

(e) collaboration in the solution of problems of handling, storage, conservation and distribution of the food products;

(f) technical and financial assistance for agricultural colonization;

(g) betterment of the conditions of nutrition of the populations in the areas in which this Agreement is carried out.

CLAUSE THIRD. For the execution of this Agreement, the Brazilian Government assumes the following obligations:

[1] Not printed.

1. To contribute, through the immediate opening of a special appropriation, five thousand contos of reis.

2. To orient, in the sense of this Program the continuance of the application of the:

(a) five thousand contos of reis allocated for the emergency development of production throughout the Northeast;

(b) three thousand forty-six contos of reis of the ordinary budget of the Division for the Development of Vegetable Production during the present fiscal year, ending December 31, 1942;

(c) eight thousand four hundred seventy-five contos of reis of funds deposited in the Bank of Brazil, for the disposition of this Division, for the execution of the Joint Services during this fiscal year, in accordance with contracts signed between the Union and the States of the aforesaid regions, cited in the present Agreement.

3. To include in the Federal budget to be approved for the next fiscal year, from January 1st to December 31, 1943, the sum of seven thousand seven hundred contos of reis, as well as to assure the inclusion of an appropriation of three thousand eight hundred fifty contos of reis in the budgets of the States which maintain contracts with the Union, for the execution of the joint services, for the same period, in the regions provided for in this agreement. The application of these funds will be oriented in the sense of this Agreement.

4. To contribute, in the year 1943, the resources of personnel and material provided for in the ordinary budget of the Ministry of Agriculture, destined to the development of vegetable and animal production in the regions provided for in this Agreement, a total of not less than five thousand contos of reis.

5. To deposit the funds provided for in obligations nos. 1 and 3, in the Bank of Brazil, to be applied in accordance with instructions which will be approved by the Minister of Agriculture.

6. To assure the utilization, in the execution of this plan, of all fields, installations and equipment of the Division for the Development of Vegetable Production, as well as the technical collaboration of all other agencies of the Ministry of Agriculture as may become necessary.

CLAUSE FOURTH. The Coordinator of Inter-American Affairs, on his part, assumes the following obligations:

1. To contribute the amount of one million dollars, for the first year of operation of this Agreement, in two sums of one-half million dollars, the first after the signing of this contract, and the other when the Brazilian Government deposits with the Bank of Brazil the amount of five thousand contos of reis, in accordance with the obligation in item no. 1, Clause 3, assumed by the same.

2. To contribute one million dollars, during the first half of September, 1943.

3. To send and to maintain in Brazil, during the duration of the present Agreement, North-American technicians specialized in the matters pertaining to this Agreement, paying their salaries, traveling expenses and per diem.

4. To facilitate, as far as possible, the acquisition of specialized material which may be necessary for the execution of this Agreement.

5. To deposit the contributions stipulated in Items 1 and 2 of this Clause, with the Bank of Brazil, at the disposal of the Minister of Agriculture, in a special account for the Brazilian-American Food Production Commission, to be expended in accordance with provisions of Clause 5, letters c and d.

CLAUSE FIFTH. For the execution of this Agreement:

(a) There will be constituted a special Commission which shall be called the Brazilian-American Food Production Commission, composed of:

> 1 — The Director of the Division for the Development of Vegetable Production who will serve as President of the Commission;
>
> 2 — the Chief Food Production Specialist designated by the Coordinator of Inter-American Affairs.

(b) The seat of the Brazilian-American Food Production Commission will be in Rio de Janeiro, being subject to transfer to another city in the judgment of the Minister of Agriculture.

(c) The application of the resources at the disposition of the Brazilian-American Commission, and its presentation of accounts will be in accordance with instructions to be drawn up by said Commission and to be approved by the Minister of Agriculture.

(d) The expenditures made for the account of the Brazilian and American contributions, consisting of item 1 of Clause 3, and items 1 and 2 of Clause 4, will be duly recorded in appropriate accounting procedure, to be submitted for the approval of the Minister of Agriculture after having been duly examined and passed upon by the two members composing the Brazilian-American Commission.

(e) The vouchers of the expenditures incurred by the Division for the Development of Vegetable Production from the funds set forth in item 2 letters a and c, and item 3 of clause 3 will be subject to the accounting procedure set forth in the regulations now in effect, it being understood that a special copy of all of the vouchers will be supplied for the information of the American member of the Brazilian-American Food Production Commission.

(f) The voucher of the expenditures incurred under the ordinary budget, consisting of item 2, letter b, and item 4, of clause 3, will be made in accordance with the requirements of Brazilian public accounting, there being sent, however, to the Brazilian-American Food Production Commission a copy of the distribution of the credits made to the Fiscal authorities of the States included in the area of the present Agreement.

(g) It is understood that all improvements made under the provisions of the present Agreement will remain the property of the Brazilian Government.

CLAUSE SIXTH. The present Agreement will be for the duration of two years, counting from the date of its signature, and may be extended in the judgment of the contracting parties.

In witness whereof, the undersigned, duly authorized thereto, sign and seal the present Agreement in duplicate in the English and Portuguese languages.

[SEAL]   JEFFERSON CAFFERY
          NELSON A. ROCKEFELLER
[SEAL]   OSWALDO ARANHA
          APOLONIO SALES

(3) Economic Cooperation with Mexico

(a) Agreement between the Governments of the United States and the United Mexican States Providing for Temporary Migration of Mexican Agricultural Workers, Effected by Exchange of Notes, Signed August 4, 1942 [1]

The Department of State announced on August 6 that an arrangement had been made between the Government of the United States and the Government of Mexico to make possible the temporary migration of Mexican agricultural workers to the United States to meet the increasing demand for farm labor caused by the war emergency.

At the request of the Department of Agriculture, the War Manpower Commission, and other appropriate agencies of this Government, and after the United States Employment Service had certified to the existence of certain shortages of agricultural workers in the Southwest, the Department of State proposed to the Mexican Government a plan for this migration. It was pointed out by the Department of Agriculture and other agencies that the enrolment of men in the armed services, the movement of farm workers into industry, and the Government's program to increase agricultural production to meet wartime needs were causing a shortage of agricultural labor which could not be met by the recruiting of workers in the United States.

The arrangement made with the Mexican Government is administered by the Farm Security Administration of the Department of Agriculture in cooperation with other interested agencies.[2]

(i) The Mexican Minister of Foreign Affairs (Padilla) to the American Ambassador (Messersmith), August 4, 1942

[Translation]

No. 312

MR. AMBASSADOR:

I have the honor to refer to the matter presented by the Embassy worthily in Your Excellency's charge regarding the possibility that the Government of Mexico authorize the departure of Mexican workers for the United States and the conditions under which such emigration can be effected.

[1] Executive Agreement Series 278.
[2] Department of State, Bulletin, VII, p. 689.

This Department considers itself under the obligation, first of all, of pointing out the importance for the country at the present moment of conserving intact its human material, indispensable for the development of the program of continental defense to which the Government of Mexico is jointly obligated and in which, by very urgent recommendation of the Head of the Executive Power, the intensification of activities and especially agricultural production take first rank. Nevertheless, the need for workers which exists in some parts of the United States having been laid before the President of the Republic himself, and the First Magistrate, being desirous of not scanting the cooperation which he has been offering to the Government worthily represented by Your Excellency in the measure that the Nation's resources permit, has been pleased to decide that no obstacles be placed in the way of the departure of such nationals as desire to emigrate, temporarily, for the performance of the tasks in which their services may be required and that no other essential conditions be fixed than those which are required by circumstances and those established by legal provisions in force in the two countries.

For the purpose of determining the scope of this matter it was agreed, as Your Excellency is aware, to treat it as a matter between States, and in order to examine it in all its aspects, it was deemed necessary to hold a meeting of Mexican and American experts, who have just completed their task, having already submitted the recommendations which they formulated and which, duly signed, are sent enclosed with this communication.

The conclusions in reference have been examined with all care, and the Government of Mexico gives them its full approval. I beg Your Excellency to be good enough to take steps that the Government of the United States of America may, if it sees fit, do likewise, in order that this matter may be concluded and that the proper instructions may be issued, consequently, to the various official agencies which are to intervene therein, and in this way the arrangement which has been happily arrived at may be immediately effective.

I avail myself of the opportunity to renew to Your Excellency the assurances of my highest and most distinguished consideration.

(ii) The American Ambassador (Messersmith) to the Mexican Minister of Foreign Affairs (Padilla), August 4, 1942

No. 503

EXCELLENCY:

I have the honor to acknowledge the receipt of Your Excellency's Note No. 312 of August 4, 1942, regarding the temporary migration of Mexican workers to the United States to engage in agricultural work, the subject-matter of which was presented by the Embassy some days ago.

Due note has been taken of the considerations expressed in Your Excellency's Note under acknowledgment with respect to the maintenance of indispensable labor within the Republic of Mexico for the development of the Continental Defense Program, especially agricultural production, to which the Government of Mexico is committed. My Government is fully conscious of these commitments and at the same time is deeply appreciative of the attitude of His Excellency President Manuel Ávila Camacho for the sincere and helpful manner in which he has extended the cooperation of the Government of Mexico within the resources of the nation to permit Mexican nationals temporarily to emigrate to the United States for the purpose of aiding in our own agricultural production.

In order to determine the scope of the conditions under which Mexican labor might proceed to the United States for the purpose set forth above, it was agreed that the negotiations should be between our two Governments, and Your Excellency was kind enough to arrange for the meeting of Mexican and American representatives to submit recommendations which they have duly completed. Your Excellency was good enough to enclose a copy of these recommendations in the Spanish with your Note under reference.

My Government accepts these recommendations as a satisfactory arrangement, and I am authorized to inform Your Excellency that my Government will place this arrangement in effect immediately, and in confirmation thereof I attach hereto the English text of the arrangement as agreed upon.

Accept, Excellency, the renewed assurances of my highest and most distinguished consideration.

(iii) *Recommendations of Mexican and American Commissioners, dated July 23, 1942*

In order to effect a satisfactory arrangement whereby Mexican agricultural labor may be made available for use in the United States and at the same time provide means whereby this labor will be adequately protected while out of Mexico, the following general provisions are suggested:

(1) It is understood that Mexicans contracting to work in the United States shall not be engaged in any military service.

(2) Mexicans entering the United States as a result of this understanding shall not suffer discriminatory acts of any kind in accordance with the Executive Order No. 8802 issued at the White House, June 25, 1941.[1]

(3) Mexicans entering the United States under this understanding shall enjoy the guarantees of transportation, living expenses and repatriation established in Article 29 of the Mexican Labor Law.

(4) Mexicans entering the United States under this understanding shall not be employed to displace other workers, or for the purpose of reducing rates of pay previously established.

In order to implement the application of the general principles mentioned above the following specific clauses are established.

(When the word "employer" is used hereinafter it shall be understood to mean the Farm Security Administration of the Department of Agriculture of the United States of America; the word "sub-employer" shall mean the owner or operator of the farm or farms in the United States on which the Mexican will be employed; the word "worker" hereinafter used shall refer to the Mexican farm laborer entering the United States under this understanding.)

CONTRACTS

a. Contracts will be made between the employer and the worker under the supervision of the Mexican Government. (Contracts must be written in Spanish.)

b. The employer shall enter into a contract with the sub-employer, with a view to proper observance of the principles embodied in this understanding.

ADMISSION

a. The Mexican health authorities will, at the place whence the worker comes, see that he meets the necessary physical conditions.

[1] 6 *Fed. Reg.*, p. 3109.

TRANSPORTATION

a. All transportation and living expenses from the place of origin to destination, and return, as well as expenses incurred in the fulfillment of any requirements of a migratory nature shall be met by the employer.

b. Personal belongings of the workers up to a maximum of 35 kilos per person shall be transported at the expense of the employer.

c. In accord with the intent of Article 29 of the Mexican Federal Labor Law it is expected that the employer will collect all or part of the cost accruing under (*a*) and (*b*) of transportation from the sub-employer.

WAGES AND EMPLOYMENT

a. (1) Wages to be paid the worker shall be the same as those paid for similar work to other agricultural laborers in the respective regions of destination; but in no case shall this wage be less than 30 cents per hour (U. S. currency); piece rates shall be so set as to enable the worker of average ability to earn the prevailing wage.

a. (2) On the basis of prior authorization from the Mexican Government salaries lower than those established in the previous clause may be paid those emigrants admitted into the United States as members of the family of the worker under contract and who, when they are in the field, are able also to become agricultural laborers but who, by their condition of age or sex cannot carry out the average amount of ordinary work.

b. The worker shall be exclusively employed as an agricultural laborer for which he has been engaged; any change from such type of employment shall be made with the express approval of the worker and with the authority of the Mexican Government.

c. There shall be considered illegal any collection by reason of commission or for any other concept demanded of the worker.

d. Work for minors under 14 years shall be strictly prohibited, and they shall have the same schooling opportunities as those enjoyed by children of other agricultural laborers.

e. Workers domiciled in the migratory labor camps or at any other place of employment under this understanding shall be free to obtain articles for their personal consumption, or that of their families, wherever it is most convenient for them.

f. Housing conditions, sanitary and medical services enjoyed by workers admitted under this understanding shall be identical to those enjoyed by the other agricultural workers in the same localities.

g. Workers admitted under this understanding shall enjoy as regards occupational diseases and accidents the same guarantees enjoyed by other agricultural workers under United States legislation.

h. Groups of workers admitted under this understanding shall elect their own representatives to deal with the employer, but it is understood that all such representatives shall be working members of the group. The Mexican consuls in their respective jurisdiction shall make every effort to extend all possible protection to all these workers on any questions affecting them.

i. For such time as they are unemployed under a period equal to 75% of the period (exclusive of Sundays) for which the workers have been contracted they shall receive a subsistence allowance at the rate of $3.00 per day.

For the remaining 25% of the period for which the workers have been contracted during which the workers may be unemployed they shall receive subsistence on the same bases that are established for farm laborers in the United States.

Should the cost of living rise this will be a matter for reconsideration.

The master contracts for workers submitted to the Mexican Government shall contain definite provisions for computation of subsistence and payments under this understanding.

j. The term of the contract shall be made in accordance with the authorities of the respective countries.

k. At the expiration of the contract under this understanding, and if the same is not renewed, the authorities of the United States shall consider illegal, from an immigration point of view, the continued stay of the worker in the territory of the United States, exception made of cases of physical impossibility.

SAVINGS FUND

(*a*) The respective agency of the Government of the United States shall be responsible for the safekeeping of the sums contributed by the Mexican workers toward the formation of their Rural Savings Fund, until such sums are transferred to the Mexican Agricultural Credit Bank which shall assume responsibilities for the deposit, for their safekeeping and for their application, or, in the absence of these, for their return.

(*b*) The Mexican Government through the Banco de Credito Agricola will take care of the security of the savings of the workers to be used for payment of the agricultural implements, which may be made available to the Banco de Credito Agricola in accordance with exportation permits for shipment to Mexico with the understanding that the Farm Security Administration will recommend priority treatment for such implements.

NUMBERS

As it is impossible to determine at this time the number of workers who may be needed in the United States for agricultural labor employment, the employer shall advise the Mexican Government from time to time as to the number needed. The Government of Mexico shall determine in each case the number of workers who may leave the country without detriment to its national economy.

GENERAL PROVISIONS

It is understood that, with reference to the departure from Mexico of Mexican workers, who are not farm laborers, there shall govern in understandings reached by agencies of the respective Governments the same fundamental principles which have been applied here to the departure of farm labor.

It is understood that the employers will cooperate with such other agencies of the Government of the United States in carrying this understanding into effect whose authority under the laws of the United States are such as to contribute to the effectuation of the understanding.

Either government shall have the right to renounce this understanding, giving appropriate notification to the other Government 90 days in advance.

This understanding may be formalized by an exchange of notes between the

Ministry of Foreign Affairs of the Republic of Mexico and the Embassy of the United States of America in Mexico.

MEXICO CITY, the 23rd of July 1942.

MEXICAN COMMISSIONERS

<table>
<tr>
<td>E. HIDALGO
acting as representative of the Foreign Office.</td>
<td>ABRAHAM J. NAVAS
acting as representative of the Department of Labor and Social Provision.</td>
</tr>
</table>

AMERICAN COMMISSIONERS

J. F. McGURK

Counselor of the American Embassy in Mexico

<table>
<tr>
<td>JOHN O. WALKER
Assistant Administrator Farm Security Administration. (Department of Agriculture.)</td>
<td>DAVID MEEKER
Assistant Director Office of Agricultural War Relations. (Department of Agriculture.)</td>
</tr>
</table>

An agreement between the Governments of the United States and Mexico to make possible the temporary migration of non-agricultural workers to the United States has also been concluded.[1] The first workers to be brought in under the new agreement were 6,000 maintenance-of-way workers for southwestern railroads, the need for whom had been certified by the War Manpower Commission. Like the agreement of August 4, 1942 for the bringing in of agricultural workers, the new agreement provided guaranties as to wage rates, living conditions, and repatriation for the Mexican workers and specified that they were not to be employed to replace other workers or for the purpose of reducing rates of pay previously established in any industry in which they might be employed. The arrangement also provided that, as temporary residents of the United States, workers brought in under the agreement should be exempted from compulsory military service in the armed forces of the United States.

Negotiations leading to the agreement, dated April 30, 1943, were opened with the Mexican Government at the request of the War Manpower Commission and other interested agencies, and the selecting and contracting of workers thereunder are administered by the War Manpower Commission. In requesting the Department of State to open negotiations with the Mexican Government, the interested agencies pointed out that serious shortages of manpower existed in certain industries because of the enrolment of men in the armed services and because of the expansion of defense industries, and stated that these shortages could not be met by recruiting workers in the United States.

The agreement of August 4, 1942 for the temporary migration of Mexican agricultural workers to the United States was modified by an exchange of notes, also dated April 30, 1943.[2] The modifications represented no basic changes in

[1] Department of State, *Bulletin*, VIII, p. 376.

[2] The date of the exchange is given as April 26 in an announcement in *ibid.*, IX, p. 86.

principles laid down in the original agreement but consisted in writing into the text thereof clearer statements of procedures than were provided for under the original agreement.

(b) Agreement between the United States and Mexico on Rehabilitation of Certain Mexican National Railways, Effected by Exchange of Notes between the Mexican Minister of Foreign Relations (Padilla) and the American Ambassador (Messersmith), Signed November 18, 1942 [1]

(i) *The Mexican Minister of Foreign Relations (Padilla) to the American Ambassador (Messersmith)*

MR. AMBASSADOR:

In conformity with Resolution II of the Third Consultative Meeting of the Ministers for Foreign Affairs of the American Republics held at Rio de Janeiro from the 15th to the 28th of January of the present year, the Mexican Government has used all the resources which it has at its disposal to bring about the mobilization of the economic resources of the Republic, particularly in so far as concerns the production of strategic materials necessary for the defense of the hemisphere. In this regard I am pleased to inform Your Excellency that this production is being achieved at a constantly accelerated pace for it is the firm intention of Mexico to unite its action with that of the United Nations in order to bring about definitive victory against the powers of the Axis.

With this in view agreements have been made through which Mexico furnishes to the United States its exportable surplus of a long list of essential products.

I have the satisfaction, at the same time, to inform Your Excellency that Mexican economy has reacted favorably to the constantly accelerated strain to which it has been subjected as a consequence of this increase in production and also that there are indications which permit the assumption that the materials which will be furnished in 1943 will exceed by far the quantities which have been made available during the current year.

Unfortunately, the capacity which Mexico has to produce articles which are needed with so much urgency is greater than the possibilities of the Mexican system of transport to carry them from the mines, fields or forests where they are extracted or produced to the places where they are exported, manufactured or consumed.

[1] *Executive Agreement Series* 289; Department of State, *Bulletin*, VII, p. 954.

The burden which is now being borne by the National Railways surpasses by far the maximum freight limit which it could reasonably have been supposed that they would carry in time of peace. If the United Nations in general, and Mexico and the United States of America in particular, are to benefit to the maximum by our common effort, it will be necessary that they take rapid and effective steps to put the National Railways of Mexico in a position to transport a war-time burden much larger in volume than that which they actually can move.

In synthesis, the matter of transport is today the real key to the Mexican-American program of joint production and economic cooperation in the prosecution of the war.

In my opinion, the best proof that the Government of the United States recognizes the fundamental importance of this question of transport is the careful attention which Your Excellency has personally given to it as well as the attitude of your Government in sending to Mexico at the suggestion of my Government, a mission of technical railway men who will put the fruit of their experience at the service of the officials of the Mexican Railways for the purpose of bettering conditions of their operation and maintenance as well as to expedite the current of traffic.

However, in order that our efforts may be crowned with the desired success it is urgent to carry out basic improvements in the lines themselves, in their equipment and in their motive power. For this the collaboration of the Government as well as the industry of the United States is indispensable.

I think at the same time that the operation of the railways should be improved in order to obtain the greatest efficiency in the utilization of the resources already existing and of those which may be obtained.

My Government, consequently, would be gratified if the Government of the United States of America would consider it possible to strengthen the present mission of railway technicians including in it for a period of six months — or for a longer time, which would be determined officially by means of an exchange of notes at the expiration of the term here foreseen — an official of a high category possessing ample knowledge of this subject; also a limited number of specialists who could assist him in carrying out a complete examination of the National Railways of Mexico who could likewise make available to them the results of their investigations and who could aid them with their advice.

I desire to assure Your Excellency that the Government of Mexico on its part will see to it that the necessary steps are taken — from the point of view of the organization and functioning of the National Railways — to obtain the maximum efficiency. With regard to this it would gratefully receive the suggestions of the North American Railway mission.

I take [etc.]

(*ii*) *The American Ambassador (Messersmith) to the Mexican Minister of Foreign Relations (Padilla)*

EXCELLENCY:

I acknowledge with appreciation Your Excellency's cordial note of November 18, 1942 outlining the constructive work which the Government of Mexico has accomplished in implementing Resolution II of the Third Meeting of Ministers of Foreign Affairs of the American Republics at Rio de Janeiro through the mobilization of its economic resources, particularly in the production of strategic materials essential for the defense of the hemisphere. Your Excellency has indicated that the production of Mexico of materials for use in the prosecution of the war in which both of our countries are now engaged is being pressed to the limit, but you appropriately point out that unless certain basic changes and improvements are made in the structure and operation of the Mexican National Railways, these lines will not be able to carry the unusual wartime peak load which is now and which will be increasingly placed upon them. It is made clear that unless this situation is promptly corrected, the war interests of our two countries and of the other United Nations will suffer. You refer to the joint efforts to improve the situation which have already been made through the cooperation of our two governments and request that this collaboration be extended materially.

The Government of the United States is in full accord with the thoughts expressed in Your Excellency's note under acknowledgment, and desires promptly to extend the added measure of collaboration which is essential to solve our mutual problems. Agencies of the Government of the United States have agreed to purchase from Mexican producers extensive quantities of a long list of strategic commodities. These are materials which are urgently needed by the United States in providing raw materials for the manufacture of war equipment for its own forces, for those of Mexico, and for those of the other United Nations. Were it not for the augmented strain being placed on the Mexican National Railways because of United States purchases of strategic materials for its armed forces, the extensive rehabilitation of certain parts of the system and the furnishing of additional technical assistance and labor would not be necessary for the normal needs of the railway lines. My Government considers that it would not be fair to expect Mexico to bear this disproportionate burden. Consequently, my Government is prepared to pay for its equitable share of the cost of the improvements which must be made in order that the materials in question may be transported to American war plants.

I have noted with gratification that, in consideration of the assistance by my Government, the Mexican Government will on its part see to it that there are taken, from an organizational and operating point of view, all measures necessary to achieve optimum efficiency of the Mexican National Railways and that in this connection it will welcome the suggestions and advice of the United States Railway Mission.

It is my understanding, from the informal conversations thus far held on the subject, that it will be acceptable to the Mexican Government if my Government undertakes, through the Office of the Coordinator of Inter-American Affairs, the following measures of rehabilitation on certain sections of the Mexican Railways:

(1) The lines to be covered are —
 (a) Main line extending south from United States border at Laredo, Texas, via Monterrey-Saltillo-San Luis Potosí to Mexico;
 (b) East-west line from Torreón via Paredon to Monterrey;
 (c) Main line southward from Cordoba and Puerto Mexico via Jésús Carranza and Ixtepec through Suchiate on the Guatemalan border;
 (d) Line from Chihuahua to Torreón;

(2) Bear the cost of all materials and equipment which the United States Railway Mission shall agree with the Mexican Government to be necessary for the rehabilitation of the aforedescribed lines, and which material and equipment must be obtained in the United States;

(3) Pay for such rails and fastenings produced in Mexico and agreed between the United States Railway Mission and the Mexican Government to be necessary for this same undertaking;

(4) Furnish without cost to Mexico the United States technicians agreed between the United States Railway Mission and the Mexican Government to be necessary;

(5) Bear the cost of repairing in the United States such Mexican National Railways motive power and other equipment which shall be mutually agreed upon shall be sent to the United States for repair under this particular rehabilitation program;

(6) Bear the cost of such additional Mexican road gangs as the Mexican Government and the Railway Mission mutually agree are necessary to put into adequate operating condition the road-bed of the lines aforementioned. Expenditures for this purpose will, of course, be ones of a character which the Mexican National Railways could not be expected to bear for normal maintenance purposes.

I am confident that it will be appreciated that for fiscal and accounting reasons it is necessary that the expenditures which the Governments of Mexico and the United States agree are desirable be first approved by the Chief of the United States Railway Mission in Mexico City so that he can certify to the appropriate agency of my Government that in his judgment the expenditures are necessary at a given time and in the amount stipulated. I have every confidence that there will be at no time major differences of opinion concerning the time or extent of aid which cannot be resolved by the frank and friendly consultative procedure which has so happily characterized the relationships between our two Governments.

In addition to the materials and equipment, which in the opinion of the two Governments it will be necessary to secure from the United States, there will undoubtedly be equipment and materials which the facilities of Mexican industry can supply, which would be furnished for the rehabilitation program by the Mexican Government.

My Government fully agrees with the view of the Mexican Government that this rehabilitation program must go forward with optimum rapidity unless our joint war efforts are to suffer.

I avail myself [etc.].

To facilitate the free and unrestricted use of Mexican railroad equipment for the transportation of necessary war material, the Treasury Department on February 4, 1943 issued regulations barring all legal and other proceedings which might interfere with such use and operation of Mexican railroad equipment within the United States.[1] This action was taken at the request of the Government of Mexico, the State Department, the Board of Economic Warfare, and other interested Government agencies.

The new regulations were intended to remove an important bottleneck in the transportation of materials from Mexico to the United States. At that time there was a large volume of war materials which was brought to the Mexican border on Mexican freight cars and there unloaded and reloaded into United States freight cars. This procedure, officials stated, was both time-consuming and wasteful of the nation's wartime freight car capacity.

Treasury officials said that this Government had been negotiating with the Government of Mexico for several months regarding the possibility of materials moving from Mexico to the United States on Mexican railroad equipment. One of the major stumbling blocks to this important wartime measure, however, had been the fear that such equipment might be seized by creditors.

To meet this wartime necessity, the Foreign Funds Control of the Treasury Department, after full consultation with the State Department, the Board of Economic Warfare and the Mexican authorities, issued General Ruling No. 15. Under this Ruling, all Mexican railroad equipment within the United States was accorded immunity against claimants seeking to attach or otherwise seize such property. Moreover, under this Ruling no legal, equitable or possessory interest could be obtained in such rolling stock and equipment by virtue of any judicial process unless a Treasury license was first obtained.

Officials stated that a specific exemption from the immunity granted by this Ruling was made in favor of service and repair charges and other claims arising

[1] Treasury Department, *Documents Pertaining to Foreign Funds Control*, p. 104; 8 *Fed. Reg.*, p. 1674.

out of the operation within the United States of Mexican railroad property on or after the date of this Ruling.

It was pointed out that since this property would not otherwise be brought into the United States, the General Ruling worked no hardship on American creditors. Also, it was stated by Treasury representatives that this Ruling protected only Mexican railroad property, as defined therein, and did not apply to any other assets.

General Ruling No. 15 was issued pursuant to section 5 (*b*) of the Trading with the Enemy Act, as amended by the First War Powers Act, 1941.

(c) Agreement Reached by the President of the United States (Roosevelt) and the President of the Republic of Mexico (Ávila Camacho), During Reciprocal Visits. Department of State Announcement, April 29, 1943 [1]

As a result of the welcome opportunity afforded by the reciprocal visits made by President Roosevelt and President Ávila Camacho, respectively, in Mexican and United States territory, the two Presidents reached the following agreement:

1. It is considered desirable that expert economists undertake the study of disturbances in the balance of international payments and the related economic situation of the Republic of Mexico resulting from the peculiar circumstances of war economy in order to recommend appropriate measures of regulation and adjustment.

2. Such measures would have as their objective the handling of economic relationships between the two countries in such a way that the production of strategic materials by Mexico should not be prejudiced and that their quantity should not be lessened and in order to ensure the stability of such production and its possible development, it is recognized that the cooperation of the United States will be indispensable.

3. To this end and in order to assure that the economic relations between the two countries be continued on the most equitable basis, it has been decided:

I. To create an economic committee made up of two representatives from each country which will study the balance of international payments and the resulting economic situation of the Republic of Mexico and formulate as the result of such study a program for economic cooperation.

II. This committee will fix as its place of meeting either Mexico City or Washington and in the course of its studies the committee will be afforded by both governments all necessary information.

III. This committee will commence its studies May 15 and will conclude its deliberations not later than June 15 of the present year.

---

[1] Department of State, *Bulletin*, VIII, p. 376.

On May 19 President Roosevelt announced the appointment of the Honorable Wayne Chatfield Taylor, Under Secretary of Commerce, and Mr. Harry D. White, Assistant to the Secretary of the Treasury, as the experts of this Government to serve with the two experts appointed by the Mexican Government, Mr. Valentin R. Garfias, a well-known mining engineer, and Mr. Evaristo Araiza, general manager of the Monterrey Steel Works, to formulate a program for economic cooperation between the two Governments.[1]

3. PRODUCTION AND PROCUREMENT OF RUBBER

[See *Documents, IV, 1941–42*, p. 378.]

Agreements along the lines of the Agreement of June 16, 1942 with Costa Rica,[2] have been signed since July 1, 1942 to secure for the United Nations war effort the maximum possible amount of rubber produced in the Western Hemisphere with the following countries: Colombia, July 3; Bolivia, July 15; Ecuador, July 21; Honduras, August 3; Trinidad and British Guiana, August 12; British Honduras, August 18; El Salvador, August 24; Guatemala, September 10; Mexico, September 11; Panama, September 14; and Venezuela, October 16.[3]

Under an exchange of notes announced on February 19, 1943 a Colombian-American Commission was established charged with the direction of a general policy of procurement of rubber in that country.[4]

A supplementary agreement to that entered into April 23, 1942 was signed on February 18, 1943 by Peru and the United States, providing for an air-transportation network to facilitate the rubber program.[5]

On April 3, 1943, notes were exchanged between the American Chargé d'Affaires ad interim at San José and the Secretary of State for Foreign Affairs of Costa Rica, effecting a supplementary agreement[6] relating to cooperative rubber investigations in Costa Rica for the purpose of defining more clearly certain procedures affecting the sale of products grown on the lands used by the rubber experiment station and in order to facilitate the continued development of rubber investigations and demonstration plantings in Costa Rica. The supplementary agreement is to remain in force as though it were an integral part of the agreement between the United States and Costa Rica effected by an exchange of notes signed April 19 and June 16, 1941, between the American Chargé d'Affaires ad interim at San José and the Secretary of State for Foreign Affairs of Costa Rica,[7] which provided for cooperation between the Governments of the two countries in conducting investigations with respect to the methods of rubber-cultivation, the development of superior strains of rubber, disease control, use of intercrops, and other matters, with a view to the successful establishment of a self-sustaining rubber-culture industry. The agreement became effective on June 16, 1941, to remain in force until six months from the day on which either Government shall have given written notice to the other Government of its intention to terminate the agreement, provided, however, that the agreement shall not remain in force after June 30, 1943, except at the option of the United

---

[1] *Ibid.*, p. 457.
[2] *Documents, IV, 1941–42*, p. 378.
[3] Department of State, *Bulletin*, VII, p. 650, 690, 698, 713, 723, 752, 773, and 838.
[4] *Ibid.*, VIII, p. 174.
[5] *Ibid.*, p. 175.
[6] *Ibid.*, p. 353; *Executive Agreement Series* 318.
[7] *Executive Agreement Series* 222.

States Department of Agriculture, which option shall be notified to the Government of Costa Rica by the Government of the United States at least one month prior to that date.

In a note addressed to the Costa Rican Secretary of State by the American Ambassador on June 21, 1943, the desire to exercise the above option was made known, but in view of the fact that notice had not been given within the one month period specified, it was suggested that the two Governments by exchange of notes record their understanding that the agreement of April 19, 1941, as amended, "shall continue in force after June 30, 1943, and shall remain in force thereafter subject to termination on a notice of six months given by either Government." This suggestion was agreed to by the Government of Costa Rica in a note dated July 1, 1943.[1]

4. COFFEE MARKETING AGREEMENT

(1) *Non-Signatory Quota. Department of State Release, July 17, 1942* [2]

[See *Documents, III, 1940–41*, p. 97 and *IV, 1941–42*, p. 380.]

Executive Order 8863 of August 21, 1941,[3] allocating for the present quota-year the quota provided by Article VII of the Inter-American Coffee Agreement for countries which are not signatories of the agreement, terminates on September 1, 1942, one month before the end of the quota-year. It has been decided not to allocate the non-signatory quota for the year beginning October 1, 1942. The effect of this decision will be to facilitate the entry into the United States of coffee from non-signatory countries which are in a position to supply it under the non-signatory quota.

The Bureau of Customs announced that beginning September 1, 1942 provisions would be made at customs ports of entry to permit importers to present entries for consumption covering coffee produced in countries not signatories of the agreement.

It was announced that no order would be issued allocating the non-signatory quota for the year beginning October 1, 1942. The unexhausted portion of the quota as of August 15, 1942 was said to be approximately 15,000,000 pounds.[4]

5. CONTROL OF EXPORTS TO THE AMERICAN REPUBLICS

The system of export control developed under the authority of the Act of July 2, 1940, underwent a radical change in the course of the period under review. The changes were introduced on the basis of agreements with the countries concerned, negotiated by the Department of State and the Board of Economic Warfare acting jointly. The main objective of these agreements was to secure precise requirements figures for each country in order to provide greater assurance that the limited shipping facilities currently available are utilized to the best advantage. For details, see Chapter II, p. 137.

[1] *Ibid.*, 335.
[2] Department of State, *Bulletin*, VII, p. 635.
[3] 6 *Fed. Reg.*, p. 4319; *Documents, IV, 1941–42*, p. 382.
[4] Department of State, *Bulletin*, VII, p. 724.

6. STABILIZATION AGREEMENTS

(1) *Agreement with Brazil, Signed July 6, 1942, Extending the Stabilization Agreement of July 15, 1937. Statement of the Secretary of the Treasury (Morgenthau), July 6, 1942* [1]

On July 6, 1942 the Secretary of the Treasury, Henry Morgenthau, Jr., and the Chargé d'Affaires of the United States of Brazil in Washington, Fernando Lobo, signed an agreement extending to July 15, 1947 the Stabilization Agreement entered into on July 15, 1937.[2]

Under this agreement, as extended, the United States will make dollar exchange available to the Government of the United States of Brazil for the purpose of stabilizing the Brazilian milreis — United States dollar rate of exchange up to a total amount of $100,000,000 and will sell gold to the United States of Brazil at such times and in such amounts as the Brazilian Government may request, also to a total amount of $100,000,000. In the agreement as originally drafted these two amounts were $60,000,000.

The extension of this Agreement between the Treasuries of the United States of America and the United States of Brazil and the increase in the facilities made available to Brazil under the Agreement, are a further evidence of the close and friendly relations existing between the two countries and constitute an assurance of continued cooperation between the two Treasuries.

The friendship and understanding symbolized by this and other agreements with our great sister republic in South America promise much for both a joint attack on the problems of the war and a solution for our common problems in the peace.

A similar agreement was signed with the Government of Cuba on the same date, in which it was provided that the unpaid-for-amount of gold should not at any time exceed $5,000,000.[2]

D. Transportation and Communications

1. INTER-AMERICAN HIGHWAY

(1) *Completion of the Inter-American Highway as a Pioneer Road. Department of State Release, July 28, 1942* [3]

[See *Documents, IV, 1941–42*, p. 407.]

Arrangements have been concluded with Guatemala, El Salvador, Honduras, Nicaragua, Costa Rica, and Panama for the immediate linking by a pioneer road of the already-constructed segments of the Inter-

[1] *Ibid.*, p. 623.
[2] See *Treaty Information Bulletin*, No. 94, July 1937, p. 17.
[3] Department of State, *Bulletin*, VII, p. 661.

American Highway between the Mexican-Guatemalan border and Panamá City. This will permit road traffic at an early date from the end of the existing standard-guage railway in Mexico to the Canal Zone. The necessary surveying is already under way, and construction work will shortly be started, at the expense of the United States Government.

The plans which have now been approved call for the construction of approximately 625 miles of new all-weather pioneer road to link about 1,000 miles of road which have already been constructed in Central America and Panama. The proposed minimum construction standards for these new links provide for a roadway width of from 10 to 16 feet with an 8-inch gravel surface, average maximum grades of 10 per cent, and average maximum curvature of 30 meters.

The completion of this road will not only be of strategic importance, in that it will link the continental United States with the Canal Zone by a wholly overland transportation system, but also it will alleviate in some degree the transportation difficulties of the Central American countries, which have hitherto depended in large measure upon water transportation. It is also expected that the contemplated construction will ease the economic difficulties which the Central American countries are facing as a result of the disruption of their foreign trade caused by the war. Arrangements have been made for the fullest possible use of local facilities, including labor, equipment, and materials.

The plan to complete the Inter-American Highway as a pioneer road will not modify the plan to construct a permanent Inter-American Highway contemplated by the act of December 26, 1941. By this act Congress authorized the expenditure of $20,000,000 toward the construction of a permanent Inter-American Highway in collaboration with the Central American Republics. The present plan will, however, permit through traffic at a much earlier date than originally contemplated and will facilitate the construction of the permanent highway, on the line of which the pioneer road is to be built.

The Secretary of Commerce and the Sub-Secretary of Finance and Public Credit of Mexico jointly announced on August 12, 1942 [1] that an agreement has been reached whereby the Mexican Highway credit of $30,000,000, announced on November 19, 1941, may be used in installments exceeding $10,000,000 a year in order to expedite the completion of roads now under construction, including the Inter-American Highway from Mexico City to the border of Guatemala.

Completion of the Highway through Honduras was assured by an agreement signed at Washington, September 9 and October 26, 1942 in an exchange of notes between the Minister of Honduras and the Secretary of State (*Executive Agreement Series* 296).

[1] *Ibid.*, p. 704.

E. Cultural and Humanitarian Relations

[See *Documents, IV, 1941–42*, p. 411.]

1. HEALTH AND SANITATION

(1) *Agreement with Bolivia Effected by Exchange of Notes, July 15 and 16, 1942.*[1] *Announcement of the Department of State, August 15, 1942*[2]

By an exchange of notes dated July 15 and 16, 1942 an agreement was entered into between the Government of the United States of America and the Bolivian Government for the cooperative development of a health and sanitation program in Bolivia.

Under the terms of the agreement the Government of the United States, through the agency of the Coordinator of Inter-American Affairs, will provide an amount not to exceed $1,000,000 to be expended toward the development of the program. A group of medical and sanitation experts from the United States will work in close cooperation with the appropriate officers of the Bolivian Government, and technical advice and expert assistance by medical and sanitation specialists will be made available by the United States to the Bolivian Government should the need for such consultation arise. Arrangements for the detailed execution of each project, and the expenditure of the funds for the purpose, will be agreed upon by the Chief Medical Officer and the appropriately designated officer of the Bolivian Government. The projects include:

1. General disease control by epidemiological procedures and by clinics and public education.

2. Malaria control.

3. Yellow-fever control.

4. Care of lepers.

5. Environmental sanitation.

The agreement was concluded in accordance with resolution XXX of the Third Meeting of the Ministers of Foreign Affairs of the American Republics, which met at Rio de Janeiro from January 15 to January 28, 1942. The resolution reads as follows:

[For text see *Documents, IV, 1941–42*, p. 324.]

(2) *Eleventh Pan American Sanitary Conference. Announcement of the Department of State, October 17, 1942*[3]

The Eleventh Pan American Sanitary Conference, which was held at Rio de Janeiro from September 7 to 18, 1942 at the invitation of the

---

[1] *Executive Agreement Series* 300; by an exchange of notes of February 18, 1943 Venezuela entered into a similar agreement (*Bulletin*, VIII, p. 354).

[2] *Ibid.*, VII, p. 703.   [3] *Ibid.*, p. 839.

Brazilian Government, was considered one of the most successful in this long series of important inter-American meetings. The Conference emphasized problems connected with the war situation and especially those related to continental defense.

Seventy-eight official delegates were present and all the 21 American Republics were represented. A group of officials of the Pan American Sanitary Bureau, headed by Dr. Hugh S. Cumming, Director of the Bureau and former Surgeon General of the United States Public Health Service, also attended. The Bureau is the permanent central organization of these Pan American Sanitary Conferences. Certain individuals affiliated with the Rockefeller Foundation, the Office of the Coordinator of Inter-American Affairs, and the Office of Vital Statistics, Bureau of the Census, were also present in their private capacities.

The United States delegation was as follows: Surgeon General Thomas Parran, Public Health Service; *chairman of the delegation;* Dr. E. L. Bishop, Director of Health, Tennessee Valley Authority; Surgeon Gilbert L. Dunahoo, Public Health Service, Chief of the Quarantine Office at the Port of Miami, Miami, Fla.; Dr. George C. Dunham, Director, Health and Sanitation Division, Office of the Coordinator of Inter-American Affairs; Brig. Gen., Medical Corps, United States Army; Surgeon W. H. Sebrell, Jr., Public Health Service; Capt. Charles S. Stephenson, Medical Corps, U.S.N., Bureau of Medicine and Surgery, United States Navy; Dr. Abel Wolman, School of Public Health, Johns Hopkins University, Baltimore, Md.; Philip P. Williams, Third Secretary, American Embassy, Rio de Janeiro, Brazil; *secretary of the delegation.*

The most important action taken by the Conference was the approval of Resolution I concerning continental defense and public health. This resolution provides for surveys to conserve and develop resources of medical supplies, to ascertain the geographic distribution of communicable diseases, to collect current health and epidemiological data, to inventory available stocks of supplies essential to the maintenance of health in order to assure their equitable domestic utilization and to make all surpluses available for continental defense, and to ascertain the medical and sanitary requirements in order to determine the essential needs which must be met from external sources. The Pan American Sanitary Bureau is charged with the responsibility of appointing a Committee of Experts, which will be available to consult with each country in order to assist in organizing these surveys. The resolution further provides that in the event of an actual or threatened epidemic in any country other countries upon request will furnish under the auspices of the Pan American Sanitary Bureau such assistance as may be possible; and, finally, the respective governments are urged to adopt extraordinary and precise methods to prevent the spreading of diseases through insect vectors and common carriers, utilizing the fullest cooperation between civil and military health authorities.

The Conference also took action to further the protection of public health on this continent in the interest of defense by adopting other resolutions dealing with military medical services, sanitary engineering, nutrition, milk, housing, standard national sanitary codes, the Pan American Highway, vital statistics, malaria, yellow fever, plague, exanthematic typhus fever, precautions against Chagas disease, influenza, tuberculosis, leprosy, and diarrhea and enteritis.

The Conference reelected Dr. Hugh S. Cumming as director of the Pan American Sanitary Bureau and decided that its next meeting should be held at Caracas, Venezuela, in 1946.

2. SOCIAL PLANNING

(1) *Inter-American Congress on Social Planning. Announcement of the Department of State, November 28, 1942* [1]

The Inter-American Congress on Social Planning was held at Santiago, Chile, from September 10 to September 16, 1942 at the invitation of the Chilean Government. The meeting was called in accordance with resolutions of the Inter-American Committee on Social Security established at Lima, Peru, in December 1940 by a group of persons who were guests of the Peruvian Government at the dedication of the Bank of Social Security Funds and the opening of the Workers' Hospital. The Committee was organized to make possible a systematic and continuous exchange of information among the social-security institutions of the American Republics, and it was planned that it would cooperate with the International Labor Office in attaining its objectives.

The organization of the Congress was entrusted to an Organizing Committee appointed by the Chilean Government and headed by the Chief of the Division of Social Welfare. The International Labor Office cooperated in the preparations for the meeting, and Mr. Oswaldo Stein of that Office was designated as a member of the Organizing Committee.

· · · · · · ·

At the invitation of the Chilean Government the Governing Body of the International Labor Office was represented by a tripartite delegation composed of Mr. Paul van Zeeland, former Premier of Belgium (Government Group), Mr. Clarence G. MacDavitt, of the United States (Employers' Group), and Mr. Robert J. Watt, of the United States (Workers' Group).

· · · · · · ·

[1] *Ibid.*, p. 970.

The principal results of the Congress were (1) the adoption of a declaration consisting of 16 resolutions concerning the extension and development of social security; and (2) the adoption of a resolution providing permanent statutes for the "Inter-American Conference on Social Security." This resolution also set up machinery designed to perfect and make permanent the organization of the Inter-American Committee on Social Security.

The Congress in its declaration took cognizance of the inalienable right of human beings to be afforded physical and economic protection against social and economic risks and adopted among other measures resolutions on the following subjects: Extension of social insurance to agricultural workers, domestic servants, and the self-employed; extension of social insurance to intellectual workers; social insurance against industrial accidents and occupational diseases; efficacy and economy of medical and pharmaceutical benefits in health-insurance plans; disability insurance; participation of employers and workers in the administration of social security; maintenance of insurance rights of mobilized persons; unification of biostatistical information; and protection of maternity, childhood, and adolescence.

The resolution establishing the Inter-American Conference on Social Security as a permanent agency of cooperation provided that the permanent Inter-American Committee on Social Security should give effect to the resolutions and recommendations adopted by the First Congress, should formulate the agenda for future meetings, and should contribute by every means to the attainment of the purposes of the Inter-American Conference on Social Security. The resolution further provided that the Permanent Committee shall consist of one regular member and at least one substitute member from each country represented at the Congress who are to be appointed by their respective governments.

3. EXCHANGE OF STUDENTS

(1) Cooperative Training Program for Peruvian Students in the United States. Department of State Release, November 18, 1942 [1]

The Department of State announces that an exchange of notes [signed at Washington, August 4 and 24, 1942] [2] has been effected with the Government of Peru whereby the two Governments confirm an understanding designed to initiate a cooperative program for the training of Peruvian students in the United States.

In accordance with this arrangement, the Government of Peru has set aside the sum of 380,000 *soles* to be used to pay subsistence expenses

---

[1] *Ibid.*, p. 950.
[2] *Executive Agreement Series* 298.

of a selected group of students who will be brought to the United States on travel grants awarded by the Department of State. The Institute of International Education, 2 West Forty-fifth Street, New York, N.Y., and the Bolivarian Society of the United States, New York, N.Y., are cooperating in obtaining tuition scholarships from American universities to round out the contributions of the Peruvian and United States Governments to this program.

The Peruvian Government has indicated its intention to select students in the following fields: Iron and steel metallurgy (2), technical processing of petroleum (2), geology (1), mechanical engineering, (1), industrial chemistry (1), electrical engineering (1), forestry (1), fisheries (1), horticulture (1), city planning (1), medicine (2), veterinary medicine (1), and port-works construction (1). Terms of study will be one year, to be extended in special cases to two years.

A committee has been appointed in Lima to select the most promising candidates for these scholarships, and it is hoped that the persons chosen will be able to begin their studies with the next term of the present academic year. The members of the selection committee are: Dr. Francisco Tudela, chairman; Dr. Carlos Monge, Dr. Enrique Laroza, Dr. Arthur Dewey, Mr. C. J. Billwiller, Mr. Ples Harper, administrative secretary.

The Department of State expresses its gratification that, with the cooperation of American institutions, it has been possible to work out this first cooperative arrangement with a government of one of the other American Republics for the planned training in useful fields of a larger number of young persons than has been possible under previous arrangements.

(2) *Suspension of Exchange Fellowships and Travel-Grant Awards to United States Students. Department of State Release, December 29, 1942* [1]

Notes have been addressed by the Department of State to the diplomatic missions of the other American Republics in Washington, informing them that the increasingly exigent demands of the war upon the manpower supply in the United States make it necessary for this Government to suspend, for the duration of the war, the award of official scholarships, fellowships, and travel or maintenance grants to students from the United States.

In transmitting this information to the diplomatic missions of the other American Republics, the Secretary of State has informed them that the Government of the United States believes, as they are aware, that all the country's energies in human, material, and spiritual re-

---

[1] Department of State, *Bulletin*, VIII, p. 8.

sources must be directed solely toward the winning of the war. In practical terms this means that most of the persons who would otherwise be eligible for appointment as exchange students or recipients of student travel grants under Government programs will be engaged in the armed forces of the nation, in the manufacture of war materials, or in other activities closely related to the war effort.

Fellowships and student travel or maintenance grants awarded to citizens of the United States up to the date of the notification to the diplomatic missions will be honored, but no grants will be made after that date. They will, of course, be resumed as soon as feasible.

The Secretary of State has also emphasized that in adopting this policy the Government of the United States has no intention or thought of suspending or discontinuing the award of fellowships and travel and maintenance grants to citizens of the other American Republics for study in the United States. On the contrary, he has expressed the hope that the situation in other American countries will permit the continuance of this program and that panels under the Convention for the Promotion of Inter-American Cultural Relations will be submitted by other participating countries in accordance with the standing procedure. He has added that the Department of State and other agencies in this Government will request funds for the 1944 fiscal year to continue this treaty arrangement, the award of travel and maintenance grants, and similar activities such as the in-service training programs of certain Government departments.

The Secretary of State recognizes in his communication to the diplomatic missions of the other American Republics that it is undoubtedly desirable, for the future of inter-American and international relations, to build up as large a group as possible of well-trained people who are skilled in special techniques and speak the languages of other American countries. He points out that, so far as the United States is concerned, many persons with special training are at present receiving experience in the other American Republics through the Auxiliary Foreign Service and the foreign activities of the emergency economic and supplies agencies. It is the view of the Department that these persons will undoubtedly make an important contribution to inter-American understanding in their present positions and will furnish for the post-war period a body of well-informed persons in many technical and professional fields.

F. Relations with Individual Countries

1. ARGENTINA

Dr. Roberto M. Ortiz was elected President of Argentina in September 1937, but relinquished the office on July 3, 1940 for an indefinite period because of ill-health, and was succeeded by the Vice-President, Dr. Ramón S. Castillo, as

Acting President. Congress accepted the resignation of Dr. Ortiz and on June 27, 1942, Dr. Castillo became President. Dissatisfaction in the United States, as well as in Argentina, with the policies of the Castillo Government, particularly with the dissolution of Congress and the declaration of a state of siege, had existed since the Rio de Janeiro Conference of January 1942.

Dr. Enrique Ruiz Guiñazú, Argentine Foreign Minister, accepted Resolution XV of the Conference which "recommended" the breaking off of relations with the Axis powers, but no action has been taken by the Government under its terms. Of the 21 American Republics Argentina alone has insisted upon maintenance of neutrality and has followed a policy of noncollaboration with the other Republics of the Western Hemisphere in the war.

Argentina's official attitude toward the rupture of relations with the Axis powers was expressed by Foreign Minister Guiñazú in July 1942 when he indicated to a session of the Chamber of Deputies that the United States' refusal to sell arms to the military mission sent to Washington unless the Argentine Government provided a naval convoy, and the subsequent ending of negotiations, had determined Argentina's position.

On September 28 the Chamber of Deputies approved a resolution recommending a break in diplomatic relations with the Axis but President Castillo in a message to the President of the Chamber "took note" of it but reminded him that the conduct of foreign affairs was in the hands of the executive branch of the government.[1]

The Argentine Government received from the United States Government on November 3 [2] memoranda on Axis espionage activities, which were centered in Buenos Aires. On the same day the Inter-American Emergency Advisory Committee for Political Defense published a memorandum, presented four months before, June 30, 1942, to the American Ambassador to Chile, on Nazi spy activities. Action was taken immediately by the Ministry of the Interior for the suppression of activities harmful to American security, but President Castillo refused to abandon "prudent neutrality." His internal policies and repressive measures in the decree of December 14, 1942 created much dissension and the situation became further complicated as the time for Presidential elections approached.

A military revolutionary committee, headed by General Arturo Rawson and General Pedro Ramírez, War Minister in the Cabinet of President Castillo, seized power on June 4, 1943, and the Castillo Government surrendered and resigned the next day.

The hope that Argentina would align itself with the United Nations was based on the first proclamation of the Committee which read in part: "We will fight to maintain the real and integral sovereignty of the nation, to fulfill its historic tradition, to make effective and absolute the true, loyal union of American collaboration, and to comply with international pacts and promises." [3]

On June 7 General Arturo Rawson resigned as president and that office was taken over by General Ramírez, who issued a statement of maintenance of neutrality in the war "for the present" but favored closer cooperation with the other American Republics.

The United States was informed by note on June 8 of the creation of the new Argentine Government and on June 11, in a ceremony in the Foreign Ministry at Buenos Aires, formal recognition was accorded by the delivery of a note by the American Ambassador. Recognition by other American Republics, Great Britain, Canada and a number of European countries was extended immediately.

The new Government stated on June 14 [4] that it was ready to sign an agreement with the United States on equipment for production of petroleum to

[1] *New York Times*, October 2, 1942.
[2] *Ibid.*, November 14, 1942.
[3] *Ibid.*, June 5, 1943.
[4] *Ibid.*, June 14, 1943.

supply neighboring republics. Negotiations had been in progress for nine months. A suggestion to send a special mission to Washington to discuss political, economic and military questions was also made, but the United States had indicated that lend-lease aid would not be given until the Axis diplomatic missions left Buenos Aires.

(1) Recognition of New Government. The United States Ambassador (Armour) to the Argentine Foreign Minister (Storni), June 11, 1943 [1]

EXCELLENCY:

I have the honor to acknowledge receipt of your Excellency's communication, dated June 8, 1943, informing me that General Pedro P. Ramírez has assumed the provisional Presidency of the nation and has designated Rear Admiral Saba H. Sueyro to perform the duties of Vice President and as members of the several Government departments officials whose names you were so good as to enumerate.

In reply I take pleasure in informing your Excellency that, taking note of the friendly sentiments which animate the Government in which your Excellency occupies such an important position, my Government desires to maintain with the new Government of the Argentine Republic those cordial relations which have ever so happily existed between our two countries.

I look forward with most pleasant expectation to cooperating with your Excellency in the discharge of my mission, which I am happy to assure your Excellency will continue to be directed toward bringing those relations ever closer.

I avail myself of this occasion to express my highest consideration.

(2) Recognition of New Government. Department of State Announcement on Remarks of the Secretary of State (Hull) at His Press Conference, June 11, 1943 [2]

Recognition of the new Government of Argentina, headed by Gen. Pedro P. Ramírez, was extended by the Government of the United States on June 11, 1943, in a note delivered to the Argentine Government by the American Ambassador.

At the press conference on June 11, the Secretary of State was asked by a correspondent if the recognition carried with it any change in relations between the Government of the United States and the Government of Argentina. The Secretary pointed out that recognition is one of the usual, ordinary steps taken, somewhat of a routine nature, when there is a change of government. Asked if he had any comment about the new Government in Argentina, the Secretary replied that he had nothing.

[1] *Ibid.*, June 12, 1943.   [2] Department of State, *Bulletin*, VIII, p. 520.

He added that we had the benefit of their public declarations of future policy.

Questioned as to whether the step was taken in concert with the Government of the United Kingdom, the Secretary stated that we acted primarily on our own initiative but had conferred with the other American Republics. He concluded that we had collaborated only with them.

The Secretary was asked if it was to be anticipated that all the American Republics which had so far refrained from giving recognition would now act together. Mr. Hull again remarked that, while we collaborate, each government acts on its own individual initiative. He added that it was his best impression that all the American Governments which had not previously extended recognition would do so.

Brazil, Chile, Paraguay, and Bolivia recognized the new Argentine Government on June 9. The remainder of the American Republics represented in Buenos Aires, except Cuba, did so on June 10 and 11. Cuba announced recognition on June 15.

2. BOLIVIA

(1) *Letter from the Under Secretary of State (Welles) to Ernesto Galarza, Chief of Division of Labor and Social Information, Pan American Union, on False Allegation Regarding Activities of the American Ambassador to Bolivia (Boal), December 31, 1942* [1]

MY DEAR MR. GALARZA:

I have received your letter of December 21, 1942,[2] in which you allege that Mr. Pierre de L. Boal, United States Ambassador to Bolivia, made certain observations to the President of Bolivia intended to diminish the prospect of the passage of a labor code which would have created procedures under which labor in Bolivia could improve its status.

At the outset, I must state my surprise that you not only made this charge but circulated it widely without having made any endeavor to verify its accuracy with this Department which is charged with the conduct of the foreign relations of the United States.

As soon as I received your letter, I had the charge thoroughly investigated. The allegation, as I expected, proved to be without foundation. The Secretary has already made this clear in answer to an inquiry made of him at his press conference yesterday. For your convenience a copy of the Secretary's remarks is enclosed herewith. I desire to make a few additional remarks to those contained in the Secretary's statement.

For you who have followed with greatest care every development of the Good Neighbor policy it is scarcely necessary to reiterate that that policy is founded upon the principle of non-interference in the internal affairs of other countries. This policy, now embodied in an inter-

---

[1] *Ibid.*, p. 5.   [2] Not printed herein.

American treaty, has been scrupulously adhered to. With respect to the particular matter under reference, the Department specifically instructed Mr. Boal on December 2, 1942, to avoid carefully any statements or actions which might be construed as an attempt to influence Bolivian legislation.

It has also been a fundamental principle of our policy to give all assistance possible to the other American Republics to raise their standard of living, particularly to improve the living standards of labor. This has been done time and time again on a cooperative basis and, of course, without unilateral interference by this Government. In this regard, a United States economic mission, in agreement with the Bolivian Government, made a study of ways in which the Bolivian economy might be improved.[1] As a result of the recommendations of that mission arrangements are being completed for the granting of specific financial and technical assistance which will enable certain vitally important public works and agricultural and industrial development to be carried out. It is my expectation that as a result of this cooperative activity the production of foodstuffs and other essential products in Bolivia will be stimulated for the benefit of Bolivian agriculturists and laborers.

Although I never doubted for a minute that Ambassador Boal had strictly adhered to this Government's basic policies I immediately asked him for a report on your charge that he had taken action to diminish the prospects of passage of the labor code.

Ambassador Boal replied that he had never at any time taken any action that could be considered as intended to influence action on the labor code. He did not discuss with the President, as alleged, or with any other Bolivian official, the new administrative expenses that would be imposed upon the companies under the decree, the question of paying earned wages on time, collective bargaining, or any other procedure for handling labor problems in connection with the mining industry. Mr. Boal did not make any suggestion regarding the approval of the bill by the President or with respect to its enforcement. Since it was obvious that the new code would increase the production cost of metals, rubber, and other products being bought by the United States Government in furtherance of the war effort, Mr. Boal asked the President the simple question of what he thought the effect of the code would be on these costs. This entirely proper question was designed to gather information that would be useful to the various Government agencies concerned in the purchase of strategic materials.

Although it would not be appropriate for me to attempt to forecast what attitude the Government buying agencies might take with respect to price changes resulting from the new labor code, it is of record that this Government, on account of the rising cost of living and shortage of

[1] See this volume, p. 385.

goods in Bolivia, has paid generous prices for materials produced in Bolivia and that prices for tin and tungsten have heretofore been revised upward by agreement of the Bolivian and United States Governments.

You doubtlessly know that the labor code was promulgated on December 8, 1942 by the Chief Executive of Bolivia and is now in effect. You may not know that the Government of Bolivia has officially denied that Ambassador Boal intervened in any way with respect to this matter.

I regret that you chose to disseminate over the country an unfounded allegation without having made any attempt to verify the true situation with the Department. The last ten years of the Good-Neighbor Policy should have been convincing proof, first, that this Government long ago gave up interference in the internal affairs of other countries, and, secondly, that this Government reflects in its foreign policy the objective of its domestic policy, namely, improvement in the standard of living in which all elements will participate, but particularly those heretofore ill-clothed, badly housed, and poorly fed.

[Enclosure]

Excerpt from the Press Conference of the Secretary of State (Hull), Monday, December 28, 1942

Our Ambassador to Bolivia cables that he did not engage in any acts or utterances which could be construed at all as an attempt to influence the labor plans and proposals and programs that were pending in Bolivia; that he once made inquiry about the effect of the proposed labor code on production costs of the strategic materials that we were securing from Bolivia; that there was nothing in that inquiry which was not in line with his duty to report all economic facts to his Government or that could be construed in any unfavorable light and nothing was so intended.

I think the fact of our Good Neighbor policy with all of its philosophies and principles and programs as enunciated at Montevideo and carried forward with most every kind of cooperation with each country in the Americas — political, economic, social, moral and cultural — I think the progress that has been made steadily in that straight course of cooperation with noticeable improvement in the welfare and the betterment of the people here and everywhere is sufficient witness to what we have always stood for during these ten years and what we shall continue to stand for.

3. BRAZIL

(1) *Meeting in Brazil of President Roosevelt and President Vargas. White House Release, January 30, 1943* [1]

President Roosevelt made his return from the Casablanca Conference, January 14–26, at which important questions of war strategy had been discussed

[1] Department of State, *Bulletin*, VIII, p. 95.

with Prime Minister Churchill, by way of West Africa and Brazil. In the course of his stop in Brazil, he conferred with President Vargas.

The President of Brazil and the President of the United States met on January 28 at an unannounced location in Brazil. The two Presidents had lunch together and inspected and reviewed Army, Navy, and air forces of the two nations. They passed the evening in conference on problems of the World War as a whole and especially the joint Brazilian-United States effort. They discussed the continuing submarine danger from the Caribbean to the South Atlantic. President Vargas announced greatly increased efforts on the part of his country to meet this menace. President Roosevelt informed his colleague of the very significant results of the conference in Casablanca and of the resolve that the peace to come must not allow the Axis to attack civilization in future years. Mr. Roosevelt demonstrated that the North African expedition has for the present eliminated the possibility of the threat of a German-held Dakar to American freedom at the narrow point of the Atlantic. Both President Vargas and President Roosevelt are in complete agreement that it must be permanently and definitely assured that the coasts of West Africa and Dakar never again under any circumstances be allowed to become a blockade or an invasion threat against the two Americas.

The two Presidents said:

"This meeting has given us an opportunity to survey the future safety of all the Americas. In our opinion each of the Republics is interested and affected to an equal degree. In unity there is strength. It is the aim of Brazil and of the United States to make the Atlantic Ocean safe for all. We are deeply grateful for the almost unanimous help that our neighbors are giving to the great cause of democracy throughout the world."

The above statement is supplemented by the following "Memorandum for the Press" from President Roosevelt:

President Roosevelt believed that the Casablanca Conference was so vital to the war effort that he should delay for a short time his return to the United States so that he might talk informally to President Vargas of Brazil about the conference and discuss several details of additional mutual aid. President Roosevelt on his journey to Africa and on his return has had many opportunities to visit and inspect vital points of the "Ferry Command" which is doing a most difficult job every day in sending planes and quantities of vital equipment from America to the Middle East, to North Africa, to Russia, to the air squadrons in China, and to the Burma front.

The Presidents of the two nations, the United States and Brazil, are old friends, and their talks were timely and profitable in every way.

4. CHILE

(1) *Projected Visit of the President of Chile to the United States. Exchange of Telegrams between the President of the United States (Roosevelt) and the President of the Republic of Chile (Rios), August 13–14, 1942* [1]

Chile and Argentina were the only two Latin-American Republics which had not by July 1, 1942 broken off diplomatic relations with the principal Axis powers in accordance with the recommendations contained in Resolution I adopted at the Rio de Janeiro Meeting of Foreign Ministers in January 1942.[2] Opinion in the United States took a more tolerant view of the failure of the Chilean Government to take the recommended action than of the inaction of the Argentine authorities, in view of the fact that Chile's long and exposed coast placed her territory and vital shipping in special danger of attack from the sea. The projected visit of President Rios of Chile to Washington was, however, looked to as the probable occasion for discussions and agreements leading to the severance of diplomatic relations by the Chilean Government.

(a) *The President of the United States (Roosevelt) to the President of Chile (Rios), August 13, 1942*

It would give me the greatest pleasure were Your Excellency to find it possible to visit this country as the guest of the Government of the United States. In times like these when the Republics of the Americas need more than ever before to cooperate in the defense of the Western Hemisphere and in order to insure the preservation of the liberties of the peoples of the Americas, I believe that the opportunities afforded for personal meetings between the Presidents of the American Republics serve a singularly valuable purpose. It would give me the greatest satisfaction to be afforded the opportunity of receiving Your Excellency as our guest in Washington and thus be enabled to confer with you with regard to problems which vitally affect the interests of our two countries and the interests of the Americas.

If it were possible for you to leave Chile at that period, I would suggest the coming month of October as a most agreeable time for your suggested visit.

I trust that it may be possible for you to honor us by the acceptance of this invitation.

Please accept [etc.]

(b) *The President of Chile (Rios) to the President of the United States (Roosevelt), August 14, 1942*

[Translation]

I deeply appreciate the high honor which Your Excellency has paid me in inviting me to make a visit to the United States as a guest of the Government, and I feel that the generous spontaneity of that invitation is

---

[1] *Ibid.*, VII, p. 701.　　　　[2] *Documents, IV, 1941–42*, p. 392.

most significant of understanding and deference toward my Government and me. I share without reservations Your Excellency's opinion that interviews of Chiefs of State, in circumstances as highly serious as those under which the world is living, serve a lofty purpose of cooperation and, on a cordial plane of mutual respect, promote a frank and sincere interchange of viewpoints on the weighty problems which so vitally concern our nations and the whole American continent. With this conviction, I am very honored to accept the invitation which Your Excellency is good enough to extend to me for conferences in Washington during the month of October, and anticipating the pleasure of exchanging views with Your Excellency, whose vigorous, democratic personality is so justly admired in Chile, I shall be very happy immediately to seek from the National Congress the constitutional authorization which will allow me to leave the country for so lofty a purpose.

I renew [etc.]

(2) *Postponement of Visit of the President of Chile to the United States. Exchanges of Messages between the President of Chile (Rios) and the President of the United States (Roosevelt), October 11 and 14, 1942* [1]

In his address of October 8 before the National Foreign Trade Convention at Boston, Under Secretary of State Welles stated that two of the twenty-one American Republics had refrained from carrying out the unanimous recommendation of the Rio de Janeiro Conference that all the American Republics sever their diplomatic relations with the Axis, and "are still permitting their territory to be utilized by the officials and the subversive agents of the Axis as a base for hostile activities against their neighbors." [2] Specific reference was made to ships that had been sunk as the result of these activities.

It was reported from Santiago, Chile, under date of October 9, that the Foreign Ministry had asked the Chilean Ambassador in Washington to deny to President Roosevelt the charges made by Mr. Welles and to point out that unless a satisfactory explanation was forthcoming from Washington, the visit of President Rios to the United States scheduled to start on October 14 would probably be postponed or canceled. A statement issued by the Chilean Foreign Ministry on the night of October 9 read in part as follows: [3]

"On the eve of the departure of President Rios to the United States Sumner Welles' speech, with unlooked-for statements, attempts to exhibit our country in an unpleasant position before other nations of the continent, throwing on her shoulders responsibilities that we cannot accept.

"Only a few days ago we received from other authoritative North American sources statements of respect and understanding concerning the collaboration of Chile with the war effort of the United States, the delivery of important quantities of essential strategic materials.

"President Roosevelt's invitation, asking President Rios to pay him a visit, was formulated as proof of the confidence in the friendly disposition of the Chilean Government and was accepted as a demonstration of loyalty in our intentions.

[1] Department of State, *Bulletin,* VII, p. 838.
[2] See this volume, p. 16.
[3] *New York Times,* October 10, 1942.

"In spite of this Mr. Sumner Welles has publicly thrown the responsibility for the sinking of ships and the loss of lives on remote seas on Chile and suggests that our attitude is not in accordance with our continental obligations."

On October 12, the Chilean Ambassador notified the Department of State of the "postponement" of President Rios' visit.

(a) The President of Chile (Rios) to the President of the United States (Roosevelt), October 11, 1942

I profoundly appreciate the friendly and understanding statements which Your Excellency has been so good to formulate to Ambassador Michels concerning the cordial spirits in which you will receive the visit of the President of Chile whose sincere American feeling, disposition and that of his Government Your Excellency so kindly recognized; but I find myself in the regrettable necessity of stating to Your Excellency that the last official information released in the United States concerning the international position of my country which has created an unfavorable atmosphere, counsels me to postpone, for the present, the honor of visiting Your Excellency.

Your Excellency can be sure that this in no way alters the decided intention of my Government to continue cooperating with the United States and the other sister nations of America in the defense of the continent.

I renew to Your Excellency the expression of my sincere gratitude for your honored invitation and seeing myself forced to defer my voyage for cause so foreign to my desire, reiterate to Your Excellency the homage of my admiration and respect.

(b) The President of the United States (Roosevelt) to the President of Chile (Rios), October 14, 1942

I wish to acknowledge Your Excellency's message stating that you have decided to postpone, for the present, your visit to the United States.

I am sorry to learn of Your Excellency's decision and I want you to know also of my deep personal regret in not having the opportunity of meeting and knowing you personally.

I was looking forward to exchanging views with you regarding the implementation of the desire of Chile, mentioned in your message, to cooperate with the United States and the other Republics of the Americas in the defense of the Western Hemisphere.

I have always felt that it is extremely difficult for heads of nations to discuss pending and difficult questions only by letter or telegram, and that almost all problems can be solved by personal meetings and by what we in the United States call "sitting around the table as personal friends."

That is why I very much hope that you will come to Washington a little later and that I can consider your visit is merely postponed for a short time.

As you probably know, I had planned to visit Santiago in the autumn of 1939 but after the World War broke out, and especially since the United States became a party to that war, I have been unable to leave Washington.

May I renew [etc.]

_____

President Roosevelt in his reply to the protest of the Chilean Ambassador,[1] stated that Mr. Welles' speech contained no accusation that the Chilean Government or its authorized representatives were participating in or sponsoring Axis agents' activities in Chile detrimental to the security of the Western Hemisphere; that the facts set forth in Mr. Welles' address referring to subversive activities in Chile could not be disputed; that the visit of President Rios to the United States would be useful in the highest degree in the interests of both countries and that when President Rios came to Washington, he [President Roosevelt] would give the Chilean Executive many additional details regarding the scope and character of the activities to which Mr. Welles referred which would show the seriousness of the danger; that he [President Roosevelt] hoped very much that President Rios would be able to make the visit and that when he came to Washington the two chiefs of state could sit down and discuss all fundamental problems in which the two countries were vitally interested.

While the proposed visit of President Rios did not materialize, the Chilean Government did take energetic and vigorous steps, publicly acknowledged by Secretary of State Hull on November 5,[2] to smash the operating center in Chile of Axis espionage, sabotage and subversive activities. On January 20, 1943, Chile severed diplomatic relations with the principal Axis powers.[3] This action was welcomed by Secretary of State Hull in a public statement.[4]

5. DOMINICAN REPUBLIC

(1) *Customs Agreement with the Dominican Republic. Exchange of Notes between the Dominican Minister of Foreign Relations (Despradel) and the American Minister (Warren), November 14, 1942* [5]

The Government of the United States has agreed not to invoke the pertinent provisions of the agreement with the Dominican Republic of September 25,

---

[1] Not disclosed to the press until November 2, though the Chilean Government had been given authority to publish the reply earlier. *Christian Science Monitor*, November 3, 1942.

[2] *New York Times*, November 6, 1942.

[3] See this volume, p. 359.

[4] Department of State, *Bulletin*, VIII, p. 83.

[5] *Ibid.*, VII, p. 952.

1924, according reciprocal unconditional most-favored-nation treatment in customs matters (Treaty Series 700),[2] for the purpose of claiming the benefit of reductions in customs duties which are accorded by the Dominican Republic exclusively to Haiti and which are specifically provided for in the treaty of commerce between those countries signed on August 26, 1941, as modified by an exchange of notes on March 24, 1942.

The products concerned are empty sisal sacks; commercialized natural medicinal waters; rugs, bags, and other novelty articles of sisal and henequen; peanuts in the shell; millet; certain types of rum; certain types of prepared cocktails; aerated waters; manufactures of tortoise shell, lignum-vitae, and mahogany; ginned cotton; and sisal fiber.

(a) *The Dominican Minister of Foreign Relations (Despradel) to the American Minister (Warren)*

[Translation]

MR. MINISTER:

I have the honor to inform Your Excellency that on August 26, 1941 a Commercial Agreement was signed in the City of Port-au-Prince, by means of which the Dominican Republic and the Republic of Haiti, in their situation as contiguous countries, established a special treatment in the commercial relations existing between both peoples. The exchange of the ratifications of this Commercial Agreement took place in this capital on March 23 of this year.

This agreement, among other stipulations, establishes the reduction of Dominican import customs duties according to a list specifying the products which, upon being imported from Haiti, are to be introduced into our country with the reductions of the Dominican import tariffs set forth in the said list.

The Government of the Dominican Republic has always supported the multilateral development of international commerce on the basis that the nations should enjoy access to the said commerce under equal conditions and be able to obtain, within those conditions, the raw materials which they require for the satisfactory and prosperous development of their respective economies.

In that connection, I have the honor to refer to the formula for contractual tariff preferences between contiguous countries which the Inter-American Financial and Economic Advisory Committee has recommended. In accordance with the spirit of that recommendation of the said Inter-American body, the Commercial Agreement referred to was concluded between the Dominican Republic and that of Haiti.

On March 24, 1942 notes were exchanged between both Governments, by which some products were added to the lists originally agreed upon.

[1] *Treaties, Conventions*, etc. IV, 1923–1937, p. 4088.

Since the *modus vivendi* agreed upon between the Dominican Republic and the United States of America, dated September 25, 1924, provides that the tariff reductions which our country grants to other countries should benefit, in the manner indicated by the principles relating to the most-favored-nation clause, similar products of United States manufacture and origin, I request Your Excellency to inform this Chancery if the Government of the United States of America, in view of all the aforesaid considerations, will consent not to invoke the clauses of the convention of September 25, 1924, already mentioned, for the purpose of claiming the benefit of the tariff preferences granted the contiguous state of Haiti, which (preferences) my Government considers as adjusted to the conditions of the formula recommended by the Inter-American Financial and Economic Advisory Committee.

(b) *The American Minister (Warren) to the Dominican Minister of Foreign Relations (Despradel)*

Excellency:

I have the honor to acknowledge the receipt of Your Excellency's note of today's date in which you reiterate the adherence of your Government to the principle of promoting the multilateral development of international trade on the unconditional most-favored-nation basis and refer to the exclusive tariff reductions to the Republic of Haiti specifically provided for in the Commercial Agreement between the Dominican Republic and that country signed on August 26, 1941, as modified by an exchange of notes on March 24, 1942 by which certain products were added to the list specified in the Commercial Agreement. In this connection you mention the contractual formula for tariff preferences to contiguous countries recommended on September 18, 1941 by the Inter-American Financial and Economic Advisory Committee, and inquire whether, in view of the Committee's recommendation and considering the special and unusual conditions affecting the trade between the Dominican Republic and Haiti, my Government would be willing to refrain from claiming, under the provisions of the *modus vivendi* between our two countries of September 25, 1924, the benefit of the tariff preferences to the Republic of Haiti specifically provided for in the Commercial Agreement of August 26, 1941 as modified by the exchange of notes of March 24, 1942.

I have the honor to inform Your Excellency that my Government, in view of the considerations set forth, agrees not to invoke the pertinent provisions of the *modus vivendi* for the purpose of claiming the benefit of such tariff preferences.

6. HAITI — FINANCIAL ARRANGEMENTS

[See *Documents, IV, 1941–42*, p. 415.]

(1) *Arrangement between the Governments of the United States and Haiti. Exchange of Notes between the Haitian Minister (Dennis) and the Secretary of State (Hull)* [1]

(a) *The Haitian Minister (Dennis) to the Secretary of State (Hull), September 17, 1942*

MR. SECRETARY:

I have the honor, upon the instructions of my Government, to inform Your Excellency that the Government of the Republic of Haiti desires to arrange for a credit not to exceed $500,000 from the Export-Import Bank of Washington. The advances under this credit are to be made to the National Bank of the Republic of Haiti and will bear the unconditional guarantee of the Government of the Republic of Haiti.

In this connection I refer to Article VII, paragraph 2 of the Executive Agreement between our two countries signed at Port-au-Prince on September 13, 1941,[2] and I should be glad if Your Excellency would confirm the understanding of my Government that no objection is entertained by the Government of the United States to the proposed credit.

Please accept [etc.]

(b) *The Secretary of State (Hull) to the Haitian Minister (Dennis), September 21, 1942*

SIR:

I have the honor to acknowledge the receipt of your note of September 17, 1942 with reference to the arrangements which your Government is making with the Export-Import Bank of Washington, for a credit not to exceed $500,000. By this arrangement the credit would be extended by the Export-Import Bank of Washington to the National Bank of the Republic of Haiti, and will bear the unconditional guarantee of the Government of the Republic of Haiti.

With respect to your reference to Article VII, paragraph 2 of the Executive Agreement of September 13, 1941 between the United States and Haiti, I take pleasure in informing you that the Government of the United States is agreeable to this transaction and to the increase in the public debt of the Republic of Haiti by the amount and in the manner indicated.

Accept [etc.]

[1] *Executive Agreement Series* 290.
[2] *Ibid.* 220; 55 Stat. 1348.

(2) Supplementary Agreement between the Governments of the United States and Haiti, Signed September 30, 1942 [1]

This agreement extends the moratorium on the payment of amortization charges on the Haitian debt to and including September 30, 1943, and extends for one year the agreement signed on September 30, 1941 (*Executive Agreement Series* 224).

The provisions of Articles I and II of the Executive Agreement of September 30, 1941,[2] shall continue in effect from and after October 1st, 1942 to and including September 30, 1943, except that

(1) All the receipts of the Haitian Government shall be deposited without deduction at the Banque Nationale de la République d'Haiti, which bank shall make the payments provided for by the loan contracts of 1922 and 1923, in accordance with the procedure outlined in Article VI of the Executive Agreement of September 13, 1941; [3]

(2) The Government of the Republic of Haiti agrees to pay $20,000 U. S. currency during the period October 1, 1942, to September 30, 1943, inclusive, on account of the amounts required to be paid under the loan contracts of October 6, 1922 and May 26, 1925 for the amortization of the loans of 1922 and 1923, the provisions of the paragraph designated (2) of Article VI of the Executive Agreement of September 13, 1941, and those of the subsequent paragraphs of the said article, notwithstanding.

Signed at Port-au-Prince, in duplicate, in the French and English languages, this 30th day of September, nineteen hundred and forty-two.

J. C. WHITE

[SEAL]   *Envoy Extraordinary and Minister Plenipotentiary of the United States of America*

7. MEXICO

A. Settlement of Claims

(1) An Act to Provide for the Settlement of Certain Claims of the Government of the United States on Behalf of American Nationals against the Government of Mexico, Approved December 18, 1942 [4]

This act provides for adjudication and awards to claimants entitled to participate in the distribution of a lump-sum settlement recently effected by the Department of State whereby the Republic of Mexico pays 40 million dollars to the United States in settlement of claims. Participating claims have originated

---

[1] *Executive Agreement Series* 299; Department of State, *Bulletin*, VII, p. 1002.

[2] *Executive Agreement Series* 224; 55 Stat. 1385.

[3] *Executive Agreement Series* 220; 55 Stat. 1348.

[4] Public Law 814, 77th Cong., originated as S. 2528, Senate Rept. No. 1615; Hearings before Subcommittee of Senate Committee on Foreign Relations, June 30, July 1, 2, 6, 10 and 14, 1942; passed by House with amendments, Senate disagreed; Conference report, House Rept. No. 2679.

over a long period extending from 1868 to 1940 and include claims for the expropriation of lands and mines, confiscation or destruction of personal property, injuries to individuals, and miscellaneous instances of alleged denial of justice. Included are all claims not heretofore finally adjudicated in which the Government of Mexico is alleged to have become responsible to the United States for injuries to American nationals, excepting claims concerning petroleum properties and certain claims arising from default of payment on Mexican bonds.

The members of the American-Mexican Claims Commission, appointed by the President pursuant to the provisions of the act of Congress known as the "Settlement of Mexican Claims Act of 1942," were Edgar E. Witt, of Texas, chairman; Samuel M. Gold, of New York; and Charles F. McLaughlin, of Nebraska.

Be it enacted by the Senate and House of Representatives of the United States of America in Congress assembled, That this Act may be cited as the "Settlement of Mexican Claims Act of 1942."

SEC. 2. (*a*) There is hereby established a commission to be known as the American Mexican Claims Commission (hereinafter referred to as the "Commission") and to be composed of three persons to be appointed by the President, by and with the advice and consent of the Senate. Each member of the Commission shall receive a salary at the rate of $10,000 a year. One of such members shall be designated by the President as Chairman of the Commission. Two members of the Commission shall constitute a quorum for the transaction of business. Any vacancy that may occur in the membership of the Commission shall be filled in the same manner as in the case of an original appointment.

(*b*) The Commission may, without regard to the civil-service laws, employ a secretary, and such legal, clerical, and technical assistants as may be necessary to carry out its functions under this Act, and shall fix their compensation without regard to the Classification Act of 1923, as amended.

(*c*) The Commission is authorized to make such rules and regulations as may be necessary to carry out its functions under this Act.

(*d*) The authority of the Commission under this Act, and the terms of office of its members, shall terminate at the expiration of two years after the date on which a majority of its members first appointed take office, but the President may by Executive order fix an earlier termination date. Upon the termination of the authority of the Commission, all books, records, documents, and other papers in the possession of the Commission shall be deposited with the Department of State.

SEC. 3. (*a*) The Commission shall have authority to examine and render final decisions in the following categories of claims on behalf of American nationals against the Government of Mexico —

(1) Agrarian claims which arose between January 1, 1927, and August 30, 1927, inclusive, and which were not filed with the General Claims Commission established pursuant to the Convention between

the United States and Mexico signed September 8, 1923 (43 Stat. 1730);[1]

(2) Agrarian claims which are predicated upon provisional expropriation decrees signed between August 31, 1927, and December 1, 1938, inclusive, but not published prior to December 1, 1938, and which were not filed with the Agrarian Claims Commission established pursuant to the agreement between the United States and Mexico effected by exchange of notes signed on November 9 and November 12, 1938, respectively (hereinafter referred to as the Agrarian Claims Agreement of 1938);

(3) Agrarian claims which arose between December 1, 1938, and October 6, 1940, inclusive, and which were not filed with the Agrarian Claims Commission on or before July 31, 1939;

(4) All other claims which arose between January 1, 1927, and October 6, 1940, inclusive, and which involve international responsibility of the Government of Mexico as a consequence of damage to, or loss or destruction of, or wrongful interference with, property of American nationals; except (A) claims predicated upon acts of Mexican authorities in relation to petroleum properties; and (B) claims which were not filed with the General Claims Commission prior to August 31, 1927, and which are predicated upon default of payment of the principal or interest on bonds issued or guaranteed by the Government of Mexico;

(5) Claims or parts of claims which were filed with the General Claims Commission, and also with the Special Claims Commission, established pursuant to the Convention between the United States and Mexico signed September 10, 1923 (43 Stat. 1722),[2] and with respect to which no final determination on the merits has been made; and

(6) Any claim in which a decision was not rendered by the General Claims Commission in conformity with the rules of procedure adopted by such Commission.

(b) All claims in the categories specified in subsection (a) may be presented for any losses or damages suffered by American nationals by reason of losses or damages suffered by any foreign corporation, company, association, or partnership in which such nationals have, or have had, a substantial and bona fide interest: *Provided*, That in all such cases the claimant shall present to the Commission either an allotment to him by the corporation, company, association, or partnership of his proportionate share of the loss or damage suffered, or other evidence thereof which is satisfactory to the Commission.

(c) All decisions by the Commission with respect to the claims in the categories specified in subsection (a) shall be based upon such evidence and written legal contentions as may be presented within such period

---

[1] *Treaties, Conventions*, etc., IV, 1923–1937, p. 4441.
[2] *Ibid.*, p. 4445.

as may be prescribed therefor by the Commission, and upon the results of such independent investigation with respect to such claims as the Commission may deem it advisable to make; except that with respect to any claim referred to in paragraph (6) of subsection (a), the Commission shall decide the case upon the basis of the record before the General Claims Commission.

Sec. 4. (a) The Commission shall also have authority, within its discretion, as hereinafter provided to examine and render final decisions (1) in those cases in which the two Commissioners designated by the United States and Mexico, respectively, pursuant to the General Claims Protocol between the United States and Mexico signed April 24, 1934 (48 Stat. 1844), failed to reach agreements and the Commissioner so designated by the United States made appraisals, and (2) in those cases in which appraisals were made by the Commissioner designated by the United States pursuant to the Agrarian Claims Agreement of 1938.

(b) In connection with such cases, the Commission shall, as soon as practicable, notify each claimant, or his attorney, by registered mail to his last-known address, of the appraisals so made. Within a period of thirty days after the mailing of such notice, the claimant shall notify the Commission in writing whether the appraisal so made is accepted as final and binding, or whether a petition for review will be filed as provided in subsection (c). If the claimant fails to so notify the Commission in writing within such period, or if the Commission is notified within such period of the final acceptance of such appraisal, it shall, at the expiration of such period, enter an award on the basis of such appraisal and certify such award to the Secretary of the Treasury.

(c) In any case in which the Commission is so notified in writing that a petition for review will be filed, the Commission shall prescribe a reasonable period, which may be extended in the discretion of the Commission, within which such petition, together with written legal contentions in support thereof, shall be filed. If no petition for review is filed within the period or any extension thereof prescribed by the Commission, it shall enter an award on the basis of the appraisal in such case and certify such award to the Secretary of the Treasury.

(d) In any case in which a petition for review is filed within the period prescribed in subsection (c), the Commission shall, if it determines to review such case, decide the case upon the basis of (1) the record before the Commissioner at the time his appraisal in such case was made, and (2) the written legal contentions filed with such petition or in connection therewith: *Provided*, That the Commission may, in its discretion, receive and consider additional evidence with respect to any claim in which it is established to the satisfaction of the Commission that it was impossible for either the claimant or his attorney, despite the exercise of due diligence, to obtain and file such evidence within any period prescribed for such filing by or in accordance with the applicable agreements between the Government of the United States and the Government of Mexico, or by or in accordance with the applicable rules adopted pursuant to such agreements.

SEC. 5. (a) All claims decided by the Commission shall be decided in accordance with the applicable provisions of the Convention of September 8, 1923, the Convention of September 10, 1923, or the Agrarian Claims Agreement of 1938, as the case may be; and all claims decided by the Commission which are not within the purview of either of such Conventions or such Agreement shall be decided in accordance with the applicable principles of international law, justice, and equity.

(b) Each decision by the Commission pursuant to this Act shall be by majority vote, shall state the reasons for such decision, and shall constitute a full and final disposition of the case in which the decision is rendered.

(c) In connection with any claim decided by the Commission pursuant to this Act in which an award is made, the Commission may, upon the written request of the claimant or any attorney heretofore or hereafter employed by such claimant, determine and apportion the just and reasonable attorneys' fees for services rendered with respect to such claim, but the total amount of the fees so determined in any case shall not exceed 10 per centum of the amount of the award, unless in special circumstances the Commission shall find that a larger fee is just and reasonable. Any fees so determined shall be entered as a part of such award, and payment thereof shall be made by the Secretary of the Treasury. Any person who accepts any compensation for services rendered with respect to such claim which, when added to any amount previously received on account of such services, will exceed the amount of fees so determined by the Commission, shall, upon conviction thereof, be fined not more than $1,000.

(d) The Commission shall, upon the completion of its work, certify in duplicate to the Secretary of State and to the Secretary of the Treasury the following —

(1) A list of all claims disallowed;

(2) A list of all claims allowed, in whole or in part (together with the amount of each claim and the amount awarded thereon) which have not been previously certified under section 4 (b) or 4 (c); and

(3) A copy of the decision rendered in each case.

SEC. 6. (a) For the purposes of this Act, the following determinations heretofore made with respect to claims on behalf of American nationals against the Government of Mexico shall be regarded as final and binding —

(1) Decisions rendered by the General Claims Commission, except in the cases referred to in paragraph (6) of section 3 (a) of this Act;

(2) Appraisals agreed upon by the Commissioners designated by the Governments of the United States and Mexico, respectively, pursuant to the General Claims Protocol between the United States and Mexico signed April 24, 1934 (48 Stat. 1844);

(3) Appraisals made by the Commissioner designated by the Government of the United States in those cases in which the two Commissioners designated pursuant to said Protocol failed to agree upon appraisals, except where such appraisals are reviewed by the Commission pursuant to section 4; and

(4) Appraisals made by the Commissioner designated by the Government of the United States pursuant to the Agrarian Claims Agreement of 1938, except where such appraisals are reviewed by the Commission pursuant to section 4.

(b) The Secretary of State shall, as soon as possible, certify to the Secretary of the Treasury lists of the awards and appraisals made in favor of American nationals in the cases referred to in paragraphs (1) and (2) of subsection (a).

SEC. 7. For the purposes of this Act, appraisals made in favor of American nationals in terms of Mexican currency shall be converted into currency of the United States at the exchange rate of $0.4985 and in any case in which an award or appraisal made in favor of an American national bears interest, such interest shall be simple interest computed at 6 per centum per annum and shall run from the date specified in such award or appraisal to November 19, 1941.

SEC. 8. (a) There is hereby created in the Treasury of the United States a special fund to be known as the "Mexican Claims Fund," hereinafter called the "fund." All payments authorized under section 9 of this Act shall be disbursed from the fund, and all amounts covered into the Treasury to the credit of the fund, less the amount of the deduction provided for in section 10 (b), are hereby permanently appropriated for the making of the payments authorized by such section.

(b) The Secretary of the Treasury is authorized and directed to cover into the fund —

(1) the sum of $3,000,000, representing the total amount of payments heretofore made by the Government of Mexico under the Agrarian Claims Agreement of 1938;

(2) the sum of $3,000,000 which was paid by the Government of Mexico upon exchange of ratifications of the Convention signed November 19, 1941;

(3) such other sums as are paid by the Government of Mexico pursuant to the provisions of the said Convention; and

(4) the sum of $533,658.95, which is hereby authorized to be appropriated, out of any moneys in the Treasury not otherwise appropriated, and which represents the total amount of awards

and appraisals, plus interest, made with respect to the claims on behalf of Mexican nationals against the Government of the United States which were filed with the General Claims Commission.

(c) The Secretary of the Treasury is authorized and directed, out of the sums covered into the fund pursuant to subsection (b) of this section, and after making the deduction provided for in section 10 (b), to make payments on account of awards and appraisals certified pursuant to sections 4 (b), 4 (c), and 6 (b) of this Act, of an amount not to exceed 30 per centum of the award or appraisal in each case, exclusive of interest.

(d) The Secretary of the Treasury is authorized and directed, to the extent that it may be possible to do so out of the sums covered into the fund pursuant to subsection (b) of this section, and after making the deduction provided for in section 10 (b) —

(1) to make similar payments of not to exceed 30 per centum on account of the principal amount of the awards certified pursuant to section 5 (d) of this Act.

(2) after completing the payments prescribed by paragraph (1) of this subsection, to make payments, from time to time and in ratable proportions, on account of all awards and appraisals certified pursuant to the provisions of this Act, according to the proportions which the respective awards and appraisals, exclusive of interest, bear to the total amount in the fund available for distribution at the time such payments are made; and

(3) after payment has been made of the principal amounts of all such awards and appraisals, to make pro rata payments on account of accrued interest on such awards and appraisals as bear interest.

SEC. 9. (a) Subject to the limitations hereinafter provided, payments pursuant to section 8 of this Act, the Act approved April 10, 1935 (49 Stat. 149), and the joint resolution approved August 25, 1937 (50 Stat. 783), and applications for such payments, shall be made in accordance with such regulations as the Secretary of the Treasury may prescribe.

(b) Such payments shall be made only to the person or persons on behalf of whom the award or appraisal is made, except that —

(1) if such person is deceased or is under a legal disability, payment shall be made to his legal representative: *Provided*, That if the amount to be disbursed at any one time is not over $500 and there is no qualified executor or administrator, payment may be made to the person or persons found by the Secretary of the Treasury to be entitled thereto, without the necessity of compliance with the requirements of law with respect to the administration of estates;

(2) if an award or appraisal is made to the estate of a deceased person, and if there has been no administration of such person's estate, or if the administration of such person's estate has been terminated,

payment may be made to the person or persons found by the Secretary of the Treasury to be entitled thereto;

(3) in the case of a partnership or corporation, the existence of which has been terminated and on behalf of which an award or appraisal is made, payment shall be made, except as provided in paragraphs (4) and (5), to the person or persons found by the Secretary of the Treasury to be entitled thereto;

(4) if a receiver or trustee for any such partnership or corporation has been duly appointed by a court of competent jurisdiction in the United States and has not been discharged prior to the date of payment, payment shall be made to such receiver or trustee or in accordance with the order of the court;

(5) if a receiver or trustee for any such partnership or corporation, duly appointed by a court of competent jurisdiction in the United States, makes an assignment of the claim, or any part thereof, with respect to which an award or appraisal is made, or makes an assignment of such award or appraisal, or any part thereof, payment shall be made to the assignee, as his interest may appear; and

(6) in the case of an assignment of an award or an appraisal, or any part thereof, which is made in writing and duly acknowledged and filed, after such award or appraisal is certified to the Secretary of the Treasury, payment may, in the discretion of the Secretary of the Treasury, be made to the assignee, as his interest may appear.

(c) Whenever the Secretary of the Treasury shall find that any person is entitled to any such payment, such finding shall be an absolute bar to recovery by any other person against the United States, its officers, agents, or employees with respect to such payment.

(d) Any person who makes application for any such payment shall be held to have consented to all the provisions of this Act.

(e) The decisions of the Secretary of the Treasury in making such payments shall be final and conclusive and shall not be subject to review by any other officer of the Government.

(f) Nothing in this Act shall be construed as the assumption of any liability by the United States for the payment or satisfaction, in whole or in part, of any claim on behalf of any American national against the Government of Mexico.

SEC. 10. (a) There is hereby authorized to be appropriated, out of any money in the Treasury not otherwise appropriated, such sums as may be necessary to enable the Commission to carry out its functions under this Act.

(b) There shall be deducted from the amount of each payment made from the fund pursuant to subsections (c) and (d) of section 8, as reimbursement for the expenses incurred by the United States, an amount equal to 5 per centum of such payment. All amounts so deducted shall be covered into the Treasury to the credit of miscellaneous receipts.

SEC. 11. (a) The Secretary of the Treasury shall continue to distribute to the beneficiaries of the final awards rendered by the Special Mexican Claims Commission all moneys heretofore or hereafter received from the Government of Mexico pursuant to the Convention signed April 24, 1934, including interest on deferred payments.

(b) So much of the Act approved April 10, 1935, and of the joint resolution approved August 25, 1937, as may be inconsistent with this Act, is hereby repealed.

SEC. 12. Nothing in this Act is intended, or shall be deemed or construed, to apply to any claim or part of claim based upon or arising out of any international arbitral award rendered prior to the effective date of the Convention between the United States and Mexico signed September 8, 1923.

SEC. 13. As used in this Act —

(a) The term "person" includes an individual, partnership, or corporation.

(b) The term "United States," when used in a geographical sense, includes the United States, its Territories and insular possessions (including the Philippine Islands), and the Canal Zone.

(c) The term "American national" includes (1) any person who is a citizen of the United States, and (2) any person who, though not a citizen of the United States, owes permanent allegiance to the United States.

SEC. 14. The following provisions of law are hereby repealed —

(a) So much of the Department of State Appropriation Act, 1936 (49 Stat. 76), of the Department of State Appropriation Act, 1937 (49 Stat. 1320), and of the Department of State Appropriation Act, 1938 (50 Stat. 271), as reads as follows: "*Provided further,* That from any sums received from the Mexican Government in settlement of a general claim of an American citizen against it, there shall be deducted and deposited in the Treasury of the United States as miscellaneous receipts, 5 per centum thereof in reimbursement of the Government of the United States of expenses incurred by it in respect of such claim."

(b) That portion of the joint resolution approved April 10, 1939 (53 Stat. 573), reading as follows: "*Provided,* That any expenditures from the amount herein authorized to be appropriated shall become a first charge upon any moneys received from the Government of Mexico in settlement of the respective claims, and the amount of such expenditures shall be deducted from the first payment by the Mexican Government and deposited in the Treasury of the United States as miscellaneous receipts."

On November 27, 1942, the Ambassador of Mexico formally presented to the Secretary of State the Mexican Government's check for $2,500,000 representing the first annual instalment due to the United States under the Claims Convention concluded November 19, 1941.[1]

Under the terms of the Convention, Mexico agreed to pay the United States $40,000,000 in settlement of certain property claims of citizens of the United States against the Government of Mexico, as described in the Convention. Payments heretofore made amounted to $6,000,000. With the above payment of $2,500,000 the balance remaining amounted to $31,500,000, to be liquidated over a period of years by the annual payment by Mexico of not less than $2,500,000.

On January 2, the Ambassador presented his Government's check for $500,000 in payment of the ninth annual instalment, due January 1, 1943,[2] in accordance with Article II of the Convention between the United States of America and the United Mexican States, signed at Mexico City on April 24, 1934, providing for the *en bloc* settlement of claims presented by the Government of the United States to the Commission established by the Special Claims Convention, concluded September 10, 1923.

The Ambassador of Mexico also presented a check covering interest due under Article III of the Convention of April 24, 1934.

B. *Military Service*

(1) *Agreement with Mexico Regarding Military Service by Nationals of Either Country Residing in the Other, Effected by Exchange of Notes between the Mexican Foreign Minister (Padilla) and the American Chargé in Mexico (Bursley), Signed at Mexico City, January 22, 1943* [3]

(a) *The Mexican Foreign Minister (Padilla) to the American Chargé in Mexico (Bursley)*

[Translation]

MR. CHARGÉ D'AFFAIRES:

I have the honor to refer to the negotiations effected for the purpose of reaching an agreement regulating certain aspects of the performance of military service by nationals of our two countries residing in the territory of the other country.

The conversations held to date elicit not only the natural interest with which the authorities of both nations view this matter but also their determination to reach a satisfactory agreement which will coincide with the excellent relations which bind our two republics.

In view of the foregoing I beg to propose for the consideration of the Government of the United States of America, through your esteemed mediacy, the following proposed arrangement:

I. The nationals of either country resident within the territory of the other may be registered and inducted into the armed forces of the

---

[1] Department of State, *Bulletin*, VII, p. 968.
[2] *Ibid.*, VIII, p. 7.
[3] *Executive Agreement Series* 323; Department of State, *Bulletin*, VIII, p. 87.

country of their residence on the same conditions as the nationals thereof unless otherwise provided herein.

II. Nationals of either country residing in the other shall be accorded the same rights and privileges as nationals of the country of residence. In the selection and induction into their armed forces of nationals of the other country the authorities of the respective countries shall take into account on the same basis as if their own nationals were involved the physical condition and health of the individuals concerned, their civil status, their financial dependents, regardless of the place of residence, and any other circumstances which under the laws and regulations in force in the country of residence would apply in selecting and inducting nationals of the latter country.

III. Nationals of either country in the territory of the other country for purposes of study and with the intention of returning to the country of which they are nationals upon the termination of such study shall upon establishing such facts in accordance with existing selective service laws and regulations be relieved from the obligation of military service.

IV. Nationals of either country who under the immigration laws of the other country are technical residents of that country known as "border crossers" shall for military service purposes be considered residents of the country in which they actually live.

V. Officials and employees of either country residing in the other whose official status has been notified to the Government of the country in which they are residing and accepted by that Government shall not be considered for military service purposes as residents of the country in which they are residing.

VI. Each Government in so far as necessities imposed by the war effort permit will furnish the other Government with information concerning its nationals who have registered for or been inducted into the military service.

VII. Nationals of either country serving in the armed forces of the other country shall receive the same treatment and have equal opportunities with respect to commissions, promotions and other incidents of military service as are accorded by that country in conformity with military law and practice to its nationals.

VIII. Representatives of either Government shall have the right to assist their nationals serving in the military forces of the other in all matters relating to their welfare including, but not limited to, the payment of pensions, gratuities, indemnities or other benefits to them or their dependents wherever the latter may be resident.

IX. Nationals of each country who have been registered for or inducted into the army of the other country, in accordance with the military service laws of the latter, and who have not declared their intention to acquire the citizenship of the country in which they reside, shall, upon being designated by the country of which they are nationals, and with their consent, be released for military service in its forces provided that this has no prejudicial effect on the common war effort. The procedure for the transportation and turning over of these persons will be agreed upon by the appropriate authorities of the two countries who are empowered to bring about the objectives desired.

X. The understandings in the foregoing arrangement shall be in effect as of today for the duration of the present war and six months thereafter.

Should the Government of the United States of America be in agreement with the foregoing text I consider that your affirmative reply to the present note shall be sufficient for the arrangement to enter immediately into effect.

I take [etc.]

(b) *The American Chargé in Mexico (Bursley) to the Mexican Foreign Minister (Padilla)*

EXCELLENCY:

I have the honor to refer to Your Excellency's note of January 22, 1943 concerning an agreement between the Governments of Mexico and the United States of America relating to military service of the nationals of either country residing in the other country, which reads textually, in translation, as follows:

I. The nationals of either country resident within the territory of the other may be registered and inducted into the armed forces of the country of their residence on the same conditions as the nationals thereof unless otherwise provided herein.

II. Nationals of either country residing in the other shall be accorded the same rights and privileges as nationals of the country of residence. In the selection and induction into their armed forces of nationals of the other country the authorities of the respective countries shall take into account on the same basis as if their own nationals were involved the physical condition and health of the individuals concerned, their civil status, their financial dependents, regardless of the place of residence, and any other circumstances which under the laws and regulations in force in the country of residence would apply in selecting and inducting nationals of the latter country.

III. Nationals of either country in the territory of the other country for purposes of study and with the intention of returning to the country of which they are nationals upon the termination of such study shall upon establishing such facts in accordance with existing selective service laws and regulations be relieved from the obligation of military service.

IV. Nationals of either country who under the immigration laws of the other country are technical residents of that country known as "border crossers" shall for military service purposes be considered residents of the country in which they actually live.

V. Officials and employees of either country residing in the other whose official status has been notified to the Government of the country in which they are residing and accepted by that Government shall not be considered for military service purposes as residents of the country in which they are residing.

VI. Each Government in so far as necessities imposed by the war effort permit will furnish the other Government with information concerning its nationals who have registered for or been inducted into the military service.

VII. Nationals of either country serving in the armed forces of the other country shall receive the same treatment and have equal opportunities with respect to commissions, promotions and other incidents of military service as are accorded by that country in conformity with military law and practice to its nationals.

VIII. Representatives of either Government shall have the right to assist their nationals serving in the military forces of the other in all matters relating to their welfare including, but not limited to, the payment of pensions, gratuities, indemnities or other benefits to them or their dependents wherever the latter may be resident.

IX. Nationals of each country who have been registered for or inducted into the army of the other country, in accordance with the military service laws of the latter, and who have not declared their intention to acquire the citizenship of the country in which they reside, shall, upon being designated by the country of which they are nationals, and with their consent, be released for military service in its forces provided that this has no prejudicial effect on the common war effort. The procedure for the transportation and turning over of these persons will be agreed upon by the appropriate authorities of the two countries who are empowered to bring about the objectives desired.

X. The understandings in the foregoing arrangement shall be in effect as of today for the duration of the present war and six months thereafter.

The above text has been submitted to my Government and has been found entirely acceptable. It is the belief of the United States Government that this agreement adds further testimony to the mutual desire of our respective countries to unite their efforts as members of the United Nations in prosecuting the war and achieving the victory.

Accept [etc.]

C. Visit of the President of the United States to Mexico

(1) Addresses of the President of Mexico (Ávila Camacho) and of the President (Roosevelt), Monterrey, Mexico, April 20, 1943 [1]

The President of the United States and the President of Mexico met in Mexico's northern industrial city, Monterrey, on April 20, 1943. When President Roosevelt's special train crossed the Rio Grande, it was the first time in 34 years that an American President touched Mexican soil, and it was the first time that the Presidents had met. At a dinner held at the Monterrey Army Base, the two Presidents broadcast their joint messages to their fellow citizens and to the world. President Ávila Camacho spoke first.

(a) Address of the President of Mexico (Ávila Camacho)

MR. PRESIDENT:

Because of the fundamental virtues which distinguish you and because of the significance of the solemn moment in which your visit to Mexico . . . is being carried out, this occasion is not only a motive of deep satisfaction for my country but also an incontrovertible proof of the progress attained by our two peoples in their desire to know each other, to understand each other, and to collaborate, without interruptions or falterings, in order to achieve the democratic aspirations which unite them.

Mexico has not been obliged to alter in the slightest degree her basic policy in order to find herself at the side of those nations which are fighting for the civilization of the world and for the good of humanity. Our true path has not varied. Our historic sense of honor continues the same as that to which we gave expression in the past with our arms in order to defend our territory and to sustain our institutions.

If our position of solidarity with your country in the present emergency had implied for us some unforeseen change in our course, our cooperation would not enjoy the unanimous support which it has been granted by Mexican public opinion.

What, then, are the causes of our firm and sincere cordiality? Your Excellency personally is giving me the best reply to this inquiry.

In effect, neither Your Excellency nor I believe in negative memories, because we both place our hope in the soundness of principles, in the perfectibility of men, and in the constructive capacity of ideals.

You furnish us with an eloquent witness of a similar capacity of the spirit which for some years has guided your country and which has led it to strengthen by all possible means the generous systems of equality and independence. In this process — which owes so much to your ability as

[1] *Bulletin of the Pan American Union*, LXXVII, p. 303; *New York Times*, April 21, 1943.

a leader — the United States has not been obliged to seek a foreign model.

In order to feel that your true greatness is not based upon dominance but rather upon the respect of sovereignties and on harmony under the law, it was sufficient for you to return with precision to the lesson of your greatest heroes. Washington, Jefferson and Lincoln are present in the current decisions of your country. And among your other claims to fame Your Excellency undoubtedly possesses that of having inflexibly fought to apply to the relations between the countries of this hemisphere the teachings of the liberators.

Mexico will never forget your participation in the structure of that new American policy which, because it is so much in agreement with our national purpose, we could without boastfulness proclaim as ours. Good neighbors. Good friends. That is what we have always wished to be for all the peoples of the earth.

It was certainly not hatred which caused us to enter the war in which we find ourselves. Nor was it a petty interest in possible practical advantages. We know perfectly well that any struggle is strenuous and that nothing durable can be created without constancy in privations and without steadfastness and severity in sacrifice.

With the same clarity we know the only conquests which the United Nations will obtain will be the moral conquests of dignity in thought, of autonomy in conduct, and of the overthrowing of might by right. And Your Excellency understands all this especially well, you to whom — as the champion of the Atlantic Charter — there is reserved a transcendent role in this time of unprecedented importance.

Our countries do not wish for a mere strategic truce obtained simply so that the world may again tomorrow fall into the same old faults of ambition, of imperialism, of iniquity and of sordid privilege.

We desire to live together free of the perpetual threats which derive from those who seek supremacy. Free from the supremacy in the domestic field which — as we were able to note during the period in which this war was prepared — led certain elements to place their class interests above the interests of the whole group. And free from the supremacy in the foreign field, the constant results of which are violence, death and the ruin of culture.

In order to bring about such a living together, we must above all destroy the machinery of barbarism constructed by the dictators. Circumstances will determine for each one of us the degree of direct participation in active combat which this obligation may warrant. But there is one thing which is in reach of all: the immediate waging of the fight at home against those evils which offend and concern us in others.

A campaign of such universal extension is not won alone in the trenches of the enemy. It is also won at home through greater unity, through more work, through greater production and through the benefit of pure democracy in which our brothers, our comrades and even our enemies may discover a promise capable of giving to their lives a better content.

The difficulties with which we will be confronted will be very great. I recognize it. However, the energies of the people who are fighting against Nazi-Fascism and the honesty of the statesmen who direct them are high pledges that the faith of which I speak will not be destroyed in the deliberations over the peace.

In order to contribute to the work of the post-war period the United States and Mexico are placed in a situation of undeniable possibilities and obligations. Geography has made of us a natural bridge of conciliation between the Latin and the Anglo-Saxon cultures of the continent. If there is any place where the Good Neighborhood policy may be proved, it is right here in the juxtaposition of our countries.

Our successes and our errors will have in the future a tremendous significance, because they will represent not only the successes or failures of Mexico and the United States but rather an example, a stimulus or a disillusionment for all America. There is our primary responsibility. And thus there can best be appreciated the usefulness of these interviews which permit us to consider at close range our problems and try to solve them with the best and clearest understanding.

You have been witness of the enthusiasm with which my fellow countrymen have assumed the burden assigned them by these strenuous times both in the carrying out of military service and in the multiple activities required by the industrial and agricultural mobilization of the country. At this table you see gathered together diverse representatives of a particularly enthusiastic and hardworking region. The other regions of the Republic of Mexico have also united in the rhythm of a production which is continually furnishing a quantity of aid to the Allied arsenal.

With the same spirit our workmen, every day in greater numbers, are going to the fields of the United States to lend their assistance in tasks which for the time being have had to be abandoned by farmers who have been drafted. This assistance, which is being coordinated with United States mobilization is — in addition to a symbol in which we understand the duties of reciprocal aid between peoples — a demonstration of the strong will which animates us.

For my part I am glad to express to you the admiration with which we in Mexico observe the prodigious effort being made by your country to hasten the end of the war. The enthusiasm with which your young men have rushed to battle areas and their bravery in offering their lives for the redemption of the oppressed awake in us an austere continental pride.

At the same time I congratulate myself on this opportunity of shaking the hand of a loyal friend. I repeat to you, Mr. President, together with the sentiments of solidarity of my country and our wish for the success of our common cause, the desire that the relations between Mexico and the United States of America may develop — always — along the channels of mutual esteem and unceasing devotion to liberty.

(b) Address of the President of the United States (Roosevelt) [1]

MR. PRESIDENT:

Your Excellency's friendly and cordial expressions add to the very great pleasure which I feel at being here on Mexican soil.

It is an amazing thing to have to realize that nearly 34 years have passed since Chief Executives of our two nations have met face to face. I hope that in the days to come every Mexican and every American President will feel at liberty to visit each other just as neighbors visit each other — just as neighbors talk things over and get to know each other better.

Our two countries owe their independence to the fact that your ancestors and mine held the same truths to be worth fighting for and dying for. Hidalgo and Juárez were men of the same stamp as Washington and Jefferson. It was, therefore, inevitable that our two countries should find themselves alined together in the great struggle which is being fought today to determine whether this shall be a free or a slave world.

The attacks of the Axis powers during the past few years against our common heritage as free men culminated in the unspeakable and unprovoked aggressions of December 7, 1941 and May 14, 1942 and the shedding of blood on those dates of citizens of the United States and of Mexico alike.

Those attacks did not find the Western Hemisphere unprepared. The 21 free republics of the Americas during the past 10 years have devised a system of international cooperation which has become a great bulwark in the defense of our heritage and our future. That system, whose strength is now evident even to the most skeptical, is based primarily upon a renunciation of the use of force and the enshrining of international justice and mutual respect as the governing rule of conduct by all nations.

In the forging of that new international policy the role of Mexico has been outstanding. Mexican Presidents and Foreign Ministers have appreciated the nature of the struggle with which we are now confronted at a time when many nations much closer to the focus of infection were blind.

The wisdom of the measures which the statesmen of Mexico and the United States and of the other American Republics have adopted at inter-American gatherings during recent years has been amply demon-

[1] Department of State, *Bulletin*, VIII, p. 348.

strated. They have succeeded because they have been placed in effect not only by Mexico and the United States but by all except one of the other American Republics.

You and I, Mr. President, as Commanders in Chief of our respective armed forces, have been able to concert measures for common defense. The harmony and mutual confidence which has prevailed between our Armies and Navies is beyond praise. Brotherhood in arms has been established.

The determination of the Mexican people and of their leaders has led to production on an all-out basis of strategic and vital materials so necessary to the forging of the weapons destined to compass the final overthrow of our common foe. In this great city of Monterrey I have been most impressed with the single-minded purpose with which all the forces of production are joined together in the war effort.

And Mexican farm workers, brought to the United States in accordance with an agreement between our two Governments, the terms of which are fully consonant with the social objectives we cherish together, are contributing their skill and their toil to the production of vitally needed food.

Not less important than the military cooperation and the supplies needed for the maintenance of our respective economies, has been the exchange of those ideas and of those moral values which give life and significance to the tremendous effort of the free peoples of the world. We in the United States have listened with admiration and profit to your statements and addresses, Mr. President, and to those of your distinguished Foreign Minister. We have gained inspiration and strength from your words.

In the shaping of a common victory our peoples are finding that they have common aspirations. They can work together for a common objective. Let us never lose our hold upon that truth. It contains within it the secret of future happiness and prosperity for all of us on both sides of our unfortified border. Let us make sure that when our victory is won, when the forces of evil surrender — and that surrender shall be unconditional — then we, with the same spirit and with the same united courage, will face the task of the building of a better world.

There is much work still to be done by men of good-will on both sides of our border. The great Mexican people have their feet set upon a path of ever greater progress so that each citizen may enjoy the greatest possible measure of security and opportunity. The Government of the United States and my countrymen are ready to contribute to that progress.

We recognize a mutual interdependence of our joint resources. We know that Mexico's resources will be developed for the common good of humanity. We know that the day of the exploitation of the resources and the people of one country for the benefit of any group in another country is definitely over.

It is time that every citizen in every one of the American Republics recognizes that the Good-Neighbor policy means that harm to one republic means harm to every republic. We have all of us recognized the principle of independence. It is time that we recognize also the privilege of interdependence — one upon another.

Mr. President, it is my hope that in the expansion of our common effort in this war and in the peace to follow we will again have occasion for friendly consultation in order further to promote the closest understanding and continued unity of purpose between our two peoples.

We have achieved close understanding and unity of purpose. I am grateful to you, Mr. President, and to the Mexican people for this opportunity to meet you on Mexican soil and to call you friends.

You and I are breaking another precedent. Let these meetings between Presidents of Mexico and the United States recur again and again and again.

D. Disturbances in Los Angeles

(1) Department of State Release, June 16, 1943 [1]

In Los Angeles, California, during the week of June 7, 1943, there was rioting between United States sailors and young Americans, most of them of Mexican descent, clad in zoot suits.[2] At the height of the disturbances it seemed certain that hundreds of zoot suiters who had committed no crime and hundreds of sailors who had not been molested were fighting over incidents about which they knew little or nothing. A harassed City Council, in an effort to stop the struggle, prohibited the wearing of zoot suits. The Navy declared Los Angeles "out of bounds" for sailors. The Army warned of "harsh punishment" for soldiers found guilty of riotous conduct.

The Mexican Ambassador called upon the Secretary of State on June 15 in order to express the concern of his Government at the recent disturbances in Los Angeles and vicinity. The Secretary assured the Ambassador that the Department of State had been closely following the situation as it has developed since these disturbances first began. He assured the Ambassador that the local authorities, in cooperation with the military and naval authorities, have been doing everything possible to ameliorate the situation. He also stated that full investigation of these incidents is being conducted by Federal and local authorities. If as a result of those investigations it is found that there are cases involving Mexican citizens (and none has yet been found), the resulting

---

[1] Ibid., p. 545.
[2] A zoot suit comprises a flat hat with a very wide brim, and over-long jacket, trousers bagged out at knees and tied in at the ankles, a watch chain almost long enough to trip the wearer and shoes sharply pointed and with thick soles (New York Times, June 13, 1943, p. 2E).

claims will be expeditiously handled by this Government in accordance with principles of international law and the principles of justice and equity which the two Governments jointly uphold.

8. PANAMA — OBLIGATIONS UNDER THE TREATIES OF 1903 AND 1936

Under the provisions of the Canal Convention of 1903, the United States acquired the right to install water and sewerage systems in the cities of Colón and Panamá, with the understanding that these were to revert to and become the properties of these cities in 1957. The United States also acquired extensive real estate titles, including reversionary rights to certain properties owned by the Panama Canal Company.

The possession by the United States Government of these property rights in Panama has long been a source of friction and misunderstanding in the relations between the two countries. The treaty of March 2, 1936, effective July 27, 1939, went far to put relations on a more satisfactory basis so far as their respective national interests and desires were concerned. Following the attack at Pearl Harbor and the declarations of war by Germany and Italy on the United States, Panama declared war on the principal Axis powers. By Executive Agreement of May 18, 1942,[1] certain areas necessary for the defense of the Canal were leased to the United States by the Government of Panama. Thus relations between the two countries were such as to inspire confidence by us in the possibility of placing the defense of the Canal on a cooperative basis.

It was against the background of increased confidence and cooperation in the relations between the two countries, that the President made the request that the United States voluntarily make certain concessions to Panama, not required by any legal commitment. The proposed concessions included (1) the conveyance to Panama of the water and sewerage systems of the cities of Panamá and Colón; (2) the relinquishment of extensive real estate holdings in the cities of Panamá and Colón, insofar as these were not essential to the operation and protection of the Canal; and (3) the liquidation of a credit of two and one-half million dollars made available to Panama by the Export-Import Bank for the construction of Panama's share of the Chorrera-Rio Hato highway. The President's request was accompanied by the draft of a Joint Resolution for giving effect to his recommendations.

The Joint Resolution was originally introduced in the House as H. J. Res. 342, 77th Cong., and was favorably reported by the House Foreign Affairs Committee on September 30, 1942.[2] The companion measure in the Senate was S. J. Res. 162 which was amended and reported favorably by the Senate Committee on Foreign Relations on November 25, 1942[3] and further amended and adopted by the Senate on December 4, 1942. Due to the lack of a quorum during the last few weeks of the 77th Congress, final consideration could not be given to the measure by the House. Upon the opening of the new Congress on January 6, 1943, this resolution as amended in the Senate was reintroduced in the House as H. J. Res. 14, reported favorably by the House Committee on Foreign Affairs on March 22, 1943,[4] and passed by the House on April 13. The Senate Committee on Foreign Relations reported the resolution favorably on April 22,[5] Senators Johnson and Nye again submitting a minority report[6] and the resolution was adopted by the Senate on April 26, yeas 37, nays 19, not voting 40.[7]

[1] *Documents, IV, 1941–42,* p. 344.
[2] House Rept. No. 2498, 77th Cong., 2d sess.
[3] Senate Rept. No. 1720, 77th Cong., 2d sess. A minority report was filed by Senators Johnson and Nye, *ibid.,* part 2.
[4] House Rept. No. 271, 78th Cong., 1st sess.
[5] Senate Rept. No. 201, 78th Cong., 1st sess.
[6] *Ibid.,* part 2.
[7] *Congressional Record,* vol. 89, pt. 3, p. 3755.

Apart from certain questions of a technical nature relating to the protection of American interests, the principal question that was discussed in the Senate was the propriety of dealing with the matter by joint resolution and executive agreement instead of by treaty. The opposition to the joint resolution was chiefly based on the argument, stated in the minority report of Senators Nye and Johnson, that the whole matter should be handled by treaty requiring the consent of two-thirds of the Senate. An excerpt from the minority report is given below.

(1) *Message of the President (Roosevelt) to the Congress, August 13, 1942* [1]

To the Congress of the United States:

The Treaty of Friendship and Cooperation between the United States of America and the Republic of Panama, effective on July 27, 1939,[2] was a definitive step in the clarification of this Government's relations with the Republic of Panama. The Panamanian Government has demonstrated its willingness to assume promptly and wholeheartedly the burdens imposed upon it as partner in the defense of the Panama Canal, a responsibility which was accepted by that Government under the provisions of the new treaty.

The attitude of the Panamanian Government in the present international crisis has been thoroughly cooperative. On March 5, 1941 the President of the Republic of Panama issued a manifesto making available for use by the United States certain defense sites in the territory of that Republic. Pending the conclusions of final arrangements regarding the terms on which these sites are to be used, the Panamanian Government has permitted our armed forces to occupy and develop them. Immediately following the attack by the Japanese on Pearl Harbor Panama declared war on the three major Axis powers, and since has taken numerous protective steps to cooperate with the other American Republics in the interest and security of the Panama Canal and the defense of this hemisphere.

This attitude is tangible evidence that the relations between the two countries are now firmly based upon a recognition of mutual interest and a disposition to assume common responsibilities.

In my opinion, the time has come for this Government to make certain concessions which have been desired by the Republic of Panama over a period of years, and in this manner to correct certain factors in the relations between the two countries which do not make for confidence and friendship between our two countries.

Accordingly, I deem it advisable that this Government convey to Panama the water and sewerage systems in the cities of Panamá and Colón; that it relinquish its extensive real estate holdings in the cities

[1] Department of State, *Bulletin*, VII, p. 698.
[2] United States *Treaty Series* 945.

of Colón and Panamá, so far as these holdings are not essential to the operation and protection of the Canal; and that it liquidate the credit of two and a half million dollars made available to the Republic of Panama by the Export-Import Bank for the construction of Panama's share of the Chorrera-Rio Hato Highway, a road essential to our defense requirements and constructed in accordance with standards made essential by these requirements.

It will be recalled that the interest of the United States in the sanitation of the Canal Zone, together with that of the cities of Panamá and Colón, has been of outstanding importance. Concurrent with the construction of the Panama Canal, through agreement with Panama, the United States installed water and sewerage systems in the cities of Panamá and Colón, and throughout subsequent years has been responsible for the operation and maintenance of these systems and for the sanitation of the two cities.

I now propose to the Congress, that since in accordance with Article VII of the Canal Convention of 1903,[1] the "system of sewers and waterworks shall revert to and become the properties of the cities of Panamá and Colón" in the year 1957, it authorize the Government to convey all its right, title and interest in the Panama and Colón water and sewerage systems to the Republic of Panama; *Provided, however,* that the Republic of Panama shall pay quarterly a rate of B/0.09 per one thousand gallons or a reasonable rate to be agreed upon by both Governments to the appropriate Canal Zone authorities for water supplied at the Canal Zone boundary; and *provided,* also, that the turning over to the Government of the Republic of Panama of the physical properties of the water and sewerage systems and the administration thereof, including the collection of the water rates, does not in any way modify the existing arrangement for the responsibility for the public health services of the cities of Panamá and Colón as specified in the second paragraph of Article VII of the Convention between the United States of America and Panama, signed at Washington, November 18, 1903, which reads as follows:

The Republic of Panama agrees that the cities of Panamá and Colón shall comply in perpetuity with the sanitary ordinances whether of a preventive or curative character prescribed by the United States and in case the Government of Panama is unable or fails in its duty to enforce this compliance by the cities of Panamá and Colón with the sanitary ordinances of the United States the Republic of Panama grants to the United States the right and authority to enforce the same.

This Government, in continuing to maintain the health services in the cities of Panamá and Colón, will ask the Government of the Republic of Panama to cooperate fully with the appropriate Canal Zone officials in

[1] United States *Treaty Series* 431; *Treaties, Conventions,* etc., II, 1776–1909, p. 1349.

carrying out the proposal regarding increased participation of Panamanian personnel in sanitation activities in those cities as provided for in the exchange of notes [1] accompanying the General Treaty of March 2, 1936.

You will recall that the Panama Railroad Company, a corporation whose stock is now wholly owned by the United States, acquired the Island of Manzanillo (the present site of the city of Colón) through concessionary contracts with the Republic of New Granada, signed in 1850, 1856, and 1867. The railroad's interest in this property was acquired for ninety-nine years from August 1867, or until August 1966. The reversionary rights to these lands remained originally with the Republic of Panama, which, however, in the Canal Convention concluded between the United States and Panama in 1903, conveyed these rights to the United States. Thus until August 1966, the Panama Railroad Company enjoys the usufruct of the lands on which the city of Colón stands, and thereafter the United States will acquire title thereto, in perpetuity. As an element of such ownership the railroad company has, of course, over a period of years rented the property in Colón to Panamanian citizens — merchants, business men, and residents, and is, in fact, the principal landlord in Colón. For obvious reasons this is unsatisfactory.

I think, therefore, that this Government should promptly withdraw from the real estate business in the Republic of Panama and convey to that country its rights, title and interest, as well as its reversionary rights, to all the Panama Railroad Company land in the cities of Panamá and Colón which is not needed for the operation of the railroad or for the operation, maintenance, sanitation or protection of the Canal.

I also wish to invite your attention to the Act approved July 20, 1939 (Public Numbered 200, Seventy-sixth Congress, Chapter 335, First Session) [2] authorizing an appropriation of not to exceed $1,500,000 "to meet such expenses as the President, in his discretion, may deem necessary to enable the United States to cooperate with the Republic of Panama in connection with the construction of a highway between Chorrera and Rio Hato in the Republic of Panama."

I also wish to refer to the Act approved August 9, 1939 (Public Numbered 361, Seventy-sixth Congress, Chapter 633, First Session) [3] entitled "An Act Making Appropriations to Supply Deficiencies in Certain Appropriations for the Fiscal Year Ending June 30, 1939 and June 30, 1940 and for Other Purposes," which contains under the heading "Corps of Engineers" the following appropriation:

Chorrera and Rio Hato road, Republic of Panama: To enable the United States to cooperate with the Republic of Panama in connection with the construc-

---

[1] Published as a corporate part of the treaty, which was signed on March 2, 1936 and proclaimed on July 27, 1939 (*Treaty Series* 945).
[2] 53 Stat. 1071.　　　　　　　　　　　　　　[3] 53 Stat. 1301.

tion of a highway between Chorrera and Rio Hato, in the Republic of Panama, as authorized by the Act approved July 20, 1939 (Public Numbered 200, 76th Congress), $1,500,000 fiscal year 1940, to remain available until expended.

It is to be noted that, while the appropriation of the United States for its share of the cost of the highway amounted to $1,500,000, the Export-Import Bank, in a contract signed February 21, 1940 with the Banco Nacional of Panama and the Republic of Panama agreed, under specific conditions, to cooperate in the financing of the Panamanian share of the construction cost to the extent of $2,500,000.

In accordance with the provisions of the aforesaid Acts of Congress and the arrangements made by Panama with the Export-Import Bank the Ambassador of Panama in Washington, representatives of the War Department, of the Export-Import Bank, and of the Public Roads Administration, Federal Works Agency, in 1940 reached a mutually acceptable basis on which the two governments would cooperate in this work, and which provided that responsibility for the construction of the highway would be in the hands of Panamanian authorities but with the advice of engineers of the Public Roads Administration.

The War Department, through the Public Roads Administration, in 1941 stressed the urgency of rapidly completing the Rio Hato Highway and asked that every effort be made immediately to transfer the responsibility for this work from the Panamanian Government to the Public Roads Administration.

The Panamanian Government agreed to this request and the transfer of responsibility was effected on December 29, 1941, with a request by the Panamanian Government that, in accordance with conversations held between the Panamanian Foreign Minister and the Under Secretary of State in June 1941, Panama's indebtedness arising out of a credit made available by the Export-Import Bank be liquidated at the earliest possible date.

With a view to effecting the proposed changes indicated, I recommend to the Congress its consideration of a draft Joint Resolution which is hereto annexed.[1]

FRANKLIN D. ROOSEVELT

(2) *Minority Views of Senator Nye (for Himself and Senator Johnson of California) from the Senate Committee on Foreign Relations Report, to Accompany H. J. Res. 14, April 22, 1943*[2]

[Excerpts]

. . . .

The minority of your committee quite agrees that every step proper to take should be taken to remove possible sources of irritation and mis-

[1] H. J. Res. 342, 77th Cong., 2d sess.
[2] Senate Rept. No. 201, 78th Cong., 1st sess., part 2.

understanding in the relationships between our country and the Republic of Panama. But irritation is a condition that can prevail on the part of the United States as well as upon the part of the Government of Panama, and we feel that there is substantial ground for irritation because of the manner in which the agreements undertaken between our country and Panama are, and are not, submitted to the Congress of the United States. The failure to submit the subject matters of agreements to the Congress of the United States constitutes an attempt to guide the foreign policy of the country by Executive agreements, without consultation with Congress and without the approval of the people of the United States, whose representatives the Senate and House of Representatives are. It seems exceedingly dangerous to grant that the President may make Executive agreements even though those agreements are not legal, because foreign governments do not make that distinction. The Constitution contains no provisions relative to Executive agreements such as that which relates to treaties. Congress cannot ignore these trends if our constitutional government is to endure. We cannot too jealously guard against encroachments upon constitutional and representative government.

TREATY INSTEAD OF RESOLUTION

Why should not the Congress of the United States be consulted and advised with and its consent obtained for such a policy as has been pursued by our Government in Panama in connection with these agreements, these undertakings of May of last year? The people of Panama, through their Congress, are of necessity being consulted with respect to at least a part of the May agreements. It would seem to us that in this day of our leadership in the cause of preserving democratic ways, we are being out-distanced, in example at least, by Panama. The Congress of the United States is ignored in this particular agreement and told, in effect, that Congress is no longer of any force or effect in agreements which its Government may enter into internationally, while those governments with which we make the international agreements are under requirement to submit them for ratification to the representatives of the people.

The fact that we are enjoying full measure of cooperation in Panama so far as our war needs are concerned, and the further fact that the Panamanian Congress has not yet ratified the so-called agreement of last May, is ample cause for us to be less solicitous about speeding these contracts to a conclusion without thorough deliberation. Goodwill and good neighborliness are not in any wise or degree at stake if we would seem to move slowly in our consideration of what has been done and in doing what we are asked to do by passing Senate Joint Resolution 14.

. . . .

SUBJECT DESERVES DIGNITY OF TREATY

We submit that this joint resolution involves a subject not properly dealt with in a legislative bill. All contracts and agreements between independent nations are, according to legal and constitutional definition, treaties. The joint resolution before us is a subject of a treaty nature under that definition. Indeed, the title of the joint resolution describes its subject matter as being a treaty insofar as it declares that the joint resolution authorizes "the execution of certain obligations under the treaties of 1903 and 1936 with Panama." Surely an instrument to supplement a treaty can be of no less dignity than the parent instrument itself, and if a further supplemental agreement is to be made with Panama, it must be with the dignity of a treaty and must come before the Senate in that form. Under the Constitution we cannot properly act on the proposed bill except in the constitutional way, in the way provided by the Constitution itself. The bill should be referred back to the Executive who is empowered under the Constitution to negotiate treaties and after a treaty has been negotiated by the Executive, it is then proper that it be presented to the Senate for its advice and consent. We are in honor bound to abide by the procedure provided for in the Constitution.

We believe that the Senate should insist that matters involved in Senate Joint Resolution 14, which should properly be in a treaty, be handled as a treaty. The founding fathers felt that the matter of assuming obligations or making promises to do something in the future for foreign nations was of sufficient importance to require that the proposal have the support of two-thirds of the Senators elected to the Senate.

A further point is properly raised with reference to the title of Senate Joint Resolution 14, which reads as follows: "Authorizing the execution of certain obligations under the treaties of 1903 and 1936 with Panama, and other commitments." It is pointed out that neither the treaty of 1903 nor the treaty of 1936 provided for the transfer of real estate as set forth in section 2, nor the cancellation of Panama's debt, covered by section 3 of Senate Joint Resolution 14, and in the case of the transfer of the water and sewer systems did not make this effective until 1957, despite the fact that the title of the measure before the Senate flatly states that this measure is merely "authority to the Executive to carry out certain obligations" under the previous agreements. We object to this language as an attempt to mislead the Senate and House into the impression that they are merely carrying out existing obligations — contrary to fact.

.   .   .   .

(3) *Joint Resolution Authorizing the Execution of Certain Obligations under the Treaties of 1903 and 1936 with Panama, and Other Commitments, Approved May 3, 1943* [1]

Resolved by the Senate and House of Representatives of the United States of America in Congress assembled, That the President of the United States be, and is hereby, authorized to transfer to the Republic of Panama all of the right, title, and interest of the United States in and to water and sewerage systems installed by the United States in the cities of Panamá and Colón: *Provided, however,* That pending the establishment of an independent water-supply system, and so long as the Republic of Panama desires to utilize a supply of water from the Canal Zone, it shall pay quarterly to the appropriate Canal Zone authorities the rate of B/0.09 per one thousand gallons or such other reasonable rate as may be agreed upon by both Governments: *And provided further,* That the turning over to the Government of the Republic of Panama of the physical properties of the water and sewerage systems and the administration thereof, including the collection of the water rates, does not in any way modify the existing arrangement in respect to responsibility for the public health services of the cities of Panamá and Colón as specified in the second paragraph of article VII of the Convention between the United States of America and Panama, signed at Washington, November 18, 1903.

Sec. 2. The Panama Railroad Company is hereby authorized to convey to the Republic of Panama, in whole or in part, all of its right, title, and interest in and to so much of the lands of the Panama Railroad Company located in the cities of Panamá and Colón as, in the opinion of the Secretary of War, are no longer needed for the operation of the Panama Railroad or for the operation, maintenance, sanitation, or defense of the Panama Canal: *Provided,* That any such instruments of conveyance shall contain a provision under which the Panama Railroad Company and any of its successors in interest agrees to fully protect the Government of the United States against any claims for damages or losses heretofore or hereafter incurred by any lessee of any of the lands covered by such conveyance. The authority conferred by this section shall not be exercised after June 30, 1944.

(a) Any conveyance of any land in pursuance of the authority contained herein shall be deemed to release any and all reversionary rights of the United States in said property.

(b) The provisions of the joint resolution entitled "Joint resolution authorizing the disposal of certain lands held by the Panama Railroad Company on Manzanillo Island, Republic of Panama," approved July 10, 1937, so far as they may conflict with the provisions of this joint resolution, are hereby modified accordingly.

[1] Public Law 48, 78th Cong.

Sec. 3. There is hereby authorized to be appropriated out of any moneys in the Treasury, not otherwise appropriated, a sum not to exceed $2,700,000, to enable the Secretary of the Treasury to pay to the Republic of Panama an amount equivalent to the principal and interest paid by that government on account of the credit of $2,500,000 made available to it by the Export-Import Bank for the construction of Panama's share of the Chorrera-Rio Hato Highway, and to pay to the Export-Import Bank an amount sufficient to liquidate the remaining obligation of the Republic of Panama to that bank on account of the aforesaid credit.

(4) *Entry into Force of Agreement for Lease of Defense Sites between Panama and the United States, Signed May 18, 1942. Department of State Release, May 22, 1943* [1]

[For text of agreement see *Documents, IV, 1941–42,* p. 344.]

By a despatch dated May 12, 1943 the American Embassy at Panamá informed the Secretary of State that on May 10, 1943 the National Assembly of Panama approved the agreement between the United States and Panama which was signed at Panamá on May 18, 1942, providing for the lease to the United States of defense sites in Panama, and that on May 11, 1943 the National Executive Power of Panama signed Panamanian Law No. 141 by which the agreement was approved.

It is provided in the agreement that it will enter into effect when approved by the National Executive Power of Panama and the National Assembly of Panama.

2. CANADIAN–AMERICAN RELATIONS

A. Prosecution of the War

1. MILITARY SERVICE

[See *Documents, IV, 1941–42,* p. 446.]

(1) *Service in the United States Armed Forces of American Citizens Residing in Canada. Exchange of Notes between the Canadian Minister at Washington (McCarthy) and the Secretary of State (Hull), September 30, 1942* [2]

Through an exchange of notes at Ottawa on March 18 and 20, 1942 [3] the Canadian Government agreed to the transfer to the armed forces of the United States of certain United States citizens and former United States citizens who were serving in the Canadian armed forces. To facilitate the return of these men

[1] Department of State, *Bulletin,* VIII, p. 459.
[2] *Ibid.,* VII, p. 789.
[3] *Documents, IV, 1941–42,* p. 446.

the Canadian-American Military Board, composed of members of the various branches of the armed services, was set up. Between May 5 and June 3 the Board visited many of the principal military camps across Canada and effected the transfer of over 2,000 Americans.[1]

The following notes were exchanged on September 30, 1942 between the Canadian Minister at Washington and the Department of State in regard to a procedure under which American citizens residing in Canada who had not declared their intention of becoming naturalized in Canada might elect to serve in the United States forces in lieu of service in the Canadian forces.

(a) The Canadian Minister at Washington (McCarthy) to the Secretary of State (Hull)

Sir:

I have the honor to refer to your note of April 8, 1942,[2] in reply to my note No. 222 of April 6 [3] concerning the application of the United States Selective Training and Service Act of 1940, as amended, to Canadian nationals residing in the United States, and stating that the Government of the United States assures the Government of Canada full reciprocity with respect to the regime outlined in your note of March 30 under which Canadian nationals in the United States who have not declared their intention of becoming United States citizens may elect to serve in the naval, military or air forces of Canada in lieu of service in the armed forces of the United States. In your note you further state that the Government of the United States agrees to the understandings, limitations and assumptions set forth in numbered paragraphs 4 to 9 inclusive of my note.

2. One of these understandings is that the Government of the United States is agreeable to the Canadian Government imposing a liability to compulsory military service on United States citizens residing in Canada. A second understanding is that while non-declarant United States citizens in Canada will, prior to their induction into the naval, military or air forces of Canada, be granted an opportunity of electing to serve in the armed forces of the United States, this opportunity will not be granted to declarant United States citizens in Canada.

3. In accordance with these understandings the Canadian Government has recently imposed on United States citizens residing in Canada a liability to compulsory military service identical with that imposed on British subjects ordinarily resident in Canada, and the Canadian Government now desires to initiate a procedure satisfactory to the Government of the United States under which United States citizens in Canada who have not declared their intention of applying for naturalization in Canada may elect to serve in the armed forces of the United States, in lieu of service in the armed forces of Canada, at any time prior to enrolment in the Canadian Army.

[1] Department of State, *Bulletin* VII, p. 711.
[2] *Documents, IV, 1941–42*, p. 453.   [3] *Ibid.*, p. 450.

4. The following proposals are made by the Canadian Government:

(a) Individuals who elect for service with the armed forces of the United States will be physically examined by the Canadian Army. The results of the examination will be forwarded to the proper authorities of the United States. On receipt from these authorities of notification that an individual is acceptable the competent Canadian authority will send the individual to a designated reception point for induction into the armed forces of the United States. If, on arrival at the reception point, the individual is found to be not acceptable to the armed forces of the United States, he shall be liable to be enrolled immediately in the Canadian Army.

(b) In order that non-declarant United States citizens in Canada may be informed of the conditions of service in the armed forces of the United States, the Canadian Government suggests that the United States authorities give the Canadian authorities copies of a pamphlet setting forth the conditions of service so that the pamphlets may be made available to non-declarant United States citizens who are called up for military service by Canada.

(c) United States citizens in Canada who elect to serve in the armed forces of the United States and are accepted by one of those forces and who return to Canada for permanent residence within six months after the termination of their service with the United States armed forces will not lose any rights they may have previously acquired under the Immigration and Naturalization Acts of Canada.

5. Acceptance by the United States of these proposals will not be construed by the Canadian Government as imposing any obligation on the United States Government to return to Canada United States citizens who may be deemed to be defaulters under the National War Services (Recruits) Regulations of Canada.

6. If these proposals are acceptable to the Government of the United States, this note and your reply thereto accepting the proposals shall be regarded as placing on record the understanding arrived at between the two Governments concerning this matter. The practical details may then be arranged directly between the appropriate governmental agencies.

Accept [etc.]

(b) *The Secretary of State (Hull) to the Canadian Minister at Washington (McCarthy)*

Sir:

I have the honor to acknowledge the receipt of your note no. 638 of September 30, 1942 proposing an arrangement under which American citizens residing in Canada, who have not declared their intention of applying for naturalization in Canada, and who may become subject to enrolment in the armed forces of Canada will, prior to such enrolment, be given an opportunity of electing to serve in the armed forces of the United States. You also state that acceptance of the proposals will not be construed by your Government as imposing any obligation on the Government of the United States to return to Canada any citizens of the United States who may be deemed to be defaulters under the National War Services (Recruits) Regulations of Canada. Your proposals are made on the understanding that the United States Government is agreeable to the Canadian Government imposing a liability to compulsory military service on United States citizens residing in Canada, and that the opportunity of electing to serve in the armed forces of the United States will be granted only to American citizens residing in Canada who have not declared their intention of applying for naturalization in Canada.

I am pleased to inform you that the Government of the United States agrees to the Canadian Government imposing a liability to military service on United States citizens residing in Canada, and that the proposed arrangement as outlined in your note under acknowledgment is satisfactory to this Government.

Accept [etc.]

2. MOVEMENTS OF PERSONS AND GOODS ACROSS THE BORDER

(1) Free Movement of Persons, Property, and Information Into and Out of the United States. Message of the President (Roosevelt) to the Congress, November 2, 1942 [1]

The recommendations contained in the President's message were referred in the House to the Committee on Ways and Means,[2] and in the Senate to the Committee on Judiciary.[3] No further action was taken. There appeared to be a widespread feeling that the recommendations were broader than the war emergency justified and pointed in the direction of long-range modifications of national policy which Congress at the time was not prepared to undertake.

To THE CONGRESS OF THE UNITED STATES:

On December 23, 1941 I approved a statement of war production policy for Canada and the United States,[4] which contained the following recommendation.

Legislative and administrative barriers, including tariffs, import duties, customs, and other regulations or restrictions of any character which prohibit, prevent, delay, or otherwise impede the free flow of necessary munitions and war supplies between the two countries should be suspended or otherwise eliminated for the duration of the war.

[1] Department of State, *Bulletin*, VII, p. 892.
[2] *Congressional Record*, vol. 88, pt. 7, p. 8792; House Doc. 882, 77th Cong., 2d sess.
[3] *Congressional Record*, vol. 88, pt. 7, p. 8697.
[4] Department of State, *Bulletin*, V, p. 578; *Documents, IV, 1941–42*, p. 439.

The needs of the war effort have multiplied our demands for a maximum and integrated war production not only at home and in Canada but in every country of the United Nations. We must further take advantage of possibilities of procurement from every available source, foreign or domestic. Speed and volume of war output have become more than ever before in our history the primary conditions of victory.

To achieve an all-out war production effort, we must implement and supplement the steps already taken by the Congress and the President to eliminate those peacetime restrictions which limit our ability to make the fullest and quickest use of the world's resources. At my direction, the Government agencies have already removed and are engaged in removing, wherever possible, numerous administrative requirements and formalities affecting the movement of war goods, information, and persons into or out of the United States. There remain, however, many legislative obstacles to that movement which impede and delay our war production effort.

These obstacles fall into two classes: Those directly affecting the movement to and from the customs territory of the United States of *matériel*, information, and persons needed for the war effort, such as customs duties and the laws, and the administrative supervision required by law affecting movement of persons and property at our borders and ports; and those which impose limitations on the procurement, acquisition, or use of non-American articles or the transportation of supplies in non-American bottoms, such as restrictions on the use, under construction differential subsidy contracts, of non-American materials in the construction of vessels under the Merchant Marine Act of 1936, as amended; on the procurement of any article of food or clothing not grown or produced in the United States or its possessions; on the acquisition for the public use, public buildings, or public works of non-American articles; or the transportation by sea of Navy supplies except in vessels of the United States.

I have already exercised by Executive order the power granted under the First War Powers Act to extend to the Government procurement agencies the authority granted to the Secretary of the Navy to make emergency purchases abroad of war materials and to enter them free of duty. This has measurably assisted our war effort, but it only partially eliminates the obstacles prescribed by law which I have already mentioned.

I, therefore, recommend early enactment by the Congress of legislation to the extent required for the effective prosecution of the war, the free movement of persons, property, and information into and out of the United States. I do not now recommend that the Congress repeal or amend any of these peacetime restrictive laws. It is my judgment that the problem can best be dealt with by giving to the President for the duration of the war, but no longer, the power on a selective and flexible basis to suspend the operation of all or any such laws, in such a way as to meet new and perhaps unforeseen problems as they may arise, and on such terms as will enable the Chief Executive and the Government agencies to work out in detail parallel action in other countries.

FRANKLIN D. ROOSEVELT

(2) Simplification of Border-Crossing Regulations on the Canadian Border. Department of State Release, February 12, 1943 [1]

The United States and the Canadian Governments, with a desire to simplify travel across the border, have agreed on changes which will exempt Canadian citizens and British subjects legally resident in Canada from the necessity of obtaining passports for visits of not more than 29 days. Entry to the United States for longer periods and for other groups will continue as at present.

Under the plan which will go into effect on February 15, 1943, a new type of non-immigrant border-crossing identification card that does not require a passport will be issued by United States consular officers in Canada and will bear an endorsement by a Canadian immigration officer guaranteeing the readmissibility of the bearer to Canada. This card will be valid for any number of visits during a period of one year from the date of its issue, provided that no one visit shall exceed 29 days. To prevent any inconvenience arising during the changeover, the non-immigrant border-crossing cards already issued will retain their validity until date of expiry and if desired may be renewed as in the past so long as the Canadian passport remains valid.

Persons desiring to obtain a border-crossing card of the new type must apply in person at an American consular office in Canada carrying three photographs, $1\frac{1}{2}''$ square, on non-glazed paper, showing full front views without head covering. They should also carry whatever evidence they have available as to birthplace, nationality, and the period of their residence in Canada. In the Consulate they will complete an application form in triplicate.

If the application is approved by the Consul, he will issue the border-crossing card and deliver both application and card to the Canadian immigration officer in the same center. The applicant will then call at the Canadian office for the endorsation of the crossing card guaranteeing readmission to Canada and will be given the card and one copy of the application form, the latter to be left with the United States immigration authorities at port of entry to the United States.

[1] Department of State, Bulletin, VIII, p. 154.

3. WAIVER OF CLAIMS

(1) *Agreement between the Governments of the United States and Canada, Effected by Exchange of Notes, Signed at Washington, May 25 and 26, 1943* [1]

(a) *The Secretary of State (Hull) to the Canadian Minister at Washington (McCarthy), May 25, 1943*

SIR:

With reference to recent communications between the Government of the United States of America and the Government of Canada in relation to the making of an agreement between the two Governments providing that each Government shall bear the cost of damages to its own vessels arising from collisions between United States warships and ships of the Royal Canadian Navy, I have the honor to inform you that the Government of the United States of America, with a view to facilitating the conduct of the war, is prepared to give effect to an agreement in the following terms:

ARTICLE I. The Government of the United States of America and the Government of Canada agree that when a vessel of war of either Government shall collide with a vessel of war of the other Government, resulting in damage to either or both of such vessels, each Government shall bear all the expenses which arise directly or indirectly from the damage to its own vessel, and neither Government shall make any claim against the other Government on account of such damage or expenses.

ARTICLE II. This Agreement shall apply in respect of claims arising since December 7, 1941, but remaining unsettled on the day this Agreement enters into force, as well as in respect of claims arising on or after such day and during the period in which the Agreement shall remain in force.

ARTICLE III. This Agreement shall remain in force until the expiration of six months from the day on which either Government shall have given to the other Government notice in writing of an intention to terminate the Agreement.

I have the honor to inform you that if an Agreement in accordance with the foregoing terms is acceptable to the Government of Canada, the agreement shall be considered by the Government of the United States of America to have been concluded and to be in effect as of the date of a corresponding note from you indicating that the Government of Canada is prepared to give effect to the Agreement.

Accept, Sir, the renewed assurances of my highest consideration.

[1] *Executive Agreement Series* 330.

(b) *The Canadian Minister (McCarthy) to the Secretary of State (Hull),*
   May 26, 1943

No. 276

SIR:

I have the honor to refer to your note of May 25, 1943 proposing an
agreement which the Government of the United States is prepared to
make with the Government of Canada for the waiver of claims arising
as a result of collisions between ships of the Royal Canadian Navy and
United States warships.

Under instructions from my Government I have the honor to inform
you in reply that the Canadian Government undertakes to give effect
to the agreement set forth in your note and understands that the agreement will come into force as of the date of this note; namely, May 26,
1943.

Accept, Sir, the renewed assurances of my highest consideration.

B. Economic Relations

(1) *Agreement between the Governments of the United States and*
   Canada Regarding Post-War Economic Settlements. Exchange
   of Notes between the Secretary of State (Hull) and the Canadian
   Minister at Washington (McCarthy), November 30, 1942 [1]

In this exchange of notes the two Governments formally record their concurrence that post-war settlements must be of a sort which will promote mutually
advantageous economic relations between them and the betterment of world-wide
economic relations.

In indicating the objectives of such post-war settlements the agreement follows
the underlying principles set forth in Article VII of the mutual-aid agreements
which have been negotiated with the United Kingdom and a number of other
countries. The two Governments indicate their readiness to cooperate in formulating a program of agreed action, open to participation by all other nations of
like mind.

To that end the agreement provides for the early commencement of conversations, within the framework which it outlines, between the Governments of
the United States and Canada and with representatives of other United Nations,
with a view to establishing now the foundations upon which may be created
after the war a system of enlarged production, exchange, and consumption
of goods for the satisfaction of human needs in our country, in Canada, and in all
other countries willing to join in this effort.

The agreement particularly emphasizes the similarity of interests on the part
of the United States and Canadian Governments in post-war international
economic policy and the collaboration for mutual aid in defense and in economic
matters which has been provided through the Ogdensburg and Hyde Park
Agreements [2] and subsequent arrangements.

[1] Department of State, *Bulletin*, VII, p. 977.
[2] *Documents, III, 1940–41*, p. 160–1.

(a) **The Secretary of State (Hull) to the Canadian Minister at Washington (McCarthy)**

SIR:

I have the honor to set forth below my understanding of the conclusions reached in conversations which have taken place from time to time during the past year between representatives of the Government of the United States and the Government of Canada with regard to post-war economic settlements.

Our two Governments are engaged in a cooperative undertaking, together with every other nation or people of like mind, to the end of laying the bases of a just and enduring world peace securing order under law to themselves and all nations. They have agreed to provide mutual aid both in defense and in economic matters through the Ogdensburg and Hyde Park Agreements and subsequent arrangements. They are in agreement that post-war settlements must be such as to promote mutually advantageous economic relations between them and the betterment of world-wide economic relations.

To that end the Governments of the United States of America and of Canada are prepared to cooperate in formulating a program of agreed action, open to participation by all other countries of like mind, directed to the expansion, by appropriate international and domestic measures, of production, employment, and the exchange and consumption of goods, which are the material foundations of the liberty and welfare of all peoples; to the elimination of all forms of discriminatory treatment in international commerce, and to the reduction of tariffs and other trade barriers; and, in general, to the attainment of all the economic objectives set forth in the Joint Declaration made on August 14, 1941,[1] by the President of the United States of America and the Prime Minister of the United Kingdom.

Our Governments have in large measure similar interests in post-war international economic policy. They undertake to enter at an early convenient date into conversations between themselves and with representatives of other United Nations with a view to determining, in the light of governing economic conditions, the best means of attaining the above-stated objectives by agreed action on the part of our two Governments and other like-minded Governments. In the conversations to be undertaken between the Governments of the United States of America and of Canada they will seek to furnish to the world concrete evidence of the ways in which two neighboring countries that have a long experience of friendly relations and a high degree of economic interdependence, and that share the conviction that such reciprocally beneficial relations

[1] *Ibid., IV, 1941–42*, p. 209.

must form part of a general system, may promote by agreed action their mutual interests to the benefit of themselves and other countries.

If the Government of Canada concurs in the foregoing statement of conclusions, I would suggest that the present note and your reply to that effect should be regarded as placing on record the understanding of our two Governments in this matter.

Accept [etc.]

(b) *The Canadian Minister at Washington (McCarthy) to the Secretary of State (Hull)*

SIR:

I have the honor to refer to your note of November 30th, 1942, setting forth your understanding of the conclusions reached in conversations between representatives of the Government of Canada and the Government of the United States with regard to post-war economic settlements. That understanding is as follows.

Our two Governments are prepared to cooperate in formulating a program of agreed action, open to participation by all other countries of like mind, directed to the expansion, by appropriate international and domestic measures, of production, employment, and the exchange and consumption of goods, which are the material foundations of the liberty and welfare of all peoples; to the elimination of all forms of discriminatory treatment in international commerce, and to the reduction of tariffs and other trade barriers; and, in general, to the attainment of all the economic objectives set forth in the Joint Declaration made on August 14th, 1941, by the President of the United States of America and the Prime Minister of the United Kingdom.

Our Governments have in large measure similar interests in post-war international economic policy. They undertake to enter at an early convenient date into conversations between themselves and with representatives of other United Nations with a view to determining, in the light of governing economic conditions, the best means of attaining the above-stated objectives by agreed action on the part of our two Governments and other like-minded Governments. In the conversations to be undertaken between the Governments of Canada and of the United States of America they will seek to furnish to the world concrete evidence of the ways in which two neighboring countries that have a long experience of friendly relations and a high degree of economic interdependence, and that share the conviction that such reciprocally beneficial relations must form part of a general system, may promote by agreed action their mutual interests to the benefit of themselves and other countries.

I am instructed to inform you that the Government of Canada concur in the foregoing statement of conclusions and agree to your suggestion that your note of November 30th, 1942, and this reply should be regarded as placing on record the understanding of our two Governments in this matter.

Accept [etc.]

(2) *Air Transport Services. Exchange of Notes between the Acting Secretary of State (Welles) and the Canadian Minister at Washington (McCarthy), March 4, 1943* [1]

By an exchange of notes on August 18, 1939 [2] the United States and Canada entered into an arrangement in regard to the operation on a reciprocal basis of air transport services between the two countries. Article III provided that the details of the application of the principle of reciprocity should be the subject of amicable adjustment between the competent aeronautical authorities of the parties to the arrangement.

By a further arrangement between the United States and Canada entered into by an exchange of notes effective December 3, 1940 [3] an agreement was reached as to routes allocated to United States air carriers and those allocated to Canadian air carriers. It was specifically provided that this agreement would be effective until December 31, 1942 and that at least six months prior to that date a further conference of representatives of the competent aeronautical authorities of the two Governments would be called for the purpose of considering any revision or modification of their recommendations, as embodied in the 1940 agreement, and any new problems pertaining to air-transport services which may have arisen in the interim. In view of the fact that it was impracticable because of the war situation for the aeronautical authorities of the two countries to hold another meeting prior to the expiration of the 1940 arrangement, an agreement between the United States and Canada was entered into on March 4 through an exchange of notes continuing the 1940 arrangement in force under the conditions set forth in these notes.

(a) *The Acting Secretary of State (Welles) to the Canadian Minister at Washington (McCarthy)*

I have the honor to refer to negotiations which have recently taken place between the Government of the United States of America and the Government of Canada for the conclusion of a reciprocal undertaking continuing in force the arrangement between the two Governments, entered into by an exchange of notes dated November 29, 1940 and December 2, 1940, for the purpose of giving effect to Article III of the Air Transport Arrangement between the two Governments concluded on August 18, 1939.

It is my understanding that it has been agreed in the course of the recent negotiations, now terminated, that the undertaking referred to in the preceding paragraph shall be as follows:

Having in mind the fact that because of the war situation it was impracticable for the aeronautical authorities of the United States and

---

[1] Department of State, *Bulletin*, VIII, p. 210.
[2] *Executive Agreement Series* 159.
[3] *Ibid.*, 186.

Canada to hold a meeting six months prior to December 31, 1942, as contemplated by the arrangement between the two Governments entered into by an exchange of notes dated November 29, 1940, and December 2, 1940, for the purpose of drawing up new recommendations relating to the allocation of air transport routes to United States and Canadian air carriers for operations between the United States and Canada, it is now agreed that, subject to the provisions of the succeeding paragraph, the 1940 arrangement as herein referred to shall be considered to have remained in force from December 31, 1942, and shall continue in force until the end of the war. It is also agreed that after the termination of the war a conference between representatives of the two Governments will be held for the purpose of reviewing the situation as it may then exist with respect to the application of the terms of the arrangement covered by the exchange of notes dated November 29, 1940 and December 2, 1940.

Notwithstanding the foregoing provisions, it is agreed that the present undertaking may be terminated at any time on six months' notice given in writing by either Government to the other Government for important reasons of public policy when the conditions thereof or the actual practice thereunder is no longer regarded by the Government of the country giving such notice as being in its interest. Such notice of termination shall be given by either Government to the other only after consultation between the two Governments for a period of at least sixty days.

I shall be glad to have you inform me whether it is the understanding of your Government that the terms of the undertaking agreed to in the recent negotiations, now terminated, are as above set forth. If so, it is suggested that the undertaking become effective on this date. If your Government concurs in this suggestion the Government of the United States will regard the undertaking as becoming effective on this date.

(b) The Canadian Minister at Washington (McCarthy) to the Acting Secretary of State (Welles)

I have the honor to refer to your note of March 4 setting forth your understanding of the reciprocal undertaking, agreed to in the course of the recent negotiations between the Government of Canada and the Government of the United States of America, to continue in force the arrangement between the two Governments entered into by an exchange of notes dated November 29, 1940 and December 2, 1940, for the purpose of giving effect to Article III of the Air Transport Arrangement between the two Governments concluded on August 18, 1939.

The Canadian Government confirms your understanding of the reciprocal undertaking and agrees that the undertaking shall be effective from the date of your note, namely March 4, 1943.

C. Fisheries

(1) *Approval of Halibut Regulations by the Canadian and United States Governments, January 29 and February 15, 1943. Department of State Announcement, March 13, 1943* [1]

The *Federal Register* of March 2, 1942 (Vol. 8, No. 42) contains on pages 2608–2610 the text of the regulations which, referred to as the 1943 Halibut Fishery Regulations, were prepared by the International Fisheries Commission pursuant to Articles I and III of the Convention between the United States and Canada for the preservation of the halibut fishery of the northern Pacific Ocean and Bering Sea signed at Washington January 29, 1937 (Treaty Series 917).[2]

The regulations, having been signed by the four members of the Commission, were, pursuant to the above-mentioned articles of the Convention, submitted for approval to the President of the United States of America and to the Governor General of Canada. The regulations were approved on behalf of Canada by an Order in Council of January 29, 1943 and by the President of the United States on February 15, 1943. They will supersede the 1942 regulations approved by the President on March 25, 1942 which were published in the *Federal Register* of April 16, 1942.

(2) *Report of the International Board of Inquiry for the Great Lakes Fisheries. Department of State Release, October 21, 1942* [3]

After two years of intensive investigation the International Board of Inquiry, established February 29, 1940 by the United States and Canada to study conservation of fisheries in the Great Lakes,[4] has submitted its report.[5] The report recommends that, based on the results of common studies of these fisheries, regulations for their management be formulated and tested by a joint agency of the two countries.

Establishment of the International Board of Inquiry grew out of a series of interstate and international conferences held during the past few years by the Council of State Governments for the conservation of the Great Lakes fisheries. The problem of conserving these fisheries had also long engaged the attention of the Governments of Canada

[1] Department of State, *Bulletin*, VIII, p. 224.
[2] *Treaties, Conventions*, etc., IV, 1923–1937, p. 4014.
[3] Department of State, *Bulletin*, VII, p. 858.
[4] *Ibid.*, II, p. 273.
[5] *International Board of Inquiry for the Great Lakes Fisheries. Report and Supplement.* Washington, Government Printing Office. 1943. 213 p.

and the United States, the Province of Ontario, and the States bordering on the Great Lakes. The production of certain species of Great Lakes fish had reached low levels.

During its two-year investigation the Board conducted hearings and meetings in 29 cities on the Great Lakes in which more than 1,500 commercial fishermen, public officials, and sportsmen participated. Facts brought out at the meetings were supplemented by information from 4,000 questionnaires mailed to commercial fishermen in the area.

The recommendations made by the full Board follow:

(1) That there be common investigation of the fisheries of the Great Lakes.

(2) That, so far as investigation shows fisheries to be dependent upon a common stock or to have the same conditions, regulations for management of these fisheries be formulated and tested by a common or joint agency.

(3) That where investigations are not conclusive such common regulations be applied and the results therefrom carefully determined until there is adequate proof of their effectiveness for the purpose.

(4) That the attention of the agencies concerned be drawn to the need (a) for accurate statistics of the take and of the fishing effort, (b) for separate statistics for each species of fish, and (c) for separate statistics for each of such districts as may be defined in common agreement.

(5) That thorough tests be made of the effectiveness of planting fish in a lake or lakes in order to determine whether the present planting of fish should or should not be continued or altered.

In a separate supplemental report [1] the United States members reviewed past efforts of the States and of the Federal Government to develop effective conservation measures for the Great Lakes fisheries, called attention to certain jurisdictional aspects of the problem, and presented extensive data on production in the fisheries investigated. The supplemental report of the United States representatives suggests a form of agreement which would vest control in established agencies in Canada and the United States, with regulation handled through the concurrent action of Federal and State Governments.

The report, together with a supplemental report by the United States representatives, was submitted to the Secretary of State and Prime Minister King. Members of the Board were Hubert R. Gallagher, Assistant Director, Council of State Governments, Chicago, Ill., *chairman;* A. G. Huntsman, Consulting Director, Fisheries Research Board of Canada, Toronto, Ont.; John Van Oosten, United States Fish and Wildlife Service, Ann Arbor, Mich.; and D. J. Taylor, Deputy Minister, Game and Fisheries Department, Toronto, Ont.

[1] *Ibid.*, p. 27.

3. EUROPEAN POSSESSIONS IN THE WESTERN HEMISPHERE

A. British Caribbean Possessions

(1) *The United States Section of the Anglo-American Caribbean Commission. Department of State Release, December 19, 1942* [1]

The announcement of the establishment of the Anglo-American Caribbean Commission was made by a joint communiqué, issued in London and Washington, March 9, 1942. For text, see *Documents, IV, 1941–42*, p. 459. The purpose of the action was announced to be the encouragement and strengthening of "social and economic cooperation between the United States of America and its possessions and bases in the area known geographically and politically as the Caribbean, and the United Kingdom and the British colonies in the same area, and to avoid unnecessary duplication of research in these fields."

The State Department has defined as follows the relation between the Anglo-American Caribbean Commission and the Caribbean Office of the Department of State.[2]

The Anglo-American Caribbean Commission has been set up by agreement between the Governments of the United States and Great Britain.[3] The United States Section, of which Mr. Charles W. Taussig is chairman, is directly responsible to the President, paralleling a similar organization set up by and responsible to the British Government to handle matters relating to the Caribbean area.

For reasons of administrative convenience, the United States Section of the Commission will be considered an integral unit of the Department.

The Caribbean Office of the Department, headed by Mr. Coert duBois since its establishment by Departmental Order 984, of October 9, 1941, in addition to such other duties as have already been specifically assigned or may hereafter be directed by the Secretary or the Under Secretary of State, to whom this Office is directly responsible, shall serve as the Executive Agency for the United States Section of the Anglo-American Caribbean Commission, the duties of which include the initiation and successful accomplishment of projects dealing with the public health and welfare of the possessions and territories of the United States and Great Britain in the Caribbean area. The Caribbean Office in the discharge of its function as Executive Agency will (1) furnish technical assistance on plans or projects worked up by the Commission, (2) maintain liaison jointly in behalf of the Department and the Commission with other offices of the Department and other departments and agencies of the Government concerned with common or related problems, and (3) keep the Commission appropriately apprised of all developments

[1] Department of State, *Bulletin*, VII, p. 1011.
[2] Departmental Order 1117, of December 14, 1942.
[3] Department of State, *Bulletin* VI, p. 229; *Documents, IV, 1941–42*, p. 459.

in its field of activity, as well as of plans, projects, or procedures developed on its own initiative and of common interest.

B. French West Indies and Guiana

Negotiations with Admiral Georges Robert, French Commissioner in the West Indies, with a view to clarifying the status of French possessions in the Caribbean and safeguarding American security interests, were first undertaken in May 1942, with the arrival of a mission consisting of Rear Admiral John H. Hoover, Commander of the Caribbean Sea Front, and Mr. Samuel Reber, Assistant Chief of the Division of European Affairs of the Department of State.[1] Agreement was apparently reached at an early date for the immobilization of the warships and merchant ships at Martinique,[2] but other issues proved highly difficult. Negotiations apparently became more difficult following the American invasion of French North Africa, November 8, 1942, and the subsequent severance of relations between Washington and the Vichy Government. Admiral Robert remained loyal to the Vichy regime and refused to cooperate with General Giraud.

On November 21, it was announced in a French radio broadcast that an agreement had been finally reached.[3] This was confirmed by Secretary of State Hull at his press conference on November 23.[4] While the Secretary said he was not yet in a position to reveal details of the new agreement, he made it clear that its primary purpose was to ensure American security and its secondary purpose was to improve the economic life of the residents of the French territories in the area.[5] The agreement, it was stated, covered Martinique and other French islands in the Caribbean and French Guiana on the South American mainland. It was made solely with Admiral Robert as the spokesman for French islands in the Caribbean, and did not involve any discussions between the United States and the Vichy Government. The Secretary indicated that the agreement seemed sufficiently satisfactory to make United States occupation of the French islands unnecessary.

Apparently either Admiral Robert refused at the last minute to sign the agreement,[6] or the agreement proved in actual operation to be less satisfactory than was expected.[7] Early in March, the report came from Martinique that Admiral Robert and the United States Government were still negotiating in order to "find a formula more adapted to certain war necessities." [8] On March 8, Acting Secretary of State Welles announced that no food had gone from the United States to Martinique since the landing of Allied forces in North Africa on November 8.[9] Subsequently, it was reported from Washington that this ban on the shipment of food was the result of Admiral Robert's refusal to cooperate with the United States in some affirmative program that would facilitate the conduct of the war by the United Nations.

On March 18, the announcement was made at Cayenne and by the French Military Mission in Washington, that French Guiana had broken away from Admiral Robert and had pledged its allegiance to General Giraud.[10] On March 20, the announcement was made in London at Fighting French headquarters that French Guiana had adhered to the cause of General de Gaulle.[11] Admiral Robert still retained his authority in Martinique and the other islands in the West Indies and continued his non-cooperative attitude toward the United States.

[1] *Documents, IV, 1941–42*, p. 460. [2] *New York Times*, March 9, 1943.
[3] *Ibid.*, November 22, 1942. [4] *Ibid.*, November 24, 1942.
[5] *Ibid.* [6] Article by "Pertinax," *ibid.*, February 18, 1943.
[7] *Ibid.*, March 9, 1943. [8] *Ibid.* [9] *Ibid.*
[10] *Ibid.*, March 19, 1943. [11] *Ibid.*, March 21, 1943.

(1) *Conditions Set by Admiral Robert to His Joining the Struggle against Germany. Letter to Mr. Joseph E. Dynan of the Associated Press, April 16, 1943* [1]

[Excerpt — Translation]

. . . .

1. Why does the High Commissioner [Admiral Robert] at Martinique remain aloof from what might be a concerted drive to liberate Metropolitan France from her German invaders?

Answer: Because his participation in that action under present circumstances risks placing the interests of the French Antilles in danger without by that step advancing by one day the liberation of France.

2. Especially when the rest of the empire has joined this fight?

Answer: The manner in which the French who believed that the moment had come to join the United Nations have been treated by the Allies only confirms me each day in my prudence.

3. What would be necessary, such as guarantees, for example, to induce the High Commissioner to join the struggle?

Answer: That this act would not mean the necessity of rebellion against the French Government. That the Allies permit the French who are fighting — instead of constituting two factions, one dominated by Britain and the other by the American Government — to form a unity under one single authority vested with sovereign rights. That this act safeguards the interests of the French Antilles such as I have been able to conserve them up to the present.

. . . .

(2) *Termination of Informal Relations with the French Antilles. Note Delivered on Instruction of the Secretary of State (Hull) to the French High Commissioner (Robert) by the American Consul General at Martinique (Malige), April 26, 1943* [2]

In November of last year,[3] the Government of the United States informed the French High Commissioner that it was prepared to maintain its relations with the French territories in the Western Hemisphere on an informal basis. It pointed out, however, that in view of the imminent full German occupation of France, it regarded any regime which the Germans might permit to function in Metropolitan France as being under the complete domination of Hitler. This view was later confirmed by the completion of the German occupation of all French metropolitan territory and the final extinguishment of French authority in France.

[1] *Ibid.*, April 17, 1943.
[2] Department of State, *Bulletin*, VIII, p. 359.
[3] See this volume, p. 540.

The Government of the United States also made it abundantly clear, in November and subsequently, that the new and changing situation would require a current reexamination with the French High Commissioner of problems of mutual interest and concern.

Almost six months have passed and today the French islands in the Caribbean are the only French territories physically free from Axis domination which have no part in the struggle for French liberation and which profess allegiance to a regime under the direct control of Germany.

It is a matter of common knowledge that the territory of Metropolitan France, contrary to the wish of the French people, is being used in an ever-increasing degree for active military operations against the United States and that the Vichy regime is now an integral part of the Nazi System. The Government of the United States does not recognize Vichy nor will it recognize or negotiate with any French representative in the Antilles who remains subservient to or maintains contact with the Vichy regime.

In the circumstances the Government of the United States does not consider effective or binding any informal understanding with respect to the French Antilles based upon past discussions and conditions, nor does it consider that those discussions can serve as a basis for either present or future relations with the French Antilles.

For this reason the American Consul General at Fort-de-France is being instructed to return to the United States, leaving the Consulate in charge of a Consular Officer whose activities will be restricted to the protection of American interests and who will not be authorized to enter into or conduct any negotiations of a political character.

(3) *Note of the French High Commissioner (Robert) to the Secretary of State (Hull), May 1, 1943* [1]

[Translation]

I have the honor to acknowledge the receipt of your note of April 26.

About six months have elapsed since Mr. [Samuel J.] Reber's note dated November 13, 1942, establishing a basis for our relations under the present situation of Metropolitan France and North Africa. Since that time I have exerted every effort toward amending that agreement in the directions that you have requested and at the same time toward protecting the interests with the care of which I am charged.

Since that time the acts of your Government have been such as to drive the people of these colonies to hunger. Now the American Government exploits its reasons for breaking all relations with the territories under my control, misfortunes that it was physically impossible for France to avoid.

[1] *New York Times*, May 1, 1943.

In the name of the French Government, I protest against this unjust decision, taken in a hasty manner. This is not a question of opinion. Some day history will show what has been averted from the people of France, as the Marshal [Henri Philippe Pétain] indicated in his message of April 4, 1943.[1] That was not the speech of a leader enslaved by a conqueror.

I protest in the name of the Frenchmen of the Antilles, whom you have subjected to blockade and, by the violation of your engagements, to the abusive action of force.

I protest in my own name, for, being charged with the foreign relations of these colonies, I have always been "a good neighbor" to the United States and have always deserved to be treated as such.

With regret I observe that the cirumstances of war seem to conceal from the American Government and from American public opinion what is for us a living reality. I regret this on behalf of the French people and also on behalf of the American people, who may one day have to pay the price of their obliviousness.

Provisionally, I accept the continued presence of the naval observers at Martinique and Guadeloupe.

It was reported from Washington on May 4 that the future of Martinique and Guadeloupe had been left to the Navy Department by the State Department.[1] Following the termination of informal relations, an American vice-consul and naval observers remained at Fort-de-France but with no power to conduct political negotiations. On July 14, it became known that Admiral Robert had withdrawn as French High Commissioner. On July 16, he handed over his authority to Henri-Étienne Hoppenot, representing the French Committee of National Liberation.[2]

[1] *New York Times*, May 6, 1943.
[2] *Free France*, August 1, 1943, p. 79–80.

CHAPTER VI

EASTERN ASIA AND THE PACIFIC AREA

A considerable portion of the chapter on Eastern Asia and the Pacific Area in the volume for 1941–42 was devoted to a documentary review of events leading up to the Japanese attack on American forces on December 7, 1941 (*Documents, IV, 1941–42*, p. 533). The story told in the documents there presented has since been considerably elaborated and further documented by two publications of the Department of State covering the development of American foreign policy during the period 1931–41. The first of these, *Peace and War: United States Foreign Policy, 1931–1941*, Department of State Publication 1853 (Government Printing Office, Washington, 1942), issued January 2, 1943, gave a running account of the development of American policy during this period, with four chapters devoted exclusively to our relations with Japan. The second volume, with the same title, Department of State Publication 1983 (Government Printing Office, Washington, 1943), contained a reprint of the earlier publication, followed by 274 supporting documents. The Department also published in 1943 in its series *Papers Relating to the Foreign Relations of the United States* two volumes carrying the subtitle *Japan: 1931–1941*.

For the period covered in this volume, all documents bearing upon our belligerent relations with Japan are in Chapter III (The Axis Powers), p. 169.

1. PRINCIPLES OF AMERICAN POLICY

(1) *Address by the Former American Ambassador to Japan (Grew), New York City, October 10, 1942* [1]

[Excerpt]

Following his return from Japan where he had served as United States Ambassador from February 1932, to the outbreak of war, the Hon. Joseph C. Grew made a series of addresses in which he sought to give the American people a better understanding of the nature of and the issues involved in the war with Japan. A brief discussion of principles to guide our future policy in the Pacific area is included here, on the ground that even though it does not represent the established policy of the Government it does present the point of view of one whose opinions, because of his official position and his background of experience, cannot but carry weight in the formulation of policy. In the earlier address on September 18, Mr. Grew had briefly expressed himself on the subject of the treatment of Japan (p. 174).

The Pacific and the Far East, when we have cleared them of the scourge of war, will justify the effort and the sacrifices involved in that achievement. We and the nations in that area that are resisting militarism and aggression are fighting not only for freedom but for world peace, world democracy, and world prosperity. Beyond the general aims of our war

[1] Department of State, *Bulletin*, VII, p. 797.

for survival there are positive high objectives in the Pacific and Far East to which we can and shall attain.

First, once Japan is destroyed as an aggressive force, we know of no other challenging power that can appear in the Pacific. The nations now members of the Pacific Council in Washington are quite simply fighting primarily for freedom — to live their own national and individual lives and to let live. No one of these powers has serious strategic claims or designs upon the independence or territory of another. There are no frontiers stained with centuries of the bloodshed of international war. The Pacific nations have clear geographical limits, sufficient natural resources, and a proven disposition to cooperate. Once militant Japan is out of the picture, there should remain no threat of further war in the Pacific area. I say this advisedly. Japan is the one enemy, and the only enemy, of the peaceful peoples whose shores overlook the Pacific Ocean.

Second, the winning of the war will bring its own rewards in uniting the Pacific peoples. Friendships and opportunities for mutual education and enrichment, both material and spiritual, possess limitless possibilities for good. The share of the Chinese in the new Pacific is bound to be a great one. Our collaboration with China will be made the easier by the sympathy which United China Relief and its related organizations have shown the Chinese people.

Third, we can hold out the hope of a liberated Japan. A population as great as that of the German Reich waits to be freed not only from its militarist masters but from itself. The Japanese have great cultural assets with which they could continue to contribute to the happiness and civilization of mankind. But they have — particularly in recent years — been led along a road of militarism and overweening extremist ambition which have directed Japanese civilization into a blind alley of potential ruin. We and our allies of the United Nations can free those people of Japan who yearn in secret merely to be allowed to pursue their normal beauty-loving lives, in peace, in their own homes, and in their own cultural surroundings. But we must realize that the captivity in which they are held is no mere temporary phenomenon of an occupying force or of a police control suddenly grown tyrannical: it is the despotism of tradition through the centuries, grown corrupt, savage, and untrue even to its own followers. Whatever desire some of the more enlightened elder statesmen of Japan may have had for peace, they have in recent times been completely overridden by the utterly ruthless extremist elements in the country. Even during the period of our internment in Tokyo the scorn in which they held the Foreign Office was only too evident, and whatever effort was made by the latter to bring our treatment into accord with international usage was in many cases arbitrarily overruled by the military and metropolitan police who dealt with us in the Embassy not merely as prisoners but as though we were criminal prisoners.

In this, again, the role of China is of fundamental import — by reason of China's propinquity to Japan, by reason of China's cultural leadership of the Far East. For almost three thousand years Chinese civilization has been the stabilizer and illuminator of Far Eastern life.

In the Pacific war we are, therefore, not only fighting for progress, for democracy, for the four freedoms of the Atlantic Charter. We are fighting to free the richest cultural heritage of East Asia, and in this fight we are proud of our indispensable ally, China, and of her leader, Generalissimo Chiang Kai-shek.

. . . .

(2) *Bases in the Pacific. Report of Remarks Made by the Acting Secretary of State (Welles) at His Press Conference, March 8, 1943* [1]

At his press conference on March 8 the Acting Secretary of State, Mr. Welles, replying to a question of a correspondent concerning reports in congressional circles that informal assurances have been received from some of our Pacific allies concerning permanent rights to bases after the war, stated that that raised a very important general question and he thought the most helpful way he could approach it was along the lines that our whole policy is directed toward assuring ourselves that the security of this country and the security of the people of the United States would be completely safeguarded at the end of this war. Certainly one of the elements in that policy, Mr. Welles said, is the unconditional surrender and the complete disarmament of Japan. Mr. Welles continued that his belief was that emphasis should be placed on the means of international security that can be achieved in the future so that the Pacific will be as safe for all law-abiding nations and peaceful nations that are interested in the Pacific as for the United States. Not that the United States should claim that the Pacific should be a lake under American jurisdiction, but rather, Mr. Welles said, that it should be a peaceful lake equally secure and equally safe for all powers and particularly for all powers interested in the Pacific. Mr. Welles concluded that naturally the question which the correspondent asked was a question which he thought all the United Nations would wish to discuss — and particularly all the nations which are interested in the Pacific would wish to discuss.

2. RELATIONS WITH CHINA

A. Aid in the Prosecution of the War

The most urgent and pressing question in relations between China and the United States in the period under review was that of American, and more generally Anglo-American, aid in the prosecution of the war. The entrance of the United States and the British Empire into the war on the side of China

[1] *Ibid.*, VIII, p. 217.

against Japan had the immediate effect of weakening instead of strengthening China's position, since it made possible and was followed by the cutting of the Burma Road by the Japanese, thus making impossible the further use of this relatively important route for supplying the hard-pressed Chinese forces.

The question was essentially one of over-all war strategy, and yet the issue was one that concerned our political relations with the Chinese as they were naturally inclined to expect from us a maximum of assistance as evidence of our professed friendship and the sincerity of our declared purposes in the war. It was generally recognized that a precondition to sending more material aid to China was the successful conclusion of military operations designed to open up new and more efficient communication and transportation routes. This involved the assignment to the Far East area of substantial quantities of men and equipment for carrying out such operations, at a time when the American and British Governments were apparently in agreement on the immediate importance of mounting the attack against Fascist forces in Europe and when we were in fact committed to important military operations in North Africa and the Mediterranean area.

A Chinese Military Mission, sent to Washington by Generalissimo Chiang Kai-shek, presumably with a view to giving China adequate representation in discussions of war strategy, was recalled by the Generalissimo on December 30, 1942.[1] In an interview given by Dr. F. S. Ho, official spokesman for the Mission, it was made clear that the Chinese had not been given the opportunity to participate in important discussions of war strategy and that they felt that the requirements of the Pacific War were being neglected.[2]

Action and words to reassure the Chinese and to strengthen their resistance were not lacking, even though not fully meeting Chinese desires. On July 7, 1942, an Order of the Day issued by the Secretaries of War and Navy, the first since December 7, 1941, paid special tribute to the Chinese on the 5th anniversary of their resistance to Japanese aggression and pledged "firm determination to expel the aggressor from every foot of Chinese soil."[3] On July 11, 1942, it was announced that the agreement of April 1, 1941, under which the United States Stabilization Fund undertook to purchase Chinese yuan to the amount of $50,000,000 and under which the Stabilization Board of China was established, had been extended for a period of one year beyond June 30, 1942.[4] On July 30, Lauchlin Currie, personal representative of President Roosevelt in China, stated in Chungking that operations in Europe would not prevent the United States from providing increasing military assistance to China.[5]

Further reassurances came following the announcement that the Chinese Military Mission had been recalled. On December 31, 1942, Secretary of the Treasury Morgenthau announced that the stabilization arrangements of July 14, 1937, under which the Central Bank of China had been enabled to obtain up to $50,000,000 in United States dollar exchange had been extended for a period of six months beyond December 31, 1942.[6] In his Annual Message to Congress on January 7, 1943, President Roosevelt gave assurance that we would get the necessary equipment to China and that the year 1943 would see the United States pass from the defensive to the offensive (see below, p. 478). While the Chinese Government was not represented at the Casablanca Conference, January 14–26, 1943, it was stated in the official communiqué that complete agreement had been reached "upon war plans and enterprises" to be undertaken during 1943 against Japan as well as Germany and Italy. It was also stated that President Roosevelt and Prime Minister Churchill had been in communication with Generalissimo Chiang Kai-shek.[7]

[1] *The China Monthly*, February 1943, p. 7.   [2] *Ibid.*
[3] *New York Times*, January 8, 1942.
[4] Department of State, *Bulletin*, VII, p. 623.
[5] *New York Times*, July 31, 1942.
[6] *Ibid.*, January 1, 1943.
[7] See this volume, p. 251.

In the face of these reassurances and the apparent dissatisfaction of the Chinese with the emphasis placed upon European operations, the visit of Mme. Chiang Kai-shek to the United States and the general tenor of her public statements assumed great significance. Especially significant was Mme. Chiang's warning contained in her address to the House of Representatives on February 18, 1943, against underrating the strength of Japan and allowing Japan too much time to exploit her occupied areas.

While there appeared to be a general willingness in the country and in Congress to recognize that the European emphasis in our over-all war strategy was sound, increasing concern was expressed over the possibility that in our proper concentration of attention and forces on the European front we were dangerously neglecting the Japanese front and running the risk that China, exhausted and dispirited, would be forced out of the war. When the Lend-Lease Act was up for extension, and again when Lend-Lease appropriations were under consideration by Congress, it was made abundantly clear that Congress was in favor of more effective aid to China, and the statement made by Mr. Stettinius (see below) was intended to give assurance on this point.[1] Additional assurance was given by Prime Minister Churchill in his address to the two houses of Congress on May 19, 1943.[2]

(1) *Message of the President (Roosevelt) to the Congress on the State of the Nation, January 7, 1943* [3]

[Excerpt]

. . . .

In the attacks against Japan, we shall be joined with the heroic people of China, whose ideals of peace are so closely akin to our own. Even today we are flying as much lend-lease material into China as ever traversed the Burma Road, flying it over mountains 17,000 feet high, flying blind through sleet and snow. We shall overcome all the formidable obstacles, and get the battle equipment into China to shatter the power of our common enemy. From this war China will realize the security, the prosperity, and the dignity, which Japan has sought so ruthlessly to destroy.

The period of our defensive attrition in the Pacific is passing. Now our aim is to force the Japanese to fight. Last year, we stopped them. This year, we intend to advance.

. . . . . .

(2) *Address by Mme. Chiang Kai-shek to the House of Representatives, February 18, 1943* [4]

[Excerpt]

. . . . . .

[1] On amount of Lend-Lease aid to China down to June 30, 1943, see *ibid.*, p. 480.
[2] *Ibid.*, p. 258.
[3] *Congressional Record*, vol. 89, pt. 1, p. 45; Department of State, *Bulletin*, VIII, p. 15.
[4] *Congressional Record*, vol. 89, pt. 1, p. 1108–9.

Sun-tese, the well-known Chinese strategist said:

In order to win, know thyself and thy enemy.

We have also the saying:

It takes little effort to watch the other fellow carry the load.

In spite of these teachings from a wise old past, which are shared by every nation, there has been a tendency to belittle the strength of our opponents.

When Japan thrust total war on China in 1937 military experts of every nation did not give China even a ghost of a chance. But when Japan failed to bring China cringing to her knees as she vaunted, the world took solace in this phenomenon by declaring that they had overestimated Japan's military might. Nevertheless, when the greedy flames of war inexorably spread in the Pacific following the perfidious attack on Pearl Harbor, Malaya, and lands in and around the China Sea, and one after another of these places fell, the pendulum swung to the other extreme. Doubts and fears lifted their ugly heads and the world began to think that the Japanese were Nietzschean supermen, superior in intellect and physical prowess, a belief which the Gobineaus and the Houston Chamberlains and their apt pupils, the Nazi racists, had propounded about the Nordics.

Again, now the prevailing opinion seems to consider the defeat of the Japanese as of relative unimportance and that Hitler is our first concern. This is not borne out by actual facts, nor is it to the interests of the United Nations as a whole to allow Japan to continue not only as a vital potential threat but as a waiting sword of Damocles, ready to descend at a moment's notice.

Let us not forget that Japan in her occupied areas today has greater resources at her command than Germany.

Let us not forget that the longer Japan is left in undisputed possession of these resources, the stronger she must become. Each passing day takes more toll in lives of both Americans and Chinese.

Let us not forget that the Japanese are an intransigent people.

Let us not forget that during the first $4\frac{1}{2}$ years of total aggression China has borne Japan's sadistic fury unaided and alone.

The victories won by the United States Navy at Midway and the Coral Sea are doubtless steps in the right direction — they are merely steps in the right direction — for the magnificent fight that was waged at Guadalcanal during the past 6 months attests to the fact that the defeat of the forces of evil though long and arduous will finally come to pass. For have we not on the side of righteousness and justice stanch allies in Great Britain, Russia, and other brave and indomitable peoples? Meanwhile the peril of the Japanese juggernaut remains. Japanese military might must be decimated as a fighting force before its threat to civilization is removed.

. . . .

(3) Lend-Lease in Action — China. Eighth Quarterly Report to Congress on Lend-Lease Operations, for the Period Ended March 11, 1943 [1]

[Excerpt]

. . . .

The Chinese are now holding a 3,000-mile front against the invading armies of the Japanese. This line is a crucial battlefront of the war. We are determined to provide the aid to China which is necessary to enable her to drive the Japanese from her soil.

The fall of Burma and the seizure of the southern portion of the Burma Road by the Japanese closed a supply route to the improvement of which we had devoted a large proportion of our lend-lease aid to China during the year 1941. The closing of the Burma Road left air transport as the only effective means of getting supplies into China. Constant efforts have been made to enlarge this air service but up to now the amount of lend-lease supplies that we have been able to get into China itself has been very small.

There is much more to the story of lend-lease aid for China than the quantity of goods which have been actually sent into China. The Chinese troops which retreated into India after the fall of Burma have been issued new weapons and other equipment under lend-lease and have been instructed in the use of this equipment by American Army officers. The British also have made available supplies and facilities to Chinese troops in India. In addition to Chinese pilots now training in India, over four hundred Chinese student pilots have come to this country to go through the standard U. S. Army Air Corps training; more are coming. A hundred of these have completed the course and returned to China to aid in the struggle against Japan.

In addition, arrangements are now under way for making available to China cargo ships which will be manned by Chinese seamen.

In estimating our aid to China, there must be considered also the large amounts of supplies sent to allied forces under the command of General Wavell and General Stilwell in China, India and Burma. These forces are cooperating with the Chinese in operations looking toward eventual reopening of the Burma supply routes. Military operations to open these routes, as well as other military measures, may well be considered the most important type of aid which we could possibly render China at the present time.

United States air forces under General Chennault, stationed in China

[1] House Doc. No. 129, 78th Cong., 1st sess., p. 30.

itself, are maintaining the control of the air over unoccupied China which the famous Flying Tigers won in December 1941 and which has never been lost since. The supplies sent by the British and American Governments to their forces in this area and the actual services of those forces are not recorded in the lend-lease figures.

The air route into China is being flown by planes of both the China National Aviation Corp. and the U. S. Army Air Transport Command. Cargo planes have been supplied to CNAC under lend-lease and additional planes are now being made available. However, the large majority of the planes on the India-China run are flown by the Air Transport Command. The value of this service, carried on over wild and mountainous country under most difficult weather conditions by U. S. Army personnel with U. S. Army equipment, is not reflected in the statistics of lend-lease aid.

The problem of lend-lease to China has always been more than anything else a problem of securing adequate routes of supply. Almost half of the lend-lease supplies sent from the United States for China are now in storage in India. The volume of lend-lease supplies getting into China cannot be expanded until the supply routes are expanded. American efforts are being concentrated, therefore, on enlarging the capacity of the air routes to China, on exploration and development of new routes, and on preparations for recapturing those which have been seized by the enemy.

It takes many months to manufacture supplies in the United States and transport them to India. We are therefore planning to have a balanced reserve of supplies in India to be sent into China as fast as the supply routes can handle them.

Recent lend-lease aid to India will play an important part in future aid to China. As India assumes more and more the role of a supply reservoir for the Burma-China-India war front, more emphasis is being placed in lend-lease operations on the development of India's own natural resources, her factories and arsenals, and her transportation system. One-fifth of the $595,000,000 of aid rendered to India from March 11, 1941 to March 1, 1943, represents machinery, tools, and raw materials.

India is the second largest producer of iron ore in the British Empire. She has the largest single steel plant in the British Empire. Labor is plentiful there. With the aid of the machines, tools, and raw materials which we are sending her, India can step up her production of arms, military vehicles, lumber for war construction, textiles for uniforms and tents, and she can improve her internal transportation system so as to get these supplies more quickly to the battlefronts.

With the industrial and transportation facilities thus provided, the factories and arsenals of India can produce many vital war supplies for China. This will free much shipping over the long route from the United States for additional supplies for China.

The lend-lease aid we have extended to Australia and New Zealand, totaling $591,000,000 up to March 1, 1943, is also directed against the Japanese. The President has said, "There are many roads which lead right to Tokyo. We shall neglect none of them."

.   .   .   .

(4) *Statement of the Administrator of Lend-Lease (Stettinius), before the Subcommittee of the House Committee on Appropriations, on Lend-Lease Aid to China, May 6, 1943* [1]

We are requesting only . . . for China. This appears to be a relatively small amount for an important war theater. It does not, however, reflect the full extent of lend-lease aid scheduled for China during the coming months. China's greatest need is for finished ordnance and ammunition and other combat equipment such as is provided from funds appropriated to the War Department. Effective use of the limited transportation facilities available for the delivery of goods to China requires the assignment of transport priority to finished munitions. Such items constitute the major part of the program for the China theater during the coming fiscal year.

In arriving at the final request for funds for China under the present appropriation, the Lend-Lease Administration first made a careful study of all the means of transportation into China that are likely to be available during the fiscal year 1943–44 and the months immediately following and estimated the total tonnage of all types of material that could be transported. The program under the lend-lease appropriation was then adjusted to the balance of transport capacity remaining after allowance had been made for the transportation of the tonnage of finished munitions to be supplied by the War Department.

If there should be an increase beyond our present expectations in the capacity of transport facilities into China, this possibility is one of those upon which is based our request for the contingency fund of $377,000,000 in category 9.

We intend to give China as much aid as can possibly be sent to her.

B. Jurisdiction over Criminal Offenses by Armed Forces

(1) *Jurisdiction over Criminal Offenses by Armed Forces of the United States and China. Agreement Recorded by Exchange of Notes between the Governments of China and the United States, Chungking, May 21, 1943* [2]

[1] *Hearings before the Subcommittee of the House Committee on Appropriations, on the Defense Aid (Lend-Lease) Supplemental Appropriation Bill, 1943,* 78th Cong., 1st sess., p. 159.

[2] Department of State, *Bulletin,* IX, p. 114; *Executive Agreement Series* 360. For agreement with the United Kingdom, see this volume, p. 517.

(a) The American Chargé at Chungking (Atcheson) to the Chinese Political Vice Minister in Charge of Ministerial Affairs, Ministry of Foreign Affairs (Wu)

EXCELLENCY:

Confirming the understanding reached in the conversations which have taken place in Chungking between representatives of our two Governments, I have the honor to inform Your Excellency that it is the desire of the Government of the United States that the service courts and authorities of its military and naval forces shall during the continuance of the present conflict against our common enemies exercise exclusive jurisdiction over criminal offenses which may be committed in China by members of such forces.

If cases arise in which for special reasons the service authorities of the Government of the United States may prefer not to exercise the above jurisdiction, it is proposed that in any such case a written statement to that effect shall be sent to the Chinese Government through diplomatic channels, in which event it would be open to the Chinese authorities to assume jurisdiction.

Assurance is given that the service courts and authorities of the United States forces in China will be willing and able to try, and on conviction to punish, all criminal offenses which members of the United States forces may be alleged on sufficient evidence to have committed in China and that the United States authorities will be willing in principle to investigate and deal appropriately with any alleged criminal offenses committed by such forces in China which may be brought to their attention by the competent Chinese authorities or which the United States authorities may find have taken place.

Insofar as may be compatible with military security, the service authorities of the United States will conduct the trial of any member of the United States forces for an offense against a member of the civilian population promptly in open court in China and within a reasonable distance from the place where the offense is alleged to have been committed so that witnesses may not be required to travel great distances to attend the trial.

The competent United States authorities will be prepared to cooperate with the authorities of China in setting up a satisfactory procedure for affording such mutual assistance as may be required in making investigations and collecting evidence with respect to offenses alleged to have been committed by members of the armed forces of the United States. As a general rule it would probably be desirable that preliminary action should be taken by the Chinese authorities on behalf of the United States authorities where the witnesses or other persons from whom it is desired to obtain testimony are not members of the United States forces. In prosecutions in Chinese courts of persons who are not members of the United States forces, but where members of such forces are in any way concerned, the service authorities of the United States will be glad to render such assistance as is possible in obtaining testimony of members of such forces or in making appropriate investigations.

Inasmuch as the interests of our common cause will best be served by provision that the foregoing arrangement may be placed on a reciprocal basis, the Government of the United States will be ready to make like arrangements to ensure to such Chinese forces as may be stationed in territory under United States jurisdiction a position corresponding to that of the United States forces in China.

It is proposed that the foregoing arrangement shall be in effect during the present war and for a period of six months thereafter.

If the above arrangement is acceptable to the Chinese Government, this note and the reply thereto accepting the provisions outlined shall be regarded as placing on record the understanding between our two Governments.

I avail [etc.]

(b) The Chinese Political Vice Minister in Charge of Ministerial Affairs, Ministry of Foreign Affairs (Wu) to the American Chargé at Chungking (Atcheson)

MONSIEUR LE CHARGÉ D'AFFAIRES:

I have the honor to acknowledge receipt of your Note of to-day's date reading as follows:

[Here follows full text of Chargé's note, printed above.]

I have the honor to inform you that I am authorized to confirm, on behalf of the National Government of the Republic of China, that the understanding arrived at between our respective Governments regarding jurisdiction over criminal offenses which may be committed by members of the United States armed forces in China, with a provision for placing the said understanding on a reciprocal basis to ensure to such Chinese forces as may be stationed in territory under United States jurisdiction a position corresponding to that of the United States forces in China, is as set forth in your Note under reply.

The present Note and your Note under reply will accordingly be regarded as placing this understanding on record.

I avail myself [etc.]

(c) Statement of the Chinese Ministry of Foreign Affairs, Chungking, May 21, 1943 [1]

According to international law and international practice, when the armed forces of the Allied nations are stationed in the territory of another

---

[1] Made in connection with the publication of the exchange of notes.

for the purpose of undertaking joint military operations, exclusive criminal jurisdiction over members of such forces is exercised by the military or naval courts or authorities of the country to which such forces belong. This practice was followed in the last world war. Last year, when the United States despatched armed forces to territories under British jurisdiction, the United States and the British Governments reached an agreement whereby the armed forces of the United States stationed in British territory are formally placed under the exclusive jurisdiction of the United States military or naval courts or authorities in respect of criminal offenses.

Inasmuch as all nationals of the United States in China, including those belonging to its armed forces, enjoyed extraterritorial rights, there was no need for any special regulations. However, as the exchange of ratifications of the new Sino-American treaty has already taken place,[1] United States nationals in China are henceforth subject to our jurisdiction. Therefore, the necessity has been felt that the question of criminal jurisdiction over members of the armed forces of the United States in China should be clearly defined.

Accordingly, the Political Vice Minister in charge of Ministerial Affairs of the Ministry of Foreign Affairs, Dr. K. C. Wu, on behalf of the Chinese Government, and the Chargé d'Affaires ad interim, of the United States, Mr. George Atcheson, on behalf of the United States Government, have reached an understanding, on the basis of equality and reciprocity which has been placed on record by an exchange of notes on May 21, 1943, to the effect that jurisdiction over criminal offenses committed by members of the armed forces of the United States in China shall be exclusively exercised by the service courts and the military and naval authorities of the United States, and that the United States Government shall make like arrangements to ensure to such Chinese forces as may be stationed in territory under United States jurisdiction a position corresponding to that of the United States forces in China.

C. Relinquishment of Extraterritorial Rights and Privileges

The treaty of January 11, 1943 between the Governments of the United States and China terminated the extraterritorial and other special rights which had been exercised by the United States for one century.[2] Beginning with the Chinese-British supplementary treaty of commerce and navigation signed October 8, 1843 [3] (following the treaty of Nanking of August 29, 1842 with Great Britain),[4] the American treaty of Wanghia, July 3, 1844,[5] and the French treaty of Whampoa [6] of October 24 of the same year, both of which defined

---

[1] See this volume, p. 489.
[2] Department of State, *Bulletin*, VIII, p. 59.
[3] 31 *British and Foreign State Papers* (1842–43), p. 132.
[4] 30 *ibid.* (1841–42), p. 389.
[5] *Treaties, Conventions*, etc. I, 1776–1909, p. 196.
[6] Martens, G. de, *Nouveau Recueil Général de Traités*, etc., VII (1844), p. 431.

and elaborated provisions of the British supplementary treaty, the citizens of all the other "most-favored-nations" eventually came to enjoy freedom from the jurisdiction of Chinese Courts and were subject only to the control of their own consuls, their own laws, and their own courts.[1]

Particularly since 1900, China has earnestly endeavored to rid herself of foreign jurisdiction, chiefly by sporadic revision of her own juridical system to meet Western standards. As early as 1903 a commercial treaty between the United States and China provided *inter alia* for the former's relinquishment of extraterritorial rights whenever the United States Government was satisfied that the state of Chinese laws, arrangements for their administration, and other considerations warranted it in so doing.[2]

Chinese efforts in this direction, however, only began to meet a slight measure of success in the 'twenties. On the whole its efforts at unilateral abrogation of the rights of the "treaty-powers" proved abortive. In 1926 a Commission on Extraterritoriality appointed by the Washington Conference on the Limitation of Armaments of 1921–1922 [3] suggested certain modifications in the system and practice of extraterritoriality in spite of conditions which did not warrant its immediate abolition.[4]

Following this report China began to revise and recodify her laws in accordance with the Commission's recommendations, while the other nations attempted concretely to effect suggestions for modification of extraterritoriality by agreeing in 1927 to a provisional return to Chinese jurisdiction of the Mixed Court in the International Settlement in Shanghai, control of which had been taken over in 1911 by the Shanghai consular body without treaty sanction.

Late in 1928 the Chinese National Government began to increase its efforts to abolish extraterritoriality. Already Germany, Austria and Hungary had lost their special rights by the treaties of peace. Soviet Russia had renounced its special rights by the Peking treaty of May 1924. Sweden and Switzerland had promised to relinquish such rights whenever the other treaty-powers should do likewise.[5] At the close of the year Belgium, Denmark, Italy, Portugal and Spain made similar promises and also renounced extraterritoriality in principle.[6] Finally in an exchange of notes in October and November, 1929, Mexico declared that it would not demand in the future extraterritorial privileges in China.[7]

The Chinese Government, therefore, felt its position sufficiently strengthened to request on April 27, 1929, that the United States, Great Britain, France, Brazil, Norway, and the Netherlands relinquish their special privileges as soon as possible,[8] and to ask on May 8 that the Shanghai Provisional Court be placed under the direct and undivided control of the Nanking Government.[9]

These governments, and Belgium, Denmark, Japan, Italy, Portugal, Spain and Sweden in addition, replied to the latter Chinese communication by proposing that a commission composed of representatives of all the countries involved

---

[1] For the general statement by Caleb Cushing of the basis of extraterritoriality in China, see *The Chinese Repository*, XIV, p. 525–6.

[2] Department of State, *Bulletin*, VIII, p. 245; see also *Treaties, Conventions*, etc. I, 1776–1909, p. 261.

[3] *Conference on the Limitation of Armament*, Washington, D. C., Government Printing Office, 1922, p. 1644.

[4] *Report of the Commission on Extraterritoriality in China*, Peking, September 16, 1926 (Washington, D. C., Government Printing Office, 1927), recommendations, p. 107–9.

[5] Provisions of their treaties with China in 1908 and 1918, respectively.

[6] For text of treaties, see *Chinese Social and Political Science Review*, Public Documents, Supplement XIII (January 1929), p. 7–51.

[7] *Ibid.*, XIV (1930, No. 2), p. 19–22.

[8] *Ibid.*, XIII (January 1929), p. 64.

[9] *Ibid.*, p. 66–7; see also Johnstone, William C., *The Shanghai Problem*, Stanford University, 1937.

should examine the question of the reorganization of the Court.[1] A note of July 3 from the Chinese Foreign Minister declined the proposal and suggested immediate negotiations [2] which finally resulted in the opening of a conference at Nanking on December 9, 1929. On February 17, 1930, an agreement was concluded between China and the Governments of the United States, the United Kingdom, France, Norway, Brazil, and the Netherlands which authorized China to set up a district court and a branch high court, declared that all Chinese laws were applicable, provided for appeals to the Supreme Court of China, and abolished the use of foreign deputies.[3] An almost identical agreement for the rendition of the Mixed Court in the French Concession was reached on July 31, 1931.[4]

But Chinese hopes for an early end to extraterritoriality as expressed in the April 27 note were not so readily fulfilled as the later request regarding the Provisional Court. In replies dated August 10, 1929, the United States and the other leading "treaty-powers" refused to abandon completely their special privileges in view of the failure of the Chinese Government fully to carry out the 1926 recommendations of the Commission on Extraterritoriality concerning reform of the Chinese juridical system.[5]

As a consequence, however, of a further exchange of notes, China was encouraged to issue on December 28, 1929 a sweeping mandate without legal provision, which stated that from January 1, 1930 all nationals of treaty-powers on Chinese soil should "abide by the laws, ordinances, and regulations duly promulgated by the central and local governments of China." [6] The United States considered that the mandate merely fixed the date for beginning the gradual process of relinquishing extraterritorial rights.[7]

In 1930 Great Britain began to negotiate with China in an attempt to arrive at some constructive plan of relinquishment while the American and Japanese Governments advanced proposals along similar lines. Although these negotiations for a treaty on the subject continued, nevertheless the Chinese Government issued on May 4, 1931 a new mandate declaring that the regulations contemplated in the December 28, 1929 mandate should come into force on January 1, 1932.[8] Before that date the invasion of Manchuria by the Japanese in September 1931, and natural catastrophes, postponed indefinitely the enforcement of the regulations, and also caused the suspension of the discussions on extraterritoriality between China and the United States and each of several other countries.[9]

In 1934 President Roosevelt, and the Department of State on several occasions, expressed their willingness "when conditions should be favorable therefor to negotiate with the Chinese Government for the relinquishment of the extraterritorial and related rights and privileges hitherto possessed by the United States in China." [10] In 1937, for example, the United States Government was prepared to "give favorable consideration to the question," but on July 7, 1937 the occupation of areas in North China by Japanese armies resulted in disruption of Chinese control.[11]

[1] Ibid. (July 1939), p. 73–4.

[2] Ibid., p. 74–5.

[3] Tyau, M. T. Z., Chinese Diplomatic Relations, 1931–1932: A Survey, China Institute of Pacific Relations, p. 15–17.

[4] For text, see Chinese Social and Political Science Review, Public Documents Supplement XV (1931), p. 466–74.

[5] Ibid., XIII (1929), p. 158–62.

[6] Ibid., XIV (1930, No. 2), p. 2.

[7] Bisson, T. A., "The United States and the Orient," Pacific Affairs, III (December 1933), p. 1129.

[8] Chinese Social and Political Science Review, Public Documents Supplement, XV (1931), p. 456–8.

[9] Department of State, Bulletin, VII, p. 806.   [10] Ibid., p. 805.   [11] Ibid., p. 806.

In a note to the Japanese Government on December 31, 1938, Sumner Welles, Acting Secretary of State, mentioned progress toward the relinquishment of certain rights of a special character which the United States together with other countries had long possessed in China.[1] These issues were clarified by Mr. Welles on July 18, 1940.[2]

"It has been this Government's traditional and declared policy and desire to move rapidly by a process of orderly negotiation and agreement with the Chinese Government, whenever conditions warrant, toward the relinquishment of extraterritorial rights and of all so-called 'special rights' possessed by this country as by other countries in China by virtue of international agreements . . ."

Similarly in a response to a letter of May 29, 1941 from the Chinese Minister of Foreign Affairs, which emphasized among other things the support by China of principles of equality of treatment among nations,[3] Secretary of State Hull stated[4] that this principle "comprehends equality in international relations in a juridical sense . . . It goes without saying that the Government of the United States in continuation of steps already taken toward meeting China's aspirations for readjustment of anomalies in its international relations, expects when conditions of peace again prevail to move rapidly by processes of orderly negotiation and agreement with the Chinese Government, toward relinquishment of the last of certain rights of a special character which this country, together with other countries, has long possessed in China by virtue of agreements providing for extraterritorial jurisdiction and related practices."

Evidently as a result of its entrance into the war on December 7, 1941, the United States Government did not feel it necessary to wait for "conditions of peace." On October 9, 1942, the Acting Secretary of State, Mr. Welles, informed the Chinese Ambassador in Washington that the United States was prepared to negotiate promptly with the Chinese Government "a treaty providing for immediate relinquishment of extraterritorial rights in China and for the settlement of related questions . . . ,"[5] and on October 24 Secretary of State Hull handed to the Chinese Ambassador a draft treaty designed to accomplish this purpose.[6] The treaty and the accompanying exchange of notes were signed on January 11, 1943, at Washington.[7]

On the same day the Secretary of State reported the objectives and more important provisions of the treaty to the President.[8] Consideration of the treaty (Executive A, 78th Cong., 1st sess.) by the Senate Committee on Foreign Relations[9] followed a letter of February 1, 1943 by the President to the Senate, asking its advice and consent to ratification of the treaty and supplementary notes.[10] The committee reported favorably and without amendment to the Senate on February 11,[11] and on the same day a unanimous resolution by that body gave its advice and consent to ratification.[12]

On May 4, 1943 the President of the United States ratified the treaty and supplementary notes,[13] the Secretary of State and the Chinese Ambassador exchanged ratifications on May 20,[14] and on May 24 the President issued a formal proclamation of the American-Chinese treaty.[15] This action together with a British-Chinese treaty also signed on January 11, 1943, at Chungking,[16] and the virtual relinquishment of special rights by all the remaining "treaty-powers" completed the long process of restoring and recognizing the full sovereignty of China.

[1] *Ibid.*   [2] *Ibid.*   [3] *Ibid.*, p. 806–7.   [4] *Ibid.*, p. 807–8.
[5] *Ibid.*, p. 805.   [6] *Ibid.*, p. 854.   [7] *Ibid.*, p. 240–5.   [8] *Ibid.*, VIII, p. 239.
[9] *Ibid.*, p. 245.   [10] *Ibid.*, p. 238.
[11] *Ibid.*, p. 245–6; Executive Report No. 2, 78th Cong., 1st sess.
[12] Department of State, *Bulletin*, VIII, p. 160.
[13] United States *Treaty Series* 984.
[14] Department of State, *Bulletin*, VIII, p. 458.   [15] *Ibid.*, p. 475.
[16] *United Kingdom, Parliamentary Papers*, China No. 1 (1943). Cmd. 6417; *American Journal of International Law*, vol. 37, no. 2 (April 1943), p. 57.

A specific application of the treaty may be seen in the request by the President to the Congress on February 19, 1943 that no funds be appropriated for the United States Courts for China for the fiscal year 1944 in view of the signature of the treaty of January 11, 1943.[1]

(1) Treaty between the United States of America and the Republic of China for the Relinquishment of Extraterritorial Rights in China and the Regulation of Related Matters, Signed at Washington, January 11, 1943 [2]

In force, May 20, 1943.

The United States of America and the Republic of China, desirous of emphasizing the friendly relations which have long prevailed between their two peoples and of manifesting their common desire as equal and sovereign States that the high principles in the regulation of human affairs to which they are committed shall be made broadly effective, have resolved to conclude a treaty for the purpose of adjusting certain matters in the relations of the two countries, and have appointed as their Plenipotentiaries:

The President of the United States of America,

Mr. Cordell Hull, Secretary of State of the United States of America, and

The President of the National Government of the Republic of China,

Dr. Wei Tao-ming, Ambassador Extraordinary and Plenipotentiary of the Republic of China to the United States of America;

Who, having communicated to each other their full powers found to be in due form, have agreed upon the following articles:

ARTICLE I. All those provisions of treaties or agreements in force between the United States of America and the Republic of China which authorize the Government of the United States of America or its representatives to exercise jurisdiction over nationals of the United States of America in the territory of the Republic of China are hereby abrogated. Nationals of the United States of America in such territory shall be subject to the jurisdiction of the Government of the Republic of China in accordance with the principles of international law and practice.

ARTICLE II. The Government of the United States of America considers that the Final Protocol concluded at Peking on September 7, 1901, between the Chinese Government and other governments, including the Government of the United States of America, should be terminated and agrees that the rights accorded to the Government of the United States of America under that Protocol and under agreements supplementary thereto shall cease.

---

[1] House Doc. No. 114, 78th Cong., 1st sess.
[2] United States *Treaty Series* 984; Department of State, *Bulletin*, VIII, p. 240.

The Government of the United States of America will cooperate with the Government of the Republic of China for the reaching of any necessary agreements with other governments concerned for the transfer to the Government of the Republic of China of the administration and control of the Diplomatic Quarter at Peiping, including the official assets and the official obligations of the Diplomatic Quarter, it being mutually understood that the Government of the Republic of China in taking over administration and control of the Diplomatic Quarter will make provision for the assumption and discharge of the official obligations and liabilities of the Diplomatic Quarter and for the recognition and protection of all legitimate rights therein.

The Government of the Republic of China hereby accords to the Government of the United States of America a continued right to use for official purposes the land which has been allocated to the Government of the United States of America in the Diplomatic Quarter in Peiping, on parts of which are located buildings belonging to the Government of the United States of America.

ARTICLE III. The Government of the United States of America considers that the International Settlements at Shanghai and Amoy should revert to the administration and control of the Government of the Republic of China and agrees that the rights accorded to the Government of the United States of America in relation to those Settlements shall cease.

The Government of the United States of America will cooperate with the Government of the Republic of China for the reaching of any necessary agreements with other governments concerned for the transfer to the Government of the Republic of China of the administration and control of the International Settlements at Shanghai and Amoy, including the official assets and the official obligations of those Settlements, it being mutually understood that the Government of the Republic of China in taking over administration and control of those Settlements will make provision for the assumption and discharge of the official obligations and liabilities of those Settlements and for the recognition and protection of all legitimate rights therein.

ARTICLE IV. In order to obviate any questions as to existing rights in respect of or as to existing titles to real property in territory of the Republic of China possessed by nationals (including corporations or associations), or by the Government, of the United States of America, particularly questions which might arise from the abrogation of the provisions of treaties or agreements as stipulated in Article I, it is agreed that such existing rights or titles shall be indefeasible and shall not be questioned upon any ground except upon proof, established through due process of law, of fraud or of fraudulent or other dishonest practices in the acquisition of such rights or titles, it being understood that no right or title shall be rendered invalid by virtue of any subsequent change in the official procedure through which it was acquired. It is also agreed that these rights or titles shall be subject to the laws and regulations of the Republic of China concerning taxation, national defense, and the right of eminent domain, and that no such rights or titles may be alienated to the government or nationals (including corporations or associations) of any third country without the express consent of the Government of the Republic of China.

It is also agreed that if it should be the desire of the Government of the Republic of China to replace, by new deeds of ownership, existing leases in perpetuity or other documentary evidence relating to real property held by nationals, or by the Government, of the United States of America, the replacement shall be made by the Chinese authorities without charges of any sort and the new deeds of ownership shall fully protect the holders of such leases or other documentary evidence and their legal heirs and assigns without diminution of their prior rights and interests, including the right of alienation.

It is further agreed that nationals or the Government of the United States of America shall not be required or asked by the Chinese authorities to make any payments of fees in connection with land transfers for or with relation to any period prior to the effective date of this treaty.

ARTICLE V. The Government of the United States of America having long accorded rights to nationals of the Republic of China within the territory of the United States of America to travel, reside and carry on trade throughout the whole extent of that territory, the Government of the Republic of China agrees to accord similar rights to nationals of the United States of America within the territory of the Republic of China. Each of the two Governments will endeavor to have accorded in territory under its jurisdiction to nationals of the other country, in regard to all legal proceedings, and to matters relating to the administration of justice, and to the levying of taxes or requirements in connection therewith, treatment not less favorable than that accorded to its own nationals.

ARTICLE VI. The Government of the United States of America and the Government of the Republic of China mutually agree that the consular officers of each country, duly provided with exequaturs, shall be permitted to reside in such ports, places and cities as may be agreed upon. The consular officers of each country shall have the right to interview, to communicate with, and to advise nationals of their country within their consular districts; they shall be informed immediately whenever nationals of their country are under detention or arrest or in prison or are awaiting trial in their consular districts and they shall, upon notification to the appropriate authorities, be permitted to visit any such nationals; and, in general, the consular officers of each country shall be accorded the rights, privileges, and immunities enjoyed by consular officers under modern international usage.

It is likewise agreed that the nationals of each country, in the territory of the other country, shall have the right at all times to communicate with the consular officers of their country. Communications to their consular officers from nationals of each country who are under detention or arrest or in prison or are awaiting trial in the territory of the other country shall be forwarded to such consular officers by the local authorities.

ARTICLE VII. The Government of the United States of America and the Government of the Republic of China mutually agree that they will enter into negotiations for the conclusion of a comprehensive modern treaty of friendship, commerce, navigation and consular rights, upon the request of either Government or in any case within six months after the cessation of the hostilities in the war against the common enemies in which they are now engaged. The treaty to be thus negotiated will be based upon the principles of international law and practice as reflected in modern international procedures and in the modern treaties which the Government of the United States of America and the Government of the Republic of China respectively have in recent years concluded with other governments.

Pending the conclusion of a comprehensive treaty of the character referred to in the preceding paragraph, if any questions affecting the rights in territory of the Republic of China of nationals (including corporations or associations), or of the Government, of the United States of America should arise in future and if these questions are not covered by the present treaty, or by the provisions of existing treaties, conventions, or agreements between the Government of the United States of America and the Government of the Republic of China not abrogated by or inconsistent with this treaty, such questions shall be discussed by representatives of the two Governments and shall be decided in accordance with generally accepted principles of international law and with modern international practice.

ARTICLE VIII. The present treaty shall come into force on the day of the exchange of ratifications.

The present treaty shall be ratified, and the ratifications shall be exchanged at Washington as soon as possible.

Signed and sealed in the English and Chinese languages, both equally authentic, in duplicate, at Washington, this eleventh day of January, one thousand nine hundred forty-three, corresponding to the eleventh day of the first month of the thirty-second year of the Republic of China.

CORDELL HULL [SEAL]

WEI TAO-MING [SEAL]

(2) Supplementary Exchange of Notes between the Chinese Ambassa-dor (Wei) and the Secretary of State (Hull), January 11, 1943

(a) The Chinese Ambassador (Wei) to the Secretary of State (Hull) [1]

EXCELLENCY:

Under instruction of my Government, I have the honor to state that in connection with the treaty signed today by the Government of the Republic of China and the Government of the United States of America, in which the Government of the United States of America relinquishes its extraterritorial and related special rights in China, it is the under-standing of the Government of the Republic of China that the rights of the Government of the United States of America and of its nationals in regard to the systems of treaty ports and of special courts in the Inter-national Settlements at Shanghai and Amoy and in regard to the employ-ment of foreign pilots in the ports of the territory of China are also relinquished. In the light of the abolition of treaty ports as such, it is understood that all coastal ports in the territory of the Republic of China which are normally open to American overseas merchant shipping will remain open to such shipping after the coming into effect of the present treaty and the accompanying exchange of notes.

It is mutually agreed that the merchant vessels of each country shall be permitted freely to come to the ports, places, and waters of the other country which are or may be open to overseas merchant shipping, and that the treatment accorded to such vessels in such ports, places, and waters shall be no less favorable than that accorded to national vessels and shall be as favorable as that accorded to the vessels of any third country.

It is mutually understood that the Government of the United States of America relinquishes the special rights which vessels of the United States of America have been accorded with regard to the coasting trade and inland navigation in the waters of the Republic of China and that the Government of the Republic of China is prepared to take over any American properties that may have been engaged for those purposes and to pay adequate compensation therefor. Should either country accord the rights of inland navigation or coasting trade to vessels of any third country such rights would similarly be accorded to the vessels of the other country. The coasting trade and inland navigation of each country are excepted from the requirement of national treatment and are to be regu-lated according to the laws of each country in relation thereto. It is agreed, however, that vessels of either country shall enjoy within the

[1] *Ibid.*, p. 243.

territory of the other country with respect to the coasting trade and inland navigation treatment as favorable as that accorded to the vessels of any third country.

It is mutually understood that the Government of the United States of America relinquishes the special rights which naval vessels of the United States of America have been accorded in the waters of the Republic of China and that the Government of the Republic of China and the Government of the United States of America shall extend to each other the mutual courtesy of visits by their warships in accordance with international usage and comity.

It is mutually understood that questions which are not covered by the present treaty and exchange of notes and which may affect the sovereignty of the Republic of China shall be discussed by representatives of the two Governments and shall be decided in accordance with generally accepted principles of international law and with modern international practice.

With reference to Article IV of the treaty, the Government of the Republic of China hereby declares that the restriction on the right of alienation of existing rights or titles to real property referred to in that article will be applied by the Chinese authorities in an equitable manner and that if and when the Chinese Government declines to give assent to a proposed transfer the Chinese Government will, in a spirit of justice and with a view to precluding loss on the part of American nationals whose interests are affected, undertake, if the American party in interest so desires, to take over the right or title in question and to pay adequate compensation therefor.

It is mutually understood that the orders, decrees, judgments, decisions and other acts of the United States Court for China and of the Consular Courts of the United States of America in China shall be considered as *res judicata* and shall, when necessary, be enforced by the Chinese authorities. It is further understood that any cases pending before the United States Court for China and the Consular Courts of the United States of America in China at the time of the coming into effect of this treaty shall, if the plaintiff or petitioner so desires, be remitted to the appropriate courts of the Government of the Republic of China which shall proceed as expeditiously as possible with their disposition and in so doing shall in so far as practicable apply the laws of the United States of America.

It is understood that these agreements and understandings if confirmed by Your Excellency's Government shall be considered as forming an integral part of the treaty signed today and shall be considered as effective upon the date of the entrance into force of that treaty.

I shall be much obliged if Your Excellency will confirm the foregoing.

I avail [etc.]

(b) **The Secretary of State (*Hull*) to the Chinese Ambassador (*Wei*)** [1]

EXCELLENCY:

In connection with the treaty signed today between the Government of the United States of America and the Government of the Republic of China in which the Government of the United States of America relinquishes its extraterritorial and related special rights in China, I have the honor to acknowledge the receipt of your note of today's date reading as follows:

[Here follows the text of the above note from the Chinese Ambassador.]

I have the honor to confirm that the agreements and understandings which have been reached in connection with the treaty signed today by the Government of the United States of America and the Government of the Republic of China are as set forth in the above note from Your Excellency.

I avail [etc.]

(3) **Report of the Secretary of State (*Hull*) to the President (*Roosevelt*), January 18, 1943** [2]

The undersigned, the Secretary of State, has the honor to lay before the President, with a view to its transmission to the Senate to receive the advice and consent of that body to ratification, if his judgment approve thereof, a treaty and supplementary exchange of notes between the United States of America and the Republic of China for the relinquishment of extraterritorial rights in China and the regulation of related matters. The treaty was signed at Washington on January 11, 1943.

This treaty constitutes an application in practice of principles which are fundamental in our foreign policy. It represents the taking of a step to which this Government and the Chinese Government have long looked forward.

The treaty, which has now been signed, provides for the relinquishment by this country of extraterritorial and other special rights in China and stipulates that American nationals in China shall be subject to the jurisdiction of the Chinese Government in accordance with the principles of international law and practice. If any question should arise in future, affecting rights of American nationals or of the American Government in China which are not covered by this treaty or by subsisting provisions of other treaties between the United States and China, these questions are to be decided in accordance with the principles of international law and practice. The treaty also provides that at a suitable time negotia-

[1] *Ibid.*, p. 244.　　　　[2] *Ibid.*, p. 239.

tions shall be entered into by the two countries for the conclusion of a comprehensive modern treaty of friendship, commerce, navigation, and consular rights.

A similar treaty with supplementary exchange of notes was signed by Great Britain with China on January 11, also, and other countries have indicated their intention of taking action along the same lines.

In brief summary, the more important matters to which the treaty between the United States and China relates are the following:

Under Article I all those provisions of treaties or agreements which authorize this Government to exercise extraterritorial jurisdiction in China are abrogated.

Article II relates to the termination of American rights under the Boxer Protocol of 1901, including the right to station troops between Peiping and the sea and rights in the diplomatic quarter at Peiping. Special provision is made in the treaty for the continued use by this Government for official purposes of the land in the Diplomatic Quarter at Peiping which was allocated to the United States in accordance with that protocol and upon which stand buildings belonging to the United States Government including the buildings which formerly housed the American Embassy.

Article III provides for the cessation of this Government's rights in relation to the International Settlements at Shanghai and Amoy.

Provision is made in Articles II and III for cooperation between the United States and China for the reaching of any necessary agreements with other governments for the transfer to the Chinese Government of the administration and control of the Diplomatic Quarter at Peiping and of the International Settlements at Shanghai and Amoy, it being expressly understood that the Chinese Government in taking over such administration and control will provide for the assumption and discharge of the official obligations and liabilities of the Diplomatic Quarter and the settlements and for the recognition and protection of all legitimate rights therein.

Article IV makes provision for the protection of existing rights and titles to real property in China held by American nationals, including corporations and associations, or by the Government of the United States, which might be affected by relinquishment of extraterritorial jurisdiction.

In Article V the Chinese Government agrees to accord to American nationals in China rights similar to those long accorded to Chinese nationals in the United States to travel, reside, and carry on trade throughout the whole extent of the United States. Hitherto, American and other foreign nationals in China have been subject to restrictions upon the areas in which they might travel, reside, and carry on trade. In Article V, also, each country agrees to endeavor to have accorded to nationals of the other country treatment no less favorable than that enjoyed by its own nationals in regard to legal proceedings, the administration of justice and the levying of taxes.

Article VI provides on a reciprocal basis for the enjoyment by the consular officers of each country in the territory of the other country of the rights, privileges, and immunities enjoyed under modern international usage, including the right to interview and to visit nationals who may be under detention or in prison.

Article VII contains the provisions already referred to with regard to the negotiation of a comprehensive modern treaty and with regard to the settlement in accordance with the principles of international law and practice of any questions affecting the rights of American nationals or of the American Government which may arise in future.

Article VIII provides for the ratification of the treaty and the exchange of ratifications and for entry into force on the day of the exchange of ratifications.

The treaty is accompanied by an exchange of notes in which the United States relinquishes the special rights hitherto possessed by its naval vessels in Chinese waters, and special rights which vessels of the United States have had in relation to inland navigation and the coasting trade. Each country is to be accorded the rights which are customary and normal in modern international relations in regard to the admission of merchant vessels into ports open to overseas merchant shipping, the treatment of merchant vessels in such ports, and visits by naval vessels. If either country accords rights of inland navigation or coasting trade to vessels of any third country such rights would similarly be accorded to the vessels of the other country. In the light of the abolition of treaty ports as such, all coastal ports in Chinese territory which are normally open to American overseas merchant shipping will remain open to such shipping after the coming into effect of the treaty. Provision is also made in the notes with regard to certain other matters, such as the continuing validity of past orders and decisions of the United States Court for China and the United States consular courts, and the disposition of cases pending before such courts.

This treaty between the United States and China is directed toward accomplishing two main objectives: First, the abolition of the extra-territorial system in China; and, second, the regulation of certain related matters, for which provision is made in a manner consonant with the long-established practices of this country.

Respectfully submitted.

(4) *Letter of the President (Roosevelt) Transmitting to the Senate the Treaty between the United States and China, February 1, 1943* [1]

To the Senate of the United States:

I transmit herewith a treaty between the United States of America and the Republic of China for the relinquishment of extraterritorial rights in China and the regulation of related matters signed at Washington by the Secretary of State and the Ambassador of China on January 11, 1943, and a supplementary exchange of notes also concerning matters related to extraterritorial rights which was signed by them at the same time and which, according to its terms, is made an integral part of the treaty.

I enclose for the information of the Senate a copy of the report of the Secretary of State laying the treaty before me, in which its provisions are reviewed.

The two main objectives of the treaty, as pointed out in the concluding paragraph of the Secretary's report, are the abolition of the extraterritorial system in China and the regulation of certain related matters. The more important among the latter are restated from the treaty and the exchange of notes in the report of the Secretary of State.

The treaty and the exchange of notes have my approval.

Accomplishment of the abolition of the extraterritorial system in China is a step in line with the expressed desires of the Government and the people of the United States. The spirit reflected by the treaty will, I am sure, be gratifying to the Governments and the peoples of all the United Nations.

I ask the advice and consent of the Senate to the ratification of the treaty, together with the exchange of notes which accompanies it.

(5) *Report of the Senate Committee on Foreign Relations, February 11, 1943* [2]

The Senate Committee on Foreign Relations, having had under consideration Executive A, Seventy-eighth Congress, first session, a treaty between the United States of America and the Republic of China for the relinquishment of extraterritorial rights in China and the regulation of related matters signed at Washington on January 11, 1943, and a supplementary exchange of notes also concerning matters related to extraterritorial rights which was signed at the same time and which is made an integral part of the treaty, hereby report the same favorably to the Senate without amendment with the recommendation that it advise and consent to its ratification.

The system of extraterritorial jurisdiction in China began with the conclusion of treaties in 1842 and 1843 between China and Great Britain

[1] *Ibid.*, p. 238.　　　　[2] *Ibid.*, p. 245.

and a treaty in 1844 between China and the United States. In those treaties and in treaties later concluded between China, Great Britain, and the United States and many other countries, were provisions whereby nationals of the various foreign governments in China were made subject in most respects to courts of their own countries, those courts functioning under and according to the laws of their various countries respectively.

Provisions similar to these had appeared earlier and have appeared later in treaties to which there have been parties on the one hand various Occidental countries and on the other hand, various Oriental countries. Such provisions have in many cases been terminated during the past four decades, but in several cases some of such provisions still survive.

At the time when provision for extraterritorial jurisdiction was made in the treaties of a century ago — and in earlier times — adoption of those provisions was not construed as a derogation of sovereignty. Extraterritorial jurisdiction was regarded as an expedient for the facilitating of contacts and relations between parties and groups whose history, philosophy, political organization, jurisprudence, and administration of justice were widely dissimilar; it was intended to diminish friction, minimize causes of conflict, and contribute to maintenance of conditions of law and order. In the course of time there developed in connection with it various abuses, and it made possible some types and not a few cases of injustice; but at the same time and on balance, it served usefully through many decades the essentially constructive and mutually beneficial purposes for which it was intended. With the passage of time, however, conditions changed, and in the light of changes such steps as those that are now being taken toward bringing to an end this system in China have been regarded as logical developments in the interest of all countries concerned.

Shortly after the beginning of the present century, there began to be discussion of discontinuing these provisions in treaties with China. When there was concluded in 1903 a new commercial treaty between the United States and China, provision was made that the United States would be "prepared to relinquish extraterritorial rights (in China) when satisfied that the state of the Chinese laws, the arrangements for their administration, and other considerations warrant it in so doing." A similar provision appeared in a treaty between Great Britain and China concluded at approximately the same time. At the time of the Peace Conference in Paris, the question of extraterritorial jurisdiction was considered, and at that time the extraterritorial rights of the Central European Powers in China were terminated by the treaties whereby the peace settlement was effected. At the Washington Conference in 1921–22, there was adopted by the nine powers that were parties to that conference a resolution in consequence of and pursuant to which an International Commission on Extraterritoriality went to China in 1925, made a study of the Chinese system of administration of justice, and submitted, under date of September 16, 1926, a report thereon.

In the period from 1903 to 1922 China was undergoing a period of transition which was marked by a change from empire to republic and by efforts of the republic to make its authority effective throughout China. Also, in this period normal international relations were disrupted by the First World War.

From 1925 until 1928 the revolutionary movement in China gained impetus and culminated in 1927–28 in the establishment of the present government, the National Government of the Republic of China.

In 1929 discussions were entered into between China and each of several other countries, among which were the United States and Great Britain, on the subject of extraterritorial jurisdiction in China. By 1931 these discussions were far advanced when they were suspended in consequence of Japan's invasion of Manchuria. Japan's subsequent movements of aggression in Shanghai and in North China during the next few years made it not opportune to resume discussions of the matter with the Chinese Government.

In 1937 this Government was giving renewed favorable consideration to the question when Japan embarked on large-scale military operations in China. Subsequently, there did not again develop until a number of months ago a situation deemed favorable to renewing negotiations on this subject. As soon as it became apparent that an opportune moment had again arrived, there were begun the conversations and negotiations which led to the signing of the treaty now under consideration. Such negotiations were carried on simultaneously between the American Government and the Chinese Government and the British Government and the Chinese Government. Treaties similar in general character were signed between the American and the Chinese Governments and the British and the Chinese Governments respectively, on the same day, January 11, of this year.

The purpose, the nature, and the conditions of the American-Chinese Treaty are set forth in the letter addressed by the Secretary of State to the President under date of January 18, 1943.

This treaty was intended to be and is a brief and simple document. Its provisions are limited to the two objectives of terminating the extraterritorial system in China and regulating certain related matters. Its political and legal purport is indicated in its preamble, which reads:

The United States of America and the Republic of China, desirous of emphasizing the friendly relations which have long prevailed between their two peoples and of manifesting their common desire as equal and sovereign states that the high principles in the regulation of human affairs to which they are committed shall be made broadly effective, have resolved to conclude a treaty for the purpose of adjusting certain matters in the relations of the two countries, etc.

In brief summary, the more important matters to which the treaty between the United States and China relates are the following:

[Here follows summary contained in letter of Secretary of State given above, p. 495.]

The British-Chinese treaty is similar to this treaty both as regards the principal document and the supplementary exchange of notes. These two treaties pave the way for complete termination of the system of extraterritorial jurisdiction in China. Various other countries have during recent years either lost their extraterritorial provisions or indicated their intention of giving them up. Several countries are at present either negotiating with China on this subject or about to begin such negotiations.

In line with the spirit of abrogation by the United States of extraterritorial rights in China, it is important to note that under Articles II and III of the treaty herein discussed, it is provided that the United States agrees to cooperate with China in reaching agreements with other Governments for the transfer to the Chinese Government of the administration and control of the Diplomatic Quarter at Peiping and of the administration and control of the International Settlement at Shanghai and Amoy.

As stated by the President in his letter of transmittal, accomplishment of the termination of the extraterritorial system in China is a step in line with the expressed desires of the Government and the people of the United States, and the spirit reflected by the treaty will, it is believed, be gratifying to the Governments and peoples of all the United Nations.

D. Cultural Relations

(1) *Building Our Relations with the Far East. Address by Haldore Hanson, Division of Cultural Relations, Department of State, at the National Convention of the National Council for Social Studies, New York City, November 28, 1942* [1]

[Excerpt]

. . . . . .

On January 14, 1942 President Roosevelt at the request of the Secretary of State set aside a modest amount of money with which to inaugurate the China cultural-relations program. The adoption of cultural relations as an instrument of American foreign policy is a comparatively new development. A program of cultural relations with the other American Republics was set up in 1937. The China program began one month after Pearl Harbor although the Department had been preparing plans for more than one year before the Japanese attack. Programs for other parts of the world are still in the discussion stage.

[1] *Ibid.*, VII, p. 964.

A definition of cultural relations as conducted by our Government is not easily given. Let me first point out what cultural relations are not. There are certain instruments of foreign policy with which cultural relations should not be confused.

For example, cultural relations are not a wartime publicity program. The Office of War Information, under Mr. Elmer Davis, has been charged by the President with the dissemination of war information. In China the staff of the OWI is carrying on its work through local newspapers, radio stations, motion-picture theaters, and libraries. Their job is to deliver war information.

Secondly, cultural relations are not a form of military assistance. The Lend-Lease Administration handles that function for our Government.

Thirdly, cultural relations are not a relief program. The President has appointed a War Relief Administrator, who will distribute American food, clothing, and medicines in foreign countries. In China, it should be noted, too, United China Relief and the American Red Cross have made available millions of dollars worth of relief supplies from the private citizens of the United States.

Finally, cultural relations are not designed for the promotion of American goods. Before the war our Government maintained in China commercial and agricultural officers. Their duties included the study of possible markets for American products.

All these activities may be excluded from the field of cultural relations. We may expect that in the building of relations with the Far East our Government will continue to use publicity. It will continue to give military supplies. It will continue to give civilian relief, and ultimately it will assist in the revival of international commerce.

Now where do cultural relations fit in? In broad terms cultural relations are the exchange of ideas and techniques which will enable nations mutually to enrich the lives of their citizens. The kind of knowledge which we seek to exchange is not limited to the arts and other cultivated intellectual interests, as the word *cultural* is often interpreted. Cultural relations may be concerned with music, with painting, and with literature, but the full scope of the program is much broader. Under cultural relations our Government wishes to exchange knowledge of public health, of better agriculture, better education, better engineering, better scientific research. In short, cultural relations aim to give other nations the same kind of knowledge and trained personnel which have enabled this nation to improve the lives of its people; and we wish to bring from foreign lands those skills and ideas which will enrich the lives of Americans.

The techniques of cultural relations are various. Knowledge can be spread through the exchange of professors and students, through the distribution of books and educational motion pictures, through the meetings of professional societies, through the exchange of visits by distinguished citizens. For example, to assist with public-health problems in the other American Republics our Government has sent some of our best health specialists southward, has brought South American medical students northward, and has distributed medical books to universities in the other republics.

The program for China was set up within the framework of the definition which I have given.

The Government recognized at the outset that private American citizens had been engaged in some phases of cultural relations with China for nearly a century. Missionaries by the thousands have spent their lives in China. Along with their religious work they have conducted many secular activities. Several hundred of the best high schools in China were established by missionaries. At least 14 Chinese colleges were founded by Americans. More than a hundred hospitals and a dozen agricultural experiment stations can be traced back to missionaries. Most of these institutions are now administered by Chinese, and many of them no longer receive financial aid from American churches. But the institutions remain as monuments to the friendship between the American and the Chinese people.

Two results of American missionary education should be noted especially. First, English has become the second language in China. The study of English is now a requirement in most high schools under the supervision of the Ministry of Education. The importance to cultural relations of this language study can well be appreciated by those who have worked for better relations with Latin America, where French, not English, is the secondary language. We can thank the missionaries for promoting the language tool whereby the Chinese today are able to read about the United States in our own language.

Secondly, missionary schools have led many Chinese students to come to the United States for advanced study. From 1900 to 1941 our universities were privileged to receive each year a fresh migration of Chinese. None has come this year, but approximately 1,000 Chinese who arrived in recent years are still in this country. The original stimulus for this migration of students came largely from the missionaries.

Religious workers were not the only American citizens who became interested in cultural relations. Great philanthropic organizations have invested millions of dollars in China. In 1924, for example, the Rockefeller Foundation financed the merger of several missionary medical schools to form the Peking Union Medical College, which is generally regarded as the finest medical training center in eastern Asia.

If I were to do full justice to the enterprises of our private citizens, I should be compelled to mention nearly 100 American groups which have carried on educational, health, and research work in China.

The Government in drafting its plans for cultural relations undertook certain projects which could not easily be performed at this time by private citizens. Let me tell you, for example, about our microfilm project. Many Chinese university professors have relied in the past upon American scientific and technical journals for a part of their classroom materials. This was a natural tendency because so many Chinese professors were educated in the United States. When Japanese submarines and military planes fanned out along the coast of southern Asia, regular mail to China was interrupted and airmail was uncertain. American technical journals failed to arrive at Chinese universities.

One of our first tasks under the China cultural-relations program was to arrange for the microfilming of approximately 60 American periodicals. A microfilm, as you may know, is the same as a 35-mm. motion-picture film. Each frame of the film, although less than an inch wide, contains the reproduction of 2 printed pages. A pound of film can reproduce 1,600 pages from a magazine or book. The Department of State is now sending more than 3,000 pages a month of microfilmed materials to China. Five copies of each film are made for distribution to universities, and the negative is also sent to enable the Chinese to make additional copies. The film can be read by the use of a small wall projector which enables about 15 persons to read the film at one time. That is one of our Government projects.

Another is the assistance given to some of the Chinese students in this country. About 600 of the 1,000 students have encountered financial difficulty during the past 12 months because the war has cut off their financial aid from China. Our Government has provided small living allowances for about 200 of these students. The Chinese Government has aided about an equal number, and the others have been befriended by American universities or have been given salaried employment.

The Department of State has recently appointed an employment counselor for Chinese students. He will seek to place the students, as they graduate from universities, in paid positions where they will be able to continue their training. This placement work is comparatively easy for students of engineering and science. It is more difficult for those who have specialized in education, history, or economics. During the next year we hope to find a solution whereby those students may receive useful training until they are able to return to China.

A third Government project for cultural relations is the sending of American technical experts to assist the Chinese Government. Last spring the Chinese Foreign Office was asked what kinds of specialists that Government needed most urgently. The Chinese sent a list of their requirements in such fields as public health, education, engineering, and agriculture. Seven Americans have already been appointed by the Department of State to go to China under this project. Others will follow.

Nearly all these Americans are expected to remain abroad for a minimum of one year.

I have given you three examples of projects under our cultural-relations program, all of which are calculated to be of assistance to the Chinese war effort. The program is still in its infancy. Its activities will undoubtedly be altered after the war, but its purpose will continue to be the exchange of knowledge and of skill which will be of mutual benefit to the peoples of the United States and China.

3. INDIA

The failure of Sir Stafford Cripps to achieve agreement between the British Government and the principal Indian groups on a plan of self-government for India was documented in *Documents, IV, 1941-1942*, pp. 544-573. The Working Committee of the Congress Party adopted a resolution, which was published on July 14, 1942, calling on the British to end their rule in India and threatening to resort to a campaign of civil disobedience if their demand was refused.[1] The Committee's resolution was submitted for ratification by the All-India Congress Committee, meeting at Bombay, on August 7, 1942, and was endorsed and approved with only 13 dissenting votes, on August 8.[2] The British Government, in the meantime, made it clear that it would not yield to violence and would take every possible step to meet the situation.[3] A last-minute appeal was made by Sir Stafford Cripps on August 5.[4] The Viceroy's Executive Council met immediately after the endorsement of the Working Committee's resolution and issued two Defense of India rules. With the outbreak of civil disobedience, the leaders of the Congress Party, including Gandhi and Nehru, were arrested and placed under detention.[5] A unanimous resolution was issued on August 20 by the Working Committee of the All-India Moslem League condemning the "open rebellion" of the Congress Party and offering cooperation in forming a provisional government for the duration of the war provided the demands of Moslem India were conceded. The Council of the All-India Moslem League adopted without amendment the resolution on November 9.

Sir Stafford Cripps in an article in the *New York Times* of August 23 stated that there were at least 160 million Indians who did not support the Congress Party resolution and that for the British to walk out of India immediately would mean that India would be left without any Constitution or any Government. "I fully realize and sympathize with the desire of the Indian people for self-government," Sir Stafford wrote, "but they will not attain it by admitting the Japanese or any other Axis power. The war must first be won by the United Nations, and I believe that the majority of the Indian people know and realize the truth of that fact."

Prime Minister Churchill on September 10 made a statement in the House of Commons on India in which he said that the broad principles of the British declaration which formed the bases of Sir Stafford Cripps' mission must be taken "as representing the settled policy of the British Crown and Parliament." [6]

[1] *Bulletin of International News*, XIX (1942), p. 674.

[2] *Ibid.*, p. 732.

[3] Statement by Leopold S. Amery, Secretary of State for India, to the House of Commons, July 30, 1942, *New York Times*, July 31, 1942.

[4] *Ibid.*, August 6, 1942.

[5] A White Paper (Cmd. 6430) was published March 24, 1943, giving a statement published by the Government of India in February on "The Responsibility of the Congress Party for the Disturbances in India 1942-43."

[6] *Bulletin of International News*, XIX (1942), p. 856.

At his press conference on October 27, Secretary of State Hull, in reply to questions regarding Mr. Willkie's remarks about India, stated that the Government was much interested in the situation there and was watching for opportunities "to give it the fullest attention feasible." [1]

On December 11, it was announced that the President had appointed Mr. William Phillips "as his Personal Representative to serve near the Government of India." [2] In a statement made on his arrival in New Delhi, Mr. Phillips said: "I have come to study and learn as much as I can of India today and the India of the future which has such an important role to play in world affairs. I shall report my findings to Washington." [3] On the eve of his departure from New Delhi, at his final press conference, April 25, 1943, Mr. Phillips disclosed that he had asked permission to see Mohandas K. Gandhi and Pandit Jawaharlal Nehru, but that his request had been refused by the Viceroy.[4]

Under Secretary of State Welles on April 10 in reply to questions contained in a letter from Professor Ralph Barton Perry stated that "the future constitutional status of India is a tremendously complicated and delicate problem. The United States Government is, of course, anxious to give full assistance to its solution. The people of India have been most solemnly assured that as soon as the necessities of war permit they will be given the opportunity to choose freely the form of government they desire." He also added, "But to make active intervention in the Indian situation a test of liberalism, as some have done, presupposes a definition of liberalism which I must confess is beyond my comprehension." [5]

(1) *Orders to American Military Forces in India, Released to the Press, August 12, 1942* [6]

[Excerpt]

The following statement of this Government's policy has been made a part of the orders to the American military forces in India:

1. The sole purpose of the American forces in India is to prosecute the war of the United Nations against the Axis powers. In the prosecution of the war in that area the primary aim of the Government of the United States is to aid China.

2. American forces are not to indulge to the slightest degree in activities of any other nature unless India should be attacked by the Axis powers, in which event American troops would aid in defending India.

3. American forces in India will exercise scrupulous care to avoid the slightest participation in India's internal political problems, or even the appearance of so doing.

4. In event of internal disturbances American forces will resort to defensive measures only should their own personal safety or that of other American citizens be endangered or for the necessary protection of American military supplies and equipment.

[1] *Ibid.*, p. 1056.
[2] Department of State, *Bulletin*, VII, p. 998.
[3] *New York Times*, January 9, 1943.
[4] *Ibid.*, April 26, 1943.
[5] Department of State, *Bulletin*, VIII, p. 319.
[6] *Ibid.*, VII, p. 697.

(2) *Joint Statement by the Governments of the United States and India Regarding the Submission of the Final Report of the Technical Mission to India, Released to the Press, September 12, 1942* [1]

[See *Documents, IV, 1941–42*, p. 543, for statement regarding the creation of the Mission.]

The final report of the American Technical Mission has been submitted by its Chairman, Dr. Henry F. Grady, to the Governments of India and the United States. The report contains much factual data concerning the production of India of essential war materials and the recommendations of the Mission for the expansion of such production. The two Governments are now engaged in studying the Mission's report and the manner in which its various recommendations may be implemented.

The function of the Mission was to investigate the industrial resources of India and to recommend ways and means by which these resources could be developed to augment production for war purposes. The work of the Mission, therefore, was directly related to the common war effort of the United Nations and was not connected with the post-war industrial and commercial problems of India. The report of the Mission contains a survey of the principal industries of India ancillary to the war effort and its principal industrial requirements. For each of these, the Mission made recommendations suggesting action by either the Government of India or the Government of the United States. In those instances in which additional output was shown to be required, the Mission recommended the erection of new plants or the installation of additional machinery in existing plants. It also suggested the rearrangement of existing machinery in order that maximum efficiency in production might be attained. The congestion at certain Indian ports received the attention of the Mission, which made various recommendations designed to expedite the loading, unloading, and repair of ships. In addition, it called attention to the overburdened condition of the railways and suggested measures for its alleviation. Vigorous steps have already been taken by the Government of India to implement some of the recommendations contained in the preliminary report of the Mission; and in this program it is being assisted by equipment and material from the United States and the United Kingdom.

With the full approval of the Government of India, the Mission recommended that a number of production engineers and technicians be sent from the United States to advise and assist in increasing the industrial production in India. Steps have already been taken to secure the services of these experts and a number of them will soon be departing to undertake their new and important assignments.

[1] *Ibid.*, p. 749.

The Governments of India and the United States have been impressed with the comprehensive character of the Mission's report. Its recommendations appear to be both constructive and timely. The Governments concerned will determine the extent to which the Mission's program is to be implemented and will seek promptly to execute their decision.

4. THE NETHERLANDS EAST INDIES

[See *Documents, IV, 1941-42*, p. 573.]

In view of the importance which the future of the Netherlands East Indies has for the people of the United States and the inevitability of our having a large responsibility for determining it, it seems appropriate to include in this volume a statement by Her Majesty Queen Wilhelmina outlining plans for the creation of a Commonwealth of the Netherlands, Indonesia, Surinam and Curaçao. To make this statement fully intelligible, the text of the statement of the Netherlands Government of January 27, 1942, to which reference is made, is also given.

These two statements are to be read against the background of the Queen's radio address of July 30, 1941,[1] in which she stated that upon the return of the Cabinet to the Netherlands, it intended to "tender its resignation so as to enable me to appoint new Ministers of the Crown" and that the new government would undertake a revision of the Constitution with a view to bringing about changes "in the Netherlands proper as well as in the relations between the constituent parts of the Kingdom as a whole"; and the statement of Foreign Minister E. N. van Kleffens at the Inter-Allied Meeting in London, on September 24, 1941,[2] expressing the adhesion of the Netherlands Government to the principles of the Atlantic Charter.

(1) *Plans for the Creation of a Commonwealth of the Netherlands, Indonesia, Surinam and Curaçao. Radio Address by H. M. the Queen of the Netherlands (Wilhelmina), December 6, 1942* [3]

Today it is a year ago that the Japanese, without previous declaration of war, launched their treacherous attack on our Allies. At that time we did not hesitate for a moment to throw ourselves into the struggle and to hasten to the aid of our Allies, whose cause is ours.

Japan had been preparing for this war and for the conquest of the Netherlands Indies for years and in so doing sought to follow the conduct of its Axis partners in attacking one country after another. This plan we were able to prevent, thanks to our immediate declaration of war. After a year of war we can bear witness that the tide is turning and that the attacker, who had such great advantages, is being forced on the defensive.

It is true that the Netherlands Indies, after defending themselves so heroically, are, for the most part, occupied by the enemy, but this phase

---

[1] *New York Times*, July 31, 1941; *Netherlands News*, vol. 1, no. 3 (August 15, 1941), p. 105.

[2] *United Kingdom, Parliamentary Papers*, Misc. No. 3 (1941), Cmd. 6315; *War and Peace Aims of the United Nations*, ed. by Louise W. Holborn, Boston (World Peace Foundation), 1943, p. 509.

[3] Netherlands Information Bureau, New York City.

of the struggle is only a prelude. The Japanese are getting ever nearer the limit of their possibilities as our ever-growing might advances towards them from all sides. They have not been able to break China's courage and endurance and Japan now faces the ebbing of her power in this self-willed war, which will end with her complete downfall.

At this moment my thoughts are more than ever with my country and my compatriots in the Netherlands and the Netherlands Indies. After an age-old historical solidarity, in which had long since passed the era of colonial relationship, we stood on the eve of a collaboration on a basis of equality when suddenly we were both confronted by the present ordeal. The treacherous aggression on the Netherlands in 1940 was the first interruption in the process of development; the heroic battle of the Netherlands Indies, followed by the occupation of the major part of this territory in 1942 was the second.

At the time when the Indies were still free and only Holland was occupied, the vigor of our unity became apparent and on both sides a feeling of stronger kinship developed more rapidly than it could have in peacetime. Now, however, this mutual understanding has been deepened still further because the same struggle is shared in all its agony and the same distress is suffered in all its bitterness. In the Netherlands as well as in the Netherlands Indies the enemy, with his propaganda for the so-called new order, has left nothing untried to lure the spirit of the people and to disguise his tyranny and suppression with the lies of his promises for the future. But these lies and this deceit have been of no avail because nearly all have seen through them and have understood that our enemies have as their aim nothing but slavery and exploitation and that as long as they have not been driven out and defeated there can be no question of freedom.

In previous addresses I announced that it is my intention, after the liberation, to create the occasion for a joint consultation about the structure of the Kingdom and its parts in order to adapt it to the changed circumstances. The conference of the entire Kingdom which will be convoked for this purpose, has been further outlined in a Government declaration of January 27, 1942. The preparation of this conference, in which prominent representatives of the three overseas parts of the Kingdom will be united with those of the Netherlands at a round table, had already begun in the Netherlands Indies, Surinam and Curaçao, the parts of the Kingdom which then still enjoyed their freedom. Especially in the Netherlands Indies, detailed material had been collected for this purpose and it was transmitted to me in December 1941 by the Governor General. The battle of the Netherlands Indies disrupted these promising preparations.

We can only resume these preparations when everyone will be able to speak his mind freely.

Although it is beyond doubt that a political reconstruction of the Kingdom as a whole and of the Netherlands and the Overseas Territories as its parts is a natural evolution, it would be neither right nor possible to define its precise form at this moment. I realize that much which is great and good is growing in the Netherlands despite the pressure of the occupation; I know that this is the case in the Indies where our unity is fortified by common suffering. These developing ideas can only be shaped in free consultation in which both parts of the Kingdom will want to take cognizance of each other's opinions. Moreover, the population of the Netherlands and of the Netherlands Indies has confirmed through its suffering and its resistance, its right to participate in the decision regarding the form of our responsibility as a nation towards the world and of the various groups of the population towards themselves and one another.

By working out these matters now, that right would be neglected, and the insight which my people have obtained through bitter experience would be disregarded.

I am convinced, and history as well as reports from the occupied territories confirm me in this, that after the war it will be possible to reconstruct the Kingdom on the solid foundation of complete partnership, which will mean the consummation of all that has been developed in the past. I know that no political unity nor national cohesion can continue to exist which are not supported by the voluntary acceptance and the faith of the great majority of the citizenry. I know that the Netherlands more than ever feel their responsibility for the vigorous growth of the Overseas Territories and that the Indonesians recognize, in the ever-increasing collaboration, the best guarantee for the recovery of their peace and happiness. The war years have proved that both peoples possess the will and the ability for harmonious and voluntary cooperation.

A political unity which rests on this foundation moves far towards a realization of the purpose for which the United Nations are fighting, as it has been embodied, for instance, in the Atlantic Charter, and with which we could instantly agree, because it contains our own conception of freedom and justice for which we have sacrificed blood and possessions in the course of our history. I visualize, without anticipating the recommendations of the future conference, that they will be directed towards a commonwealth in which the Netherlands, Indonesia, Surinam and Curaçao will participate, with complete self-reliance and freedom of conduct for each part regarding its internal affairs, but with the readiness to render mutual assistance.

It is my opinion that such a combination of independence and collaboration can give the Kingdom and its parts the strength to carry fully their responsibility, both internally and externally. This would leave no room for discrimination according to race or nationality; only the ability of the individual citizens and the needs of the various groups of the population will determine the policy of the government.

In the Indies, as in the Netherlands, there now rules an oppressor who, imitating his detestable associates and repudiating principles which he himself has recognized in the past, interns peaceful citizens and deprives women and children of their livelihood. He has uprooted and dislocated that beautiful and tranquil country; his new order brings nothing but misery and want. Nevertheless, we can aver that he has not succeeded in subjugating us, and as the evergrowing force of the United Nations advances upon him from every direction, we know that he will not succeed in the future.

The Netherlands Indies and the Netherlands with their fighting men on land, at sea and in the air, with their alert and brave merchantmen and by their dogged and never-failing resistance in the hard struggle, will see their self-sacrifice and intrepidity crowned after the common victory with the recovery of peace and happiness for their country and their people in a new world. In that regained freedom they will be able to build a new and better future.

(a) *Statement of the Netherlands Government, January 27, 1942* [1]

The present political structure of the Kingdom of the Netherlands as well as the relations between the Motherland and her Overseas Territories are based on the Constitution of 1922 and the Constitutions of the Netherlands Indies, Surinam and Curaçao built thereon.

Since 1922 the spiritual and material development of these Overseas Territories, especially the Netherlands Indies, has been unusually rapid. In consequence, the thoughts of the Motherland and the Indies, in and outside their representative bodies, during the latter years have been especially focused on constitutional measures for a greater emancipation within the Empire of these Overseas Territories.

The excellent attitude and spiritual energy that these parts displayed under the leadership of their Governors and notwithstanding the rupture of their ties with the Motherland, proofs given in these times of their ability to stand on their own legs, have stimulated the processes of spiritual and political emancipation in ever-growing groups of overseas populations.

In order to direct these deserving aspirations, aiming at the improvement of relationships between Netherlands territories in accordance with gradually grown circumstances, Her Majesty Queen Wilhelmina announced in a radio speech on May 10, 1941 that an Imperial Conference would be convened after the war.

The Crown now has made its decision in regard to calling this post-war conference in order to prepare the way of carrying through political reforms. The conference will be composed of prominent persons from all the four Netherlands territories who will be expected to represent various spiritual movements in these parts.

Participation will be as follows: from the Netherlands, 15 members; Netherlands Indies, 15 members; and Surinam and Curaçao each three. Of the 15 members from the Netherlands Indies, 10 will be appointed by the Government of the Netherlands Indies on recommendation of the People's Council and five

[1] Netherlands Information Bureau, New York City.

by the Government of the Netherlands Indies independently. Members from Surinam and Curaçao will be appointed by the Governor, two on recommendation of the States and one of the Government.

Appointment of the members for the East Indies and West Indies will be made now in order to enable the appointees to study and prepare their subject freely and thoroughly. The Governor-General of the Netherlands Indies and the Governors of Surinam and Curaçao have been asked to publish the Queen's decision with all possible speed and to appoint deputies for their territories.

The conference's task will be of an advisory nature and the conference itself will be in the nature of a round-table discussion which will consider all wishes and opinions in regard to the position of the various territories within the structure of the Empire and will make recommendations on the basis of these discussions.

5. THE PHILIPPINES

(1) *Radio Address of the President of the United States (Roosevelt), November 15, 1942* [1]

This address was delivered on the occasion of the seventh anniversary of the Government of the Commonwealth of the Philippines.

Though the alien flag of a treacherous aggressor flies temporarily over the Commonwealth of the Philippines, it is with supreme confidence in ultimate victory that the United Nations commemorate this birthday of its youngest member.

It was just seven years ago that this Commonwealth was established. By that time the United States had maintained sovereignty of the Philippine Islands for almost forty years. But as I said in 1935 when the present Commonwealth was inaugurated, "The acceptance of sovereignty was but an obligation to serve the people of the Philippines until the day they might themselves be independent and take their own place among the nations of the world."

Let me go back to the days when Admiral Dewey won the battle of Manila Bay, and American sovereignty was established over the Islands. To a very large part of the American people, it seemed incongruous and unwise that the United States should continue a colonial status over many millions of human beings who had already shown a desire for independence.

However, the United States and the leaders of the Filipino people soon undertook a long-time process of providing facilities in the Islands for education, health, commerce, and transportation, with the definite thought that the day would come when the people would be able to stand on their own feet. At the same time, we granted them a greater and greater degree of local self-government.

---

[1] From the Office of the Secretary to the President.

By the year 1934 sympathetic conferences between Philippine and American leaders reached the conclusion that the time for complete independence could be definitely set, — to follow a ten-year period of complete local autonomy under a Commonwealth form of government with its own Constitution.

This status was duly set up in 1935 under the Presidency of my old friend, Manuel Quezon. It succeeded so well that by December 7, 1941 we were jointly at work preparing for the consummation of complete independence in 1946. Both nations and peoples had kept faith with each other during all these years. Confidence in each other's good faith was firmly established — and it was cemented into place during the bitter months of ordeal which followed the treachery of Japan.

The brave peoples of the Philippines — their Army and their civilians — stood shoulder to shoulder with the Americans in the fight against overwhelming odds — resolute to shed their blood in defense of their liberty. Richly do they deserve that liberty!

I like to think that the history of the Philippine Islands in the last forty-four years provides in a very real sense a pattern for the future of other small nations and peoples of the world. It is a pattern of what men of good-will look forward to in the future — a pattern of a global civilization which recognizes no limitations of religion or of creed or of race.

But we must remember that such a pattern is based on two important factors. The first is that there be a period of preparation, through the dissemination of education and the recognition and fulfillment of physical and social and economic needs. The second is that there be a period of training for ultimate independent sovereignty, through the practice of more and more self-government, beginning with local government and passing on through the various steps to complete statehood.

Even we in the United States did not arrive at full national independence until we had gone through the preliminary stages. The town meetings in the New England colonies, and the similar local organizations in other colonies, gradually led to county government and then to state government. That whole process of political training and development preceded the final formation of the permanent Federal Government in 1789.

Such training for independence is essential to the stability of independence in almost every part of the world. Some peoples need more intensive training and longer years; others require far less training and a shorter period of time.

The recent history of the Philippines has been one of national cooperation and adjustment and development. We are sure now, if ever we doubted, that our Government chose the right course.

The pattern which was followed there is essentially a part and parcel of the philosophy and the ideals of the United Nations. The doctrine which controls the ambitions and directs the ruthlessness of our enemies — that there is one master folk destined to rule all other people — is a doctrine now on its way to destruction for all time to come.

The United States and the Philippines are already engaged in examining the practical economic problems of the future — when President Quezon and his Government are re-established in the Capital of Manila. He and I, in conference last week, agreed to set up a Joint Commission of our two countries, to study the economic situation which will face the nation which is soon to be, and to work out means of preserving its stability and security.

This typifies the highest form of good faith, which now exists between our two Governments.

It is more than that. It is a realistic symbol of our grim determination and of our supreme confidence that we shall drive the Japanese Army out of the Philippines — to the last man.

President Quezon — on this auspicious anniversary — I salute, through you, the people of the Philippine Islands. I salute their courage. I salute their independence.

6. AUSTRALIA AND NEW ZEALAND

Concerning agreements of September 3, 1942, specifying the principles and procedures applicable to the provision of aid to the United States and its armed forces by the Governments of Australia and New Zealand, see Chapter IV, p. 234, 245-6.

CHAPTER VII

EUROPE, AFRICA AND WESTERN ASIA

1. RELATIONS WITH PARTICULAR EUROPEAN COUNTRIES

A. United Kingdom

During the period under review, the relations between the United States and the United Kingdom have been largely carried on within the framework of the United Nations concept and for the purpose of achieving common United Nations purposes. For that reason, even though these relations have in most cases been conducted on a bilateral basis, they have been described and documented in Chapter IV (The United Nations). Consequently, the exhibits presented here are few in number and fragmentary in the story they tell, thus by themselves giving a quite inadequate idea of the importance and scope of relations between the two countries. To aid in the use of the documents bearing on Anglo-American relations contained in this volume, cross references are extensively given, so that one approaching these relations from the strictly Anglo-American angle will not be too greatly handicapped.

1. POST–WAR RELATIONS

(1) *Address by the Prime Minister (Churchill), Guildhall, London, June 30, 1943* [1]

[Excerpt]

. . . .

But now I must speak of the great Republic of the United States whose power arouses no fear and whose pre-eminence excites no jealousy in British bosoms.

Upon the association and the intimate alignment of the policy of the United States and the British Commonwealth and Empire depends, more than upon any other factor, the immediate future of the world.

If we walk, or, if need be, march together in harmony and in accordance with the moral and political conceptions to which English-speaking peoples have given birth and which are frequently referred to in the Atlantic Charter, all will be well. If they fall apart and wander astray from the lines of their destiny, there is no end or measure to the miseries and confusion which would mark modern civilization.

This is no rhetorical extravagance in genial sentiment for a festive occasion; it is hard, cold, vindictive truth. Yet there are many light and

[1] *New York Times*, July 1, 1943.

wayward spirits in both our countries who show themselves by word and action unmindful of this fundamental fact.

It is a fact in no way derogatory to that mighty nation now fighting at our side or to any nation, great or small, making its way through the perils of the present age.

We have seen no narrow or selfish combination. We presume not at all upon the lawful interests and characteristics of any ally or friendly state. We nourish the warmest feelings of fellowship toward the valiant Russian people, with whom we have made a twenty years' treaty of friendship and mutual aid.

We foresee an expanding future to the long-enduring Republic of China. We look forward to a revival of the unity and true greatness of France. We have the loyal, faithful comradeship of all. Nevertheless the tremendous and awe-inspiring fact stares the British and American democracies between the eyes, that acting together we can help all nations safely into harbor and that if we divide all will toss and drift for a long time on dark and stormy seas.

It is fitting in a singular manner to speak upon this theme of fraternal association of Britain and the United States here amid the proud monuments and the prouder ruins of the City of London, because nothing ever made a warmer feeling between the British and American people than the unflinching resistance of London to the formidable and prolonged assault of the enemy.

. . . .

2. PROSECUTION OF THE WAR

For text of the agreement of February 23, 1942, between the Governments of the United States and the United Kingdom for mutual aid pursuant to the Lend-Lease Act of March 11, 1941, see *Documents, IV, 1941-42*, p. 235. Three supplementary agreements were subsequently entered into during the period under review: (1) Agreement for Reciprocal Lend-Lease Aid to the United States and its Armed Forces, Concluded between the Governments of the United Kingdom and the United States of America by Exchange of Notes, dated September 3, 1942 (see p. 234); (2) Agreement between the Governments of the United States of America and the United Kingdom for the Interchange of Patents Rights, Information, Inventions, Designs, or Processes, signed at Washington, August 24, 1942 (see p. 220); and (3) Agreement between the Governments of the United States of America and the United Kingdom Regarding Certain Problems of Marine Transportation and Litigation, signed at London, December 4, 1942 (see p. 225).

For data on the amount of Lend-Lease aid given to the United Kingdom by the United States, see p. 131; for data on reverse Lend-Lease aid received by American forces in the United Kingdom, see p. 242.

On conferences of British and American officials, especially President Roosevelt and Prime Minister Churchill, on questions of policy and over-all strategy, see p. 248-60.

On other measures, largely administrative in character, for the better coordination of the war efforts of the two countries, see *Documents, IV, 1941-42*, p. 239 ff. and this volume, p. 248.

(1) Jurisdiction over Members of the Military and Naval Forces of the United States of America. Agreement Recorded by Exchange of Notes between the Governments of the United Kingdom and the United States, July 27, 1942 [1]

(a) The United Kingdom Secretary of State for Foreign Affairs (Eden) to the United States Ambassador (Winant)

YOUR EXCELLENCY:

Following the discussions which have taken place between representatives of our two Governments, His Majesty's Government in the United Kingdom are prepared, subject to the necessary Parliamentary authority, to give effect to the desire of the Government of the United States that the Service courts and authorities of the United States Forces should, during the continuance of the conflict against our common enemies, exercise exclusive jurisdiction in respect of criminal offenses which may be committed in the United Kingdom by members of those Forces, and they are ready to introduce in Parliament the necessary legislation for this purpose.

2. It is appreciated, however, that cases may arise where for particular reasons the American authorities may prefer that their courts should not exercise the above jurisdiction, and His Majesty's Government would accordingly propose that in any case in which a written communication to that effect is received from the Diplomatic Representative of the United States it should be open to the appropriate British authority to restore the jurisdiction of the courts of the United Kingdom to deal with that case.

3. In view of the very considerable departure which the above arrangements will involve from the traditional system and practice of the United Kingdom there are certain points upon which His Majesty's Government consider it indispensable first to reach an understanding with the United States Government. I have accordingly the honor to invite Your Excellency to be so good as to lay the following enquiries and observations before your Government and to inform me of their attitude thereupon.

4. In the first place, the readiness of His Majesty's Government in the United Kingdom to agree to the exercise by United States Service courts of exclusive jurisdiction in respect of offenses by members of their Forces is based upon the assumption that the United States Service authorities and courts concerned will be able and willing to try and, on conviction, to punish all criminal offenses which members of the United States Forces may be alleged on sufficient evidence to have committed in the United Kingdom, and that the United States authorities are agreeable in principle to investigate and deal with appropriately any alleged criminal

---

[1] *United States of America (Visiting Forces) Act, 1942*, 5 & 6 Geo. 6, ch. 31, Schedule. London, H. M. Stationery Office, 1942; (U. S.) *Executive Agreement Series* 355.

offenses committed by members of the United States Forces in the United Kingdom which may be brought to their notice by the competent British authorities, or which the American authorities may find to have taken place.

5. Secondly, His Majesty's Government will be glad if Your Excellency will confirm their understanding that the trial of any member of the United States Forces for an offense against a member of the civilian population would be in open Court (except where security considerations forbade this) and would be arranged to take place promptly in the United Kingdom and within a reasonable distance from the spot where the offense was alleged to have been committed, so that witnesses should not be required to travel great distances to attend the hearing.

6. Thirdly, His Majesty's Government propose that no member of the United States Forces should be tried in the United Kingdom by a Service Court of the United States of America, for an offense committed by him before 7th December, 1941.

7. Fourthly, while His Majesty's Government in the United Kingdom would not wish to make the arrangements in regard to jurisdiction over members of the United States Forces in this country dependent upon a formal grant of reciprocity in respect of United Kingdom Forces in the territory of the United States of America, I feel that Your Excellency will appreciate that the considerations which have convinced His Majesty's Government in the United Kingdom that the interests of our common cause would be best served by the arrangements which they are prepared to make as regards jurisdiction over American forces in the United Kingdom would be equally applicable in the case of British forces which in the course of the war against our common enemies may be stationed in territory under American jurisdiction. It would accordingly be very agreeable to His Majesty's Government in the United Kingdom if Your Excellency were authorized to inform me that in that case the Government of the United States of America will be ready to take all steps in their power to ensure to the British forces concerned a position corresponding to that of American forces in the United Kingdom under the arrangements which His Majesty's Government are willing to make. The considerations indicated in paragraph 2 above would naturally apply and His Majesty's Government would be prepared to authorize the Diplomatic Representative of His Majesty in the United States to notify the competent American authorities in cases where the appropriate British authorities preferred not to exercise jurisdiction.

8. Fifthly, the proposal to ensure to the United States Service courts and authorities by legislation the exclusive exercise of jurisdiction in respect of criminal offenses by members of the United States Forces in the United Kingdom is based upon the further assumption that satisfactory machinery will be devised between the competent American and

British authorities for such mutual assistance as may be required in making investigations and collecting evidence in respect of offenses which members of the United States Forces are alleged to have committed, or in which they are alleged to be concerned. His Majesty's Government have no doubt that the United States Government will agree that it would as a general rule be desirable that such preliminary action should be taken by the British authorities, on behalf of the American authorities, where the witnesses or other persons from whom it is desired to take statements are not members of the United States Forces. Conversely, His Majesty's Government trust that they may count upon the assistance of the American authorities in connection with the prosecution before British courts of persons who are not members of the United States Forces where the evidence of any member of these Forces is required or where the assistance of the American authorities in the investigation of the case (including the taking of statements from the American Forces) may be needed.

9. His Majesty's Government in the United Kingdom are prepared to extend the proposed legislation where necessary to British Colonies and Dependencies under their authority, other than those British territories in which are situated the United States Military and Naval Bases leased in pursuance of the Agreement of 27th March, 1941, where the question of jurisdiction is already regulated by that Agreement.[1] I accordingly propose that the foregoing paragraphs of this note, and your eventual reply, should be regarded as extending also to the arrangements to be made in the British Colonies and Dependencies to which the proposed legislation may be applied.

10. Finally, His Majesty's Government propose that the foregoing arrangements should operate during the conduct of the conflict against our common enemies and until six months (or such other period as may be mutually agreed upon) after the final termination of such conflict and the restoration of a state of peace.

11. If the foregoing arrangements are acceptable to the United States Government, I have the honor to propose that the present note and Your Excellency's reply be regarded as constituting an agreement between the two Governments to which effect shall be given as from the date on which the legislation to which I have already referred takes effect.

I have the honor to be, [etc.]

(b) *The United States Ambassador (Winant) to the United Kingdom Secretary of State for Foreign Affairs (Eden)*

SIR,

I have the honor to refer to your note of July 27, 1942, in which you inform me that His Majesty's Government in the United Kingdom is

[1] *Documents*, III, 1940–41, p. 216.

prepared, subject to the necessary Parliamentary authority, to give effect to the desire of the Government of the United States that American authorities have exclusive jurisdiction in respect to criminal offenses which may be committed in the United Kingdom by members of the American Forces. I now have the honor to inform you that my Government agrees to the several understandings which were raised in your note.

In order to avoid all doubt, I wish to point out that the Military and Naval authorities will assume the responsibility to try and on conviction to punish all offenses which members of the American Forces may be alleged on sufficient evidence to have committed in the United Kingdom.

It is my understanding that the present exchange of notes is regarded as constituting an agreement between the two Governments to which effect shall be given as from the date on which the necessary Parliamentary authority takes effect.

Accept, Sir, the renewed assurance of my highest consideration.

(2) *An Act to Give Effect to an Agreement Recorded in Notes Exchanged between His Majesty's Government in the United Kingdom and the Government of the United States of America, Relating to Jurisdiction over Members of the Military and Naval Forces of the United States of America, August 6, 1942* [1]

The bill to give effect to the Agreement of July 27, 1942 was passed through all stages at one sitting by each House of Parliament.[2] In the House of Commons there was considerable criticism of the bill on the grounds of its unprecedented character and its infringement upon the common law principle of the territorial basis of jurisdiction.

The recognized principle of international law, as stated by Chief Justice Marshall in 1812, is that in the case of a foreign army passing through the territory of a state by permission, the grant of a free passage "implies a waiver of all jurisdiction over the troops during their passage, and permits the foreign general to use that discipline, and to inflict those punishments, which the government of the army may require." [3] The situation of a foreign army stationed within a friendly or allied country, where the members of the armed forces while on leave are free to mingle with the civilian population, is obviously different. During World War I, the British Government made the same claim in the case of the British forces in France as was made by the United States Government in this instance, and received for their military authorities the right to exercise a similar jurisdiction.[4]

WHEREAS His Majesty, in exercise of the powers conferred on Him by subsection (3) of section one of the Allied Forces Act, 1940,[5] and of all other powers enabling Him in that behalf, has been pleased, by Order in Council, to make provision defining the relationship of the authorities

---

[1] *United States of America (Visiting Forces) Act, 1942.* 5 & 6 Geo. 6, ch. 31.
[2] *New York Times*, August 5, 1942.
[3] Schooner Exchange v. McFaddon (1812), 7 Cranch, 116, 119.
[4] Statement of the Secretary of State for Home Affairs (Morrison) in the House of Commons. *Parliamentary Debates, Commons* (1941–42), vol. 382, p. 877.
[5] 3 & 4 Geo. 6, ch. 51.

and courts of the United Kingdom to the military and naval forces of the United States of America who are or may hereafter be present in the United Kingdom or on board any of His Majesty's ships or aircraft, and facilitating the exercise in the United Kingdom or on board any such ship or aircraft of the jurisdiction conferred on the service courts and authorities of the United States of America by the law of that country:

AND WHEREAS the Notes relating to jurisdiction over members of the said forces set out in the Schedule to this Act have been exchanged between His Majesty's Government in the United Kingdom and the Government of the United States of America:

AND WHEREAS it is expedient to give effect to the agreement recorded by the said Notes:

Now, therefore, be it enacted by the King's most Excellent Majesty, by and with the advice and consent of the Lords Spiritual and Temporal, and Commons, in this present Parliament assembled, and by the authority of the same, as follows: —

1. — (1) Subject as hereinafter provided, no criminal proceedings shall be prosecuted in the United Kingdom before any court of the United Kingdom against a member of the military or naval forces of the United States of America:

Provided that upon representations made to him on behalf of the Government of the United States of America with respect to any particular case, a Secretary of State may by order direct that the provisions of this subsection shall not apply in that case.

(2) The foregoing subsection shall not affect any powers of arrest, search, entry, or custody, exercisable under British law with respect to offenses committed or believed to have been committed against that law, but where a person against whom proceedings cannot, by virtue of that subsection, be prosecuted before a court of the United Kingdom is in the custody of any authority of the United Kingdom, he shall, in accordance with such general or special directions as may be given by or under the authority of a Secretary of State, the Admiralty, or the Minister for Home Affairs in Northern Ireland, for the purpose of giving effect to any arrangements made by His Majesty's Government in the United Kingdom with the Government of the United States of America, be delivered into the custody of such authority of the United States of America as may be provided by the directions, being an authority appearing to the Secretary of State, the Admiralty, or the Minister, as the case may be, to be appropriate having regard to the provisions of any Order in Council for the time being in force under the Act hereinbefore recited and of any orders made thereunder.

(3) Nothing in this Act shall render any person subject to any liability whether civil or criminal in respect of anything done by him to any member of the said forces in good faith and without knowledge that he was a member of those forces.

2. — (1) For the purposes of this Act and of the Allied Forces Act, 1940, in its application to the military and naval forces of the United States of America, all persons who are by the law of the United States of America for the time being subject to the military or naval law of that country shall be deemed to be members of the said forces:

Provided that no person employed in connection with the said forces, not being a citizen or national of the United States of America, shall be deemed to be a member of those forces unless he entered into that employment outside the United Kingdom.

(2) For the purposes of any proceedings in any court of the United Kingdom, a certificate issued by or on behalf of such authority as may be appointed for the purpose by the Government of the United States of America stating that a person of the name and description specified in the certificate is, or was at a time so specified, subject to the military or naval law of the United States of America, shall be conclusive evidence of that fact.

(3) For the purposes of any proceedings in any court of the United Kingdom in which the question is raised whether a party to the proceedings is, or was at any time, a member of the military or naval forces of the United States of America, any such certificate as aforesaid relating to a person bearing the name in which that party is charged or appears in the proceedings shall, unless the contrary is proved, be deemed to relate to that party.

(4) Any document purporting to be a certificate issued for the purposes of this section, and to be signed by or on behalf of an authority described as appointed by the Government of the United States of America for the purposes of this section, shall be received in evidence, and shall, unless the contrary is proved, be deemed to be a certificate issued by or on behalf of an authority so appointed.

3. — (1) His Majesty may by Order in Council direct that the foregoing provisions of this Act shall, subject to such adaptations and modifications as may be specified in the Order, have effect in any colony or in any British protectorate or in any territory in respect of which a mandate on behalf of the League of Nations is being exercised by His Majesty's Government in the United Kingdom, in like manner as they have effect in the United Kingdom.

(2) An Order in Council under this section may be revoked or varied by a subsequent Order in Council.

4. This Act may be cited as the United States of America (Visiting Forces) Act, 1942.

3. POST-WAR PROBLEMS

On cooperation between the Governments of the United States and the United Kingdom in the study of the international refugee problem, see p. 286.

On exchange of views between technical experts of the two Governments on proposals for exchange stabilization, see p. 649.

B. Union of Soviet Socialist Republics

1. PROSECUTION OF THE WAR

During the period under review, a principal concern of Anglo-American diplomacy was to bring the leaders of the Soviet Union into more effective cooperation in the prosecution of the war. For material on conferences with that end in view and some of the difficulties encountered, see p. 248. The United States Government continued to give Lend-Lease aid to Soviet Russia, in increasing amounts (see p. 131).

(1) *United Press Report of Statements of the United States Ambassador to Moscow (Standley) at a Press Conference, Moscow, March 8, 1943* [1]

While the aid given the Soviet Union in the form of supplies was substantial, and while military operations in North Africa no doubt had a valuable diversionary influence, the Soviet leaders continued their demand for a "real second front." In fact Soviet insistence on a second front and failure to acknowledge the amount of aid actually received, both private and governmental, combined with apparent Soviet disinclination to share military information with British and American military representatives, threatened to create considerable resentment in the United States at a time when the extension of Lend-Lease was before Congress. Admiral Standley's frank personal statement, in the course of a press conference, served to clear the atmosphere.

Admiral William H. Standley, United States Ambassador, said today that news of important American aid was being kept from the Russian people and he suggested that Russian authorities sought to give the impression that Russia was fighting the war entirely alone.

Admiral Standley said also by implication that Russia was reluctant to exchange information on the conduct of the war and that unless Congress felt that it was helping Russia, it might be inclined to hesitate before it passed the pending lend-lease extension bill.

"It is not fair to mislead Americans into giving millions from their pockets, thinking that they are aiding the Russian people, without the Russian people knowing about it," Admiral Standley said at a press conference.

Admiral Standley, the blunt Navy man sent here on a key diplomatic assignment after a distinguished career of nearly forty years that took him to the high post of Chief of Naval Operations, made his statement when he was asked about the fact that British and American, but not Russian, newspapers had published an acknowledgment by the Russian Red Cross of American aid.

"Well, there is no question that people in America know the facts and that here the people don't," Admiral Standley said.

[1] *New York Times,* March 9, 1943.

"Ever since I have been here, I have been carefully looking for recognition by the Russian press of the fact that they are getting material help through America, not only through lend-lease but through the Red Cross and the Russian-American Relief. And I have yet failed to find any acknowledgment of that.

"The American people are giving aid out of a friendly feeling for the Russians, but the Russian people do not know about it."

Asked whether there had been any progress in the exchange of information between the Russian and United States Governments, Admiral Standley said there had been no obvious change in Russia's attitude concerning exchange of information dealing with the conduct of the war.

When asked why he thought the Russian authorities were not informing their people regarding the aid received, Admiral Standley said:

"They seem to be trying to create the impression at home as well as abroad that they are fighting the war alone.[1]

"There appears to be a desire on the part of the Russians to create the impression that they are fighting the war with their own resources rather than acknowledge help from any one."

In a discussion of extension of the Lend-Lease Act, Admiral Standley said that the bill to that effect had passed the House Foreign Affairs Committee and the Senate Foreign Relations Committee.[2]

"But as those familiar with legislative procedure know," he continued, "it is a long way from the Foreign Affairs Committee to enactment. The American Congress is rather sensitive. It is generous and bighearted as long as it feels that it is helping some one. But give it the idea it is not helping, and it might be a different story."

(2) *Statement of the Acting Secretary of State (Welles) at His Press Conference, March 9, 1943* [3]

I have cabled Ambassador Standley, asking him to let us have the text of what remarks he may have made. I have not yet received a reply, and for that reason, until I have received a reply from the Ambassador, I am not going to comment in any detail on what was said or alleged to have been said. I think I should make it clear, however, that whatever was said in this reported press conference was said without prior consultation with or reference to this Government. The understanding which exists between the United Nations in this great enterprise in which they are joined for the purpose of defeating utterly the Axis tyrannies and for the purpose of insuring the security and the liberties of the peoples of the United Nations would not be worth very much if it were not based upon

[1] According to the Associated Press report, Admiral Standley said: "I find no political motive to this. It is only an effort to create the impression with their own people that they are pulling themselves through by their own bootstraps."

[2] See this volume, p. 123, 127.

[3] Department of State, *Bulletin*, VIII, p. 217.

complete trust and understanding between all of them. I believe that that understanding and trust exists, and I am perfectly confident that anything that Ambassador Standley may have said could not have been intended to and did not cast any doubt on that trust and understanding. For the time being, I am going to limit myself to that brief statement.

In a report announced by Mr. Welles on March 11, the Ambassador said that he had spoken in his personal capacity and not for the Government. His report, according to Mr. Welles, did not differ in any essential details from press reports.[1]

(3) Address of the Ambassador of the Soviet Union (Litvinov) at a Luncheon Given by the Executive Staff of the Lend-Lease Administration, March 11, 1943 [2]

The address of the Ambassador was one of several public recognitions given by the Government of the Soviet Union to the importance of American assistance following Ambassador Standley's statement. The publication in the Soviet Union of several statements of Mr. Stettinius, Lend-Lease Administrator, also contributed to this result.[3]

I am very happy to be the guest today of the executive staff of Lend-Lease, and to have this opportunity of testifying publicly to the pleasure I have had in cooperating with it. I should like also to use the opportunity to express my admiration for the untiring labor and devotion to the cause of those members of the personnel dealing with supplies for the Soviet Union. In particular I should like to mention the extremely valuable cooperation of Mr. Harry Hopkins, Mr. Edward Stettinius, General Burns, and the heads of all those offices upon which the successful fulfilment of the Lend-Lease program for the Soviet Union devolved.

The Soviet Union has been waging war without the slightest lull for twenty months now, along a continuous front of 2,000 miles. It is hardly possible for the mind even to grasp the enormous quantities of all the varieties of armaments and supplies used by the Red Army during this period. Although much the largest part of these supplies has had, of course, to be provided by the Soviet Union itself, supplies received through Lend-Lease have been an enormous help, and as such deeply appreciated by the people of the Soviet Union, who are fully aware of its extent. Unfortunately I have no statistics at my disposal which would enable me to quote the exact proportion of American supplies used in any particular battle, and such statistics are hardly likely to be obtainable. I can, however, say that war materiél received from the U. S. A. has been used during both the defensive and the offensive operations of the Red Army, and that American fighters, notably Airacobras, have given a

---

[1] New York Times, March 12, 1943.
[2] Embassy of the Union of Soviet Socialist Republics, Information Bulletin, No. 26, March 13, 1943, p. 1.
[3] New York Times, March 11, 15, 1943.

specially good account of themselves. I can quote you a few examples known to me of the independent part played by American armaments:.

There is a regiment in the air force of the Red Army, flying Airacobras, which has been given the title of a Guards regiment for its distinguished services. During the last three months this regiment, at first on the Voronezh Front, and then on the Northwest, in the Demyansk area, brought down during air fights 43 enemy planes, itself losing only three. One of our aviation units, using American B–25 bombers, achieved, in difficult meteorological conditions, 380 combat fights during January last, without losing a single plane. One of the results of these raids was the destruction of a railway junction of the utmost importance to the enemy for the transfer of troops to the south, where the Red Army was then launching an offensive. Five trains of war materiél, two troop trains, and a number of locomotives, were destroyed at the junction.

Of great assistance to the Red Army's mobility have been American trucks, which have been used for the traction of artillery guns, as well as for the carrying of troops. The American jeep has also been most useful for the traction of low-caliber guns, and for liaison purposes in all weather and all road conditions.

I need hardly say how welcome the foodstuffs received from the U. S. A. are proving, at a time when the fertile Ukrainian lands are still in enemy hands, and the newly-liberated North Caucasian and Central regions are in a state of devastation. And medicaments have benefited both Red Army soldiers and the civilians in the newly-liberated territories.

I hope the originators of Lend-Lease, and those contributing to its realization, will find satisfaction in the conviction that they could hardly have found an investment yielding better dividends than the share of Lend-Lease in the results of the Red Army's operations. These results may be summed up as a considerable weakening of the common foe by the obliteration of scores of his divisions, the destruction of the faith of his army and people in their "invincibility," the lowering of Hitler's prestige in the satellite and neutral countries, the diversion of his forces from other fronts, and the facilitation of operations in which the other partners in the common war are engaged, or are likely to be engaged. Thus has been created the prerequisite for the final victory over the common foe, a victory indispensable for the survival of all freedom-loving countries. Its attainment presupposes the unity of aims and purposes of the United Nations.

One of the symbols and manifestations of this unity is that new form of international military cooperation which we know as Lend-Lease.

2. THE DISSOLUTION OF THE COMINTERN

The propaganda and revolutionary activities of the Communist International have from the beginning presented a serious problem to those governments desirous of pursuing friendly relations with the Government of the U.S.S.R. Not only has Moscow been the seat of the Comintern but also there has been a considerable overlapping in the membership of the executive and policy determining organs of the Comintern and the Government of the Soviet Union. In Mr. Litvinov's note of November 16, 1933, to President Roosevelt, at the time of the establishment of normal diplomatic relations, it was stated to be the "fixed policy" of the Government of the Union of Soviet Socialist Republics "to restrain . . . all organizations of the government or under its direct or indirect control, including organizations in receipt of any financial assistance from it, . . . from . . . any agitation or propaganda having as its aim . . . the bringing about by force of a change in the political or social order of the whole or any part of the United States, its territories or possessions," and "not to permit the formation or residence in its territory of any organization or group, or of representatives or officials of any organization or group — and to prevent the activity on its territory of any organization or group, or of representatives or officials of any organization or group — which has as an aim the overthrow or the preparation for the overthrow of, or the bringing about by force of a change in, the political or social order of the whole or any part of the United States, its territories or possessions." [1]

In spite of this very specific undertaking the fear or suspicion of subversive activities by the Comintern in the United States has been a disturbing factor in relations between the two governments. Also, and particularly, since we have become allies in the war against Germany and her European satellites, there has been concern over the possibility that the Comintern will be used as an instrument for extending communism and Soviet influence into the occupied and even the enemy countries. The announcement of the dissolution of the Comintern therefore was an event of considerable importance.

(1) Resolution of the Presidium of the Executive Committee of the Communist International, Moscow, May 22, 1943 [2]

The historic role of the Communist International, which was founded in 1919 as a result of a political union of the great majority of the old pre-war working-class parties, consisted in upholding the principles of the working-class movement, in helping to promote consolidation in a number of countries of the vanguard of the foremost workers in the real working-class parties, and in helping them mobilize workers for the defense of their economic and political interests, and for the struggle against Fascism and the war which the latter was preparing, and for the support of the Soviet Union as the chief bulwark against Fascism.

The Communist International from the first exposed the real meaning of the Anti-Comintern Pact as a weapon for the preparation of war by the Hitlerites. Long before the war it ceaselessly and tirelessly exposed the vicious, subversive work of the Hitlerites, who masked it by their screams about so-called interference of the Communist International in the internal affairs of these states.

But long before the war it became more and more clear that, with increasing complications in internal and international relations of various countries, any sort of international center would encounter insuperable

[1] *American Journal of International Law*, Supplement, XXVIII (1934), p. 3.
[2] *New York Times*, May 23, 1943; *The United Nations Review*, III (1943), p. 268.

obstacles in solving the problems facing the movement in each separate country.

Deep differences of the historic paths of development of various countries, differences in their character and even contradictions in their social orders, differences in the level and the tempo of their economic and political development, differences finally in the degree of consciousness and organization of workers, conditioned different problems affecting the working class of the various countries.

The whole development of events in the last quarter of a century and the experience accumulated by the Communist International convincingly showed that the organizational form of uniting workers, chosen by the First Congress of the Communist International, answered conditions of the first stages of the working-class movement, but it has been outgrown by the growth of this movement and by the complications of its problems in separate countries and has even become a drag on the further strengthening of the national working-class parties.

The World War that the Hitlerites have let loose has still further sharpened the differences in the situation of the separate countries and has placed a deep dividing line between those countries that fell under the Hitlerite tyranny and those freedom-loving peoples who have united in a powerful anti-Hitlerite coalition.

In countries of the Hitlerite bloc the fundamental task of the working class, toilers and all honest people consists in giving all help for the defeat of this bloc by sabotage of the Hitlerite military machine from within and by helping to overthrow the governments guilty of war.

In countries of the anti-Hitlerite coalition the sacred duty of the widest masses of the people, and in the first place of foremost workers, consists in aiding by every means the military efforts of the governments of these countries aimed at the speediest defeat of the Hitlerite bloc and the assurance of the friendship of nations based on their equality.

At the same time the fact must not be lost sight of that the separate countries that are members of the anti-Hitlerite coalition have their own particular problems. For example, in countries occupied by the Hitlerites that have lost their state of independence the basic task of the foremost workers and of the wide masses of people consists in promoting the armed struggle developing into a national war of liberation against Hitlerite Germany.

At the same time the war of liberation of freedom-loving peoples against the Hitlerite tyranny, which has brought into movement the masses of people, uniting them without difference of party or religion in the ranks of the powerful anti-Hitlerite coalition, has demonstrated with still greater clearness that the general national uprising and mobilization of people for the speediest victory over the enemy can be best of all and most fruitfully carried out by the vanguard of the working-class movement of each separate country, working within the framework of its own country.

Already the Seventh Congress of the Communist International meeting in 1935, taking into account the change that had taken place both in the international situation and in working-class movements that demanded great flexibility and independence of its sections in deciding the problems confronting them, emphasized the necessity for the Executive Committee of the Communist International, in deciding all questions of the working-class movement arising from concrete conditions and peculiarities of each country, to make a rule of avoiding interference in the internal organizational affairs of the Communist parties.

These same considerations guided the Communist International in considering the resolution of the Communist party of the United States of America of November 1940, on its withdrawal from the ranks of the Communist International.

Guided by the judgment of the founders of Marxism and Leninism, Communists have never been supporters of the conservation of organizational forms that have outlived themselves. They have always subordinated forms of organization of the working-class movement, and methods of working of such organization, to the fundamental political interest of the working-class movement as a whole, to peculiarities of the concrete historical situation and to problems immediately resulting from this situation.

They remember the example of the great Marx, who united foremost workers in the ranks of the Working Men's International Association, and when the First International had fulfilled its historical task of laying the foundations for the development of working-class parties in the countries of Europe and America, and, as a result of the matured situation creating mass national working-class parties, dissolved first the International, inasmuch as this form of organization already no longer corresponded to the demands confronting it.

In consideration of the above and taking into account the growth and the political maturity of Communist parties and their leading cadres in separate countries, and also having in view the fact that during the present war some sections have raised the question of the dissolution of the Communist International as the directing center of the international working-class movement, the Presidium of the Executive Committee of the Communist International, in the circumstances of the World War, not being able to convene a Congress of the Communist International, puts forward the following proposal for ratification by the sections of the Communist International:

The Communist International, as the directing center of the international working-class movement, is to be dissolved, thus freeing the sections of the Communist International from their obligations arising from the statutes and resolutions of the Congresses of the Communist International.

The Presidium of the Executive Committee of the Communist International calls on all supporters of the Communist International to concentrate their energies on the whole-hearted support of and active participation in the war of liberation of the peoples and the states of the anti-Hitlerite coalition for the speediest defeat of the deadly enemy of the working class and toilers — German Fascism and its associates and vassals.

(2) *Statement of the Secretary of State (Hull) at His Press Conference, May 24, 1943* [1]

The dissolution of the Communist International is welcome news. The elimination of that organization from international life and the cessation of the type of activity in which that organization has in the past engaged is certain to promote a greater degree of trust among the United Nations and to contribute very greatly to the whole-hearted cooperation necessary for the winning of the war and for successful post-war undertakings.

(3) *Letter of the Premier of the U.S.S.R. (Stalin) to Mr. Harold King, Moscow Correspondent of Reuters, May 29, 1943* [2]

I have received your request to answer questions referring to the dissolution of the Communist International. I am sending you my answer.

Question — The British comment on the decision to wind up the Comintern has been very favorable. What is the Soviet view of this matter and of its bearing on future international relations?

Answer — The dissolution of the Communist International is proper and timely because it facilitates the organization of a common onslaught of all freedom-loving nations against the common enemy — Hitlerism.

Dissolution of the Communist International is proper because:

(*a*) It exposes the lie of the Hitlerites to the effect that "Moscow" allegedly intends to intervene in the life of other nations and to "bolshevize" them. An end is now being put to this lie.

(*b*) It exposes the calumny of adversaries of Communism within the labor movement to the effect that Communist parties in various countries are allegedly acting not in the interest of their people but on orders from outside. An end is now being put to this calumny, too.

(*c*) It facilitates the work of patriots in freedom-loving countries for uniting the progressive forces of their respective countries, regardless of party or religious faith, into a single international camp for the fight

[1] Department of State, *Bulletin*, VIII, p. 473.
[2] *The United Nations Review*, III (1943), p. 270.

against world domination by Hitlerism, thus clearing the way to future organization of a companionship of nations based upon their equality.

I think that all these circumstances taken together will result in further strengthening of the united front of the Allies and other nations in their fight for victory over Hitlerite tyranny.

I feel that the dissolution of the Communist International is perfectly timely because it is exactly now, when the Fascist beast is exerting its last strength, that it is necessary to organize a common onslaught of the freedom-loving countries to finish off this beast and to deliver the peoples from Fascist oppression.

3. RELATIONS WITH POLAND

The active part taken by the Government of the United States in the establishment of a free and independent Poland at the end of the last war, the continued recognition of the Government of Poland after Polish territory had been divided between Germany and the Soviet Union by the treaty of September 29, 1939,[1] and our interest in and at least implied commitment to the re-establishment of a free and independent Poland after this war, together with the growing recognition of the importance of agreement among the United States, the United Kingdom and the Soviet Union on basic post-war issues, make the question of Soviet relations with the Polish Government-in-Exile a matter of direct concern to the Government of the United States.

Following the German attack upon the Soviet Union on June 22, 1941, there was a definite improvement in Soviet-Polish relations, evidenced by the successful conclusion of the Agreement of July 30, 1941 [2] in which the Soviet-German treaty of September 29, 1939 was recognized as invalid, followed by the Joint Declaration of Friendship and Mutual Aid of December 4, 1941, by the heads of the two Governments, General Sikorski and Marshal Stalin.[3]

Certain difficulties, however, still persisted. For one thing, it was not made clear that the Soviet Union was prepared to renounce its claim to the territory which it had acquired under the 1939 treaty with Germany and it soon became clear that the Soviet leaders had no immediate intention of doing so. Furthermore, difficulties arose over the question of the release of Poles who had been made prisoners of war or who had come under other forms of Soviet control as the result of the occupation of Polish territory in 1939. The question of the whereabouts of certain Polish officers was a matter which especially agitated relations between the two Governments.

On April 17, 1943 the Polish Government issued a statement [4] in London concerning German allegations that thousands of Polish officers had been killed by the Russians two years earlier at Smolensk and that their bodies had been buried in a grave recently discovered by the Germans. The Polish Government, while denying the right of the Germans to make capital of the fate of the Poles, demanded an investigation by the International Red Cross.[5] The request brought an immediate repercussion in the severance of diplomatic relations by the Soviet Government on April 25 and brought into the open a fundamental conflict which it was definitely in the interest of British and American diplomacy to remove. Efforts to heal the breach, however, were complicated by the Polish demand for the release of 800,000 Poles in the U.S.S.R. and by a statement in Moscow by Andrey Y. Vishinsky, Deputy Commissar of Foreign Affairs,

---

[1] *Documents, II, 1939–1940*, p. 359.
[2] *Ibid., IV, 1941–1942*, p. 260. [3] *Ibid.*, p. 261.
[4] *The United Nations Review*, III (1943), p. 213; *Bulletin of International News*, XX (1943), p. 412. [5] *Ibid.*

accusing the Polish Government-in-Exile of being "under the influence of pro-Hitlerite elements."[1] This statement appeared the day after the publication of Stalin's reply to the questions put to him by Mr. Ralph Parker of *The New York Times*.

On April 28, the Union of Polish Patriots in the U.S.S.R. published in *Izvestia* a five-point declaration criticising the Polish Government in London and stating that its policy was aimed at causing a rift between Britain, the U. S. A. and the Soviet Union.[2] A message of good wishes was sent to the Union of Polish Patriots by Marshal Stalin on June 17 praising them for "reinforcing the friendship between the peoples of Poland and the U.S.S.R." and assuring them that Russia would do everything to aid the re-birth of a strong, independent Poland.[3]

General Sikorski in a broadcast to Poland on May 4, 1943 stated that "friendly relations with Soviet Russia has been and continues to be one of the main guiding principles of the Polish Government and the Polish Nation. Therefore, the facts that are separating us must be removed as soon as possible."[4]

During his trip to the Middle East to review Polish troops, General Sikorski broadcast from Beirut, Syria on June 27, giving assurance that there would be no division of Europe into spheres of interest against the will of the interested parties.[5] A sealed personal letter from President Roosevelt had been handed to him the day before.[6] On July 2, just two days before he was killed in an air crash off Gibraltar on his return journey, General Sikorski made a statement in Cairo on Polish-Soviet relations in which he declared that the two essentials for the restoration of relations were: first, the release of 150,000 Polish women and children, still detained in Russia, and secondly, acceptance of the minimum terms contained in the agreement of December 1941, which was the charter of future relations between the two nations. He later told the press that it was imperative that East Prussia and Danzig should come under Polish control after the war, otherwise they would be an object of future wars.[7]

(1) *The People's Commissar of Foreign Affairs of the Union of Soviet Socialist Republics (Molotov) to the Polish Ambassador (Romer), April 25, 1943* [8]

MR. AMBASSADOR,

On behalf of the Government of the Union of Soviet Socialist Republics, I have the honor to notify the Polish Government of the following:

The Soviet Government considers the recent behavior of the Polish Government with regard to the U.S.S.R. as entirely abnormal, violating all regulations and standards of relations between two allied States. The slanderous campaign, hostile to the Soviet Union, launched by the German fascists in connection with the murder of Polish officers which they themselves committed in the Smolensk area on territory occupied by German troops, was at once taken up by the Polish Government and is being fanned in every way by the Polish official press.

[1] *Ibid.*, p. 472.   [2] *Ibid.*, p. 470.
[3] Embassy of the Union of Soviet Socialist Republics, *Information Bulletin*, No. 46, May 1, 1943, p. 6.
[4] *The United Nations Review*, III (1943), p. 260.
[5] *Bulletin of International News*, XX (1943), p. 637.   [6] *Ibid.*   [7] *Ibid.*, p. 622.
[8] Embassy of the Union of Soviet Socialist Republics, *Information Bulletin*, No. 45, April 29, 1943, p. 1.

Far from offering a rebuff to the vile fascist slander of the U.S.S.R., the Polish Government did not even find it necessary to address the Soviet Government with any inquiry or explanation on this subject.

Having committed a monstrous crime against the Polish officers, the Hitlerite authorities now stage a farcical investigation, and for this staging they made use of certain Polish pro-Fascist elements whom they themselves picked in occupied Poland where everything is under Hitler's heel and where an honest Pole cannot openly have his say. For the "investigation" both the Polish Government and the Hitlerite Government invited the International Red Cross, which is compelled, in conditions of a terroristic regime with its gallows and mass extermination of the peaceful population, to take part in this investigation farce staged by Hitler. Clearly such an "investigation," conducted behind the back of the Soviet Government at that, cannot evoke the confidence of people possessing any amount of honesty.

The fact that the hostile campaign against the Soviet Union commenced simultaneously in the German and Polish press and is conducted along the same lines — this fact leaves no doubt as to the existence of contact and accord in carrying out this hostile campaign between the enemy of the Allies — Hitler, and the Polish Government.

While the peoples of the Soviet Union are bleeding profusely in the hard struggle against Hitlerite Germany and strain every effort for the defeat of the common enemy of the Russian and Polish peoples and all freedom-loving, democratic countries, the Polish Government, to please Hitler's tyranny, deals a treacherous blow to the Soviet Union.

The Soviet Government is aware that this hostile campaign against the Soviet Union was undertaken by the Polish Government in order to exert pressure upon the Soviet Government by making use of the Hitlerite slanderous fake for the purpose of wresting from it territorial concessions at the expense of the interests of the Soviet Ukraine, Soviet Byelorussia and Soviet Lithuania.

All these circumstances compel the Soviet Government to recognize that the present Government of Poland, having slid to the path of accord with Hitler's government, has actually discontinued allied relations with the U.S.S.R. and has adopted a hostile attitude toward the Soviet Union.

On the strength of all the above, the Soviet Government has decided to sever relations with the Polish Government.

Please accept, Mr. Ambassador, assurances of my very high esteem.

(2) *Statement of the Polish Government-in-Exile, London, April 28, 1943* [1]

The Polish Government affirm their policy aiming at a friendly understanding between Poland and Soviet Russia on the basis of integrity and

[1] *The United Nations Review*, III (1943), p. 214; *New York Times*, April 29, 1943.

full sovereignty of the Polish Republic, which was and continues to be fully supported by the Polish nation.

Conscious of their responsibility toward their own nation and toward the Allies, whose unity and solidarity the Polish Government consider to be the cornerstone of future victory, they were the first to approach the Soviet Government with the proposal for a common understanding in spite of the many tragic events which had taken place from the moment of the entry of Soviet armies on the territory of the Republic on September 17, 1939.

Having regulated their relations with Soviet Russia by the agreement of July 30, 1941, and by the understanding of December 4, 1941, the Polish Government have scrupulously discharged their obligations.

Acting in close union with their Government, the Polish people, making extreme sacrifice, fight implacably in Poland and outside the frontiers of their country against the German invader. No traitor Quisling has sprung from Polish ranks. All collaboration with the Germans has been scorned.

In weight of facts known throughout the world the Polish Government and the Polish nation have no need to defend themselves from any suggestion of contact or understanding with Hitler.

In a public statement the Polish Government categorically denied to Germany the right to abuse the tragedy of Polish officers for her own perfidious schemes. They unhesitatingly denounce Nazi propaganda designed to create mistrust between the Allies. About the same time a note was sent to the Soviet Ambassador accredited to the Polish Government asking once again for information which would help to elucidate the fate of the missing officers.

The Polish Government and people look to the future. They appeal in the name of solidarity of the United Nations and elementary humanity for the release from the U.S.S.R. of thousands of families of the Polish armed forces, engaged in the fight or preparing in Great Britain and the Middle East to take their part in the fight, and tens of thousands of Polish orphans and children, for the education of whom they would take full responsibility and who now — in view of the German mass slaughter — are particularly precious to the Polish people.

The Polish Army, in waging war against Germany, will also require for reinforcement all the fighting Polish males who are now on Soviet soil and the Polish Government appeal for their release.

They reserve their right to plead the cause of all these persons to the world.

In conclusion, the Polish Government ask for continuation of relief welfare for the mass of Polish citizens who will remain in the U.S.S.R.

In defending the integrity of the Polish Republic which accepted war with the Third Reich, the Polish Government never claimed and do not claim in accordance with their statement of February 25, 1943, any Soviet territories.

It is and will be the duty of every Polish Government to defend the rights of Poland and of Polish citizens. The principles for which the United Nations are fighting, and also the making of all efforts for strengthening their solidarity in this struggle against the common enemy, remain the unchanging basis of policy of the Polish Government.

(3) *Letter of the Premier of the U.S.S.R. (Stalin) to Mr. Ralph Parker of* The New York Times, *May 4, 1943* [1]

[Officially authorized translation]

DEAR MR. PARKER:

On May 3 I received your two questions concerning the Polish-Soviet relations.

Here are my answers:

1. *Question:* "Does the Government of the U.S.S.R. desire to see a strong and independent Poland after the defeat of Hitler's Germany?"

Answer: Unquestionably, it does.

2. *Question:* "On what fundaments is it your opinion that the relations between Poland and the U.S.S.R. should be based after the war?"

Answer: Upon the fundament of solid good neighborly relations and mutual respect, or, should the Polish people so desire, upon the fundament of an alliance providing for mutual assistance against the Germans as the chief enemies of the Soviet Union and Poland.

C. France

1. VICHY GOVERNMENT

[See *Documents, IV, 1941–42*, p. 623–32.]

The United States Government maintained technically correct relations with the Government at Vichy (although Ambassador Leahy was recalled from his post at Vichy in August 1942) until the severance of diplomatic relations by Vichy on November 8 following the American invasion of French North Africa on November 7. Except for the resumption of the exchange of goods with North Africa under the terms of an economic accord of August 1942,[2] however, these relations were featured predominantly by protests and recriminations.

On the whole an anti-collaborationist line of policy was clearly visible in United States relations with Vichy. Repeated attempts were made to safeguard the French fleet; the controversy involving the disposition of French warships at Alexandria, for example, occurred in July 1942 as a result of American efforts to place the ships under protective custody in a French port in the Western Hemisphere.[3]

[1] *New York Times*, May 6, 1943; Embassy of the Union of Soviet Socialist Republics, *Information Bulletin*, No. 49, May 8, 1943, p. 1.

[2] Department of State, *Bulletin*, VII, p. 713; *New York Times*, August 14, 1942.

[3] Department of State, *Bulletin*, VII, p. 631; *New York Times*, July 10, 1942. For report of further negotiations, see *ibid.*, February 24, 1943.

Vichy protests that the support of the Fighting French group by the United States constituted aid and comfort to the "outlaws" of a country whose Government was recognized by the United States as the legal government of France were ignored by this Government.[1]

Stringent anti-Jewish laws of the Vichy Government which attempted to purge France of allegedly undesirable Jewish expatriates [2] were met by the criticism of Secretary Hull and the filing of a strong protest at Vichy on September 4, 1942.[3]

The forced labor decrees issued by Vichy which established compulsory labor for all men between eighteen and fifty and for all women between twenty and thirty in employment "the government will judge useful to the nation" [4] drew further protest from the State Department.[5] Secretary of State Hull warmly praised the resistance of the French people to enforcement of these laws and likewise applauded the Jeanneney-Herriot declaration denouncing Marshal Pétain (September 12, 1942).[6] On frequent occasions Mr. Hull also felt free publicly to compare M. Pierre Laval with Reichsfuehrer Hitler.[7]

Strong protests by the French Government against American participation in R.A.F. bombings of occupied France were met by appeals to the French people and by the explanation that such bombings were "aimed only for the Germans and the installations working for them . . ." [8]

Vichy failed, too, in its efforts to obtain acceptable terms for a suspension of the hostilities begun in Madagascar on May 5, 1942 [9] and the British policy was approved by the American Government in a statement of September 10, 1942.[10] Shortly after the collapse of resistance on the island on December 5, Madagascar was formally handed over to the French administration of the French National Committee in London.[11]

Finally, on November 8, 1942, Secretary Hull issued a comprehensive statement to enable "all those people concerned about the Vichy policy of the United States Government to see clearly and fully its entire content." [12] Already on October 21, 1942, he had said:

"I think you will recall that this Government . . . took the lead in protecting and keeping alive all the doctrines and policies and ideals of what was once the great free French Republic and in condemning all pro-Hitler acts of M. Laval just as we condemn Hitler himself." [13]

(1) French Ships at Alexandria, Egypt. Summary of Remarks of the Under Secretary of State (Welles) at His Press Conference July 14, 1942 [14]

In his press conference on July 14, Under Secretary of State Welles outlined statements which the United States Government has made to

[1] Free France, II (1942), p. 91.
[2] New York Times, September 12 and December 20, 1942.
[3] Ibid., September 5, 1942.
[4] Ibid., September 15, 1942.   •
[5] Department of State, Bulletin, VII, p. 770.
[6] Ibid., p. 751.
[7] New York Times, October 22, 1942.
[8] Ibid., October 8, 1942.
[9] Ibid., September 17 and 18, 1942.
[10] Ibid., September 11, 1942.
[11] Ibid., December 15, 1942.
[12] Department of State, Bulletin, VII, p. 903.
[13] New York Times, October 22, 1942.
[14] Department of State, Bulletin, VII, p. 631.

the French Government at Vichy with regard to French warships at Alexandria. He pointed out at the outset that these French warships at Alexandria are understood by the United States Government as being outside the provisions of the Armistice agreement entered into between the French Government at Vichy and Germany. Mr. Welles said that these warships were in Alexandria at the time of the Armistice signature and were there in accordance with naval understandings between the French Government and its then ally, Great Britain. The Under Secretary said that, on July 3, in view of the situation which existed at that time in North Africa, President Roosevelt made the following proposal to the French Government at Vichy. The President made it clear that he hoped that the French ships at Alexandria could be placed in the protective custody of the United States, to include passage of the French ships through the Suez Canal, thence to a secure and remote part of this hemisphere for the duration of the war, either in a port of the United States or in some neutral port, with a guaranty of the return of these ships to France at the end of the war. The President said, Mr. Welles added, that he felt that this proposal was in the interest of France; he stated further that if this offer on behalf of the United States was not accepted by the French Government, the British, knowing of this offer, would of course be properly and wholly justified in ordering the French ships through the Suez Canal, and, if the order was not obeyed, they would be wholly justified in destroying the ships to prevent them from falling into the hands of the enemy. Mr. Welles said the offer made at that time by the President was rejected by the French Government. On July 9, the Under Secretary continued, the President made a further proposal to the French Government. He proposed that if the French Government agreed that the French naval units now at Alexandria be withdrawn by way of the Suez Canal, the Government of the United States by agreement with the British Government would grant safe passage to Martinique, where they would not be used by either of the two belligerent Governments, namely, the United States and Great Britain, but where they would be immobilized for the duration of the war on the same basis as other French warships now at Martinique, with the assurance that at the end of the war they would be restored to the French people. The two Governments would further agree, Mr. Welles said, to periodical relief and repatriation of the crews after they had reached Martinique, on the same basis which would have obtained had they remained at Alexandria. The President made this proposal in view of his belief that no matter what military situation might develop in North Africa, these French ships would be in imminent danger because of the possibility of enemy attack, and said specifically that in the opinion of this Government, since these ships have from the beginning occupied a special, and are now in a precarious, situation, they are not within the operative provisions of the Armistice agreement, and hence the arrangement proposed by the President would not violate the said agreement, Mr. Welles added. The Under Secretary said he was sorry to say that that offer of the President has also been refused by the French Government at Vichy, which is insisting that the French ships proceed to a nearby French port. In other words, Mr. Welles said, the French Government at Vichy is refusing the proposal solely on the ground that the French port suggested by the President is not nearby, and apparently not sufficiently close to German and Italian hands. The Under Secretary said that he felt certain that the French people themselves will regard this offer made by the President as very much in their interest, since it would have assured the safety of the crews of those vessels and would have assured the French people themselves that at the end of the war these French naval vessels would have been returned to them.

(2) *Letter of the Under Secretary of State (Welles) to Morris D. Waldman, General Secretary of the American Jewish Committee, Protesting the Policy of the Vichy Government Toward Jews, Released to the Press, September 4, 1942* [1]

I have received your communication of August 27, 1942, enclosing a letter, signed by the President of the American Jewish Committee, the American Jewish Congress, the B'nai B'rith and the Jewish Labor Committee, in regard to the mass deportation of Jewish refugees from unoccupied France.

I am in complete agreement with the statements made concerning this tragic situation, which provides a new shock to the public opinion of the civilized world. It is deeply regretted that these measures should be taken in a country traditionally noted for adherence to the principles of equality, freedom and tolerance.

The American Embassy at Vichy has reported fully to the Department concerning developments in regard to these deportations and, in compliance with instructions sent by the Department, has made the most vigorous representations possible to the highest authorities at Vichy. I assure you that the Department and the Embassy will take an active interest in this matter.

(3) *Reported Plans for Conscription of French Labor for Use in Germany. Statement of the Secretary of State (Hull) at His Press Conference, September 15, 1942* [2]

Naturally this Government has been observing with special interest the recent reports about plans of the French Government at Vichy to

[1] *New York Times*, September 4, 1942.   [2] Department of State, *Bulletin*, VII, p. 770.

send many thousands of French laborers into Germany for the purpose of furnishing labor to the German Government. This action, if carried out, would be of such aid to one of our enemies as to be wholly inconsistent with France's obligations under international law. The Government here is naturally observing closely this more recent announcement about the conscription of French labor, with a view to seeing whether it is part of the plan or purpose of the original undertaking which seems to have failed, according to reports, of getting great numbers of French laborers into Germany. This Government is accordingly observing, as I say, the developments with the same special interest as the first reports to which I have referred.

I think today too is the deadline as it is called in relation to another policy which itself is astonishing and that relates to measures taken during recent weeks by the same governmental authorities against a large number of unfortunate people who sought to obtain refuge in France in accordance with its traditional hospitality. These policies include the delivery of these unhappy people to enemies who have announced and in considerable measure executed their intention to enslave, maltreat, and eventually exterminate them under conditions of the most extreme cruelty. The details of the measures taken are so revolting and so fiendish in their nature that they defy adequate description.

(4) *Reply to French Protest against Bombings in France. Department of State Release, September 8, 1942* [1]

The American Chargé in Vichy, Mr. S. Pinkney Tuck, on September 7 was called in by Monsieur Laval who said that in recent bombings of Le Havre and Rouen by combined military forces of the United Nations a number of people were killed and others wounded and that he, M. Laval, desired to enter a protest to the American Government since it was reported some American flyers participated. Mr. Tuck's immediate reply was that these air forces were bombing military plants in the employ of Germany and that, of course, the Americans do not desire to see the French people suffer any more than can be avoided since they have already suffered to an incalculable extent under German occupation but that M. Laval must be assured that the military plants operated by or for Germany and other German military properties in France will be bombed at every opportunity in the future.

(5) *British Military Operations in Madagascar. Statement of the Department of State, September 10, 1942* [2]

The Government of the United States has been informed by the Government of the United Kingdom that developments in Madagascar

[1] *Ibid.*, p. 750.   [2] *Ibid.*

subsequent to the occupation of Diégo-Suarez have not resulted in adequate safeguards against Axis penetration in other parts of the island. In the circumstances the British Government, with the approval of the United States, has deemed it absolutely necessary to undertake further military operations in that area.

The Government of the United States recognizes that military considerations must be paramount in reaching such a decision. The penetration or occupation of any part of Madagascar by the Axis powers would constitute a definite and a serious danger to the United Nations. The full military occupation of the island by British forces will therefore not only contribute to the successful conduct of the war against the Axis forces but will be in the interest of the United Nations.

As stated in the State Department's announcement of May 4, 1942,[1] the Governments of the United States and the United Kingdom are in accord that Madagascar will be restored to France after the war or at any time that the occupation of the island is no longer essential to the common cause of the United Nations.

(6) *Summary of Remarks of the Secretary of State (Hull) on the Purposes of United States Policy toward Vichy, at His Press Conferences, November 8 and 9, 1942. Department of State Release, November 9, 1942* [2]

In response to questions by the newspaper correspondents at a press conference held on November 8, the Secretary of State said that the people who have been concerned about the Vichy policy of the United States Government will now be able to see clearly and fully its entire content. He added that liberation of French Morocco by American military forces carries forward the various purposes and objectives of this Government in pursuing its policy toward Vichy. This policy, he said, has been directed toward the ultimate liberation of France from her German captors. The American, British, and Canadian Governments have whole-heartedly favored and supported this policy, he added.

The more important of those purposes, Secretary Hull pointed out, have been: (1) opportunity for the Government of the United States to get from week to week highly important information virtually from the inside of German-controlled territory and from North Africa regarding Axis subversive activities and other important phases of the international situation; (2) the maintenance of close relations with the French people and encouragement of leadership in opposition to Hitlerism wherever it exists; (3) the keeping alive of the basic concepts of freedom of the French people, looking toward ultimate restoration of free institutions for France as they existed before the German occupation;

[1] *Documents, 1941–42, IV*, p. 688.   [2] Department of State, *Bulletin*, VII, p. 903.

(4) the retention of the closest personal touch on the ground with all phases of the French and German situation under the armistice prevailing between Germany and France; resistance to increased German pressure on France to go beyond the armistice provisions and to collaborate with Germany; constant effort to prevent delivery of the French fleet or any part of it into German military hands or to give military support to German arms; that also includes French bases all along the Mediterranean and the Atlantic coast; and (5) last, but most important, paving the way and preparing the background, in the most effective manner possible, for the planning and sending of the military expedition into the western Mediterranean area, and assisting the movements supporting present British operations farther east.

The Secretary of State was asked, at his press conference on November 9, whether he would care to say whether he felt that the traditional friendship which had existed between the peoples of this country and France for so long would make it impossible for the Vichy Government to turn the French people against us in view of the developments in North Africa.

The Secretary permitted the press to quote him directly on the following statement:

"The Vichy Government did all — reached its maximum stage by its plan and efforts to mislead the French people many months ago. The French people, I think, to the extent of not less than 95 per cent understand fully that the Laval government at Vichy has been a most willing puppet of Hitler and Hitler agencies, with the result that instead of being influenced in that Hitler direction by the Laval government, they — the French people — will, on the contrary, be most grateful for our having come to the relief of French Africa, which is the first and preliminary step in our plans, so far as I understand, to come to the relief of all enslaved peoples in Europe, including France proper. The French people will continue, I am sure, to be grateful to us for our policies and be wholly cooperative with us to the extent within their power."

2. FIGHTING FRANCE

[See *Documents, IV, 1941–42*, p. 632–5.]

(1) *Appointment of Representatives to Consult with the Free French in London. Statement of the Department of State, with Text of Memorandum Handed to General de Gaulle, July 9, 1942* [1]

The President of the United States, in a letter to the Lend-Lease Administration dated November 11, 1941,[2] stated that the defense of

---

[1] *Ibid.*, p. 613.   [2] *Documents, IV, 1941–42*, p. 178, n. 1.

those French territories under the control of Free French forces is vital to the defense of the United States. In the spirit of the President's letter, and consistent with the policy of the United States Government in aiding all peoples who are resisting Axis aggression to maintain and uphold their own liberty, the Government of the United States and the Free French National Committee in London have closely maintained cooperation in those areas where such cooperation would further the war objectives.

To make this cooperation more effective in the prosecution of the war, Admiral Harold R. Stark and Brigadier General Charles L. Bolte have been designated as this Government's respresentatives to consult with the French National Committee in London on all matters relating to the conduct of the war. A memorandum on the subject, the text of which is printed below, has been handed to General de Gaulle.

In this connection the following message has been received from the French National Committee in London:

"General de Gaulle has read the memorandum with pleasure. He is most gratified by its terms and he warmly welcomes the decision of the United States Government to appoint Admiral Stark and General Bolte as representatives of the United States Government to consult with the National Committee."

Memorandum

The Government of the United States is subordinating all other questions to the one supreme purpose of achieving military success in the war and carrying it forward to a successful conclusion. The French National Committee has the same objective and is undertaking active military measures for the preservation of French territory for the French people.

The Government of the United States recognizes the contribution of General de Gaulle and the work of the French National Committee in keeping alive the spirit of French traditions and institutions and believes that the military aims necessary for an effective prosecution of the war, and hence the realization of our combined aims, are best advanced by lending all possible military assistance and support to the French National Committee as a symbol of French resistance in general against the Axis powers. The Government of the United States whole-heartedly agrees with the view of the British Government, which is also known to be the view of the French National Committee, that the destiny and political organization of France must, in the last analysis, be determined by free expression of the French people under conditions giving them freedom to express their desires unswayed by any form of coercion.

In pursuing the common war objective, the Government of the United States will continue to deal with the local Free French officials in their respective territories where they are in effective control. Realizing the need for coordinating their common efforts the Government of the United States perceives every advantage in centralizing the discussion of those matters relating to the prosecution of the war with the French National Committee in London. An essential part of the policy of the Government of the United States for war collaboration is assistance to the military and naval forces of Free France, which is being extended under the terms of the President's statement of November 11, 1941, that the defense of those French territories under the control of Free French forces is vital to the defense of the United States.

In harmony with the foregoing observations the Government of the United States is prepared to appoint representatives in London for purposes of consultation.

DEPARTMENT OF STATE,
   Washington.

(a) Telegram from General de Gaulle to the Secretary of State (Hull), July 10, 1942 [1]

[Translation]

It is with great satisfaction that the French National Committee welcomes in London the distinguished representatives of the Government of the United States. I thank you for the personal part you have taken in this decision. The confident collaboration which the France which has remained faithful to the Allies and to the great American democracy will thus establish will certainly contribute in an effective manner to the final victory of the United Nations.

(2) Text of Letter of the President (Roosevelt) to the Lend-Lease Administrator (Stettinius) on Aid to Fighting France, October 6, 1942 [2]

For text of the Reciprocal Lend-Lease Agreement of September 3, 1942, between the Government of the United States and the French National Committee, see this volume, p. 237.

MY DEAR MR. STETTINIUS:

In order that Lend-Lease aid to the French National Committee (now Fighting France) may be more effectively rendered, my letter to you of November 11, 1941,[3] is hereby amended to remove the provision that such aid be arranged for "by way of retransfer from His Majesty's Government in the United Kingdom or their allies," and you are hereby authorized to arrange for Lend-Lease aid directly to the authorities of the French National Committee (Fighting France).

[1] *Ibid.*, p. 614.
[2] *Ibid.*, p. 84.
[3] *Documents, IV, 1941–42*, p. 178, n. 1.

(3) *Statement of General de Gaulle Protesting American Dealings with Admiral Darlan, November 16, 1942* [1]

General de Gaulle and the French National Committee announce that they are taking no part whatsoever in or assuming any responsibilities for the negotiations in progress in North Africa with the representatives of Vichy.

Should these negotiations result in arrangements that would in effect establish a Vichy regime in North Africa such decisions could obviously not be accepted by Fighting France.

The union of all French territories overseas in the struggle for liberation should be achieved in conditions consonant with the will and dignity of the French people.

3. THE NORTH AFRICAN INVASION

The decision to land Anglo-American forces at various points on the French North and West African Coasts was apparently taken in Washington at the conference beginning June 19, 1942 between President Roosevelt and Prime Minister Churchill.[2] Preceded by weeks of intensive staff study in the British and American capitals, the meeting had been arranged for the purpose of "obtaining the earliest maximum concentration of Allied power upon the enemy."

The final phase of preparation necessitated sending a secret mission to North Africa to "establish first-hand contacts with pro-Allied factions and obtain vital military information."[3] This mission was accomplished successfully by General Mark Clark and his staff. Disembarking at midnight, October 21, 1942 from a submarine waiting off the North African shore, they met with prominent French officials at a farmhouse seventy-five miles from Algiers. Little new military information was obtained but important confirmations were made.[4]

The activities of our consular officers and special representatives in Algeria, Tunisia, and Morocco also adroitly paved the way for the entry of our troops and were a most significant contribution to lessening the resistance offered by French forces.[5] The State Department representative in Algiers, Robert D. Murphy, reached an agreement for the cooperation of General Giraud through the aid of General Charles Mast and in other ways (both economic and political) helped lay the groundwork "on which it was possible to plan an operation of immense tactical value . . ."[6]

The actual landings by American forces in North Africa[7] caused an immediate break in diplomatic relations between the United States and Vichy on November 8.[8] The United States took protective custody of all Vichy ships in American

---

[1] *New York Times*, November 17, 1942.

[2] See *Documents. IV, 1941–42*, p. 241.

[3] *New York Times*, Section 4, November 15, 1942, p. 1.

[4] Knight, Ridgeway B., "General Clark's Secret Mission to Algeria on October 21, 1942," *American Foreign Service Journal*, XX (1943), p. 122–3, 154–6.

[5] Villard, Henry S., "Action in North Africa," *American Foreign Service Journal*, XIX (1942), p. 637.

[6] *Ibid.*, p. 690. For defense of Robert Murphy by Under Secretary of State Welles, see *New York Times*, January 20, 1943.

[7] See Baldwin, Hanson W., "Political Pitfalls of Our African Landing," *New York Times*, May 15, 1943.

[8] Department of State, *Bulletin*, VIII, p. 903.

harbors, froze all her accounts, and extended trade and communications restrictions of the Trading with the Enemy Act to cover unoccupied France. Secretary of State Hull declared, however, that our relations with Martinique remained unchanged and that trading restrictions applied only to continental France and not her colonies.[1] French consular officials were placed under close surveillance on November 10,[2] and on November 16 announcement was made that arrangements were proceeding for the exchange of diplomatic and consular personnel.[3]

Meanwhile, President Roosevelt had spoken to the French people directly by radio over the head of the Vichy Government.[4] He had also addressed messages to the Resident-General [5] and the Bey of Tunis,[6] the Governor-General of Algeria,[7] and the Sultan of Morocco,[8] in which he requested that they give cooperation and assistance to American forces.

The occupation of all France by the Germans on November 11 [9] did not discourage Marshal Pétain from appealing to all French officers in North Africa to obey his orders and "resist any Anglo-Saxon invasion." [10] As a result of the German move, however, Pétain virtually abdicated in favor of Pierre Laval. Secretary of State Hull promptly denounced Laval as a Hitlerite and the latter in turn rebuked President Roosevelt and prophesied a Nazi victory.[11]

The political situation in North Africa was confused. Originally General Giraud had been chosen to lead in French North Africa [12] (apparently the Fighting French in London had never been consulted on the invasion at any time), but the American military command considered that Darlan was the only man who could conclude an effective armistice with them. Giraud had obviously failed in his radio broadcast, at the beginning of the invasion, to halt resistance and to rally around him active support for American forces. Thus, although Giraud appears to have been promised by General Eisenhower himself full responsibility for all military and civil affairs in the French North Africa area,[13] the Admiral was able to proclaim himself "Protector" of all French interests in North Africa, while Giraud occupied a slightly subordinate position as Commander-in-Chief of all French forces.[14] Outlawed in a message by Pétain who excluded him from the "national community" and cancelled all his powers [15] (although Darlan had asserted his loyalty to the Marshal just previously and had expressed the opinion that Pétain had fallen completely into the clutches of the Germans against his will),[16] Darlan succeeded, nevertheless, in bringing French West Africa into the Allied camp,[17] and in joining units of the French fleet stationed at Alexandria, Dakar,[18] and North African ports to the Allied cause, and also made plans to train an army of 300,000 troops. Both his and

---

[1] *New York Times*, November 19, 1942.

[2] *Ibid.*, November 11, 1942.

[3] Department of State, *Bulletin*, VII, p. 939.

[4] *New York Times*, November 19, 1942.

[5] Department of State, *Bulletin*, VII, p. 907.

[6] *Ibid.*

[7] *Ibid.*

[8] *Ibid.*, p. 961.

[9] For text of Reichsfuehrer Hitler's letter of explanation to Marshal Pétain, see *New York Times*, November 28, 1942.

[10] *Ibid.*, November 20, 1942.

[11] *Ibid.*, November 21, 1942.

[12] *Ibid.*, November 9, 1942.

[13] *Ibid.*, November 10, 1942.

[14] *Ibid.*, November 16, 1942.

[15] *Ibid.*, November 17, 1942.

[16] *Ibid.*, November 16, 1942.

[17] For text of agreement between the United States and Governor-General Boisson of West Africa, see *Free France*, II (1942), p. 346-7.

[18] *New York Times*, December 9, 1942.

General Eisenhower's efforts to bring the French fleet at Toulon to the British naval base at Gibraltar were frustrated.[1] On November 27 a large part of the fleet was scuttled by its officers.[2] This action followed the announcement that Hitler had ordered German forces to occupy Toulon and to "prevent the ships from leaving or to annihilate them."

Particularly significant was the announced intention of Pierre Boisson, Governor-General of French West Africa, to intervene against Germany as soon as Dakar and the rest of the territory received materials and equipment from America.[3] It would appear that the Germans had never succeeded in infiltrating there or in using it as a naval base, largely because of the stubborn resistance of most of the French officials.[4]

Admiral Darlan further consolidated his position by setting up an Imperial Council to advise him and to negotiate with American officers for the supply of munitions, food, and equipment under lend-lease arrangements.[5] American military officials expressed themselves as satisfied with the Admiral's cooperation.[6] President Roosevelt also implied his approval by commenting that "the people of North Africa have allied themselves on the side of liberalism." [7]

Bitter criticism was leveled at the whole Allied policy in America and especially in Great Britain, where it was charged that General de Gaulle and the Fighting French had been betrayed. Underneath the various protests lay perhaps these chief fears: "(1) that Anglo-American forces in North Africa were taking a great military risk in embarking on a campaign while a man of uncertain loyalty controlled the civil authority at their bases; (2) that the United States' association with Admiral Darlan would impair the morale of French democrats; (3) that Admiral Darlan would use his authority to build a fascist organization in North Africa and attempt to foist it on Metropolitan France when the Germans were driven out." [8]

The Secretary of State sought to allay these fears by conferring with representatives of General de Gaulle in Washington [9] and by explaining that the political arrangement in North Africa was a temporary expedient for military purposes.[10]

Admiral Darlan himself explained that his sole purpose was to save French Africa, help free France and then return to private life, and that he was helpless to oppose the Nazis before the Allied stroke in North Africa.[11] The assassination of Admiral Darlan on Christmas Eve was condemned by Secretary Hull and President Roosevelt. "Of Admiral Darlan, it may be repeated that the part he played in North Africa related primarily to the military situation and was of incalculable aid to the Allied armies in the battle which is still raging," declared Mr. Hull.[12]

---

[1] *Ibid*, November 12, 13, 1942.

[2] *Ibid.*, November 29, 1942.

[3] *Ibid.*, December 10, 1942.

[4] Wasson, Thomas C., "The Mystery of Dakar: An Enigma Resolved," *American Foreign Service Journal*, XX (1943), p. 169–74, 214–18.

[5] *New York Times*, December 2, 1942.

[6] *Ibid.*, December 12, 1942.

[7] *Ibid.*, December 17, 1942.

[8] *Ibid.*, Section 4, December 13, 1942.

[9] *Ibid.*, for Hull's reassurance of Fighting French; for article by Arthur Krock, see *ibid.*, December 9, 1942.

[10] Department of State, *Bulletin*, VII, p. 935, and p. 1008.

[11] *New York Times*, December 20, 1942.

[12] Department of State, *Bulletin*, VII, p. 1017; for comprehensive review of the North African background of invasion and of the reasons behind State Department policy before and after the invasion, see Metz, Bernard, "The North African Imbroglio," *American Foreign Service Journal*, XX (1943), p. 561–5, 599, 601–08.

A. Rupture of Diplomatic Relations with Vichy as a Result of American Military Operations in French North Africa

(1) Radio Message of the President (Roosevelt) to the French People, November 7, 1942 [1]

My friends, who suffer day and night, under the crushing yoke of the Nazis, I speak to you as one who was with your Army and Navy in France in 1918. I have held all my life the deepest friendship for the French people — for the entire French people. I retain and cherish the friendship of hundreds of French people in France and outside of France. I know your farms, your villages, and your cities. I know your soldiers, professors, and workmen. I know what a precious heritage of the French people are your homes, your culture, and the principles of democracy in France. I salute again and reiterate my faith in Liberty, Equality, and Fraternity. No two nations exist which are more united by historic and mutually friendly ties than the people of France and the United States.

Americans, with the assistance of the United Nations, are striving for their own safe future as well as the restoration of the ideals, the liberties, and the democracy of all those who have lived under the Tricolor.

We come among you to repulse the cruel invaders who would remove forever your rights of self-government, your rights to religious freedom, and your rights to live your own lives in peace and security.

We come among you solely to defeat and rout your enemies. Have faith in our words. We do not want to cause you any harm.

We assure you that once the menace of Germany and Italy is removed from you, we shall quit your territory at once.

I am appealing to your realism, to your self-interest and national ideals.

Do not obstruct, I beg of you, this great purpose.

Help us where you are able, my friends, and we shall see again the glorious day when liberty and peace shall reign again on earth.

Vive la France éternelle!

(2) Statement of the President (Roosevelt) Concerning American Military Operations in French North Africa, November 7, 1942 [1]

In order to forestall an invasion of Africa by Germany and Italy, which, if successful, would constitute a direct threat to America across the comparatively narrow sea from western Africa, a powerful American force equipped with adequate weapons of modern warfare and under American command is today landing on the Mediterranean and Atlantic coasts of the French colonies in Africa.

[1] Department of State, *Bulletin*, VII, p. 891.

The landing of this American Army is being assisted by the British Navy and air forces and it will, in the immediate future, be reinforced by a considerable number of divisions of the British Army.

This combined allied force, under American command, in conjunction with the British campaign in Egypt is designed to prevent an occupation by the Axis armies of any part of northern or western Africa and to deny to the aggressor nations a starting point from which to launch an attack against the Atlantic coast of the Americas.

In addition, it provides an effective second-front assistance to our heroic allies in Russia.

The French Government and the French people have been informed of the purpose of this expedition and have been assured that the allies seek no territory and have no intention of interfering with friendly French authorities in Africa.

The Government of France and the people of France and the French possessions have been requested to cooperate with and assist the American expedition in its effort to repel the German and Italian international criminals, and by so doing to liberate France and the French Empire from the Axis yoke.

This expedition will develop into a major effort by the allied nations, and there is every expectation that it will be successful in repelling the planned German and Italian invasion of Africa and prove the first historic step to the liberation and restoration of France.

(3) *Message of the President (Roosevelt) to the Chief of the French State (Pétain), November 8, 1942* [1]

MARSHAL PÉTAIN:

I am sending this message to you as the Chef d'État of the United States to the Chef d'État of the Republic of France.

When your Government concluded the Armistice Convention in 1940, it was impossible for any of us to foresee the program of systematic plunder which the German Reich would inflict on the French people.

That program, implemented by blackmail and robbery, has deprived the French population of its means of subsistence, its savings; it has paralyzed French industry and transport; it has looted French factories and French farms — all for the benefit of a Nazi Reich and a Fascist Italy under whose Governments no liberty loving nation could long exist.

As an old friend of France and the people of France, my anger and sympathy grows with every passing day when I consider the misery, the want, and the absence from their homes of the flower of French manhood. Germany has neglected no opportunity to demoralize and degrade your great nation.

[1] *Ibid.*, p. 903.

Today, with greedy eyes on that Empire which France so laboriously constructed, Germany and Italy are proposing to invade and occupy French North Africa in order that they may execute their schemes of domination and conquest over the whole of that continent.

I know you will realize that such a conquest of Africa would not stop there but would be the prelude to further attempts by Germany and Italy to threaten the conquest of large portions of the American Hemisphere, large dominations over the Near and Middle East, and a joining of hands in the Far East with those military leaders of Japan who seek to dominate the whole of the Pacific.

It is evident, of course, that an invasion and occupation of French North and West Africa would constitute for the United States and all of the American Republics the gravest kind of menace to their security — just as it would sound the death knell of the French Empire.

In the light of all the evidence of our enemy's intentions and plans, I have, therefore, decided to dispatch to North Africa powerful American armed forces to cooperate with the governing agencies of Algeria, Tunisia and Morocco in repelling this latest act in the long litany of German and Italian international crime.

These indomitable American forces are equipped with massive and adequate weapons of modern warfare which will be available for your compatriots in North Africa in our mutual fight against the common enemy.

I am making all of this clear to the French Authorities in North Africa, and I am calling on them for their cooperation in repelling Axis threats. My clear purpose is to support and aid the French Authorities and their administrations. That is the immediate aim of these American armies.

I need not tell you that the ultimate and greater aim is the liberation of France and its Empire from the Axis yoke. In so doing we provide automatically for the security of the Americas.

I need not again affirm to you that the United States of America seeks no territories and remembers always the historic friendship and mutual aid which we have so greatly given to each other.

I send to you and, through you, to the people of France my deep hope and belief that we are all of us soon to enter into happier days.

(4) *Message of the Chief of the French State (Pétain) to the President (Roosevelt), November 8, 1942* [1]

It is with stupor and sadness that I learned tonight of the aggression of your troops against North Africa.

I have read your message. You invoke pretexts which nothing justifies. You attribute to your enemies intentions which have not ever been

[1] *Ibid.*, p. 905.

manifested in acts. I have always declared that we would defend our Empire if it were attacked; you should know that we would defend it against any aggressor whoever he might be. You should know that I would keep my word.

In our misfortune I had, when requesting the armistice, protected our Empire and it is you who acting in the name of a country to which so many memories and ties bind us have taken such a cruel initiative.

France and her honor are at stake. .

We are attacked; we shall defend ourselves; this is the order I am giving.

(5) *Statement of the President* (*Roosevelt*) *Concerning United States Policy toward the Vichy Government, November 9, 1942* [1]

The representative of this Government at Vichy has reported that last evening M. Laval, Chief of the Government at Vichy, notified him that diplomatic relations between Vichy and this Government had been severed. I regret this action on the part of M. Laval.

He is evidently still speaking the language prescribed by Hitler.

The Government of the United States can do nothing about this severance of relations on the part of the Vichy Government.

Nevertheless, no act of Hitler, or of any of his puppets, can sever relations between the American people and the people of France. We have not broken relations with the French. We never will.

This Government will continue as heretofore to devote its thought, its sympathy, and its aid to the rescue of the forty-five million people of France from enslavement and from a permanent loss of their liberties and free institutions.

B. Political Arrangements in French North and West Africa

(1) *Statement of the President* (*Roosevelt*) *Regarding the Temporary Political Arrangements in North and West Africa, November 17, 1942* [2]

I have accepted General Eisenhower's political arrangements made for the time being in Northern and Western Africa.

I thoroughly understand and approve the feeling in the United States and Great Britain and among all the other United Nations that in view of the history of the past two years no permanent arrangement should be made with Admiral Darlan. People in the United Nations likewise would never understand the recognition of a reconstituting of the Vichy Government in France or in any French territory.

[1] *Ibid.*, p. 903.
[2] *Ibid.*, p. 935.

We are opposed to Frenchmen who support Hitler and the Axis. No one in our Army has any authority to discuss the future Government of France and the French Empire.

The future French Government will be established, not by any individual in Metropolitan France or overseas but by the French people themselves after they have been set free by the victory of the United Nations.

The present temporary arrangement in North and West Africa is only a temporary expedient, justified solely by the stress of battle.

The present temporary arrangement has accomplished two military objectives. The first was to save American and British lives on the one hand, and French lives on the other hand.

The second was the vital factor of time. The temporary arrangement has made it possible to avoid a "mopping-up" period in Algiers and Morocco which might have taken a month or two to consummate. Such a period would have delayed the concentration for the attack from the west on Tunis, and we hope on Tripoli.

Every day of delay in the current operation would have enabled the Germans and Italians to build up a strong resistance, to dig in and make a huge operation on our part essential before we could win. Here again, many more lives will be saved under the present speedy offensive than if we had had to delay it for a month or more.

It will also be noted that French troops, under the command of General Giraud, have already been in action against the enemy in Tunisia, fighting by the side of American and British soldiers for the liberation of their country.

Admiral Darlan's proclamation assisted in making a "mopping-up" period unnecessary. Temporary arrangements made with Admiral Darlan apply, without exception, to the current local situation only.

I have requested the liberation of all persons in Northern Africa who had been imprisoned because they opposed the efforts of the Nazis to dominate the world, and I have asked for the abrogation of all laws and decrees inspired by Nazi governments or Nazi ideologists. Reports indicate that the French of North Africa are subordinating all political questions to the formation of a common front against the common enemy.

(2) *Statement of the President (Roosevelt), Including Declaration by Admiral Darlan, Concerning Support of the United Nations by the French in North Africa, December 16, 1942* [1]

Since November 8 the people of North Africa have accomplished much in support of the war effort of the United Nations, and in doing so have

[1] *Ibid.*, p. 1007.

definitely allied themselves on the side of liberalism against all for which the Axis stands in government. I am informed in this connection by General Eisenhower that Admiral Darlan has made the following declaration:

"French Africa with the Allies must make the maximum military effort for the defeat of Germany and Italy. This will be accomplished by the unity of all citizens, regardless of their political or religious opinions, in an orderly and cohesive fashion.

"At last liberated from German and Italian restrictions, the French authorities in Africa will adjust the situation which has existed in accordance with French national traditions. Once France and the French Empire is free from the Axis yoke, the French people themselves will decide freely the form of government and national policy they desire.

"In actual accomplishment the high commissioner has already granted full and complete amnesty to all against whom any action had been taken because of sympathy to the Allies. Certain of these have been given important posts in the High Commissariat. He has restored to their proper ranks and emoluments all Army officers who had been suspended from office because of rendering aid to the Allies. He is now organizing a body of representative private citizens to work with him in an advisory and consultative capacity in carrying on official business. Prisoners and internees of the United Nations were promptly released and their travel to seaboard expedited.

"The High Commissioner has begun the restoration of rights to those persons from whom these had previously been taken because of race. Measures have been taken to stop immediately whatever persecution of the Jews may have resulted from the laws passed in France under German pressure. His announced purpose is to give just treatment to all elements making up the complex North African population to the end that all can dwell and work together under laws insuring mutual tolerance and respect for rights.

"There is little industrial development in North Africa and Vichy laws prejudicial to labor unions had little or no application and all reports show no serious problem here. Censorship of the press and radio in which Allied authorities participate is only that which is necessary for the security of military operation.

"On the practical military side, General Giraud has conducted the most active participation of the Armed Forces of North and West Africa in the Allied war effort. Units of substantial size under the leadership of General Giraud are fighting side by side with the United Nations in Tunisia against the Germans and Italians. All posts and airfield facilities including the services of officials and technicians have been made freely available for use by the Allies. North African shipping is already entering the services of the Allied Nations. Railroads, motor trucks, communications, public and private buildings and everything that North Africa has to give have been freely offered to the Allied Forces, wherever a military need exists.

"I have stated emphatically and repeatedly to the Commander-in-Chief, General Eisenhower, that in leading North and West Africa against Germany and Italy and into the ranks of the United Nations, I seek no assistance or support for any personal ambitions. I have announced that my sole purpose is to save French Africa, help free France and then retire to private life with a hope that the future leaders of France may be selected by the French people themselves and by no one else."

(3) Statement of the Secretary of State (Hull) on French Unity, December 17, 1942 [1]

At his press conference December 17, the Secretary of State was asked the following question by a correspondent:

"Apart from Admiral Darlan's statement, do you think that those French leaders who are eager to help us in bringing about the defeat of the Axis should now try to cooperate with one another in the common effort?"

In reply the Secretary made the following statement:

I have had only one view with respect to the two central points in the international situation as they address themselves especially to the Allied nations, and that view applies universally and not to any one country or one people any more than another. The first central point is that every person in sympathy with the cause of the United Nations and every group of persons and every other one concerned should strive to unify their efforts in the support of the Allied military cause until final success. That is the supreme and the immediate question that addresses itself to each and all of us alike in every part of the world. We need all the help we can get.

With the victory won and freedom restored to those who have lost it or who are seeking it, there would then arise under point three of the Atlantic Charter the fullest opportunity for each people to select their leaders and their forms of government. These two central points of the world situation have been expressed heretofore by myself and others.

4. FRENCH COMMITTEE OF NATIONAL LIBERATION

The election of General Henri Honoré Giraud to the post of High Commissioner of French North Africa only two days after the death of Admiral Darlan was welcomed by Secretary of State Hull as a "selection which would lend to greater unification of all (French) groups." [2] Immediately following his election, Giraud announced plans for cooperation with Fighting France in the war to liberate Metropolitan France. He also pledged full cooperation with the Allies and declared that "France has the fullest confidence in America. I pray that

[1] *Ibid.*, p. 1008.   [2] *Ibid.*, VIII, p. 5.

America will have confidence in France." [1] Asked for comment with regard to the political situation in North Africa, Giraud replied: "I am a soldier." [2]

Both Secretary Hull and General Giraud seemed to be agreed in their exclusive dedication to the military defeat of Germany.[3] Most questions concerning the political situation in North Africa were, therefore, viewed in the light of military expediency.[4] This line of policy is illustrated by a statement of President Roosevelt that the problem in North Africa "is essentially military"; [5] by a statement of Secretary Hull on February 8, 1943; [6] and also by a letter of Sumner Welles, Under Secretary of State to Professor Ralph Barton Perry of Harvard University on April 2.[7]

The somewhat cautious policy of the United States Government in stressing order and subordinating political to military considerations may be seen, too, in President Roosevelt's defense of the Jewish-Moslem policy of the Giraud administration,[8] and in Under Secretary Welles' letter to Baron de Rothschild defending Giraud's promulgation of an ordinance continuing the denaturalization of Algerian Jews carried out by the Vichy Government through the abrogation of the Crémieux decree of 1870.[9] General Giraud based his action on the ground that he was eliminating racial discontent between the Jews and the Moslems.[10] It was justified as a military measure "designed to forestall wide discontent among the Moslems," who constituted 80 per cent of the French North African Army.[11]

One apparent political objective in North Africa was to broaden the base of political cooperation and thus create a healthier political atmosphere in North Africa. As early as November 17, 1942, President Roosevelt had asked for the liberation of political prisoners,[12] and in February a commission was organized to deal with such prisoners.[13] All signs of liberalization of the existing political organization in North Africa were welcomed by the United States Government.[14] Such liberalization was called a "move in the right direction" by both Robert D. Murphy and Harold Macmillan, American and British Ministers to French North Africa, respectively.[15] In accordance with the policy of putting military ahead of political matters, it is worthwhile to note that officially Mr. Murphy was the chief diplomatic official in North Africa acting under the direction and supervision of General Eisenhower.

The British and American Governments gave many indications of their desire for French unity. In January, President Roosevelt and Prime Minister Churchill had brought together Generals de Gaulle and Giraud at the Casablanca Conference. The British and American leaders had agreed on the necessity for the full use of the fighting potentialities of all Frenchmen, although neither country aimed (openly, at least) to impose any particular leader or form of government on the French people.[16]

In spite of the desire of the State Department for French unity, serious division

[1] *New York Times*, December 26, 1942, exclusive interview by Walter Logan.
[2] *Ibid.*
[3] See this volume, p. 560, 565.
[4] *New York Times*, January 21, 1943.
[5] *Ibid.*, February 3, 1943.
[6] See this volume, p. 567.
[7] *Ibid.*, p. 568.
[8] *New York Times*, February 3, 1943.
[9] See this volume, p. 566.
[10] *New York Times*, March 19, 1943.
[11] *Ibid.*, March 22, 1943.
[12] Department of State, *Bulletin*, VII, p. 935.
[13] *New York Times*, February 6, 1943.
[14] *Ibid.*, March 9, 1943.
[15] *Ibid.*, February 8, 1943.
[16] *Ibid.*, Section 4, April 4, 1943, p. 2.

among the French in North Africa persisted. Hardly had Giraud assumed power when he ordered the arrest of twelve Frenchmen (alleged to be Allied sympathizers by the Fighting French), whom he accused of plotting the assassination of high French officials and of Robert Murphy as well.[1] The appointment of Marcel Peyrouton, former Minister of the Interior in the Vichy Government as Governor-General of Algeria provoked another storm of protest from the de Gaulle group.[2]

The struggle between Giraud and de Gaulle appeared to be in part a continuation of the old struggle between Right and Left which had plagued the Third Republic. The North African situation was further complicated by the activities of local political groups and by Arab unrest and nationalism.[3] A striking illustration of the difficulties created by French internal conflict in the carrying out of the American program of assistance in the prosecution of war was afforded in the affair of the French warships.

In February of 1943, the French warships *Richelieu* and *Montcalm* arrived in the Port of New York. Secretary of the Navy Knox announced that these ships would operate under French command, although under Allied leadership in whatever area assigned.[4] Shortly after their arrival, twelve sailors from the *Richelieu* were held by immigration authorities at Ellis Island as a result of a request by the Giraud mission to the Navy Department to round up "deserters." The Fighting French group in London asked for their freedom on the ground that the sailors did not trust their Giraudist officers and that they had become de Gaullists.[5] But the United States Government, fearing the immobilization of the warships,[6] decided to classify the deserting sailors as undesirable aliens illegally in this country, and subject therefore to action by the immigration authorities.[7] Thus the matter ended officially. In April, however, the head of the Fighting French Military Mission in New York stated again that the sailors had no confidence in officers who had collaborated with Vichy, and that they voluntarily went over to the Fighting French "because de Gaulle was the only man they could trust because he never stopped fighting."[8]

Despite many such points of conflict, despite wide diversities of view, General Giraud and General de Gaulle made attempts to reach a common ground almost from the first. On Christmas Day, 1942, immediately after the assassination of Admiral Darlan, de Gaulle addressed a letter to Giraud asking him to meet him on French soil to discuss the establishment of a central provisional government in Algiers uniting all the forces of the French Empire.[9] De Gaulle repeated his request three times between then and January 7, 1943,[10] and on January 8 Giraud agreed to such a meeting. On January 26 the Generals finally conferred at Casablanca; both expressed "their entire agreement on the end to be achieved, which is the liberation of France, and the triumph of human liberties by the total defeat of the enemy."[11]

These words seemed to imply a postponement until after the war of the deep divisions that split the French community.[12] Unofficial reports stated that de Gaulle had asked for a declaration of the reestablishment of democracy in France. Giraud was said to have refused on account of his belief that many of France's

[1] *Ibid.*, December 31, 1942.
[2] *Ibid.*, January 24, 1943.
[3] *Ibid.*, Section 4, January 10, 1943, p. 2.
[4] *New York Times*, February 18, 1943.
[5] *Ibid.*, March 12, 1943.
[6] *Ibid.*, March 14, 1943.
[7] *Ibid.*, March 13, 1943.
[8] *Ibid.*, April 4, 1943.
[9] *Ibid.*, Section 4, January 3, 1943, p. 1.
[10] *Free France*, III (1943), p. 2.
[11] *Ibid.*, p. 321.
[12] *New York Times*, Section 4, January 31, 1943, p. 1.

misfortunes could be attributed to the weaknesses of the democratic regime.[1] The real differences, therefore, seemed to hinge on political considerations; it was partly a matter of the relation of the organization in French North Africa to the problem of France as a whole.[2] Such, at least, was the de Gaullist view.

Nevertheless, the Casablanca Conference did bear certain fruits. An agreement was reached to exchange missions to work out cultural, economic, and financial problems.[3] Giraud took his first step in the re-establishment of political liberties in North Africa by releasing twenty-seven political prisoners, some of whom were Communists, others, de Gaullists, or both. On February 5, he changed the name of the Imperial Council to that of "War Council" and left the door at least partially open for the entrance of de Gaulle. The latter, however, suspected the assertion that "General Giraud (now) has in his hands all the vital interests of the country at war" and complained that the new Committee had been set up without consulting him.[4] Giraud also proceeded to appoint a prominent de Gaullist to high office in North Africa for the first time when he named Charles Brunel head of the newly created Permanent Council of War Economy.[5] Soon after, another supporter of de Gaulle replaced a Vichyite as Secretary of Information and Propaganda.[6]

General de Gaulle clarified his views in a speech on February 9 at a Conference in London in which he particularized the conditions necessary for the union of the French Empire.[7] Two important principles he considered a *sine qua non:* (1) The union of the French Empire in the spirit of Metropolitan France where all are united against the Germans; and (2) the restoration of the laws of the Republic in French North Africa, with liberty of the press, of assembly, of opinion, and of the individual included.[8]

On February 28, General Georges Catroux, head of the Fighting French mission with General Giraud, presented to Giraud a Memorandum adopted by the French National Committee in London on February 23, more specifically stating the conditions of union "in accordance with the will of the French people."[9] Briefly, the Memorandum demanded that the 1940 Armistice between Germany and France be rejected, that all Vichyites be ejected from the French North African Government, that there be a return to the laws of the Republic, and that a "Central Power" be set up as the governing body.[10]

A few days later General Giraud made a speech which did not contribute anything new to the question of unity but wherein he stated the adherence of French North Africa to the principles of the Atlantic Charter.[11] In his "Alsace-Lorraine Speech" of March 14, however, he declared: "I give to the people of France my most solemn assurances that their sacred right to determine by themselves their own government shall be fully conserved. . . ."[12]

Giraud gave more concrete evidence of a policy of gradual liberalization by repudiating the publication in the *Journal Officiel* on March 2 of two Vichy decrees relating to the status of Jews in North Africa. The Vichy supporter who was responsible was dismissed from membership in the Government-General of Algeria.[13] Not only were all post-Armistice laws against Jews and Moslems

[1] *Ibid.*, article by Edwin L. James, Section 4, February 7, 1943, p. 3.
[2] *Ibid.*
[3] *Ibid.*
[4] *Ibid.*
[5] *Ibid.*, Section 4, February 14, 1943, p. 2.
[6] *New York Times*, February 22, 1943.
[7] *Free France*, III (1943), p. 104.
[8] *New York Times*, article by Tania Long, Section 4, February 14, 1943, p. 4.
[9] *Free France*, III (1943), p. 189.
[10] *Ibid.*, this volume, p. 571.
[11] *Free France*, III (1943), p. 198.
[12] See this volume, p. 562.
[13] *New York Times*, Section 4, March 14, 1943, p. 1.

repealed,[1] but all mementos of Pétain were barred,[2] de Gaullists were permitted openly to demonstrate in the streets of Algiers,[3] and finally the local elected assembly in North Africa which had held office up to June 22, 1940 was re-established and its powers prolonged until the French people could vote again.[4] Only French Morocco practised a policy of obstructionism against these new decrees of Giraud.[5] Closely connected with these liberalizing measures was an invitation addressed to General de Gaulle by Giraud on March 15 for a meeting in Algiers.

On April 1 General Giraud finally replied to the Memorandum of the French National Committee of February 23. He proposed to reject the Armistice entirely, to set up a French Committee of Overseas Territories, a program for Metropolitan France as well, and set forth conditions necessary for establishing a provisional Liberation Government by putting into effect the Tréveneuc Law of 1872 under the authority of the French Military Commander-in-Chief.[6]

General de Gaulle then accepted the March 15 invitation of Giraud for a meeting, and was preparing to leave for Algiers when General Eisenhower requested a postponement of his visit because of exigencies of military operations in the North African Theatre.[7] The French National Committee immediately protested on April 5 that any prolonged delay in the proposed meeting would seriously impair the achievement of unity.[8]

On April 15 the French National Committee replied to Giraud's Memorandum of April 1 by demanding again that all Vichy legislation be annulled. It also stressed the desirability of a National Consultative Council which would include representatives of French movements of resistance in Metropolitan France. The military power responsible for order in France was to be subordinated to the civilian authority. And, finally, the discussions had to be held on French soil.[9]

In a letter of April 27 Giraud again proposed a meeting with de Gaulle outside of Algiers, but on May 4 de Gaulle repeated his opinion that Algiers, the capital of the North African Empire, was the only proper place of *venue*.[10] A few days later, May 7, 1943, the French National Committee also repeated its view that French public opinion should be represented in any "Central Power."[11]

Evidently in a further effort to pave the way for a meeting, General Giraud ousted the Bey of Tunis on May 10,[12] issued a decree repealing all Vichy labor laws,[13] and restored the full freedom of the press at the end of the month.[14] In a letter to General de Gaulle, dated May 17, General Giraud stated that he was convinced that "the hour of action and of our common responsibilities has come." [15] On May 29, General de Gaulle and his advisers boarded a plane for Algiers.

On June 4, 1943, only a few days after discussions had begun,[16] a communiqué was issued announcing the formation of a National Council of Liberation with Generals de Gaulle and Giraud as co-chairmen. Both Washington and London welcomed the news; it was well known that President Roosevelt and Prime

[1] *Ibid.*, Section 4, March 21, 1943, p. 1.
[2] *New York Times*, March 17, 1943.
[3] *Ibid.*, Section 4, March 21, 1943, p. 1.
[4] *Ibid.*
[5] *New York Times*, March 31, 1943.
[6] *Free France*, III (1943), p. 281; see this volume p. 578.
[7] *New York Times*, Section 4, April 4, 1943, p. 2.
[8] *Free France*, III (1943), p. 323.
[9] *Ibid.*, p. 285; see this volume p. 579.
[10] *Free France*, III (1943), p. 315.
[11] *Ibid.*, p. 319.
[12] *New York Times*, May 11, 1943.
[13] *Ibid.*, May 20, 1943.
[14] *Ibid.*, Section 4, May 30, 1943, p. 2.
[15] See this volume, p. 586.
[16] *New York Times*, June 4, 1943.

Minister Churchill had canvassed the situation in Washington at their meeting in May 1943.[1]

It was announced at the White House on June 28 that General Giraud would soon visit the United States as the guest of the Government, but would come in his military capacity rather than as joint leader of the Committee of National Liberation. General Giraud arrived in Washington on July 7 and was received by President Roosevelt.

A. General Giraud as High Commissioner of French North Africa

(1) Statement of the Secretary of State (Hull) on Selection of General Giraud as High Commissioner of French North Africa, December 28, 1942 [2]

The selection of General Giraud to his new post is a most fortunate choice and one that will, I am sure, receive the enthusiastic commendation of all. General Giraud is one of the great military commanders of the world today, and his recent selection will result in greater unification of all groups and elements behind his military leadership and will go far to insure the common victory with the restoration of French liberty everywhere.

(2) Statements of General Giraud Regarding Problems in French North Africa, as Reported by Mr. Guy Ramsey in the London News Chronicle. Department of State Release, February 2, 1943 [3]

During his press conference of February 2, 1943, President Roosevelt invited attention to this interview.

In this interview Ramsey states that Giraud "spoke with amazing frankness of many of his problems for he believes it is essential that Britain and Washington should fully understand both what those problems are and his methods of solving them — methods which he states may be open to criticism from people who are not so intimately acquainted with France and with French Africa as he is." . . . And then, Ramsey goes on: "half the population of Algiers still calls de Gaulle 'traitor' because they believe his only reason for coming to Britain was to gain decorations, high rank or money (yes, this is what a considerable proportion of the people here genuinely believe) and while it is commonly said that the two French generals are like a couple of prima donnas manoeuvring for the centre of the stage General Giraud said bluntly: 'the British are right to support de Gaulle. He is the only Frenchman who has spoken for two years with the voice of France. I am not only in accord with him, I am one of his greatest admirers as a soldier and for what he has done from London.' Here is a second

---

[1] Ibid., article by Edwin L. James, Section 4, June 13, 1943, p. 3.
[2] Department of State, Bulletin, VIII, p. 5.
[3] Ibid., p. 118.

example of General Giraud's grip on problems. 'Doubtless,' he said, 'it is being asked why I do not clear out every man of Vichy from my Government. I will tell you why. In the first place I need trained administrators. There are not so many trained men in North Africa available. In the second place not all men who have held office under Vichy are, in the sense one uses the phrase, men of Vichy. For instance, Laval is a man of Vichy and so is Peyrouton. That is, both held office under the Vichy regime. Peyrouton knows this country. He is an able man. The man he replaced was not sufficiently energetic.'" (Algiers is the location of the replacement.) "'Do you think I would have called in a man like Laval no matter how able? There are good men, decent men, who have worked for Vichy — and it is folly to call them men of Vichy merely because they have held office. Peyrouton for example is no man of Vichy in that sense — if he had been I would not have sent for him.

"'Boisson (the Governor of Dakar) is another. I have been down to French West Africa. It is magnificently administered — I have been to the Ivory Coast and all the other colonies under his jurisdiction and all are equally well governed — and Boisson although holding office under Vichy never allowed a *boche* in Dakar. Do you think I am going to throw out men like that, men who are capable patriots?'"

Urging necessity of proceeding gradually in order to avoid "revolution" and unnecessary bloodshed Giraud went on to say to Ramsey: "I have the Moslem problem and the Jewish problem and I am dealing with both progressively. I am not going to try to solve them either by a stroke of the pen or a stroke of the sword: I know North Africa — I have made my career here — and I know that too swift reversals in this country mean trouble. I do not want trouble. The only trouble I want is trouble for the *boche*." Giraud went on to emphasize that he would use members of the Sol, Communists, Conservatives or anyone under the sole criterion that they want to fight Germans and not engage in politics. (Here the President said this was not a bad line for any country these days.) He made an eloquent plea for modern arms for his army as soon as possible — "I believe I am convinced, they will come." (At this point the President again interpolated mentioning "raised sights.") He went on: "as for me I am not thinking only of North Africa. I am thinking of France herself and I am thinking of one million two hundred thousand Frenchmen imprisoned in Germany. I have been a prisoner and every day those men remain prisoners, every day that France remains enslaved and occupied, every one of those days for me counts double. I have seen my men fight, I say. They are fighting now and they are fighting well but with what? . . . but with what equipment and especially when they see British and American equipment beside them and know they have got to be helped in every action by British or American troops for the very reason of this equipment — what will happen to their morale if they have to wait too long? For look, I have been in France since my escape from Germany. I know that France is ready to rise and fight as we are fighting. I know my own men are highly trained enough to handle rapidly whatever modern weapons are given them.

"And it is right that France should fight to free herself. It is not the duty of Britain and America to free France — it is the duty of France to free herself with British and American help.

" France must regain not only her country and her empire: France must regain her old Frenchness, her old confidence. Then only will France really be free. Above all, it is necessary for Britain and America to understand our problems and even my problems. For that very reason I am hoping to send to London and Washington a small commission of first-class men, who know England and the English and know the Americans, to create a real liaison. Meantime, if you can do anything to present the true facts in their true colors you will not only be the friend of France but you will help more than a little to win the war."

(3) *Address by General Giraud to the Alsace-Lorraine Society, Algiers, March 14, 1943* [1]

[Translation]

DEAR FRIENDS:

I cannot tell you how glad I am to find myself today amidst Frenchmen so resolutely patriotic, convinced of the legitimacy of our cause and prepared to sacrifice all to guarantee its success.

Alsace and Lorraine have been incorporated into Germany. Not a single voice in France has been raised to protest this.

But here we protest. All the world must know that France does not accept that annexation. Alsace and Lorraine shall again become French within a completely liberated France.

Certain ones among you may have had doubts after the catastrophe, but you never swayed, you never yielded to the lying promises or the brutal threats. For you France is but one and indivisible.

Whether you were born here or over there, whether you have lived in Mulhouse or in Thionville, in Paris or in Algiers, you are still Alsatians, you are Lorrainers, and above all you are Frenchmen. This is what those beyond the Rhine have never understood. Despite the defeat, you are still Alsatians and Lorrainers among us, who are believers in the eternal France. France has been defeated in body, but never has she suffered defeat in spirit. Let us not forget that since June 1940, she has been silent and gagged.

[1] *New York Times*, March 15, 1943.

I have the right to speak to you about the people of France. I lived their life for two years: first with the prisoners, eating their bread with them, drinking their water, then for eight months in the "free zone," as a victim of ceaseless supervision. I have seen the sons of France forcibly deported. I have seen the heroic struggle against the [German] forced-labor conscription. I have seen children odiously torn from their parents, families torn apart and youth prematurely aged by its trials. Such are the essential elements of national resistance. We owe them our support. These will be the vital factors tomorrow for the new dawn of France. I have seen the heroism of hostages who were proud to die so that the spirit of resistance might be kept up, and the workers go on stoically under the bombardments of their plants by Allied aircraft.

Germany thought she could crush and debase France. While the breath of humiliation and misfortune fanned across the land, in every village, in every factory and in every school, a heroic France rose against the indignity of serfdom. The people of France have not accepted the Armistice. In their hearts the people of France were sustained during these tragic hours by the heroic resistance of the English people, who stood alone in the struggle against the common foe.

The heroes of resistance, those who remained loyal in the hour of need, those who kept their faith at the time of despair, have been and are now the real expression of France. Those who died in these terrible fights, those who suffer in torture camps and in prisons are the advance guard of the nation. The citizens and soldiers without uniforms who are fighting in France, the soldiers of the French Army who are battling on the war front of liberation, the soldiers of the army of Africa fight with the same spirit, as one, and die for the same ideals. It is an astonishing spectacle to see France, at the very moment when our enemies would like to tear her to pieces and to suppress her completely, stand up everywhere, on the desecrated soil of the mother country as well as abroad.

Tomorrow, in the streets of our villages alongside the war memorials, people will revere the monuments of francs-tireurs, of saboteurs, of hostages, of those who were deported and of the heroic multitude of those who fell for liberty.

As Lincoln said at Gettysburg:

"The world will little note nor long remember what we say here, but it can never forget what they did here." There exists but one catastrophe, for individuals as well as for nations: self-renunciation. France has never known this catastrophe.

The French people remain true to themselves. They have never given up. Each time France has known invasion, whatever her internal dissensions or conflicting ideologies, she has found again her unity and her foe has been driven out.

It was Philippe Auguste at the head of his advisers, it was Joan [of Arc] with her arms in hand, it was Henri IV with the white plume, it was Richelieu by his inflexible will, it was the volunteers of '92 [1792] and the poilus of 1918 and now it will be the liberators of tomorrow. The French army of victory, with its Allies, will join the people of France to liberate our mother-country. England and America are throwing all their force into the battle, and the Russians are presenting to the astonished world the most magnificent example of patriotism.

Have no fear, gentlemen: The French Army, too, knows how to fight. You have seen its soldiers at Bir Hacheim, at Medjez-el-Bab, at Ksar Rhilane and at Metlaoui. Fifty thousand of them now face the Germans in Tunisia while others come up from Libya and the Chad Territory and will soon join hands.

There will be but one French Army, but one French Navy fighting Germany, whether it arrives from Algeria or from Libya, whether in the course of recent events it resisted the Americans or whether in obedience to my orders it cooperated with them.

Many still await arms. These weapons are arriving. Our friends do all they can to help us. But by improvisation one does not within a few days equip an army of 300,000 that was completely disarmed by the Armistice Commissions but that today resumes the battle against the Germans.

It is not too great a task to produce war material with the prodigious American capacity. But to distribute it among the Allies is a problem when China, Russia and France, as well as England, are to be supplied.

I am glad to announce that, as a result of the very cordial and very realistic conversations at Casablanca, I found most loyal and understanding partners; not only were deliveries agreed upon in principle, but such deliveries have begun in actuality, thus carrying on the help that my friend General Eisenhower, if I may be permitted to call him that, has given us.

As all France shares with her allies the victory of the cause for which she suffered, France shall resume her place among the victorious nations. The people of France will then be the masters of her destiny. The essential conditions precedent for the free expression of France's sovereignty will be restored in France. The people of France will form their provisional government in accordance with the constitutional laws of the republic. The expression of the sovereignty of the French people has been interrupted by German occupation and it will be re-established only when France has been liberated.

I give to the people of France my most solemn assurances that their sacred right to determine by themselves their own government shall be fully conserved. I promise them that all conditions permitting them to make such a choice in lawful order, with all their liberties re-established, shall be assured. I assure them that such a situation will be created as soon as France has been freed.

I am the servant of the people of France. I am not their master.

All the Frenchmen gathered around me — all of us from myself to the last soldier of the army of victory — are the servants of the people of France. Tomorrow we shall be the servants of the government that will be freely chosen and we shall undertake to hand over to it our authority.

After June 22, 1940, the will of the French people ceased to express itself freely. By occupying two-thirds of France and her capital, by controlling the government and all public services, by directing the economy, openly as well as secretly, by limiting or deforming intellectual life, by uprooting social life, by imposing discriminatory legislation intolerable to the French conscience, Germany has prohibited the French people from voicing its opinion.

The free will of the people alone forms a basis for law. Without it all codes of law are nullified. Then they are either doctrinary constructions without collective significance or they are commands of the occupying power under the cloak of national legislation.

In the absence of a legitimate foundation, which alone can be given by the free will of the French people, legislation subsequent to June 22, 1940, whether originating from the régime within or dictated from abroad, is without legal force. It may be considered null and void, as issued and promulgated without the consent of French people and against their interests.

In such a situation we can draw conclusions, concerning both the texts [of the decrees] and the men [who issued them]. We repudiate the tyranny imposed on the French people. Measures have already been taken and others will follow, to re-establish the French nation.

Nevertheless, life continued after June 22, 1940. There were temporary situations to be regulated and new conditions to be met. To ignore this fact would only create disorder in French overseas territory and confusion that would increase the present difficulties.

We shall begin to work immediately to re-establish a situation of order. To accomplish this we shall take progressive measures adapted to the entanglements and complexities that our economic life imposes. Everybody understands that it is impossible to abolish laws and decrees by the stroke of a pen without having first organized an adaptation to new conditions. To act otherwise would mean to run counter to the purpose that we are pursuing.

And now the measures that have already been taken:

The municipal assemblies and the General Councils will resume their traditional role. The laws of racial discrimination, imposed on France by the Nazis, exist no more. The order has been promulgated declaring null and void the law of June 2, 1941, and the decrees connected with it.

The abrogation of these laws and decrees has restored the French tradition of human liberty and the return to equality of all before the law. Without such equality there exists no French liberty. This abolition wipes out that mark of shame that in their work of persecution the Nazis wished to inflict on France by forcibly associating her with their own perversion.

With the same desire to eliminate all racial discrimination, the Crémieux decree, which established in 1870 the different status between native Moslems and native Jews, is abrogated.

Mohammedans should not lend their ears to one-sided advice lavished upon them by German-Italian propaganda. Germans as well as Italians have too often demonstrated how they treat non-Aryans for one to be misled by their word.

Regarding relations between Moslems and Jews, they must be those of men who are destined to complement each other in economic life; the latter work in their shops and the former on the soil, without one being better than the other, as France assures them both security and tranquility.

I have lived a long time in North Africa and I find this possible — even easy. I have confidence in the intelligence of all to see it realized.

It is in this spirit and in accordance with this principle that we shall administer the possessions and the interests of France, with which task we were charged. We shall preserve intact these territories to which France has brought civilization. France will end this war as a victorious nation, taking her place in the peace discussions, free and in possession of all her overseas territories.

France, battered in the flesh, will emerge spiritually as the eternal France, the France of human liberty, the France of noble ideals. The people of France, like their ancestors, are inspired by the breath of liberty. In peace, at the commencement of a new era for the world, she will contribute her ideals, inspired by the fundamental principles that from the time of their inception have united the American and French democracies.

France will contribute the fruit of her reflections, ripened in suffering, to help in the end to build a better Europe — a Europe at peace. I feel certain that such a vital contribution will be made by France. It will come forth from Frenchmen, united and free; from the prisoners, my countrymen, of whom I think incessantly, whose souls, as a youth from the North told me in captivity, were forged better than their weapons.

My brother Frenchmen: With all my heart I wish the union of us all. This union must be whole-hearted and effective. It will band together not only Frenchmen in France, now bent under the enemy yoke, but equally those Frenchmen who, like ourselves, are outside France.

This union is indispensable. It is a question of life and death for our country. Disunity is the evidence of defeat, unity the mark of victory. For my part, I am ready to cooperate with all those who, accepting the basic and traditional principles of which I have spoken, joining in the solemn oath that I give to the people of France, are participating in the battle against the enemy.

And now, in conclusion, my dear friends, permit me to ask the Lord for an early victory and that it prevent the return of such horrors as we have lived through and through which we still live. May it give to men of good-will the gift of living together in tolerance, understanding, mutual aid and — dare I say — loving one another.

Surely this is the commandment that comes down to us from on High and that we have so often scorned. After this tragic trial, let us try to forget it less often and to apply it better.

This is not a philosophy of weakness. Take the word of one who escaped from Koenigstein.

(a) Statement of the Secretary of State (Hull) Commending the Speech of General Giraud, March 15, 1943 [1]

General Giraud has now confirmed the hopes of this Government that his selection as the Commander-in-Chief of the French forces fighting in North Africa would make possible a greater unification of all groups behind his military leadership. This should insure the proper place for a victorious France in the restoration of liberty everywhere.

General Giraud, like a true soldier, has devoted all the time available to him from his military duties to the careful and patient study of the problems involved in the French territories. He has reached the point where, with no material disturbance to his military effort, he has been able to remove discrimination in the treatment of those living under his jurisdiction. He has now made it possible for all elements who desire the defeat of the Axis powers and the liberation of French territory to unite in their will to rid French soil of the weight of the Axis yoke. He has based his authority firmly upon the principle of the free expression of liberated Frenchmen and, forseeing all France once more mistress of her destiny, has swept aside laws and decrees which were contrary to her traditional republican institutions.

(b) Statement of the Prime Minister of the United Kingdom (Churchill) Commending the Speech of General Giraud, March 17, 1943 [1]

His Majesty's Government in the United Kingdom warmly welcome General Giraud's speech, in particular his abolition of French legislation

[1] Department of State, *Bulletin*, VIII, p. 229.

subsequent to June 22, 1940, his abrogation of all race distinction between native Moslems and Jewish inhabitants, and his decision that municipal assemblies and *Conseils Généraux* will resume their traditional role with their members elected by the people. In order to achieve the liberation of France through victory, Frenchmen everywhere must be united and, above all, all Frenchmen outside Nazi power should act loyally against the common enemy without a day's needless delay. This object has been promoted by General Giraud's speech and the National Committee memorandum, since these show that no questions of principle divide these two bodies of Frenchmen.

In commenting on the statement of Prime Minister Churchill, Mr. Hull said that the Government of the United States was "in the heartiest accord with this timely and splendid statement of the British Prime Minister and finds satisfaction in strongly commending this further step toward French unity." [1]

(4) Letter Addressed to Baron Edouard de Rothschild by the Under Secretary of State (Welles) with Regard to the Position of Jews in North Africa, March 27, 1943 [2]

MY DEAR BARON DE ROTHSCHILD:

You will recall that last week you were good enough to send me the text of a statement which you had prepared for publication regarding the general position of the Jewish community in North Africa and, more particularly, the abrogation of the Crémieux Decree of 1870 in relation to the speech made by General Giraud on March 14.

I felt so strongly that your statement gave a completely erroneous picture of the position of Jews in North Africa and of General Giraud's measures in their behalf that I immediately telegraphed a summary of it to our representatives there. The following comment, prepared in consultation with an unbiased specialist familiar with the various legal points involved, has just been received. I hasten to send it to you in the belief that you will not wish to allow an erroneous impression of the situation to prevail.

1. The laws relating to the Jews which were of Nazi inspiration were abolished by General Giraud by an ordinance of the fourteenth of the current month. The Jews are guaranteed the right to practice the liberal professions including the holding of public office, the right to own property and freely to manage their property, assets and all business enterprises, and the right to attend institutions of learning of all degrees. The Jew is no longer indicated as of a race apart in the civil registry records. By ordering the reinstatement of all public officials, agents and employees excluded because they were Jews, General Giraud effaced an odious past. The order that property sequestered under provisional administration would be restored to the Jews and that the sales of real property and other assets would be null and void was given with the same objective. Con-

[1] *Ibid.*   [2] *Ibid.*, p. 255.

sequently, Baron de Rothschild's affirmation that the decisions of General Giraud are obscure and insufficient is untrue.

2. French citizenship is retained by Jews born in France or descendants of parents born in France. Baron de Rothschild's affirmation that they lose their citizenship is untrue.

3. Only native Algerian Jews are affected by the Crémieux Decree. The Decree is abrogated but in the near future a procedure will be established whereby native Algerian Jews who desire to become citizens may acquire citizenship. It may be remembered that, following the precedent of 1914–1918, elections are deferred until the end of the war, that is to say until Metropolitan France is liberated. Consequently, native Algerian Jews who desire to participate in those elections will have ample time to become citizens. The affirmation of Baron de Rothschild that Jews will be unlawfully deprived of voting power is likewise absolutely untrue.

Believe me,

B. Official Statements of the Policy of the United States toward French North Africa

(1) Statement of the Secretary of State (Hull) Regarding the Diplomatic Situation in North Africa before the Subcommittee of the Committee on Appropriations of the House of Representatives, February 8, 1943 [1]

[Excerpt]

Mr. CARTER. Mr. Secretary, have you any statement you care to make on the diplomatic situation in North Africa?

Secretary HULL. There is not much to that whole thing except talk about politics and conditions among Frenchmen and others on the political side. We have never had but one policy there, and that was to deal militarily and help militarily everybody who was fighting the Axis powers. If the Frenchmen there were fighting or opposing the Axis powers we would work with them and help them militarily, as we did with the de Gaulle group when we gave them lease-lend recognition. That was from the very beginning.

We knew we would get into a hopeless tangle if we stopped fighting to take up politics.

I think they had 25 or 30 different political parties as they moved into the war. We figured that the thing for us to do was to devote all of our attention, that is, for the Army, the Navy, and the State Department, to devote all possible attention to winning battles and winning the war. So the only complaint that anybody has against the Government or the State Department is that it did not lend itself to the political ambitions and desires of some of the fine, patriotic Frenchmen. We

[1] *Department of State Appropriation Bill for 1944, Hearings before the Subcommittee of the Committee on Appropriations, House of Representatives,* 78th Cong., 1st sess., p. 17.

know that we must win this war and let everybody have their freedom, and then let them have a fair opportunity to select their own leaders and their own form of government. All of this talk has been because we did not abandon that policy and plunge into this political maelstrom.

(2) Letter from the Under Secretary of State (Welles) to Professor Ralph Barton Perry of Harvard University Explaining the United States Government's North African Policy, April 2, 1943 [1]

[Excerpt]

MY DEAR PROFESSOR PERRY:

Thank you for your letter of February 20, 1943. I am, of course, aware of the many criticisms directed against the State Department. It is inevitable, and desirable, that the policies of a democratic government should be subject to full public criticism. Obviously, the better informed discussion can be, the better will it further the public interest. The responsibility for seeing that such discussion is well-informed rests upon the government as well as upon a vigilant and independent press.

However, in time of war there are necessary limitations upon the amount of information a government can make public. In the field of foreign affairs especially, there are great practical difficulties in the way of disclosing all the information bearing on a given subject. Certain of the information which guides a democratic government must be kept secret, to protect the source and, perhaps, to preserve friendly relations with another power. Foreign Offices in democratic countries are particularly exposed to criticism, partly because of this need for secrecy, and partly because they must often, in the nature of their task, act in ways which go against the grain of the average citizen. For example, the average citizen likes to think of his country as all-powerful. He does not see why his country should not say bluntly what is right and what it wants done — and see that it is done. He is apt to be impatient over delays in reaching the goal, and he is eager to proclaim his principles to the world at all times. The diplomat, on the other hand, must be aware not only of his country's power but of the limitations of its power and the demands of innumerable contingencies which it faces. He must always guard against committing his country to more than it can do. He must be patient, and must welcome each small point gained, even when his fellow-citizens, in their chagrin over the failure to make rapid progress, do not recognize the gain. And he may, on occasions, have to refrain from proclaiming his beliefs, as the private citizen is free

[1] Department of State, *Bulletin*, VIII, p. 319.

to do, simply in the interest of furthering their acceptance. His freedom of speech is limited by the nature of his duties.

Criticisms of the Government's North African policy must be viewed in the light of certain further considerations. First, we must bear in mind that they concern one aspect of a major military operation. This operation has already achieved great successes. We may confidently expect that it will, before long, succeed in its ultimate objective — to expel Axis forces from the continent of Africa and thus open the way for an invasion of southern Europe. The citizen is free to speculate, after the event, on what he might have done differently. But the commander in the field has to act, and is responsible for the success or failure of his actions. Usually, he is faced with the choice not between a good plan and a bad plan, but between a number of courses, all of which have disadvantages.

I believe that much of the criticism of our North African policy has arisen because surface developments have been taken as indications of basic policy when they were in fact merely temporary steps in the process of achieving that policy. When there are delays or incidental errors, which are inevitable in the confusion of a complex and obscure situation, some people assume that those in authority do not wish to reach certain approved objectives. General Giraud's speech of March 14, 1943, and the issuance on March 17, 1943 of decrees repealing the discriminatory legislation of the Vichy government in North Africa and confirming the authority of the French Republic have, I hope, gone far to eliminate misunderstandings of this sort.

Our wartime foreign policy has two purposes which override all others. First, we must do all we can to win absolute victory as quickly as possible, with the least possible loss of life. I believe that our North African policy saved the lives of many American boys, and of many North African soldiers and civilians. Secondly, we must work to establish a just and lasting peace. I believe that it is important in the interest of lasting peace that the French people should be free, under their own Republican laws, to choose their government after the Nazis have been driven out of France. Until that day, French forces will, I hope, fight side by side in harmony against the common enemy. These are our stated policies, and they are also the stated policies of General de Gaulle and General Giraud.

. . . .

———

In his address before the White House Correspondents' Association in Washington, February 12, 1943, President Roosevelt made an important statement on United States policy regarding the liberation of France, which had a definite application to the North African situation (see p. 42).

C. Negotiations between General Giraud and General de Gaulle

(1) Statement of General de Gaulle Suggesting a Meeting with General Giraud to Discuss Plans for Achieving French Unity, London, January 2, 1943 [1]

[Translation]

Internal confusion is steadily increasing in French North and West Africa. The reason for this confusion is that French authority has no basic point following the collapse of Vichy, since the great force of national fervor, coherence and experience that constitutes fighting France and that has already returned to war and restored to the Republic a large part of the Empire, is not officially represented in these French territories.

The results of this confusion are, first, a situation that is and will be embarrassing for the operation of the Allied armies; second, the fact that France at this decisive moment is deprived of that powerful trump card that would be represented by union for the prosecution of the war by her vast empire in liaison with the movement of resistance in France herself.

Finally — and perhaps most important of all — is the amazement of the French people, staggered in their misery by the strange fate of that part of the Empire most recently liberated.

The remedy for this situation is the establishment in French North and West Africa, as in all other French territories overseas — of a temporary and enlarged central power founded on national union, inspired by the spirit of war and of liberation, with laws that are the laws of the Republic, to last until such time as the nation has made known her will.

Such is the tradition of French democracy.

It was thus that, in 1870, after the fall of the Empire, men of national defense provisionally took power in the name of the Republic in order to direct the war effort of the nation.

On December 25, 1942, in full agreement with the [French] National Committee and the Council for Defense of the Empire, I suggested to General Giraud that we should meet immediately on French soil in order to study the means of attaining this object.

I believe in fact that the situation in France and the general situation of the war admit of no delay.

(2) Communiqué Issued in Algiers Reporting the Results of the Casablanca Conference with Respect to French Unity, January 27, 1943 [2]

[Translation]

An important Inter-Allied conference has taken place on our soil. On this occasion, General Giraud met President Roosevelt and the

[1] *New York Times*, January 3, 1943.　　[2] *Free France*, III (1943), p. 118.

British Prime Minister, Mr. Churchill, as well as the military leaders of the Allied armies. Important gains were secured by France. The United Nations have recognized in France an ally who has never ceased fighting, either by continuing the struggle outside the Metropolis, or by making ready for a new battle on her own soil. France's action in Tunisia demonstrates her wish to free her territory. Under the title "military agreements," agreements have been concluded in all domains. In particular, they anticipate furnishing by priority to the French forces of Africa the arms which are indispensable to them and which include the most modern matériel. The permanent defense of French interests in France and outside is organized under the title "economic and financial agreements."

Moreover, on the occasion of this conference General Giraud met General de Gaulle. This personal contact permitted a first examination of the conditions under which France's effort could be organized in the war of liberation. Exchanges of views on this subject are being continued. It has been decided to establish from now on a permanent liaison.

(3) *Memorandum from the French National Committee Proposing a Provisional Union, Adopted February 23, 1943, and Sent to General Giraud on February 27, 1943* [1]

[Translation]

At a time when its mission is about to begin its functions in North Africa, the National Committee wants to make clear its intentions with regard to the union of the French Empire and of French forces in the war that France has waged against the powers of the Axis since September 3, 1939.

The National Committee notes first with satisfaction that, in the course of their meeting at Anfa, General Charles de Gaulle and General Henri Giraud were in agreement on the aim to be achieved: the liberation of France and the triumph of human liberties by the total defeat of the enemy. But, in order that France may enjoy the advantages of her war effort from a national and international point of view and one day of her participation in victory of the United Nations, it is necessary that a unification of all her fighting and resistant forces be realized as much inside as outside the country. This implies unity on the basis of one legislation, of direction of efforts by one and the same organization.

Since June 18, 1940, and before the events created by the arrival of the Allied forces in North Africa, a single directing organization existed. General de Gaulle and the French National Committee have, in fact,

---

[1] *Ibid.*, p. 189; *New York Times*, March 14, 1943. The memorandum was adopted by the National Committee in London on February 23, forwarded to General Giraud a few days later, and published on March 13.

conducted in war, in fighting and resistance French forces within and without the land ever since the fall of the last government of the French Republic.

A natural procedure for unification with regard to North and West Africa would be their incorporation within Fighting France and the enlargement of the National Committee in accordance with the new conditions. The National Committee considers that this is the most efficient and most justified solution.

In fact, with the support of the Allies, certain French forces existing in North Africa have returned to the war, but at the same time the unity of the French war effort is at present shattered. The result in North Africa is confusion, which represents an obstacle to the coherent participation of this territory in the war, unquestionable anxiety and dissatisfaction inside the French nation and certain qualms in the public opinion of democracies.

The National Committee is certainly not concerned with any rivalry of persons, which should not and do not exist, but with the grouping of the French people and Empire in the war by the sides of all the Allies and, with the triumph of the aims pursued by the French nation, it is determined to make every effort to remedy this regrettable situation and to seek all means of obtaining unification. To obtain that, certain conditions are indispensable.

A. First of all, the so-called "armistice" concluded against the will of France by the pseudo-government, which has provoked against itself the animosity of French resistance, must be officially held in French North and West Africa as null and void and as not engaging the nation. This truth lies at the basis of the national war effort. It suffices, but it is necessary to admit it to recognize that duty toward the nation demands and has always demanded struggle against the enemy by the side of all the Allies to discern the political and moral impossibility of leaving in the principal posts of direction men who have assumed a large personal responsibility in capitulation and in collaboration with the enemy.

B. The French nation struggles particularly to recover at home and to contribute to the reign everywhere of human liberties — that is, of the fundamental principles that are at the basis of France's own institutions and of which the United Nations are seeking to obtain a triumph in the world against the principles of Nazism and Fascism. The result is that, in all French territories as they are liberated, these fundamental liberties must be restored. They apply particularly, with only the reserve of restrictions really necessitated by the state of war, to liberty of thought, liberty of the press, liberty of assembly and liberty of association, and the equality of all citizens in the eyes of the law to guarantee against arbitrary measures of justice or police.

This obviously implies the immediate liberation of all citizens detained in violation of these liberties and the dissolution of organizations of Fascist inspiration, such as the Legion of Combatants and its annexes.

C. As long as the enemy occupies part of the territory and more than 1,000,000 Frenchmen are prisoners, the pursuit of political aims and notably the change of the fundamental institutions and laws of France as they existed on June 16, 1940, constitute an attack against the union of citizens and war effort of the nations. In consequence, the transformation of the republic into a "French State" and the so-called legislative measures inspired by Nazi or Fascist ideology and imposed on the people by usurpatory power must be considered null and void.

Republican legality must be reestablished. Local Republican institutions must be restored. Changes, which no doubt will have to be made in our political institutions, can be so made only by the French people in full and free exercise of its sovereignty.

D. No doubt should remain as to the determination of any French authority to help in assuring, immediately after liberation, the free expression of popular will by the election, with universal suffrage, or a national representation that in turn will alone be empowered to establish a constitution of France, to designate her government and to judge finally the acts accomplished by any organization that would have assumed the provisional management of national interests.

It must be made clear in particular that no agreement with a foreign power could have consequences outlasting the duration of the war unless it is specially ratified by this assembly. While we await the total liberation of our territory — although proclaiming that at the present time no organization could to any extent substitute itself for the national sovereignty — it will be advantageous, as soon as a provisional central power shall have been constituted, wherein various opinions and activities will be represented, to create by the side of this power a consultative council of French resistance. This council could be formed, for example, with delegates mandated by organizations of resistance in metropolitan France, with fighting elements, with members of Parliament who do not symbolize capitulation and collaboration with the enemy, with elected bodies of those territories liberated in the Empire, with economic trade, unionist and university groups existing in the Empire and with associations of French citizens abroad.

The function of this council would be to give expression to the opinion of Frenchmen as far as they are able to make themselves heard in the present circumstances. These are the lines along which the national committee judges it possible to realize the effective union of all combatant and resistant forces. In any case, in the superior interest of the country, the national committee considers it necessary that cooperation, as extensive as possible, be immediately established with the French in

North and West Africa for the solution in common of certain problems of the war on condition that the intentions manifested at Anfa be given in these territories at the commencement of execution.

These problems are of three kinds:

a. In the military sphere, it is necessary to assure the cooperation of French forces on land, on the sea and in the air and the utilization of all human and material resources of the Empire. It is also necessary to effect the return to war of those French forces available but still held away from it.

b. In the diplomatic sphere, it is indispensable to reach an agreement, to have represented abroad the general interests of France, to adopt a common attitude in diplomatic questions, to unify the French representation with foreign governments and at international or Inter-Allied conferences.

c. It is necessary, finally, to reach a common settlement on concrete problems of finance, economy, health, supply, transport, intellectual and material exchange and legislative and administrative coordination, which are those facing all Frenchmen in the struggle today, and to study in accord the practical problems affecting the life of the French people as the enemy is chased out of France and the Empire.

(4) *Memorandum from General Giraud to General de Gaulle, Proposing a Basis of French Unity, April 1, 1943* [1]

[Translation]

OBJECTS: The discussions which are about to begin have as their essential object the union of all Frenchmen, whether at home or abroad, in a common effort to fight against the invader, to liberate France, to safeguard French liberties, to establish a French government under orderly conditions in conformity with the laws freely established by the French people, to preserve French territories overseas and, when peace comes, to restore France, which will take its part in the victory, to its historic position with respect to England, America, Russia and the world.

In order that these objects may be achieved it is essential that the unification of all the fighting and resisting forces of France, both at home and abroad, take place. This implies unity on the basis of a common legislation and under the control of a single organization.

Only in this way will the territories overseas be able to participate to the utmost in the war effort of the Allied nations and France be able to bring to the work of world peace its traditional contribution.

This union can be obtained only if a real agreement is reached on the

[1] *Free France*, III (1943), p. 281.

basis of well-defined principles and on the program of action which will be the expression thereof.

These principles are indispensable in order that the same conviction may animate Frenchmen both in France and abroad. This program of action is indispensable in order that those who will direct the French central organization, created as a result of the agreement, may carry out this leadership with a common good-will and without divisions between them which might be fatal.

PRINCIPLES: These principles are set forth in General Giraud's speech of March 14 [1] and in the memorandum of the French National Committee of February 27.[2]

Essentially, these principles are: That the armistice is repudiated and that the expression of the sovereignty of the French people has been suspended by the German occupation. It will be resumed only when France is liberated. Consequently, the legislation promulgated after June 22, 1940, was not established by the French people in the free exercise of their sovereignty. It has no legal value.

The only legislation having legal force is legislation enacted prior to June 22, 1940, and, after necessary adjustment, laws subsequent to that date which will have been validated as in conformity with French tradition. Situations of fact must be maintained when applied to individual cases.

Oaths or pledges of allegiance, public or secret, to individuals are barred. The laws of France, as defined above, alone may govern the acts of each individual and any pledges to the contrary must be annulled.

This restoration of traditional French law constitutes a return to respect of the law, the expression of the people's will, a return to the restoration of French liberties.

After their liberation the people of France will become master of their destinies. The process by which the will of the French people will be expressed is laid down in existing law.

This respect of French law fixes the limits within which the French central organization to be created will operate. This body will have the responsibility of governing French territories and interests overseas. It will exercise French sovereignty in the French departments of Algeria, in all territories overseas and in all French territories as they are liberated. It will direct, in a common effort, the French contribution to the liberation of France and the victory of the United Nations. It will contribute to the preparation of the peace treaty negotiations. It will surrender its powers to the provisional government as soon as the latter is constituted in accordance with French law and will be accountable to it for its administration of affairs.

[1] See this volume, p. 560.
[2] *Ibid.*, p. 571.

ORGANIZATION OF THE FRENCH COUNCIL OF OVERSEAS TERRITORIES: The following principles and the program of action indicated hereafter will govern the constitution of the French organization. The best form would appear to be a formula taking its inspiration from the one adopted by the British Government in wartime: namely, the creation of a council composed principally of governors or residents and commissioners responsible for administration, as well as a limited executive committee.

The council could, for example, be called the "French Council of Overseas Territories."

PROGRAM OF ACTION: Organization of the French Council of Overseas Territories as it has just been defined:

All overseas territories and metropolitan territories, as and when they are liberated, will be placed under the authority of the Council. This also implies that certain territories, such as Martinique, will have to submit without delay to this authority. Indo-China will adhere when liberated.

The Council will exercise national sovereignty over these territories until such a time as it can deliver its powers to the provisional government. This situation will involve the subordination of local French authorities to the Council.

In North Africa this will in particular involve a revision of the present status of the Allied authorities established by the Clark-Darlan agreement.

The Council exercising French sovereignty, will consequently grant the Allied authorities certain facilities and will delegate to them certain rights and powers necessary to the conduct of the war.[1] The administrative autonomy of the different overseas territories will be maintained under the Council, which will be responsible for administration as a whole and coordination which will give the maximum efficiency to the war effort of these territories.

The Council will make necessary agreements with the Allied or foreign powers as regards all metropolitan and overseas territories. The Council should be accorded recognition by the Allies as administrator and trustee of all French interests abroad and be treated as an Allied power formally accepted as one of the United Nations.

The Council will establish and maintain relations with Allied and foreign governments through the appointment of representatives. It will negotiate the necessary agreements with the Allied governments and in particular a lend-lease agreement with the United States. It will centralize questions of a financial nature; it will control expenditures and the granting of subsidies.

The establishment and equipment of a single French army will be

---

[1] This is purely a military agreement relating only to billeting, requisitions and similar activities.

undertaken as quickly as possible. The necessary arrangement will be made for the French command effectively to participate in the Allied General Staff so that the French command as well as the French army will form an integral part of the Allied armies. Furthermore, the French army must effectively participate in the Allied operations for the liberation of Europe.

ROLE IN PEACE ENVISAGED: When peace comes it is impossible to conceive that France should not take its place at the peace table alongside England, the United States, Russia and China with an equal footing, and should not be a member of the Supreme Council of the United Nations which will establish the peace and determine the conditions, both European and universal, which will govern the world after the war.

France, an ally at the beginning, succumbed under the weight of armies double its own and a superior armament. Resuming the struggle, it will participate in the victory and, in full possession of the overseas territories which it held in June 1940, will again take its place in the discussions looking toward a free peace, at the point where defeat overtook it.

Bruised but true to itself, it will rejoin its allies. It will contribute to world order, inspired by the principles of the traditional liberty of France, and to the organization of a Europe in which not only will peace be maintained but in which conditions will be established which will make peace the normal state.

The Council will follow, in cooperation with the United Nations, the evolution of post-war projects and will prepare the participation in the peace discussions of the representatives who will be named by the provisional government of liberated France for this purpose.

RELIEF PLANS INCLUDED: The Council, in collaboration with the Allies, will make preparations for the immediate relief and the necessary feeding of the people of liberated France.

Through maintenance of continuous contact with occupied France the Council will endeavor to aid and coordinate the resistance efforts of the French people, not allowing this organization of resistance to be linked to any political formula or purposes. It will inform the French people of the program of action adopted by the Council. It will strengthen their feeling of self-confidence, faith in victory, pride in the army, and their conviction that they alone will determine the constitution of their provisional government, in accordance with the laws of the Republic. It will make clear that the Council and the army to be created are the servants of the French people and will be the servants of the provisional government, to which they will deliver their powers. It will make it clear to France that, in re-entering the struggle, when victory comes it will recover the place it had in the world at the moment when defeat overtook it. It will make it clear that any necessary modifications of the French constitutional mechanism will be determined by the French people themselves.

In other words, it is necessary that the French people be convinced of the total political disinterestedness of the Council, that they believe in victory, in liberty, in the reconstruction of France under orderly conditions, and in the continuation of France's traditions of democracy and its historical role. Finally, it is necessary that they be convinced that the defeat will be effaced.

PROPAGANDA EMPHASIZED: To this end, the Council will be responsible, through a single administration, for the information and propaganda services of the various French organizations. Moreover, it should endeavor to insure a complete coordination between those propaganda services and the United Nations services. If such is the Council's effort in the war, it cannot be doubted that the memory of the defeat will be effaced from world public opinion and that the true figure of France will thus be reestablished.

When the Allied armies enter France, the French High Command will insure order. The latter will provisionally appoint, by delegation from the Council, the military authority in each liberated department which will be responsible for both the execution of administrative functions and police powers within the framework of the law. These appointments will in their essence be of a non-political character.

The executive committee and the necessary administrative groups will proceed to France in order to insure the administration of the territories, the feeding of the population, etc. The Council will appeal for the cooperation of representative Frenchmen in the liberated zones. The committee will immediately reestablish French legislation in accordance with the laws of the Republic, following the principles and the practices already in force in North Africa. The similarity of the legal establishments in the Algerian departments and those of metropolitan departments will facilitate these measures. The fundamental liberties will be restored.

In each department the Conseil Général, reconstituted in conformity with the legislation in force on June 22, 1940, will assist the committee and the provisional departmental authorities. It will constitute the main assembly. In the cases of those Conseilers Généraux who have been compromised through their relation with the enemy, necessary steps will, of course, be taken to exclude them in the interest of national unity.

1872 LAW TO BE INVOKED: When all of the departments of Metropolitan France are liberated, the law of February 15, 1872 (the Tréveneuc Law), will be applied. The entry in force of this law provides the only means of giving France at the time of its liberation the indispensable lawful political authority which is provided by French legislation.

In fact, the law of February 15, 1872, applies when the lawful powers of the government and the National Assembly have ceased to exist. An assembly of the delegates of the Conseils Généraux, as provided by the law of February 15, 1872, the text of which is attached, "is charged with taking, in all of France, those urgent measures required for the maintenance of order and in particular those which have as their object the restoration to the National Assembly of its full independence and exercise of its rights. The Assembly will make provisional arrangements for the general administration of the country."

The assembly of the delegates of the Conseils Généraux will meet in a place to be determined. The first act of this assembly will be to provide for a provisional government. The provisional government will then exercise its powers and will be the lawful political authority of France until the election of the National Assembly. It will represent France in the Allied councils, as mentioned above. From the time of its constitution it will have authority over the Commander-in-Chief and the Council will deliver its powers to it.

The assembly of the delegates of the Conseils Généraux will also arrange general elections, setting the date thereof, and will specify that the National Assembly to be elected will have the task of establishing the new Constitution of France. The formula should be as broad as possible. The date of the elections should be so fixed as to make it certain that the prisoners and the workers in Germany will have returned home, that French liberties, as set forth above, will all be reestablished and that this essential popular consultation will be put into operation under conditions of peace and confidence in the future.

When the National Assembly is in session, the French people make their own decisions and all prevision ceases.

(5) *Note from the French National Committee to General Giraud, April 15, 1943* [1]

[Translation]

The French National Committee, having carefully read the memorandum that General Giraud sent to it in answer to its own memorandum of February 23, notes with satisfaction that there is agreement on certain essential points.

General Giraud admits, in effect, that the armistice is null and void; he recognizes that the exercise of French sovereignty has been suspended by the constitution of a government under enemy control and that consequently the Vichy legislation must be abolished; he proclaims invalid any oath of allegiance to one man; he affirms, finally, that the central power to be formed outside Metropolitan France can be only

[1] *Free France*, III (1943), p. 285; *New York Times*, April 22, 1943.

the servant of the French people, to whom it will give back its powers on the day of liberation so that the nation may, freely and by herself, decide her destiny.

General Giraud desires that the war should be continued in close collaboration with all the Allies, that the central power to be formed should represent the permanent interests of the nation among foreign nations, that it should obtain for France recognition as an Allied power, that it should administer liberated colonial and metropolitan territories and exercise in them full French sovereignty, at the same time granting to the Allied armies the rights and facilities necessary to the pursuit of the common war.

These are the very principles that since June 18, 1940, have served as immutable bases of action for the course taken in the French war effort by General de Gaulle and the French National Committee, principles that they have never failed to apply.

About the application of these principles, as it is envisaged by General Giraud, the French National Committee, certain of being in agreement with the general feeling of the nation, has formulated the following observations:

1. There must be a complete abolition of Vichy legislation and no existing situation must stand in the way of the moral recovery required by the people of France. Groups inspired by totalitarian ideologies such as the Légion des Combattants [War Veterans Legion], must be immediately and effectively dissolved. On the other hand, the fact that the so-called armistice is null and void implies, in particular, that the main positions of authority cannot be given to men who have had a personal responsibility in the capitulation and the collaboration with the enemy.

2. At the time of the liberation the departmental administrators should not be appointed by the military authority. Such a proviso would be, in fact, contrary to law and would not be accepted by the French population, organized for resistance, which knows the local situation and whose feelings should not be ignored. The prefectoral authority must issue from the central authority and not from the Commander-in-Chief of the Army.

3. Having to exercise French sovereignty in the liberated territories, having to represent the permanent interests of the nation abroad and having to direct the war effort of France by a unification of all the forces fighting at home or outside the national territory, the central authority acts not only in the name of and for the Empire, but also in the name of and for the whole nation. It must therefore play, in fact and by interim, the role of a governmental agency. A complete distinction must exist between the central authority and the agencies of executive administration, such as Governors, residents, etc. These are subordinated to the central authority and act upon its instructions. They

should not be party to it. They come under this authority through the intermediary of the ministerial departments under which they normally come in the republican regime. However, the advisory council of the Empire, composed of the residents and Governors and of competent persons, should give its advice on the general problems concerning the life, administration and defense of the Empire.

4. Furthermore, the actual commander-in-chief or the actual commanders-in-chief of the armies must be subordinated to the central authority and should not participate in it. To add the functions of commander-in-chief to those of member of the central authority would be contrary to the Constitution and to the 1938 law concerning the organization of the nation in wartime, as well as to the secular tradition of the French State — with the sole exception of the period of the Consulate and of the Napoleonic Empire. Such a regime would certainly be disavowed by the French people after the experience that they had with the personal power, both civilian and military, imposed by Vichy.

5. The French National Committee is convinced of the necessity of avoiding abuses of power. A legal council should pass on the legality of the decrees and administrative decisions according to the procedures on the excess of power. A national advisory council must be constituted — as indicated by the French National Committee in its memorandum of February 23 — to provide the means for the expression of Frenchmen's opinion in so far as they can express themselves in the present circumstances.

6. To sum up, the French National Committee, in accordance with the spirit of French institutions, believes that the central provisional authority must be established and must include the essential ministerial departments that have traditionally constituted the agencies of the French Government; the heads of these departments would have, in fact and by interim, the individual and collective functions normally given to Ministers.

As to the choice and appointments of persons in the aforesaid framework, this will have to be discussed and settled on French soil and among Frenchmen. Since December 25, 1942, the French National Committee has considered it necessary that its President and several of its members be given the opportunity to go to Algiers.

(6) *Letter from General Giraud to General de Gaulle, April 27, 1943* [1]

[Translation]

General Catroux has handed me the text of the note setting forth the views of the National Committee with respect to my *aide-mémoire* of

[1] *Free France*, III (1943), p. 315; *New York Times*, May 10, 1943.

April 1.[1] The object of the latter was to draw up the principles and the program of action for the establishment of the unity of our efforts, which is so vital to France.

(1) The National Committee's note makes interesting observations in regard to the *aide-mémoire*. The annex to this letter [2] answers these observations and contains proposals to resolve the differences in regard to the settlement of the present situation of fact, division of labors, etc. I have no doubt that we can rapidly reach an understanding on all these questions. As regards the settlement of our personal positions, I accept the proposal that General Catroux made to me and include it in the annexed note.

(2) There is one point on which our complete agreement is essential — namely, that the French people, from the moment of their liberation, should establish a provisional government by legislative means under the indispensable legitimate authority derived from the fact of its origin in law. In order to solve this fundamental problem, the *aide-mémoire* of April 1 proposed to insure the return to legality at the time of the re-entry into France by leaving the appointment of the provisional government to an assembly of delegates from the Conseils Généraux in conformity with the Tréveneuc Law of February 15, 1872. Frenchmen drew up this law to defend themselves against arbitrary action at a time when they were anxious to maintain their liberties. For my part, after studying the situation carefully, I see no other way for France, in accord with its laws, to return to a normal, legitimate and free regime. We cannot leave this path, because others would lead us into unknown dangers.

Since the National Committee, in its note of April 15,[3] offered no objection to this course, I have no doubt of obtaining its full agreement on this question, which is at the same time a point of departure for our union and the goal of our common efforts.

Consequently, I consider that one of the first acts of the Council, as soon as it is established, must be to address a proclamation to the people of France that will give solemn undertaking to the nation that the law of February 15, 1872, will be put into operation when French territory has been liberated under the conditions set forth in my memorandum of April 1. Our agreement on those principles conforms with the spirit of the undertakings of our allies to restore to France her integrity, her liberties and her territory. The French people will be informed in advance of the stages by which the country will recover its rights, will take comfort in these assurances for the future and have new reasons for confidence and hope. We shall thus give assurances of the disinterestedness of the Council and the proof of its will to re-establish republican laws and to be governed by them. Doubts and fears will disappear.

---

[1] See this volume, p. 574.   [2] *Ibid.*, p. 583.   [3] *Ibid.*, p. 579.

(3) Since we have now exchanged views of essential points, I believe that we should now reach our agreement by means of direct conversation. This work can be done rapidly together. I therefore propose to you that we should meet as soon as it is possible for you after May 5 at Marrakesh or Biskra. When it is known that our agreement has been reached we can return together to Algiers and begin to work without reticence or reserve.

In order that our conversations may retain the character that they should have, I suggest that each of us should be accompanied only by indispensable collaborators, two or three at the most.

(a) Proposals on French Unity Contained in Annex to Letter from General Giraud to General de Gaulle, April 27, 1943 [1]

[Translation]

I. SETTLEMENT OF THE PRESENT SITUATION IN FACT

A. THE COUNCIL

1. *Composition.* The council will be formed of secretaries of departments, Governors, Resident Generals, etc., and qualified individuals without special administrative functions. Within this council, a small executive committee will be created, composed of de Gaulle and Giraud, the secretaries general of the departments essential for the war effort, and a few individuals without administrative posts. The executive committee will meet periodically and have the responsibility for the general direction of affairs. The committee should have collective responsibility and discuss all essential decisions. The choice of original members would be decided between Giraud and de Gaulle and afterward any new or additional appointment would be made by the full council.

2. *Our Respective Positions.* The two generals shall preside in turn over the meetings of the committee and of the council. There is no question of a duumvirate. On the contrary, their responsibilities are merged in the collective responsibility of the committee and of the council. They shall sign decrees together and participate on the same level as the other members in the deliberations and decisions of the two bodies.

3. *The Council and the Future Provisional Government.* The distinction must be maintained between a council having its origin in necessity and a provisional government resulting from the laws of France. The council will represent a national effort and will continue to depend for the liberation of France on American and British assistance. Liberated France, represented by persons accredited by a provisional government,

[1] *Free France,* III (1943), p. 316; *New York Times,* May 11, 1943.

will have its historic place equal to that of England, the United States and Russia.

4. *Relations Between the Council and the Commander-in-Chief.* Giraud recognizes that it is in accordance with the tradition of France to subordinate the Commander-in-Chief to the central power. However, the present exceptional circumstances justify and make necessary the participation in the council of the Commander-in-Chief.

B. ABOLITION OF VICHY LEGISLATION

It must be complete. Giraud proclaimed it on March 14. It is only in order to insure public order and the continued functioning of the administration and life of the community that the rules and regulations made since June 22, 1940, are to be reviewed.

C. TOTALITARIAN ASSOCIATIONS

These should be suppressed or prohibited. The Légion des Combattants [War Veterans Legion] will be dissolved at once.

D. PEOPLE WHO HAVE TAKEN PART IN THE CAPITULATION OR HAVE COLLABORATED WITH THE ENEMY

The question of individuals is to be examined and decided by the executive committee. By "collaboration" should be understood the action of those who by their attitudes or actions have helped the enemy. One should not include in this term Frenchmen who have resisted the enemy while remaining at their posts and whose task has often been more difficult than those who have left France and served her abroad.

E. CONSULTATIVE BODIES

Full account has been taken of the remarks of the French National Committee's memorandum on this point and it is proposed (1) to create a national advisory committee; (2) to change the functions of the Supreme Council of Legislation; (3) to create a committee for the coordination of resistance; (4) to establish an information committee.

1. *National Advisory Committee.* While it is important to keep in close touch with French public opinion and representative organizations in the Empire, care should be taken not to give to any bodies that we set up the appearance of elected bodies. These can be only advisory. Giraud suggests that the advisory committee be composed of sixty to eighty members, divided into sections — for example, finance, agriculture, et cetera. The sections will meet periodically. They would also meet in plenary session.

2. *Supreme Council on Legislation.* One has already been set up in Algiers to insure that legislation and executive action are in conformity with the laws of June 22, 1940. It is composed of a permanent committee of three members and of persons appointed on account of their functions

in North African territories. The permanent committee, whose president alone has so far been chosen, could be transformed into a body having definite jurisdiction and decide appeals in cases of abuse of power in conformity with the procedure followed before the Conseil d'État.

3. *Committee for the Coordination of Resistance.* Giraud agrees with the National Committee's proposal for the constitution of such a committee, composed of representatives of resistance groups and of persons qualified to deal with the military and other questions involved in the organization and maintenance of resistance in France.

4. *Information Committee.* This would include representatives of French resistance.

II. PROGRAM OF ACTION FOR THE RETURN TO FRANCE

There is a misunderstanding in Paragraph Two of the National Committee's memorandum of April 15. The intention was that, when the Allied armies entered France, the French Commander-in-Chief should be responsible to the Allied High Command for the maintenance of order in the liberated territories and that he should be empowered by the Council to specify the military authority temporarily charged with the prefectural duties and police powers. It is understood that the departmental administration will not be nominated by the military authority. Giraud's original formula assumed the application of the legislation concerning the state of siege.

It follows:

A. That, as the French military authority will take responsibility for the maintenance of order to the Allied High Command, the Allied armies will, in the eyes of the French people, be unmistakably armies of liberation and not occupying troops.

B. That the departmental administration is not nominated by the military authority. In every case the central power will appoint the prefects. The Conseil Général and the Commission Départementale, being elected bodies, will be composed of the members functioning on June 22, 1940, subject to those who may be subsequently eliminated according to the normal procedure.

C. Application of the Tréveneuc Law: The procedure of this law to be followed as indicated in my memorandum of April 1.

(7) *Declaration Communicated by General Giraud to the American Minister (Murphy) and the British Minister (Macmillan) in North Africa, April 28, 1943* [1]

[Translation]

As regards this period I consider myself bound by the provisions of French law that are explained in my *aide-mémoire* of April 1 and my

---

[1] *Free France*, III (1943), p. 318; *New York Times*, May 11, 1943.

letter of April 27 to General de Gaulle. These provisions give to Frenchmen guarantees for the preservation of their liberties and for the rapid constitution of a provisional government, which it is our strictest duty to maintain and respect.

I consider that it is essential that the Council, as soon as it is established, should address a proclamation to the French people on this subject. I have no doubt that there is complete agreement between General de Gaulle and myself on this point. However, in order to avoid any misunderstanding, I was anxious to define to you, as I did to General Georges Catroux yesterday, my position on this point.

(8) *Letter from General Giraud to General de Gaulle, May 17, 1943* [1]

[Translation]

In his reply of May 7 (10)[2] to General Giraud's letter and memorandum of April 27, General de Gaulle reaffirmed his view that the military authority should be subordinated to the civil authority, that the civil authority should be organized so as to be as representative as possible of French public opinion, and that the necessary consultations should be held at Algiers.

Thank you for your letter of May 10 which replies to my letter and memorandum of April 27.

This latest exchange of views convinces me that our preliminary discussions have come to an end and that the hour of action and of our common responsibilities has come. Time presses and, among other questions, the rapid fusion of all the French forces in a single army of victory is urgent.

I propose that we should pass to action and immediately bring about our union. The method is simple and can be rapid.

It is sufficient for us to form immediately the central executive committee and at the same time to record our agreement on its essential bases — namely, that its responsibility should be collective and that its life should be limited. Thus we shall conform to the tradition and to the laws of the Republic.

Thus established, the executive committee will meet immediately at Algiers.

The formation of the executive committee. The committee is the central authority. It possesses the general direction of and the responsibility for all matters at present within the scope of the National Committee or of the Civil and Military High Command at Algiers. It will discuss all the other questions that have been the subject of our exchange of views based on the notes that we have exchanged. In particular, it will organize the national consultative council and the committee on resistance, appoint the commissioners, fix their functions, etc.

[1] *Free France*, III (1943), p. 351; *New York Times*, May 24, 1943.
[2] *Free France*, III (1943), p. 318, gives the date of the reply as May 7, while in General Giraud's letter of May 17, the date is given as May 10.

The responsibility of the executive committee must be collective. All the essential decisions will be discussed and taken by the executive committee acting as a whole. In accordance with the proposal made by General Catroux, you and I will preside in turn; our responsibilities will be merged in the collective responsibility of the executive committee. With the commissioner or commissioners who may be responsible, we shall together sign the decrees or ordinances that may be discussed and decided in the committee.

The duration and the functions of the committee must be limited. In the action that we are now taking we are convinced that we are acting according to the wish of the French people. However, we must recognize that our authority derives from a situation of fact. We are not and cannot be the government of France.

As soon as the executive committee begins its functions, it should solemnly make known to the French people that it will hand over its powers to the provisional government that, as soon as the country has been liberated, will be constituted in France according to the Law of February 15, 1872. The application of this law is contemplated when the legislative assemblies have ceased to function, as is the case today, and can be adapted by having recourse to other elected bodies on the advice of the national consultative council and of the council of legislation, taking into account the changes brought about by the action of the enemy or by the development of the situation in France (i.e. since the Law of 1872 was passed).

If I have correctly represented the essential points of the subject, I beg you to give me the agreement on these points that is essential for the establishment of our union. At the same time we can rapidly agree upon the composition of the committee. To begin with, it will consist of two members proposed by you and two members proposed by me, making the first members of the executive committee six in all. I suggest that three places should be left vacant in order that the executive committee may fill them later.

D. Formation of French Committee of National Liberation

(1) Communiqué Announcing Formation of French Committee of National Liberation, Algiers, June 3, 1943 [1]

The Committee of National Liberation is constituted. It is comprised of Generals Giraud and de Gaulle as presidents, General Catroux, General Georges, MM. René Massigli, Jean Monnet and André Philip as members.

[1] *Free France*, III (1943), p. 387; *New York Times*, June 4, 1943.

Secondly: The committee nominated General Catroux, Commissioner for Coordination of Moslem Affairs.

Thirdly: The committee designated General Catroux, Commissioner of Moslem Affairs, as Governor General of Algeria.

Fourthly: The committee decided upon the nomination of General Bouscat as commander of air forces in North Africa and in French West Africa, replacing General Mendigal, who had already resigned by an earlier decision of the Commander-in-Chief.

Generals de Gaulle and Giraud as presidents, General Catroux, General Georges, MM. René Massigli, Jean Monnet, and André Philip, as members, constitute the French Committee of National Liberation. It will later be completed by the addition of other members.

The so-constituted committee is the French central power. The committee directs the French effort in the war in all forms and in all places. As a result it exercises French sovereignty on all territories placed beyond the enemies' power. It assures the administration and defense of all French interests in the world. It assumes authority over the territory, and the land, naval and air forces which have up to the present time been under the authority of either the French National Committee or under the civilian and military Commander-in-Chief.

All the measures necessary to a realization of the fusion of the administrations of these two organizations will be taken by the committee without delay. In conformity with the letters exchanged between Generals Giraud and de Gaulle, the committee will turn over its powers to the temporary government, which will be constituted in conformity with the laws of the Third Republic as soon as the liberation of the metropolitan territory permits it, and, at the latest, at the total liberation of France.

The committee will continue, in close cooperation with all the Allies, the common fight with a view to the integral liberation of the French territories and the Allied territories until the final victory over all the enemy powers. The committee solemnly commits itself to reestablish all the French liberties, the laws of the Republic and the republican regime, completely destroying the arbitrary regime and the personal power that is imposed on the country today.

The committee wishes to serve the people of France, for whom the war effort, the resistance, the trials, as well as the necessary renovation, require unity of all national forces. It calls all Frenchmen to follow it, so that France may take again in battle and in victory her liberty and her greatness and her traditional place among the great Allied powers, and so that in the peace negotiations she may bring her contribution to the council of the United Nations, which will determine the conditions of Europe and the world after the war.

(2) *Reception Accorded by the Secretary of State (Hull) to Representatives of the French Committee of National Liberation. Department of State Release, June 9, 1943* [1]

Acting under instructions from the French National Council of Liberation sitting at Algiers, Messrs. Hoppenot and Baudet have formally informed the Secretary of State of the formation of the Council and of the transfer to it of all the functions heretofore carried on by the elements composing it.

Secretary Hull replied that, as was well known, this Government had continuously hoped for the unification of all French resistants in a common effort against Axis aggression wherever it might be found throughout the world. He warmly welcomed, therefore, the spirit in which the French National Council of Liberation had been formed.

Concluding, the Secretary expressed his deep appreciation of the spirit of sacrifice which had made the union of true French interests possible and added the conviction that the same spirit would continue to animate all Frenchmen in meeting the problems still to be faced for the liberation of continental France.

(3) *Statement of the British Prime Minister (Churchill) to the House of Commons, June 9, 1943* [2]

Formation of this committee, with its collective responsibility, supersedes the situation created by the correspondence between General de Gaulle and myself in 1940. Our dealings, financial and otherwise, will henceforward be with the committee as a whole.

There is a further and larger question, namely, the degree of recognition of this committee as representatives of France. These questions require consideration from the British and the United States Governments, but if things go well I should hope that a solution satisfactory to all parties may shortly be reached.

D. Finland

[See *Documents, IV, 1941–42*, p. 637.]

The United States Government has attempted throughout the war to preserve friendly relations with Finland and at the same time to obtain the withdrawal of Finland from the war against the Soviet Union. At first the Government followed methods of diplomatic persuasion in its efforts to terminate the hostilities between the Soviet Union and Finland.[3] But as the gravity of the Russian

---

[1] Department of State, *Bulletin*, VIII, p. 514.
[2] *New York Times*, June 10, 1943.
[3] See *Documents, IV, 1941–42*, p. 642.

military situation on the Eastern Front during the summer of 1942 increased and Russian pressure for a rupture of American-Finnish relations reportedly became more insistent,[1] relations between the two Governments steadily deteriorated.

(1) Cancellation of Consular Representation between Finland and the United States. Department of State Release, July 16, 1942 [2]

Under the terms of Article XXIII of the Treaty of Commerce and Consular Rights of February 13, 1934 between Finland and the United States of America,[3] American consular officers "may, within their respective consular districts, address the authorities, National, State, Provincial or Municipal, for the purpose of protecting their countrymen in the enjoyment of their rights accruing by treaty or otherwise."

However, in a note dated July 17, 1941 the Finnish Foreign Ministry informed the American Legation in Helsinki that "in view of wartime conditions" consular matters should be handled entirely through the Finnish Foreign Ministry rather than directly with local authorities. This action of the Finnish Foreign Ministry had the direct effect of denying to American consular officers in Finland the specific treaty rights mentioned above.

Furthermore, the Finnish Foreign Ministry in a note dated July 9, 1942 informed the American Legation that with reference to the Foreign Ministry's note of July 17, 1941 it was preferable to postpone to a subsequent date the question of an exequatur for a career officer of the American Foreign Service whom the American Government had recently commissioned as a vice consul in Helsinki and for whom the American Legation had requested provisional recognition in accordance with established custom in such cases.

The American Legation, acting on instructions from its Government, informed the Finnish Foreign Ministry in a note dated July 16, 1942 that the request which the American Legation had made for the provisional recognition of the consular officer referred to above was withdrawn. The Legation further informed the Finnish Foreign Ministry that by the latter's action in regard to the withholding of recognition of the consular officer referred to and in denying American consular officers presently in Finland their treaty rights in connection with the representation of American interests in Finland the Finnish Government had undermined the basis upon which American consular representation was maintained in Finland. Accordingly, the Foreign Ministry was informed that the consular commissions of the American consular officers at present in Finland had been canceled and the consular section of the

---

[1] *New York Times*, July 17, 1942.

[2] Department of State, *Bulletin*, VII, p. 632.

[3] *Treaties, Conventions*, etc. IV, 1923–37, p. 4138.

American Legation in Helsinki was being closed immediately, and that this action had been taken by the American Government to put an end to the present untenable situation involved in maintaining American consular representation in Finland in the face of the attitude adopted by the Finnish Government in the matter. The Finnish Government was requested by the American Legation to close all Finnish consular offices in the United States not later than August 1, 1942.

The Finnish Government continued to express a desire to maintain peaceful relations with the United States. In this country Hjalmar J. Procopé, Finnish Minister, attempted to make public the Finnish case for the war with the Soviet Union. On September 19, he stated that Finland "wants to cease fighting as soon as the threat to her existence has been averted and guarantees obtained for her lasting security." [1] He emphasized especially that Finland had entered the war "not owing to any alliances or political commitments, but because she was forced by the Communist attack"; that she sought no imperialistic ends; that her political and social system had not changed to a fascist dictatorship, and that Finland's hope for the future lay in keeping "her land in her own hands until a lasting peace built up on real guarantees comes." [2]

Finnish Prime Minister J. W. Rangell, in a press conference on December 31, 1942, flatly declared that "Finland will never declare war on the United States of America. I hope that nothing will happen during the coming year to give America any reason to take the step of declaring war against our country. . . ." [2]

"Our relations with the American people have long been so good that they should understand the situation in which we find ourselves through no fault of our own." [3]

The breach had already widened still farther, however, when the State Department ordered that the Finnish Information Center in New York cease issuing news releases and pamphlets, and stated that the American Legation in Helsinki had stopped sending out bulletins and material furnished by the Office of War Information. [4]

Finnish President Risto Ryti summarized the situation in an address to the closing session of the 1942 session of the Riksdag: [5]

"An unfortunate influence on our relations with the United States arises from the delicate circumstance that while we fight a defensive war against the Soviet Union, the United States has become Russia's ally, while Germany and her ally, our brothers-in-arms, are locked in a war against the Soviet Union and have therefore also been precipitated into a war with the United States. . . . Thus consular relations have been broken [but] . . . diplomatic relations are still maintained and we warmly hope that our relations with the United States will again become as good and confident as they had been in the past."

Nevertheless, even the status of diplomatic relations was poor, since H. F. Arthur Schoenfeld, United States Minister to Finland, was called home for consultation in December 1942 and did not return. [5]

Soon after the presidential election in Finland, Under Secretary of State Sumner Welles expressed the hope that the Government of Finland would cease

[1] *New York Times*, September 22, 1942.
[2] *Ibid.*, January 4, 1943. [3] *Ibid.*, January 5, 1943.
[4] *Ibid.*, December 30, 1942. [5] *Ibid.*, January 27, 1943.

giving military aid on the side of Germany (February 23, 1943). In effect he implied that Washington believed that the Finnish people desired peace more strongly than their Government, and that he hoped that the new government would be more in line with popular sentiment in Finland.[1]

But relations grew even more strained in April 1943, when the State Department suddenly ordered the reduction of the American Legation staff in Helsinki to a single diplomatic official (Robert M. McClintock, chargé d'affaires) and a small clerical force.[2] The State Department offered only the explanation that this was "an administrative move" arising out of the general situation. As the start of the spring and summer campaigns in Russia grew near, the State Department repeatedly made known its concern over the continued military aid given by Finland to Germany, especially because of Finland's position on the flank of the northern supply route to the Soviet Union.[2]

In spite of such increasingly bad relations, however, the Finnish Minister in Washington, Mr. Procopé, continued at his post and the Finnish Government maintained its uninterrupted record of paying semi-annual installments on its World War I relief debt to the United States.

E. Portugal

The day after the American invasion of French North Africa on November 7, 1942, the President of the United States released to the press the text of a message which he had sent to the President of the Republic of Portugal, General Antonio Oscar de Gragoso Carmona, in order to reassure the Portuguese Government that American military operations were in no way to be considered a threat to any part of Portuguese territory.

(1) Message of the President (Roosevelt) to the President of Portugal (Carmona), Released to the Press, November 8, 1942 [3]

MY DEAR MR. PRESIDENT:

The Republic of Portugal and the United States of America have long enjoyed the full and complete friendship of each other. Because of this great friendship, and our mutual desire to insure its continuation, I desire to relate to you the urgent reasons that have compelled me to despatch to the assistance of the friendly French Possessions in North Africa a strong Army of the United States.

I have been advised by very reliable sources of information that in the near future it is the intention of Germany and Italy to occupy the French North African Colonies with a large military force.

I know that it will be quite clear to you that prompt and effective action should be taken to deter such an attempt by the Axis Nations, with its inherent danger to the defenses of the Western Hemisphere.

To forestall occupation by the Axis Nations of the French North African Possessions and Protectorates, and thus to insure the defense of American Nations, is the only reason which prompts the despatch of powerful United States forces to the Area. It is hoped that French

---

[1] Ibid., February 24, 1943.   [2] Ibid., April 24, 1943.
[3] Department of State, Bulletin, VII, p. 905.

North Africa will not suffer in any way from the destruction of war on its own soil.

I desire to reassure you fully that the presence of American Military Forces in French North Africa presages in no manner whatsoever, a move against the people or Government of Portugal or against any of Portugal's Continental or Island Possessions. Since I realize that Portugal really desires above all else to avoid the horrors and devastation of war, I hope that you will accept my solemn assurance that your country should have no fear of the motives of the United Nations.

(2) *Message of the President of Portugal (Carmona) to the President of the United States (Roosevelt), November 12, 1942* [1]

MR. PRESIDENT:

I received from the hands of His Excellency the United States Minister the message with which Your Excellency honored me, conveying to me the motives for the military operations undertaken in French North Africa.

In the same message it was Your Excellency's wish in view of that new fact again to assure me categorically that the presence of military American forces in the North of Africa do not forebode any attempt against the people and Government of Portugal or against Continental or Insular Portugal.

I do not wish to lose any time in thanking Your Excellency for the friendly tenor and spirit of your communication and further for the solemn assurances that my country has nothing to fear from the intentions of the United States, which is another proof of the unalterable and confident friendship existing between our two nations.

The Government and the people of Portugal learned with sincere appreciation of the contents of the message and join me in conveying to Your Excellency the thanks and the wishes I hereby express for Your Excellency's personal prosperities and those of your people.

Following the passage of United Nations military planes over Portuguese territory as a result of the exigencies of the Allied campaign in North Africa, the Portuguese Government made a diplomatic protest on November 17, 1942, to both the United States and British Governments.[2] The Government of Portugal maintained a position of strict neutrality at all times and on January 15, 1943 eleven American fighter planes and their crews were interned when they were forced to land at the Lisbon airport.[3]

[1] *Ibid.*
[2] *New York Times*, November 18, 1942.
[3] *Ibid.*, January 16, 1943.

F. Spain

On August 28, 1942, President Roosevelt announced a plan to rehabilitate the art treasures, the manuscripts, literature, and famous buildings of Spain, and to encourage the movement of tourists from the twenty-one American Republics to Spain. The President qualified his statement, however, with the warning that such a plan was predicated on the Spanish Government's remaining neutral in the war, "as this country hoped it would remain." [1]

(1) *Message from the Head of the Spanish State (Franco) to the President of the United States (Roosevelt), Released to the Press, November 13, 1942* [2]

Immediately following landings by American troops in North Africa, President Roosevelt addressed a letter to the head of the Spanish State, Generalissimo Francisco Franco, which duplicated his assurances to Portugal.[3] General Franco had reportedly informed both the Axis and the United Nations that Spain immediately would accept aid from the other side if any of her sea and air bases were seized.[4] On November 19, 1942, the Spanish Ambassador in Washington, acting under instructions from the Spanish Foreign Office, had reiterated to Under Secretary of State Welles the attitude of his Government in its continued maintenance of absolute neutrality.[4]

MY DEAR MR. PRESIDENT:

I have received from the hands of your Ambassador the letter in which, actuated by the relations of friendship which unite our peoples, and which in their benefit should be preserved, you explain to me the reasons which induced Your Excellency to send troops of the American Army to occupy the territories of the French possessions and protectorates in North Africa.

I accept with pleasure and I thank you for the assurances which Your Excellency offers the Government and the people of Spain to the effect that the measures adopted are not in any manner directed against their interests, or against their territories, metropolitan or overseas, or against the protectorate in Morocco, and I confidently hope that the relations among the Moroccan peoples of both zones likewise will in the future be maintained in the same spirit of peace and of reciprocal confidence which have characterized them up to now.

I can assure you that Spain knows the value of peace and sincerely desires peace for itself and for all other peoples.

On this occasion I am pleased to reciprocate the same friendly sentiments you expressed to me and to express my intention of avoiding anything which might disturb our relations in any of their aspects, and I reiterate with a salutation the expression of my personal esteem and sincere friendship.

[1] *Ibid.*, August 29, 1942.
[2] Department of State, *Bulletin*, VII, p. 906.
[3] *Ibid.*
[4] *New York Times*, November 20, 1942.

(2) *United States Trade with Spain. Statement of the Acting Secretary of State (Welles), March 1, 1943* [1]

Speaking on the twenty-fifth anniversary of the American Chamber of Commerce in Madrid, on February 26, 1943, Carlton J. H. Hayes, United States Ambassador to Spain, asserted that the amount of petroleum products available in Spain at that time was "considerably higher than the present per capita distribution to the people of the Atlantic Seaboard of the United States itself"; [2] he also mentioned that the United States was exporting cotton, food, and other products to Spain. Discussing the general line of American policy toward Spain and the purposes behind it, Ambassador Hayes was reported to have declared: [3]

"The United States stands ready to continue and extend any help it can to Spain, which itself is doing so much with such obvious success to develop a peace economy that can, and will, carry this country safely into a future of world peace. . . . Our foreign policy for ten years long has been the policy of the good neighbor. . . . The good neighbor policy in the international field cannot be effective unless it is reciprocal. . . . My Government is convinced that this [aid to Spain] is a much more efficacious and sensible way of eradicating those social and political inequalities which in the past have given rise to such phenomena as Nazism and Communism. The complete prosperity of the Iberian peninsula awaits only freer access to raw materials and markets. These materials and markets will be available to Spain after hostilities cease."

Bearing upon Ambassador Hayes' remarks concerning petroleum exports the State Department revealed on the same day that all Spanish oil supplies had been moved in Spanish tankers from the Caribbean area rather than in United States ships or from the United States proper. [3]

In an effort to clarify American policy toward Spain, Under Secretary Welles gave a statement to the press on March 1, 1943.

At the time American forces landed in North Africa the President gave the Spanish Government unqualified assurances that no action would be taken by our forces which would call for any departure by the Spanish Government from its position of neutrality in the war. The Spanish Government, on our invitation, gave us unqualified assurances that for its part the Spanish Government was determined to continue its policy of neutrality and that it would resist by force any external aggression against its territories from whatever source.

Our trade with Spain is a two-way trade, and there are certain commodities in Spain which are needed in our war effort. It is naturally in our interest that those Spanish commodities needed in this country should reach the United States rather than fall into enemy hands, and to accomplish this a trade program is necessary. The trade program with Spain has been carefully reviewed by the Joint Chiefs of Staff.

Trade between the United States and Spain is of course subject to the control system jointly maintained by the United States and the British Governments, since the British are likewise engaged in a two-way trade program with Spain. The interchange of goods with Spain is a matter of joint discussion and programing between United States

[1] Department of State, *Bulletin*, VIII, p. 201.
[2] *New York Times*, February 27, 1943.
[3] *Ibid.*

and British authorities. Before any goods from outside of Spain are permitted by the United States and British authorities to proceed to their destination the fullest assurances satisfactory to both the British and the United States Governments must be given by the importers and the Spanish Government that the goods will not be allowed to reach enemy hands, directly or indirectly.

As regards wartime trade between the United States and Spain, it must be recognized that this trade can be maintained only to such extent as both countries believe to be in their respective national interests. Naturally in the case of the United States all considerations in respect to foreign trade are definitely subordinated to the conduct of the war.

Spain requires a determinable minimum amount of petroleum from the Western Hemisphere to maintain her economic life. The carefully restricted quantity of petroleum which has been cleared by the two Governments destined to Spain has with the exception of packaged lubricants been obtained from sources outside of the United States and has been transported exclusively in Spanish tankers. This had had no effect whatsoever on the quantity of petroleum available to any consumers in the United States. The restricted volume of petroleum imports into Spain has provided for minimum current needs and makes the accumulation of stocks impossible. No petroleum products of aviation grade have been included.

(3) *Exportation of Petroleum Products. Letter of the Under Secretary of State (Welles) to the Chairman of the House Committee on Foreign Affairs (Bloom), March 11, 1943* [1]

Congressional criticism of the Government's petroleum export policy resulted in a resolution by the House of Representatives requesting the President to furnish information as to the amount of petroleum products sent to Spain. In response to Under Secretary of State Welles' letter of March 11 to the Committee on Foreign Affairs giving such information together with an explanation of the Government's policy, the Committee reported unfavorably upon the resolution.[2]

In a letter of April 2, 1943 to Professor Perry of Harvard University,[3] Mr. Welles commented further on American policy toward Spain:

"It is always easier in wartime to make enemies than friends. We do not share, of course, the social and political philosophy of the Spanish State. But the Spanish people and the Spanish economy are capable of helping. There are certain commodities in Spain which are needed in our war effort. The trade program in Spain has been carefully reviewed by the Joint Chiefs of Staff and is subject to the control system maintained jointly by the United States and Great Britain, which carries on similar trade and for similar purposes."

My Dear Mr. Bloom:

Your letter of March 8 enclosing copies of House Resolution 150 requesting the President to furnish the House information as to the

---

[1] Department of State, *Bulletin*, VIII, p. 218.
[2] House Report No. 245, 78th Cong., 1st sess.
[3] Department of State, *Bulletin*, VIII, p. 321.

amount of petroleum products sent to Spain, which has been referred to the Committee on Foreign Affairs, has been received.

The exportation of petroleum products to Spain from the United States during the past 2 years have been: 1941, 227,347 metric tons; 1942, 17,771 metric tons. These are the only shipments made from the United States in the last 2 years. The last bulk shipment from this country occurred on February 19, 1942.

However, by arrangement between the Governments of the United States and Great Britain, Spain has been permitted in her own vessels to carry through the blockade certain limited quantities of oil bought by Spain in South American ports and transported under the Spanish flag. The movement envisaged in the arrangement was estimated to meet essential needs, especially public utilities and transportation. Under this procedure Spain does not have in stock at any one time a supply for those minimum needs for longer than a 60-day period with respect to any petroleum products except lubricating oil, of which a 90-day limited supply is allowed. Adequate guarantees have been furnished by the Spanish Government to satisfy the British and United States Governments that none of these petroleum products will leave Spain or Spanish territories. The arrangement for the shipment of these quantities of oil was for the purpose of permitting the continuance at a minimum level of the economic life of Spain, Spanish Morocco, and Spain's island possessions in the Atlantic. The program of shipments has received the approval of the Joint Chiefs of Staff.

No future sales to Spain from the United States are in contemplation except small quantities of lubricating oils unobtainable in South America.

Any future shipments by Spain from South America will be subject to the agreement of the British and American Governments and the approval of the Joint Chiefs of Staff.

As can be seen from the foregoing, the transportation of petroleum products in Spanish vessels from ports outside of the United States has no relation to the quantity of petroleum products available to the eastern seaboard of this country.

2. THE OCCUPIED TERRITORIES

A. The Governments-in-Exile

During the period from July 1, 1942, to June 30, 1943, there was no significant change in the status of Governments-in-Exile of occupied European territories. The heads of certain of these governments — King Peter II of Yugoslavia, Queen Wilhelmina of the Netherlands, and President Beneš of Czechoslovakia — made visits to this country, in the course of which they were the official guests of President Roosevelt in Washington and problems of mutual concern were discussed.

On the question of Lend-Lease aid to Governments-in-Exile, see p. 215. For text of Mutual Aid Agreement of July 1, 1942 with the Government of

Poland and information regarding other agreements with Governments-in-Exile, see p. 217. A Supplementary agreement was entered into on July 11, 1942, with the Government of Norway regarding the Norwegian merchant fleet (see p. 228).

B. Territorial and Other Problems

On the question of Polish-Soviet relations, see this volume, p. 531.

The position of the United States with regard to the restoration of the political independence and territorial integrity of the occupied countries has been indicated by repeated reassertions of the principle of non-recognition, by numerous statements made by the President, the Secretary of State, and the Under Secretary of State, by our support of the principles of the Atlantic Charter.

C. Relief to Occupied Countries

The position of the Government of the United States with regard to the supplying of relief to occupied countries was stated in a letter from Secretary of State Hull to Senator George, June 19, 1941.[1] An exception to the general practice has been made in the case of Greece.[2] The following two Department of State releases give essential facts regarding the operation of the program of Greek relief.

On steps taken by the Government of the United States with a view to organizing work of relief and rehabilitation in occupied areas, and proposals made for a United Nations Relief and Rehabilitation Administration, see p. 285.

(1) Greek Relief. Department of State Release, August 7, 1942 [3]

On the initiative of the Swedish Red Cross, negotiations were undertaken some months ago through the Swedish Government regarding relief for the starving population of Greece. The Swedish Government having expressed its willingness that Swedish vessels lying in Swedish ports be employed for this purpose, the United States, British, and Canadian Governments immediately declared themselves ready to authorize monthly shipments of 15,000 tons of wheat or flour from North America to Greece, subject to appropriate conditions governing the distribution of these imports and of Greek native produce in the interests of the Greek people and on the understanding that a neutral commission would receive the necessary control and reporting facilities from the occupying powers. Following the negotiations conducted by the Swedish Government, the German and Italian Governments agreed to this proposal. The belligerent powers have accordingly granted safe conducts for the voyages of the Swedish vessels which will be used. The first three, the *Formosa*, the *Eros*, and the *Camelia*, have already loaded and are scheduled to leave Montreal on August 7 for Greece. A Swedish-Swiss commission has been set up to handle the actual distribution of the supplies, under the general supervision of the existing organization of the International Red Cross Committee, in Greece.

[1] *Documents, IV, 1941–42*, p. 659.
[2] *Ibid.*, p. 660.
[3] Department of State, *Bulletin*, VII, p. 687.

The Greek Government, the American and Canadian Red Cross Societies, and the Greek War Relief Association are actively supporting and cooperating in the operation of this plan.

Reports reaching the Department of State from Greece have portrayed conditions of suffering from inanition and death from starvation appalling almost beyond belief.

Information has also been received through American officials recently returning from Europe confirming that the small quantities of foodstuffs which have been sent to Greece during the past year under the United Nations' auspices and with the cooperation of the Turkish Government have been effectively distributed through the agency of the International Red Cross Committee and consumed by the Greek people only. The reports of these officials indicate, however, that although these supplies have unquestionably saved many persons from death they have been inadequate to prevent further deterioration of the general food-supply situation.

(2) *Greek Relief. Department of State Release, April 19, 1943* [1]

Inquiries have been received by the State Department regarding the operation of the Greek-relief scheme, resulting from the publication in the press of a report alleging that "Greek refugees who have recently fled to North Africa have reported to American officials there that the leakage [of relief foodstuffs] into enemy hands has been nearly 40 percent."

No such reports have reached this Department or other interested agencies from any American Government or Red Cross officials in North Africa, or from any other source. On the contrary, this Government and the British Government have received regular reports through the Swedish Government, which has generously assumed responsibility for this scheme, under the general auspices of the International Red Cross Committee, confirming that the foodstuffs sent into Greece are being distributed to the Greek population without interference by the occupation authorities and that there has been no diversion of these supplies to the enemy. Furthermore, these reports indicate that the Axis authorities have entered into agreement with the Swedish-Swiss Relief Commission for the implementation of their pledge, given to the Swedish Government in connection with the negotiations preceding the initiation of the scheme, that Greek native produce would be reserved solely for normal peacetime residents of Greece except so far as local foodstuffs consumed by the armed forces or officials of the occupying powers are replaced by equivalent foodstuffs imported from Axis sources for the Greek population.

[1] *Ibid.*, VIII, p. 347.

This Government's approval of the Greek-relief scheme was announced to the press by the Department of State on August 7, 1942,[1] on which date the first of the eight Swedish vessels engaged for the purpose departed from Montreal for Piraeus. These vessels, charter-hire on which is now being met principally by this Government, are carrying monthly quantities of 15,000 tons of wheat donated by the Canadian Government; 3,000 tons of dried vegetables and 300 tons of evaporated milk supplied by this Government; medical supplies furnished principally by the American Red Cross; and miscellaneous supplies and equipment donated by the Greek War Relief Association.

These relief supplies are distributed to the Greek people by a Neutral Relief Commission of 30 Swedish and Swiss nationals under the chairmanship of the distinguished Swedish jurist, Emil Sandstrom. The Commission is aided in its task by some 800 carefully selected Greek employees.

To insure its independent mobility, the Commission has been supplied with its own motor vehicles. It is in a position to insure close surveillance and control over the distribution of all relief supplies received and to report fully thereon to this Government and the British Government, which will of course agree to the continuance of the scheme only so long as they are satisfied that it is not in fact benefiting the enemy.

D. Execution of Hostages and Other Acts of Cruelty

For the statement of President Roosevelt on August 21, 1942, regarding crimes against civilian populations in occupied countries, see p. 176. This was followed by a statement of the President on October 7, 1942, indicating the intention of the Government of the United States to cooperate with the United Nations Commission to Investigate War Crimes (see p. 177).

3. AFRICA AND WESTERN ASIA

A. Liberia

Shortly before the American invasion of North Africa on November 7, 1942, confirmation of reports was received that United States troops had been stationed since July in the Negro Republic of Liberia, situated 750 miles from Dakar at the strategic "Atlantic Narrows" where the bulge of Africa faces the bulge of Brazil.[2] On December 3 it was officially announced that a defense agreement was signed on March 31, 1942 at Monrovia by the Liberian Secretary of State (Simpson) and the Special Representative of the President of the United States (McBride). The Government of Liberia granted to the Government of the United States for the duration of the war the right to construct, control, operate, and defend airports in Liberia and to assist also in the protection and defense

[1] See this volume, p. 598.
[2] *New York Times*, November 5, 1942.

of any part of the Republic which might be liable to attack during the war. At the same time, by an exchange of letters between President Barclay and Lt. Col. McBride, the United States agreed to extend certain defense aids to the Government of Liberia and to assist in the improvement and extension of its road system.[1]

It was announced on December 3 that American forces, chiefly composed of Negro troops, were then stationed in Liberia in execution of the agreement, and that the German Consul and his staff had recently departed from Monrovia at the request of the Liberian Government, thus eliminating Axis interests from the country.[2]

The close and friendly relations between the two countries was further emphasized in January 1943 when President Roosevelt paused in Liberia on his way back from the Conference at Casablanca to visit President Barclay and review American troops.[3] The Liberian President returned the call in a visit to the White House in May.[4]

(1) Agreement between the Governments of the United States and Liberia, Signed March 31, 1942 [5]

WHEREAS:

The situation of Liberia is made critical by the existing war and there is danger of attack or aggression by unfriendly powers; and

2. additional protection is necessary in order that the independence and security of the Republic may be safeguarded; and

3. the Government of Liberia has requested that the Government of the United States because of its traditional friendly interest in the welfare of Liberia, give such aid as may be possible in the circumstances in the defense of the Republic; and

4. the Government of Liberia has granted the Government of the United States in this emergency the right to construct, control, operate and defend at the sole cost and expense of the latter and without charge to the Republic of Liberia, such military and commercial airports in the Republic as in consultation with the Government of the Republic of Liberia may mutually be considered necessary; and the right also to assist in the protection and defense of any part of the Republic which might be liable to attack during the present war, said grant to include the right to construct access roads from Monrovia to the airport at Roberts Field on the Farmington River and the seaplane facilities at Fisherman Lake in the County of Grand Cape Mount; and

[1] Department of State, *Bulletin*, VII, p. 979.
[2] *Ibid.*
[3] *New York Times*, January 29, 1943.
[4] *Ibid.*, May 29, 1943.
[5] Department of State, *Bulletin*, VII, p. 979. The text of the agreement was released to the press on December 3, 1942; *Executive Agreement Series* 275.

On June 8, 1943 the two Governments signed a Mutual Aid Agreement. The exchange of notes of the same date, confirmed the specific applications of the general principles of the agreement of March 31, 1942 (see this volume, p. 231).

5. the above-mentioned rights have been granted as of February 14, 1942 to become effective from that date and to remain in effect for the duration of the existing war and for a period not to exceed six months thereafter;

THEREFORE:

the undersigned to wit:

HARRY A. McBRIDE, Special Representative of the President of the United States of America, acting on behalf of the Government of the United States; and

CLARENCE L. SIMPSON, Secretary of State of the Republic of Liberia, acting on behalf of the Government of Liberia, have agreed as follows:

ARTICLE 1. The grants of rights specified above shall also include the right to improve and deepen channels, to construct connecting roads, communication services, fortifications, repair and storage facilities and housing for personnel, and generally the right to do any and all things necessary to insure the efficient operation, maintenance and protection of such defense facilities as may be established;

ARTICLE 2. The Republic of Liberia retains sovereignty over all such airports, fortifications and other defense areas as may be established under the rights above granted. The Government of the United States during the life of this Agreement shall have exclusive jurisdiction over any such airports and defense areas in Liberia and over the military and civilian personnel of the Government of the United States and their families within the airports, fortifications and other defense areas, as well as over all other persons within such areas except Liberian citizens.

It is understood, however, that the Government of the United States may turn over to the Liberian authorities for trial and punishment any person committing an offense in such defense areas. And the Liberian authorities will turn over to the United States authorities for trial and punishment any of the United States military or civilian personnel and their families who may commit offenses outside such defense areas. The Liberian authorities and the United States authorities will take adequate measures to insure the prosecution and punishment in cases of conviction of all such offenders, it being understood that the relevant evidence shall be furnished reciprocally to the two authorities.

ARTICLE 3. It is agreed that the Government of the United States shall have the right to establish and maintain postal facilities and commissary stores to be used solely by the military and civilian personnel of the United States Government and their families stationed in Liberia in connection with this Agreement and with such aid in the defense of Liberia as the Government of the United States may furnish.

ARTICLE 4. All materials, supplies and equipment for the construction, use and operation of said airports of the United States Government and for the personal needs of the military and civilian personnel and their families, shall be permitted entry into Liberia free of customs duties, excise taxes, or any other charges, and the said personnel and their families shall also be exempt from all forms of taxes, assessments and other levies by the Liberian Government and authorities, including exemption from Liberian regulations pertaining to passports, visas and residence permits.

The Government of the United States undertakes to respect all legitimate interests of Liberia and of Liberian citizens, as well as all the laws, regulations and customs relating to the native population and the internal administration of Liberia. In exercising the rights derived from this Agreement, the Government of the United States undertakes to give sympathetic consideration to all representations made by the Liberian authorities with respect to the welfare of the inhabitants of Liberia.

In respect of the commercial use of such airports, passengers, mail and cargo entering or leaving Liberia by air shall have transit over such airports to and from a Liberian customs station established adjacent to said airports and under the exclusive jurisdiction of the Government of Liberia.

ARTICLE 5. The Government of the United States undertakes to extend to the Government of Liberia such aid as may be possible in the circumstances in the protection of the Republic, including necessary equipment for road construction, certain monetary aids for defense purposes, certain assistance in the organization and training of the Liberian military forces and certain other assistance of a similar nature.

ARTICLE 6. The Government of the United States undertakes, at the end of the war and the additional period provided in Paragraph 5 of the Preamble to this Agreement, to withdraw all military forces of the United States. It is mutually understood and agreed that the jurisdiction hereby conferred on the Government of the United States over any airports and defense areas, and over military and civilian personnel under the provisions of Article 2 of this Agreement, shall continue until all matters calling for judicial determination, but undisposed of after the termination of this Agreement, shall have been disposed of by the United States authorities, or, alternately, until the withdrawal of the United States forces shall be complete.

ARTICLE 7. The Government of Liberia and the Government of the United States agree that at this time the above Agreement shall apply to the air facilities at Roberts Field on the Farmington River, and at Fisherman Lake in the County of Grand Cape Mount. If other defense areas of this kind are deemed necessary in the future, their location will be fixed by mutual agreement.

ARTICLE 8. For the purposes of this Agreement, a Defense Area shall be construed as the actual areas of said airports and such additional areas in the immediate neighborhood upon which installations necessary for defense may be established by agreement between the United States Commanding Officer and the Liberian Government.

Signed, at Monrovia, Liberia, in duplicate, the texts having equal force, this 31st day of March, 1942

HARRY A. McBRIDE
*Special Representative of the President
of the United States of America*
C. L. SIMPSON
*Secretary of State of the Republic
of Liberia.*

B. Afghanistan

(1) *Presentation of Letters of Credence by the Minister of Afghanistan (Aziz) to the President (Roosevelt), June 4, 1943* [1]

MR. PRESIDENT:

I have the honor to hand to Your Excellency the letters of credence by which His Majesty, my beloved King, appoints me as his Envoy Extraordinary and Minister Plenipotentiary near Your Excellency.

I am highly gratified that this responsible duty of being the first Afghan Minister in the United States of America has been entrusted in me. I can assure Your Excellency that it will be my constant endeavor to promote, maintain, and strengthen the friendly relations and good understanding subsisting between our two countries. I take this opportunity to convey to Your Excellency and to the noble American nation the greetings and good wishes with which my august Sovereign has been pleased to charge me.

In conclusion allow me to express my sincere good wishes for Your Excellency's health and the happiness and prosperity of your great nation.

(2) *Reply of the President (Roosevelt) to the Remarks of the Minister of Afghanistan (Aziz), June 4, 1943* [1]

MR. MINISTER:

It gives me great pleasure to receive from you the letters by which your august Sovereign, His Majesty Mohamed Zaher, King of Afghanistan, has accredited you as Envoy Extraordinary and Minister Plenipotentiary to the United States.

That you are the first Minister of Afghanistan accredited to the United States makes this occasion especially memorable, and the establishment of diplomatic missions in Kabul and Washington by our

[1] *Ibid.,* VIII, p. 495.

respective Governments marks, I am confident, the beginning of an era of understanding and friendship between our two peoples which should contribute much to the well-being of both nations.

I know that those of my countrymen who have visited Afghanistan have been deeply impressed by the courage and fortitude of the Afghans, by their love of freedom and their determination to tolerate no acts of aggression against their country. You will find, I am sure, Mr. Minister, that the love of freedom upon which we in the United States so pride ourselves is similar to your own and that there is much in the mutual idealism of our two peoples to cement the friendship now being manifest.

You may rest assured, Mr. Minister, that in the execution of your high mission you will receive the sincere cooperation of the officials of this Government and my own personal support.

I shall be grateful if you will convey to your Sovereign my deep appreciation of the cordial message which you have voiced, my pleasure at your arrival in our capital, and warm greetings and best wishes for His Majesty's personal happiness and for the prosperity of Afghanistan.

C. Iraq

United States relations with Iraq became increasingly friendly during the period under review. The Prime Minister of Iraq, Nuri es-Said addressed an open letter to President Roosevelt on November 18 congratulating him on the successful operations in North Africa.[1] "The whole Mediterranean scene has been changed in a few days and all the friends of the United Nations and particularly the Arab races of North Africa and the Near East are full of rejoicing . . .," wrote the Prime Minister.[2] The President replied in a message to the Prime Minister of Iraq (released to the press on November 25, 1942) that the United States was proud to feel that it had "the sympathy and cooperation of Iraq and of all the Arab peoples." [3]

On January 16, 1943, Iraq declared war on Germany, Italy, and Japan, on the ground of open interference by Germany in particular in the domestic affairs of Iraq. American troops had already been in Iraq for some time according to European reports.[4]

(1) *Communication from the Minister of Iraq (Jawdat) to the Secretary of State (Hull) Informing the United States of a State of War between Iraq and the Axis Powers, January 16, 1943* [5]

SIR:

I have the honor to inform you that this Legation has received the following important communication from the Ministry for Foreign Affairs in Iraq, to be transmitted to the Department of State.

Inasmuch as the German Government has interfered most openly and in every way in the domestic affairs of Iraq and has been responsible

[1] Cf. messages of Presidents of American Republics, *ibid.*, VII, p. 908, 936.
[2] For text see *ibid.*, p. 938.
[3] *Ibid.*, p. 962.
[4] *New York Times*, January 17, 1943.
[5] Department of State, *Bulletin*, VIII, p. 42.

for the instigation and promotion of outright rebellion against the duly constituted Government of Iraq, and whereas the Government of Germany has continued in an open manner without cessation in its hostile acts directed at Iraq by the dissemination through radio broadcasts of untruthful rumors and prevaricating reports, of vile slanders directed against the royal family, and of direct encouragement to unrest and disaffection, the Government of Iraq declares that Iraq regards itself, as from midnight on January 16–17, 1943, as being at war with Germany.

And, inasmuch as the Government of Italy, in collaboration with the German Government, has committed the same acts constituting interference in the domestic affairs of Iraq and has been guilty of grave provocation directed against Iraq until the present time, it is declared by the Government of Iraq that Iraq regards itself, as of midnight January 16–17, 1943, as being at war with Italy.

And, inasmuch as the Government of Japan has been guilty of the flagrant violation of the neutrality of Iraq by lending assistance to the German and Italian Governments in the interference by those Governments in Iraqi domestic matters, and inasmuch as the Government of Japan has since joined these Governments openly in their provocative acts directed against Iraq, the Government of Iraq declares that, as of midnight on January 16–17, 1943, a state of war exists between Iraq and Japan.

I take this opportunity to renew to you the assurances of my highest consideration.

(2) Rights of United Nations Forces in Iraq. Department of State Announcement, March 16, 1943 [1]

By a despatch dated March 16, 1943 the American Legation at Baghdad transmitted to the Secretary of State the text of Law No. 24 of the Government of Iraq, approved March 7, 1943, in which it is promulgated that the Government may grant the forces of the United Nations, for the period of their presence in Iraq for purposes of the present war, the right to enjoy the immunities and privileges pertaining to judicial and financial matters which are enjoyed by British forces under paragraph 2 of the annex to the Treaty of Alliance between Iraq and Great Britain, concluded on June 30, 1930.[2]

By a despatch dated March 22, 1943 the Legation reported that Iraqi regulations had been issued in accordance with Law No. 24.

[1] Ibid., p. 421.
[2] League of Nations, Treaty Series, CXXXII, p. 363.

D. Palestine

In commemoration of the twenty-fifth anniversary of the publication of the Balfour Declaration by the British Government on November 2, 1917,[1] a memorandum was presented to the Secretary of State by a group of Rabbis. Secretary Hull observed that the United States had followed with interest and sympathy the work done under the Declaration, in which American citizens played a useful part, and continued as quoted below.

(1) *Anniversary of the Balfour Declaration. Remarks of the Secretary of State (Hull), Released to the Press, October 31, 1942* [2]

This country was shocked and outraged, when tyranny and barbarity again commenced their march, at the brutality which was inflicted on certain races, and particularly on the Jewish populations of Europe. Apparently no form of abuse has been too great, and no form of torture or oppression too vile, to be meted out to these populations by the Nazi despots. And in taking this attitude toward the Jewish race they have made it plain by concrete acts that a like attitude would be taken toward any other race against whom they might invent a grievance.

The Jews have long sought a refuge. I believe that we must have an even wider objective; we must have a world in which Jews, like every other race, are free to abide in peace and in honor.

We meet today when the battle for freedom is being carried on in the East and in the West and our every effort is concentrated on a successful issue. We can with confidence look forward to the victory when liberty shall lift the scourge of persecution and the might of the United Nations free mankind from the threat of oppression.

Of all the inhuman and tyrannical acts of Hitler and his Nazi lieutenants, their systematic persecution of the Jewish people — men, women, and children — is the most debased. The fate of these unhappy people must be ever before us in the efforts we are making today for the final victory; at the moment of triumph under the terms of the Atlantic Charter the United Nations will be prepared not only to redeem their hopes of a future world based upon freedom, equality, and justice but to create a world in which such a tragedy will not again occur.

E. Syria and Lebanon

[See *Documents, IV, 1941–42*, p. 667.]

The United States Government had declared in November 1941 that it was hopeful that, as soon as international conditions should permit, negotiations could be undertaken enabling the United States Government to extend formal recognition to Syria and Lebanon.[3] The first concrete step in the recognition of

---

[1] 1917 *Foreign Relations*, Supp. 2, p. 317n.

[2] Department of State, *Bulletin*, VII, p. 886.

[3] *Documents, IV, 1941–42*, p. 673.

the two Republics by the United States (although Great Britain and the Fighting French had already recognized their independence) was taken on October 2, 1942, when President Roosevelt nominated George Wadsworth of New York to be Diplomatic Agent and Consul General near the Government of the Republic of Lebanon at Beirut, and near the Government of the Republic of Syria at Damascus.[1] The following day Under Secretary of State Welles commented that the United States Government had consistently received with sympathy the aspirations of the people of Syria and Lebanon.[2] The nomination was confirmed by the Senate on October 8, 1942.[3]

[1] *New York Times*, October 3, 1942.
[2] *Ibid.*, October 4, 1942.
[3] Department of State, *Bulletin*, VII, p. 828.

CHAPTER VIII

TRADE AND FINANCE

In view of the particular purpose of trade and financial controls adopted in time of war for the more effective prosecution of the war effort, it has seemed wise to transfer from this chapter to Chapter II, *Defense and the War Effort*, documents bearing upon Export Control, Foreign Funds Control, Blocked Nationals and Trading with the Enemy.

As a consequence, this chapter is limited to documents and other material bearing upon economic and financial policies and measures not vested with a special war purpose and therefore more directly concerned with normal peacetime relations with foreign countries.

1. PRINCIPLES OF POST-WAR ECONOMIC POLICY

(1) *Address by the Under Secretary of State (Welles) before the Chamber of Commerce of the State of New York, New York City, April 1, 1943* [1]

[Excerpts]

. . . .

The greatest single interest, the greatest single objective of the American people is to prevent the recurrence of war, to create a reliable and permanent peace. The thing that lies nearest the hearts of all of us is to avoid again sacrificing our young men on the field of battle, to avoid the untold suffering, heartache, and bereavement of war, and to avoid the huge economic cost of war and the social chaos that inevitably follows in the wake of all wars.

I have no illusions whatever as to the difficulty of this task. In attempting to put an end to war we face a problem that the human race has never yet been able to solve. But of one thing I am perfectly sure: the greatest obstacle to success is defeatism — the assumption that nations are by nature so antagonistic, that foreign peoples are so untrustworthy, or that the technical problems of constructing peace machinery are so great that the task is a hopeless one. For my part I do not consider it hopeless. I believe that from the moment its hopelessness is generally denied, from the moment people abandon a defeatist attitude and begin searching for ways to solve the problems presented rather than for reasons why they can't be solved, from that moment we will be well on the way to success in this greatest of all human undertakings.

[1] Department of State, *Bulletin*, VIII, p. 280.

And I am even more convinced that unless the American people are willing to assume their fair share of responsibility for the maintenance of peace in the world of the future, by joining in the exercise of police powers when that may be determined by international agreement to be necessary, and by participating in such other forms of international co-operation as may effectively prevent the rise of economic or political dangers, the peace of the world cannot be maintained.

When the war is over we shall be faced with domestic problems of the utmost difficulty. We have enormously expanded our productive facilities in many lines of industry and agriculture. We shall be faced with the problem of maintaining the present level of employment and at the same time re-absorbing millions of demobilized soldiers. As a result of the war we shall have incurred an enormous debt and our people must bear the heaviest burden of taxation in their history.

In the field of our international relations it will be necessary, in order to preserve the peace in which we have so much at stake, to supply our fair share of immediate relief for the millions of people left destitute in the wake of war. We must do this not only for humanitarian reasons but for reasons of purest self-interest. If we want the world in which we are to live to be a peaceful one, we must prevent international anarchy. There are no more disrupting forces than starvation and pestilence.

The provision of our fair share of relief will help to keep our productive facilities employed, but this will be at the expense of the already-burdened taxpayer. In his interest the relief period must be made as short as possible, which means that peoples in the devastated countries must be placed upon a self-reliant and a self-sustaining basis as rapidly as possible. From this standpoint wise trade policies are essential. Foreign countries can attain a self-sustaining basis only if there are markets for their products. Full employment of our men and resources can be maintained only if there are markets for our products. In a larger sense, also, sound international trade policies are essential in relation to our vital interests. They are essential, above all, from the standpoint of constructing a durable peace.

Any organization whereby the nations who want peace will cooperate to enforce it would fall apart if the economic underpinning were unsound. Unemployment, poverty, and declining living standards will not be tolerated for long. Short-sighted measures will be resorted to. Peoples will in desperation take any action which promises momentary relief even if it means the destruction of world order and world peace.

From whatever standpoint our domestic or our international problems are approached, it becomes apparent that in the post-war world an expansion of international trade is indispensable. Consider for a moment in elementary terms why this must be so.

What would happen to the living standards of any of our States if their trade with the other States were shut off? The answer is obvious. Cut off any of our States from commercial intercourse with the other States, or seriously interfere with it, and you would create so grave a political issue as to threaten the destruction of the Union. Under such conditions would these United States continue to act as a unit?

Is it stretching the point in the least to ask similar questions about international trade? Suppose the trade of any one of the United Nations with the others were cut off or seriously disrupted. Would that nation, with unemployment lines growing and living standards sinking, cooperate whole-heartedly with the other United Nations in any common objective? It is highly significant that the tragic period between the wars was characterized by widespread trade warfare and by the fact that the spirit of cooperation among peace-loving nations was so weak that they did not unite against the Axis until war was actually upon them and their very existence was at stake.

My purpose in mentioning these considerations is to focus your attention on a question which must be acted upon by the present Congress of the United States. I refer to the fact that the Trade Agreements Act, which provides an effective means for international trade cooperation by the United States with other countries, in our own national interest, will expire in June unless the Congress shall meanwhile have renewed it. I doubt whether the vital importance of this legislation in relation to the crisis which lies ahead is fully realized by our people. Its importance goes beyond trade and employment; it is the first concrete test of whether we really intend to cooperate with the rest of the world in a matter that is essential not only to the full solution of our domestic problems but to the construction of a durable peace.

Let me recall to your minds the nature and significance of this piece of legislation. It was adopted in 1934 following the disastrous effects of successive tariff acts which closed this market to many foreign products without regard to the interests of other countries and without regard to the interests of American producers for export, of American consumers, and of the Nation as a whole. It was adopted at a time when our own policy and that of other countries consisted of cutthroat trade warfare, each country seeking by acts of economic desperation to benefit itself at the expense of others. It was enacted in a period of stark international trade anarchy which was part of a developing state of general anarchy in international affairs out of which grew the catastrophe of another world war. That was a period characterized by high and rising tariffs, quotas, exchange-controls, depreciated currencies, clearing agreements, discriminations, and every conceivable device for waging trade warfare that the ingenuity of man could devise. Our trade-agreements program represented one spark of sanity in a world outlook that seemed wholly and hopelessly dark.

We, as well as other countries, had seen our export industries all but destroyed, our surpluses backed up on the domestic market with ruinous effects on prices. Our export industries were sick and the buying power of the large and important interests dependent on foreign trade was rapidly shrinking. We saw the sickness spread throughout our economy. The decline of our foreign trade had contributed materially to creating the worst depression in our history.

It was in these circumstances that the Trade Agreements Act of 1934 was passed. It authorized the Executive to enter into agreements reducing our tariffs, within specified limits, in return for corresponding reductions in the barriers erected against our trade by foreign countries. In brief, it sought to substitute commercial peace for trade war.

.   .   .   .

In connection with the administration of the act, let me refer to one point on which there is a good deal of misconception. People often speak of the trade agreements "made by the State Department." Failure to recognize the part played by the Tariff Commission and the Departments of Commerce, Agriculture, and Treasury in the formulation of these agreements does serious injustice to those agencies and to the numerous highly qualified and devoted experts whose work has made this program the success it has been. Indeed the factual material, the expert analysis of it, and the recommendations as to what action should be taken are predominantly the work of these other agencies rather than that of the State Department. The role of the Department of State is to mobilize and coordinate the resources and effort of all the other agencies of the Government that may be concerned and, with the assistance of these agencies, to perform its function of carrying on the international negotiations involved. The terms of the agreement which are the subject of the negotiations are not by any means solely of the State Department's making. Any offer to a foreign government with respect to a reduction in our tariff or any request to a foreign government for a reduction in a trade-barrier against American exports, or any other provision of these agreements, no matter how detailed, is referred for recommendation to the Trade Agreements Committee, upon which all of the agencies concerned are represented. The negotiations take place on the basis of a detailed draft prepared by this committee and approved by the Secretary of State and by the President. The State Department in the course of the negotiations does not deviate in the least from that draft without referring any proposed deviation to the Trade Agreements Committee and getting its decision upon it.

When agreement has been reached and the new rates are put into effect, the act provides that they "shall apply to articles, the growth, produce or manufacture of all foreign countries," with, of course, appropriate provision for suspension in the case of any country which discriminates against our products. Under this provision we extend to all friendly foreign countries the concessions that we grant to any one, and we expect and ask them each to do the same for us. The only exception on our side is for our special preferential arrangement with Cuba. This provision constitutes the so-called "unconditional most-favored-nation clause," which could better be described as the clause against discrimination. It has been somewhat criticized, as a result of what I can only think of as a misunderstanding of its purpose and effect.

That purpose and effect is simply to prevent discrimination. The policy against discrimination in international trade was not invented at the time the Trade Agreements Act was passed. It goes back to our first commercial legislation, in the time of President Washington, and has been followed, with some vacillation, ever since. The recent occasion on which the policy was most thoroughly discussed was in the administration of President Harding, when Mr. Hughes was Secretary of State. The correspondence of 1923 and 1924 between Secretary Hughes, President Harding, Chairman Culbertson of the Tariff Commission, and Senator Lodge, then chairman of the Foreign Relations Committee of the Senate, has been published and is most illuminating. Mr. Hughes summed the whole matter up accurately in one of his incisive sentences: "Either we are to have a policy of discrimination or a policy of obtaining immunity from discrimination." Needless to say, the second alternative was the course which was adopted. The Trade Agreements Acts embodies the same view. I cannot believe that any businessman would prefer the other policy. For if we applied two tariff rates, depending on the place of origin of goods, we would discriminate against every country whose goods took the higher rate, and we could properly expect them to do the same toward us. I know of nothing so calculated to disrupt the orderly conduct of private trade as such a system of reciprocal discriminations.

There is one further general aspect of the Trade Agreements Act and of the agreements concluded under it to which I wish to invite your particular attention. This is a matter of first and fundamental importance to every American businessman. You will look in vain for any provision whereby the Government of the United States, as a government, undertakes to buy or to sell anything. You will look in vain for any provision whereby this Government or any agency of it participates in the conduct of business. The Trade Agreements Act is based upon the philosophy that it is the function of private enterprise to develop our foreign trade. It is based on the idea that the profit motive coupled with American efficiency, ingenuity, and enterprise will create for us the largest and best foreign commerce, from which the whole Nation will benefit. You will find from a thoughtful examination of the agreements concluded under this authority that all the Government has done has been to reduce in so far as practicable governmental obstacles to private trade, to create opportunities for American businessmen who may want to take advantage of such opportunities.

I may add that even during the unsettled period during which these agreements were negotiated, American businessmen did take advantage extensively of the opportunities created for them, with benefit to themselves, to our whole economy, and to the foreign countries with which the agreements were concluded.

There is no question whatsoever that both in the interest of American prosperity and living standards and in the interest of creating conditions conducive to peace we must foster trade with other countries. These are vital interests, for reasons which I have indicated. They are compelling and overriding considerations. Any person or party in a position of responsibility must face them. There has been vigorous but misguided opposition to these agreements by special interests who insist on a virtually complete monopoly of the domestic market and who object to facing any foreign competition at all.

If the effort to develop a thriving foreign trade in the traditional American way, as contemplated in the Trade Agreements Act, should be thwarted by such opposition, other ways inevitably will have to be found to meet the over-riding requirements I have mentioned. Doubtless there are some who would favor actual government trading. If private interests will not let private enterprise do what is essential in the national interest, then pressure of necessity will force the adoption of other methods. For my part, I consider it of vital importance to the continued functioning of this democracy that American foreign trade, as well as other economic activities, be handled in the American way.

I am revealing no state secret when I say to you that one of the gravest doubts which exists in the minds of our partners of the United Nations today is the doubt as to what the policy of the United States will be when the victory is won. They remember that when the victory of 1918 had been achieved, this great country of ours withdrew from almost every form of practical cooperation with its former allies in the great task of constructing that kind of world in which we and all other peace-loving and liberty-loving peoples could securely and profitably live. In very truth, we won the war and made no effort to win the peace.

Our allies are asking themselves now whether we will again follow that same course. In a very real sense the decision that will be made with regard to the renewal of the Trade Agreements Act will be regarded by peoples throughout the world as an acid test of our future intentions. They will see in that decision a clear indication as to whether the people of the United States have determined upon a policy of international cooperation for the future or whether they will once more turn back to that road of isolation which leads to inevitable disaster.

(2) *Statement of the Secretary of State (Hull) in Connection with National Foreign Trade Week, May 15, 1943* [1]

For a fuller statement by the Secretary of State on principles of United States economic policy, see Radio Address of July 23, 1942, given on p. 1 of this volume.

The great military operations which have taken place during the year that has elapsed since the last observance of Foreign Trade Week have made clear to the world that the United Nations have learned to work together and that together their power is irresistible. Much hard fighting lies ahead. The winning of the war is our most immediate task, and by united effort we shall win it.

Whether the victory will bring a long and fruitful peace or merely another uneasy interlude between ever more destructive wars will depend upon whether or not the United Nations, having learned to cooperate in war, will continue to cooperate through and beyond victory to make it possible for men everywhere to raise their standards of living in a world secure from economic cataclysm and safeguarded against the specter of war. The United States is vitally interested in the effort to achieve such a world.

We are a great trading nation. Our producers require many foreign raw materials, and they need foreign markets for the products of agriculture and industry. Our consumers need many foreign articles, both crude and manufactured. The creation of conditions favorable to full production in each country and the mutually beneficial exchange of goods and services between countries is indispensable to our economic well-being and is essential to the achievement of a securely peaceful world.

The trade-agreements program is a major contribution of this country to the creation of such a world. Its continuance or non-continuance as an effective instrument of action poses some questions which we must ask ourselves now and which the world is asking.

Does the United States intend to continue to promote greater cooperation and expansion of mutually advantageous international trade, or is the economic giant among nations going to throw its influence in the other direction and attempt once again, as after the last war, to withdraw into a shell of economic isolation?

Have we as a nation arrived at the realization that we are not only *in* this world but are *of* this world; that we cannot live apart from our neighbors but in our own self-interest must assume our fair share of the responsibility for making possible a peaceful, secure, and prosperous world economy?

[1] *Ibid.*, p. 430.

The resolving of these questions will not wait for the conclusion of the war. They are before us now. Our answers to them must be clear if there is to be confidence in the future.

For the present most of our foreign commerce is directed to the immediate needs of supplying our forces and our allies overseas with the materials of war. The most efficient serving of this immediate objective requires import and export controls of various kinds. Governmental agencies have undertaken to increase and speed up the procurement and importation of needed materials, and a large part of our export trade is carried on under lend-lease. These are indispensable war measures. But, when the victory has been won, only through the retention of the reciprocal-trade-agreements program and through the application of the experience gained under it shall we be able to make our contribution toward achieving greater freedom and greater opportunity for vigorous and healthy private commercial activity to play its indispensable part in helping to create a better secured and increasingly fruitful world of peace.

2. TRADE AGREEMENTS

[See *Documents, I, 1938–39*, p. 334; *II, 1939–40*, p. 448; *III, 1940–41*, p. 459; *IV, 1941–42*, p. 693.]

A. Extension of the Trade Agreements Act of 1934

The Trade Agreements Act of 1934 (An Act to Amend the Tariff Act of 1930, approved June 14, 1934) [1] was extended in 1937 and 1940 for terms of three years. It came up for renewal in 1943 at a time when, on the one hand, the foreign trade situation was dominated by war requirements with the result that the proportion of our trade affected by the trade agreements program was of declining importance, while, on the other hand, the United States was committed under the provisions of the Atlantic Charter and Article VII of the Master Lend-Lease Agreements to the elimination of all forms of discriminatory treatment in international commerce and the reduction of tariff and other trade barriers in the period after the war.

H. J. Res. 111, as introduced in the House, provided for the extension of the authority of the President under the original act for a period of three years. It was referred to the House Ways and Means Committee before which extensive hearings were held from April 12 to 23, 1943.[2] It was reported out on May 5, 1943 with an amendment, amending Section 350 (a) (2) of the Tariff Act of 1930 by inserting after "because of its discriminatory treatment of American commerce or because of other acts" the words: "(including the operations of international cartels)."[3] Of the numerous amendments offered on the floor of the House, only that of Representative West (Texas) reducing the term of the extension from 3 years to 2 years was adopted, by a vote of 155 to 132. It was clear from the debate that the purpose which the House had in mind was to limit the extension to the approximate duration of the war and to leave the way open

---

[1] 48 Stat. 943; *Documents, I, 1938–39*, p. 334.
[2] *Hearings before the Committee on Ways and Means, House of Representatives, on H. J. Res. 111 (Extension of Reciprocal Trade Agreements Act)*, 78th Cong., 1st sess.
[3] House Report No. 409, 78th Cong., 1st sess.

for the reconsideration of the issue when the war is over.[1] This was the one respect in which Secretary of State Hull's plea for "a clear-cut continuance of the Trade Agreements Act for the customary three-year period"[2] was disregarded. After extensive debate, the resolution passed the House on May 13, yeas 343, nays 65, not voting 25.

In its amended form the resolution was referred by the Senate to the Senate Finance Committee. After brief hearings,[3] an amendment requiring that every agreement should be subject to termination six months after the cessation of hostilities by joint resolution of the Congress or by the President was adopted by the Committee, and the bill as amended was reported favorably to the Senate.[4] This amendment was subsequently eliminated by the Senate by a vote of 51 to 33.[5] The resolution as passed by the House was approved by the Senate on June 2 by a vote of yeas 59, nays 23, not voting 14. The joint resolution was signed by the President on June 7.

(1) Statement of the Department of State on the Reciprocal-Trade-Agreements Program in War and Peace, February 20, 1943 [6]

The reciprocal-trade-agreements program is based upon the Trade Agreements Act of June 12, 1934, which has twice been extended by Congress for additional 3-year periods, from June 12, 1937 to June 12, 1940 and again from June 12, 1940 to June 12, 1943. Further extension of this program will be considered by the Seventy-eighth Congress.[7]

Why It Was Adopted

Purpose. To increase foreign markets for products of the United States is the primary purpose of the trade-agreements program. This purpose is sought through reciprocal adjustment of excessive trade barriers. The general objectives of the program are to substitute economic cooperation for economic warfare in our relations with other countries; to give economic substance to our good-neighbor policy; and to create the kind of international economic relations upon which a structure of durable peace can be erected.

Necessity. Normally the United States can and does produce more of a great number of farm and industrial products than can profitably be sold in the American market.

[1] See particularly remarks of Representative Wadsworth (New York), *Congressional Record*, vol. 89, pt. 3, p. 4294.

[2] Statement by the Secretary of State on April 24, 1943, Department of State, *Bulletin*, VIII, p. 350.

[3] *Hearings before the Committee of Finance, United States Senate, on H. J. Res. 111 (Extension of Reciprocal Trade Agreements Act)*, May 17, 18, 19, and 22, 1943, 78th Cong., 1st sess.

[4] Senate Report No. 258, 78th Cong., 1st sess.

[5] *Congressional Record*, vol. 89, pt. 4, p. 5109.

[6] Department of State, *Bulletin*, VIII, p. 169; Department of State Publication 1893.

[7] See this volume, p. 632.

When large quantities of such goods cannot be exported, our agricultural products pile up in unmarketable surpluses and our industrial production slows down. The result is felt throughout the country in depressed prices, unemployment, reduced wages, and poorer home markets for American producers.

Trade between nations declined sharply after 1929, largely because most nations, including the United States, set up excessive barriers against imports. By thus making it difficult for its people to buy things they needed and desired from other countries, each country made it difficult — in many cases impossible — for its own producers to sell their exportable surpluses in other countries.

The value of the foreign trade of the United States fell even more rapidly than did that of the world as a whole; it dropped from $9,640,-000,000 in 1929 to $2,934,000,000 in 1932.

As world trade diminished, employment and incomes fell and the world-wide economic depression was deepened and prolonged. Between 1929 and 1932 our foreign trade dropped nearly 70 per cent; national income, 43 per cent; cash farm income, 58 per cent; wages and salaries in manufacturing industries, 53 per cent.

Benefits of Foreign Trade. Expansion of our trade with foreign countries benefits the whole country:

1. It benefits directly the great branches of American agriculture and the many industries, large and small, that have products to sell in foreign markets.

2. It benefits directly American producers who use imported raw materials or semi-manufactured products in making their finished products.

3. It benefits millions of workers dependent upon these branches of agriculture and industry for their livelihood.

4. It improves domestic markets for American producers not directly interested in export or import trade; American farmers and manufacturers who can sell more of their goods in foreign markets — and their employees as well — are better customers for the goods and services of Americans not in the business of exporting or importing.

5. It raises living standards by providing more employment, more purchasing power, and more goods for American consumers at reasonable prices; it increases, to our mutual advantage, the exchange of products we grow or manufacture to better advantage than other countries, for products that other countries can grow or manufacture to better advantage than we can.

Foreign Trade Is Two-Way. Foreign trade *necessarily* is two-way trade. We cannot export unless we import; we cannot import unless we export. Our exports provide purchasing power for the things we import; our imports provide purchasing power to foreign countries for the things they buy from us. People in foreign countries can buy our products only to the extent that they can acquire United States dollars to pay for them, and the only way they can acquire dollars is through the sale in this country of their products (including gold and silver) and services or by borrowing. Loans, even if available to them, merely postpone the ultimate necessity for payment in the form of commodities or services. If such payment is prevented, defaulted debts are inevitable.

How the Program Works

Direct negotiation with other countries is the method prescribed by the Trade Agreements Act for reducing excessive barriers standing in the way of expansion of our foreign trade. This method was chosen as more practicable and more effective than general downward revision of the United States tariff alone. Even if feasible, such a revision would not insure the reciprocal reduction by other countries of their tariffs and other barriers, including discriminations, against our export trade.

Method. Specifically, the act empowers the President, in order to obtain from other countries concessions on American exports, to modify excessive United States tariff rates, to bind existing tariff rates against increase, and to guarantee continued duty-free entry of products now on the free list.

The act does *not* empower the President to modify tariff rates except under a trade agreement; it does *not* empower him to reduce the duty on any foreign product under a trade agreement by more than 50 per cent or to transfer any item from the dutiable list to the free list.

It *does* require that trade agreements be concluded only after the President has sought the advice of the Departments of State, Agriculture, and Commerce, the Tariff Commission, and other appropriate agencies of the Government, and only after public notice and full opportunity for presentation of information and views by any interested person.

All Government agencies concerned with foreign commerce cooperate, through interdepartmental committees, in studying all pertinent facts and views. Before any trade agreement is concluded, public notice is given of all products on which concessions by the United States will be considered and public hearings are held by representatives of the Government agencies concerned. Resulting recommendations in regard to trade agreements are submitted to the President through the Secretary of State.

Concessions Obtained. The United States, in negotiating a trade agreement, asks a foreign country to lower its excessive tariff rates on our exports, or to liberalize quota or exchange restrictions on them.

Such concessions and assurances against higher trade barriers have been obtained from countries which are important customers for thousands of American products, both agricultural and non-agricultural, comprising one third of all United States exports.

Concessions Granted. Under trade agreements the United States has agreed to tariff reductions or to the continuance of existing tariffs or free entry in the case of imported products needed or desired by American producers and consumers. Concessions are granted on imported products more or less similar to those produced in the United States when they are in the national interest and when reciprocal concessions are obtained in return — but only after exhaustive study has indicated that such concessions will not cause serious injury to American producers. In appropriate cases imports of such products permitted to enter at the reduced tariff rates are limited in amount or restricted to seasons when similar American products are not marketed in quantities sufficient to satisfy the needs of American consumers.

"Most-Favored-Nation" Clause. The traditional trade policy of the United States is not to discriminate between foreign nations but to extend equality of tariff treatment to all who do not discriminate against the trade of this country. This policy is embodied in the Trade Agreements Act. Under it a lower rate of duty on a given product in a trade agreement with a foreign nation (other than Cuba) applies also to the same product from any third nation, unless that third nation is found to discriminate against the products of the United States. This policy enables the United States to require other countries, as well as the other party to the trade agreement, to give our exports non-discriminatory treatment.

This policy of fair treatment on a reciprocal basis pays large dividends in dollars and cents to American producers who are thus protected against foreign tariff and other discriminations. It promotes peaceful commercial relations. Discriminatory trade policies create resentment and invite retaliation.

Beneficial Results of the Program

The United States has concluded agreements with 26 foreign countries.[1] These countries, in the order in which the agreements were signed, are: Cuba, Brazil, Belgium, and Luxemburg, Haiti, Sweden, Colombia, Canada, Honduras, the Netherlands, Switzerland, Nicaragua,[2] Guatemala, France, Finland, Costa Rica, El Salvador, Czechoslovakia,[3] Ecuador, the United Kingdom of Great Britain and Northern Ireland, Turkey, Venezuela, Argentina, Peru, Uruguay, and Mexico.

[1] See table p. 633.

[2] The reciprocal duty concessions and certain provisions of this agreement ceased to be effective March 10, 1938.

[3] The operation of this agreement was suspended April 22, 1939.

About 65 per cent of the total foreign trade of the United States is carried on with the countries with which reciprocal trade agreements have been concluded. The United Kingdom and Canada are, respectively, the largest and the second largest customers for American exports.

Agreements with American Republics. Trade agreements have been concluded with all the other American Republics except Bolivia, Chile, the Dominican Republic, Panama, and Paraguay. Negotiations with Bolivia are under way. Over 90 per cent of the trade of the United States with the other American Republics is with the trade-agreement countries.

Trade Increases. The trade-agreements program contributed substantially to the increase in United States foreign trade between the inauguration of the program and the outbreak of war in 1939. Other factors have also, of course, affected the volume and the nature of our trade.

During the 2-year period 1934–35 United States total foreign trade averaged 4.1 billion dollars a year. In the 2-year period 1938–39 the average was 5.3 billion dollars.

The contribution of the trade-agreements program to the increase in our foreign trade is indicated by a comparison of United States trade with agreement and with non-agreement countries.

In the 2-year period 1938–39, when 16 trade agreements were in effect, United States exports to the countries covered by these agreements averaged 62.8 per cent greater than in 1934–35, when only 1 agreement was in effect for a year or more. In 1938–39 our exports to all other countries were only 31.2 per cent greater than in 1934–35.

Our imports from the 16 agreement countries averaged 21.6 per cent greater in 1938–39 than in 1934–35, but our imports from other countries averaged only 11.1 per cent greater.

These comparisons reinforce the common-sense conclusion that the reduction of excessive tariffs and other barriers to the exchange of our goods for those of other nations tends to support and enlarge our foreign trade.

Improved Trade Relations. Trade agreements improve trade relations generally between the United States and the foreign country concerned. The agreements themselves provide a basis for consultation in regard to matters dealt with in the agreements. Beyond this the cordial atmosphere fostered by the agreements paves the way for friendly discussion of other trade and economic matters not directly involved in the agreements.

Improved General Relations. Economic cooperation through mutually beneficial trade agreements tends to promote good relations with other countries. The trade-agreements program has helped us to win back, to our great advantage, some of the friendships we lost by our short-sighted tariff and war-debt policies after the last war. Today the trade agreements with the other American Republics are one of the strongest pillars in the structure of hemispheric solidarity and of our global good-neighbor policy.

The Program in War and Peace

During the War. Our existing trade agreements with the United Kingdom and Canada entered into force on January 1, 1939, the year in which war began in Europe. The agreement with Turkey took effect in May of that year. During the war period five new agreements have become effective with: Venezuela in December 1939; Argentina in November 1941; Peru in July 1942; Uruguay on January 1, 1943; and Mexico on January 30, 1943. During this period four supplementary agreements (two each with Canada and Cuba) were concluded.

Wartime trade controls, scarcity of shipping, and military considerations have come to dominate the nature and extent of our foreign trade. Nevertheless, a considerable amount of trade continues to be influenced primarily by economic considerations. The trade-agreements program exerts a beneficial influence on our trade relations with friendly countries and on our own war effort.

The agreements provide valuable insurance, now, against a repetition of the tidal wave of trade barriers and discriminations that swept over the world after the last war. They provide, now, a solid foundation for resumption of mutually beneficial trade after the war, when so many of our agricultural and industrial producers will need foreign markets if they are to avoid curtailment of production and ruinously low prices, and when American industry and consumers will need imported raw materials and semi-manufactured and finished products.

Trade agreements, old as well as new, help to bring about close economic cooperation between this country and the other United Nations in the joint effort to achieve complete victory. These agreements stand today for economic cooperation in war and in peace — for a world in which men everywhere can produce in accordance with their ability and exchange their goods on a fair and reasonable basis. For this reason, an active trade-agreements program during the war strengthens the determination of the United Nations to win a victory that will be worth the cost; it inspires confidence that the United States will do its share in creating conditions favorable to prosperity and security after victory.

After the War. Secure peace after victory must be built upon the solid foundation of economic cooperation. Economic insecurity and social unrest, caused in considerable part by excessive trade barriers and discriminatory trade policies, helped to spawn a Hitler and to plunge the world into this greatest of all wars before it had recovered from the last one. After this war, economic cooperation, not economic warfare, must be the rule.

The governments of the United Nations, in subscribing to the Atlantic Charter, agreed "to further the enjoyment by all States, great or small, victor or vanquished, of access, on equal terms, to the trade and to the raw materials of the world which are needed for their economic prosperity"; and affirmed their "desire to bring about the fullest collaboration between all nations in the economic field with the object of securing, for all, improved labor standards, economic advancement, and social security."

In Article VII of the mutual-aid (lend-lease) agreement of February 23, 1942 the Governments of the United States and of the United Kingdom agreed that "In the final determination of the benefits to be provided to the United States of America by the Government of the United Kingdom in return for aid furnished under the Act of Congress of March 11, 1941, the terms and conditions thereof shall be such as not to burden commerce between the two countries, but to promote mutually advantageous economic relations between them and the betterment of world-wide economic relations. To that end, they shall include provision for agreed action by the United States of America and the United Kingdom, open to participation by all other countries of like mind, directed to the expansion, by appropriate international and domestic measures, of production, employment, and the exchange and consumption of goods, which are the material foundations of the liberty and welfare of all peoples; to the elimination of all forms of discriminatory treatment in international commerce, and to the reduction of tariffs and other trade barriers; and, in general, to the attainment of all the economic objectives" of the Atlantic Charter.

Similar Article VII provisions are contained in mutual-aid agreements with China, the Soviet Union, Belgium, Poland,[1] the Netherlands, Greece, Czechoslovakia, Norway, and Yugoslavia. Australia and New Zealand have accepted these principles, and Canada, although not a recipient of lend-lease aid, has subscribed to them.

The trade-agreements program, if extended by the Congress prior to June 12, 1943, will be one of the most effective means of applying, in cooperation with other countries, these agreed-upon principles for the attainment of the economic basis of an enduring peace.

(2) *Statement of the Secretary of State (Hull) before the House Ways and Means Committee, April 12, 1943* [2]

MR. CHAIRMAN, MEMBERS OF THE COMMITTEE:

This is the third occasion on which the Congress undertakes a periodic review of the operation of a great national policy, which has been carried

---

[1] See p. 217.

[2] Department of State, *Bulletin*, VIII, p. 329; *Hearings before the Ways and Means Committee, House of Representatives on H. J. Res. 111 (Extension of Reciprocal Trade Agreements Act)*, 78th Cong., 1st sess., p. 2.

forward for the past nine years by cooperative action of the legislative and executive branches of the Government. In a profound sense, the present is the most momentous of these occasions.

At the time when the policy was inaugurated in 1934, our country and all countries were suffering from the disastrous consequences of excessive restrictions and obstructions to trade, commerce, and credit. The resulting intensive and destructive economic warfare caused a far-reaching disruption of world trade and was in large measure responsible for the collapse of domestic economies, including ours. Vigorous and determined action was needed to reverse the fatal trend toward ever-mounting obstructions. That action was undertaken through the adoption of the reciprocal-trade-agreements policy.

It was clear to us that satisfactory economic recovery was impossible without a restoration and expansion of healthy foreign trade. It was clear that our foreign trade and international trade as a whole could be restored and could expand only through a reduction here and abroad of unreasonable and excessive trade barriers. It was equally clear that the most advantageous method of accomplishing this was to negotiate with other countries mutually beneficial trade agreements based upon a reciprocal reduction of trade barriers.

It was also clear from the beginning that a revival of world trade was an essential element in the maintenance of world peace. By this I do not mean, of course, that flourishing international commerce is of itself a guaranty of peaceful international relations. But I do mean that without prosperous trade among nations any foundation for enduring peace becomes precarious and is ultimately destroyed.

The reason for this is not far to seek. The political and social instability caused by economic distress is a fertile breeding ground of agitators and dictators, ready to plunge the peoples over whom they seize control into adventure and war. Economic warfare, which destroys trade and thus works havoc on production, employment, prices, values, and standards of life within nations, is always a powerful factor of rivalry, dissension, and strife between nations.

All these explosive elements were present in the international situation at the time when we embarked on the trade-agreements program. Through the trade program our country made a determined effort to provide leadership in international cooperation and to point the way forward in the economic field. We attained a measure of success in spite of the colossal difficulties that stood in the way. Unfortunately, the momentum of deterioration in other fields of international relations was already so great that even the progress that was being made toward placing international economic relations on a sound basis was finally engulfed in the overwhelming catastrophe of a new World War.

It is well for us to bear in mind these facts and considerations as we begin this periodic review of our trade-agreements policy. In them lie lessons for the future. To ignore them can only lead to recurrent and widespread disasters.

II

The trade-agreements program was enacted nine years ago in exactly the form in which it has been twice renewed for three-year periods, and is now before the Congress for renewal for another period of three years.

The original purpose of the act of 1934, as stated in its first section, was to expand foreign markets for the products of the United States, and so to create added employment and added income in this country. This was to be done by a process of negotiation and agreements, by which this country would obtain reductions in foreign restrictions against American products by granting similar reductions in American restrictions against foreign products. The concessions were to be adjusted "in accordance with the characteristics and needs of various branches of American production." The act looked forward to increased trade in both directions, to the benefit of employment, income, and living standards both in this country and abroad.

By the act of 1934 the President was authorized by the Congress to enter into trade agreements with other countries and, through the proclaiming of such agreements, to grant to foreign countries reductions in our tariff rates in exchange for benefits extended to our trade by the other countries. It was specifically provided that no duty could be reduced by more than 50 per cent; that no article could be transferred between the dutiable and the free lists; that while the proclaimed duties would be applicable to imports from all countries, their application could be suspended in the case of countries which discriminate against American goods. It was likewise specifically provided that no agreement could be concluded for more than three years. Each agreement would thereafter be subject to termination upon not more than six months' notice. Provision was made for full collaboration of the Tariff Commission and the Departments of Commerce, Agriculture, and State in the carrying out of the program. Finally, it was provided that reasonable public notice should be given of intention to negotiate an agreement and full opportunity be afforded for the presentation of views by any interested person.

During the years that the act of 1934 has been in force we have concluded agreements under it with 27 countries. I shall not undertake to discuss the unquestionably impressive commercial results of these agreements carefully concluded under the safeguards prescribed by the Congress. These results attained under peace conditions were examined fully by your Committee three years ago, and I assume will be examined again in these hearings. My associates will be glad to furnish you any data which you may desire to have for that purpose.

Important as was the trade-agreements program in the past, important as it has been and will be from a broader point of view, it will be more significant than ever, from the viewpoint of our own material interest, when the present fighting stops. When that happens almost every metal-making plant in the United States and many other factories and mines and farms will be faced with the termination of war orders and will be looking urgently for markets for their peacetime products. Foreign markets will be very important to us then and will continue to be essential as far as anyone can see ahead. It will be well to have in being and in working order a tested and tried instrument for obtaining the reduction of foreign-trade barriers and the elimination of discriminations against our products.

It will be well, too, to carry on the process of negotiated reduction of trade barriers wherever clearly feasible even during the war years, as we have already found it possible to do in some instances with appropriate safeguards against unforeseeable contingencies. In this way our producers will find it possible to develop their foreign business as smoothly and rapidly as possible when the war ends. To negotiate effectively to either of these ends this country will need the kind of authority the Trade Agreements Act provides. The extension of that authority, and the intelligent and careful use of it, are the best available insurance against new and old discriminations and restrictions on the foreign markets open to American enterprise and American products.

The trade-agreements program is not only a thoroughly tested instrument but also a flexible one. Plainly, after the war all manner of conditions will need to be taken into account, arising out of new forms of trade, changed values of currency, and shifting currents of commerce. The flexibility of operation which the Trade Agreements Act makes possible will enable us to adjust our commercial policy to the actual conditions of our post-war economic situation in all its branches.

III

Of the 27 countries with which we have concluded trade agreements, only tragic Finland is at war today with any of our allies, and even she is not at war with us. Of the others, 16 are now by our side, at war with our enemies. They are Belgium, Brazil, Canada, Costa Rica, Cuba, Czechoslovakia, El Salvador, France, Great Britain, Guatemala, Haiti, Honduras, Luxemburg, Mexico, the Netherlands, and Nicaragua. Six of the remaining 10 have broken off relations with the Axis countries and are cooperating on our side in many ways. These 6 are Colombia, Ecuador, Iran, Peru, Uruguay, and Venezuela. The remaining 4 are neutral (Argentina, Sweden, Switzerland, and Turkey), and one of these, Switzerland, has undertaken the heavy duty of representing American interests, including the interests of American prisoners of war, in the places which our enemies control.

The nations which entered into trade agreements did so because they were peace-loving nations, seeking peaceful relations in all respects, economic and political. It is no accident, therefore, that in the searching test to which individuals and nations are being subjected in this war, those nations which have entered into a cooperative economic relationship with us through the conclusion of trade agreements are on the side of opposing rather than aiding the forces of aggression.

As we look into the future, it is this theme of international cooperation that should be uppermost in our minds if we really want to make sure that another world conflict is not to be ahead of us after we win this war.

When the day of victory comes, we and other nations will have before us a choice of courses to follow. Basically, that choice will be, as it was in 1918, between, on the one hand, extreme nationalism, growing rivalries, jealousies, and hatreds, with the ultimate certainty of another and even more devastating war; and, on the other hand, increased international cooperation in a wide variety of fields, and at least the hope of secure peace for our children.

No one can give a promise that secure peace will really prevail. It is much harder to make the peace secure than it is to wage successful war. Many wars have been fought and won, by many nations, but not yet has any nation made its peace secure and enduring. No one nation, no two nations can do this. For war is an international affair; in a world of many nations its prevention requires international collaboration. In the new world of the airplane all nations are the near neighbors of all others. In such a world any one strong industrial country has power to plunge the world into war with devastating suddenness and violence. To keep the peace secure will require the resolute and continuous collaboration of all law-abiding nations. It is a hard way and a long way, but it is the only hopeful way there is to prevent war.

Of the various necessary fields of international collaboration one of the most essential is the field of economic life. The goods and services by means of which men live must be abundant, and they must be well distributed. If the material basis of civilization fails, we must not anticipate that human beings will be civilized or peaceful. Solid and lasting friendships between large groups of people require mutual willingness to cooperate in the fundamental business of earning a living. That is why it is so essential, in the words of the Atlantic Charter, "to bring about the fullest collaboration between all nations in the economic field with the object of securing, for all, improved labor standards, economic advancement, and social security." This objective, and the balance of the Charter, have now been endorsed by all the United Nations. That action was taken by the hard-headed and realistic men who guide these Governments, not by reason of humane sentiments alone but because they recognize that the only way to attain these ends is through cooperative action.

Stable peace and economic warfare will not mix. We know that now from bitter experience. Just as we must work together to set up and operate the necessary machinery to maintain peace, we must work together to make the years of peace fruitful for ourselves and for others.

One of the most essential subjects of international cooperation in the years that lie ahead is this very one of trade and the various trade restrictions to which the act refers. What happens to international commerce has an intimate effect on many of the things that lie closest to the minds of the people of every country. The price of crops, the chance of paying off the mortgage, or of getting or holding a job, the supply and price of common articles on merchants' shelves — these are the things that foreign trade affects in every country. If both reason and experience teach anything, they teach the necessity for more trade between nations.

It has long since become axiomatic that international trade cannot be a one-way affair. The problems which it presents can, therefore, be dealt with wisely only by international cooperation of governments and of peoples.

Nations have various ways of managing the production and exchange of goods and services. In this country we prefer that our combined domestic and international economy rest primarily on a system of free enterprise. The trade-agreements program is designed to promote this end.

International trade is regulated and is necessarily affected by the tariffs, regulations, and economic institutions of the various countries. What the trade-agreements program proposes is that this complex system of trade-regulation, both our own and that of others, shall be administered and guided, as far as our influence extends, not in the direction of regimentation and scarcity but in the direction of increased production, better distribution, and more abundant consumption.

That is neither Republican nor Democratic doctrine. It is American doctrine, and the greater the extent to which we can get it accepted by other nations, the better will be the prospect for our own future prosperity and peace. I am confident that the more the subject is discussed the more clearly these facts will be seen by all of us and the more nearly unanimous we shall be in our support not only of the measure now before us but of all measures that make possible, in our own hard-headed self-interest, fuller international cooperation against the common scourges of poverty, social and political instability, and war, and for greater abundance, social and political stability, and secure peace.

IV

The foundations of international cooperation must be laid now, and they must be built out of mutual confidence, mutual respect, and common interest. Today we are engaged in the greatest cooperative enterprise in history. In this struggle for human freedom, 31 United Nations, large and small, are banded together in a brotherhood of self-preservation and 12 other nations are associated with them. While bending their utmost energy to the attainment of complete military victory and enduring the immense sacrifices which the war imposes upon them, these nations are meantime laying plans for the future.

All these hope-inspiring plans for international cooperation will come to nothing more than pious expressions unless there is confidence that the countries which participate in them are determined to have ready for immediate use, whenever needed, the necessary instruments of effective action. So far as our nation is concerned, the continued existence of the trade-agreements machinery is the most important of these instruments. It is the central and indispensable point in any feasible program of international cooperation. The only alternative is for nations to travel the same extremely narrow economic road that was traveled so disastrously during the years following the last war.

The many peoples who look toward this country with hope are watching our action on this act with profound interest. What we do about it will be looked upon as a signpost pointing to the path they can expect us to follow. Repudiation of the trade-agreements program, or the curtailment of it in scope or time by amendment, would be taken as a clear indication that this country which in war is bearing its full share of responsibility will not do so in peace. This might well weaken the ties which hold together the group of nations with which we are so vitally associated in the prosecution of the war. Extension of the program without change will mean not only that we understand the kind of commercial relationships which, from a purely business point of view, lead to our mutual well-being but that we recognize the deeper implications of our great strength and commensurate responsibility for good or ill in the world.

Strong non-partisan support of this non-partisan legislation would have a most heartening effect on people here and everywhere who look forward with profound hope to a world rich in economic and spiritual opportunities for all.

(3) *Report of the Committee on Ways and Means, House of Representatives, to Accompany H. J. Res. 111, May 5, 1943* [1]

[Excerpt]

On the basis of the foregoing, and of the other testimony offered before it, and of its own consideration, the committee has concluded that:

First. It is desirable to continue in existence this tested and sound instrument of international cooperation, in the interest both of unity in the war effort, of a secure peace hereafter, and of American prosperity;

Second. It is desirable to make the vote as large and bipartisan as possible, in order that our allies and the citizens of the United States may be assured that international cooperation in post-war reconstruction is not a party matter;

Third. It is desirable that the extension be in the form and for the term that has formerly been used, in order that no unnecessary doubts may be created.

The committee therefore recommends that the bill which the committee has reported pass without further amendment, and it bespeaks bipartisan support for this proposal.

(4) *Statement of the Secretary of State (Hull) before the Senate Finance Committee, May 17, 1943* [2]

[Excerpt]

In the debate on the floor of the House, amendments were offered requiring approval by Congress of agreements entered into under the terms of the Act. The term of the extension was actually reduced by House amendment from 3 to 2 years in order to reduce our commitment in the post-war period. That part of the statement of the Secretary of State before the Senate Committee on Finance devoted particularly to the proposal for Congressional approval is given here.

It has been suggested that the trade-agreements program be retained but the agreements negotiated under it be made subject to approval by the Congress. Let me recall briefly some pertinent history.

During the entire history of this country only three reciprocity tariff treaties have been ratified and made effective. All of these were of a special character and were with countries with which the United States had particularly close political or geographic ties: Canada (1854), Hawaii (1875), and Cuba (1902).

Twenty-two other reciprocity tariff treaties have been negotiated by the Executive, 10 under the general treaty-making powers and 12 pursuant to the express statutory provision in section 4 of the Tariff Act of 1897, but not a single one of these became effective. Seventeen of these were either rejected by or failed to come to a vote in the Senate, one was rejected by the foreign government because of amendments by the Sen-

---

[1] House Report No. 409, 78th Cong., 1st sess.

[2] Department of State, *Bulletin*, VIII, p. 443; *Hearings before the Committee on Finance, United States Senate, on H. J. Res. 111*, 78th Cong., 1st sess., p. 1.

ate, one failed to receive Congressional legislation necessary to place it in effect, and three were withdrawn.

In contrast to the record of reciprocity *treaties* requiring Senate or Senate and Congressional approval, is the record of *executive agreements* negotiated under authority delegated by the Congress and not subject to subseqent approval by the Senate or Congress. Under the McKinley Tariff Act of 1890, 12 reciprocity agreements were made effective, and under section 3 of the Dingley Tariff Act of 1897, 15 such agreements were brought into force.

In 1933 the United States Tariff Commission, after summarizing the reciprocity experiences of this country up to that time, concluded:

"The past experiences of the United States with respect to the difficulty of obtaining reciprocal tariff concessions by means of *treaties* and the greater success in negotiating *executive agreements* under previous authorization by the Congress may be significant as a guide to future policy regarding methods of tariff bargaining." [1]

Since the Trade Agreements Act has been in operation 30 agreements have been negotiated and made effective. One agreement, that with Iran, signed on April 8, 1943, has not as yet become effective.

No one in his right senses would dream of asking the Congress for an unlimited grant of authority to adjust our tariff rates. No Congress would ever dream of making such a grant of power — and no Congress ever has. The Trade Agreements Act involves a strictly and specifically limited delegation of power, with the terms of which you are all familiar. Its periodic review by the Congress is a fully effective safeguard against the abuse even of these limited powers. In the light of the record of disastrous experience which I have just recited, a demand for Congressional action on trade agreements is a demand for the abandonment of the whole program without which our country's hands will be tied in a field in which it must either act or accept overwhelmingly disastrous consequences.

I shall not dwell on other equally important reasons why it is imperative that the program be continued in its present form without weakening change. Many of us, both within and outside the Government, including the almost unanimous voice of the public press, have strongly urged such action as an early indication to other nations of our post-war intentions. We have all referred to the interest and anxiety with which other nations would follow the debates in Congress on this question. Developments since the introduction of the legislation in the House have confirmed this. Reports received from country after country, particularly in the neighboring American Republics, reveal the marked attention by government officials, the press, and the public to this legislation. The universally expressed hope — except in the Axis countries — is for the

[1] U. S. Tariff Commission, *Tariff Bargaining Under Most-Favored-Nation Treaties*, p. 13.

trade-agreements program to be extended, both for its practical significance and for the reaffirmation of the principles of cooperation and fair dealing which it embodies.

When post-war economic readjustments are sought we shall need to be in a position, in our own national self-interest, to play our part in establishing conditions favorable to mutually beneficial trade, full employment, and generally to fruitful and friendly relations between the peoples of the world. Only through enlarged market opportunity abroad and at home shall we be able to establish and maintain our peace-time economic activity and the employment and living standards of our people on anything like a satisfactorily high level.

The experience of the two decades which elapsed between the end of the World War and the outbreak of a new war in Europe has brought out in sharp relief the validity of two basic propositions. The first of these is that our nation, and every nation, can enjoy sustained prosperity only in a world which is at peace. The second is that a peaceful world is possible only when there exists for it a solid economic foundation, an indispensable part of which is active and mutually beneficial trade among the nations. The creation of such a foundation is a primary objective of the trade-agreements program, which seeks the advancement of our domestic prosperity and the promotion of world peace.

These great objectives cannot, of course, be accomplished by trade agreements alone. But they cannot be accomplished without them.

(5) Joint Resolution to Extend the Authority of the President under Section 350 of the Tariff Act of 1930, as Amended, Approved June 7, 1943 [1]

Resolved by the Senate and House of Representatives of the United States of America in Congress assembled, That the period during which the President is authorized to enter into foreign-trade agreements under section 350 of the Tariff Act of 1930, as amended by the Act (Public, Numbered 316, Seventy-third Congress) approved June 12, 1934, is hereby extended for a further period of two years from June 12, 1943.

SEC. 2. Section 350 (a) (2) of the Tariff Act of 1930 (U. S. C., 1940 edition, title 19, sec. 1351 (a) (2)) is amended by inserting after "because of its discriminatory treatment of American commerce or because of other acts" the following: "(including the operations of international cartels)".

B. Status of Trade Agreements Program as of June 30, 1943

During the period July 1, 1942 to June 30, 1943 trade agreements were signed with Uruguay on July 21,[2] with Mexico on December 23 [3] and with Iran

[1] Public Law 66, 78th Cong.

[2] *Executive Agreement Series* 276. For analysis of provisions, see Department of State, *Bulletin,* VII, p. 654C.

[3] *Executive Agreement Series* 311. For analysis of provisions, see Department of State, *Bulletin,* VII, p. 1033.

on April 8, 1943.[1] A supplementary proclamation was issued by the President on December 11, 1942 to the effect that the agreement with Argentina, signed on October 31, 1941, and which had entered provisionally into force on November 15, 1941, should enter into force on January 8, 1943.[2]

Formal notices of intention to negotiate agreements with Iceland, Bolivia and Paraguay have been published.

(1) Reciprocal Trade Agreements Entered into Under the Trade Agreements Act of 1934 [3]

COUNTRY	DATE SIGNED	DATE EFFECTIVE	EXECUTIVE AGREEMENT SERIES
Cuba	Aug. 24, 1934	Sept. 3, 1934	67
Belgium	Feb. 27, 1935	May 1, 1935	75
Haiti	Mar. 28, 1935	Jun. 3, 1935	78
Sweden	May 25, 1935	Aug. 5, 1935	79
Brazil	Feb. 2, 1935	Jan. 1, 1936	82
Canada (see revised agreement below)	Nov. 15, 1935	Jan. 1, 1936	91
Kingdom of the Netherlands (Netherlands in Europe, Netherlands India, Surinam, and Curaçao) . .	Dec. 20, 1935	Feb. 1, 1936	100
Switzerland	Jan. 9, 1936	Feb. 15, 1936	90, 193
Honduras	Dec. 18, 1935	Mar. 2, 1936	86
Colombia	Sept. 13, 1935	May 20, 1936	89
Guatemala	Apr. 24, 1936	Jun. 15, 1936	92
France and its colonies, dependencies, and protectorates other than Morocco	May 6, 1936	Jun. 15, 1936	146
Nicaragua [4]	Mar. 11, 1936	Oct. 1, 1936	95, 120
Finland	May 18, 1936	Nov. 2, 1936	97
El Salvador	Feb. 19, 1937	May 31, 1937	101
Costa Rica	Nov. 28, 1936	Aug. 2, 1937	102
Czechoslovakia [5]	Mar. 7, 1938	Apr. 16, 1938	147
Ecuador	Aug. 6, 1938	Oct. 23, 1938	133
United Kingdom, including Newfoundland and the British Colonial Empire	Nov. 17, 1938	Jan. 1, 1939	164
Canada (revision of agreement of 1935)	Nov. 17, 1938	Jan. 1, 1939	149, 170
Turkey	Apr. 1, 1939	May 5, 1939	163
Venezuela	Nov. 6, 1939	Dec. 16, 1939	180
Cuba (supplementary agreement) .	Dec. 18, 1939	Dec. 23, 1939	165
Canada (supplementary agreement)	Dec. 30, 1939	Jan. 1, 1940	184
Canada (supplementary agreement)	Dec. 13, 1940	Dec. 20, 1940	216
Argentina	Oct. 14, 1941	Nov. 15, 1941[6]	277
Cuba (supplementary agreement) .	Dec. 23, 1941	Jan. 5, 1942	229
Peru	May 7, 1942	Jul. 29, 1942	256
Uruguay	Jul. 21, 1942	Jan. 1, 1943	276
Mexico	Dec. 23, 1942	Jan. 30, 1943	311
Iran	Apr. 8, 1943	[7]	

[1] For analysis of provisions, see *ibid.*, VIII, p. 299.
[2] *Ibid.*, VII, p. 1001.   [3] Table from Department of State.
[4] Certain provisions of the trade agreement ceased to be in force as of March 10, 1938.
[5] The operation of this agreement was suspended as of April 22, 1939.
[6] Effective definitively January 8, 1943.
[7] Effective 30 days after exchange of formal documents.

(2) Trade Agreements in Process of Negotiation, as of June 30, 1943 [1]

COUNTRY	DATE OF ISSUANCE OF PUBLIC NOTICE	LATEST DATE FOR SUBMITTING WRITTEN STATEMENTS	OPENING DATE OF PUBLIC HEARINGS
Iceland	Nov. 17, 1941	Dec. 8, 1941	Dec. 15, 1941
Bolivia	Apr. 4, 1942	May 4, 1942	May 18, 1942
Paraguay	Jun. 23, 1943	Jul. 23, 1943	Aug. 4, 1943

C. Trade Agreement with the Soviet Union

(1) Exchange of Identic Notes. The Secretary of State (Hull) to the Ambassador of the Union of Soviet Socialist Republics (Litvinov), July 31, 1942 [2]

This exchange of notes continued in force the commercial agreement between the United States of America and the Union of Soviet Socialist Republics, which was proclaimed on and became effective August 6, 1937 [3] and which was renewed for successive periods of one year on August 5, 1938,[4] August 2, 1939,[5] August 6, 1940,[6] and August 2, 1941.[7]

At the time this extension was agreed to, it was publicly stated to be the official expectation that for the ensuing year the character and amount of United States trade with the Soviet Union would be governed largely by the military requirements of the United States and of the Soviet Union and other countries struggling against the forces of armed aggression, rather than by the usual commercial considerations.

In accordance with the conversations which have taken place, I have the honor to confirm on behalf of my Government the agreement which has been reached between the Governments of our respective countries that the agreement regarding commercial relations between the United States of America and the Union of Soviet Socialist Republics recorded in the exchange of notes of August 4, 1937, which came into force on August 6, 1937, and which was renewed on August 5, 1938, August 2, 1939, August 6, 1940, and August 2, 1941 shall remain in force until August 6, 1943. It shall continue in force thereafter, unless superseded by a more comprehensive commercial agreement, subject to termination on six months' written notice by either Government.

The present agreement shall be proclaimed by the President of the United States of America and approved by the Council of People's Commissars of the Union of Soviet Socialist Republics.

Accept [etc.]

[1] Copy from Department of State.
[2] Department of State, *Bulletin*, VII, p. 663; *Executive Agreement Series* 265.
[3] *Documents*, I, *1938–39*, p. 384; E. A. S. 105.
[4] *Ibid.*; E. A. S. 132.
[5] *Ibid.*, II, *1939–40*, p. 492; E. A. S. 151.
[6] *Ibid.*, III, *1940–41*, p. 469; E. A. S. 179.
[7] *Ibid.*, IV, *1941–42*, p. 711; E. A. S. 215.

3. INTERNATIONAL COMMODITY CONTROL

A. Sugar

(1) *Protocol to Enforce and to Prolong after August 31, 1942, the International Agreement of May 6, 1937 Regarding the Regulation of Production and Marketing of Sugar, Signed at London, July 22, 1942* [1]

On May 9, 1931, a producers' agreement on the marketing of sugar, known as the Chadbourne Agreement, was concluded at Brussels. In 1933, a subcommission of the Economic Commission of the World Economic and Monetary Conference proposed a special conference on the production and marketing of sugar, [2] which met at London from April 5 to May 6, 1937. The agreement of May 6, 1937 [3] was signed by the representatives of 21 Governments, including the Government of the United States. Mr. Norman H. Davis, the United States representative, also signed "in respect of the Commonwealth of the Philippines."

The agreement was not ratified by all the signatory Governments by September 1, 1937, the date specified in Article 48 of the Agreement. It entered into force, provisionally, as of that date, in so far as states which had ratified it were concerned. [4]

The International Sugar Council by a resolution adopted on August 29, 1941 recommended that steps be taken to insure the continuance after August 31, 1942 of the International Agreement Regarding the Regulation of Production and Marketing of Sugar, signed at London on May 6, 1937. [5] Pursuant to this resolution a draft protocol was drawn up and transmitted by the British Government to the governments which were signatory to the agreement of May 6, 1937, with a request that they signify their willingness to sign the protocol. The British Ambassador at Washington by a note dated March 27, 1942 transmitted the draft protocol to this Government and under date of June 19, 1942, the American Ambassador at London was authorized to sign the protocol for the Government of the United States of America and to sign separately in respect of the Commonwealth of the Philippines. At the request of the Haitian Government the American Ambassador was subsequently authorized to sign the protocol in the name of and in respect of the Haitian Government.

By a telegram dated July 24, 1942 the Department was informed by the Ambassador that the protocol had been signed on July 22, 1942 by the following countries: United States of America, Australia, Belgium, Cuba, Czechoslovakia, Dominican Republic, Haiti, Netherlands, Peru, Commonwealth of the Philippines, Union of South Africa, Union of Soviet Socialist Republics, and United Kingdom. Subsequently the protocol was signed by Brazil and Portugal. [6]

WHEREAS an Agreement regarding the Regulation of Production and Marketing of Sugar (hereafter referred to as the Agreement) was signed in London on the 6th May, 1937; and

WHEREAS Article 48 of the Agreement provides as follows:

(a) The present Agreement shall come into force on the 1st September, 1937, if at that date it has been ratified by all the signatory Governments.

[1] Department of State, *Bulletin*, VII, p. 679.

[2] League of Nations, *Official Journal*, vol. 14 (1933), p. 1488.

[3] For text, see *Treaties, Conventions*, etc., IV, 1923–1937, p. 5599.

[4] Manley O. Hudson, *International Legislation*, VII, p. 651.

[5] This and the following portions of this note are based on a statement appearing in the Department of State, *Bulletin*, VII, p. 678.

[6] *Ibid.*, p. 841.

(*b*) If by the above-mentioned date the instruments of ratification of all the signatories have not been deposited, the Governments which have ratified the Agreement may decide to put it into force among themselves;

and

WHEREAS the ratifications of all the signatories were not deposited by the 1st September, 1937; and

WHEREAS the Agreement has been ratified by the Governments of the following countries: Union of South Africa, Commonwealth of Australia, Brazil, Belgium, United Kingdom of Great Britain and Northern Ireland, Cuba, Czechoslovakia, Dominican Republic, Germany, Haiti, Hungary, India, Netherlands, Peru, Poland, Portugal, Union of Soviet Socialist Republics, United States of America; and

WHEREAS it seems desirable that the said Agreement should be put in force between those Governments which have ratified it, the Governments of the Union of South Africa, the Commonwealth of Australia, Brazil, Belgium, the United Kingdom of Great Britain and Northern Ireland, Cuba, etc.

Now, therefore, the undersigned being duly authorized by their respective Governments have agreed as follows:

ARTICLE 1. The Agreement shall be regarded as having come into force in respect of the Governments signatories of the present Protocol, on the 1st September, 1937.

ARTICLE 2. After the 31st August, 1942, the Agreement shall continue in force among the said Governments for a period of two years from that date.

ARTICLE 3. The present Protocol shall bear this day's date and shall remain open for signature until the 31st August, 1942. It shall take effect in respect of each signatory Government on the date of signature.

In witness whereof the undersigned, being duly authorized thereto by their respective Governments, have signed the present Protocol and have affixed thereto their seals.

Done in London on the 22nd day of July, 1942, in a single copy which shall be deposited in the archives of the Government of the United Kingdom of Great Britain and Northern Ireland, and of which certified copies shall be furnished to the signatory Governments.

B. Wheat

[On considerations leading to the convening of, and the antecedents of, the Washington Wheat Meetings of July 10–August 4, 1941, and subsequent dates, see *Documents, IV, 1941–42*, p. 713.]

The Memorandum of Agreement [1] signed by representatives of the Governments of Argentina, Australia, Canada, the United Kingdom and the United States, on April 22, 1942 provided that pending the conclusion of a wheat agreement at an international wheat conference, impracticable to convene at that

[1] *Documents, IV, 1941–42*, p. 714.

time because of the war, certain provisions of the Draft Convention,[1] formulated for submission to the proposed international wheat conference, should be regarded as in force among the signatories for the purpose of dealing with the emergency situation existing during hostilities and likely to exist after the cessation of hostilities. The provisions thus referred to are specifically enumerated and defined in the Minutes of the Final Session of the Washington Wheat Meeting, April 22, 1942.[2]

Under paragraph 4 of the Memorandum, the five countries agreed to regard as in effect among themselves, pending the conclusions of an international wheat conference, "those arrangements described in the attached Draft Convention which are necessary to the administration and distribution of the relief pool of wheat and to the control of production of wheat other than those involving the control of exports." Paragraph 1 of the Minutes of the Final Session identified these arrangements as follows: paragraph 3 of Article II (Production Control), Articles VI (Relief Pool), VII (The Council) except paragraph 6, X (Finance), XVII (Definitions), and should the Council at any time so decide, Article VIII (The Executive Committee).

Under paragraph 5 of the Memorandum, the five countries agreed that in the period following the cessation of hostilities and pending the conclusion of an international wheat agreement, the arrangements in the Draft Convention "which relate to the control of production, stocks and exports of wheat and to the administration thereof will be brought into effect among themselves." The arrangements are to come into effect on such date "as may be unanimously agreed." Paragraph 2 of the Minutes of the Final Session identifies these arrangements as the following: Articles VII (except paragraph 6), VIII, X and XVII (referred to above), paragraphs 1 and 2 of Article II (Production Control), Article III (Stocks), Article IV (Export Control) except the provisions of paragraphs 10 and 12 relating to the obligations of importing countries, Article IX (Reports to the Council) and Article XVI (Territories).

Under paragraph 6 of the Memorandum, the five countries, "on the cessation of hostilities or such earlier date as they may agree, will regard as in effect among themselves the arrangements described in the attached Draft Convention for the control of the price of wheat." It was provided that the determination should be by unanimous consent. By paragraph 3 of the Minutes of the Final Session, "cessation of hostilities" was defined as "the earliest date at which none of the five countries is engaged in substantial belligerent operations." The arrangements referred to were identified in paragraph 4 of the Minutes of the Final Session as the provisions of Article V.

Paragraph 7 of the Memorandum provided that in taking any decisions under the Memorandum or the arrangements of the Draft Convention, each of the five countries "will have one vote and a two-thirds majority will be required for decision except as otherwise provided herein." Paragraph 6 of the Minutes of the Final Session provided that the seat of the Council should be in Washington during the period when the Memorandum of Agreement is in force, unless the Council should otherwise decide.

In view of the growing importance of the Draft Convention as the basis of international cooperative action involving the United States, its text, not reprinted in *Documents, IV, 1941–42*, is given here.

(1) *Draft Convention, Adopted by Washington Wheat Meeting, April 22, 1942* [3]

PREAMBLE

1. The prospects with regard to the production and marketing of wheat are such that accumulation of wheat surpluses threatens to result in grave post-

---

[1] Department of State, *Bulletin*, VII, p. 584.

[2] *Documents, IV, 1941–42*, p. 716.

[3] Department of State, *Bulletin*, VII, p. 584.

war difficulties for the economies of the producing countries and hence, because of the interdependence of nations, for the economies of all countries. It is also to be expected that, unless appropriate action is taken, such accumulation will recur.

2. A solution of the problem thus presented must be regarded as an essential part of any program of world economic reconstruction and will call for cooperative action by all countries concerned in international trade in wheat. It will involve national and international measures for the regulation of wheat production in both exporting and importing countries, for the orderly distribution of wheat and flour in domestic and international trade at such prices as are fair to consumers and provide a reasonable remuneration to producers and for the maintenance of world supplies which shall be at all times ample for the needs of consumers without being so excessive as to create a world burden of unwanted surpluses.

3. Cooperative action is also necessary to meet the need for relief in the war-stricken areas of the world by the supply and distribution of gifts of wheat.

4. The benefits of abundant world supplies of wheat cannot be assured to consumers unless there is a substantial decrease in uneconomic incentives to high-cost production, a lowering of barriers to world trade and the charging of prices to consumers not substantially higher than the price of wheat in international trade.

5. In many countries the standard of living would be improved by increasing the consumption of wheat through a lowering of prices. In all countries the standard of living would be improved by stimulating the consumption of foods rich in vitamins, proteins and minerals. The increased production of such foods would offer a more valuable use for land which has at times been used uneconomically for high-cost production of wheat.

6. Producers of an international commodity such as wheat are directly affected by standards of living throughout the world, by international purchasing power and by prevailing policies and practices affecting international trade generally. There can be no basic solution of the problem of export surpluses without a general reduction of import barriers and no measure should be taken or maintained which has the effect of retarding such reduction or of preventing in any way the fullest possible development of international trade.

Accordingly the contracting Governments have agreed as follows:

ARTICLE I (EXPANSION OF TRADE). 1. The contracting Governments agree that an essential element of a solution of the world wheat problem is that consumers should have the opportunity and means of increasing their purchases of wheat from areas which are equipped to produce it economically. They agree that such opportunity and means depend not only on the lowering of barriers to the importation of wheat but also on making available to wheat importing countries increased outlets for the exportation of goods which they in turn are equipped to produce economically. They agree that this requires the adoption and pursuit of national and international policies aimed at a fuller and more efficient use among nations of human and natural resources and thereby a worldwide expansion of purchasing power.

2. Recognizing therefore that much that is called for transcends the scope of a wheat agreement and requires action on a broad international basis, but that much also can be accomplished by national measures and by agreements with each other and with other countries, the contracting Governments undertake to further in every way possible the attainment of the foregoing objectives.

3. The Council shall from time to time submit to the contracting Governments a review of international trade in wheat and invite them to consider, in the light of the foregoing, what measures may be adopted for the expansion of such trade.

ARTICLE II (PRODUCTION CONTROL).[1] 1. The Governments of Argentina, Australia, Canada and the United States of America shall adopt suitable measures to ensure that the production of wheat in their territories does not exceed the quantity needed for domestic requirements and the basic export quotas and maximum reserve stocks for which provision is hereinafter made.

2. Should nevertheless production in any country be found to have exceeded in any crop-year the quantity above prescribed, the Government of that country shall before the end of that crop-year take such action as will result in the disappearance of the excess production within its territories before the end of the following crop-year or shall otherwise deal with such excess production as the Council may direct, except that if any part of the excess production is shown to the satisfaction of the Council to be due to a yield above the average of the preceding 20 years the Government of the country concerned may carry that part as provided in paragraph 3 (a) of Article III or deal with it in such other manner as may be agreed with the Council.

3. Pending the coming into force of paragraphs 1 and 2 of this Article, the Governments of Argentina, Australia, Canada and the United States of America shall adopt or maintain positive measures to control production with the object of minimizing the accumulation of excessive stocks.

ARTICLE III (STOCKS). 1. The Governments of Argentina, Australia, Canada and the United States of America shall, subject to the provisions of paragraphs 2, 3, 4 and 5 of this Article, ensure that stocks of old wheat held at the end of their respective crop-years are not less than 35, 25, 80 and 150 million bushels respectively, and not more than 130, 80, 275 and 400 million bushels respectively. Any stocks not in excess of the specified maximum are hereinafter called "reserve stocks."

2. Stocks of old wheat in any country may be permitted to fall below the specified minimum (a) if the new crop together with the carry-over from the previous crop-year is insufficient to meet domestic requirements and leave at the end of that crop-year the minimum reserve stocks specified, in which case those stocks may be reduced by the amount necessary fully to meet domestic requirements, and (b) in so far as the Council decides that exports from the minimum reserve stocks of that country are required fully to meet the world demand for imported wheat.

3. Stocks of old wheat may exceed the maximum by (a) the quantity of permitted excess stocks ascertained under paragraph 4 of this Article and (b) the quantity of permitted surplus stocks ascertained under paragraph 5 of this Article.

4. Such part of excess production in the first crop-year in which it occurs following the crop-year in which Article IV comes into force as may be shown under paragraph 2 of Article II to be due to above average yields shall be permitted excess stocks at the end of that crop-year. The permitted excess stocks at the end of each succeeding crop-year shall be ascertained by the Council by deducting from the permitted excess stocks, if any, at the end of the preceding crop-year any quantity by which production in the crop-year then ending was

[1] NOTE: This Article to be expanded, when further international consideration of the subject is possible, to include provisions for production control in other exporting countries and in importing countries. [Footnote in original.]

less than the maximum prescribed in paragraph 1 of Article II or by adding thereto such part of any excess production in that crop-year as may be shown under paragraph 2 of Article II to be due to above average yields.

5. Stocks in excess of the maximum, as ascertained by the Council, at the end of the crop-year in which announcement is made of the date on which the provisions of Articles II, III and IV will come into effect shall be permitted surplus stocks, unless that announcement is made less than 45 days prior to the beginning of the seeding period for the next harvest in which case stocks in excess of the maximum at the end of the succeeding crop-year shall be permitted surplus stocks. Permitted surplus stocks at the end of each succeeding crop-year shall be ascertained by the Council by deducting from the permitted surplus stocks at the end of the preceding crop-year (a) any secondary or supplementary export quotas allocated in the crop-year then ending and (b) any quantity by which production in that crop-year plus the permitted excess stocks at the end of the preceding crop-year was less than the maximum production prescribed in paragraph 1 of Article II.

6. Should it be shown to the satisfaction of the Council that, owing to insufficient or defective storage facilities, any part of the permitted surplus stocks in any country has been destroyed or has been disposed of by governmental measures in a manner clearly constituting extraordinary use such part shall nevertheless be counted as permitted surplus stocks for the purposes of paragraphs 3 and 4 of Article IV so long as any other permitted surplus stocks remain in that country.

7. The Council shall —

(a) at its regular August meeting ascertain the permitted surplus stocks in Canada and the United States of America at the end of their preceding crop-years and estimate such stocks in Argentina and Australia at the end of their current crop-years and

(b) at its regular January meeting ascertain the permitted surplus stocks in Argentina and Australia at the end of their preceding crop-years and estimate such stocks in Canada and the United States of America at the end of their current crop-years.

ARTICLE IV (EXPORT CONTROL). 1. The contracting Government of each exporting country shall adopt the measures necessary to ensure that net exports of wheat, including flour expressed in terms of its wheat equivalent, from its territories in each quota-year shall not, subject to the provisions of paragraph 11 of this Article, exceed the basic, secondary and supplementary export quotas for which provision is hereinafter made. It is recognized in principle that, within the framework of this Agreement, wheat from each exporting country should continue to find its way into its normal markets.

2. The basic export quotas for Argentina, Australia, Canada and the United States of America shall, subject to the provisions of paragraph 3 of this Article, be 25, 19, 40 and 16 percent respectively of the Council's latest published estimate of the total volume of international trade in wheat and flour in each quota-year less (a) such basic export quotas for other exporting countries as may be agreed under Article XIV and (b) reasonable allowances, having due regard to exports in past years, for net exports from the territories of Governments not parties to the Agreement.

3. Should the residual quantity ascertained under paragraph 2 of this Article exceed 500 million bushels in any quota-year, the excess shall be allocated to Argentina, Australia, Canada and the United States of America as secondary export quotas. Allocations made in the first half of the quota-year shall be in proportion to permitted surplus stocks as determined under paragraph 7 (a) of

Article III and allocations made in the second half of the quota-year shall be in proportion to permitted surplus stocks as determined under paragraph 7 (*b*) of Article III. Should there be no permitted surplus stocks in any of those four countries the excess shall be allocated to those countries as secondary export quotas in proportion to their basic export quotas.

4. If the Council is satisfied that any part of any country's export quota or of the allowance made for its exports for any quota-year will not be exported by that country in that quota-year, it shall, subject to the provisions of paragraph 6 of this Article, re-allocate that part as supplementary export quotas to the other exporting countries in accordance with the procedure prescribed in paragraph 3 of this Article for the allocation of secondary export quotas. Should there be no permitted surplus stocks in any of those countries that part shall, unless the Council otherwise decides, be re-allocated as supplementary export quotas to those of the other exporting countries which have percentage export quotas in proportion to those quotas.

5. No decisions taken by the Council pursuant to paragraph 4 of this Article shall prejudice the right of any country to export its full export quota within the quota-year to which it relates.

6. Should it be shown to the satisfaction of the Council that the failure of any country to ship any part of its export quota during the first quota-year is due to shortage of shipping, the amount of the supplementary export quotas allocated to other countries in respect of such part shall be deducted from the basic export quotas of those countries for the second quota-year and added to the afore-mentioned country's basic export quota for the second quota-year.

7. No export quota or part thereof shall be exported in any quota-year other than that to which it relates, except as otherwise provided in this Article. Should it nevertheless be shown to the satisfaction of the Council that, owing to unavoidable delay in the arrival or departure of ships, part of an export quota had not been shipped at the end of the quota-year that part may be shipped in the following quota-year but shall be deemed to have been shipped in the quota-year to which it relates.

8. No export quota or part thereof shall be ceded, transferred or loaned by any country except as provided in this Article or with the unanimous approval of the contracting Governments of exporting countries.

9. When it appears that any country is approaching the limit of its export quota, the Chairman of the Council on the recommendation of the Executive Committee shall request the Government of that country to control loadings for export during the remainder of the quota-year and to telegraph each week to the Council the gross exports and gross imports of wheat and of wheat flour from and into its territories during the preceding week.

10. When the Chairman of the Council after consultation with the Executive Committee finds that any country has exported its export quota for any quota-year he shall immediately make a declaration to that effect. The contracting Government of the exporting country concerned shall thereupon announce that the exportation of wheat or flour from its territories will not be permitted after seven days from the date of the Chairman's declaration and the contracting Government of each importing country shall not permit the importation into its territories of wheat or flour shipped from that exporting country during the current quota-year more than seven days after the date of the Chairman's declaration.

11. Should it be found that, owing to practical difficulties of closely controlling shipments, exports from any country have exceeded its export quota, that country shall not be deemed to have infringed the provisions of paragraph 1 of

this Article so long as the excess is not more than 5 percent of the quota, but the amount of that excess up to 3 percent of the quota and three times the amount of that excess above 3 percent of the quota shall be deducted from that country's export quota for the following quota-year.

12. The contracting Governments recognize that international trade in wheat should be distributed on a fair and equitable basis among all countries which export wheat and they agree that the effective operation of the Agreement should not be impaired by abnormal exports from countries that have not acceded to it. Accordingly the contracting Governments shall cooperate in taking, on the advice of the Council, such practicable measures as may be necessary to attain this end.

ARTICLE V (PRICE CONTROL). 1. The Council shall fix and publish prior to the coming into force of Article IV and thereafter at each regular August meeting a basic minimum price and a basic maximum price of wheat, c.i.f. United Kingdom ports, and schedules of prices, c.i.f. and/or f.o.b., equivalent thereto for the various wheats sold in world markets. These prices shall take effect on such date as may be determined by the Council and shall remain in force until the effective date of the prices fixed by the Council at its next regular August meeting but shall be subject to such adjustments as the Council may find necessary to meet substantial changes in freight or exchange rates or as may be made in accordance with the provisions of paragraph 3 of this Article.

2. The prices fixed under paragraph 1 of this Article shall be such as will in the opinion of the Council (a) return reasonably remunerative prices to producers in exporting countries, (b) be fair to consumers in importing countries, (c) be in reasonable relationship to prices of other commodities and (d) make appropriate allowance for exchange rates and transportation costs.

3. Should the Council so decide the basic minimum and maximum prices of wheat and the schedules of prices equivalent thereto shall be adjusted at monthly or other intervals to allow for carrying charges.

4. The Governments of Argentina, Australia, Canada and the United States of America shall not, after the coming into force of paragraph 1 of this Article, sell or permit the sale of wheat for export, or to millers for producing flour for export, at prices below the minimum equivalents fixed by the Council under paragraph 1 or 3 of this Article.

5. The Governments of Argentina, Australia, Canada and the United States of America shall ensure that wheat for export is at all times on sale at f.o.b. prices not in excess of the maximum equivalents fixed by the Council under paragraph 1 or 3 of this Article.

ARTICLE VI (RELIEF POOL). 1. The Governments of Argentina, Australia, Canada, the United Kingdom and the United States of America shall establish a pool of wheat which will be available for intergovernmental relief in war-stricken countries and other necessitous areas of the world, where circumstances in the view of those Governments make such relief practicable.

2. The Governments of Canada, the United Kingdom and the United States of America shall give to the pool, as and when required by the Council, 25, 25 and 50 million bushels respectively of wheat, or its equivalent in whole or part in flour, f.o.b. seaboard port in the country of origin.

3. The Governments of Argentina, Australia, Canada and the United States of America shall, as and when required by the Council, give to the pool in addition to the contributions prescribed in paragraph 2 of this Article a quantity of wheat or its equivalent in whole or part in flour, f.o.b. seaboard port, to be determined by them in consultation with the Council and on such basis as may be agreed among them.

4. The Council shall be responsible for the administration of the relief pool and shall, wherever possible, arrange for the distribution of relief wheat through such intergovernmental relief body as may be set up and given general responsibility for the distribution of relief. Should the Council decide to make relief wheat or flour available to any necessitous area in which the intergovernmental relief body has not the organization necessary for the distribution of such wheat or flour the Council shall arrange with the appropriate authorities to distribute such wheat or flour in that area. Any arrangements for the distribution of relief wheat shall be such as to minimize, so far as the provision of sufficient relief permits, the reduction of the effective demand for wheat on sale.

5. The United Kingdom Government may, if so agreed by the Council after consultation with the intergovernmental relief body, contribute transportation of relief wheat or flour in lieu of part or all of its contribution under paragraph 2 of this Article.

6. Any contributing Government shall, if the Council after consultation with the intergovernmental relief body so requests and upon such terms of replacement as may be agreed with the Council, make, pending the arrival of contributions by other Governments, advances of such wheat or flour as that Government may consider practicable to release for immediate relief.

7. Should the Council consider or be advised by the intergovernmental relief body that the quantity of relief wheat contributed under paragraphs 2, 3, and 5 of this Article appears likely to prove insufficient, the Council shall make recommendations to the contracting Governments regarding additional contributions.

8. The Council shall instruct the Executive Committee (a) to facilitate the transfer of relief wheat and flour from the national wheat-handling organizations of the contributing Governments to the intergovernmental relief body, (b) to maintain effective liaison between the national wheat-handling and shipping organizations of the contributing Governments and international shipping and transport controls and (c) generally to consult with the intergovernmental relief body regarding all transactions relating to the relief pool.

9. Should the Council receive, at any time after the completion of the relief to which the provisions of paragraphs 1 to 8 of this Article relate, an appeal for relief wheat or flour from any Government to relieve famine in any area within the jurisdiction of that Government, the Council shall investigate the possibilities of meeting such an appeal and report to the contracting Governments its findings together with its recommendations.

ARTICLE VII (THE COUNCIL) [1] 1. This Agreement shall be administered by an International Wheat Council consisting of one or more delegates of each contracting Government.

2. The Council shall have the powers specifically assigned to it under the Agreement and such other powers as are necessary for the effective operation of the Agreement and for the carrying out of its provisions.

3. The Council may, by unanimity of the votes cast, delegate the exercise of any of its powers or functions to such persons or bodies as it thinks fit.

4. The Council shall elect, for such periods and upon such conditions as it may determine, a Chairman and a Vice Chairman, who need not be delegates of contracting Governments.

5. The Council shall appoint a Secretary and such other employees as it considers necessary and determine their powers, duties, compensation and duration of employment

---

[1] NOTE: This Article to be expanded, when further international consideration of the subject is possible, to include provisions for voting. [Footnote in original.]

6. The seat of the Council shall be in London unless the Council should otherwise determine.

7. The Council shall meet in January and August of each year and at such other times as it may determine. The Chairman shall convene a meeting of the Council if so requested (a) by the Executive Committee or (b) by the delegates of five contracting Governments or (c) by the delegates of contracting Governments with a total of not less than —— votes.

8. Notices of all meetings shall be dispatched so as to ensure receipt by delegations of contracting Governments at least fourteen days in advance of the date fixed for the meeting.

9. Any contracting Government may designate the delegation of any other contracting Government to represent it and to vote on its behalf at any meeting of the Council or on any particular question. The terms of any such delegation of authority shall be communicated in writing by the delegating Government to the Chairman of the Council.

10. The Council may take decisions, without holding a meeting, by correspondence between the Chairman and the delegations of the contracting Governments, unless any delegation objects. Any decisions so taken shall be communicated forthwith to all the delegations and shall be recorded in the Minutes of the next meeting of the Council.

11. The Council shall make at the earliest practicable date all possible arrangements with international shipping controls to facilitate the exportation of wheat.

12. The Council shall instruct the Executive Committee (a) to cooperate with bodies engaged in the task of improving human nutrition, (b) to investigate the possibilities of increasing wheat consumption and (c) to examine and report upon any proposals made to the Council by any contracting Government designed to facilitate the attainment of the objectives of the Agreement.

13. The Council shall ascertain and make public the carry-over of wheat in Argentina, Australia, Canada and the United States of America at the end of each of their respective crop-years.

14. The Council shall, upon the request of any contracting Government of an exporting country, investigate the possibility of meeting the needs of that country for wheat storage facilities to maintain in a good state of preservation such stocks of wheat as may accumulate prior to the coming into force of Article IV. The Council shall report to the contracting Governments its findings together with its recommendations.

15. The Council shall at its regular August meeting make and publish, with such detail as it considers desirable, an estimate of the total volume of international trade in wheat and flour in the current quota-year and shall from time to time review that estimate and publish such revised estimates as it may make.

16. The Council shall publish an annual report on the operation of the Agreement which shall include a summary of relevant statistics and such other material as the Council may determine. The Council may authorize the publication of such other reports as it considers appropriate. Reports shall be published in English and in any other languages that the Council may determine.

17. Pending the establishment of the Executive Committee under Article VIII, the Council shall itself perform the functions assigned by the Agreement to that Committee.

18. The Council may arrange to take over the assets and liabilities of the Wheat Advisory Committee upon the dissolution of that body on such terms as may be agreed with it.

ARTICLE VIII (THE EXECUTIVE COMMITTEE). 1. The Council shall, when it considers it desirable to do so, establish an Executive Committee which shall work under its general direction.

2. The Chairman of the Executive Committee shall be appointed by the Council for such period and upon such conditions as it may determine. He need not be a delegate of a contracting Government to the Council or a member of the Committee.

3. The Secretary of the Council shall be the Secretary of the Executive Committee.

4. In addition to the specific duties for which provision is made in this Agreement, the Executive Committee shall be charged with the general duty of keeping under review the working of the Agreement and of reporting to the Council from time to time on the manner in which the provisions of the Agreement are being carried out.

5. The Executive Committee may be convened at any time by its Chairman.

6. The decisions of the Executive Committee shall be taken by a simple majority of the total votes held by its members.

ARTICLE IX (REPORTS TO THE COUNCIL). 1. Each contracting Government shall make to the Council such reports as the Council may from time to time request on the action which that Government has taken to carry out the provisions of this Agreement.

2. Each contracting Government shall upon request telegraph each month to the Council the gross exports and gross imports of wheat and of wheat flour from and into its territories in the preceding month, and shall supply such other information as the Council may from time to time request for the purposes of the Agreement.

ARTICLE X (FINANCE). 1. The contracting Governments shall share proportionally to the votes which they hold in the Council any expenses incurred by the Council in administering this Agreement.

2. The Council shall at its first meeting approve its budget for the period prior to the first day of the month of August after its first regular January meeting and assess the contribution to be paid by each contracting Government for that period.

3. The Council shall at each regular January meeting approve its budget for the following August–July period and assess the contribution to be paid by each contracting Government for that period.

4. The initial contribution of any Government acceding to the Agreement after the first meeting of the Council shall be assessed proportionally to the number of its votes in the Council and to the number of full months between its accession and the beginning of the first August–July period for which it is assessed under the provisions of paragraph 3 of this Article, but the assessments already made upon other Governments shall remain unaltered.

5. The Council shall publish an audited statement of all moneys received and paid out during the period referred to in paragraph 2 of this Article and during each August–July period thereafter.

6. Consideration shall be given by each contracting Government to the possibility of according to the funds of the Council and to the salaries paid by the Council to its employees who are nationals of other countries treatment in respect of taxation and of foreign exchange control no less favorable than that accorded by such Government to the funds of any other Government and to salaries paid by any other Government to any of its accredited representatives who are its nationals.

7. The Council shall determine the disposal, on the termination of the Agreement, of any funds which remain after meeting its obligations.

ARTICLE XI (DATE UPON WHICH THE AGREEMENT COMES INTO FORCE).[1]

ARTICLE XII (DURATION OF THE AGREEMENT). This Agreement shall remain in force for four years after the last day of the month of July following the date upon which it comes into force. The Council shall inquire of the contracting Governments at least six months before the Agreement is due to expire whether they desire to continue it and shall report to the contracting Governments the results of such inquiry together with its recommendations.

ARTICLE XIII (RELATION TO OTHER AGREEMENTS). 1. So long as this Agreement remains in force it shall prevail over any provisions inconsistent therewith which may be contained in any other agreement previously concluded between any of the contracting Governments.

2. Should any contracting Government be party to an agreement with a non-contracting Government containing any provision inconsistent with this Agreement, that contracting Government shall take all reasonable steps to procure the necessary amendment of such agreement at the earliest date which it deems practicable.

ARTICLE XIV (ACCESSIONS). This Agreement shall at any time be open to accession by the Government of any country on the terms contained therein so far as they are applicable to that Government and on such other terms not inconsistent therewith as may be agreed with the Council. It shall accede as the Government either of an exporting country or of an importing country as may be agreed with the Council and if it accedes as the Government of an exporting country it shall have such basic export quota as may be agreed with the Council.

ARTICLE XV (WITHDRAWALS). 1. The contracting Government of any country which considers its national security endangered as a result of hostilities may apply to the Council for the suspension of any of its obligations under Articles II, III, IV and V of this Agreement. If the application is not granted within 30 days after the date thereof, such Government may within 15 days after the end of that period withdraw from the Agreement on written notice to the Council.

2. If it is shown to the satisfaction of the Council that the Government of Argentina, of Australia, of Canada or of the United States of America has failed to carry out its obligations under paragraph 1 of Article IV or paragraph 4 of Article V, the contracting Government of any exporting country may within 90 days withdraw from the Agreement on 30 days' written notice to the Council.

3. If the Government of Argentina, of Australia, of Canada or of the United States of America withdraws from the Agreement, the Agreement shall thereupon terminate, unless the Council, by three-fourths of the total votes held in the Council, decides to maintain the Agreement with whatever modifications it may deem necessary.

ARTICLE XVI (TERRITORIES). 1. The rights and obligations under this Agreement of the Government of Argentina apply to the Customs territory thereof; those of the Government of Australia to Australia and her territories; those of the Government of Canada to the Customs territory thereof; those of the Government of the United Kingdom of Great Britain and Northern Ireland to Great Britain and Northern Ireland; and those of the Government of the United States of America to the Customs territory thereof.

2. In the event of the Government of any other country acceding to the Agreement under Article XIV, the Council shall agree with the said acceding Government as to the territories to which the rights and obligations of the said acceding Government under the Agreement shall apply.

[1] NOTE: The text of this Article to be determined when further international consideration of the subject is possible. [Footnote in original.]

ARTICLE XVII (DEFINITIONS). For the purposes of this Agreement:

1. "Bushel" means sixty pounds avoirdupois.

2. "Carrying charges" means the costs incurred for storage, interest and insurance in holding wheat.

3. "Carry-over" means the aggregate of the stocks in any country, as ascertained by the Council under paragraph 13 of Article VII, of old wheat at the end of the crop-year held (a) in all elevators, warehouses and mills, (b) in transit or at railroad sidings and (c) on farms, except that in the case of Canada "carry-over" means in addition the stocks of wheat of Canadian origin held in bond in the United States of America.

4. "Council" means the International Wheat Council for which provision is made in Article VII.

5. "Crop-year" means in respect of Argentina and Australia, the period from December 1 to November 30; in respect of Canada, the period from August 1 to July 31; and in respect of the United States of America, the period July 1 to June 30.

6. "Domestic requirements" means all use of wheat and flour during any crop-year within the territories of each contracting Government for human and animal consumption, for industrial purposes, and for seed, and waste.

7. "Equivalent," with reference to the measurement of flour in terms of wheat, means a quantity calculated in the ratio of such number of pounds of flour to 100 pounds of wheat as the Council shall determine.

8. "Executive Committee" means the Executive Committee established by the International Wheat Council under Article VIII.

9. "Exporting country" means Argentina, Australia, Canada, the United States of America or any country that may accede as such to the Agreement under Article XIV.

10. "Export quota" means basic export quota together with any secondary or supplementary export quota allocated under Article IV.

11. "Extraordinary use" means use which the Council is satisfied would not have taken place but for the governmental measures referred to in paragraph 6 of Article III.

12. "Gross exports" means the total quantity of wheat, including flour expressed in terms of its wheat equivalent, shipped from the territories of any Government, except that in the case of Canada "gross exports" means the overseas clearances of Canadian wheat from seaboard ports in Canada and the United States of America, plus imports of wheat from Canada into the United States of America for consumption and for milling in bond, plus flour expressed in terms of its wheat equivalent shipped from Canadian territories.

13. "Gross imports" means the total quantity of wheat, including flour expressed in terms of its wheat equivalent, imported into the territories of any Government.

14. "Importing country" means the United Kingdom or any country that may accede as such to the Agreement under Article XIV.

15. "Net exports" means gross exports minus gross imports.

16. "Net imports" means gross imports minus gross exports.

17. "New crop" means wheat harvested not more than two months prior to the beginning of the current crop-year.

18. "Old wheat" means wheat harvested more than two months prior to the beginning of the current crop-year.

19. "Quota-year" means the period ending July 31 following the date upon which the Agreement comes into force and thereafter the period from August 1 to July 31.

20. "Seaboard port" means any sea or river port at which a sea-going ship of 6000 tons gross can load.

21. "Shipped" means transported in any manner.

22. "Territories" means territory, or group of territories, to which the rights and obligations of the Agreement apply in accordance with the provisions of Article XVI.

23. "The beginning of the seeding period for the next harvest" means in respect of Argentina, May 1; in respect of Australia and Canada, April 1; and in respect of the United States of America, September 1.

24. "Total volume of international trade in wheat and flour" means the aggregate of the net export from each country of the world.

25. "Wheat Advisory Committee" means the Committee established under the Final Act of the Conference of Wheat Exporting and Importing Countries held in London at the Offices of the High Commissioner for Canada, from August 21 to 25, 1933.

26. "Yield" means quantity of production per unit of sown area.

Following the announcement on July 2 of the approval of the Memorandum of Agreement regarding international trade in wheat between the Governments of Argentina, Australia, Canada, the United Kingdom, and the United States, the five Governments named as their delegates to the Council the following officials:

Argentina:
Señor A. M. Viacava, Commercial Counselor, Argentine Embassy (London)
Señor Miguel E. Quirno-Lavalle, Commercial Counselor, Argentine Embassy (Washington)

Australia:
Mr. E. McCarthy, Assistant Secretary, Department of Commerce (Canberra)
Mr. F. L. McDougall, Economic Adviser to the Australian Government (London)

Canada:
Mr. Lester B. Pearson, Minister Counselor, Canadian Legation (Washington)
Mr. A. M. Shaw, Director of Marketing Service, Department of Agriculture (Ottawa)
Mr. C. F. Wilson, Chief, Agricultural Branch, Dominion Bureau of Statistics (Ottawa)
Mr. J. J. Deutsch, Special Wartime Assistant to the Department of External Affairs (Ottawa)

United Kingdom:
Mr. Noel Hall, British Minister to the United States (Washington)
Mr. E. Twentyman, British Food Mission to the United States (Washington)

United States:
Mr. Paul Appleby, Under Secretary of Agriculture (Washington)
Mr. Leslie A. Wheeler, Director, Office of Foreign Agricultural Relations, Department of Agriculture (Washington)
Mr. N. E. Dodd, Director, Western Division, Agricultural Adjustment Administration, Department of Agriculture (Washington)
Mr. R. M. Carr, Assistant Chief, Division of Commercial Policy and Agreements, Department of State (Washington).

The first meeting of the International Wheat Council, held August 3–5 in Washington, was largely devoted to questions of organization. Mr. Paul Appleby was elected chairman of the Council. The Council established an

Executive Committee, under the chairmanship of Mr. Leslie A. Wheeler, consisting of one delegate from each of the five Governments. Mr. Andrew Cairns was appointed secretary of the Council.

The Council discussed the positive measures contemplated to control production in 1943 with the object of minimizing the accumulation of excessive stocks and instructed the Secretariat to prepare, under the direction of the Executive Committee, a comprehensive report on the measures being employed in each country to control production. The Council took note of recent increases in yields per acre in several producing areas, and the Executive Committee was asked to consider the influences bearing on any trends in this connection.[1]

The next regular meeting was held in Washington, January 28–29, 1943. The Council appraised the present and prospective supply position in Argentina, Australia, Canada and the United States and concluded that, despite the heavy demand in both Canada and the United States for wheat to feed to livestock, the aggregate stocks of wheat in these four countries at the end of their 1942–43 crop-years would be the highest on record, about 1,750 to 1,800 million bushels compared with the previous record high figure of about 1,325 million bushels at the end of their 1941–42 crop-years.

The delegates discussed the plans being made to control wheat production in 1943 and concluded that these would probably result in a further substantial reduction in wheat acreage in each of the four countries, particularly in those countries where the greatly increased livestock population and the national campaigns to promote increased production of special war crops would facilitate the diversion of wheat lands to other uses.

The members of the Council exchanged views on preparations to ensure that there should be no delay in the provision of wheat and wheat flour for intergovernmental relief in war-stricken and other necessitous areas as soon as circumstances permitted. With a view to facilitating the provision of such relief the Council empowered its Executive Committee, of which Mr. L. A. Wheeler is Chairman, to assume, upon the establishment of the intergovernmental relief body envisaged in the International Wheat Agreement, the Council's authority to call upon the governments concerned to give their already agreed contributions to the relief pool. The Council instructed its Executive Committee to request the Governments of Canada, the United Kingdom and the United States to deliver part or all of their initial contributions of 25, 25 and 50 million bushels respectively at the times, rates and places and in the forms recommended by that Committee after consultation with the intergovernmental relief body.[2]

4. EXCHANGE STABILIZATION

A. International Agreement for Exchange Stabilization

(1) *Statement of Secretary of the Treasury (Morgenthau) before the Senate Committees on Foreign Relations and Banking and Currency and the Special Committee on Post-War Economic Policy and Planning, April 5, 1943* [3]

For some time we in the Treasury have been deeply concerned with the threat of international monetary chaos at the end of this war.

---

[1] Department of State, *Bulletin*, VII, p. 688.

[2] Press Communiqué issued by the International Wheat Council, Washington, D. C., January 29, 1943.

[3] From the Treasury Department.

We feel that international currency stability is essential to reconstruction in the post-war period and to the resumption of private trade and finance. It is generally held that this formidable task can be successfully handled only through international cooperation.

I think further that most of us would agree that the establishment of a program adequate to deal with the inevitable post-war monetary problems should not be postponed until the end of hostilities. It would be ill-advised, if not dangerous, to be unprepared for the difficult task of international monetary cooperation when the war ends. No one knows how long or how short the war will be. We therefore believe it is desirable to begin now to devise an international monetary agency adequate to cope with the problems with which we shall be confronted when the war does end.

The completion of such a task is certain to take many months at the least. Specific and practical proposals must be formulated and must be carefully considered by the policy-shaping officials of the various countries. In each country acceptance of a definitive plan can follow only upon legislative or executive action. And even when a plan is finally adopted, much time will be consumed in establishing an organization capable of beginning effective work.

There is another important reason for dealing with this problem now. A plan for international monetary cooperation can be a factor in winning the war. It has been suggested, and with much cogency, that the task of assuring the defeat of the Axis powers would be made easier if the victims of aggression, actual and potential, could have greater assurance that a victory of the United Nations will not mean in the economic sphere a repetition of the exchange instability and monetary collapse that followed the last war. That assurance should be given now. The people in all of the United Nations must be encouraged to feel themselves on solid ground. They must be given to understand that a victory of the United Nations will not usher in another two decades of widespread economic disruption. The people must know that we at last recognize the fundamental truth that prosperity, like peace, is indivisible.

With these points in mind the technical experts of the Treasury and other agencies of the Government for some time have been studying methods by which post-war monetary stability can be achieved. No specific plan has as yet been considered by this Government, but preliminary suggestions of our technical experts have been formulated and have been made available for exploratory study of the experts of other interested Governments. The technical men of other Governments have likewise been studying the problem.

Our own thinking along the lines of currency stability has not been addressed to concocting some panacea that will automatically cure all the economic ailments of a post-war world. Rather, we have attempted to address ourselves to the specific problem of foreign exchange stability and the common-sense way of achieving this end.

Our views are based on the rich experience that this country has had in cooperating with other Governments in our attempts to maintain exchange stability. We have tried to adapt that experience to the broader and more difficult currency problems confronting the world during the post-war years. We have also kept in mind the pattern laid down by the Tripartite Agreement and our own stabilization agreements.

Our tentative proposal is to establish an international stabilization fund in which all the United Nations and those nations which are associated with them in this war would participate. This Fund would constitute an international agency with powers and resources adequate to promote the maintenance of currency stability. The cooperating Governments who would participate in the program would, among other things, undertake not to engage in competitive depreciation of their currencies. This stability would be in large measure secured by fixing the value of currencies in terms of gold, and by providing that changes could not be made without consultation with other members.

The resources of the Fund that we have in mind would be provided by the participating governments in an amount and form suited to each nation. Participation would be in the form of gold and local currency and public obligations of the member countries. The operations of the Fund would include buying and selling of foreign exchange under adequate safeguards.

The Fund would deal only with Treasuries and central banks. It would not compete with private banks or existing agencies. Its operations would be maintained only to supplement the efforts made by each member government to maintain monetary stability. The established channels of international trade and international banking would be retained in full for all international transactions.

We have given special attention to the solution of certain troublesome monetary problems growing out of the war and have included suggestions for the handling of such problems. In particular, the Fund would facilitate the restoration of free exchange markets and liberate the abnormal balances which have accumulated in some of the countries as a consequence of war conditions.

The control of the operations of the Fund would be in the hands of an international board appointed by the governments of the member countries and the voting power on that board would be related to the contribution which each country makes to the required revolving fund.

The creation of an international agency of the character that we are contemplating is a logical development of the various tentative steps which have been made in the direction of stabilization of currencies during the immediate pre-war years.

I have been anxious to discuss this matter with you and to keep you informed of developments. Obviously, we are still in the early stages of our thinking and discussions. However, I did want you to know what we are doing and I do want to feel free to come back from time to time and discuss the subject with you and obtain your views and advice.

(2) *Letter from the Secretary of the Treasury (Morgenthau) to the Ministers of Finance of Thirty-Seven Foreign Countries,*[1] *Released to the Press, April 7, 1943* [2]

The Preliminary Draft Outline of Proposal for a United and Associated Nations Stabilization Fund [3] was drawn up by technical experts in the Treasury Department under the direction of Dr. Harry D. White, Director of Monetary Research. It came subsequently to be referred to as the White Plan. The purpose of the scheme was declared to be to stabilize the value of the currencies of member countries. To achieve this stability, the establishment of a Fund was proposed which would, with adequate safeguards, meet the legitimate needs of member countries for foreign exchange for their current transactions. The Fund would be established by subscriptions by member countries, of at least $5 billion, initial payments of one-half of the subscription being in the form of gold, currency and government securities. Exchange control by individual countries would be largely eliminated, and where allowed, would be brought under international control. The Fund would be given extensive power to buy and sell gold, currencies, and, with their approval, the securities of member countries. It would deal only with treasuries, central bank or fiscal agents of member states, or with international banks owned predominantly by member countries. The proposal provided for an international gold monetary unit called the Unitas, equal in value to $10. The Fund would be managed by a Board of Directors representing the member governments, each country having voting power related to its subscription to the Fund, but no country having more than 25 per cent of the total votes. Most decisions would be by a majority vote except that for certain important decisions a four-fifths vote would be necessary.

The publication of the draft prepared by United States Treasury experts (White Plan) was followed immediately by the publication on April 8 of British Proposals for an International Clearing Union.[4] The proposals were the result of study by Treasury experts in consultation with other departments. Because of the conspicuous role of Baron Keynes in the drafting of them, they came to be referred to as the Keynes Plan. It was stated in a prefatory note that "H. M. Government is not committed to the principles or details of the scheme. . . . It is hoped that these proposals will afford a basis for discussion, criticism and constructive amendment, together with similar plans, having similar objectives which may be prepared by experts of other governments. On these terms it has

---

[1] The countries to whose Finance Ministers the letters were addressed are the following: Australia, Belgium, Brazil, Canada, China, Costa Rica, Cuba, Czechoslovakia, Dominican Republic, El Salvador, Ethiopia, Great Britain, Greece, Guatemala, Haiti, Honduras, India, Iraq, Luxemburg, Mexico, Netherlands, New Zealand, Nicaragua, Norway, Panama, Poland, Union of South Africa, Union of Soviet Socialist Republics, Yugoslavia, Bolivia, Colombia, Chile, Ecuador, Paraguay, Peru, Uruguay, Venezuela.

[2] From the Treasury Department.

[3] *Preliminary Draft Outline of a Proposal for An International Stabilization Fund of the United and Associated Nations.* Washington, U. S. Treasury, April 7, 1943.

[4] *International Clearing Union. Text of a Paper Containing Proposals by British Experts for an International Clearing Union.* British Information Services, N. Y., April 8, 1943.

been presented for technical examination by experts of the U. S. Government. . . ."

Apart from form and style the provisions of the Keynes Plan which distinguished it most sharply from the White Plan were (1) emphasis upon the clearing function; (2) proposal of a mutual credit pool instead of an initial fund; (3) more liberal and flexible provisions for borrowing; and (4) voting power based on volume of foreign trade.

It was made clear in the official statements of both the British and American Governments that the two plans were submitted as bases for further discussion between technical experts and were not to be regarded as reflecting the considered views of the two Governments.

My dear Mr. Minister:

I am sending for your examination a preliminary draft of a Proposal for an International Stabilization Fund of the United and Associated Nations. This draft was prepared by the technical staff of the United States Treasury in consultation with the technical experts of other departments of this Government.

The document is sent to you not as an expression of the official views of this Government but rather as an indication of the views widely held by the technical experts of this Government. I hope you will examine the draft and submit it for critical study by the technical experts of your Ministry and your Government. After you and your experts have had opportunity to study it, you may wish to send one or more of your technical experts to Washington to give me your preliminary reaction to the draft proposal, and to discuss with our technical experts the feasibility of international monetary cooperation along the lines suggested therein, or along any other lines you may wish to suggest. We are informed that the technical experts of the British Government have also been studying the question and will doubtless make their views available.

It seems to me that the enclosed draft proposal points the way to an effective means of facilitating through cooperative action the maintenance of international monetary stability and the restoration and balanced growth of international trade. It is my hope that as a result of unofficial discussion involving no commitments, we may find a sufficient area of agreement to warrant proceeding on a more formal basis.

Officials of the Canadian Government after examining the United States Treasury Department Preliminary Draft Outline of a Proposal for a United and Associated Nations Stabilization Fund and the Proposals of British Experts for an International Clearing Union held discussions with both British and American officials which were entirely exploratory in character. It was stated that the Canadian Government had not been committed to any course of action as a result of these conversations. The American and British experts, for their part, had laid stress on the fact that their proposals were tentative in character, and had made it clear to representatives of the Canadian Government (as well as to those of other governments) that they would welcome critical comment and constructive suggestions. Canadian experts who had been studying the British and the American proposals were therefore led to make General Observations [1] and to submit an alternative plan. Like the British and the American plans, the proposals of the Canadian experts were provisional and tentative in character; they incorporated important features of both the American and the British plans and added to them certain new elements. The following statement of purpose and summary of these observations indicates the general content:

"4. The establishment of an international monetary organization is no substitute for the measures of international relief and rehabilitation which will be required as the war draws to its conclusion and afterwards; and in the view of the Canadian experts any monetary organization which is set up should not be called upon to finance transactions of this nature. Some continuing and stable arrangements regarding international long-term investment are also clearly essential if equilibrium is to be achieved and maintained. Nor should it be thought that the proposed international monetary institution is merely an instrument of the transition period from war to peace. True, it has special importance in this period, but it should be designed as a permanent institution and not as a stop-gap to function during a relatively short period of time."

.   .   .   .

"13. To sum up these general observations, it is suggested that:—

(a) An international agreement for the establishment of an international monetary organization which involves the extension of credit is essential if international cooperation in the post-war world is to be achieved.

(b) Such machinery will deal with only one of the numerous problems which must be faced, but it is a logical and convenient starting place for joint international action.

(c) The credit made available through the international monetary organization should be adequate to deal with that portion of current account surpluses and deficits which is not met by relief and other concerted international action in the years immediately after the war; it should be sufficient to provide a firm basis on which multilateral world trade can be reestablished after the war; and it should provide time to countries which find their international accounts unbalanced to take the necessary corrective measures to adjust their position.

(d) The extension of credit is not a cure-all; it merely provides time for adjustments; and unless unbalanced positions (except those accompanying long-term capital movements) are brought into equilibrium, any arrangements made will break down.

(e) No country participating in the arrangements loses control over the size of its international commitments, since it can determine their size by its own action, if it wishes to do so.

(f) No country participating in the arrangements loses control over its domestic economic policies."

B. National Stabilization Fund

(1) *An Act to Extend the Time Within Which the Powers Relating to the Stabilization Fund May Be Exercised, Approved April 29, 1943* [2]

The Gold Reserve Act of 1934, approved January 30, 1934, conferred upon the President certain powers relating to the alteration of the gold content of

[1] *Tentative Draft Proposals of Canadian Experts for an International Exchange Union*, Ottawa, June 1943.   [2] Public Law 42, 78th Cong., 1st sess.

the dollar and the establishment of a stabilization fund to assist in maintaining the stability of international exchange. These powers were conferred for two years, subject to the right of the President to extend them for one year which he did in January 1936. In 1937, 1939 and 1941 these powers were extended by Congress for additional two-year periods.

Under the provisions of Congressional enactments, the powers conferred were due to expire automatically June 30, 1943 unless renewed by Congress. On April 12, Senator Wagner (New York) introduced S. 991 (A bill to extend the time within which the powers relating to the stabilization fund and alteration of the weight of the dollar may be exercised).[1] The Committee on Banking and Currency, to which the bill was referred, held public hearings and reported it with amendments.[2] In its amended form, provision for the extension of the President's power to devalue further the dollar was omitted. With a corresponding amendment of title the bill was passed.[3]

The bill was referred to the House Committee on Coinage, Weights and Measures and reported out on April 21 with amendment.[4] In his testimony before the House Committee Secretary of the Treasury Morgenthau stated that, while under the Act as it stood his legal experts had advised him that the fund might be used to provide the United States contribution to an international stabilization fund, he had no intention of taking such action without securing the approval of Congress. To confirm this understanding, and to make it impossible for such action to be taken by any other official not so pledged, an amendment providing that "such fund shall not be used in any manner whereby direct control and custody thereof passes from the President and the Secretary of the Treasury" was introduced and adopted.[5] In its amended form, the bill was adopted by the House, April 21.[6] The Senate concurred on April 22.[7] In both houses, it was made clear in brief debate that it was not intended to pass judgment on the merits of any proposal for international exchange stabilization, but simply to make certain that any such proposal should be submitted to the Congress for approval and that it should not be possible to take advantage of a possible legal interpretation of the Gold Reserve Act of 1934 to put the proposal into operation by purely executive action.

Be it enacted by the Senate and House of Representatives of the United States of America in Congress assembled, That subsection (b) of section 10 of the Gold Reserve Act of 1934, approved January 30, 1934, as amended, is amended by inserting after the second sentence thereof the following new sentence: "Such fund shall not be used in any manner whereby direct control and custody thereof pass from the President and the Secretary of the Treasury."

SEC. 2. Subsection (c) of section 10 of the Gold Reserve Act of 1934, approved January 30, 1934, as amended, is amended to read as follows:

"(c) All the powers conferred by this section shall expire June 30, 1945, unless the President shall sooner declare the existing emergency ended and the operation of the stabilization fund terminated."

---

[1] *Congressional Record*, vol. 89, pt. 3, p. 3264.
[2] Senate Report No. 200, 78th Cong., 1st sess.
[3] *Congressional Record*, vol. 89, pt. 3, p. 3467.
[4] *Ibid.*, p. 3638.
[5] House Report No. 374, 78th Cong., 1st sess.
[6] *Congressional Record*, vol. 89, pt. 3, p. 3641.
[7] *Ibid.*, p. 3673.

CHAPTER IX

TRANSPORTATION AND COMMUNICATIONS

1. ACQUISITION OF FOREIGN MERCHANT SHIPS

(1) *Executive Order No. 9350 Conferring Certain Additional Authority upon the Administrator of the War Shipping Administration, June 10, 1943* [1]

By virtue of the authority vested in me by the act entitled "An Act to authorize the acquisition by the United States of title to or the use of domestic or foreign merchant vessels for urgent needs of commerce and national defense, and for other purposes," approved June 6, 1941 (55 Stat. 242), as extended by the act of June 16, 1942, 56 Stat. 370, it is ordered as follows:

1. The Administrator of the War Shipping Administration is hereby authorized to exercise until six months after the termination of the present war shall have been proclaimed the authority vested in him by Executive Order No. 9054 of February 7, 1942,[2] to purchase, requisition, charter, requisition the use of, or take over the title to, or the possession of, foreign merchant vessels lying idle in the waters within the jurisdiction of the United States, including the Philippine Islands and the Canal Zone; and any such vessel so acquired may be documented under the laws of the United States or of any foreign country.

2. All acts of the Administrator of the War Shipping Administration subsequent to June 30, 1942, with respect to any matters or things authorized by paragraph 1 hereof are hereby ratified.

2. USE OF AVAILABLE SHIPPING FACILITIES

On December 4, 1942 the United States and Great Britain signed an agreement regarding problems of marine transportation and litigation aimed primarily at eliminating losses of tonnage and manpower in useless litigation. In general, each Government agreed to waive claims against the other arising out of collisions, damage to cargo, and the rendering of salvage services.[3] See this volume, p. 225, for the full text of the agreement. A similar agreement was entered into with the Canadian Government by an exchange of notes on May 25, 26, 1943 (see p. 461).

Also intended to further the more efficient use of vital shipping facilities was the action of Great Britain in suspending the International Load Line Con-

---

[1] 8 *Fed. Reg.*, p. 7887.

[2] 7 *ibid.*, p. 837; see also *Documents, IV, 1941–42*, p. 776.

[3] Department of State, *Bulletin*, VIII, p. 28.

vention for the duration of the emergency, as the United States had already done on August 9, 1941.[1] On August 8, 1942 the American Ambassador at London informed the Secretary of State he had received a note from the British Foreign Office calling attention to the expiration on August 31, 1942 of the Modifications of the Convention, which were announced in August 1941.

The note stated that "we propose to continue the application of the declaration to United Kingdom ships for the period of the national emergency, i.e., until the end of six months after the cessation of hostilities between the United Kingdom and Germany. . . . We are notifying accordingly all Governments which we invited to join us in making the declaration in question and we are suggesting to them that they extend similarly the measure which they have taken."[2]

The British Government specifically suggested as modifications that ships may be permitted to load:

(a) To their tropical marks instead of their summer marks when the latter are applicable under the provisions of the said Convention;

(b) To the fresh water tropical marks instead of the existing tropical marks when the latter are applicable under the provisions of the said Convention.

3. THE POST-WAR MERCHANT MARINE POLICY

In February 1943 the annual report of the Chamber of Shipping of the United Kingdom forecast that the British merchant marine would eventually have to yield leadership to the United States. This view was implicitly confirmed by a speech of Rear Admiral Emory S. Land in June 1943 in which he laid down a concrete program of post-war shipping policy. He advocated reversal of former United States Maritime Commission policy regarding tramp shipping by making it a definite part of the maritime economy; private ownership, private operation, and private construction; shipment of "a liberal percentage of our overseas traffic" in American bottoms; establishment of proper routes, lines, and services with a minimum of American competition necessary; and maintenance for the duration of the Commission's present policy of holding title to new ships.[3]

(1) *Address by Rear Admiral Emory S. Land (U.S.N. Retired), Chairman, United States Maritime Commission, and War Shipping Administrator, at Baltimore, Maryland, June 7, 1943* [4]

[Excerpt]

•   •   •   •   •   •   •

Our post-war maritime objectives are not being overlooked because of the exigencies of war. We are not losing sight of the objective manifestly set up in the Merchant Marine Act of 1936 which gives to the Maritime Commission the duty of proper rehabilitation of the Merchant Marine. The Commission has a new economic survey well underway. We have a tentative program in formulation and a skeleton organization in being.

[1] See *Documents, IV, 1941–42*, p. 774.

[2] Department of State, *Bulletin*, VIII, p. 859.

[3] For a statement of the Maritime Commission's policy of retaining full title and control in the allocation of American-built freighters to Allies in the war, see *New York Times*, November 14, 1942.

[4] Copy received from U. S. Maritime Commission. The address was delivered before the Maryland Historical Society on the occasion of the observance of Maritime Day.

In fact, a start on that was made more than a year and a half ago by a group which is now called the American Maritime Council.

Suggestions I would make with regard to American policy covering the United States Merchant Marine, with primary reference to our after-the-war position are:

(a) Private ownership, private operation and private construction.

(b) Ship American; travel American.

(c) Our goal is to ship a liberal percentage of our overseas traffic in American bottoms.

(d) Set up proper routes, lines and services with a minimum of American competition as foreign flags will furnish all possible competition necessary.

(e) Study seriously indirect lines as other leading Maritime Nations have done. We have every right to compete on the indirect lines.

(f) Modify previous Maritime Commission policy by thoroughly considering and adopting tramp shipping.

(g) Maintain for the duration our present policy of holding title to new ships.

In order to plan properly for the after-the-war period consideration must be given to the probable fleet under American flag that will be in existence at the end of the War. We should definitely earmark for United States commerce, under United States flag, a modern fleet of from 15 to 20 million deadweight tons. As a Nation of 135 million people, we are entitled to that tonnage. As the greatest shipbuilding Nation in the world, we are entitled to have it as modern and up to date as the exigencies of the war permit.

In order to give reasonable consideration to the over-all shipping industry of the United States, we should so set our sights as to hold this fleet of about 20 million deadweight tons and in addition, even though not necessary from a world-economic point of view, it is very desirable that we lay out our plans so that our best shipyards properly distributed throughout the United States should be able to proceed with a nucleus of construction of new ships even though we may build up a reserve. While we have no excess today of shipbuilding capacity for war purposes, it is unthinkable to believe that the day the War ends it will be possible to stop immediately all ship construction in the United States. Let us plan accordingly so that we can so modify this ship construction as not to permit a collapse of the shipbuilding industry.

By the same token, it appears probable that we will have an excess of ships at the end of the War and we should so plan as to retain not only a proper Merchant Marine Fleet but also a reasonable reserve even though such action might be uneconomical at that particular time.

War causes some sacrifice on the part of every citizen in the United States from the most menial worker at home to the man who lays down his life for his country in the war zone. It must be evident to each of us that peace will also mean some sacrifice for every individual even though the sacrifice is quite different from that which obtains in War. There is no lack of patriotism in this grand country of ours from a war-time point of view; there should be no lack of intelligence and economic patriotism from a peace-time point of view.

.   .   .   .

4. CIVIL AIR TRANSPORT

For statement by Assistant Secretary of State Berle before the House Foreign Affairs Committee on the right to commercial air bases as a benefit to be received under Lend-Lease, and steps taken by the Government for the protection of post-war aviation rights, see p. 122.

CHAPTER X

TREATMENT OF PERSONS

1. PERSONS ENTERING AND LEAVING THE UNITED STATES

[See *Documents, IV, 1941–42*, p. 788.]

(1) *Summary of Report of Board of Appeals on Visa Cases to the President (Roosevelt), Released to the Press, November 29, 1942* [1]

The first report of the Board of Appeals on Visa Cases was made to the President in November 1942. On the establishment and duties of the Board, see *Documents, IV, 1941–42*, p. 792.

Robert J. Bulkley, former Senator from Ohio, and Frederick P. Keppel, former President of the Carnegie Corporation, were appointed to the Board of Appeals on Visa Cases on December 3, 1941 by the President on the joint recommendation of the Secretary of State and the Attorney General; later, Dean F. D. G. Ribble of the University of Virginia Law School was added as an alternate member of the Board.

The purpose of the appointment was "to supplement the function of investigation already efficiently conducted by the representatives of the State Department, the Army and Navy Intelligence, the Federal Bureau of Investigation, and the Immigration Service by an independent agency evaluative rather than investigative in character."

Since January first, when the present procedure was established, the Primary Committees, made up from the representatives mentioned, have cleared 2,951 applications. The Review Committees, similarly composed, which hold hearings on cases not favorably acted upon by the Primary Committees, have favorably recommended 1,782. The Board of Appeals has thus far recommended 1,283 applications in cases passed on adversely by the Review Committees and also has confirmed 736 recommendations for the issuance of visas to alien enemies, concurring with the favorable recommendations of the Review Committees. The present disturbed conditions throughout the world and the care exercised in the elimination of persons who might be harmful to the national welfare have combined to reduce the total number of admissions to less than one tenth of the admissions in a normal pre-war year.

The Committees and the Board are concerned first with the fundamental question as to whether the applicant may receive his visa with safety to the United States, and are agreed that only when adequate

[1] Department of State, *Bulletin*, VII, p. 982.

assurance of safety appears can weight be given to the second fundamental question — that of benefit. Their sympathies are daily aroused by records of suffering and distress, but sympathies must be held in control until safety and benefit are determined. The presidential proclamations prescribe a funding of benefit to the United States in the granting of visas to enemy aliens. An early finding of the Board found such benefit in maintaining the traditional American policy of providing a haven of refuge for decent people who are in distress and peril. Affirmative benefit has been found in the admission of doctors, dentists, nurses, and other professionally trained people and of those with technical and industrial skills useful in the war effort. Indirectly, the effect upon civilian and military morale within the United States is also considered, it being believed that a favorable decision, when it may safely be made, will enhance morale and an unfavorable decision will tend to lower it not only among the relatives and friends of the applicants but throughout a larger group of the same race and background now in the United States, many of them in the armed forces.

The 6,152 applications thus far examined by the Board involve more than twice as many individuals. Of these more than one fourth are now in the United States, 1 in 6 of them illegally. A tenth are or were in Cuba; about as many, elsewhere in the Western Hemisphere. Overseas nearly two fifths of the total are in detention camps; the remainder are in England, Switzerland, or more widely scattered. Birth statistics contrast sharply with those of present residence. More than two fifths of all applicants had already moved from one country to another even before the days of organized persecution or armed invasion. Thirty-one percent are German-born, 27 percent Poles, 12 percent Austrian, 6 percent each from Hungary, France, and Russia; a somewhat slighter proportion from Spain; the remainder are widely scattered. Only 1 application has come from a person of Japanese birth.

The most serious difficulty in the procedure is the frequent absence of information regarding the applicant adequate to justify the granting of a visa under war conditions. Even close relatives in this country have in many instances not seen the applicant for years, and other sponsors can furnish information only at second hand. It is a painful duty to refuse admission to people who appear to be decent and deserving, and with devoted sponsors, and to do so wholly because of the absence of information adequate to furnish the basis of an informed judgment.

The report discusses the delay in the clearing of cases, pointing out the presence of unavoidable factors under war conditions, and intimates that plans are under way for expediting the procedure wherever possible.

The hostage problem is fully discussed and also the difficulties frequently involved in determining whether or not an applicant is an enemy alien.

The report closes with the statement to the effect that the procedure may have a significance far beyond the safety and happiness of the individuals concerned. Many persons have been granted visas who by their knowledge and ability in science and the learned professions or by their skill as artisans and mechanics will contribute directly to the well-being of the Nation. Others are courageous men who in their own lands have led in the democratic opposition to the Nazis and whose admission to the United States is an evidence of confidence in and a source of encouragement to forces of democracy still working in occupied territories. Many others are persons without distinction, often very humble people, who have suffered grievously under the Nazi tyranny. Ideals of fair treatment of all decent people who are oppressed and who seek such treatment at our hands have been forcefully expressed in the declaration of the four freedoms and in the Atlantic Charter. Acts of the United States in giving relief to deserving people, the victims of tyranny, furnish present proof by deed of the good faith of these verbal declarations. They exhibit the United States before the whole world as having the strength and courage to stand firm in the common cause of humanity even in stress of war.

On March 5, 1943 the Secretary of State issued regulations relating to the transportation of subjects or citizens of an enemy or an ally-of-an-enemy by American vessels or American aircraft which revoked all previous regulations that were inconsistent.[1] On June 15, 1943, by Executive Order 9352,[2] the President prescribed regulations governing the entry of alien seamen into the United States, for the most part superseding and canceling Executive Order 8429 of June 5, 1940.

2. TREATMENT OF ENEMY ALIENS

[See *Documents, IV, 1941–42*, p. 811.]

The policy of the United States with regard to the treatment of enemy aliens followed the same general lines already laid down. On July 17, 1942, following the declaration of war against Hungary, Rumania and Bulgaria, the President issued a proclamation enjoining all natives, citizens, etc. of these countries "to preserve the peace . . . to refrain from crime against the public safety . . . and actual hostility . . ."[3] This proclamation duplicated in substance a proclamation of December 7, 1941 designating Japanese subjects as enemy aliens and setting forth rules governing their conduct.[4]

(1) *Employment of Aliens or Former Nationals of Another Country. Statement of the President (Roosevelt), July 11, 1942* [5]

In order to clarify the policy of the Government in regard to the employment of aliens and other persons of foreign birth, the President today issued the following statement:

[1] 8 *Fed. Reg.*, p. 2817–21.   [2] *Ibid.*, p. 8209.   [3] For text see 7 *Fed. Reg.*, p. 5535.
[4] See *Documents, IV, 1941–42*, p. 817.   [5] *New York Times*, July 12, 1942.

1. Persons should not hereafter be refused employment, or persons at present employed discharged, solely on the basis of the fact that they are aliens or that they were formerly nationals of any particular foreign country. A general condemnation of any group or class of persons is unfair and dangerous to the war effort. The Federal Government is taking the necessary steps to guard against, and punish, any subversive acts by disloyal persons, citizens as well as aliens.

2. There are no legal restrictions on the employment of any person (A) in non-war industries, and (B) even in war industries, if the particular labor is not on "classified" contracts, which include secret, confidential, restricted and aeronautical contracts.

The laws of the United States do provide that in certain special instances involving government contracts an employer must secure from the head of the government department concerned permission to employ aliens. Section 11 (A) of the act of June 28, 1940 (Public No. 671, 76th Congress, 3d Session) contains a provision that:

"No aliens employed by a contractor in the performance of secret, confidential, or restricted government contracts shall be permitted to have access to the plans or specifications, or the work under such contracts, or to participate in the contract trials, unless the written consent of the head of the government department concerned has first been obtained."

The Air Corps Act of 1926 has a similar provision:

"No aliens employed by a contractor for furnishing or constructing aircraft parts or aeronautical accessories for the United States shall be permitted to have access to the plans or specifications or the work under construction or to participate in the contract trials without the written consent beforehand of the secretary of the department concerned."

There are no other Federal laws which restrict the employment of aliens by private employers in national war industries. There are no Federal laws restricting the employment of foreign-born citizens of any particular national origin.

3. Where, under the law, permission to employ aliens is required from the War and Navy Departments, the alien shall go to the nearest office of the United States Employment Service, which will furnish him with application form, and assist him in filling it out. The completed form will then be submitted by the alien to the employer who will fill out the reverse side of the form, and then immediately forward same to the department concerned. Upon receipt of the application, the department will act promptly thereon, in the normal case within forty-eight hours, and give its approval or disapproval, either of which shall be subject to change at any later time.

4. In passing upon applications for permits, the department will give special and expedited consideration to nationals of United Nations and

friendly American Republics, and any other aliens, including enemy aliens, who come within the following categories:

A. Aliens who have served in the armed forces of the United States and have been honorably discharged.

B. Aliens who have, or who have had, members of their immediate family in the United States military service.

C. Aliens who have resided in the United States continuously since 1916 without having returned to the country of origin within the last ten years.

D. Aliens who have married persons who, at the time of marriage, were citizens of the United States and who have resided in the United States continuously since 1924 without having returned to the country of origin within the last ten years.

E. Aliens who have declared their intention to become citizens of the United States and who had filed petitions for naturalization before December 7, 1941.

5. Any inquiries or complaints by aliens, pertaining to specific instances of discrimination, or intentional failure to carry out the above procedure, should be referred directly to the Committee on Fair Employment Practice, Washington, D. C. This committee will consider the complaints and take such action as may be warranted in the particular case.

6. Any information concerning disloyal activities in war industries or elsewhere, or indications of disloyalty on the part of persons employed in war industries, should be reported immediately to the nearest office of the Federal Bureau of Investigation. Employees have the same duty in this matter as have employers.

(2) *Address by the Attorney General of the United States (Biddle), with Regard to Italian Aliens, Carnegie Hall, New York City, October 12, 1942* [1]

[Excerpt]

The action by the United States Government in removing Italian aliens from the enemy alien classification was apparently the first concrete step taken in an effort to drive a wedge between the Italian Government and the people. Assistant Secretary of State Berle added a sort of postscript on November 14 when, in addressing the Mazzini Society in New York, he made a special appeal to "the true Italy" as against the Fascist regime.[2]

.   .   .   .

I have an announcement to make to you tonight, that comes as a result of the splendid showing the Italians of America have made in meeting this test. It also comes as the fulfilment of my own hopes, the consummation of a project that has been very close to my heart. I now

[1] *New York Times*, October 13, 1942.
[2] See this volume, p. 170.

announce to you that beginning October 19, a week from today, Italian aliens will no longer be classed as alien enemies. From that time on the exoneration which they have so well earned will be granted them. With the approval of the President I have today issued the following order:

"Section 30.2 of the Regulations Controlling Travel and Other Conduct of Enemy Nationalities is amended by adding thereto paragraph (f), so that it will read: Classes of persons not required to comply with these regulations:

(f) Any alien of Italian nationality."

Of course, this does not mean that dangerous or disloyal persons are no longer subject to apprehension or internment. We still will take no chances. It does mean that the regulations applying, up to now, to alien enemies no longer apply to Italian aliens. Those persons, though they are still aliens, are not, from this time forth, subject to the restrictions imposed by existing regulations on alien enemies. They will be free to participate in the war effort without the handicaps that have hampered them up to now. They will be free to travel and go about their lives as any other person.

. . . .

3. COORDINATION OF RELIEF

[See *Documents, III, 1940–41*, p. 609; *IV, 1941–42*, p. 833.]

(1) *Report of the President's Committee on War Relief Agencies to the President (Roosevelt), Released to the Press, July 27, 1942* [1]

Your Committee on War Relief Agencies respectfully submits the following report.

In the foreign relief field, a degree of success has been achieved in reducing the number of agencies and coordinating the activities of those remaining. The number of active foreign relief agencies is now approximately 300 as compared with some 700 or more during the peak period in early 1941. While this is a definite improvement, further coordination and consolidation is desirable in the public interest.

Funds and contributions in kind raised by agencies registered with the Department of State from the beginning of the war to the end of May 1942 have totalled over $71,000,000. During the same period other foreign relief agencies raised a total estimated at $25,000,000. It is significant that the administrative and other costs of the agencies registered with and subject to supervision by the Department of State have averaged only about 10 percent of total receipts while those of other foreign relief agencies have averaged, on the basis of somewhat

[1] Department of State, *Bulletin*, VII, p. 657.

incomplete information, 30 percent or more. It is also significant that administrative expenses of the latter group have shown an appreciable decrease since the President's Committee requested periodic reports from them, even though the Committee has been able to exercise only advisory supervision. The present rate of collections by foreign relief agencies, other than the Red Cross, is substantially below the peak, with a resulting increase in the percentage of overhead costs, but this decrease in collections is far more than offset by the increase in domestic relief solicitations.

In the domestic relief and welfare field, the entry of the United States into the war has quite naturally resulted in the establishment of a very large number of new agencies appealing to the public for funds and contributions for the relief and welfare of our own civilian population and armed forces. As there is at present no central registration or other regulatory authority, these organizations are subject to no coordinated supervision or control and even their number can only be estimated.

While actuated by the highest humanitarian motives, these agencies tend to duplicate each other's efforts causing public confusion and uncertainty. Undue competition among themselves and between them and the foreign relief agencies leads to a waste of financial resources and manpower and thus tends to hamper the national war effort. There is a lack of correlation between the programs of the private agencies in both the domestic and foreign relief fields, and those of the Red Cross and of the several governmental agencies concerned with various phases of relief and welfare.

Certain important objectives of the Committee have not so far been accomplished, because of lack of authority. There remain, as indicated above, two important factors affecting national unity of effort in these times of emergency — (a) the public is subject to solicitation from far too many agencies representing an excessive amount of duplication and (b) the limited amount of leadership that exists for charitable, welfare and Government war bond campaigns is overly occupied and its effectiveness seriously diminished and dissipated.

The Committee believes that these facts call for a central authority with general jurisdiction and powers to bring about coordination of effort and elimination of duplication and waste. Pursuant thereto, the Secretary of State, upon whose recommendation this Committee was originally appointed, has suggested that, as the domestic relief field is now dominant, it would be in the national interest to consolidate, in such a central authority, supervision over both domestic and foreign relief agencies, including the administration of Section 8 (b) of the Neutrality Act, 1939, now vested in the Secretary of State.

The Committee recommends, therefore, that adequate powers be delegated to a central authority and suggests that this might be done by the issuance of an Executive Order.

(2) *Executive Order No. 9205 Establishing the President's War Relief Control Board and Defining Its Functions and Duties, July 24, 1942* [1]

In accordance with the recommendation of the President's Committee on War Relief Agencies, the President on July 24 signed the Executive order given below. On July 30, 1942, the President's War Relief Control Board prescribed certain regulations governing solicitation and collection of funds and contributions for war relief and welfare, which are to supersede the regulations promulgated by the Secretary of State under authority of sections 8 and 13 of the Neutrality Act of 1939 relating to relief contributions.[2]

By virtue of the authority vested in me by the Constitution and statutes of the United States, as President of the United States of America and Commander-in-Chief of the Army and Navy, because of emergencies affecting the national security and defense, and for the purpose of controlling in the public interest charities for foreign and domestic relief, rehabilitation, reconstruction, and welfare arising from war-created needs, it is hereby ordered as follows:

1. The President's Committee on War Relief Agencies, appointed by me on March 13, 1941, is hereby continued and established as the President's War Relief Control Board, hereinafter referred to as the Board. The Chairman of the Board shall be responsible to the President.

2. The Board is hereby authorized and empowered —

(*a*) to control, in the interest of the furtherance of the war purpose, all solicitations, sales of or offers to sell merchandise or services, collections and receipts and distribution or disposition of funds and contributions in kind for the direct or implied purpose of (1) charities for foreign and domestic relief, rehabilitation, reconstruction and welfare arising from war-created needs in the United States or in foreign countries, (2) refugee relief, (3) the relief of the civilian population of the United States affected by enemy action, or (4) the relief and welfare of the armed forces of the United States or of their dependents; *Provided*, that the powers herein conferred shall apply only to activities concerned directly with war relief and welfare purposes and shall not extend to local charitable activities of a normal and usual character nor in any case to intra-state activities other than those immediately affecting the war effort;

(*b*) (1) to provide for the registration or licensing of persons or agencies engaged in such activities and for the renewal or cancellation of such registration or licenses; (2) to regulate and coordinate the times and amounts of fund-raising appeals; (3) to define and promulgate ethical standards of solicitation and collection of funds and contributions in kind; (4) to require accounts of receipts and expenditures duly and

[1] 7 *Fed. Reg.*, p. 5803; Department of State, *Bulletin*, VII, p. 658.
[2] 7 *Fed. Reg.*, p. 5946.

reliably audited, and such other records and reports as the Board may deem to be in the public interest; (5) to eliminate or merge such agencies in the interests of efficiency and economy; and (6) to take such steps as may be necessary for the protection of essential local charities; and

(c) to prescribe such rules and regulations not inconsistent with law as the Board may determine to be necessary or desirable to carry out the purposes of this Order.

3. The provisions of section 2 of this Order shall not apply to (a) the American National Red Cross or (b) established religious bodies which are not independently carrying out any of the activities specified in section 2 of this Order.

4. Under the authority given me by section 13 of the Joint Resolution of Congress approved November 4, 1939 (54 Stat. 8, 11) and Title I of the First War Powers Act, 1941, approved December 18, 1941 (Public Law No. 354, 77th Congress), and pursuant to the suggestion of the Secretary of State, it is ordered that the administration of any and all of the provisions of section 8 (b) of the said Joint Resolution relating to the solicitation and collection of funds and contributions for relief purposes, heretofore by me vested in the Secretary of State, be and it hereby is transferred to the said Board. All rules and regulations and forms which have been issued by the Secretary of State pursuant to the provisions of said section 8 (b) and which are in effect shall continue in effect until modified, superseded, revoked or repealed by the Board.

5. Any and all matters within the jurisdiction of said Board which may be affected with a question relating to the foreign policy of the Government of the United States in connection with the administration of the powers vested in the Board by this Order shall be determined only after conference with the Secretary of State, to the end that any action with respect to such matters shall be consistent with the foreign policy of the United States.

6. For the purpose of economy in administration, the Board is authorized to utilize the services of available and appropriate personnel of the Department of State and other Government departments and agencies and such other services, equipment, and facilities as may be made available by these departments and agencies.

7. For the purpose of effectively carrying out the provisions of this Order, the Board may require that all war relief and welfare policies, plans, programs, procedures and methods of voluntary agencies be coordinated and integrated with those of the several Federal departments, establishments and agencies and the American Red Cross; and all these organizations shall furnish from time to time such information as the Board may consider necessary for such purposes.

8. The Board shall from time to time submit to the President such reports and recommendations regarding war charities, relief and welfare

in foreign countries and in the United States and the relationship of public and private organizations, resources and programs in these and related fields, as the public interest may require.

9. The members of the Board shall serve as such without compensation, but shall be entitled to necessary transportation, subsistence, and other expenses incident to the performance of their duties.

10. This Order shall remain in force during the continuance of the present war and for six months after the termination thereof, unless revoked by Presidential order.

———

On September 30, 1942, the President's War Relief Control Board issued to the press a tabulation of contributions collected and disbursed during the period September 6, 1939 through August 1942, as shown in reports submitted by persons and organizations registered with the Board for the solicitation and collection of contributions to be used for relief in foreign countries.[1] On February 28, 1943 it issued a further tabulation of contributions collected and disbursed from September 6, 1939 through January 1943.[2]

[1] Department of State, *Bulletin*, VII, p. 791.
[2] *Ibid.*, VIII, p. 223.

CHAPTER XI

THE DEPARTMENT OF STATE AND THE FOREIGN SERVICE

1. ORGANIZATION AND FUNCTIONS

[For general references on organization and functions, see *Documents, IV, 1941–42*, p. 845.]

A. General

The War has broadened the scope of the activities of the Department and changed some methods of procedure and operation.[1] Maintenance of close relations with our Allies involves closer relations with other government agencies in the coordination of all policies in the foreign-relations field. The Department is charged with the responsibility of carrying out these activities so far as they require action in foreign countries.

For example, the Special Division,[2] which was established on September 1, 1939 for handling special problems arising out of disturbed conditions in Europe, expanded its responsibilities to include the relations with the Swiss Government in matters of United States interests in enemy and enemy-controlled countries, such as exchanges and repatriation of American officials and civilians, and liaison with the President's War Relief Control Board for the coordination of foreign-relief operations with the foreign policy of the United States. This division also handles questions relating to prisoners of war and other matters concerning the application of the Geneva Prisoners of War Convention of 1939, the Geneva Red Cross Convention and similar international agreements and the supervision of the representation of enemy interests in the United States by third powers.

Certain administrative changes in the Department were provided in Departmental Order 1078 of August 6, 1942 [3] creating the Office of Chief Clerk and Administrative Assistant and in Departmental Order 1086 of August 31,[4] whereby the Division of Personnel Supervision and Management was abolished and its functions transferred to the newly created Division of Departmental Personnel, which was given responsibility for administrative aspects of the formulation and execution of policy within the Department under the general direction of the Assistant Secretary of State and Budget Officer.

The problems involved in dealing with non-military matters arising from the military occupation of foreign territories, in Europe and North Africa, by American forces led to the establishment, by Departmental Order 1110 of November 25, 1942, of the Office of Foreign Territories in the Division of European Affairs of the Department. Close collaboration was envisaged between this Office and the Director of the Office of Relief and Rehabilitation Operations, Herbert H. Lehman. The provisions of this order are given below. With the creation on June 24, 1943 of the Office of Foreign Economic Coordination, the Office of Foreign Territories was abolished.

[1] Department of State, *Bulletin*, VII, p. 855.
[2] *Ibid.*, VIII, p. 155.
[3] *Ibid.*, VII, p. 691.
[4] *Ibid.*, p. 743.

The planning and administration of measures for the relief and rehabilitation abroad of victims of war, including the provision of food, housing, clothing and medical supplies in territories occupied by the armed forces of the United Nations, were entrusted to the Office of Foreign Relief and Rehabilitation Operations established in the Department of State. On November 21, 1942, the President announced that Herbert H. Lehman had been appointed Director. For further information, see this volume, p. 263.

The development of the Department's political activities was placed in the hands of the Committee on Political Planning created by Departmental Order 1105 [1] on November 2, 1942 and composed of the four Advisers on Political Relations, the Adviser on International Economic Affairs and a representative of no less rank than an Assistant Chief of the following Divisions: Foreign Activity Correlation, Current Information and World Trade Intelligence. Officers of other divisions would be invited to participate in the sessions of the Committee, as occasion demanded.

To provide the basis for the planning of integrated programs in the fields of post-war economic and political reconstruction and for the formulation of appropriate policy recommendations, the need of organized special research has been recognized. By Departmental Order 1124 of January 14, 1943 a Division of Political Studies and a Division of Economic Studies were established in the Department, the functions of which are set forth below.

(1) *The Office of Foreign Territories. Departmental Order 1110, November 25, 1942* [2]

Responsibility for dealing with all non-military matters arising as a result of the military occupation of territories in Europe and North Africa by the armed forces of the United Nations and affecting the interests of the United States is hereby assigned to the Division of European Affairs.

In order that the interests of other divisions and offices of the Department in this field of operations may be effectively coordinated and their facilities fully utilized and that the necessary liaison with other departments and agencies may be maintained so far as practicable through established channels, there is hereby established as a component part of the Division of European Affairs an Office of Foreign Territories. The Adviser on International Economic Affairs and the Chiefs of the Divisions of Near Eastern Affairs, Special Research, Defense Materials, Foreign Funds Control, Commercial Policy and Agreements and the Financial Division are directed to cooperate fully with the Office of Foreign Territories and are authorized to detail personnel to that Office. Mr. Paul Appleby, who is hereby designated Special Assistant to the Secretary of State, will be in charge of the Office of Foreign Territories, the office symbol of which shall be FT.

The provisions of this Order shall be effective immediately and shall supersede the provisions of any existing Order in conflict therewith.

[1] *Ibid.*, p. 896.
[2] *Ibid.*, p. 971.

(2) *The Divisions of Political Studies and of Economic Studies. Departmental Order 1124, January 14, 1943* [1]

The Division of Political Studies shall have responsibility for the conduct of continuing and special research, for the preparation of studies required in the formulation of policies, the planning of integrated programs as a basis for action in the field of foreign political relations affecting the interests of the United States, with particular reference to the long-range implications of current policies, actions and developments in this field affecting post-war political reconstruction, and for the formulation of appropriate recommendations with respect to the foregoing. In carrying out these responsibilities, the Division of Political Studies shall cooperate fully and maintain effective liaison with other divisions and offices of the Department, in particular the Division of Economic Studies, with other departments and agencies, and with interdepartmental and intergovernmental agencies having joint interest or authority in the field of activity.

Mr. Harley A. Notter is hereby designated Chief, and Mr. Durward V. Sandifer, Mr. Philip E. Mosely, and Mr. S. Shepard Jones are hereby designated Assistant Chiefs of the Division of Political Studies, the symbol designation of which shall be PS.

The Division of Economic Studies shall have responsibility for the conduct of continuing and special research and for the preparation of studies required in the formulation of policies and the planning of integrated programs as a basis for action in the field of foreign economic relations affecting the interests of the United States, with particular reference to the long-range implications of current policies, actions and developments in this field affecting post-war economic reconstruction, and for the formulation of appropriate recommendations with regard to the foregoing. In carrying out these responsibilities, the Division of Economic Studies shall cooperate fully and maintain effective liaison with other divisions and offices of the Department, in particular the Division of Political Studies, with other departments and agencies and with interdepartmental and intergovernmental agencies having joint interest or authority in the field of activity.

Mr. Leroy D. Stinebower is hereby designated Chief, and Mr. H. Julian Wadleigh is hereby designated an Assistant Chief of the Division of Economic Studies, the symbol designation of which shall be ES.

The various divisions and offices of the Department shall cooperate fully and maintain effective liaison with the Division of Political Studies and the Division of Economic Studies and, in particular, they shall keep those divisions fully informed of current policy decisions, activities and developments in their respective political and economic fields, inviting their participation whenever feasible and appropriate in the formulation

[1] *Ibid.*, VIII, p. 63. The order was effective January 1, 1943.

of policy decisions having long-range implications, and shall route to them for their information or advice communications and other material of a policy character falling within the scope of their responsibilities or interests.

There is hereby established a Committee on Special Studies, the purpose of which shall be to facilitate the carrying out of the responsibilities defined in this Order. Mr. Pasvolsky shall be the Chairman of the Committee on Special Studies, the other members of which shall be the Chiefs of the Divisions of Political Studies and Economic Studies, and such other officers as may be designated by the Secretary of State.

The Division of Special Research is hereby abolished and its personnel, equipment and other facilities are hereby transferred to the new divisions.

(3) *Transfer of Activities on Cultural Relations from the Office of Coordinator of Inter-American Affairs to Division of Cultural Relations, Department of State*

(a) *Letter from the Under Secretary of State (Welles) to the Coordinator of Inter-American Affairs (Rockefeller), August 12, 1942* [1]

My Dear Mr. Rockefeller:

You and Mr. Harrison have generously suggested in conversations with officers of the Department the possible transfer to the Department of certain phases of the cultural-relations program now being carried on by your office. You indicated your willingness to have the Department assume responsibility for those functions in the cultural field for which the Department might receive adequate funds from the Congress to the end that the cultural-relations program might be placed on a permanent basis as a phase of Government activity, in order to assure its active continuance after the war.

In accordance with the understanding developed in these conversations, the Joint Committee on Cultural Relations, which has served so effectively to correlate the activities of your office and of the Department, considered at several meetings in May and June, budget requests of the Department for the 1944 fiscal year, for American cultural institutions abroad such as cultural institutes, American libraries and American schools; exchanges of books and other materials in the cultural field, together with production and distribution of translations in that area; vocational training; art and music interchanges.

I am attaching herewith copies of the summaries of appropriations requests which the Department proposes to submit to the Bureau of the Budget and subsequently to the Congress.

It would be helpful indeed to have from your office a statement indicating its approval of the transfer of functions indicated.

[1] *Department of State Appropriation Bill for 1944, Hearings before the Subcommittee of the Committee on Appropriations, House of Representatives*, 78th Cong., 1st sess., p. 44.

(b) *Letter from the Coordinator of Inter-American Affairs (Rockefeller)*
   to the Under Secretary of State (Welles), August 14, 1942 [1]

DEAR MR. WELLES:

Thank you for your letter of August 12 concerning transfer from our office to the Cultural Relations, Department of State, such activities as the Department has been equipped to administer efficiently and such activities as will be continued by Congress.

We feel it is highly desirable that the activities listed in your letter be placed on a permanent basis and, therefore, are in complete agreement with the transfer of the functions indicated.

As part of our war effort, we believe that it is necessary to continue certain activities in the cultural field not listed in your letter, such as the Committee for Inter-American Artistic and Intellectual Relations, which is now administered by Dr. Moe, and our inter-American training centers, until we can feel sure that these activities should be integrated into the program and may be approved permanently by Congress.

B. Economic Operations

The relations of the Department to foreign wartime economic operations are of a direct character, but the carrying out of these operations is generally entrusted to one of the operating agencies. In many cases the operating agencies must rely upon the Department not only for the broad foreign policy considerations involved in a particular problem, but also for the specific information upon which the operating decision must be based.

By June 30, 1943, there were four divisions of the Department dealing with emergency economic control and supply measures: the Division of Exports and Requirements, the Division of Defense Materials, the Division of Foreign Funds Control and the Division of World Trade Intelligence.

The Division of Exports and Requirements was created by Departmental Order 1128 [2] on February 1, 1943 to function as a component part of the Board of Economic Operations. It had responsibility for all matters of foreign policy involved in the Export Control Act of July 2, 1940 and the Lend-Lease Act of March 11, 1941 (except the negotiation of Lend-Lease Agreements and the application of Article VII thereof), the Acts of June 28, 1940 and May 31, 1941 (in so far as priorities and allocations for export were concerned), provided that where such matters involved arrangements for purchase of materials in foreign countries, the policies to be followed would be formulated by the Division of Defense Materials. The American Hemisphere Exports Office was abolished and its personnel and facilities were transferred to the Division of Exports and Requirements.

On June 24, 1943, following the establishment of the Office of Foreign Economic Coordination, these four divisions were made component parts of that Office.

The plan for coordinating the economic operations of United States civilian agencies in areas liberated from enemy control, outlined by the Bureau of the Budget on June 1, 1943, was submitted by President Roosevelt on June 3 in a letter to Secretary of State Hull. The agencies engaged in foreign economic activities included the Office of Lend-Lease Administration, the Office of Foreign Relief and Rehabilitation Operations and the Board of Economic Warfare, in addition to the State, Treasury, War and Navy Departments. On June 24,

[1] *Ibid.*
[2] *Ibid.,* VIII, p. 138.

1943, the Secretary of State issued Departmental Order 1166, creating in the Department the Office of Foreign Economic Coordination and abolishing both the Office of Foreign Territories and the Board of Economic Operations. The letter of the President, the plan and the Departmental Order are given below.

(1) *Coordination of Economic Operations of Civilian Agencies in Liberated Areas. Letter of the President (Roosevelt) to the Secretary of State (Hull), June 3, 1943* [1]

MY DEAR CORDELL:

I am enclosing a plan for the coordination of the economic operations of United States civilian agencies in areas liberated from enemy control, which has been worked out by the Budget Bureau after extended discussion with the agencies concerned. While I am told that complete agreement was not reached on every detail, I believe this plan represents a positive approach to the problem and I urge you to move ahead rapidly in its application through the operation of the State Department and the proposed interdepartmental machinery.

Our civilian agencies must be adequately prepared to assist our military forces in performing those services and activities in which they are expert. We must harness together military and civilian efforts. Only thus can we achieve full mobilization for the prosecution of the war, and adequately meet the many problems developing in the wake of our armed forces.

It is impossible, of course, to outline in detail the exact nature of those problems. Certain general functional assignments have been made to the civilian agencies. However, I am amplifying those assignments here so that you may be fully aware of your responsibilities and those of other agencies. More detailed working arrangements should be evolved through the mechanisms provided for in the enclosed plan.

The Office of Foreign Relief and Rehabilitation Operations will be responsible for the relief and rehabilitation of victims of war in certain liberated areas to be designated by me. In such areas, subject to consultation and arrangements with our allies, Governor Lehman should distribute relief goods, and goods to facilitate the production of basic civilian necessities, whether they be given away, sold, or bartered. In these areas the Office of Foreign Relief and Rehabilitation Operations should also provide technical advice and services with respect to relief and the production of civilian necessities, and should facilitate the restoration of agriculture, housing and transportation. In its work I want the Office of Foreign Relief to make full use of available personnel and facilities of other agencies. When any or all of this program is transferred to a United Nations organization, further adjustments may be necessary. In certain other areas it may prove desirable, in accordance

[1] *Ibid.*, p. 575.

with arrangements with our allies, to have civilian supplies furnished by Lend-Lease.

In this way we can maintain the single civilian supply line to each liberated region, so essential in assuring consistency in policy and administration.

I understand that the Office of Foreign Relief and Rehabilitation Operations may use a number of the services of the Office of Lend-Lease Administration. So long as Lend-Lease funds are used to finance the Relief and Rehabilitation program, allocations of goods by the allocating agencies should be made to Lend-Lease for the account of the Office of Foreign Relief. While Lend-Lease would thus act as the claimant, the presentation of requirements should be a joint undertaking. Should conditions demand shifts within Lend-Lease allocations which affect the Relief account, such changes should be made with the approval of the allocating agencies.

The Office of Lend-Lease Administration can assist the Office of Foreign Relief and Rehabilitation Operations in preparing and screening requirements and, when feasible, should detail staff members to work with Governor Lehman's staff for this purpose to insure maximum speed and efficiency. While detailed working arrangements on other functions will need to be developed, the Office of Foreign Relief *vis-à-vis* Lend-Lease might assume generally a relationship similar to that now assumed by the British. It may be desirable, however, for the Lend-Lease Administration to send a few representatives to the field to participate in the preparation of requirements and the inspection of distribution.

The Board of Economic Warfare is responsible for foreign procurement, the development of strategic and critical materials, certain industrial development, gathering economic intelligence, and other prescribed economic warfare measures. The staff of the Board should be available for technical advice and other assistance to the several agencies.

The Treasury Department is responsible for fixing exchange rates and should assist on monetary, currency control and general fiscal matters. This important work must be geared in with the plans and activities of the other agencies.

Since you are and have been responsible for determining the policy of this Government in relation to international problems, I shall rely on you to unify our foreign economic activities to the end that coherent and consistent policies and programs result. The Department of State should provide the necessary coordination, here and in the field, of our economic operations with respect to liberated areas. The attached plan properly recognizes this role of the State Department, and is similar to what I had in mind when we discussed the problems arising from the invasion of North Africa, as set forth in my letter to you referring to that discussion.

I want to emphasize the importance of selecting as Area Directors, men of administrative competence and vision — men adjustable to the complex conditions they will face. I believe that the various agencies concerned have on their staffs a number of persons of the type you will need.

The job in Washington will demand a large part of the time and energy of the Assistant Secretary you name to coordinate these activities. Because of the wide scope of the work involved, the Department should reexamine its internal organization and procedures in order that it may assume the positive leadership required.

I want the facilities of our civilian agencies operating in the international economic field utilized to the fullest extent. It is equally essential that the transition from military to civilian operations in liberated areas be consummated as speedily and efficiently as possible.

In view of the time required for preparing to meet economic problems in liberated areas and the possibility that the enemy may soon be driven from presently held territory, I urge you to take all necessary steps to fulfill your responsibilities with respect to the attached plan.

I am sending copies of this to the other interested agencies.

Sincerely yours,

FRANKLIN D. ROOSEVELT

[Enclosure]

PLAN FOR COORDINATING THE ECONOMIC ACTIVITIES OF U. S. CIVILIAN AGENCIES IN LIBERATED AREAS

The plan herein outlined for coordinating in this country and abroad, the activities of U. S. civilian agencies relative to economic affairs in liberated areas is based on the following premises:

1. Premises

a. There must be one central point in Washington for the coordination of interrelated activities of the several U. S. agencies operating abroad. Leadership in providing this coordination rests with the Department of State.

b. There must likewise be in each liberated area a central point of leadership and coordination similar to that in Washington.

c. The attainment of unity in policy and operations requires the participation of all agencies concerned through interdepartmental machinery which provides a setting for close and continuous working relationships.

d. Such provision for coordination shall not remove the responsibility or authority of each agency for carrying out its own functions.

e. A major objective of the interdepartmental machinery should be that of relating the economic plans and operations of U. S. civilian agencies for liberated areas to those of officials responsible for foreign political policies, and to those of the armed services and members of the United Nations.

f. Excepted from the scope of this memorandum are the territories and possessions of the United States now occupied by enemy forces, such as Guam and the Philippine Islands.

g. At all levels of interagency operations in Washington, the military and the political policy representatives of our government should work with the civilian operating agencies to afford proper guidance, to obviate excessive clearance, and to provide the information essential to effective planning and operations.

2. *Interdepartmental Policy Committee*

In order to develop a unified policy and to facilitate the coordination of agency activities, there is hereby established an interdepartmental Committee for Economic Policy in Liberated Areas (Policy Committee). The Chairman of this Committee shall be an Assistant Secretary of State whose designation is provided for in Section 3 of this plan. In addition to the Chairman, the Committee shall consist of the heads, or their deputies, of the following:

> State Department (Political Policy)
> Treasury Department
> War Department
> Navy Department
> Board of Economic Warfare
> Office of Lend-Lease Administration
> Office of Foreign Relief and Rehabilitation Operations

This Committee will provide a means for bringing together responsible officials of the agencies to consider policies, programs, and other matters of concern to such a group. The Committee will give final resolution, subject to the decisions of the President, to over-all policies and programs of interagency concern which have not been resolved in the Coordinating Committee (to be established).

3. *Assistant Secretary for Foreign Economic Coordination*

The Secretary of State shall designate an Assistant Secretary of State who shall coordinate our economic activities related to liberated areas and facilitate military-civilian cooperation.

In connection with these duties, he shall act as Chairman of the Policy Committee and of the Coordinating Committee to coordinate the activities of the interested agencies. To this end he shall provide a secretariat and necessary staff to serve the Policy Committee, the Coordinating Committee, and any subcommittees.

4. Coordinating and Other Subordinate Committees

The Policy Committee shall establish as a working committee a Coordinating Committee composed of representatives of the same agencies as those in the former group.

Subject to appeal to the Policy Committee, the Coordinating Committee shall review and coordinate area plans, and take such steps as may be necessary to adjust policy and area operations to meet the changing needs of the military services and to comply with working arrangements set up with our allies.

Area subcommittees, covering territories to be liberated as well as territories already liberated, may be set up, based on administrative areas determined in consultation with military officials. While the exact nature of their work cannot be definitely foreseen, it is expected that each area subcommittee will develop and coordinate interdepartmental policies and plans with respect to its area, collaborate with the prospective Area Director prior to liberation, and expedite his operations in Washington once the area is liberated. In performing these tasks, the area subcommittees may be utilized to review communications from the Area Director, and to maintain close working relationships with military groups concerned with civil affairs in the area and with similar committees and officials of our allies.

The Coordinating Committee may establish such subcommittees as it deems necessary (functional, *ad hoc*, etc.).

These various area and other subcommittees will serve under chairmen appointed by the Chairman of the Coordinating Committee in consultation with the members of the Committee.

In order to tie in recruitment and training programs, the Interdepartmental Committee for the Recruitment and Training of Personnel and its subcommittees shall be reconstituted as a Subcommittee on Recruitment and Training under the Coordinating Committee. The membership of the Subcommittee shall come from the same agencies represented on the Coordinating Committee and shall also include the representatives of the Civil Service Commission and the Office of War Information. This subcommittee will coordinate the recruitment and training activities of civilian agencies with regard to personnel for service in liberated areas and bring about a maximum use of common training facilities by both military and civilian agencies.

Placing this committee under the Coordinating Committee will facilitate close relationship between training programs and area planning, thereby increasing mutual understanding and cooperation among staffs.

5. Area Directors

For each of the areas liberated, the Secretary of State shall appoint, with approval of the Policy Committee, an Area Director. These

Directors will provide over-all direction and coordination to the economic activities of U. S. civilian agencies in their respective areas.

It is recognized that the emergency problems faced and the delay of detailed Washington clearances make it necessary to give Area Directors wide latitude in operations and ample authority to act "on the spot." It is likewise evident that the pattern for each area must be modified according to the military theatre arrangements and agreements with our allies.

In general, however, the following pattern shall obtain where a major part of economic operations are under U. S. agencies.

The Area Director will be subject to orders of the military commander of the area, and of the Assistant Secretary in accordance with policies established by the Policy or Coordinating Committees. In the field the Area Director will keep the political representative of the State Department advised of his activities and will be guided by him on matters of general political policy. That representative, however, shall intervene only when definite political policies are involved. Clearance "bottlenecks" in this respect shall be avoided throughout.

Within these limits, the Area Director shall have all the powers necessary to coordinate the field activities of the various U. S. civilian agencies concerned with the economic affairs of the area. In case of emergency, threatened breakdown of activities, or serious difficulties, these powers shall extend to directing specific operations and shifting functions and personnel, pending other arrangements in Washington to meet the situation.

The Area Director will act as the major channel of contact for the civilian economic agencies with the military and our allies in the field. He will likewise channel all communications of these agencies from the field to the Assistant Secretary in Washington for proper handling.

6. Communications and Clearance of Personnel

The Assistant Secretary shall facilitate the speedy dispatch of all communications between civilian agencies and their representatives in the field and prompt decision by the State Department on the clearance (including passports) of movements of agency personnel to and from liberated areas.

Where a delay of such communications or clearances is deemed desirable by the State Department, the relevant agency or its field representative shall be promptly notified and an effort made to settle any differences. Should an agency or its field representative thereafter insist on the delivery of a message under dispute, it will be delivered along with any companion message the State Department, the Area Director, or an agency representative may wish to send.

BUREAU OF THE BUDGET,
   June 1, 1943.

(2) *Office of Foreign Economic Coordination. Departmental Order 1166, June 24, 1943* [1]

There is hereby created in the Department an Office of Foreign Economic Coordination which shall have responsibility, so far as the Department is concerned, for the coordination of (1) activities related to economic affairs in liberated areas and the facilitation of military-civilian cooperation in regard thereto; and of (2) the foreign policy aspects of wartime economic controls and operations.

The Assistant Secretary, Mr. Acheson, shall be the Director of the Office of Foreign Economic Coordination and the Special Assistant to the Secretary, Mr. Finletter, shall be the Executive Director thereof.

There shall be three Deputy Directors of the Office of Foreign Economic Coordination, to be charged respectively with (1) the planning of economic activities related to liberated areas, (2) the recruitment and training of personnel for service in liberated areas, and (3) coordination of the foreign policy aspects of wartime economic controls and operations.

The symbol designation of the new office shall be OFEC.

The Defense Materials, Exports and Requirements, Foreign Funds Control, and World Trade Intelligence divisions shall be considered for all purposes as component parts of the Office of Foreign Economic Coordination.

The Adviser on International Economic Affairs, Mr. Feis, and the advisers on political relations shall serve as participating advisers in this work.

The chiefs of the Divisions of Economic Studies, European Affairs, Near Eastern Affairs, Far Eastern Affairs and of the American Republics shall designate ranking officers of their respective divisions who shall be responsible for maintaining liaison with the Office of Foreign Economic Coordination. Such other divisions and offices of the Department as may be concerned shall assist the Office of Foreign Economic Coordination as required in carrying out its work.

The Office of Foreign Territories and the Board of Economic Operations are hereby abolished.

2. ACTIVITIES

(1) *Statement of the Secretary of State (Hull) on the Estimates and Fiscal Needs of the State Department before the Subcommittee of the Committee on Appropriations of the House of Representatives, February 8, 1943* [2]

Secretary HULL. Mr. Chairman and members of the committee, I am pleased to participate again with you in your discussions of the

[1] *Ibid.*, p. 579.

[2] *Department of State Appropriation Bill for 1944, Hearings before the Subcommittee of the Committee on Appropriations, House of Representatives,* 78th Cong., 1st sess., p. 2.

financial needs of the Department of State, to renew old associations, and to greet the new members of this body. The committee has always been most cooperative in aiding the Department, not only in relation to its fiscal program so necessary to the discharge of its unbelievably heavy responsibilities, but also through suggestions and recommendations has assisted the Department to gear its personnel and administrative machinery adequately to meet the needs occasioned by rapidly changing world events. I anticipate and will appreciate your continued cooperation to the end that, through inadequacy of funds, we shall not fail in our proper role and sphere vigorously to combat the Axis wherever its influences may be found; to foster and, if possible, to improve our relations with our allies and friends; to prepare for the peace and restoration of order; and at the same time to carry on the manifold, important, and exacting responsibilities of our foreign relations which call for that full measure of attention, careful planning, and thorough execution that the Department endeavors to give.

In presenting to your consideration in summary fashion these budget estimates for 1944, I want you to know that I personally am satisfied that they represent our minimum, actual, and definitely foreseen requirements. I shall not attempt to give you in detail the needs for the various services, as Mr. Shaw and other competent witnesses will appear before you for this purpose. Rather, I should like to tell you briefly of some of the activities of the Department as a preface to a more detailed justification in certain cases, and in others, although no funds are now sought, so that you may know what is being done in other directions toward winning of the peace.

Somewhat over a year ago, the Axis powers declared war on the United States. The recital of the sustained efforts of this Government to avoid war in the decade immediately preceding Pearl Harbor, while still preserving our vital interests, are faithfully recorded in the introduction to a collection of documents concerning the foreign relations of the United States, separately printed under the title "Peace and War," [1] which has, I am sure, had your attention. Just recently, the President has reported to the Congress and to the people the tremendous effort that is being made and the progress which has been achieved. He has not failed to tell you, as well, of the hard road which lies ahead, and of the many things yet to be done. We have come a long way, but we all know, abundantly well, that we have a long way to go.

The Department of State, as a militant part of our fighting forces, will continue by every means at its command to put down the forces of aggression, to succor and sustain our allies and the unfortunate victims of the ruthless forces of darkness, and to demonstrate to all

[1] Department of State Publication 1983.

peoples, that they themselves may come to know that the principles for which we stand as enunciated in the Atlantic Charter and in the declaration by United Nations are not merely a play on words, but sound, workable tenets, affording through united effort a practical plan to the solution of the world's political, economic, and social ills. The importance of this I need not emphasize. Many changes in the political and economic organization of the world will be necessary to achieve a firm foundation for a lasting and enduring peace. It will not be easy, but it is not impossible. We shall strive to that end.

Not least among the many considerations necessary to an enduring peace is attainment of greater freedom in international trade. This, properly, is one of the cardinal principles of the Atlantic Charter. In the Department the Division of Commercial Policy and Agreements is generally responsible for handling all matters relating to the international commercial policy of the United States. As a result of the war the Division's responsibilities have been very considerably broadened to include — in addition to its regular functions in connection with the formulation, negotiation, and administration of commercial treaties, trade agreements and other commercial agreements, and tariff and foreign trade matters generally — the commercial policy aspects of matters directly connected with the war effort as well as the commercial policy aspects of matters relating to the broad field of international collaboration in economic reconstruction.

The primary objectives of the Division's activities at this time are, first, to strengthen our economic relations with the British Empire countries and the other United Nations which are fully associated with us in the war; second, to strengthen our economic relations with certain other countries, particularly in the Western Hemisphere, which, although not at war or not signatories of the United Nations declaration, are nevertheless closely associated with us in the war effort; and third, to formulate policy and action recommendations with regard to the commercial policy aspects of economic reconstruction.

The trade-agreements work of the Division [1] — the formulation, negotiation, and administration of reciprocal trade agreements under the authority of the act of June 12, 1934 — not only has continued during the war but has become, more than ever, of vital and fundamental importance in strengthening our relations with our allies and with other friendly countries, particularly in the Western Hemisphere, as well as in laying the bases for sound economic collaboration in the future.

Since Pearl Harbor, new or supplementary trade agreements have been entered into with four of the other American Republics, the latest

[1] See this volume, p. 616–30.

being the important agreement with Mexico which was signed on December 23, 1942 (the others are: A supplementary agreement with Cuba and agreements with Peru and Uruguay). This brings to 30 the total number of trade agreements (including supplementary agreements) which have been so far concluded with 25 countries under the 1934 act. Moreover, active negotiations are going on with three other countries (Iceland, Bolivia, and Iran), and preparatory studies continue to be made with respect to a number of other countries.

Under existing legislation, the authority to enter into trade agreements with foreign countries is due to expire in June 1943, unless this authority is further extended by the Congress.[1] However, it seems inconceivable that the Trade Agreements Act will not be extended by the Congress before that date because such legislation will be vitally needed (a) to open up foreign markets for American products during the post-war period and thereby (b) help maintain domestic prosperity and full employment during the difficult post-war readjustment period, and (c), in the light of the program and principles subscribed to by this Government in the Atlantic Charter, the United Nations Declaration, and Article VII of more than a dozen lend-lease agreements, to enable the United States to occupy the position of leadership now in laying the groundwork for post-war, world-wide economic reconstruction. Since the unity of the war effort among the United Nations depends in large degree upon unity among them in regard to peace objectives, and since unity in regard to peace objectives depends, in turn, in large degree upon this country's leadership as evidenced by its policies and actions, extension of the trade-agreement authority is needed as evidence of this country's willingness in pursuit of its vital interests to continue to bear its share of the responsibility and of its sincerity of purpose and continuity of policy as regards the peace.

In addition to its regular work in connection with trade agreements and commercial treaties and foreign trade matters generally, the Division has responsibility for important matters of commercial policy coming under the Lend-Lease Act, for the preparation of statistical and other studies needed by the Board of Economic Operations, for handling the international aspects of surplus commodity problems, and for dealing with the commercial policy aspects of numerous problems arising directly out of the war. Many of these problems will be multiplied and tremendously intensified by the termination of the war, and we must neither do too little nor be too late.

As I remarked last year, every division of the Department is performing functions that are connected directly or indirectly with the prosecution of the war or preparation for the peace to follow. The nature of

---

[1] The authority was extended June 7, 1943; see p. 632.

the work in certain of the divisions and the emphasis placed on various phases of it, while similar in character, has varied with the needs of the emergency, and has not diminished in volume but on the contrary has tended appreciably to increase. For example, when set up on September 1, 1939, to handle problems growing out of the disturbed conditions in Europe, the Special Division's activities were largely concerned with whereabout and welfare inquiries respecting American citizens abroad and the transmission to them of funds for their subsistence and eventual repatriation. More than 50,000 inquiries were handled in the first few months of the emergency, and from September 1, 1939, to December 31, 1942, more than $3,500,000 in private funds were transferred to Americans abroad through official channels. The Division has likewise been instrumental in the safe return to the United States of something in the neighborhood of 100,000 American citizens from various disturbed areas throughout the world. The Division is currently endeavoring to arrange for the repatriation of the several thousand bona fide Americans in Japanese custody, including those civilians at Wake, Guam, and the Philippine Islands, as well as the return of our official personnel from France.

The representation in enemy territory of the extensive interests of Allied belligerents (involving the disbursement of over $7,000,000 of Allied funds) before our entry into the war gave the Special Division valuable experience which, with our entry into the war, was immediately applied to the representation of American interests in enemy and enemy-occupied territories through the neutral auspices of the Swiss Government. The Department also supervises the representation of enemy interests in the United States by representatives of neutral powers protecting enemy interests here.

One of the growing responsibilities of the Special Division is that of seeing that the Geneva Prisoners of War and Red Cross Conventions are equitably applied to American prisoners of war and civilian internees in enemy hands and to prisoners of war and civilian internees of enemy nationality held in the United States.

In order to minimize misunderstandings, correct abuses, and insure correct reports on the part of representatives of the protecting powers to the enemy governments and thus minimize the possibility of retaliation and reprisals against our own nationals in enemy hands, it is necessary that the representatives of the protecting powers be accompanied by representatives of the Department of State when making to the places of internment the frequent visits of inspection which are prescribed by the Geneva Prisoners of War Convention.

The Division's responsibilities as a whole are thus seen to have far outgrown those envisaged at the time of its organization.

Similarly, other phases of the work and functions of the Department have been broadened and adapted to meet the changing needs created by the war and American participation in the war. The Department coordinates in the foreign-relations field the many complex war activities of other departments and agencies and, in large part, furnishes the means of carrying out these activities so far as they require action in foreign countries by our Foreign Service. You are generally familiar with the work of the American Foreign Service and its auxiliary service. However, I should like to emphasize the extent to which that Service has recently become a service for the entire Government of the United States. Casual appraisal of statistics relating to the dissemination and distribution of various economic and political reports and information through the Division of Commercial Affairs throughout the past year affords some indication of the extent of the coverage. These show that over 50 Government agencies were serviced and a total of 182,870 documents, many of which were in multiple copy, distributed. The Board of Economic Warfare received 49,806; the Office of Lend-Lease Administration, 5,704; the Office of Price Administration, 3,855; the War Production Board, 6,791; the Office of Strategic Services, 4,652; the Reconstruction Finance Corporation, 15,668, to mention but the more important emergency agencies which have been served. In addition to its normal peacetime role, many new wartime tasks have been assumed by the Foreign Service, among the more important of which are collaboration in enforcing control over the export of commodities from the United States, in order that limited commodities and shipping space may be used to the best advantage and may not benefit enemy or unfriendly nations, firms, or individuals. That is the work of the Division of American Hemisphere Exports and World Trade Intelligence in the Department. The Service collaborates in enforcing control over the remittance of funds between the United States and foreign nations, as a weapon against enemy or unfriendly nations, firms, or individuals. This work is conducted in the Department by the Division of Foreign Funds Control. The Service collaborates in obtaining scarce minerals and other materials abroad for our war effort, and in connection with using such materials to the best advantage. This work is conducted in the Department by the Division of Defense Materials and the Petroleum Adviser. The Service also collaborates in promoting understanding between the United States and foreign countries. This responsibility is carried on primarily by cultural relations officers and by the Division of Cultural Relations, among others.

It is recognized that much that the wartime agencies have done in the foreign field in collaboration with the Department and with the Foreign Service has contributed to the war effort, but there is need for continued vigilance and assertion of the primary responsibility in the foreign field of the Department of State which, with its Foreign

Service, is altogether capable of rendering most of the required services efficiently and promptly. This is the sound and economical way to do it.

Specifically, the Department collaborates with the military and civilian branches of the Government in the planning of broad strategies; the determination of questions of policy relating to lend-lease aid, agreements regarding post-war settlements; and phases of economic warfare, including administration of the list of proclaimed nationals, foreign-fund control, and the procurement of critical materials from abroad. Many of the higher officers of the Department serve on the various interdepartmental and international commissions, committees, and boards primarily concerned with the conduct of the war. In the program of psychological warfare, for example, the Department, through its Division of Current Information, the Division of Cultural Relations, and the geographic divisions, works in liaison with other Government agencies in the war-information field and furnishes advice to those agencies based on information assembled by the Department and its officers abroad.

To deal with particular problems arising from the military occupation of territories in Europe and North Africa by the forces of the United Nations, and affecting the interests of the United States, Herbert H. Lehman, former Governor of New York, was in December appointed Director of Foreign Relief and Rehabilitation Operations. His task is to provide the necessities of life to the peoples, whom the Axis conquerors had hoped to make slaves, by helping them to help themselves as they are liberated from the yoke of the enemy. It is a reconstruction problem of great magnitude, successful solution of which, both in terms of the occupational government phase and in terms of relief and rehabilitation, will contribute much to quicken the establishment of a firm foundation for economic reconstruction and confidence so essential both to the winning of the war and of the peace.

As an inevitable consequence of these various expansions and the need for the closest collaboration with other agencies of the Government there has resulted as well a marked increase in the work and the personnel of the several administrative and service divisions of the Department.

Personnel increases and an expansion by transfer from the Office of the Coordinator of Inter-American Affairs of additional phases of the program for cooperation with other American Republics constitute the primary increases over 1943 sought in the present budget.

The committee following its inspection trip of somewhat over a year ago observed the need for a workable plan contributing to continental economic and political solidarity. With what has since been achieved in this direction I feel you are all familiar. Our continuing efforts should be directed in cooperation with our neighbors to the end that continental solidarity may be a perpetual reality.

During the past year several developments in connection with the program of cultural relations have brought Government activities in this field under more central direction and effective coordination. The requests now before you would continue, in agreement with the Coordinator of Inter-American Affairs, the tried and proven activities of the permanent program of cooperation with the American Republics, the administrative responsibility for which was during the year unified in the Division of Cultural Relations. I am confident that the Government's activities in cultural relations with the other countries of the hemisphere and, through the use of other funds, with China, have been most effective in promoting the awareness of the purposes and principles for which we fight.

The fundamental long-range value of the cultural relations program is to be found in its contribution to the creation and maintenance of those conditions of peace which will counteract forces likely to produce disorder and nondemocratic movements. The prospect of victory in this war opens vistas of useful cooperation between nations beside which even the great advances we have made in the past few years will seem small indeed. In preparing for this task, we may remember that the program of cooperation with the other American Republics has shown the way toward the development of practical methods by which a great body of free nations may know and understand each other and cooperate among themselves.

The considerable increases being requested for expanding the program of cooperation with the American Republics are the result of careful planning over a period of years and the gradual development of an effective program. Funds are being requested only for activities which have been tried in previous programs of the Interdepartmental Committee or in the program of the Coordinator of Inter-American Affairs and have been found of definite value. In the former category is the development of the travel grant program; in the latter are the proposals to continue the exchange of books and translations; to give the cultural institutes in the other American Republics the support recommended by this committee in the report of its visit to the other American nations late in 1941; and to stimulate vocational training in the other American countries.

With respect to the promotion of teaching of the languages of the American Republics, which the committee has justly emphasized in its report and on other occasions, I may say that a coordinated program has been worked out by the Department of State, the Office of the Coordinator of Inter-American Affairs, the Office of Education, and private agencies. We have all been gratified by the progress made during the past year in the teaching of Spanish and Portuguese in the United States and the notable growth in the study of English in the other American Republics.

When victory is achieved our experience will stand us in good stead in our efforts to foster with other people in other lands a better understanding and a conviction among nations that the United States seeks to assure for all that liberty and justice which are foundation stones for peace and prosperity.

At this point it may be well for me to mention briefly another phase of international cooperation, which is closely allied to the cultural program and from which that program may be said to have sprung. I speak of the support by the United States of various international bodies, for which quotas and contributions are annually provided. Agreeable to the suggestion of this committee a most careful inquiry has been made as to the usefulness and the desirability of continuing our participation. The results are reflected in the present estimates and the sums sought are insignificant in comparison with the irreparable loss to the advancement of scientific and professional achievement which withdrawal of our support would occasion. I am thoroughly in accord with the conclusion that this Government should do everything within its power to maintain and to safeguard the effectiveness and the existence of these peacetime institutions. They are most valuable agencies of international collaboration and a remaining open door to the resumption of normal and wholesome channels of intercourse between governments and intellectual and professional leaders of the world looking to further attainment and progress.

A further factor to which I feel compelled to invite your attention is the imperative need in the face of rising living costs of providing altogether adequate allowances for the personnel of the Foreign Service. There has been a rapid, continuing and substantial price inflation in many countries which has necessitated increases in the compensation of clerks and other low-salaried employees, and the upward revision of cost of living allowances for the officers and American employees of the Foreign Service. The extent to which prices will go is problematical. Certainly the ceiling has not been reached and our employees are having a most difficult time in maintaining even that minimum standard of living required for health and efficiency. It is simple justice that their official income from all sources should reflect these factors, over which neither they nor the Department has any control and that they be assured against reduction of their official incomes to a mere pittance in terms of purchasing power in the countries of assignment.

Among other factors which must be taken into consideration in evaluating increased expenditures for general items are the greater costs of travel by air, which means of travel is alone possible to many countries at this time; the necessity of conducting to a great extent all communication to and from field offices by telegraph or by air mail; the problem of shipment or procurement of supplies and equipment at any cost; rapidly rising rentals necessary to obtain suitable quarters for expanding establishments and the necessity for continued payment of rental for various closed offices in enemy or enemy-held territory and storage charges for Government-owned property similarly situated.

Finally, I ask the grant of moneys amply to enable the Department to carry on its publication program uninterruptedly. Today as perhaps never before there is need to keep the American public informed of its Government's varied activities, and, in particular, it seems to me, is this true in the field of foreign relations. The American people are avidly interested; they are entitled to know and must know if they are intelligently to support the efforts of the Government in the winning of the war and the peace which we are but beginning to realize cannot be accomplished by complacently following our customary normal life, habits, and pursuits.

I am sure the committee will readily appreciate that to foresee all the implications of world events in terms of fiscal requirements for the year beginning next July is impossible.

The events of the coming few months may very well result in making wholly inadequate these funds which are projected as requirements for 1944. Already they are known to be deficient in various respects. Diversion of our endeavors and of funds to programs other than those proposed and the need for deficiency appropriations in larger amounts may be dictated by the course of events to come. At an appropriate time the Congress will be apprised of these requirements and will endeavor, I am sure, to meet our needs with the same sympathetic and understanding attitude this committee has evidenced toward our problems in the past. Our needs for the Department, for the Foreign Service, for the Foreign Service Auxiliary, for international obligations, and for the cooperative program are real and immediate and, I believe, fully warrant your earnest consideration. I have refrained from recital of the actual amounts and increases requested as this is carefully explained in the justifications, and witnesses will provide you with such additional information as you may desire. If any of the members have any questions they wish to ask me, I shall be glad to answer to the best of my ability. Other officers will amplify as need be these broad statements which I hope will be found helpful to your deliberations.

3. APPROPRIATIONS

(1) Comparison of Department of State Appropriations for 1944 with Appropriations for 1943 [1]

Appropriation Titles	Appropriations for 1944	Appropriations for 1943	(+) Increases, (−) Decreases for 1944
Department Proper . . .	$6,451,000	$5,926,200	+ $524,800
Foreign Service (exclusive of Emergency Fund) . . .	19,237,600	16,881,800	+ 2,355,800
Emergency Fund	1,500,000	1,500,000	——
Foreign Service Buildings .	144,000	275,000	− 131,000
International Obligations .	1,690,500	2,509,000	− 818,500
Cooperation with the American Republics	4,500,000	1,685,000	+ 2,815,000
Grand Total	33,523,100	28,777,000	+ 4,746,100

4. DIPLOMATIC REPRESENTATION

[See *Documents, III, 1940–41*, p. 763; *IV, 1941–42*, p. 862.]

(1) Changes in List of Diplomatic and Consular Offices from July 1, 1942–June 30, 1943 [2]

Establishment of New Legations

Place	Date
Beirut, Lebanon	November 19, 1942
Damascus, Syria	December 1, 1942

Establishment of Mission and Combined with Consulate General

Dakar, French West Africa	June 1943

Elevation of Legations to Rank of Embassy

Ciudad Trujillo, Dominican Republic	April 17, 1943
Guatemala, Guatemala	May 19, 1943
Managua, Nicaragua	April 14, 1943
Port-au-Prince, Haiti	April 15, 1943
San José, Costa Rica	May 20, 1943
San Salvador, El Salvador	April 16, 1943
Tegucigalpa, Honduras	April 26, 1943

[1] Department of State, *Bulletin*, IX, p. 73. As of the time of final action on the 1944 budget, and exclusive of supplemental appropriations made for 1943 subsequent to the presentation of the 1944 budget (see Table II, *ibid.*, p. 77).

The Department's appropriation act of 1944 (Public Law 105) was approved by the President on July 1, 1943.

[2] Compiled by the Department of State.

ELEVATION OF RANK OF CONSULAR OFFICES [1]

Dakar, French West Africa — From C to CG	January 1, 1943
Kunming, China — From C to CG	December 1, 1942
Lagos, Nigeria — From C to CG	July 9, 1942
Lourenço Marques, Mozambique, Africa — From C to CG	April 1, 1943
Nairobi, Kenya, East Africa — From C to CG	June 1, 1943

ESTABLISHMENT OF NEW CONSULAR OFFICES

	Type of Post	
Arica, Chile	VC	December 7, 1942
Bello Horizonte, Brazil	C	October 1, 1942
Camagüey, Cuba	C	October 24, 1942
Ceuta, Spanish North Africa	C	November 25, 1942
Ciudad Bolívar, Venezuela	VC	September 29, 1942
Cochabamba, Bolivia	C	December 2, 1942
Concepción, Chile	VC	October 11, 1942
Corumbá, Brazil	VC	November 24, 1942
Iskenderun, Turkey	C	September 12, 1942
Luanda, Angola, Africa	C	October 10, 1942
Mombasa, Kenya, East Africa	C	August 13, 1942
Monaco, Monaco	C	November 6, 1942 (Closed about November 8, 1942)
Nueva Gerona, Cuba	VC	September 8, 1942
Osorno, Chile	VC	November 24, 1942
Rosario, Argentina	VC	August 3, 1942
Tocopilla, Chile	VC	October 1, 1942 (Closed March 15, 1943)
Beira, Mozambique, Africa	C	January 15, 1943
Bone, Algeria	VC	June 4, 1943
Bucaramanga, Colombia	C	January 20, 1943
Buenaventura, Colombia	VC	April 21, 1943 (In lieu of CA)
Golfito, Costa Rica	CA	April 1, 1943
Kweilin, China	C	May 21, 1943
Malmo, Sweden	C	May 14, 1943
Manta, Ecuador	VC	January 17, 1943
Oran, Algeria	C	February 22, 1943
Quepos, Costa Rica	CA	April 3, 1943
Rabat, Morocco	C	January 15, 1943
Suez, Egypt	C	About April 1943
Tapachula, Mexico	VC	June 11, 1943
Tihwa, China	C	April 19, 1943
Tunis, Tunisia	reopened C	May 9, 1943

[1] Key to symbols used:

C	— Consulate	E	— Embassy
CA	— Consulate Agency	L	— Legation
CG	— Consulate General	VC	— Vice Consulate

OFFICES CLOSED

Asmara, Eritrea	C	May 31, 1943
Buenaventura, Colombia	CA	About April 30, 1943
Caibarien, Cuba	CA	June 30, 1943
Cucuta, Colombia	C	About January 20, 1943
Lyon, France	C	November 8, 1942
Marseille, France	C	November 8, 1942
Monaco, Monaco	C	November 8 (?), 1942
Nice, France	C	November 8, 1942
Riohacha, Colombia	VC	February 7, 1943
St. Georges, Bermuda	CA	September 30, 1942
Salina Cruz, Mexico	VC	May 17, 1943
Tocopilla, Chile	VC	March 15, 1943
Tunis, Tunisia	C	November 8, 1942
Vichy, France	E	November 8, 1942
Yarmouth, Canada	C	September 1, 1942

COMBINATION OF CONSULAR AND DIPLOMATIC OFFICES

Lisbon, Portugal	CG combined with L	March 1, 1943

5. INTERNATIONAL CONFERENCES IN WHICH THE UNITED STATES GOVERNMENT PARTICIPATED, JULY 1, 1942–JUNE 30, 1943

[Continues lists in *Documents, I, 1938–39,* p. 471; *II, 1939–40,* p. 822; *III, 1940–41,* p. 761; *IV, 1941–42,* p. 867.]

Inter-American Conference on Systems of Economic and Financial Control,
  Washington, D. C., June 30–July 10, 1942
Second Inter-American Conference on Agriculture,
  Mexico, D. F., Mexico, July 6–16, 1942
Eleventh Pan American Sanitary Conference,
  Rio de Janeiro, Brazil, September 7–18, 1942
Inter-American Congress on Social Planning,
  Santiago, Chile, September 10–16, 1942
United Nations Conference on Food and Agriculture,
  Hot Springs, Virginia, May 18–June 3, 1943

CHAPTER XII

INTERNATIONAL ORGANIZATIONS

1. GENERAL POLICY

(1) *Statement of the Chief of the Division of International Conferences (Kelchner), Department of State, February 12, 1943* [1]

The hearings before the Subcommittee of the House Committee on Appropriations had called attention to the fact that for United States contributions to international commissions, congresses, and bureaus, the appropriation for 1943 was $996,500, with a supplemental of $29,300, and with an additional supplemental for 1943 then before the Deficiency Subcommittee of $62,405, or a total of $1,088,205, and that the estimate for 1944 was $1,214,500. This amount was appropriated in the Act approved July 1, 1943, see p. 691.

All of the items included in these estimates represent obligations acquired by this Government through duly ratified treaties or conventions or by specific legislative authority. This Government has acquired membership in a number of international organizations, and these contributions and quotas are the amounts which this Government is obliged to pay during the coming fiscal year as a condition of membership in the respective international bodies.

The Department has obtained reports from its diplomatic missions in the countries in which these organizations are domiciled regarding the effectiveness of the activities being pursued by the respective organizations, as well as the steps which have been taken to adjust their programs and expenditures to the current international situation. Inquiries have also been made of the departments and agencies of the Government primarily interested in the respective activities. As a result of these studies and in deference to the realities of the present situation, the Department has again refrained from including in this request for appropriations for 1944 items for those international organizations which it is felt are not in a position to function effectively during the present emergency as autonomous and independent agencies.

It will be recalled that last year the Department, after careful consideration of the usefulness of these organizations and the desirability of continuing our participation, refrained from requesting quotas for certain organizations. Your committee in commending the Department

[1] *Department of State Appropriation Bill for 1944, Hearings before the Subcommittee of the Committee on Appropriations, House of Representatives*, 78th Cong., 1st sess., p. 149.

for this action — Report No. 1771, Seventy-seventh Congress, Committee on Appropriations of the House of Representatives — suggested that the Department continue to scrutinize the situation in the light of present conditions. Accordingly, during the past year the Department has continued to examine very carefully the operations of these organizations, and it is again refraining from requesting appropriations for all of the organizations which were not included last year as well as one other — the Cape Spartel and Tangier Light. It will also be observed that the Department has been able to obtain a reduction in the quotas of four other international organizations.

The committee will observe that only three of the quotas are in excess of the net amounts paid from the appropriations for the fiscal year 1943. These are for organizations which for the most part have expanded their duties and responsibilities incident to the prosecution of the war and the preparation for the reconstruction period.

The committee will note that the Department in accordance with the committee's recommendation has submitted the estimates this year in the amounts which approximate as nearly as possible the sums which will actually be expended to discharge the individual obligations. It will be recalled that heretofore the estimates for certain of the quotas payable in foreign currencies were entered in the regular bill for definite appropriations in the amounts of the par value of the gold franc at 19.3 cents. It was necessary, therefore, to supplement these direct appropriations by such amounts from the indefinite appropriations as were necessary to take care of the fluctuations in exchange. The amalgamation of the sums from the definite and the indefinite appropriations results, of course, in comparatively higher figures in this year's estimates from those in last year's bill. This new procedure, however, does not increase the total amounts which would actually be paid by this Government for any of these quotas. It presents a more realistic picture of the total funds actually required to discharge the obligations.

The Department is of the firm belief that this Government should do everything within its power to enable these international organizations to function throughout the present emergency. The other departments and agencies primarily responsible for activities represented in these fields are convinced that this Government should continue its support of the international agencies and organizations which are still in a position to function independently during the war. These international organizations have been built up as an integral part of that international world order for which the United Nations are now fighting. These organizations constitute the normal and wholesome channels of intercourse between the Government and intellectual and professional leaders of the world. Their ability to function during the present war will have an important bearing on their capacity to perform useful service in the reconstruction period. It is believed important that this Government do everything within its power to safeguard the effectiveness and in some instances the very existence of these valuable peacetime institutions. In fact, the failure of this Government to continue its support might result in complete collapse of the organizations with the resultant serious damaging effect to scientific progress and enlightenment.

This Government is now engaged in an all-out war effort to defend and preserve the democratic way of life and to guarantee future international relations based upon a dignified world order. These international organizations, composed of sovereign and independent nations, form an integral part of international democracy, and merit therefore the continued financial and moral support of this Government.

There are four items which show reductions and only three which indicate any increases. There are not included in this year's Budget the items for those organizations which were not included last year. These are organizations with headquarters in occupied territory and the total obligations to them represent a lump-sum reduction of approximately $100,000, which is not shown in this, because they were eliminated last year.

2. INTERNATIONAL LABOR ORGANIZATION

(1) *Statement of the Department of Labor on the Needs of the International Labor Organization, February 12, 1943* [1]

In response to questioning before the House Subcommittee of the Committee on Appropriations on the Department of State Appropriation Bill for 1944, Dr. Carter Goodrich, official representative of the United States on the Governing Body of the International Labor Organization, summarized the wartime activities of the Organization.

MR. GOODRICH. I am an official of the Department of Labor charged with looking out for the interests of the United States in this organization. It is in liaison with that organization.

This amount that is indicated here differs from last year, as indicated on the page that you have before you, page 183, and is a decrease as compared with the sum of the items in the appropriation for 1943, plus the supplementary item which is being requested and which is now before the subcommittee considering supplemental appropriations.

The total assessment of the United States for the fiscal year 1943 is $258,000. The total assessment for the United States fiscal year 1944 is $250,041 plus $6,000 traveling item, which is the same as last year.

[1] *Department of State Appropriation Bill for 1944, Hearings before the Subcommittee of the Committee on Appropriations, House of Representatives*, 78th Cong., 1st sess., p. 151.

The International Labor Organization continues to serve as the chief world center for information on labor questions. Its monthly review contains the most comprehensive collection of current data on labor measures and reconstruction plans throughout the world. Three reports recently issued, Wartime Transference of Labor in Great Britain, Food Control in Great Britain, and Joint Production Committees in Great Britain, are of particular value on immediate war problems.

The International Labor Organization has recently supplied a series of confidential memoranda requested by the Department of Labor for the use of the War Department. Material on conditions in continental Europe collected by the International Labor Organization's office at Geneva has been made use of by the Board of Economic Warfare, the Office of Strategic Services, the Department of Labor, and a number of other Government agencies in Washington. Some of this material has been microfilmed by the International Labor Organization at Geneva at the request of the Inter-Departmental Committee for the Acquisition of Foreign Publications; other material secured by the International Labor Organization has been microfilmed by the Library of Congress. The International Labor Organization has also answered a large number of inquiries, some of them confidential in character, from United States Government agencies.

The performance of these services is made possible by the maintenance of a wide network of connections in many parts of the world. The main working center was moved from Geneva to Montreal by the then director, John G. Winant, to assure freedom from totalitarian influence. The Geneva office remains open, however; there are branch offices in Chungking, New Delhi, and London, as well as in Washington; and there are correspondents in each of the principal Latin-American countries.

Beginning early in the defense program the International Labor Organization has held a series of conferences bringing together Americans and Canadians with responsibilities for manpower problems. These have been attended by operating officials of both governments, representative employers, and union leaders from the A. F. of L., C. I. O., and railroad brotherhoods. The studies of Wartime Transference, Joint Production Committees, and an earlier volume, Labor Supply and National Defense, have resulted from these meetings. The seventh of these meetings is to take place in New York City on February 13 and 14, on the subject Labor-Management Cooperation in Organizing Labor Supply for War Production.[1]

In June 1942 the Joint Maritime Commission composed of nine shipowners and nine seamen from a number of the United Nations met in London. The United States was represented by a prominent shipowner

[1] *International Labour Review*, XLVII (1943), p. 479.

and officials of both the A. F. of L. and C. I. O. unions. The commission recommended a number of measures for the protection of seamen under war conditions. Certain of these recommendations have already been adopted by the American and British Governments. As a result of this meeting, the International Labor Organization has recently issued a report on Life-Saving Measures for Merchant Seamen in Time of War.

The International Labor Organization was responsible for the organization of the First Inter-American Conference on Social Security which met in Santiago in September on the invitation of the Chilean Government.[1] Twenty-one nations of the Americas were represented. The United States delegation was headed by the chairman of the Social Security Board. Officials of the I. L. O. were called to London to give expert testimony before the Beveridge committee, and they have also assisted the governments of several of the Latin-American countries in improving their systems of social security.

The International Labor Organization has a vital contribution to make to post-war reconstruction. This judgment has been expressed by the President of the United States on a number of occasions and was reaffirmed by him in a letter to the Secretary of State on October 28, 1942. In line with this policy the United States delegation to the International Labor Conference held in New York and Washington in October and November 1941, introduced a resolution instructing the International Labor Office to undertake certain studies in the field of labor and its relationship to post-war reconstruction. It declared that the I. L. O. was peculiarly fitted to take part in this work because it "possesses the confidence of the free peoples and includes in its structure the representatives of workers and employers." It therefore instructed the I. L. O. "to study and prepare measures of reconstruction and emergency measures to deal with unemployment." This resolution which was presented by the Government, Employer, and Worker Delegates of the United States met with the unanimous and wholehearted approval of the delegations of the 34 countries represented at the conference.

The I. L. O. Emergency Committee, meeting in London in April 1942, stated the principal objects to be kept in mind in planning this program as, "the provision of full employment and a rising standard of living." The studies initiated by the office have been undertaken with these aims in view. Among the subjects already being treated are the effects of wartime displacements of population; methods of organizing the transfer of workers from wartime to peacetime industry; the planning of public works to prevent unemployment in the industrial countries and of development works in the devastated and underdeveloped countries; the problems of labor in colonial areas; the social and economic

---

[1] For work of Conference see *ibid.*, XLVI (1942), p. 661.

effects of the increased industrialization of backward countries; and the effect on labor of expanded international trade.

In accordance with the instruction given by the conference, these reconstruction studies are being carried on in cooperation "with governmental, intergovernmental, and private agencies, engaged in similar studies." As the only international agency actively functioning in this field, the I. L. O. furnishes a unique clearinghouse for pooling of the post-war plans of the various United Nations and the nations of South America. Its cooperation with United States agencies is particularly close and duplication of effort is thus avoided.

MR. RABAUT. Do you feel that the work of the International Labor Organization has made a real contribution to the war effort in which we find ourselves?

MR. GOODRICH. Yes. I wish to cite these as current purposes quite apart from the purposes that they might serve in the period of reconstruction.

---

3. PERMANENT COURT OF ARBITRATION

According to a statement released by the Department of State to the press on April 7, 1943, the President approved the designation of Mr. Green H. Hackworth, Legal Adviser, Department of State, to succeed himself as a member on the part of the United States of America of the Permanent Court of Arbitration. This designation was made in accordance with the provisions of The Hague Conventions of July 29, 1899 (Treaty Series 392) [1] and October 18, 1907 (Treaty Series 536) [2] and was for a period of six years, which will terminate on March 9, 1949.

The Court was first established in 1900, and its members constitute a panel of competent jurists from which arbitrators may be chosen by states parties to a dispute to pass upon that controversy. Members, acting as national groups, are also entitled to nominate candidates in the election of judges of the Permanent Court of International Justice.

Each signatory power can select a maximum of four members. The present membership on the part of the United States of America of the Permanent Court of Arbitration follows: Manley O. Hudson, of Massachusetts; Green H. Hackworth, of Kentucky; Henry L. Stimson, of New York; Michael Francis Doyle, of Pennsylvania.

4. INTERNATIONAL CONTROL OF NARCOTIC DRUGS

Under the International Opium Convention of January 23, 1912, the Government of the United States along with some 59 or 60 other world powers, entered into an agreement to suppress the abuse of narcotic drugs, their manufacture and their distribution.[3] Congress itself had enacted legislation restricting the importation of opium and its derivatives as early as 1909. On July 13, 1931 the United States and other nations signed at Geneva the Convention for Limiting the Manufacture and Regulating the Distribution of Narcotic Drugs.[4]

[1] *Treaties, Conventions,* etc. II, 1776–1909, p. 2016.
[2] *Ibid.,* p. 2220.
[3] *Ibid.,* III, 1910–1923, p. 3025.
[4] *Ibid.,* IV, 1923–1937, p. 5351.

Until the outbreak of war in 1939 the United States obtained most of the opium required for its medicinal and scientific needs from the Near East. The war, however, disrupted these arrangements. Recently, therefore, the cultivation of the opium poppy in this country reached proportions large enough to cause the Government to have introduced in Congress a bill to control and regulate the production of opium in order to discharge more effectively the obligations of the United States under treaties.

The bill (H. R. 7568) was introduced in the House of Representatives on September 21, 1942. After amendment by the Committee on Ways and Means (House Report No. 2528) it was passed unanimously by the House on October 21. On November 30 the Committee on Finance of the Senate reported the bill back favorably with clarifying amendments and it passed the Senate on the same day. The House agreed to the Senate amendments on December 3 and on December 11 the President signed the bill.

(1) *An Act to Discharge More Effectively the Obligations of the United States under Certain Treaties Relating to the Manufacture and Distribution of Narcotic Drugs, by Providing for Domestic Control of the Production and Distribution of the Opium Poppy and Its Products, and for Other Purposes, Approved December 11, 1942* [1]

Be it enacted by the Senate and House of Representatives of the United States of America in Congress assembled, That it is the purpose of this Act (1) to discharge more effectively the obligations of the United States under the International Opium Convention of 1912, and the Convention for Limiting the Manufacture and Regulating the Distribution of Narcotic Drugs of 1931; (2) to promote the public health and the general welfare; (3) to regulate interstate and foreign commerce in opium poppies; and (4) to safeguard the revenue derived from taxation of opium and opium products.

SEC. 2. For the purpose of this Act —

(*a*) The term "person" includes a partnership, company, association, or corporation, as well as a natural person or persons.

(*b*) The terms "produce" or "production" include the planting, cultivation, growth, harvesting, and any other activity which facilitates the growth of the opium poppy.

(*c*) The term "opium poppy" includes the plant *Papaver somniferum*, any other plant which is the source of opium or opium products, and any part of any such plant.

(*d*) The term "opium" includes the inspissated juice of the opium poppy, in crude or refined form.

(*e*) The term "opium products" includes opium and all substances obtainable from opium or the opium poppy, except the seed thereof.

SEC. 3. It shall be unlawful for any person who is not the holder of a license authorizing him to produce the opium poppy, duly issued to

[1] Public Law 797, 77th Cong.

him by the Secretary of the Treasury in accordance with the provisions of this Act, to produce or attempt to produce the opium poppy, or to permit the production of the opium poppy in or upon any place owned, occupied, used, or controlled by him.

SEC. 4. (a) Except as otherwise provided in section 7: (1) it shall be unlawful for any person who is not the holder of a license authorizing him to produce the opium poppy or to manufacture opium or opium products, duly issued to him by the Secretary of the Treasury in accordance with the provisions of this Act, to purchase or in any other manner obtain the opium poppy; and (2) it shall be unlawful for any person to sell, transfer, convey any interest in, or give away the opium poppy to any person not so licensed.

(b) It shall be unlawful for any person who is not the holder of a license authorizing him to manufacture opium or opium products, duly issued to him by the Secretary of the Treasury in accordance with the provisions of this Act, to manufacture, compound, or extract opium or opium products from the opium poppy.

SEC. 5. It shall be unlawful for any person who is not the holder of a license authorizing him to produce the opium poppy or to manufacture opium or opium products, duly issued to him by the Secretary of the Treasury in accordance with the provisions of this Act, to send, ship, carry, transport, or deliver any opium poppies within any State, Territory, the District of Columbia, the Canal Zone, or insular possession of the United States, or from any State, Territory, the District of Columbia, the Canal Zone, or insular possession of the United States, into any other State, Territory, the District of Columbia, the Canal Zone, or insular possession of the United States: *Provided*, That nothing contained in this section shall apply to any common carrier engaged in transporting opium poppies pursuant to an agreement with a person duly licensed under the provisions of this Act as a producer of the opium poppy, or as a manufacturer of opium or opium products, or to any employee of any person so licensed while acting within the scope of his employment.

SEC. 6. (a) Any person who desires to procure a license to produce the opium poppy, or to manufacture opium or opium products, shall make application therefor in such manner and form as the Secretary of the Treasury shall by rules and regulations prescribe.

(b) A license to produce the opium poppy shall be issued only to a person who, in the opinion of the Secretary of the Treasury, is determined to be a person (1) of good moral character; (2) of suitable financial standing and farming experience; (3) who owns or controls suitable farm land to be used as a production area, in such locality, as will, in the judgment of the Secretary of the Treasury, render reasonably probable the efficient and diligent performance of the operations of producing the opium poppy in appropriate number and quality; and (4) who complies with such additional requirements as the Secretary of the Treasury shall deem and prescribe as reasonably necessary for the controlled production and distribution of the opium poppy. Each such license shall be nontransferable and shall be valid only to the extent of the production area and maximum weight of opium poppy yield specified in the license, shall state the locality of the production area, and shall be effective for a period of one year from the date of issue and may be renewed, in the discretion of the Secretary of the Treasury, for a like period.

(c) A license to manufacture opium or opium products shall be issued only to a person who, in the opinion of the Secretary of the Treasury, is determined to be a person (1) of good moral character; (2) who possesses a method and facilities, deemed satisfactory to the Secretary of the Treasury, for the efficient and economical extraction of opium or opium products; (3) who has such experience in manufacturing and marketing other medicinal drugs as to render reasonably probable the orderly and lawful distribution of opium or opium products of suitable quality to supply medical and scientific needs; and (4) who complies with such additional requirements as the Secretary of the Treasury shall deem and prescribe as reasonably necessary for the controlled production, manufacture, and distribution of the opium poppy, opium, or opium products. Such license shall be nontransferable, shall state the maximum quantity of opium poppies purchasable or obtainable thereunder, and shall be effective for a period of one year from the date of issue and may be renewed, in the discretion of the Secretary of the Treasury, for a like period.

(d) All licenses issued under this Act shall be limited to such number, localities, and areas as the Secretary of the Treasury shall determine to be appropriate to supply the medical and scientific needs of the United States for opium or opium products, with due regard to provision for reasonable reserves: *Provided, however,* That nothing contained in this Act shall be construed as requiring the Secretary of the Treasury to issue or renew any license or licenses under the provisions of this Act.

(e) The Secretary of the Treasury may revoke or refuse to renew any license issued under this Act, if, after due notice and opportunity for hearing, he finds such action to be in the public interest, or finds that the licensee has failed to maintain the requisite qualifications.

SEC. 7. It shall be unlawful for any person to sell, transfer, convey any interest in, or give away, except to a person duly licensed under this Act, or for any unlicensed person to purchase or otherwise obtain, opium poppy seed for the purpose of opium poppy production: *Provided,* That the seed obtained from opium poppies produced by licensed producers may be sold or transferred by such producers to unlicensed

INTERNATIONAL ORGANIZATIONS

persons, and may thereafter be resold or transferred, for ultimate consumption as a spice seed or for the manufacture of oil.

SEC. 8. (a) Any opium poppies which have been produced or otherwise obtained heretofore, and which may be produced or otherwise obtained hereafter in violation of any of the provisions of this Act, shall be seized by and forfeited to the United States.

(b) The failure, upon demand by the Secretary of the Treasury, or his duly authorized agent, of the person in occupancy or control of land or premises upon which opium poppies are being produced or stored to produce an appropriate license, or proof that he is the holder thereof, shall constitute authority for the seizure and forfeiture of such opium poppies.

(c) The Secretary of the Treasury, or his duly authorized agent, shall have authority to enter upon any land (but not a dwelling house, unless pursuant to a search warrant issued according to law) where opium poppies are being produced or stored, for the purposes of enforcing the provisions of this Act.

(d) Any opium poppies, the owner or owners of which are unknown, seized by or coming into the possession of the United States in the enforcement of this Act shall be forfeited to the United States.

(e) The Secretary of the Treasury is hereby directed to destroy any opium poppies seized by and forfeited to the United States under this section, or to deliver for medical or scientific purposes such opium poppies to any department, bureau, or other agency of the United States Government, upon proper application therefor under such regulations as may be prescribed by the Secretary of the Treasury.

SEC. 9. (a) Nothing in this Act shall be construed to repeal any provisions of the Internal Revenue Code, except that the provisions of subchapter A of chapter 23, and part V of subchapter A of chapter 27 of the Internal Revenue Code shall not apply to the production, sale, or transfer of opium poppies, when such opium poppies are lawfully produced, sold, or transferred by persons duly licensed under this Act in conformity with the provisions of this Act and the regulations issued pursuant thereto.

(b) Nothing in this Act shall be construed to repeal any provision of the Narcotic Drugs Import and Export Act, as amended (U. S. C., title 21, secs. 171–184): *Provided*, That the Secretary of the Treasury is hereby authorized to limit further or to prohibit entirely the importation or bringing in of crude opium, to the extent that he shall find the medical and scientific needs of the United States for opium or opium products are being, or can be, supplied by opium poppies produced in accordance with this Act.

SEC. 10. (a) It shall be the duty of the Secretary of the Treasury, whenever in his opinion the medical and scientific needs of the Nation will not be met by importation or licensed production, to provide for the acquisition of opium poppy seed, for the production of the opium poppy, for the manufacture of opium or opium products, and for the use, sale, giving away, or other proper distribution of opium poppy seed, opium poppies, opium, or opium products by the United States Government either directly or through and with the approval of the head of any agency of the Government, including any Government-owned or controlled corporation.

(b) None of the prohibitions contained in this Act shall apply to any officer or employee of the United States Treasury Department, who in the performance of his official duties and within the scope of his authority engages in any of the businesses or activities herein described, nor to any other officer or employee of the United States Government, who in the performance of his official duties, within the scope of his authority and with the approval of the Secretary of the Treasury, engages in any of the businesses or activities herein described.

SEC. 11. (a) It shall be the duty of the Secretary of the Treasury to enforce the provisions of this Act, and he is hereby authorized to make, prescribe, and publish all necessary rules and regulations for carrying out the provisions hereof, and to confer or impose any of the rights, privileges, powers, and duties conferred or imposed upon him by this Act upon such officers or employees of the Treasury Department as he shall designate or appoint.

(b) It shall be the duty of the other departments, bureaus, and independent establishments, and particularly the Bureau of Plant Industry in the Department of Agriculture, when requested by the Secretary of the Treasury, to furnish such assistance, including technical advice, as will aid in carrying out the purposes of this Act.

SEC. 12. The provisions of this Act shall apply to the several States, the District of Columbia, the Territory of Alaska, the Territory of Hawaii, the Canal Zone, Puerto Rico, and the other insular possessions of the United States.

SEC. 13. (a) Any person who violates any provision of this Act shall be guilty of a felony and upon conviction thereof, be fined not more than $2,000, or imprisoned not more than five years, or both, in the discretion of the court.

(b) Any person who willfully makes, aids, or assists in the making of, or procures, counsels, or advises in the preparation or presentation of, a false or fraudulent statement in any application for a license under the provisions of this Act shall (whether or not such false or fraudulent statement is made by or with the knowledge or consent of the person authorized to present the application) be guilty of a misdemeanor, and, upon conviction thereof, be fined not more than $2,000 or imprisoned for not more than one year, or both.

SEC. 14. It shall not be necessary to negative any exemptions set forth in this Act in any complaint, information, indictment, or other writ or proceeding laid or brought under this Act and the burden of proof of any such exemption shall be upon the defendant. In the absence of the production of an appropriate license by the defendant, he shall be presumed not to have been duly licensed in accordance with this Act and the burden of proof shall be on the defendant to rebut such presumption.

SEC. 15. If any provision of this Act, or the application of such provision to any circumstance, shall be held invalid, the validity of the remainder of the Act and the applicability of such provision to other persons or circumstances shall not be affected thereby.

SEC. 16. This Act shall take effect on the sixtieth day after its enactment.

SEC. 17. The Act may be cited as the "Opium Poppy Control Act of 1942."

INDEX